The Paradoxes of Network Neutralities

Russell A. Newman

The MIT Press
Cambridge, Massachusetts
London, England

This book was set in Stone Serif and Stone Sans by Westchester Publishing Services, Danbury, CT. Printed and bound in the United States of America.

Library of Congress Cataloging-in-Publication Data

Names: Newman, Russell, 1973- author.
Title: The paradoxes of network neutralities / Russell Newman.
Description: Cambridge, MA : MIT Press, [2019] | Series: Information policy | Includes bibliographical references and index.
Identifiers: LCCN 2018060936 | ISBN 9780262043007 (hardcover : alk. paper)
Subjects: LCSH: Network neutrality--United States. | Telecommunication policy--United States. | Competition--Government policy--United States.
Classification: LCC HE7781 .N496 2019 | DDC 384.3/3--dc23
LC record available at https://lccn.loc.gov/2018060936

10 9 8 7 6 5 4 3 2 1

Contents

Series Editor's Introduction

Sandra Braman

> Media reform, as it was, is now quaint...
>
> —Russell Newman

Despite all the talk about the transition to an information economy, including analyses by scholars of media policy and the political economy of communication, it is not until reading *The Paradoxes of Network Neutralities* that the implications of developments in the nature of capital for those concerned about freedom of expression has been fully addressed. Yes, we have been talking about the profit motives driving the loss of privacy, and yes, the concept of the prosumer—the person who is, often simultaneously, both a producer and a consumer of online content—has become familiar. But Russell Newman's analysis of the fight over network neutrality plumbs the ideas, rhetoric, and processes involved to depths that are revelatory: activists who believed at the time that they were fighting neoliberalism were actually participating in its continued construction; organizations that supported network neutrality using language focused on freedoms were in reality working to ensure a continuous supply of precarious labor.

As Newman notes, the massive outpouring of public input into the 2014 round of Federal Communications Commission (FCC) decision making on network neutrality marked what has been to date the high point of genuinely mass interest in media policy—a subset of the domain of information policy that is the purview of this series—issues. Such matters have historically been almost exclusively of interest only to the *cognoscenti*, in part because the technical and legal minutiae of issues so often obscure human rights and civil liberties dimensions of what can be at stake in matters such as management of the electromagnetic spectrum, and perhaps in part because infrastructure, as Leigh Star noted, typically remains invisible until it is broken. I first witnessed the rise of popular interest in telecommunications regulation in the early 1990s when, at a meeting of the Association of American Cultures, Jeremy Rifkin described the launch of spectrum auctions by the FCC in terms that sounded as if aliens were about to land on the planet and suck all of the air away. Having been provided with no history of spectrum regulation, a subject about which there may have been three people in the room of a thousand or so with any previous knowledge, the deeply experienced audience of artists and other cultural workers from historically marginalized groups devoted to use of the arts and culture for the purpose of community development was so traumatized by what they had heard about the selling off of spectrum that the topic erupted in session after session, irrespective of planned focal topic, as individuals literally stood on chairs shouting out questions about what was going on.

There is a long history of smart, devoted, and effective nonprofit organizations pursuing media policy issues in the United States through various forms of legal and policy work, but when Free Press was formed in 2003 it was able to ride this already-rising tide of popular interest to catalyze a social movement focused on media policy issues, leading the way in stimulating popular as well as specialist engagement with issues such as media concentration. Newman worked for Free Press on network neutrality, and for a period in Congress as a staffer as well, and is to be admired for the honesty and, indeed, courage of his quite critical insights into the arguments and actions of those on both sides of the fight.

It is upon his work as a scholar and as a theorist, though, that the richnesses of this book rests. The book would be invaluable for its detailed documentation of this still-ongoing fight over the nature of the Internet (and how we can use it) alone, but there is much more. We have long thought about media policy as important as, in essence, a means to an end for those concerned about other policy issues with a focus on what it offers in terms of who can take part in which debates, but Newman makes clear that in the information, or network, or surveillance, or platform economy, media policy is now about the fundaments of how the capitalist system itself works. While in the past we distinguished content-sensitive analyses, technical decisions, and regulatory policies for the digital environment from those that take the position that "a bit is a bit is a bit," this book convincingly makes the argument that the "speech" for which those interested in free speech fight is no longer speech, or only speech, but economic *materiel*—the profit motives driving the socially disastrous political polarization via social media and diverse formations and claims of "fake news" provide vivid and important examples of why that matters.

The book is instructive when it comes to method, too. In his exhaustive mining of a wide range of types of primary and secondary resources, the author provides a model of how to "do" media policy research. The history of policy analysis has been one of ever-expanding frames. Most traditionally, policy analysis has looked at alternative solutions to an immediate problem, but over the course of the twentieth century we went on to think about stakeholder interests, to the discourses through which these interests unfold, and to competition among policymaking arenas within which these discourses take place. Newman adds another layer to this expanding onion of layers of types of policy analysis, turning our attention to ideological frames for those discourses and processes, ways in which both can be used to serve particular interests.

In the comment that provides an epigraph to this piece, Newman is talking about media reform practices and ideas as they were in play only a decade ago. In *The Paradoxes of Network Neutralities*, his piercing, disheartening, and necessary analysis provides the conceptual and theoretical tools we need to take the next steps forward. And he makes clear just why, politically, we must do so.

Acknowledgments

This book emerged from and was only possible thanks to my long-standing relationship and friendship with the people at the national nonprofit advocacy organization Free Press. I want to thank the longtime colleagues with whom I had the privilege of working, even as many of them have moved on to other pastures: Josh Silver, Craig Aaron, Amanda Ballantyne, Ben Byrne, Jordan Carduner, Candace Clement, Stevie Converse, Mary Alice Crim, Jill Fitzsimmons, Yolanda Hippensteele, Sarena Neyman, Tim Karr, Kimberley Longey, Adam Lynn, Amy Martyn, Kate McKenney, Ben Scott, S. Derek Turner, and Frannie Wellings. Others, who joined the organization after I left to join the academy, welcomed me as if I had never left on the numerous occasions I had the pleasure of joining them at such venues as subsequent National Conferences for Media Reform and beyond. In particular, I thank Robert McChesney and John Nichols, who started as intellectual inspirations before giving me an opportunity to work full-time on these issues we all cared about. McChesney was willing to take a chance on a near-complete unknown when he invited me to coedit a book with him and Ben Scott back when the network neutrality fights were getting under way in earnest. Hannah Sassaman, whom I met when she was an organizing powerhouse at the Prometheus Radio Project, was an early significant influence, as was Lauren-Glenn Davitian. Thanks are also due to a number of people from my year spent as part of Suffolk University: Rick Gregg, Bill Mosher, and Jody Santos all inspired me to take the path I have; Barbara Zheutlin in particular was a critical source of inspiration, discussion and critique. Joyee Chatterjee and Janel Schuh were instrumental in getting the original writing off the ground. A couple of really special people were a huge part of not just making this book but in shaping my own thinking as well: Brian Dolber,

Christina Dunbar-Hester, John Cheney-Lippold, Sascha Meinrath, and Victor Pickard were always grounding forces when I met them inside and outside academic settings. I'm lucky to count them as friends.

A special thanks to James Losey, who beyond being one of the most energetic people I know working on these issues, reintroduced me to Sandra Braman, with whom I ended up working at MIT Press. Sandra's suggestions and ideas were always on point and added a great deal to my own thinking as the book came together. I would go as far as to say that a number of her suggestions completely transformed elements of my research program going forward once I dug in. I'm tremendously in her debt. MIT Press has been terrific to work with overall: I offer my sincere thanks to Gita Manaktala, as well as to John Donohue at Westchester Publishing Services, who shepherded this project through to completion. My thanks to Enid Zafran for indexing and for her eagle eye. Thanks as well to the anonymous reviewers who offered substantial and thoughtful feedback on the original manuscript. Their comments were terrifically helpful and have made this a much better book as a result.

Arguments within this work were offered and honed through presentations given at the International Association for Media and Communication Research conferences as well as at those of the Union for Democratic Communication. IAMCR's political economy division has been a terrific source of inspiration and feedback. I thank in particular Wayne Hope, Peter Thompson, and Dwayne Winseck. Serving on the Union for Democratic Communications steering committee has been particularly rewarding: this community has proven an incredibly supportive environment for scholars and activists alike who seek to drill into important structural features that shape all our futures.

This project commenced nearly eight years ago at the University of Southern California's Annenberg School for Communication. I owe my doctoral committee co-chairs, Manuel Castells and Larry Gross, a tremendous thanks; I want to express an equally resounding thanks to those who rounded out my committee as it grew to fill a small conference room: Paul Adler, Jonathan Aronson, Sarah Banet-Weiser, and Ernest Wilson III. Their very productive and positive input into the initial conception of this project forced me to think very hard about where this work "fit" into the broader scheme of the field (and beyond), and it is the better for it. Their influence lasted well beyond my time with them. Larry Gross, in particular, was always a source of both support and opportunities too numerous to name. Sarah Banet-Weiser was willing to make time in her increasingly busy schedule to work through numerous issues. Her own work was foundational for me: I owe her a tremendous debt. Paul Adler was a willing participant in a madhouse independent study I proposed; he suggested bringing others aboard and turned it into one of the best experiences I had while at USC. Outside my committee proper, Herman Gray turned my entire world upside down in a matter of months. I am fortunate to have caught him during the year he spent at USC. G. Thomas Goodnight affected my thinking more than he knows.

I am incredibly lucky to count Emerson College's Institute for Liberal Arts and Interdisciplinary Studies as my institutional home. Amy Ansell, my dean, has been terrifically supportive of all my endeavors, as has the college itself. My colleagues in the Institute have similarly been a terrific source of support, as have new friends met through the Emerson Engagement Lab, which presented an opportunity to give the initial book proposal an airing. In particular, thanks to Miranda Banks, Eric Gordon, and Paul Mihailidis. I've learned a great deal from those who were hired with me: my thanks to Catherine D'Ignazio, Vincent Raynauld and Sarah Zaidan. My students at Emerson have always served as willing test subjects for new ideas; those who have taken the last few iterations of my "It's not Paranoia if They're Really after You" class on the political economy of surveillance have helped in drawing my attention to areas unexpected.

The various members of the Federal Communications Commission who granted me time to ask them sometimes naïve questions were incredibly gracious. My colleagues in Senator Dick Durbin's office, for the time I was there, were very welcoming as well: thank you. The Washington public interest community writ large was also terrifically generous with their time; I thank in particular Mark Cooper, Harold Feld, and Andrew Schwartzman. Andrew Schwartzman was kind enough to read much of the first half of the book and offer substantial feedback—this section is much the better for it. Any errors, of course, are my own. My old undergraduate colleague Jeremy Warren was generous enough to give a long out-of-touch friend on a relatively modest stipend access to his Dupont Circle digs for the fall of 2010 as I commenced the frustrating early stages of this project.

My parents, Robert and Anna Marie Newman, were stalwart bastions of support throughout. My sister, Gweneth Newman-Leigh, provided distant encouragement from across the ocean in Australia. Hands down, however, this project would have been impossible without the support of my long-time partner, Mary-Frances Cusick. She was a vital source of inspiration throughout, both directly and indirectly sparking numerous epiphanies that influenced my overall argument. She less kept me sane than made me see the bright side of chaos, and to embrace and channel it. Thank you so much.

Some arguments in the text initially appeared in "The Debate Nobody Knows: Network Neutrality's Neoliberal Roots and a Conundrum for Media Reform," *International Journal of Communication* 10 (2016): 5969–5988.

Introduction: Network Neutrality, Media Reform, and Neoliberalism

> Regulators do not really care about theory but about outcomes, along the lines determined by the political system.... [P]rices are the tool; economic theorists merely provide the rationale.
>
> —Eli Noam (from *Interconnecting the Network of Networks*)

> As in judo, the best answer to an adversary maneuver is not to retreat, but to go along with it, turning it into ones own advantage, as a resting point for the next phase.
>
> —Michel Foucault (as quoted by Jean Baudrillard in *Forget Foucault*)

> The survival of the internet as we know it is at risk. Its gravest peril originates in the White House, the current occupant of which has launched a campaign, both at home and internationally, to subjugate it to agents of government. The President ordered the chair of the supposedly independent Federal Communications Commission to impose upon the internet rules devised in the 1930s for the telephone monopoly.... We salute the Congressional Republicans who have legislatively impeded his plans to turn over the Information Freedom Highway to regulators and tyrants.
>
> —2016 Republican Party platform statement

On Thursday, December 7, 2017, hundreds of protests were taking place across the country: I was at one, in Providence, Rhode Island. Speaking to the urgency felt, this particular one had been announced not three days prior, and despite this, there were still easily twenty people on my particular corner and more arriving at regular intervals, even in the almost-bitter cold. Fellow protesters on their smartphones connected to any of the myriad others in solidarity. What I was witnessing was the result of something truly remarkable: in the first two decades of the 2000s, a remarkable shift transpired in media activism—a national mass movement focused on not just media policy but also telecommunications policy emerged. From 2005 onward, presidential candidates were forced to express a stance on consolidating media interests and on a once-obscure, seemingly arcane issue going by the name "net neutrality": that is, how much control should the owners of broadband wires possess over what passes through them? Could they speed up, slow down, or stop content on a whim (or as part of a contractual agreement)? The debate had grown from a specialist concern to a rallying cry as everyday people grew accustomed to being intertwined with the Internet and as communities that felt marginalized by big-city newspapers and broadcast networks were able to spark awareness of some event or a cry for justice. Yet, imminently, the Federal Communications Commission (FCC) was slated to undo protections from these sorts of discriminatory practices, setting the stage for broadband companies to start picking and choosing which services, content, and applications would gain safe passage and which might find themselves stuck in park. To everyone on that street corner, it was unthinkable, yet simultaneously virtually unstoppable—for now.

Millions of people had submitted comments to the FCC seeking to "save the Internet" and had called their representatives, senators, and even local officials on the issue, seeking to protect what was seen as "the First Amendment of the Internet" from destruction. Yet over the weekend, the story became little better: footage leaked of FCC chairman Ajit Pai performing a "comedy" routine at the Federal Communications Bar Association dinner, in which he showed a video featuring himself being recruited by Verizon senior vice president Kathy Grillo to be a "Manchurian candidate" for Verizon. Ajit Pai's blatant play on the notion of industry capture was brashly put on display as a joke, and he was fully aware of the optics of the performance.[1] There would be no last-minute change of heart. Net neutrality, as official policy, was scheduled to die. Corporate websites of Comcast and other incumbents quietly took down long-standing pages claiming that they had no plans to offer paid prioritization; former promises to stand by net neutrality rules started to disappear as the date of a vote drew closer. The Pai FCC, of all of the Trump administration's appendages, appeared to be among the most effective at accomplishing the core task as spoken by sometime administration official Steve Bannon: the destruction of the administrative state.

This was in horrific contrast to what had previously transpired just a few short years before, a complete quashing of years of tremendous and expensive activist effort and energy. The elevation of Barack Obama to the presidency seemingly proferred to longtime activsts, finally, a grand opportunity to institute strong nondiscrimination rules on broadband provision after years of pushback from the Bush administration and the FCC. With Obama's appointment of Julius Genachowski as chairman—someone who had interfaced with activists throughout the election campaign and seemed to share their desires—advocates for progressive-style reforms believed, much like in the late 1990s, that they might just have an ally leading the agency. For the second time in just under a decade, when it came to the large decisions regarding the next emergent dominant medium of our time, they would be wrong. When the Genachowski FCC finally issued its first "Open Internet" rules after tortuously protracted debate (FCC, 2010a), the results for network neutrality supporters were particularly frustrating. Other countries, like Australia, had investigated a national network to address deployment issues, a network that would follow "open access" policies of the ilk the United States once incompletely attempted and then discarded—and that went beyond nondiscrimination rules and created genuine competition for broadband provision. The FCC's first-attempt rules stood in contrast to such vision, noncommittal in the agency's commitments, disappointing in their outcome, declaring the agency's dedication to "one Internet" while carving it into wired and wireless segments with different rules applied to each and with loopholes yet to be explored. These rules hewed to the desires of the largest telecommunications and cable operators.

As Barack Obama won his second presidential term in November 2012, the postmortems of the first four years of activity at the FCC were being written. All struck polite tones of triumphalism or melancholy, save one. Free Press president Craig Aaron (2012) then wrote for the *Huffington Post*, "Here's the truth: [Former FCC chairman] Genachowski may pride himself on playing the 'compromiser in chief,' but his tenure has been a series of major disappointments for those expecting real change.... [Other publications portray] Genachowski as a card shark at the poker table, but his strategy at the FCC has been to fold, fold, fold anytime industry comes calling." Aaron mercilessly branded the soon-outgoing chairman a "serial capitulator." He excoriated Genachowski for not taking on the quandary of "meaningful competition" in broadband; in particular, for failure in "mov[ing] a three-year-old proposed rule to collect accurate data about the broadband market," since "you can't fix what you don't measure." But worst of all:

> Genachowski missed the opportunity to reverse failed Bush administration policies and "reclassify" broadband under the Telecommunications Act. Doing so would have ensured the FCC's authority to protect consumers from corporate malfeasance. But once again, Genachowski bowed to industry pressure—and did nothing.... This failure to act leaves FCC lawyers with a weak hand as they now try to defend the agency's Net Neutrality rules before a hostile D.C. Circuit Court of Appeals. Those rules are so watered down that even AT&T endorsed them, but Verizon still sued to have them overturned. (Aaron, 2012)

Even the weak rules promulgated by Genachowski were too much for telecommunications giant Verizon, who sued the FCC and won in 2014, thus largely scrapping them.

With a new chairman in Thomas Wheeler—an ex-lobbyist for telecommunications and cable interests, seen by many in the public interest advocacy community as the industry's darling—a second Open Internet proceeding was launched in 2014 to deal with the fallout of the court case. The public was already keyed into this issue in 2009 and 2010, submitting over a million comments into the Genachowski proceeding; this time that number grew to over four million, which remains remarkable even today—even as *that* number would be dwarfed by the number of submissions to the agency in 2017 on the same issue. To activists' delight, in 2015, the FCC voted 3–2 in favor of a set of Open Internet rules which went well beyond anything activists had dreamed would be obtainable even a year earlier, setting bright-line rules forbidding provider discrimination against disfavored content and applications (FCC, 2015). It reversed fifteen years of policy at the FCC to subject broadband networks to the same regulatory regime reserved for telecommunications networks, reestablishing a notion of "common carriage" (albeit not an exact replica of the old telephone regime) for data. Aaron said of the outcome, "Today's vote is the biggest win for the public interest in the FCC's history. It's the culmination of a decade of dedicated grassroots organizing and advocacy. Millions of people came to the defense of the open Internet to tell Washington, in no uncertain terms, that the Internet belongs to all of us and not just a few greedy phone and cable companies" (Karr, 2015). Similarly, a number of newer civil rights organizations including the Center for Media Justice, ColorOfChange.org, Presente.org, and the National Hispanic Media Coalition expressed their relief at the ruling (Chynoweth et al., 2015). During the summer of 2016, the D.C. Circuit rebuffed a challenge brought by broadband operators, and an attempt to revisit the decision was turned back once again by the same circuit: the new, stronger rules would stand, and had now even passed court muster.

In contrast to Aaron's elation, the *Wall Street Journal* (Crovitz, 2015) took a different perspective in reaction to the turnaround: in an editorial following a Technology Policy Institute conference, the paper noted, "Economist Tom Hazlett proposed a mischievous toast to 'our friend, former FCC chief economist Tim Brennan, who wrote every word' of the FCC's new regulations over the internet." Brennan responded, "Nothing the FCC says necessarily represents the views of Tim Brennan or his staff." The *Journal* notes, "He called the rules 'an economics-free zone'" (Crovitz, 2015, A11). Even as Brennan would walk back this comment later, the characterization is interesting because nothing could be further from the truth: from the commencement of the network neutrality debates of the early 2000s onward, the debate was itself instigated, continued, absolutely *imbricated* in economics. The concept's creation was itself a techno-economic formulation riding aboard particular economic foundations; the terms in which regulators debated the policy stemmed from the same. To partake in these debates, advocates themselves recognized that economics was the coin of the realm when it came to taking part. Here, "economics-free" expresses several layers of meaning that deserve exploration. If there were insufficient "economics" applied to the emergent order, Candeub (2015) augmented this diagnosis in an introduction to a series of articles on the topic entitled "Is There Anything New to Say about Network Neutrality?" Offered in the midst of the debates leading to the strong rules of 2015, he notes that the proposed rules themselves (which would be much revised in the coming year) represented an ill-fated effort to shoehorn routing into law: "[The proposed rules] still [do] not come to grips with the fundamental problem: 'network neutrality,' 'open Internet,' and 'routing fairness' are legal concepts that do not translate in any recognizable way into routing practice, network engineering, or interconnection.… Instead of dealing squarely with this fundamental conceptual problem—a problem that will haunt and likely doom any Internet regulatory regime—the FCC… once again abstracts away from it" (p. 463). The FCC is, by these diagnoses, endlessly caught in a vortex from which there is no exit when it comes to its authority over broadband networks.

This intractability is, I would argue, less genuinely immanent happenstance than something that required a great deal of material effort to construct. In all instances, to net neutrality advocates' displeasure or glee, these rules were formulated uneasily aboard currents that were already transforming the purpose to which our new networks would be put: financial and business interests wanted inexpensive access to communication and coordination while other increasingly powerful interests aboard these networks sought greater access to information about collective lived experience online and off to assist the broader sales effort—all those machinations, well beyond advertising, dedicated to clearing markets—as it was continuing its own metamorphosis (Baran & Sweezy, 1966; McChesney et al., 2009). The concerns of the likes of Dan Schiller (2007b) concerning the "hollowing out" of public telecommunications infrastructure in favor of the shifting needs of capital remain lucidly on display.

The Open Internet debates of 2017 (provocatively named "Restoring Internet Freedom" by the Pai FCC) were only the latest round of a long debate regarding common carriage (and even the notion of "universal service" itself) aboard telecommunications and cable infrastructure. In its most recent iteration, shortly after the passage of the Telecommunications Act of 1996, a series of struggles would commence under the eventual mantle of "open access." The primary question of this debate was: should owners of emergent broadband networks be required to offer common carriage to unaffiliated Internet service providers (ISPs) over their infrastructure? "Network neutrality" emerged as this first debate was being decided by FCC chairman William Kennard and his successor, Michael Powell; it coincided with and buttressed the former. The core question of network neutrality was: what, if any, steps should be taken to ensure that end users have full control over their use of the Internet, and to what extent (and to what ends) can Internet providers manage their networks in such a setting? Ironically, Michael Powell's brash actions to attempt to squelch open access (and, shortly thereafter, to loosen traditional media ownership rules in an equally bold move) would foment massive public dissent in an arena that ordinarily remained, for regulators and industry players alike, blissfully behind closed doors.

Tim Wu, who gave "network neutrality" its name and secured its foundation, would later argue that regarding the debate surrounding "blocking and discrimination" aboard the Internet, "it cannot be said that public debate was wanting" (Wu, 2011a, p. 1852). Indeed, network neutrality has spawned an immense literature: a recent Google Scholar search for the term (performed on March 15, 2018) rendered over sixteen thousand results (which was two thousand more than just over a year earlier). Nonetheless, this book is a counterpoint to Wu's assertion. Ferocious exchanges churned; millions of dollars were spent on such "debates"; the issue found its way into places where media policy discussions rarely tread, such as in mainstream venues like *The Daily Show with Jon Stewart,* user-created videos on YouTube, and beyond. From 2014 into 2015, the issue found expression through physical in-person protests outside the FCC, through users who created videos that explained why network neutrality was so important and that were broadcast on large-scale monitors to staffers inside the FCC, and again through late-night television shows such as *Last Week Tonight with John Oliver.* Even Burger King saw the issue as holding a potentially positive influence on their brand, releasing a video using "burger neutrality" as a metaphor for the debate (Burger King, 2018). The FCC's tepid response to these 2010 initiatives and the FCC's turnaround of 2015 quite reasonably leads to the questions "Who or what controls the FCC?" and "How effective or ineffective were advocates in achieving their aims?" The issue is posed quite often in terms of a battle between "open" versus "closed" architectures and corporate players versus the people; dubbed in Wu's *The Master Switch* (2011b) as "The Cycle," the emergence of nascent new open technologies and their eventual closure is taken to be the dominant trope of communications history in the United States writ large.

While these questions are important and necessary (if not inevitable), I argue here that they effectively erase some of the most important questions we should be asking, that they commence their queries too late, and that once the queries begin they take root in the wrong realms. The activities and decisions of activists who are struggling with these questions are integrally tied to the broader developments of neoliberal capitalism today; the social history of the network neutrality debate as an argument, taken as the object of analysis in its unity, provides a key to its development. The significance is less the debate itself than what it, as a *whole,* tells us about acting and activism in the prevailing neoliberal environment. This book seeks to provide a bottom-up window to its constitution and its continued *re*constitution; it is a study of a moment of transformation of debate—from open access to network neutrality proper—that reveals much more than what might appear via a shift in rhetorical and political strategy. It is an angle missed by what has become a rote story of neoliberalism itself, taken for granted: not an untrue one, but one which is in need of fresh narratives. The shift had effects that were both material and immaterial as massive resources were expended to argue on transformed terrain—terrain that, it turns out, was hardly new at all. The ground was long prepared and came readily stocked with all the implements necessary to both facilitate and contain those who would tread on it.

The true task of one seeking to explain the ambivalent yet significant achievements of this next generation of media reformers in the early 2000s is in creating a record of the material and epistemological platforms aboard which activism on all sides operated. Stories told of the network neutrality debate tend to begin either in 2002 (when the FCC originally declared cable wires "closed" to competition, unlike telephone wires) or in 2005 (when an independent ISP challenge to this order was defeated in the Supreme Court in a case shorthanded as *Brand X*). In the popular telling, all speak of a battle of activists that built coalitions to achieve a particular policy end, and as a story, it truly is remarkable, one bucking the trend that had long become the norm in regulatory matters: that these things would be decided behind closed doors by insiders. The actions the FCC took in 2015 appear unthinkable in this construct, and it truly does speak to the progress of efforts to increase public understanding on tech policy issues since the 1990s. Their reversal in 2017 is similarly revealing.

By the same token, however, looking more deeply at the *justifications and rationalizations* of the debate, when one engages recent work that interrogates the neoliberal project, this debate is revealed to be something a bit more constrained, which in turn presents a long-term conundrum with which activists will need to contend if they seek real change. In the heat of the debates, the cultural labor performed by the battles which are fought tends to go unnoticed; while 2015 was in numerous senses a dramatic victory by network neutrality advocates, when seen from a more distant perspective, it in fact represents a continuum. Perhaps, ironically, there is a cost in arguing these battles in an issue's own terms. The reasons for this go beyond the corruption of individual actors or "bought" government officials: such explanations are clean but too easy, even as, simultaneously, those issues are without a doubt part of the problem.

This was not a battle against capital (although it was never really posited that way, except in a limited sense); indeed, Pickard and Berman (2019) argue that network neutrality is but a single piece of a much larger political program that confronts the market power of broadband giants and offers more equitable access to the Internet. This is undoubtedly true, but is only scratching the surface of what these events illuminate. Rather, this entire continuing debate might be reframed as neoliberalism's own contradictions being revealed. It was, to put an even finer point on it, a struggle against the particular overarching *structure of capital* in relation to communications technologies as part of a broader game—one in which activists hoped that, by setting the playing field a particular way, conditions may improve overall for individuals and groups, acting in concert, to achieve aims of social justice. Such was the point that new media justice and civil rights organizations made in 2014 into 2015 and in earlier years. Even leaving aside their reversal in 2017, the creation of what advocates saw as "fake net neutrality" rules in 2010 and the institution of strong rules in 2015 introduces a number of important questions that beg for answers: the task is to identify the correct ones.

A grand war of maneuver was waged that garnered a significant amount of press attention and public outcry. However, the years considered most intense in the struggle for network neutrality were, in a broad historical irony, perhaps the most staid in surprising senses—arguably, in the long view, they were quite possibly even the *least* significant. In the *short* view, the possibilities of new forms of massive online organization made themselves known; these have received a tremendous amount of attention (and critique), and rightly so—they were important in their own right. By the same token, new logics were settling in. Taking these new logics into account, one realizes that the fights play out in a dynamic stasis in foundational ways featuring constant action of seeming consequence on the surface, all the while seemingly ignoring the ground moving beneath everyone's collective feet via other currents entirely. It is a perfect example of how debates find themselves "channeled" on socially and epistemologically constructed platforms, thereby avoiding some of the biggest issues of all. "Platforms" are perhaps themselves the dominant trope of our time—seemingly each day a new business to facilitate other businesses is proposed—and this is the reason network neutrality has gained its deserved pride of place in the long march of media reform efforts in the United States and, increasingly, globally (Pasquale, 2015; Schiller, 2014; Scholz, 2012). Debates regarding the future of the Internet represented one such venue that witnessed such channeling in action—that is, channeling at a systemic level. Network neutrality, as an issue and as a discourse that presented players no options but the ones they took—channeled as they were on a platform with limited weapons—stemmed from and depended wholesale on an erasure of those things which threatened the platform itself; elimination of these features obtained, the game was over before it even began.

The contradictions and ambivalences are crucial for us to note. Core issues remain undecided and untested. The fight continues, and interest has barely flagged. New openings for walls between activism and theory to be destroyed have become quite apparent: emergent popular support for those who may have once been considered fringe candidates, such as Bernie Sanders and Donald Trump, the incendiary appearance of Black Lives Matter protests, the aftermath of the Occupy movement, the emergence of new socialist journals as *Jacobin*, and more all point to neoliberalism as a central and significant flashpoint of debate today. This presents a fight beyond the bounds of open and closed (or of corporate power versus the public interest); a much bigger problematic is at stake, a class struggle of a unique variety.

At base, then, network neutrality is among the most neoliberal of neoliberal debates—and thus a debate whose roots have become pivotal to understand. I view the issue as a lens through which to examine important ways that neoliberalism renews and reconstitutes itself, the limits of particular forms of activism today, and critical avenues for further research of interest to those who desire to shape regulatory processes and policies. I argue that the creation and propagation of network neutrality as a discourse was very much of a piece of its neoliberal environment, rather than counter to it; in perverse ways, it actually served to further solidify the primacy of a commercially dominant Internet. All the same, "open Internet" activists faced little choice but to engage this issue on its own terms. The issue forces a confrontation with what media reform activism means today and what role is played by the production of knowledge in policy debates, particularly by individuals who were activated via emergent online tools.

My own stance on this fight was hardly as a detached observer. I supported the institution of strong network neutrality rules; I was as disappointed as Aaron was at the FCC's final decision in 2010 and shared his enthusiasm for the turnaround of 2015. For better or for worse, this book is personal: my own belief is that it is for the former. I was one of the original staff members of Free Press, a national nonprofit organization started by Robert McChesney, John Nichols, and Josh Silver in 2003 to push against efforts of the FCC to loosen media ownership rules; the organization would expand its purview into broadband and telecommunications policy before long. This organization, inarguably, spearheaded the drive to bring network neutrality to public consciousness. I was part of a new wing of what is rightly construed as a long-standing media reform movement, decades old, built on the shoulders of civil rights activists—a history of which was compiled in one volume (and inviting numerous more) by González and Torres (2011)—but informed by the writings of critics like Herb Schiller, Ben Bagdikian, Robert McChesney, Noam Chomsky, and countless others who called attention to the particularities of corporate structures of commercial media and their pernicious effects on journalism, democratic access to media, just representation, access to information, and civil rights. I also spent time as a COMPASS (Consortium on Media Policy Studies) Telecommunications Fellow in Senator Richard Durbin's office for a number of months in 2007. Having spent time working with community groups and activists outside Washington, what I observed there was quite striking: the arguments in play inside this office and outside were completely different. This went beyond points of rhetoric; they were substantively and semantically at odds, with entirely different understandings of the implications of one policy prerogative over another. Input from constituents had little to no bearing on technical aspects of policy decisions. Public input on telecommunications policy was worse than useless to the staffers I worked with unless it came from an established interest seen as legitimate, and even then, the input not always incorporated. I watched the office capitulate to the desires of Sam Zell as he sought to take over the Tribune Company, to disastrous (yet predictable) results now long felt. I saw, even conducted, the seeking out of public input on broadband policies—which was a terrific illusion of some new paradigm flying under the banner of "Legislation 2.0" (for which the office gained much credit) while the real action happened elsewhere.

The timidity I witnessed in Congress was assuredly an effort to avoid stirring up a powerful hornet's nest, but there was more in play which I couldn't put my finger on at the time. A much deeper understanding of the neoliberal drive is required to address it properly. I commence my own humble effort at it with this book. In the process, I seek to turn the usual literature on neoliberalism on its head—not to supplant it but to add another perspective to it. Here is an opportunity to observe the discursive yet material dimensions of this conjuncture from the point of view of activists seeking to address its worst harms—while revealing a new, multilevel struggle that must be engaged.

In this introduction, I want to air out the usual narrative surrounding the network neutrality debate in the United States. This narrative, while hardly untrue, creates several important erasures in our understanding of the construction of this policy as well as the implications of these erasures. That is, the story as told seems to make sense in its elimination of what came briefly before—debates over "open access"—even as the *transition* between these debates and what became network neutrality debates proper provide the greatest key to understanding the shifting logics of the Internet, the medium's relationship to broader systems, and its regulation to come. The difference between the two was significant. I suggest an alternative framework with which to examine the network neutrality debates as they occurred and for understanding the cultural labor they performed. Finally, I outline the work to come.

Network Neutrality's Common Narrative

When the tale of the network neutrality fights in the United States is told, it commonly follows a particular trajectory. This trajectory appears in the materials of activist organizations seeking nondiscriminatory treatment of content on the Internet, it appears in the materials of scholars arguing the issue (some advocating a side, others not), and it appears in the materials filed at the FCC in the numerous dockets related to it.[2] It is the story told in countless activist messages when shorthand is needed.

The tale sometimes begins in 2002 following the Michael Powell–led FCC's passage of a Declaratory Order and Notice of Proposed Rulemaking (FCC, 2002b), which is credited with setting the chain of events rolling. Responding to exigencies stemming from convergent broadband technologies in the wake of the Telecommunications Act of 1996, Powell sought to outright clarify that cable lines, regulated differently than telecommunications wires (yet beginning to serve the same purposes), would not be subject to the same "common carriage" rules to which telecommunications lines were subject. In plainer terms, telecommunications companies were expected to supply nondiscriminatory service to all comers—including emergent ISPs, which is why in the late 1990s and early 2000s thousands of such providers came into existence; in any particular urban locale one could expect to have a choice among them. There were also consumer protections to which these wires were subject: to facilitate connections outside a locale and to guarantee that calls went through, telecommunications providers were required to interconnect with other networks outside their region on reasonable terms. Under this and additional laws, the United States found most of its citizens connected to a telephone line (but, importantly, not all, even today), one that guaranteed access to emergency services. When cable companies started to provide Internet service that performed virtually all the same functions as telephone lines, ISPs sought the ability to ply their trade over these faster wires: Powell's order essentially meant that for no reason but regulatory fiat—not technological impossibility—this would not be the case.

This was an incendiary and brash move by Powell. While the common telling generally does not mention it, not two years prior, the former FCC chairman, William Kennard, had issued a mere Notice of Inquiry into the topic; normal procedure, after receiving public comment, would be to move to a Notice of Proposed Rulemaking that would feature specifics that, in turn, would then go through another full round of public comment. Powell's move, effectively leapfrogging public comment on proposed new rules, was procedurally "skipping steps" in favor of the cable industry. ISPs, who were seeking carriage aboard fast Internet conduits (here, cable), sued in a case that made it to the Supreme Court, and in 2005 the Court agreed with the cable companies—not on the merits but in deference to the FCC's authority to make such decisions on technical issues when statute was unclear (National Cable & Telecommunications Assn. v. Brand X Internet Services, 2005). Outside the FCC, these issues were not necessarily partisan in nature, in contrast to the way such debates have played out in Congress or in presidential politics since the latter half of the first decade of the twenty-first century and the 2010s. The majority opinion, blessing the FCC's action in favor of the cable industry, was written by Justice Clarence Thomas, while his erstwhile conservative colleague, Justice Antonin Scalia, wrote a scathing dissent that remains perhaps one of telecommunications policy's most entertaining reads, one punctuated with pizza delivery and dog-on-leash metaphors lambasting what he saw as his colleagues' misreading of the situation. This bookend often provides the second "beginning" point for other narratives of the issue: it provides a natural break and signals the true death knell of "open access" policy. From this point forward, the FCC would no longer demand that the owner of any wire must share it with competitors.

The fear, raised years earlier but now finding itself with new urgency, was that those who controlled access to end users might just try to take advantage of the situation to favor or disfavor content or applications if it meant that they could make extra profit by doing so. There were examples of such behavior, such as when the Madison River Telephone Company in North Carolina would block voice over Internet protocol (VoIP) calls from reaching their ultimate destination (this competed with their own services, of course) and the FCC admonished them for it as an example. Despite Michael Powell's efforts to "jawbone" emergent broadband operators to honor a proposed "four Internet freedoms"—freedom to access content, to use applications, to attach personal devices, and to obtain service plan information—providers would test the limits of the FCC's mettle.

With cable lines now closed to competition, telecommunications interests now were being regulated entirely differently than their coaxial-fiber hybrid brethren. In the name of regulatory symmetry, and with the Supreme Court supplying wind at their backs, the FCC then declared that telecommunications providers may similarly consider their wires closed to high-speed ISP access except on commercially negotiated terms rather than the formerly "just and reasonable" rates that law required. This was done by declaring that, similarly to cable broadband service, these services supplied over digital subscriber line (DSL) or over fiber-optic connections were to be reclassified as "information services," which had none of the explicit rules attached to telecommunications services. Information services would fall under the shorthand of "Title I" of the act, which did not subject them to any requirements in particular. The removal of these services from consideration as "telecommunications services" (and subject to rules under "Title II" of the act) thus also removed many of the consumer protections, such as nondiscriminatory interconnection on reasonable terms to other networks, privacy protections, reasonable rates, and more. One must be quick to note:

the mere declaratory force of the FCC, and not any reason specific to the technology itself, is what wrought these changes. Independent ISPs, having lost their statutory right to gain carriage over competitors' plant, were now beginning to drop like flies, leaving consumers with what amounted to a local duopoly—if they were fortunate—between the cable company and the telephone company for broadband service (Crawford, 2013).[3] For good measure, the FCC similarly reclassified Internet communications aboard wireless connections as well as the nascent and doomed "broadband over powerline" conduit.

Alongside these moves, the FCC issued an informal policy statement that enshrined Powell's former "freedoms" into a set of nonbinding principles. Consumers would be entitled to access the "lawful content of their choice"; they were "entitled to run applications and services of their choice, subject to the needs of law enforcement"; consumers were "entitled to connect their choice of legal devices that do not harm the network"; and consumers were "entitled to competition among network providers, application and service providers, and content providers" (FCC, 2005). As these were offered only as principles to guide future rulemakings and not rules themselves, they would only provide "guidance" on future proceedings. Despite even these weak assurances for public-interest advocates, Ed Whitacre of Southwestern Bell Corporation (SBC), in a moment of candor with a reporter from Businessweek, would not be able to help himself and affirmed activists' worst fears when asked about his opinion regarding such online upstarts as Vonage:

> How do you think they're going to get to customers? Through a broadband pipe. Cable companies have them. We have them. Now what they would like to do is use my pipes free, but I ain't going to let them do that because we have spent this capital and we have to have a return on it. So there's going to have to be some mechanism for these people who use these pipes to pay for the portion they're using. Why should they be allowed to use my pipes? … The Internet can't be free in that sense, because we and the cable companies have made an investment and for a Google or Yahoo! or Vonage or anybody to expect to use these pipes [for] free is nuts! (O'Connell, 2005)

The statement was so outrageous that when advocates trumpeted his words (using his pipes, no less, to circumvent a virtual news blackout on the issue) he may as well have thrown a smoldering cigarette into a dry haystack.

This provides a third, and perhaps most common, point of entry for many who were new to telecommunications and broadband policy debates. For years to come, millions of Americans would pressure the FCC and Congress to prevent the kinds of harms Whitacre presaged in his not-so-empty threat via a policy going under the name "network neutrality." It was understood, and sold, as the principle that users and users alone should determine what services, content, applications, and equipment they would use on the Internet. Those who provided Internet service should have no say in the matter beyond technical details that had to do with managing their network, and this was equated with following a technical "end-to-end" bedrock principle.[4] If network congestion should occur, network providers should be expected to solve such problems not with offers to carry some content or application provider's data in a privileged capacity for a fee but to find nondiscriminatory ways of solving the problem instead, preserving what amounted to a "best-efforts" service in the background.

The multitude of Americans who united behind the clarion call of network neutrality were of no particular political affiliation, and they were legion; following on the heels of debates in the early 2000s over efforts by the FCC to loosen media ownership rules (McChesney, 2004, 2007), these same activists turned toward the Internet, which for years had been thought as a way to circumvent a corrupt media system (Wolfson, 2014). This was a nonpartisan issue that involved the combined efforts of an odd bedfellows coalition featuring activist group MoveOn, various unions (albeit, for various reasons, not the Communications Workers of America), and even the Christian Coalition. Such seemingly contradictory coalitions led to a narrow Senate committee vote that almost, but not quite—and against all odds—would have brought the principle one step closer to being enshrined into law in 2006.

The story only intensified in the mid-2000s as, for the first time since the early 1980s, local and long-haul networks united once again under one corporate banner: AT&T was swallowed up by one of its children, SBC, and Verizon combined with long distance provider MCI. Illustrating the organizational prowess of those fighting for network neutrality, when SBC (now the "new AT&T") purchased BellSouth shortly thereafter, temporary network neutrality requirements were negotiated as part of the FCC's granting of the merger. These had long expired by the time the Open Internet debates continued into the second decade of the twenty-first century. But real outrage reigned when, in 2007, Comcast commenced interfering with and blocking its users from using the popular file-sharing protocol BitTorrent and then spent months lying repeatedly to the FCC and the press as to its doing so. The company's goodwill was further eroded when, during an FCC hearing on the issue, Comcast paid people off the street to attend the meeting so as to take up seats, relegating activists prepared with testimony to overflow rooms away from the main proceedings (Bangeman, 2008). Again, against all odds, a true consumer victory was won in the form of an FCC order forcing the company to cease its practice and institute nondiscriminatory means of dealing with congestion (FCC, 2008). Illustrating how advocates had managed to ply the system against what would rightly be considered headwinds, this occurred under a Republican FCC chairman, Kevin Martin; it would be the height of advocate achievement until 2015. Comcast ultimately sued the Commission and won, resetting the process.

The action in Congress was intense during these years, and network neutrality became the issue that potentially sank bills or elevated them. In 2008, remarkably, this seemingly arcane issue found itself in the spotlight as both parties took stands on it in the presidential election: due to popular pressure and outcry, not only had the debate been extended long past what one would have expected its expiration date to be, but it also was actually being acknowledged as an issue that could sway voters. It didn't hurt that Google was the number three donor (behind Goldman Sachs and Microsoft) to the Obama campaign and at the time was an ally on the matter (Hart, 2011, p. 433). The amount of money being spent by all sides to lobby on the issue was staggering. Obama's FCC, once in place and chaired by Julius Genachowski, issued in 2009 a Notice of Proposed Rulemaking tackling network neutrality, and in early 2010 a long-awaited National Broadband Plan that made numerous gestures toward an open Internet.

The first Open Internet Order was finally issued in late 2010 (FCC, 2010a), one that left advocates cold (this understating their feelings a great deal). The Obama FCC largely hewed to the desires of the largest telecommunications and cable operators with weak rules that at once announced their belief in "one Internet" while dividing it into two: wireline and wireless. Over wireline connections, operators would be prohibited from outright blocking content and applications. They would similarly be disallowed from instituting "unreasonable discrimination" with the exception of an experimental category of "specialized services"—albeit with some caveats that this should not be a hedge to sneakily use this category as a loophole to discriminate. Finally, they would be required to disclose their policies when it came to prioritization. Each of these provisions, advocates declared, held too many loopholes; there were no real standards set or details announced; pay-for-priority deals were not expressly disallowed. Wireless was treated as if it were a "new" technology in need of protection from oversight until it could develop: to these networks, only the no-blocking and transparency rules applied.

While AT&T approved of these rules (or at least acquiesced to them), Verizon sued the agency, ultimately winning a resounding victory in the D.C. Circuit in early 2014 and leaving intact only a spare set of transparency rules. As far as the United States was concerned, there was now nothing standing in the way of dominant telecommunications and cable interests from discriminating against Internet traffic at will, from establishing what activists had termed "fast lanes" and "slow lanes" online, from making commercial arrangements with content providers for pride of place on their services. Julius Genachowski left the FCC to seek his fortune with the Carlyle Group, where he would oversee media acquisition activity for the hedge fund in technology investments (Carlyle Group, 2014).

Advocates were further incensed when Obama appointed Thomas Wheeler to serve as FCC chairman. Wheeler had been a darling of the telecommunications and cable industry, having served as both the president of the National Cable & Telecommunications Association (NCTA) and the Cellular Telecommunications & Internet Association (CTIA) prior to this appointment, albeit some time prior. While most organizations had commenced moving on to greener, more hopeful pastures, groups like Free Press, Public Knowledge, Fight for the Future, Demand Progress, Center for Media Justice, and coalitions as MAG-Net and others kept plugging away at trying to resolve the network neutrality quandary.

What happened next might seem nothing short of miraculous—but while historical accidents certainly played a role, miracles had nothing to do with what transpired. Years of educating the public about these issues were about to pay off. In early 2014 Wheeler responded to the court decision by issuing a Notice of Proposed Rulemaking that explicitly would have allowed broadband companies to set up long-feared discriminatory mechanisms (FCC, 2014). Over the course of the coming months a remarkable turnaround took place: activism erupted outside the FCC itself as longtime inside players adopted direct action tactics; *Last Week Tonight with John Oliver* aired a segment which called renewed interest to it in a grand way and shut down the FCC's servers for a time, with public comments overwhelming the system. Even before the show, however, comments were piling in at a record clip: all told, approximately four million comments were filed in the proceeding, a then-historic record.

Advocates plied an inside-outside strategy, building coalitions of new civil rights groups, consumer groups, and emergent startups, and by November, President Obama himself issued a direct statement expressing his desire that the FCC would issue strong network neutrality rules. Come early 2015, longtime activists were elated as the FCC followed through, passing rules which far surpassed what activists ever expected to achieve. These rules reversed over a decade of policy by undoing what Powell had done in 2002 (FCC, 2015). The FCC reclassified broadband activity of all stripes as a Title II telecommunications service and simply "forbore" from enforcing certain of the Telecommunications Act's provisions that did not apply to this medium. In contrast to the 2010 proceeding, this time three "bright-line" rules applied equally to wired and wireless connections: broadband providers would be prohibited from blocking content, services, applications, and devices; broadband providers would be forbidden from impairing traffic based on the content of traffic (that is, picking favorite applications or content and slowing the rest); and broadband providers would be forbidden from offering "paid prioritization" to those who would ask for it. The FCC would even delve more deeply into the inner workings of networking and police the interconnection activities of ISPs.

In the summer of 2016, the D.C. Circuit affirmed these rules in a challenge brought by telecommunications companies; when these companies appealed, they were rebuffed yet again: the rules had now withstood court challenge twice. By the same token, the issue itself has taken on new life in other forms. As Susan Crawford (2016) was quick (and correct) to note shortly after the court affirmation of the new rules, "In the US, the net neutrality issue has been forced to bear too much weight. It stands in for a larger problem that a single law or regulation can't address." Importantly, she adds, "It's like a small white bird perched on the head of a hippo. The little bird is noticeable and interesting, but really just a side-effect of the reality of the hippo himself. And the hippo in this metaphor is the lack of competition for network access services, particularly higher-capacity services, in a fundamentally unregulated market." "Zero rating" price practices lurk where carriers offer certain favored content as free (that is, not counting toward one's data allotment) (Lomas, 2016), as do privacy implications and continued concerns about underlying interconnection arrangements; decisions overseas in the EU and elsewhere all pose continued challenges and opportunities (Orcutt, 2016). Trade deals similarly may affect the ability of the FCC to enforce network neutrality protections.

The election of Donald Trump to the presidency upended all of these developments. With the ascendancy of Ajit Pai, who was appointed initially by Obama, the FCC now had perhaps its fiercest network neutrality opponent leading the agency. He acted quickly, spending 2017 eviscerating many of the protections gained through the Wheeler FCC. In May 2017 he unveiled his own "Restoring Internet Freedom" proceeding (FCC, 2017b) that sought to reclassify broadband services back to Title I and eliminate the bright-line rules the Wheeler FCC passed. Furious activism followed, with millions upon millions of comments entered into the proceeding, but all was not well. Millions of those comments turned out to be manufactured; names and accompanying information had been stolen from hacked lists. Despite nationwide protests, the FCC would vote in December to reduce the edifice of network neutrality protections to rubble. Broadband services would be reclassified as "information" services; all the nondiscrimination rules would be eliminated. The only rule that remained was a transparency rule: if a broadband provider planned to give preferential treatment to particular applications or content, they would need to disclose this. The Federal Trade Commission (FTC) would enforce these covenants via antitrust authority. Given that the FTC only prosecutes misleading conduct, once disclosed, they would be powerless to stop any discriminatory activity online by any provider.

At the time of writing, these rules were under contest by activist organizations and state attorneys general who commenced legal proceedings against the FCC. States have passed or are considering their own laws of varying strength; one passed by California was seen as a "gold standard," and upon passage was immediately challenged by the U.S. Department of Justice. Efforts to obtain a "Resolution of Disapproval" against the rules passed the Senate but were stymied by the House of Representatives before the 2018 midterm elections. After the midterms, and with Democrats retaking the House, the chamber passed the Save the Internet Act, which would restore the FCC's rules but stood little chance of moving to the Republican-dominated Senate.

Ghosts of Former Debates and Conspicuous Absences

Writing shortly after the first Open Internet rules were issued in 2010, the account above is one similar to that offered by Hart (2011). He is a political scientist, and the questions he seeks to interrogate are to be expected from his discipline but are generally the questions that are most often asked of this entire affair:

> What are the main factors explaining the emergence of support for and opposition to net neutrality guarantees? How are politics in this area related to the broader debates over regulation and the role of the state in American politics? To what extent did outcomes depend on which party controlled the White House and/or Congress? How did the two main parties frame the issue? Was there evidence that the political influence of Internet-based services such as Google, Amazon, and Yahoo! was growing over time? Going beyond the struggle between groups with differing interests, what role did considerations of the broader public interest play in the debates? (Hart, 2011, p. 419)

I point to Hart's aging account less because there is so much wrong with such an approach than to illustrate the massive erasure it rehearses—one found throughout the broader account of the network neutrality story. This is in no small part because the arbitrary closure of Michael Powell's brash actions of the early 2000s seems an appropriate place to begin telling the tale. It is the story of activism finally bringing out from behind closed doors what otherwise would have been a continuance of the long-standing pattern of powerful players emerging victorious, having set policy in their favor, to be reverse-justified and rationalized. Not so in 2015: people and groups that had not previously been involved in communications-oriented policymaking spoke up, put up an amazing fight and, even in the wake of the Genachowski FCC's issuance of "fake net neutrality" rules, returned in force when a confluence of factors gave one side of this issue enough of an upper hand to reverse fifteen years of policymaking, going far further than advocates had ever dreamed in the initial skirmishes of the Obama administration. They returned yet again, redoubling their numbers and their efforts, when the Trump administration sought to undo their victory.

It is a natural inclination to wonder how to replicate the "lightning in a bottle" activists seemed to discover in this issue.

One of the paradoxes giving this book its name is that it turns out to be even more crucial to examine the period which preceded the intense public struggles that comprised the network neutrality debates, significant as they were. Generally ignored or discounted are the initial, crucial fights where the terms of debate were laid and during which the stage was set for the broader involvements to come with the emergence of massive advocacy campaigns that the popular Internet made possible in the early 2000s. These were the debates swirling around the issue of "multiple ISP access" or "open access" over broadband facilities to end users. Should those who own the last-mile pipe to a house or business be forced, like the dial-up telephone world, to permit numerous companies offering different services and foci to offer Internet access service to these end users? The blind spot surrounding this issue strikes me as curious, and it turns out to be quite revealing when one digs into it. What we do have from that time period is a voluminous (if useful in a narrow sense) litany of business-oriented accounts such as Malik (2003), Ferguson (2004), Handley (2005), and Goldstein (2005). The focus of these accounts is often a critique of national policy regarding telecommunications with a particular eye toward the dot-com bubble which popped shortly before Powell took over as chairman of the FCC. Yet they do not speak to policy debates outside the combat waged by telecommunications companies both against each other and against cable interests. Such accounts describe massive miscommunication, misdirected objectives, misread investment decisions, internal turmoil, overwhelming greed, and generally bad business decisions as root causes of the crash to come. Yet these still commit dramatic acts of erasure: the debates over "open access" which were still raging as Powell commenced his reign are largely treated as sidenotes, as annoyances, as something which plainly did not matter much in the broad scheme of things. Malik, for instance, largely dismisses the entire debate as a "giant hairball" predisposed to astroturf tactics by opposing corporate interests (Malik, 2003, p. 153).

Other attempts to outline in broad strokes the nuances of telecommunications and media policy going into the new millennium still undervalue this era. For instance, when Nuechterlein and Weiser (2005) attack the issue, they acknowledge an intense debate, but it is largely constrained by boundaries of technology and policy details; the frame is dominated by concerns of the constraint of monopoly power and broader competitive concerns, paying little heed to others. The frame is certainly relevant, particularly given Whitacre's statement, but it is one that leaves out much that fed into the debates of the late 2000s. Given the scope of their project, however, this is certainly understandable. This said, it is also illustrative of how debate outside of Washington in this arena was seen: a nuisance in itself by people that just didn't get it—a significant feature of the story I aim to tell.

Tim Wu, the originator of the concept of "network neutrality," added to the story in his *The Master Switch* (2011b). While intended for a broad audience and hardly his most sophisticated work, he provides an overarching view of the history of communications networks that he dubs "the Cycle": decentralization giving way to monopolization, with such moves largely bringing increased "openness" and "closedness" in respective tow. In the process, however, he largely (if surprisingly) discounts the open access struggle of the late 1990s, focusing instead on the failed marriage of AOL and Time Warner as a business relationship. The failure to integrate is given one overarching cause: "the Internet." He concludes that multiple ISP access over cable networks of the kind advocates fought for in the face of efforts by emergent cable broadband providers to create their own "walled gardens" for users would not alleviate the issue; besides, these "walled gardens" were simply and plainly technologically unsustainable given the exigencies of this new technology. Granted, he concludes by proposing as a guiding principle a more informal "separations principle" that is, perhaps, a "soft" version of a common carriage or structural separation regime, one not so far afield from "open access" principles advocates sought. All the same, even the creator of the concept of network neutrality committed his own form of erasure that will be, it turns out, on several levels.

The sheer effort that has been expended in "forgetting" this episode points to its importance in U.S. broadband history. A common tack is to remove advocates from history entirely. When in 2011 Thomas Hazlett and Joshua Wright lambasted the FCC's first 2010 *Open Internet Order*, for instance, extraordinary lengths were taken to wipe consumer advocates from history and replace their actions with the much simpler acts of "market forces." In examining years of broadband uptake data comprising the "natural experiment" of deregulation and observing that, despite the closing of networks to competition, broadband adoption continued apace, they conclude, "The implication of the evidence is that U.S. consumers responded very positively to policy choices that refrained from imposing "open access" or eliminated such rules once in place" (Hazlett & Wright, 2011, pp. 77–78). This conclusion is oddly tautological: as access to the Internet has become more and more important and ingrained in ordinary Americans' lives, one doesn't choose to gain access to a closed network; one chooses to gain access, by whatever means available, to the Internet itself. Left out of the inquiry is the nature of the Web on offer.

This was the debate that never happened in open view (and one that network neutrality seemed to address but did not): the broad discussion that should have occurred regarding the purpose to which the Internet should be put and the role of competition policy within that realm. Advocates attempted to reinstate such a debate on the national scene, but it was subsumed by what followed. Speak with advocates working the policy circuit in Washington, and a bright-line as to when the landscape shifted is usually drawn shortly after the Supreme Court decided in its *Brand X* decision that the FCC's decision to "reclassify" cable broadband networks as "information" services themselves was legitimate. The focus then turned directly to this thing called "network neutrality," even as this issue and that of "open access" had coexisted for several years. Tim Wu concocted the notion of "network neutrality" because he feared that open access solutions of the ilk consumer advocates were proposing still would not get at some of their concerns regarding the possibility of oligopolistic last-mile services discriminating in harmful ways against certain forms of content and applications. What is key with this "bright line" is that not only did debates switch to network neutrality rather than open access, but the sides were already decided and largely ceased to move regarding the issue of network neutrality from that point forward, with minor exceptions. From 2005 until the release of the first *Open Internet Order*, a cottage industry of publication regarding "open" and "closed" networks emerged. The legal and academic literature, on the surface, appears to increase our understanding of broadband networking, multiple-sided markets, and more. To be sure, numerous new features required deep thought; this said, when this body of work is read as part of a broader stream of history, it emerges as something completely different and leads to a far starker place: taken as event and examining what kind of labor this literature performed during that time, advocates seeking social justice will find that the task ahead is larger than they imagined. The victories of 2015 do not lessen the urgency—they in fact heighten it, something revealed even more starkly given the reversal since. Even with the immense growth of corporate power as a sector, this remains only a small part of the picture with which activists will need to contend. This is truly one of those moments where, in an academic twist, the secondary literature becomes, in fact, primary.

"Open access" is present via its absence in the later debates; it both figured, and did not, in impending network neutrality debates of the late 2000s. Instigated and waged by a small number of core groups in Washington, DC—primarily Consumers Union, the Consumer Federation of America, the Center for Media Education, and the Media Access Project, but in consort with others—and up against terrific odds, these actors were able to take advantage of inconvenient facets of the (neo)liberalizing aims of the Telecommunications Act of 1996: that is, the battles which ensued were effectively neoliberalism at war with itself as capital formations struggled for dominance. Consumer advocates were able to engage the struggle due to their formation of strategic alliances that on the surface were hardly anti-capital. These ambivalent positionings arose from the belief that individuals should benefit from the same competitive drive that the broader business community sought, albeit to different ends. So even while on the one hand this seems not to advance the cause of considering the broader systems that drive the rollout of these technologies, the manner in which the struggles were conducted, and what transformed them at a core level as the battles wore on, reveal a great deal about the continuing liberalization process itself that was given tailwinds in the late 1990s and emerged from the tech bubble burst in the early 2000s with intensified force, and how it was itself sustained behind activists' backs. It is a political act at a distance to write these actors back into existence for this reason alone. Doing so shifts how we view the network neutrality struggle to follow.

Digital Capitalism Settling In

The beginnings of a broader critique, the kind that is erased by the likes just described, must take into account what Foster and McChesney (2011) call the Internet's "unholy marriage to capitalism": that is, the effort to seek out new opportunities on the Internet to create scarcity and thus opportunities for profit making. More broadly, these efforts seek to draw the Web more closely and in new and surprising ways into the sales effort (see also McChesney et al., 2009). Turow (2011) and Einstein (2016) tell of the mechanics of the long-established and deepening gears of the online sales effort, and Vaidhyanathan (2011) provides similar service. Zuboff's opus, *The Age of Surveillance Capitalism* (2019), raises similar questions on a grand scale (even as Morozov [2019] offers an important warning against using the notion of surveillance capitalism as a too-expansive rubric). It is striking in this context to note that the notion of hypercommercialism—one of the original key tenets of the nascent resurgence of the media reform movement in the early 2000s (expressed in stark form in McChesney, 2004) is one of the features network neutrality sweeps under the rug. With open access, ironically, this was not the case.

Numerous scholars have commented on the ambivalent relationship of the Internet to democracy (for some examples, see Assange, 2014; Castells, 2009; Couldry, 2012; Dean, 2009)—or its miscategorization as a "public sphere" proper (Cammaerts, 2008). A shift to examining the political economic forces shaping it might get us further, then, and yet somehow this long remained shunted to the side as advocates stressed accounts such as Benkler (2006) which expressed optimism that the Internet, if not subject to outside forces which could throw its natural (theoretical) function off-kilter, would provide by the linking mechanism on a broad scale a machine that would filter and synthesize content, negating the worries of those who feared that closed communities would form and consolidate attention on a small number of sites (Hindman, 2008 expresses such concerns empirically).[5] McChesney (2013) perhaps expresses the quandary the clearest (see also Powers & Jablonski, 2015). He argues that attacking the broad problem of media reform and broadband policy itself, by necessity, must challenge the entire core economic structure of modern-day "actually existing capitalism." Given information technology accounted for (then) forty percent of nonresidential private investment in the United States, "quadrupling the figure from fifty years ago," and that "Internet-related corporations now comprise nearly one half of the thirty largest firms in the United States in terms of market value," he concludes, "If one challenges the prerogatives of the Internet giants... one is challenging the dominant component of really existing capitalism" (McChesney, 2013, p. 222). He continues:

> In my view, efforts to reform or replace capitalism but leave the Internet giants riding high will not reform or replace really existing capitalism.... [T]he Internet giants are not a progressive force. Their massive profits are the result of monopoly privileges, network effects, commercialism, exploited labor, and a number of government policies and subsidies. The growth model for the Internet giants, as one leading business analyst put it, is "harvesting intellectual property," i.e., making scarce what should be abundant. The entire range of Internet and media issues must be in the center of any credible popular democratic uprising. Given the extent to which the digital revolution permeates and defines nearly every aspect of our social lives, any other course would be absurd. (McChesney, 2013, p. 223)

This current (or, at least, a less radical version of it) was never absent by any stretch, but it seemed to figure little in Washington policy debates. Quite juxtaposed to the rhetoric of "freedom" and "competition," Schiller (2000, 2007b, 2014) proposes that the defining problem regarding telecommunications networks in general—both domestic and international—is the hollowing out of telecommunications infrastructure of public-interest purpose. "It cannot be emphasized sufficiently that this ongoing shakeup of the supply end of the telecommunications industry comprised a strategic response to a profound shift in demand. Corporate users of Internet systems and services never lost their primacy within the wider metamorphosis" (Schiller, 2000, p. 35). Further,

> Selectively bypassed by major corporate users, the existing system is being attacked for different reasons by big local-exchange carriers, cable system operators, Internet service providers, and other purveyors of new services, from voice-over-Internet companies like Vonage to makers of video-game consoles possessing Internet capabilities. Traditional forms of rate regulation and long-standing strictures of common carriage have come under fierce pressure from carriers and new industry participants demanding to supplant them with privately negotiated contracts for pricing and service. (Schiller, 2007b, p. 92)

For Schiller, it was always a fiction in political-economic terms that data, which would make increasing use of computer networks, were somehow "separate" from that which lay beneath: a collective process of liberalization that was "embraced first and foremost as a reflex of political intervention by leading banks, insurance companies, retail chains, automobile manufacturers, oil companies, aerospace firms, and other corporations, all of which sought to reorganize their business operations around networks" (Schiller, 2000, p. 7). More recently Schiller has noted how these tendencies have only intensified and shifted, particularly since the onset of the crisis of 2008; the "economic contributions made by information and communications to contemporary—digital—capitalism rendered the digital a fundamental pole of growth, akin to the nascent consumer industries of the 1930s, and that, when it arrived, the crisis could be traced not only to financial speculation but to capital's multifaceted integration of digital systems into the political economy" (Schiller, 2014, p. 9). Network enterprises and network states comprise relatively new features (Braman, 1995a, 2009; Castells, 2009), requiring the growth of internetworked technologies to manage them. Even as network technologies have been necessary to the cinching-tighter of geographic expanse, emergent transactional imperatives such as high-speed trading require the cinching-tighter of temporal span to unfathomably tiny fractions of a second as money works to transform itself into more money with no intermediary production "step" (Hope, 2006, 2009). One of the reasons that the likes of Goldman Sachs initially profited so handsomely in the midst of the 2008 crisis stems exactly from its mere ability to conduct transactions faster than others, enabling it to cash in on arbitrage opportunities before the rest of the market could catch up. These moves happen in the telecommunications shadow regions of "special access" transactions, and activists of the late 2000s worried over "specialized services" carve-outs in the emergent *Open Internet Order* of 2010 that would fall outside the new regime of "openness," in similar fashion to the newly emergent worries over "zero rating" practices of providers which subsidize certain content for customers so that it does not count toward one's data limits (Lomas, 2016). Perhaps of even more concern are the surveillance practices of broadband providers, commercial services providers, and government—with the close relationships among all three sectors as well—and the broad implications for all realms of democratic activity of these practices (Bauman et al., 2014; Diffie & Landau, 2010; Pasquale, 2015; Scheer, 2015).

Advocates who were integral to the fights of the late 2000s, in summing their difficulties, tended to lay blame at the feet of Congress for the vagaries of the Telecommunications Act itself (Ammori, 2009). But to put a heavy dose of blame on a "vague" Telecommunications Act for unnecessary uncertainty in this sector is to miss the point, as the prime object was not some coherent set of rules at the time but rather broader liberalization within the telecommunications sector itself—period. At the behest of powerful users of telecommunications networking capability, the U.S. government in the late

1990s was using venues such as the World Trade Organization and beyond to seek further liberalization of these services (McChesney & Schiller, 2003). In a document entitled *Connecting the Globe: A Regulator's Guide to Building a Global Information Community*, which was commissioned by then–FCC chairman William Kennard but in consort with regulators from around the globe, this set of "best practices" extolled "privatization, liberalization and competition" throughout the communications marketplace, "deregulation as competition develops" with goals of "universal access to communications services and technology" and "opportunity for underserved communities" featuring subsidy schemes that are "targeted, explicit and competitively neutral" (FCC, 1999a). What this meant, of course, remained to be decided. This undecidability at the time would be significant, but the undecidability only lay in which capital formation would benefit the most, not in any lack of clarity or vision.

The ability of the broad systemic critique of the commercialization of broadband networks itself to slip past all concerned in the network neutrality debates (or to be covered more obliquely) in favor of arguments about innovation and about individual freedom and consumer rights signals significant implications and new problematics. It is remarkable that advocates were able to sustain the debate as long as they did and with the visibility they did, taking advantage of novel circumstances and the newness of organizing techniques online. Their tactics, however, took the resultant first principles they offered to one of several possible logical ends: that is, while advocates were battling one form of control, another was busy settling in and cared not a whit under which regime it would need to settle.

Approach

These approaches present a start, but the concept of network neutrality cannot be analyzed outside the concept of neoliberalism in the broad. On the one hand, Harvey's (2005) formulation of neoliberalism as a primarily redistributive system of "accumulation by dispossession" (p. 159) undergirded by a strong ideological firmament has proven useful for explaining the current conjuncture; the accounts mentioned above all draw from it. What he refers to is an ongoing process of bringing new arenas of life and activity into the commercial sphere, the rise of finance as a sector and the "financialization" of economies, and the general favoring of markets as proper venues not just for the sale of goods but also in the delivery of governmental services as well (if not the elimination of services altogether). Harvey calls this a new form of primitive accumulation (2005, pp. 177–178), a form that is "fragmented and particular—a privatization here, an environmental degradation there, a financial crisis of indebtedness somewhere else." Freedman (2012), building on Harvey (2005) and Schiller (2000, 2007b), theorized network neutrality's interactions with neoliberalism as a confrontation of reductionist pro-market thinking opposed to broader questions of how we as a society desire our networks to operate. In such a context, he argues, network neutrality as a debate was reduced to traffic management issues cast in economistic logics; policymakers limited discussion to narrow topics of "ill-defined notions of transparency, competition and 'openness'" (p. 109). When the FCC issued even weak rules in 2010, he saw this as activism overcoming economistic thinking, even as "the determination of the Republicans, together with some major industry figures, to overturn the rules demonstrates the continuing presence of pro-market, anti-state ideologies" (pp. 109–110).

A great deal of attention has been paid to the epiphenomenon of the neoliberal drive; what gets neglected is its continued reconstruction. Of late I have faced my own growing frustration at the increasing overdependence upon the narrative provided by Harvey and its derivatives. His otherwise immensely useful oeuvre on neoliberalization seems, in the hands of too many scholars, to have led at times to too-easy descriptions and explanations—themselves ironically lacking explanatory force. While it is not a functionalist account by any stretch, taken as a foundation on which a great deal of other work rests, it seems sometimes to grant the neoliberal drive a systemic neofunctionalism against which activists who seek to push back against its worst ills can do little. Recent efforts to critically examine the push for network neutrality, such as that of Dolber (2013), suffer from this. Dolber draws his theoretical tie to a summary article by Neubauer (2011) that argued, borrowing from Harvey's accounts, that capitalism's "resurgence" was "best described neither by technological determinism nor a self-propelled reorganization of capitalism, but rather through the hegemonic consolidation of a very specific ideology" (p. 2), one emerging from think tanks and universities with corporate and governmental funding. He accurately points to the roles played in the development of neoliberalism today by Friedrich Hayek and the Mont Pèlerin Society, the Business

Roundtable, and more; these, too, are points that McChesney and Nichols (2013) similarly delineate in their discussion of the systemic corruption of policymaking processes. This skim, however, lacks an additional effort to drill into the ways that neoliberalism spreads, reconstitutes itself, and faces down its own contradictions. One of the means by which it does so is less via its ideas in propagation than the platforms on which they travel, which is a step beyond calling out an ideology.

Dolber's critique of latter-day policy-based media reformers is still well taken as he argues that activists, as much as corporate actors, perpetuated several "informationist" myths which serve as neoliberalism's right hand—all of which is undoubtedly true. In examining the discourses of media reformers and network neutrality supporters Free Press (as well as their partners, as part of SaveTheInternet.com)—and others who differed in view, like the Communications Workers of America and the older civil rights organizations which sided against strong network neutrality rules—Dolber notes the ties of all involved to three tenets perpetuated by the notion of informationism: the myth of the equality of labor and capital (using garage startups as exemplars of the importance of an open Internet); the myth that new technologies, in and of themselves, will enable full citizenship (a technologically deterministic notion of cosmopolitanism, even at smaller scales); and an acceptance of corporate elites within new media, such as Google, as defenders of democracy (at least in the early stages of the network neutrality fights proper). As a result, SavetheInternet's arguments "that were inherently critical of capital's relationship to technology might have resonated across the digital divide, informationist discourses allowed potential allies to view ISPs—not content companies—as the true emissaries of democracy in neoliberal societies" (Dolber, 2013, p. 151). Informationism "constricted the terms of the debate over network neutrality" (p. 157), leading to a basic question (p. 159): "Can policy discourses operate outside of informationism?"

His question is my own. His answer, however, falls victim to the illusion that the principal debates took place after the *Brand X* Supreme Court decision of 2005. What Dolber does not examine is this debate's materially constructed history: a political economy of an ideological firmament. Informationism is a static notion: what is needed is a more dynamic one. It is just too easy to castigate the political tactics of these public-interest players in performing such seemingly functionalist roles for neoliberalism:

examining the reasons for these alliances, their pragmatic aims in doing so, offers great insight about our time and activism in general. Now, lest I be misread: I believe Harvey's accounts are fantastic things and incredibly useful for analysis. Increasingly, however, the use to which they have been put—conceiving neoliberalism as a set of unified business maneuvers (in the guise of a seemingly static ideology that claims dynamism without demonstrating it beyond its own overly functionalist imperatives)—results in losing sight of what a "bottom-up" view of neoliberalism looks like, the kind of thing Dolber is trying to accomplish: a self-critique of activist action for more effective struggles to come.

Situating this informationist discourse within a historicized context would do much to point activists toward next steps: the issue could have been argued in other terms but was not. What is necessary is an examination of the uses of informationism: a more complex thing was happening, similarly accessible via discourse analysis, but in a materialist register. One needs to observe the ways that neoliberalism was itself constructed via these discourses in new form to provide a more substantive view of what was happening: this was no static notion but a further development off of longer-standing discourses. The creation and propagation of network neutrality as a discourse was very much of a piece of its neoliberal environment rather than counter to it; in perverse ways, emerging from the cocoon of open access, it actually served to further solidify the primacy of a commercially dominant Internet, but even more importantly, an overarching neoliberal "governance" (Brown, 2015). The platform aboard which network neutrality was argued *forced* activists to subsume notions of justice or the demos in particular terms, raising questions about the forms such activism will need to take moving forward.

Another of the paradoxes giving this book its name, then, is that the concept of network neutrality may have contained its own disappointment (in 2010), its success (in 2015), and even its (either temporary or permanent) eradication (in 2017) in its roots: it facilitated a very particular cultural labor in how it was both posited and how it served as empty signifier for those who would fight for it. To fully grasp how this concept performed the labor it did, it is necessary to understand the transitional period during which open access debates became network neutrality debates; one must leave behind the "heat" of the period of peak activity in the mid-to-late

2000s and return to the seemingly well-trodden period of the late 1990s and early 2000s.

My research questions stem from my interest in the "knowledge industry" surrounding media policymaking and the latter's relationship toward the continued (re)construction of neoliberalism. This book thus seeks to uncover the underlying forces by which neoliberalism, as a project, was maintained and strengthened explicitly by the arguments made about network neutrality. To the extent that such technologies require the services of cultures of interpretation (Knorr Cetina, 1999) or "interpretive communities" (which we discuss in more detail later; see Fish, 1982; Streeter, 1996) to be rendered legible, what does this portend for public discourse surrounding media and communication policy? Given the myriad "points" from which new "technologies" emerge that then circulate through the FCC, where might those who seek to affect change address their efforts so as to make institutional processes more conducive to their arguments and desires? In which ways is engagement with the agency productive, and in which ways is it not? How do we need to thus rethink the concept of "media activism" in light of this? Does it cease being "media activism" and transform into something else? What are the particular means by which these debates grew, and what was their historical foundation? What were the particular means by which we are or are not admitted to debates within Washington, DC? What cultural labor did the network neutrality debate perform writ large? What does it teach us about the continued expansion of neoliberal capitalism as its logics continue to settle in?

This book, then, aims to perform two tasks. One is to tackle the story of the fight for open access conditions on broadband networks themselves, to revisit the tale of the small group of self-described "grass-tops" organizations and advocates that, against all odds, managed to bring the United States the closest it has come to any vision of a broadband-as-common-carrier (or even public utility) model, if indirectly and by pieces. They spoke their case in terms of competition, but their aims were far broader: they were concerned not with competition for competition's sake but with the function that these networks would serve in terms of democratic norms going into the future, for social justice and for innovation. The transformation of the debate from one consisting of open access and network neutrality into network neutrality itself held implications not just for the future of the structure of broadband communications but for what these debates meant writ large. Network neutrality was simultaneously not as simple nor as complex as the literature surrounding it makes it out to be. Thus this book explicitly does not join the network neutrality debate on its own turf by any stretch. It seeks the answers to a different set of questions, ones that have less to do with media policy (although it is concerned with these) than with what media policy and activism in this regard can show us about broader forces at work.

The second task I seek to perform is much more ambitious. I seek to lay out a new problematic that activists seeking democratic ends need to face, one that the debates surrounding network neutrality served to bury in their operation, however unintentionally. This central question is, perhaps surprisingly, epistemological and material at the same time: it inquires into the material supports of knowledge-formations. If those fighting for open access upset some of these, the transition to the network neutrality debate served to restore them. Whereas network neutrality, by all indications, appeared as a fight about the future of the Web, it both was and was not: in many regards the debate ironically stymied the ability to combine the necessary issue into a united whole necessary to address the broad view. It is a story of a dramatic push by local authorities and a small cadre of activists to stop the creation of "walled gardens" by cable interests in the late 1990s and the efforts of the FCC to thwart them. With a new term coined by a then-obscure legal scholar, new life was breathed into these debates—but only by fatefully yoking them to streams of theory of old vintage, streams which sought to reshape capitalist society in its entirety in the wake of World War II and continuing through the present. The story of network neutrality as a debate is one of new, peculiar forms of activism particular to their time and, alongside, new forms of management of public opinion by these same activists, by regulators, and by capital. It is a story of how "ersatz" understandings are dealt with in a powerful modern democracy: how is input registered? When does it matter, and when does it not? Does the production of expert knowledge in regulatory debates still play the same role it may once have played, and what implications follow? Network neutrality provides a lens through which we can fruitfully examine the emergence of new forms of activism, of the production and function of knowledge production in regulatory spheres, and of the development of neoliberalism in all its guises.

How I am using the term *ersatz* to describe the input of those outside legitimated policy circles bears some explanation. Commonly taken to mean a cheap substitute of sorts, I instead borrow the term in its sense once used by Deirdre McCloskey, who wrote regarding the conceptions of "man in the street" economics in her 1985 textbook on price theory and quoted here by Amariglio and Ruccio (1999):

> The economist should persuade the open-minded noneconomist that these economic propositions are true by the same method that an astronomer would use to provide them that astronomical propositions are true: refined common sense, consistent reasoning, and ascertainable fact.... The economist faces the special obstacle that the people being persuaded are themselves economic bodies and have elaborate opinions of their own. The Earth's own opinion about the movement of the heavenly bodies would probably be that they all move around the Earth itself in circles. Untutored economic experience is a bad teacher of economics, just as the unaided eye is a bad teacher of astronomy.... Practically everything that you thought you knew about economics before studying it is wrong.... The vocabulary of such ersatz economics, the economics of the man in the street, contributes to the confusion.... This book will attack ersatz economics again and again, with ever-increasing violence. (p. 20)

Amariglio and Ruccio take this opportunity to expand upon this rather harsh pronouncement and what it means. "While McCloskey does not go so far as to claim that ersatz economics is inferior because it is vulgar, the discourse of the masses, there is no question that its informality and lack of rigor make it unsuitable for anyone serious enough about conducting economic analysis and making sound judgments about economic issues" (p. 21). Ersatz economics does not "contribute[] to economic knowledge"; it is also the reason for the "gross misconceptions that non-economists... harbor in their approaches to everyday questions of economic activity and policy" (p. 21). They note that McCloskey was hardly alone in this sentiment; "much of the jockeying for position of different economic schools in the history of economic thought has relied on various maneuvers to discredit other schools as lying closer to popular opinion, ideology, values, and the like than to rigorous science" (p. 21). Ersatz economics is even held "as a non-discourse... as a mostly random set of irrational elocutions lacking both structure and consistency" (p. 22).

One would think it would thusly be ignored completely, but that is hardly the case: "the attacks on ersatz economics are quite vitriolic, leading us to suspect that something of consequence is at stake here in the academic economists' imagination, not to mention their (our) practices" (p. 22). They sense something "transgressive" about it, something "enough to make someone as careful and respectful as McCloskey nearly foam at the mouth in expressing her reactions," something that makes "proper" economist interlocutors offer "clear warnings against the dangers of even thinking in these ways since thoughts are sometimes put into practice" (p. 22). It is knowledge that "does not need to be taken seriously, to be investigated for the knowledges which it may offer" (p. 24)—but it similarly does require response, an attack, again and again, with ever-increasing violence.

McCloskey admitted the over-the-top nature of the comment in a personal communication with Amariglio and Ruccio; similarly, she emphasized that the attack was hardly personal in nature. In her response to these comments, McCloskey herself says, "My textbook *The Applied Theory of Price* (1985) was one, long argument that 'rigor' of the Samuelsonian, Hal Varian sort is mostly a waste of mental storage space. (My argument failed to convince adopters of intermediate microeconomic textbooks; Hal got the market and the kids lost their common sense)" (1999, p. 60). (Perhaps this is a good moment to note that Varian became Google's chief economist.) Then, to correct Amariglio and Ruccio as to their charges, she offers, "The man in the street commits errors in economic thinking because he's ignorant or self-interested or just innocently confused into thinking that his self-interest is the same thing as the social good, *not* because he is 'untrained in the rigors of mainstream theory,' if 'rigors' means what it usually means in economics, namely, the pointless formality" (p. 61). However, she allows that in relation to the harsh treatment of ersatz economics, something more is certainly going on.

This formulation of the "ersatz" is quite useful in the story to follow. There are several reasons I prefer it to other terms to describe the viewpoints stemming from outside the small circles of communication policy researchers, overwhelmingly economists or lawyer-economists. The language of the official filings regarding an "Open Internet" and its antecedents (and the Orwellian "Restoring Internet Freedom" proceeding) represents a specialist dialect, even a specialist *logos*. But the story of activism, once it burst free of Washington backroom politics, was one of many interested—even informed—individuals, all of whose views were to be found under attack by those who sought to guard the realm. Those who had spent decades constructing the closed discourse in which these issues needed to be fought pushed back hard. These interlopers were clearly self-interested actors but saw in full view the implications of the closing down of net neutrality. New inputs from those outside the fold were not just ignored: outside inputs were quite viciously attacked, and not even on their own terms. They were attacked as either lacking terms, bringing inappropriate terms, or being fully ignorant of how things really worked. Those who possessed a popular, or personally derived from life experience, or even a reasonably and historically informed conception of the key issues found themselves kept out by a phalanx of well-heeled and established disciplinary gatekeepers, at least for a time; and once this wall was broken down, the irony would be that even as their influence played a role in the decisions made, their justifications were still ignored.

The story of network neutrality is the story of this gaining of access—and the moves that were then made to permanently shut them out once again, with terrifically huge ramifications. However, it is not merely "breaking in" to unsettle a discourse. There was absolutely something transgressive about the ersatz in these debates, something that could not be just ignored anymore by those who had spent years building their fortress. How the ersatz interacts with such institutions is, then, of great interest, as epistemic battles for justification were as important in supporting a broader political economic imperative and trajectory as the more commonly noted corruption of lawmakers. In the end, perhaps, the greatest obstacle to progressive change is less corruption (although this remains not insignificant) than that of *sincerity,* an ironic twist during an era in which one of the chief weapons of this form of sincerity is the promulgation of fake news, fake protesters, and fake comments that would find their way into the proceeding, rendering the Internet potentially no longer something resembling the common carriers of yore. Ironically, gaining access meant aiding in the broader quandary's construction, both discursively and materially.

This requires an historical investigation of the cultural, epistemological, and material processes that prepared the ground for the arguably quite disappointing result of the FCC's "Open Internet" proceeding of late 2010, the success of 2015, and advocacy's nadir of 2017—how we came to accept certain measures and knowledge of our media system as the basis for policy and the implications for activism going forward. My contention is that the debate itself is the unit of analysis most appropriate to examine. Is this an exercise of political economy? To the extent it is, it is a story about the efforts of (certain emergent) sectors of capital to gain a particular form of dominance. Yet that is hardly the most interesting element of the story. Is this a cultural studies story? It is an examination of dominant norms being formed; the open access debate was the training ground for new activists in the 2000s. It takes seriously Sum and Jessop's call for a "cultural political economy" (2003), that such an approach "take[s] the argumentative, narrative, rhetorical, and linguistic turns seriously in the analysis of political economy"; it "examine[s] the role of discourse in the making and re-making of social relations and its contribution to their emergent extra-discursive properties"; it accepts the "(in)stability and the interplay of objects-subjects in the remaking of social relations—and hence the importance of remaking subjectivities as part of the structural transformation and actualization of objects" (pp. 14–15). Is it, then, a tale of "science studies," in a sense? To the extent that it is a story of the material construction of a particular conceptual apparatus—one that had material effects upon the manner of policy formation in Washington, if indirect—it is that as well.

In their important book *Greening the Media*, Maxwell and Miller (2012) recall Benjamin's image of the ragpicker as "a motif for philosophical or historical method in times of chaotic change that could not be captured by social scientific controls" (p. 103). This is exactly my challenge and my method, borne of necessity. If one approaches these debates from the underside rather than from a sky-high view, network neutrality becomes but one part of a broader set of debates surrounding the development of the Internet—debates that only became more buried the more involved in the technocratic side advocates became. The continued commercialization of the Internet itself always resided in the background of these debates but never really came into view as the key question to be addressed; this is the chief argument that McChesney (2013) seeks to address. By observing the transformation of the open access debates into exclusively network neutrality debates, the material impacts of theory come into view. That is: the method I undertake is seeking the erasures of those moments and arguments that upset the broader undercurrents that comprise the modern platform of debate. In particular, my task is to outline those actions and debates that less upset neoliberal formations than reveal to them their own contradictions, leading to efforts undertaken quite naturally and without malice that nevertheless serve to erase these contradictions. This is something different than corruption, in Robert McChesney and Lawrence Lessig's sense, as well as in the sense expressed by my former colleagues; nor is it a rote "economism" in positing a direct link between specific strains of theorizing and resultant action.

I draw inspiration from historical work in the communications tradition that focuses on "critical junctures" in policy. A key feature of such work is the notion of "ideological closure," as illustrated by McChesney's (1993) classic study detailing the intense struggles over the future of radio during the late 1920s and early 1930s, as well as Pickard's more recent analyses of the Hutchins Commission and Blue Book analysis by the FCC during the following era (Pickard, 2010, 2011, 2014). Using what he terms a "neo-Gramscian" version of history, Pickard describes key struggles which occurred and importantly details the efforts following their end made by players to justify the positions taken. In McChesney's instance, following commercial media's victory in the Communications Act of 1934, David Sarnoff would deceptively and self-servingly trumpet that the result was not that of policy debates but an "American way." Pickard argued similarly regarding the importance of efforts to establish a new "common sense" in which dominant actors would emerge as the natural victors (and regulators) of their respective domains: the pushback against both the FCC's Blue Book and the findings of the Hutchins Commission—tepid as these products were—resulted in a "common sense" that a negative interpretation of the First Amendment would prevail (in a legal sense: emphasizing the "shall pass no law" part of it). Where my study differs from these is that in the story I tell, it turns out that a *lack* of ideological closure can sometimes be just as useful, if not more so. That is, the way ideological closure is ironically maintained is in its continued ambivalence in its preferred arena—and this is a historically specific conjuncture.

Pickard makes another important contribution. The debates he describes were themselves hardly radical affairs: all the same, he sees the possibility of a recovery of radical imperative from them if they could be so harnessed. What I find in my own study is a similar possibility of radical recovery: by the same token, an interpretive, discursive tack taken upon the core arguments themselves reveals an unaddressed register which points to a new problematic. A powerful engine of the growth of neoliberalism, as numerous commentators have noted, is the explosion of think tanks driving policy discourse. However, for advocates to counter with think tanks that "cancel out" their views is similarly useless, if not disastrous—neoliberalism today is promulgated by a platform of process, not the promulgation of specific ideas; running ideas counter to those offered by the neoliberals only instills them more deeply on the plane (even as the paradox may be that the creation of the same may be necessary in the short term for other reasons). Or, to be clearer: just as old strategies never die, this now becomes one more layer of activity with which activists need to contend. Activists were complicit in this but at a far deeper level than what the likes of Dolber believes. Where he sees them as always already traitors to their own purported causes (or blindly marching forward of their own volition), I see them as having had little choice in taking the actions they did, and one cannot brush them off so easily as betraying the broader cause of justice.

A microstudy of neoliberalism in its action and propagation, then, requires us to look at a wide set of artifacts to piece together the story. It is necessarily interpretive, and to the extent I have been successful here, I have provided a fresh viewpoint on these materials and how they fit into a broader, cohesive whole where once they seemed scattered and dispersed. I spent three months in Washington, DC, during the fall of 2010, leaving as the first Open Internet Order was issued. I had the good fortune of being able to interview several economists and staff from the FCC, both present and past. Many would only speak on background, and I respect their wishes here. Many of the arguments put forth by advocates of the late 1990s were housed on their websites at the time and were not necessarily turned into published journal articles. The Internet Archive allowed me to excavate the original documents that consumer advocates of the late 1990s used to make their case. I made an exhaustive search of news accounts from trade and mainstream press surrounding these debates as they transpired, and I made a detailed study of these. These accounts filled in details but were tempered with accounts from public-interest advocates. Trade press, as all historians in this realm realize, has its own institutional biases. A deep exploration of comments cast into FCC dockets relating to the cable transactions of the late 1990s provided an additional wealth of information regarding the scope of argument present. I followed up this archival research with interviews with key activists in the network neutrality fight in the late summer and fall of 2012 and then again in early 2015 and 2016. As the Trump FCC commenced its work of dismantling the Obama-era rules, I participated in the nationwide calls organized by the groups comprising the Voices for Internet Freedom that were periodically held.

My approach to these materials is to see them through the lens of what scholars as Mirowski and Plehwe (2009) have termed a "thought collective" that comprises the neoliberal project. Others, like Streeter (1996), have sought to describe clear lines in media policymaking from the early twentieth century to the present; he argues that "corporate liberalism" serves as a continuing productive force in media policymaking, still lying in the background. He borrows from Fish (1982) in thinking through the making of policy via "interpretive communities" with their own rules and conditions. While the history of policymaking in the United States has appeared to follow this thread of "corporate liberalism," and even as he is sensitive to the various changing intellectual frameworks employed in the making of policy (when research is considered at all), the ontological features of these shifts are hardly uniform (see Braman, 2003, 2004 as well). Nor are they so cleanly delineated. Starting from the notion of a thought collective allows for a more dynamic universe to appear, one that moves in numerous directions at once while maintaining a distinct trajectory. Tracing activists' involvements with these discursive streams and connecting them to shifting material conditions is remarkably revealing and adds much to how we understand the nature of media activism in policymaking. The notion of thought collectives allows us to view the ways that the voices of ordinary people are processed in broader systems; the notion of an "interpretive community" does not allow for this, as I will argue in the next chapter.

The effectiveness of these advocates during the open access debates (and, later, in network neutrality debates) stemmed from their turning of a diverse discourse into a heterogeneous one. The network neutrality debate, once engaged, effectively reversed the process in a historical accident (which, at the same time, was no accident). By these terms, I intend to use them in the sense supplied by Laclau (2005). Here, he reinvigorates his vision of "radical democracy" developed initially in Laclau and Mouffe (2001). Their critical conception of "heterogeneity" is useful for our purposes here, in which it

> does not mean pure plurality or multiplicity, as the latter is compatible with the full positivity of its aggregated elements. Heterogeneity, in the sense in which I conceive it, has as one of its defining features a dimension of deficient being or failed unicity.... We have, however, partial objects that, through their very partiality embody an ever-receding totality. The latter requires a contingent social construction, as it does not result from the positive, ontic nature of the objects themselves. This is what we have called articulation and hegemony. (pp. 223–224)

"Difference" marks for Laclau a closed "space" for politics, one easily managed. Diversity is the "death" of politics; once all have been named and "taken into account" (see, too, McRobbie, 2004), they need only be accommodated by overarching systems; the game is over. Heterogeneity hints at a pervasive sense (or dread) that the positions available are hardly exhaustive: the horizon of possibility is not clear. Decisions and judgments are rendered difficult, if not impossible, in such an environment: politics proper can thus continue. Once the horizon becomes visible, once bounds are clear, politics ends and positions are all that remain. Importantly, it is the *perception* of either which is paramount. The "radical democratic politics" envisioned by Laclau and Mouffe (2001) militates against the closure "diversity" offers. Building on this foundation, Laclau (2005) invites one to examine entire systems themselves as envisionable by their own constitutive discourses, as systems comprised of articulated elements juxtaposed against one another, importantly with an absence which has not yet made its presence known. What network neutrality would do, ironically enough, is to admit exactly this type of closure. In such a situation—in which the terms are foreclosed—what consumer advocates were able to accomplish during the open access debates would be rendered much more difficult, if not impossible, for them to do once the fight switched completely to network neutrality.

The work required to sustain such efforts—to sustain heterogeneity or to foreclose it—requires material resources. The success of advocates during the open access debates to instill this heterogeneity is illustrated by the manner in which they are forgotten by the likes of (largely) evenhanded (if counterframed) accounts, such as Nuechterlein and Weiser (2005). The problem is solved by ignoring their efforts entirely. The easy ability to commence the story of network neutrality with Powell's brash actions in the early 2000s, as Hart did (and even activists are prone to do), thus reducing the story to tactics of maneuver over the former war of position is, in Marx's words, to reveal "both the strengths and the weaknesses of the kind of criticism which knows how to judge and condemn the present, but not how to comprehend it" (Marx, 1990, p. 638n648). The framework I have described with which to examine the transition of open access into network neutrality is not merely interpretable as historical happenstance but is part of a broader pattern. The lessons to be learned from the concept's development, and the resulting fights, provide a glance at neoliberalism encountering its own roadblocks and routing around them.

Examined from a discursive, historical, and political economic perspective, a deep study of the production of the network neutrality debates themselves reveals numerous challenges faced by present-day actors in regulatory debates—why open Internet activists faced such disappointments in the first Obama administration despite every indication that this administration shared their views and, arguably, why in the second Obama term we saw what appears as success. Even with the disaster that befell them with the Trump administration, a common thread continues to be drawn. Strikingly, what emerges is less discontinuity than continuum. The combination of the use of the "thought collective" construct in concert with Laclau and Mouffe's notions of heterogeneity and diversity supplies a very powerful tool for the evaluation of activist efforts; watching for those moments when particular discourses either open up horizons or foreclose them has everything to do with how efforts to shape and reshape policy ripple across unpredictable fields of action—materially so. It allows us to move beyond facile arguments of the influence of money in politics (even as it does) and adds depth to political economic analyses of ongoing policy debates.[6] Similarly, it allows an effort to move beyond discussion of the emergence of shifting theories undergirding regulatory policy; it is a look at how such discourses are articulated to emergent policy debates themselves.[7]

This production of knowledge, and the activities which surrounded it, often reduced all markets as one, as if they all functioned the same—assuming the lessons learned in one area directly applied to the provision of broadband and telecommunications. It is useful to understand the implications of such argument. Throughout what follows, we will dissect such theorizing, taking it to its logical conclusions. The perspective taken in this book is that markets are not uniform, nor are they natural; they are constructed and require support to continue functioning. But, as we will observe, much of this theory, which is considered mainstream today and is taken very seriously in policy circles, brooks no such distinctions, yet the manner in which it does so is hardly uniform, and at times can even seem contradictory. There is even irony to this, as there is tacit acknowledgement by those who are dominant in this sphere that markets *are* constructed affairs in that they are keen to enforce their presence and our participation in them. What we will observe are exemplars that have driven decision making in regulatory institutions, in Congress, and in the courts.

However, the point is never that a particular theorization prevailed. As an example of a neoliberal debate in how it functioned, network neutrality, particularly after the open access debates, may have been written in terms of certain forms of theorizing (economic, legal, technical), but the struggle itself was hardly legible in those terms. This is perhaps the biggest facet that numerous other otherwise very useful accounts of network neutrality tend to miss. Marsden (2017), for instance, usefully focuses on policy development, competition law, technical debates (such as the implications for "specialized services"), implications for dimensions of privacy, and more, with emphasis on implementation and comparative analysis. Other compendiums compiling various opinions that have stretched over years, such as Belli & De Felippi (2016), offer the same. But such accounts take technical analyses and economic study as quests for truth, which, for numerous economists and technologists, they certainly intend. But this is to ignore the broader effects of their *production*. As Mirowski's (2013) study of the financial crisis makes clear, knowledge is never separate from political economy, but knowledge activates particular actors in ways that are sometimes unpredictable, sometimes very predictable; the articulation of knowledge to particular debates is, itself, a driver of material outcomes in surprising ways. In particular, they bred a particular strain of what I term *neoliberal sincerity* that expresses itself in ways that turn liberal institutions against themselves in order to undermine or even destroy them.

This holds terrific ramifications for media reform going forward. The strategies which were effective even ten years ago are now obsolete—yet paradoxically remain necessary to follow, even as a new layer on top of them needs to be conceived, and quickly. Neoliberal sincerity is a singularly threatening obstacle across the activist field. At its roots, activism geared toward changing the media and its operations involved a challenge to markets and their operation in the media sphere: markets produced, for these activists, distinctly skewed media coverage that favored corporate interests over others, certain privileged populations over others while immiserating or misrepresenting others still further. It is, at base, also a class struggle fought through many lenses. Battles from the 1990s forward to prevent the consolidation of broadcast and print media were about preserving nonmarket space for expression and seeking ways for noncommodified and marginalized speech to find subsidy and an audience. The Internet, to many, seemed a way to short-circuit the bottlenecks of an old media universe, and attention turned to protecting it. But perhaps the greatest impediment to addressing these things was that capitalism itself is, for all its centrality to these issues, always off limits in order to stay in polite circles. Always at the forefront of the mind was that these were technological problems not with technological solutions, but rather social ones, ones which require political will to solve. This book, then, is a call to return to basics: a return to a centering of capitalism in our analyses—but even this, and to make it matter in proper settings, will involve a new epistemic, yet material, project to counter a force constructed for decades.

Chapter Breakdown

The layout of the book is as follows. Chapter 1 establishes the necessary theoretical framework on which I build my case. I commence with outlining network neutrality in the broader context of broader efforts to liberalize the U.S. telecommunications sector throughout the twentieth century. I outline the copious effort that has gone into "understanding" network neutrality in the peak of the fights over the issue; I similarly turn to theories of regulation and regulatory process, including current "capture" theories and discursive offerings, and explain why these are effectively moribund for evaluating action around network neutrality. By turning to a strategy of thinking through "thought collectives" that underlie part of the neoliberal project, however, an entirely new set of possibilities open up.

Chapters 2, 3, and 4 commence the history of this transformative period, examining a key conjuncture in the development of what became a national debate regarding open access policies over broadband communications. This is the story of the effort of one local regulatory body—Portland, Oregon's Mt. Hood Cable Regulatory Commission—to utilize the cable franchise renewal process to foment competition on their own terms over broadband networks, a true David versus Goliath story. AT&T would respond with a vengeance, launching an epic struggle culminating in the network neutrality debate of the first two decades of the twenty-first century. Examining press coverage, meeting minutes of the Mt. Hood Cable Regulatory Commission, and corroborating documents from activists culled from the Internet Archive, I am able to paint a picture not just of a local struggle but one of the loci where neoliberal imperatives found themselves abutting and creating their own contradictions. The emergent "open access" debates were hardly radical struggles: they were competing interpretations of neoliberal writ, at once analytically ensconced on its playing field and destructive of it at the same time. I seek here to recover the inconvenient (systemically speaking) arguments of advocates for open access as they found support in local settings, only to find themselves stymied by the FCC itself. The conflicts which ensued serve to illustrate how arguments asking for an absolute divorce from "marriages of convenience" with corporate players by radicals serve to hide the ways discursive formations in the form of "dynamic/static processing" take shape (or don't). The struggle was, it turns out, the result less of entirely local initiative (although it was that) than efforts by professional advocates to insert themselves in between warring corporate factions. This was a deliberate strategy that used neoliberalism's contradictions against itself, to glean concessions while letting large corporate interests "neutralize" each other's efforts. These accounts are reconstructed from trade press, national and local newspaper accounts, documentation of arguments wrought from the Internet Archive, FCC records, and records from past conference proceedings.

In the face of defeat at the FCC, and with incoming FCC chairman Michael Powell's attempts to quash the debate once and for all, chapter 5 shifts to the salvage performed by Tim Wu's introduction of the network neutrality concept. It examines the arguments to which it responded as well as the principal arguments that were pitted against it. Here is an odd happenstance in which *secondary literature ironically provides exactly the insight necessary to tie the social history of network neutrality to the broader neoliberal imperative.* It was a necessary salvage, one that extended debate on the fate of broadband communications networks, but was at the same time of a piece with a long-standing neoliberal drive. Crucially, this is something quite aside from functionalist interpretations of neoliberal actions and policy. The debate, not the actions of individual activists or activist groups, collectively constructed a platform aboard which the drive could continue to develop while eliminating contradictory elements left over from the open access debates.

Chapter 6 offers a view of what resulted. Newly emergent is an oddly neoliberal form of activism, one that resides at several levels. It mirrors the "double truth" of the neoliberal thought collective: one set of logics would apply to those who make the rules; another would apply to those who were subject to them. In an environment in which new technologies offer new opportunities for massive input from "ersatz" understandings, activist groups themselves needed to "manage" this knowledge in sometimes discomforting ways. These are the results and lessons of the paradoxes contained in the fights that resulted and the formulation of a new problematic which, I am convinced, needs to be grappled with by those seeking to shape broadband channels toward the achievement of social justice. The presence of these understandings of network neutrality drove economists long active in such policy debates nuts: their response is illustrative of the ways in which public participation itself needed to be managed. What emerges is a terrific irony: advocates had more success in working to instill net neutrality principles under a *Republican* FCC—when Comcast was found to be blocking BitTorrent traffic—than what was to come. In 2010, an ambivalent space prevailed. Advocates were visibly shaken by the outcome of what should have been a victory: the first Obama FCC, under Julius Genachowski, instead instituted weak rules, to the chagrin of longtime activists.

If chapter 6 details the emergence of a neoliberal form of activism, chapter 7 analyzes the reactions and ramifications, lessons learned by open Internet activists in the wake of what they considered a stunning disappointment. All sides prepared for an expected court decision against the rules and the possibility of a reclassification of broadband as a telecommunications service. It was now that the role of knowledge in this debate began to shift: if debate about network neutrality had obtained a "dynamic stasis," now the role of the FCC itself was increasingly up for debate. Even as new production in this vein was under construction, with the rules struck down, activists engaged more fully in a blazing display of innovative activism. Notable were shifting (and increasingly anxious) stances by the likes of the Ad Hoc Telecommunications Users Committee and the emergence of the Internet Freedom Business Alliance. Historical accidents play numerous roles in any decision; a disastrous election for Democrats in 2014, chance encounters by particular players in the debate with administration officials certainly contributed to the president's decision in late 2014 to implore the FCC to reclassify broadband Internet service as a telecommunications service, enabling the institution of strong network neutrality protections. However, even if reading press accounts may leave one with the impression that business led the charge, this is categorically false. Activism led; capital followed its lead opportunistically. Reading *ex parte* opinions of the likes of online crafters' platform Etsy is quite revealing: their role in the current "flexibilization" of labor is argued as reason to support network neutrality. When sites such as Etsy or Tumblr turned to their users to defend net neutrality, it was a brilliant double-move. On the one hand, these sites were clearly important to their users. By the same token, having users defend Etsy or Tumblr from the vicissitudes of the largest cable and telecom incumbents stood *as defense of a particular form of platform capitalism under construction.* Still further, an analysis of supporter comments submitted appears to show that network neutrality in practice, as discourse, reconstructed a particular form of labor and instilled this form *as* freedom. The 2015 victory was hard-won by open Internet activists. Yet we might be concerned that the victory was Pyrrhic: in the end, the thought collective of old saw its greatest victory in what was now being cast as freedom online. The commercial model, emergent modes of tracking, and labor precarity all won the day.

Throughout the process of debating network neutrality, adjoining controversies have included determining whether there has been adequate rollout of broadband facilities, albeit cast in different terms than classic notions of "universal service." In fact, in perverse ways, the issue of network neutrality was *reducible* to it in the manner the FCC operationalized its Open Internet rules both in 2010 and 2015. Alongside this have been calls to "reform" the FCC that have usually indicated limiting its purview. Chapter 8 examines such controversies and rethinks universal service in light of the shifting nature of the value-subject operative in contemporary capitalism; it analyzes the changing political economic landscape of the late 2000s in the context of the economic downturn, which materially affected the environment in which the network neutrality debate operated. The role of financialization and sources of capital in these struggles is similarly examined, as are other elements of the sales effort in terms of intensified tracking and beyond with their relation to network neutrality. Universal service to broadband needs to be rethought in light of what kind of Web is on offer: issues of privacy, data collection, and beyond are salient features herein. The Republican Congress's destruction of the FCC's still-nascent privacy rules for broadband providers of 2016 signals dire happenings afoot: the value-subject operative in today's media environment is being transformed. For media reform to have continued salience, it will need to grapple with all these dimensions at once and cease seeing audiences as mere audiences (or even as mere "audience commodities") but as yet another layer of inputs into production processes, increasingly automated, increasingly invisible. Manipulation concerns are merely the tip of the iceberg; the concepts of commodification and exploited "free labor" (Terranova, 2012) don't completely capture what is happening either. This chapter explores the shifting nature of the value-subject in contemporary capitalism and its relationship to the network neutrality debates. "Universal service" today has been rendered complex indeed.

Chapter 9 tackles the Pai FCC's efforts to undo what the Wheeler FCC accomplished. In the process, we witness something completely surreal: a truly postmodern debate, one not rooted in facts or modern liberal discourse even while alluding to their existence and terms. The machinery of liberalism was weaponized against the strategies of media reformers and even itself: the strategies of the 2000s and early 2010s would no longer work against such measures. Perhaps most disturbingly, the 2017 debacle for network neutrality activists represents the pinnacle of achievement of the neoliberal thought collective: network neutrality debates were no longer even about the operation of technologies, and they were only just barely about access to broadband communications, although this was the language ascendant chairman Ajit Pai used to justify the wrecking ball he set in motion. Rather, network neutrality became merely the vehicle via which the FCC itself might potentially be neutralized, now that activists had built and institutionalized a machinery that was able to work with it. Pai's efforts may well be undone, but the general trajectories they reveal are increasingly important to understand.

I conclude with a discussion of the aftermath, including current developments and where these debates go next. I offer a summation of the proceeding chapters, arguing that the emergence of network neutrality—and the inflection point it offers—reveals new problematics for analysts and activists alike. It militates for a rethink of what "media reform" may mean in practice today and shifts our understanding of how to affect regulatory processes. We are left in a truly ambivalent place but need to accept this ambivalence to fully understand the implications of our actions. A new dimension to media reform activism and research is apparent. Network neutrality was a neoliberal debate; to counter it, a neoliberal form of organization was necessary. The debate, taken as a whole, performed tremendous cultural labor, inscribing a particular, emergent form of capitalism as freedom in ways just starting to be understood. Network neutrality is a battle of survival in neoliberal times; in the United States, on the surface, it meshed well with the goals of a vibrant free press and diverse forms of expression and experimentation. At the same time, it fed in the material and cultural manner it was fought into the continued constitution of what autonomist theorists have termed the "social factory." For these reasons, continued explorations into the connections between the development of present-day media policy debates and the activities of the efforts of the neoliberal thought collective need to be better understood and acted on. Barring this, faintly over the ballyhooed technological winds of change breathlessly described in the press, we may still sense wisps of the riotous laughter of the progenitors of the neoliberal thought collective of old, their specters still haunting the making of policy in the United States and activism that seeks to steer it toward promotion of social justice.

1 Knowledge and the Neoliberal Thought Collective: Viewing Network Neutrality through the Appropriate Lens

Network neutrality is but the latest development in a long continuum of debates surrounding the liberalization of telecommunications (and now Internet) infrastructure. Even beyond this, the copious work that has gone into the network neutrality knowledge-production "industry" similarly needs to be placed in a broader stream of understanding about telecommunications as well as that of the rights and privileges afforded to its users. The task of obtaining greater knowledge "about" network neutrality has served numerous ends.

This chapter provides the necessary background. I place the debate in the broader historical trajectory of debates concerning the tension between conduit and content inherent in the liberalization drive of the twentieth century in telecommunications as well as within thinking on communications policy itself. In examining the copious production of knowledge surrounding network neutrality and its relationship to efforts to explain regulatory outcomes, I offer an overview of present understandings of the issue and the illusion these understandings portend. I similarly seek to explain why I see theories of regulation itself unavailing for understanding the present conjuncture. I outline efforts that have attempted to view these debates discursively and show how these efforts are similarly unavailing, themselves more instances of the dominant tropes of our time than revealing of them. I briefly address the current vogue, sparked by frustration in this and other issues, of a resurgence in capture theories, of a belief that returning strictly to money in politics angles will enable democratic debate to recommence in a more just register. I also seek to tie these debates less to the interpretation of neoliberalism provided by David Harvey than the alternative, intellectual-production perspective of Philip Mirowski (1989,

2004; Mirowski & Nik-Khah, 2007; Mirowski & Sent 2002). This turn offers a striking, new way of viewing the events to come as they unfold, one that goes beyond analysis of problem frames and closed concepts as "interpretive communities" to provide something more dynamic, something which can take into account "ersatz" inputs, to ambivalent ends. I argue that the appropriate lens is to view network neutrality as indicative of its time, as the natural progression of a thought collective which came together long ago but whose legacy continues.

Conduit and Content: Liberalization and a Long-Contested Realm

Debates surrounding the control of content passed via various conduits stretch well back decades and largely (but not completely) out of public view. As networking enabled businesses to reach out to potential customers across the world in the middle of the twentieth century (and, importantly, as data became as important as voice), these businesses turned to the Federal Communications Commission (FCC) to assist in liberalizing access to communications networks (Schiller, 2000, 2007b, 2014). Individual users were hardly disinterested in these debates and were certainly involved in stirring public utility commissions to act to address rates for access to communications (Horwitz, 1989; Schiller, 2007a, 2007c; for an alternate take, see Yoo, 2013). Liberalization of telecommunications networks was in pieces as the AT&T monopoly, established in the early part of the twentieth century, was challenged in terms of long distance services, in terms of attachments to the network, and in terms of data communications.[1] Landmark struggles over the emergence of competition in long distance service commenced with FCC approval of the entry of MCI in 1967. With the FCC's *Carterfone* decision, itself following on the heels of a differently decided and fraught Hush-A-Phone controversy (of which Wu [2011b] provides a stirring telling), AT&T was forced to allow end users to plug in their own end-equipment to network wires. Without such a decision, modems would not have become possible; the foundation of "edge-oriented" innovation depended on this particular ruling.[2]

The most direct antecedent of the network neutrality debates, however, were the three Computer Inquiries conducted by the FCC—the first launched in 1966, the second in 1976, and the third in 1985, which still possesses loose ends in need of tying. Cannon's (2003) account of the inquiries was at pains to note the proactive role the FCC took in fomenting the development of the wires and services that would underlie the Internet and, in particular, fashioning regulation of data which would flow over telecommunications networks not by technology but instead by type of service, doing so by adopting the layers model which had been applied to communications internetworks: an implicit "layered model of regulation." In applying the technological metaphor of "layers" to policy, a historical tension would persist, particularly in network neutrality debates (an application of the metaphor can be found throughout M. Cooper [2004]; van Schewick [2010] notes numerous such tensions). It is curious that Cannon's account was controversial in certain quarters. From his perch as a longtime member of the FCC's Office of Strategic Planning and Policy Analysis, his goal of the piece was to debunk notions that the "Internet had never been regulated" or, more broadly, that government actors had nothing to do with its development. The agitprop value of the "Internet has never been regulated" line was simply too delicious for large telecommunications and cable companies to resist throughout the 2000s in the network neutrality debates, a brash falsehood that persisted even as the rules remained in contention through early 2015 and in similarly disingenuous fashion in 2017. Cannon was taking on a few of his own colleagues inside the agency at the time the piece was published.

At root in these Inquiries were matters of the control of providers of telecommunications over what passed through their wires. Perhaps the most important Inquiry as far as network neutrality was concerned was the model provided by the second Inquiry, which established a division of "enhanced service providers" which rode aboard "basic services." Providers of services operating "basic" services would continue to be subject to regulation as common carriers. ("Common carriers," of which telecommunications companies are but one, are required to offer their advertised services to all who request them for a fee; someone who desires service and can pay the fee must be accommodated. Telephone companies operate as common carriers, and U.S. law subjects them to conditions such as nondiscrimination, posting of rates, and more. In contrast, "private carriage" would entail negotiating with each potential customer on an individual basis, and different arrangements can be made for each one; a private carrier would also be able to turn potential business away without justification.) Providers of "basic" services would need to keep "enhanced" operations structurally separated;

this would force the carrier to set up entirely separate businesses—one to provide the basic service, one to provide the enhanced service. Those offering enhanced services would purchase necessary access to basic services as if from any other common carrier. "Enhanced services" would not be subject to common carrier rules, with the logic being that this market was competitive, whereas the "basic service" was not. The present-day equivalent is not placing rules on who must be able to gain access to a personal blog or whether all content needs to be treated on an equal basis on a website, such as a search engine.

The third Computer Inquiry moved from a "separation" model of basic services and enhanced services by market to a prototype "unbundling" scheme. The newly formed Bell Operating Companies (BOCs), created via the AT&T divestiture of 1982, had been disallowed from providing "enhanced services" without structural separation requirements. This Inquiry allowed them back into these areas explicitly. The decision to allow BOCs to enter the enhanced services market came with a requirement to publish "Comparatively Efficient Interconnection" statements—what services they were offering to their own enhanced service providers and what services they would offer to others. This was a first step toward an "open network architecture," where the Bells would break down their networks into basic units to which competitors' enhanced services could gain access so as to provide service to their own customers. In the early 1990s the Ninth Circuit, worried at the time that discrimination would still be possible by the Bells against their competitors (Cannon, 2003, p. 202), struck down parts of the resulting rules. The environment which resulted from further commission action involved a challenging landscape for enhanced service providers that depended on the Bells: unregulated industries (like emergent Internet exchanges) were to monitor the regulated one (the Bells) despite size and information discrepancies; only the Bells truly knew how they truly operated! Worse, service providers were "placed in a position of filing complaints against their sole supplier of a crucial facility" (p. 204).

Debates in the early 1990s surrounded the terms by which competitive service operators could demand interconnection with the various regional Bell facilities (Nuechterlein & Weiser, 2005, p. 66); actions taken by the FCC to address these issues kept courts busy until the signing of the 1996 Telecommunications Act, the first significant overhaul of the 1934 Communications Act in decades. In regard to telecommunications, the act borrowed heavily from the ideas contained in the third Computer Inquiry, with an eye toward attempting to open local telephony to competition, hoping that, with increased technical capacity and increased traffic, there would eventually emerge multimodal, multiprovider competition, even down to "the last mile"—the wire which physically connected destination premises to the phone company's central office. The bill specifically instituted competition as a regulatory goal as well as "the deployment on a reasonable and timely basis of advanced telecommunications capability to all Americans"; it stipulates that it was national policy to "promote the continued development of the Internet," "to preserve the vibrant and competitive free market that presently exists for the Internet," and "to encourage the development of technologies which maximize user control over what information is received by individuals, families, and schools who use the Internet and other interactive computer services." The act attempted to deal simultaneously with network effects, scale economies, and monopoly leveraging that lingered after years of localities having no real choice in telephone provider for local service (Nuechterlein & Weiser, 2005, pp. 74–75).[3]

The Telecommunications Act, combined with the Computer Inquiries, drew dividing lines between certain "zones" of activity, with the zones crucially defined via markets and driven by overriding logics geared toward fomenting some notion of "competition"—local exchange versus long distance; enhanced services versus basic services; information services versus telecommunications services. This maneuver—taking as given that competition should be equated with the public interest—has been assumed to be gospel in recent years, a data point in the story to come. Further complicating matters in the bill was a tangle of definitions whose application and reinterpretation would form the foundation of numerous legal and regulatory battles to follow. "Telecommunication services" were equivalent to "common carriers" (or "basic services" in the Computer Inquiries), distinct from "telecommunications" (the service which underlay "telecommunication services" on offer); "information services" mapped onto "enhanced services" as defined by the Computer Inquiries. The law also speaks of networks while largely ignoring how those networks operate. (It may seem odd that the Internet is never mentioned in the Act, and this has been read in other contexts as almost naïvete by lawmakers; in fact, however, the term was deliberately avoided for political reasons at the time alongside the collective oversight by all parties of how its use was primed to explode.)

Rendering the law more complex still, cable wires remained sequestered in their own title of the Communications Act, even as these wires would shortly mimic the telecommunications services on offer in terms of function. If subsequent policy choices on the telecommunications side were largely aimed at enacting the interpretation of the 1996 act with an eye toward fomenting competition in telecommunications, then cable, increasingly offering similar services, remained closed for such competition. The Telecommunications Act reaffirmed the legacy model of monopoly franchises to be negotiated locally with each cable provider; this provision would be the very thing that would precipitate the battles to come. While seeking competitive access to particular markets, the legacy of piecemeal legislation handling new technologies had resulted in a still-maintained division of law not by function, but by technology, a challenge hardly lost on the FCC (see, for instance, Esbin, 1998).

The act left the details of how to implement these laws to the FCC. Each attempt the agency made was rebuffed by communications incumbents in court, resulting in no small amount of regulatory uncertainty in the years to follow. One of the ironies Wu (2011b) notes is that telecommunications companies used the very argument of "competition" to push for an act that would allow mechanisms for its opposite to result; indeed, the regional Bells would cartelize rather than compete with each other (see perspectives in M. Cooper, 2004; McChesney, 2013). Throughout the Clinton, Bush, and Obama administrations, a law which purportedly was geared toward promoting some notion of "competition" among providers resulted in massive reconsolidation in telecommunications as the old AT&T found itself reborn arguably more powerful than ever alongside a small number of other giants wielding similar clout.

The Quandary of Network Neutrality

The construction of the present environment for investment is a crucial part of the overall picture. The late 1990s found itself in a finance-driven bubble that led to both overenthusiasm for online dot-com "get large before profit" strategies while at the same time providing the impetus for the growth of massive investment in telecommunications infrastructure itself (Crain, 2014; Schiller, 2000, 2007b). Numerous commentators have noted that low-income economies found telecommunications infrastructure far and away the largest form of foreign direct investment. Crain (2014) notes that the development of the dot-com sector, despite the crash, had a double effect—on the one hand, of companies finding ways to appropriate the use of "cookies" toward the deepening of the sales effort; on the other, setting up an overabundance of telecommunications capacity for what was expected to be massive demand. With the burst of the dot-com bubble in the early 2000s and the recession that followed, the politics of the time precluded any genuine fiscal stimulus, falling back on long-familiar efforts of what Brenner (2006) has termed "asset Keynesianism": that is, efforts to stimulate the *paper wealth* of individuals via lowering interest rates and propping up the stock market. The net effect of these moves was to create an environment in which interest rates were low alongside low yields of numerous financial instruments (Srnicek, 2017). These in turn drove the development of the housing bubble as mortgage rates became less expensive; the burst of *that* bubble in 2007–2008 precipitated much of the present environment in which the network neutrality debate found its footing.

Before and throughout these developments, the very notions of "media policy" and "information policy" were being redefined. In the mid-1990s, as the Telecommunications Act was being finalized, Braman (1995b) noted the confluence in communications policy debates of First Amendment law, broadcast regulation, and common carriage regulation; specifically up for grabs would be questions concerning federalism, access to government information, democracy and its practice, industrial policy, and "impacts of the net on policymaking processes themselves" (Braman, 1995b, p. 15). Her exhaustive review of the literature at the time (and since; see Braman, 2009) reveals the broad sweep of issues surrounding the emergent communications medium at the time as well as now. Technology policy followed its own course of history spanning several paradigms (traced by Braman, 2009) from postindustrialists such as Daniel Bell to information society theorists (Castells, 2000, 2001, 2004, 2009). Telecommunications policy was always concerned with terms of universal service and the shift toward the opening of telecommunications markets to competition, in particular in the wake of the divestiture of AT&T in the early 1980s (Horwitz, 1989; Mueller, 1997, 1999, 2013; Schiller, 2007a, 2007c). Alongside conceptualizations of concrete concerns as access to communication and globalization, others have noted the slippage of abstract principles that have been the motors driving the development of media and communications policy. Napoli (2001) discusses its foundations, thinking through temporally specific conceptions of the First Amendment, the "public interest," the "marketplace of ideas," diversity, competition, universal service, and localism: while enduring, the shifting of their meanings lead him to argue that "policy analysts need to take a more expansive and well-rounded approach to communications policy decisions" (p. 22). International concerns surrounding the terms of internetworking figured prominently, and have continued to do so, as emergent issues of Internet governance came to the fore, particularly in the 1990s with continued debates raging today (Drake & Wilson, 2008; Mueller, 2010; Schiller, 2014).

Scholarly work about network neutrality grew out of this still-expanding inventory, but one seeking to gain a grasp of the issue is easily misled by the volume of work addressing it. It is immense, providing the illusion of a gross uptick in knowledge generated about broadband communications technologies and the economics of networking. On its face, for all of its enormity, it largely accomplishes a small number of tasks. Some efforts seek to take Wu's initial concept—expressed in his "Network neutrality, broadband discrimination" (2003)—and nuance it or complicate it. Others sought to evaluate its necessity in law from either a technological standpoint (was the Internet ever really neutral?) or an economic one (what option would render greatest total welfare and minimal deadweight loss? Is the unpredictability of emerging pricing models sufficient to render any decision on the issue premature?).

Meinrath and Pickard (2008), both advocates (and partisans) in support of network neutrality, identified at the time of their writing three "waves" of scholarship on the issue. The first surrounds Wu's initial offering "where he forwarded the idea that network architectures should be neutral purveyors of data" (p. 14). This is an overgeneralization of what Wu was proposing in many ways and not really the whole truth, but this is beside the point at present. Until the Supreme Court's 2005 *Brand X* decision, "the debate simmered among a relatively small group of commentators" that was dominated by technologists and economists. Thierer (2005), of the Progress and Freedom Foundation (a close ally of large telecommunications and cable interests), argued that in lieu of mandating a particular manner in which broadband wires should operate, numerous varieties of networks should be permitted to evolve; policymakers, he argued, should be "agnostic" in regards to a preference for "smart" versus "dumb" networks. Yoo (2004) buttressed Thierer's sketch with theoretical and analytical heft, supportive of a "network diversity" policy that would foment myriad, diverse networks which would be allowed to differentiate their services. Network neutrality would effectively inhibit such activity; it would even, he argues, go as far as stifling new content aboard the Internet, by his reasoning, since new upstarts would require some form of purchasable differentiation to compete with established players in all likelihood.

A "second wave" emerged with new urgency following the Supreme Court's *Brand X* decision in 2005. As this decision represented the beginning of the end of any "unbundling" of Internet access to competition aboard not just cable wires but telecommunications wires, Yoo intensified and doubled-down on his arguments (2005, 2006) and was joined by Sidak (2006), who would provide a detailed application of welfare maximization theory to the debate. McTaggert (2006), then senior regulatory counsel for Canadian telecommunications giant TELUS, presented a pointed interrogation as to whether the Internet was ever really "neutral." Noting the various efforts to evolve the operation of Internet protocol (IP) networks, the Internet had, in his view, inexorably moved away from "neutrality" for years toward "diversity":

> As time goes on, a legislative or regulatory net neutrality rule continues to grow more incongruous with the reality of the Internet and the interests of mainstream Internet users.... Let's let the user-driven innovation of the Internet continue, and not try to pre-judge what kinds of data service offerings consumers will find attractive in the future. If changes to the way the Internet works are not anti-competitive and are not rejected by consumers in the marketplace, they should be presumed to be responsive to market demand, whether such changes diverge from the Internet's classical architecture or not. (McTaggert, 2006, p. 31)

The eagerness for "compromise" and nuance in the debate, despite the stakes, was evident at this time; Noam (2006), for instance, suggested a "third way" for network neutrality limited to last-mile providers in an editorial, making distinctions between last-mile facilities and the middle- and long-haul networks with differing rules for each.

When communications scholarship did get involved, they were "remarkably cautious given the stakes involved" (Meinrath & Pickard, 2008, p. 14), often responding to advocates for network neutrality in asking them to "nuance" their views; Sandvig (2007) is a prime example of this from within the field, calling attention to numerous varieties of discrimination which take place within broadband networks that would likely be unaddressed by a single rule or set of rules. Free Press, in consort with others under the umbrella of SaveTheInternet.com, found terrific success mobilizing the public in support of the concept at this time; new fuel was added as Wu (2007) greeted the emergence of the iPhone, at this time only available on the AT&T network, with a well-timed conception of "wireless Carterfone," noting the myriad ways that cellular telephony operators locked down end-user equipment such as their phones. (The irony was that as activists tied such control to network neutrality as an issue, they inadvertently *muddied* the issue—paradoxically to make it more tractable to the broader public—by equating network neutrality with end-user attachment problems.)

That the communications academy was increasingly paying attention was illustrated by the newly launched *International Journal of Communication* offering its own collection of articles reflecting what it considered the key arguments in the debate. Several sought to define or redefine what the debate was about (Faulhaber, 2007; Frieden, 2007; Jordan, 2007; Peha, 2007; Peha, Lehr, & Wilkie, 2007); technologists returned, with similar arguments to those who would argue that the Internet was never truly neutral (Hahn & Litan, 2007). In seeking to both clarify and nuance the issue, Clark (2007) argued that "the debate about network neutrality is a proxy for a debate about the collision of different models, all valid in their own sectors—the open nature of the Internet, and the tied content-conduit model of the entertainment industry" (p. 703). Clark tied the new debates to the abandonment of open access policies:

> One could speculate that the reason for [the emergence of network neutrality debates worldwide] is that we have abandoned the idea of increasing competition through facilities unbundling, and see (to some extent) the outcome of that decision, whereas other parts of the world are following the path of encouraging competition at the retail level through unbundling, and are thus hoping that the issues of market power at the retail level will be less pronounced. (Clark, 2007, p. 704)

He explored various ways in which discrimination can occur—featuring often-asked questions regarding "quality of service" offerings that might be applied to time-sensitive materials, holding out a guarantee that they would get priority treatment (would neutrality requirements render these illegal in all cases?); regarding the defense of old business models (is it good or bad that providers of video content operate a "separate" network alongside a "public" Internet within their systems?). He notes the complexities of interconnection agreements (private contracts determining terms between networks that agree to swap traffic) and caching (putting content on servers in numerous locations so that end users are not requesting content from one centrally located server, thus speeding up delivery), the challenge of (and challenges to) flat-rate consumer pricing. To would-be advocates of the concept, he argues that they needed to recognize the "complexity" of the debate. Such calls were enjoined by the likes of Peha (2007) who called, much like Wu (2003) did in his original paper, for ways to discern beneficial and harmful discrimination, seeking a similarly nuanced view of the issue. Lehr et al. (2007) spoke to a possible "arms race" surrounding "resource bypass" of users trying to skirt discriminatory activity, which might ironically load networks further, wrecking attempts to "manage traffic flow": "It is disingenuous of operators to state that giving priority to some traffic has no effect on the remaining traffic" (Lehr et al., 2007, p. 627). Rather, "it seems more likely to hope that access competition will emerge to make the risk of adverse discrimination less likely than to hope that such large-scale end-user bypass will become generally available" (pp. 637–638).

Numerous frameworks for some network neutrality regime emerged. "Third way" propositions, such as that of Atkinson and Weiser (2006), insisted that the debate was being focused on the "wrong issues," and needed to focus instead on "nuanced, balanced policy" since the arguments of both advocates and commercial operators appeared valid. Jordan (2007) suggested a framework for neutrality that sought to "prevent oligopoly rents" while allowing for network management. Numerous frameworks involved no frameworks at all: Bauer (2007) examined several models (absence of network neutrality rules, some nondiscrimination rules, and "full regulation") and determined that the situation was still too fluid to sketch out specific rules; a policy of monitoring for abuse was proposed. Similarly, a former chief economist of the FCC, Gerald Faulhaber (2007), long involved in telecommunications policy minutiae, relied on a wait-and-see policy due to the complexity of new pricing structures wrought by multiple-sided markets. While allowing for problems stemming from vertical foreclosure, in the end, economic theory "cannot even predict the direction of payments, much less the size of payments, which may evolve in this market. Price recognition of the two-sidedness of the broadband ISP [internet service provider] is not 'double dipping'; it is simply one of the many ways in which two-sided markets can price" (Faulhaber, 2007, p. 690). He places the blame for the state of affairs and the policy debate itself squarely on the pricing structure of the industry: new rhetorical features as "bandwidth hogs" were not being charged for their inordinate use of networks, for instance. The existence of said "bandwidth hogs" was not something empirically proven at this time (nor since), even as it provided a useful fudge for dominant broadband interests (Crawford, 2013).

It is curious to note how pro-network neutrality advocates' calls for the policy were systematically misconstrued, particularly the calls of those outside of Washington. Faulhaber (2007, p. 689), for instance, seemed convinced that they saw caching services as problematic. Caching services were never at issue: what was always at issue was the ability of the last-mile providers to usurp choice of content and applications from end users. Neutrality advocates similarly had never made any claim that the Internet, from end to end, was neutral every step of the way (and neither did Wu [2003] in his original article on the subject). While advocates for network neutrality firmly supported the concept of users having the ultimate choice in what they would and would not access, boiling it down to "the net was never neutral" served nonetheless as a useful foil. Even David Clark, a significant figure in the development of the Internet, misconstrued the argument: diving deep into the innards of communications networks, he noted that interconnection arrangements among ISPs themselves are quite opaque. ISPs "may offer reduced costs for transit [agreements to pass along content from another network] based on other business conditions that apply. Some ISP may try to charge for the privilege of peering. So there is a good deal of discrimination that can be found in today's practice of interconnection" (Clark, 2007, p. 706). Crowcroft (2007) similarly rehearsed arguments about the basic non-neutrality of the Internet (capacity as a function of round-trip time and packet loss probabilities; differing routes of return due to the business relationships of ISPs; caches nearer to certain users of certain content), all of which miss the point as far as advocates were concerned. However, when he argued that the Internet should not been seen as a "special" service but increasingly as a utility, advocates would agree, similarly with the notions that "infrastructure and bundles are incommensurable; [and that] the timescales for regulation may often be wrong (both too short and too long), and need constant revision, possibly requiring smart regulated markets rather than fixed franchises" (p. 570). However, his lens on the issue blocks what was really at stake; his "solution" involved, much like the "third way" alternatives, multiple-part definitions for network neutrality with their designs yet to be determined: "connectivity neutrality" (end-to-end service at all layers); "performance neutrality" (defined rules in a measurable, comprehensible, transparent fashion); or "service neutrality" (availability of new services that allow them to retain their differences from each other "such as multi-home, multicast, mobility, etc. in a way that allows cross-provider/cross-platform differences to exist until these services have sufficiently matured" [p. 579]). He sums up,

> The Internet's evolution has thrived on differences that through one lens may appear as non-neutral treatment while through another may appear as vigorous and healthy competition. Regulators who seek to impose a rigid or static definition of net neutrality would be well advised to heed the lessons of Internet history and the examples cited herein.... In conclusion then: We never had net neutrality in the past, and I do not believe we should engineer for it in the future. (Crowcroft, 2007, p. 579)

All the while, he misses that what was at stake was not an engineering issue but one of concerns over the increasing power of broadband players, of free speech and the ability to assemble over emergent technologies, and of implications for the ability to do so given the structural forces in play. It is surely true that policy would need to drill into details beyond these prerogatives. All the same, network neutrality was but one means to a broader end, necessary but not sufficient to achieve such aims. To reduce the issue of neutrality to theoretical welfare calculations or technicalities served to bury these concerns. Yet misconceptions seemed to march forward long of their own accord: when former FCC chairman Reed Hundt spoke to a group of scholars at the University of Southern California in early 2010, he asked the assembled audience whether network neutrality proposals should apply to services online, like Google: if activists demanded that AT&T treat all content neutrally, shouldn't it be demanded of Google's search results too? This was something advocates had never broached; the issue had always been about network providers themselves, and to muddy the waters like this was to miss the point (Hundt, 2010).

There certainly were alternative arguments to the welfare-and-utility calculators and net-was-never-neutral technologists. Van Schewick's early entry into the debate (van Schewick, 2007) offered a counter to the narratives of the economists (and legal scholars utilizing economic theory) provided by Sidak and Yoo. Communications scholarship from the field proper, looking largely through the lens of democratic theory and innovation, supported the concept as well, even if these were expressed in the domain of the law journals (Herman, 2006; Meinrath & Pickard, 2008).

By 2008, Pickard and Meinrath note a "third wave" of debate, "one that places net neutrality positions in a state of uncertainty" (Meinrath & Pickard, p. 14). That is, scholarship had become "less complacent toward the loss of net neutrality" as they wrote; they submitted that "now is precisely the moment that we should be aiming beyond mandated net neutrality for more encompassing safeguards to ensure an open Internet." It is also notable that this literature was bifurcating strongly along the lines of not just analysis, but *stance:* articles which appeared were increasingly less trying to work out details than support one side of the issue or the other. Quite in line with the likes of Frischmann in emphasizing the positive externalities which accrue to a neutrally operating Internet seen as *infrastructure*—and which are ignored by Sidak and Yoo (Frischmann, 2005; Frischmann & van Schewick, 2007)—and based on the work of Benkler (2006), Lessig (2002, 2007), Wu, and Mark Cooper of the Consumer Federation of America, they propose network neutrality as a normative principle:

> Much of the existing scholarship and commentary fails to sufficiently emphasize the import of normative principles—principles regarding the role of the Internet in a democratic society and the debt that the Internet providers owe to the public.... The fact that network neutrality is a normative principle is far too often overlooked. Industry attempts to reframe the debate, growing technological complexity, and shifting allegiances among competing actors artificially sunder democratic Internet principles that should be considered together.... [W]e envision a more open and participatory Internet. Frequently referred to as a commons-based approach to the management of communications systems, this model emphasizes cooperation and innovation as opposed to privatization and enclosure. Given that all technology is inscribed with social values that foreclose certain possibilities while encouraging others, emphasizing these linkages illuminates what is at stake with network neutrality and situates this debate within a larger vision of Internet openness. (pp. 14–15)

Their vision is revealing, consisting of ten points that would find themselves expressed yet again a few years hence as Meinrath, Losey, and Pickard (2010) would look, layer interstice by layer interstice, at emergent multiple bottlenecks in Internet infrastructure well beyond the one so often identified during the network neutrality debates to that point (that is, at the IP layer). Normative principles of network neutrality would require in their view, first and foremost, mandated common carriage. Internet architecture should "support open architecture and open source drive[n] development," including "open protocols and open standards." It should feature "an end-to-end architecture (i.e., is based upon a 'dumb network')"; while "safeguard[ing] privacy (e.g., no back doors, deep packet inspection, etc.)." Building on the concept further, it should foster "application neutrality" while "mandat[ing] low-latency and first-in/first-out." Interoperability would need to be ensured as well as remaining "business-model neutral." Finally, it would need to be "governed by its users (i.e., is internationally representative and non-Amerocentric)" (Meinrath & Pickard, 2008, p. 18). This is to say, whereas so many in the debate seen as the "prime movers" in the academic realm (and legitimated as such) were emphasizing minutiae of telecommunications operation and competition policy, it was perfectly possible to set up large goals and guidelines that would serve to determine exactly whether a particular form of discrimination was harmful or beneficial, allowing room for interpretation on specific cases but grounded in a firm normative foundation. It is revealing that the main players in the literature insist on shunting these normative notions to the side in favor of specifics.

Rethinking Regulatory Process

As the endgame of the first Open Internet Order approached in 2009, these debates had every appearance of ferocity. Once the Notice of Proposed Rulemaking (FCC, 2009a) was released, in late 2009, early 2010 and mid-2010, the FCC held a series of "workshops" inside and outside of Washington on debates long played out. On December 8, 2009, one was held entitled "Technical Advisory Process Workshop on Broadband Network Management" (FCC, 2009b); on December 15, 2009, one covering "Speech, Democratic Engagement, and the Open Internet" (FCC, 2009c); on January 13, 2010, another on "Innovation, Investment, and the Open Internet" (FCC, 2010e); on January 19, 2010, the topic was "Consumers, Transparency, and the Open Internet" (FCC, 2010c); and finally, another on April 28, 2010 was entitled "Approaches to Preserving the Open Internet" (FCC, 2010b). President Obama himself had extolled the concept at least eighty-three times across various addresses, blog posts, and beyond, and in a positive light.[4] Yet, in the end, none of these debates seemed to have moved that particular commission one way or another: as Wu (2011a) notes, the adopted rules which followed in 2010 (FCC, 2010a) did not budge much from the sentiment of the "four freedoms" speech delivered by Republican ex-chairman Michael Powell six years prior (Powell, 2004).

Revisiting the literature today, one is struck by a supreme sense of confinement. This was similarly felt even at the time; burnout on network neutrality was palpable in activist circles from 2006 to 2010 and beyond. This seemed the case as well during 2014 when the issue received new attention following the D.C. Circuit's nullification of the first *Open Internet Order* even as excitement started to build again. The reason was certainly simple: the same debates were being rehashed again and again even as certain questions appeared settled and done. Virtually identical hearings, featuring similar arguments, were held in 2014. Even as the debates raged well into 2018, advocate Harold Feld would bluntly exclaim in a blog post offering links to his past writings on the subject:

> This is one of the reasons I find this topic so frustrating. In 2006, I spent a lot of time pushing back on these arguments. Here is the first time I wrote about the importance of net neutrality to political speech. Here is when I wrote about "the tiered Internet and virtual redlining." Perhaps most centrally, here is my piece talking about what the FCC would later call the "virtuous cycle" that flows from prohibiting providers from monetizing scarce bandwidth by prohibiting prioritization ("fast lanes"). And here is my first piece summarizing all this and talking about the FCC's general authority over broadband. And I'll throw in this "Debunking Telco Disinformation" post, also from 2006, because I am still getting the same goddamn talking points from the telcos. (Feld, 2018a)

The literature is wholly unsatisfying on any number of levels, absolutely grating against the reasons I involved myself with this thing called "media reform." Feld punctuates the point with, "Have I mentioned I've been doing this for a very long time, and that there are not a lot of new arguments? As I started saying, I think back in 2010, you either believe the arguments or you don't. It's not like anyone is likely to say anything new" (Feld, 2018a). Here was an issue that struck at the heart of free-speech concerns, justice concerns, civil rights, the digital divide, and more: how narrowly it was construed, and how narrowly it continues to be construed, turns out to be one of the chief data points of this study.

Perhaps one might then run to the realm of political science, where questions of regulatory capture, administrative function, and institutional incentives of regulators have long been subjects of concern. Horwitz (1989) provides a powerful overview of many strains of thought in this regard in his thick description of the progress and ironies involved in a shift from New Deal regulatory oversight to 1980s moves to "deregulate." The core of Horwitz's argument, now decades old, is that it is an error to think of any of these agencies as originally being established to serve some notion of a "public interest" that is itself increasingly desiccated over time. He makes a thorough study of existing paradigmatic turns in the theory of regulation and regulatory capture from both the left and right, a realm every bit as immense—much more so—than the network neutrality debates themselves. When Horwitz arrives at his own iteration that seeks to avoid functionalism and oversimplification, he recognizes that agencies are often the weakest player in broader formations of power. The legal realm is itself most appropriately seen not as part and parcel of the seeming "captured" nature of agencies by dominant interests; rather, one needs to view the rationalizations and thought-processes provided by these players as semi-autonomous. This is a view also strongly illustrated by Napoli (2001). It does not help, Horwitz notes, that industry pressure and power stem from the fact that agencies act within an industrial framework that is preconstituted with generally negative forms of power available to them. They have a tendency not just to be conservative but also to avoid rulemaking altogether: instead, they bargain. Regulatory power, in his view, becomes a commodity for which parties with standing vie; administrative process becomes a forum to work out conflicts, such that their conclusions would then be enforceable by law.

The conservatism of bargaining is that it is only among those with standing, and once established, the agency is loath to disturb the new agreement; thus "basic regulatory formulas, whether rules or policies or methods, achieve a kind of settledness; they become like political constitutions which structure all rules and policies together" (Horwitz, 1989, p. 87). The move to pressure agencies to "deregulate" stemmed from an increase in parties with standing in regulatory matters: that is, who had the ability to actually have their opinions "count" in official settings. At the FCC, for instance, the battles of civil rights advocates in the late 1960s were pivotal in granting the broader public standing in matters before the commission and other federal agencies. Before this time, only those with material interests in broadcasting or other matters before the commission—not listeners, in other words—held appropriate standing to be heard. Such expansion of legal standing, however, would disrupt the "balance of formalism and bargaining historically receptive to industry interests" (p. 87). As these processes became more open and more political, industry found it more costly, time-consuming, and contentious; this actually led to increased formalism of the process. "Though formalism and bargaining are opposite tendencies, in another sense they feed on each other. Both contribute to agency conservatism" (p. 87). Further, "regulatory agencies, opened up to more democratic participation, became less able to bargain and more bound to procedural norms. Administrative rationality and economic rationality diverged, and by the mid-1970s business engaged in a wholesale revolt against regulation" (p. 89).

Horwitz's take certainly rings true for the experience of advocates for network neutrality as they experienced it: what we see in the 2010 Open Internet decision was exactly this brand of regulatory conservatism and bargaining, wrought of a formalism designed to contain the massive effort of individuals across the country to exercise their standing; this from an administration that muppeted the words of network neutrality activists themselves before their decisions would have to be made. The process which preceded the 2015 order, while distinctly different in outcome, was hardly so different; one of the things which certainly made a difference was activists' renewed emphasis on surprising efforts outside the bargaining process while hardly disengaging it. They would be aided, however, by new sectors (and logics) of capital which had had the opportunity to grow, finding themselves (if pushed and cajoled into it by activists) in new positions of potential power that could take advantage of core tenets undergirding regulatory logic of the time.

Following what many considered the disastrous outcomes of the first Open Internet debate (and, adding insult to injury, the subsequent approval of Comcast's takeover of NBC Universal fast on its heels), in the public interest community, a return of left-capture arguments rode once again to the fore; attention shifted to bought-off staffers, to revolving doors—that is, industry representatives that circulate in and out of government, perhaps finding a perch at a think tank or friendly university setting until political winds shift and they can reenter an administration. There is much truth to this: cable giant Comcast cynically hired away numerous staffers from FCC offices that had been sympathetic to media reformers' causes in its endgame. Staffers of congressional actors friendly to the concerns of activists went to work for powerful telecommunications and cable giants. Reacting to such overwhelming power, Josh Silver, one of the original founders of Free Press, left the organization to return to his old bailiwick—campaign finance reform—by founding a new organization, United Republic (later Represent.us), to address these issues head on. The long-standing frame of a bought commission, of "capture," of the public interest deferred continues to operate in the minds of Washington advocates, and not for bad reason. President Obama's selection of Tom Wheeler to take the FCC's reins from Julius Genachowski—someone seen as a darling to the cable and telecom lobbies—intensified these forebodings. With the election of Donald Trump and his subsequent appointment of regulators who saw their job as the dismantling of the agencies they led, frames of capture and corruption became central. If past officials at least attempted to maintain a veneer of distance from the industries they oversaw, this new crop was almost purposively blatant about their intentions.

In numerous regards, however, this frame seems incomplete and only partially satisfying, and not necessarily because of the apparent surprise of it being Wheeler that ushered in Open Internet rules that were stronger than any activists believed were possible to obtain. The circumstances surrounding this frame have changed, such that there is in fact a unity in both activists' failure in 2010 and their success in 2015; the thread even continues through the quick and dramatic Trump FCC reversal of their gains. Even more so, the sky-high theories of regulation that have developed over the past decades are similarly unavailing. This is because such analyses examine the actions of regulatory officials after the decisions are done: they study the actions of political movements, perhaps the key stances and their arguments as rendered at the end of the process. Left behind are these arguments in their formative state. It is to these that we need to turn: not just an analysis of "who controls the FCC," for it is quite clear by the actions of the agency that effective "control" continues to lie in the hands of those who seek to continue building the capitalist order in its own image for years to come, and here, we reach a dead end. In short, these theories of regulation and capture ask the wrong questions for our task at hand.

Discourse and Views "from Below"

What all of these theories miss is an "angle from below." How one interprets the political environment matters: it shapes how actors working purportedly for the public interest in attempting to shift national policy and beyond respond in policy settings; it shapes their understandings of what is possible; and even outside the proverbial beltway, it shapes how one views policymaking, period. Even more importantly, it shapes the kinds of activism that forms around an objective of changed policy. It is necessary to add one more narrative to a story of "capture" and money in politics. The story I tell (and my theorization of the quandary itself) is hardly meant to supersede any of the large number of theories surrounding questions of regulatory capture, structural analysis of numerous stripes, and so forth; rather, my tale acts as an overlay to such thinking.

When one looks at the arguments surrounding the "network neutrality" concept as it formed, the more one realizes that during those moments in the late 1990s and early 2000s something discernibly changed in terms of the manner in which public interest advocates were addressing the emergent broadband problem, and this stemmed from the way in which the argument itself shifted. This transformation in debate, and how it then proceeded to unfold in the halls of power in Washington, DC, was revealing in terms of how one needed to interact with policy players: the network neutrality debate revealed if not the shortcomings then the limits of activism today. Ironically, the success of advocates in 2015 is equally revealing of this. Given the role of the Internet in intensifying the broader sales effort, it seems appropriate to borrow an old notion to tackle a new issue: James Rorty, the advertising man turned radical of the Great Depression, drew a similar frustration as I have in addressing critiques of "advertising": "The advertising business is quite literally the business nobody knows; nobody, including, or perhaps more especially, advertising men.... The error here is that of mistaking a function of the thing for the thing itself" (Rorty, 2004, p. 132). What Rorty meant was that to only examine the function of a thing like advertising (to sell products) is to miss the story entirely. The advertising business encompassed all who carried ads and sold ad space as well as the advertisers themselves; the implication was that the public was part of a large-scale training exercise in consumerism. Too many critiques addressed only the offensiveness or dishonesty of specific campaigns. Similarly, theories of regulation and stories which limit their tale of network neutrality to 2005 (or even 2002) onward mistake the function of the debate for the debate itself in a similar fashion: that is, they miss what undercurrents were in play at propelling this debate forward in a seemingly inexorable direction. In order to access this dimension of it, new tacks must be taken: ones that, perhaps ironically, view discourse as a material construct and examine it as such, ones that seek to examine what arguments, actions, and beyond are structurally erased by the current conjuncture.

Discursive analyses, then, could prove enlightening; several appeared both in the midst of the original fights of the first decade of the 2000s and shortly after the issuance of the initial 2010 *Open Internet Order*. The efforts to evaluate the network neutrality debate from such a dimension (loosely defined) tend to fall victim to several errors. For one, they tend to fall victim to the timeframe error of considering post-2005 the core of the debate. For another, they become trapped within the discursive framework within which network neutrality operated, not realizing their own confinement. For instance, Cherry (2007) sought to augment arguments that material power imbalances were primarily responsible for dominant broadband players' success at pushing back against activist demands. She notes, "Although resource differentials between issue proponents and opponents may be an important factor affecting agenda success or failure, in many circumstances this explanation is insufficient" (p. 581). Rather, "symbolic and cultural strategies," as "agenda denial," were every bit as important a set of tactics whereby opponents can "define issues and their proponents in ways that make active consideration of issues less likely" (p. 581). Noting a range of strategies available, ranging from "low cost" ones (denial; nonconfrontation) to escalatory practices (discrediting advocacy groups or the issue itself; admitting problems but offering nonavailing solutions) to "high-cost strategies" (violence; economic threats), she seeks to elucidate the ways in which opponents to network neutrality committed flaws in their own reasoning. For her, the ball was in network neutrality opponents' court: "The burden within the debate may need to shift to opponents to justify their claims that failure to impose network neutrality will likely not create greater negative consequences. Similarly, they also challenge the adequacy and wisdom of the FCC's strategies of symbolic placation"

(p. 592). This conclusion is opposed to that of Clark (2007), who put the onus on activists: proponents' proposals needed to be "clear and workable," and despite shifts taking place,

> At the moment, the ball is in the court of those who favor network neutrality. They have the responsibility to propose a set of definitions for the dividing line between acceptable and unacceptable discrimination. The issue is complex, and Washington likes simple cartoons. Most of what we have seen so far (in my opinion) either greatly overreaches, or is so vague as to be nothing but a lawyer's employment act. (Clark, 2007, p. 708)

In a different vein, Powell and Cooper (2011) argued that what was needed is analysis of "the nature of the relationship between advocacy and regulation, particularly…the way that arguments flow between advocates and regulators" (p. 314). They sought to draw conclusions about the relationships between arguments offered both for network neutrality and against it, the media treatments of these arguments, and how regulatory bodies responded to such agenda setting by media entities. In the United States, the authors identify five principal themes which emerged: problems of definition, free speech and democracy, innovation and investment, competition and market forces, and history and precedent. Advocates established the frames for debate, and the media performed an agenda-setting function in selecting "specific arguments to surface in the popular press" which depended on "the substance of each particular argument" (p. 316). Regulators purportedly "incorporate[d] ideas from among the established advocacy frames and arguments reflected in the media into their own regulatory work" (p. 316). They note that with the entry of the Obama administration itself seemingly "less ideologically inclined to rely solely on market forces" (a questionable assertion itself), media narratives of the previous years which emphasized market abilities to discipline operators "became less visible in regulatory discourse" (p. 321). It "speaks to the limits of the agenda-setting function that the media can play" (p. 321). This completely misreads the situation. Mistaking lip service for impact, they state, "The competition arguments provide perhaps the greatest proof that, in some cases, regulators will do what they do regardless of external influence. In the United States, despite support for free market idealism in the mass media, the FCC's more recent statements have acknowledged the limits of the current market structure and the need for regulatory action" (p. 323).

The mistake that all here make is in their assumption that these arguments themselves are what, in the last analysis, affect the end decisions being contemplated by regulators. They are important; they must be argued; but these arguments fulfilled an entirely different function stemming from the epistemic environment in which they were couched. In Powell and Cooper's case, they get it backward: regulators do what they desire in the endgame; but the arguments themselves serve an entirely different function than informing end actions, although they could. Long-term staff at the FCC were, and are, sincerely interested in the minutiae of policy debates. One interviewee from the Office of Strategic Planning and Policy Analysis wished my project would address how to make the process actually work. The fact of the matter, however, is that these debates were all about legitimating actors in the hopes that they obtained the ear of decision makers in the end, at which point pure politics takes over.

One may rightly ask at this point, how exactly is policy made? The FCC as an institution is bound by law to fully justify the decisions that it makes. Many issues decided by the commission are fairly straightforward affairs, but on emergent issues with many stakeholders, a usual pattern is generally followed on the surface. Regarding an issue of great consequence and which might represent a shift in policy—or just to think through the applicability of law on a new technology—the agency will often first issue a Notice of Inquiry (generally abbreviated as NOI) and offer interested parties the ability to respond, including the general public. The submission of comments is now primarily done online via the FCC's "Electronic Comment Filing System" (ECFS), and this produces a searchable database anyone with Web access (and a fast-enough connection) can explore at will.[5] Various issues or proceedings are assigned their own "docket" numbers; with this, one can explore every comment submitted on an issue. If one meets with the Commission in private about an issue currently under debate in one of the agency's official dockets, one must also (by law) file what is termed an *ex parte* notice in ECFS describing one's conversation. (These, of course, can be maddeningly vague: somewhat unethically, but hardly illegally, interests may sometimes just note something as basic as "We discussed recent spectrum policy decisions with the commissioner regarding our interests" with few scant other details to enable response.) After a Notice of Inquiry, the FCC may move on to a Notice of Proposed Rulemaking (NPRM) on an issue, producing a document of proposed plans of action and offering them up for comment as well aboard ECFS. The end result of this process produces a Report and Order (R&O) in which a final decision is made and announced that (also by law) must address the comments put into the proceeding. Perhaps more questions are raised for further examination, in which case the FCC will offer a Report and Order and Further Notice of Proposed Rulemaking (or a Further Notice of Inquiry), reduced in shorthand in policy documents to the alphabet soup "R&O & FNPRM" or "R&O & FNOI." It is unusual to offer a Report and Order on a new issue (or, for that matter, a Notice of Proposed Rulemaking) before holding a Notice of Inquiry on the implications or legal justifications at stake on the issue, although it happens; and Notices of Proposed Rulemaking, particularly on network neutrality, have largely served as the vehicles for policy discussion rather than Notices of Inquiry, although NOIs have been offered. Report and Orders then simply reference outstanding and undecided NOIs in an R&O on a particular NPRM, as decisions reference anywhere from one to many dockets at once in the official record.[6] Any decision rendered via these documents can be subject to a lawsuit by interested parties in the U.S. circuit courts, and these courts have "remanded" FCC decisions numerous times, in which case the FCC must take another go at the proceeding. The process produces tremendous amounts of documentation justifying incremental (and sometimes monumental) decisions, all open to public examination.

That, of course, is the formal process; but formal processes always ride on the backs of more informal ones. The seeming staid rationality of any proceeding very effectively masks the raw political machinations undergirding it. One ex-FCC staffer, who would only speak on background, confided in me one of his experiences. One particular set of deliberations revolved around the revision of a form that companies would need to submit. A rulemaking was on offer in this regard. Involved in the making of any such policy in the end involves "the spreadsheet," quite literally an Excel spreadsheet "that describes the comments, gives quotes, page numbers, general issues also keyed to comments." The staffer didn't really know what happened "higher up the [staff] food chain," but there was generally a good-faith effort to get all offered comments in. "Now, the 'fun' part doesn't really start until late," he told me. "Often these orders aren't really ready until the last minute. On this particular proceeding, we worked until midnight—often these things really even take longer. There was a chart up on the white board put up by the deputy bureau chief. Along the top were each of the commissioners beside" the chairman's. The chairman's "own positions would be along the left side: via a check-box approach this was where the ending 'balancing' goes on." He paused for a minute. "I'll never forget that white board. In the end it comes down to the white board. Every so often the chairman's legal aide would step in and monitor the discussion, seeking enough on each side"—here, meaning Democratic or Republican—"to make the thing 'passable' even with dissentions" by other commissioners.

What the network neutrality debate exhibited all along was a form of "processing bias": the arguments themselves, in their processing by all players involved, needed to hew to a particular set of terms to matter as an actor where decisions were made. As long as one pursued the debate in these terms, one mattered; when one deviated, one ceased to be seriously considered. The process of legitimation was intimately tied to epistemic currents flowing underneath of long vintage. This book argues that these are pivotal for activists to understand, as they inform not just the legitimation process, but also the assumptions of those who get to sit at that table in the end. Calls for advocates to recognize the "complexity" of network neutrality were effectively both poison pill and an invitation to be taken seriously at one and the same time.

Yet something even deeper is in play. To wit: Cherry (2007) argues that there was an overemphasis and reliance on antitrust in these debates, but one may interpret her broader points to indicate she feels that this stemmed from a short-term discursive strategy. She would then be incorrect on two counts. For one, arguably, opponents of network neutrality turn out not to be the ones which initiated the shift: it would be its original advocate, Wu, which sturdied the bridge to this realm. For another, this was no short-term strategy; undertaken knowingly or not as such by partisans involved, it was part of a long-standing strategy, decades old, in which all actors found themselves swept up. Cherry, in particular, mistakes "agenda conflict" and "denial" for the real issue: opponents' rhetorical strategies are important but in a different sense than she believes.

In this vein, perhaps one of the more revealing documents which emerged from the debates surrounding the 2010 order was Robert Atkinson's "Economic Doctrines and Network Policy" (2011). Atkinson, as head of the Information Technology and Innovation Foundation, was one of the "think tank" actors in the network neutrality debate and largely urged a hands-off stance by the FCC on the issue. The foundation, of course, finds support (both monetary and board of directors-wise) in the corporate actors most interested in the issue. This article, however, is a key example of discourse analysis as maintenance of a particular "processing." "While many network policy issues have an engineering basis, with disagreements revolving around technical matters, much of network policy is based on economics," he argues. He adopts an undertheorized and simplistic amalgam of epistemic determinism at an individual level:

> When considering economic issues it is important to realize that much of what appears to be objective theorizing and unbiased analysis is in fact deeply shaped by the doctrine of the economist. Economists' and policy makers' beliefs about what policy works best for the economy, including their beliefs about the appropriate types and roles of network policy, are not simply independent constructs applied to new contexts; rather such beliefs constitute an area reflection of coherent world views or doctrines. Such doctrines profoundly shape how proponents view the economy, what they consider important, and most importantly, what they believe to be correct vs. misguided public policy. These economic doctrines guide thinking and help individuals make sense of a complex, rapidly evolving economy. (Atkinson, 2011, p. 414)

His revealed taxonomy would be unavailing. Tim Wu, who approached the issue (in his own words) from an evolutionary innovation perspective, is called by Atkinson "the most prominent" neo-Keynesian of the debate among a field of "conservative neoclassicals," "liberal neoclassicals," "neo-Keynesians," and "innovation economists." But no matter: a warped taxonomy is not the key issue here. No, this article attempts to perform an entirely different set of labors. First, it is an effort to divide up a field of players into "classifiable" quantities—significant in itself. Second, it performs a far grander function to boot: it hides what really amounts to a great uniformity in the thinking behind broadband policy by advocates and opponents alike under what appears to be a thesis of debate among seemingly incommensurable positions. Third, it aims to re-anchor the debate within an exclusively economic framework. To my knowledge, this article has hardly been a pivotal piece in debates that have grown since: yet as an artifact of the network neutrality struggle, it is a near-perfect illustration.

Harold Feld—a prominent advocate, now based at Public Knowledge but formerly part of Washington's now-defunct Media Access Project—noted his puzzlement at Republican inclusion of a line in their 2012 platform against network neutrality. In doing so, he provided another lens on the discursive elements of this quandary. By 2010, most of the industry participants were satisfied with the emerging outcome at the FCC (even as pro-network neutrality advocates took issue with the emerging consensus), and usually when that happens, the issue slips away. For him, a key question he wanted answered about the proceeding was: why did Congress still care, after the proceeding was over, when AT&T, Comcast, and "all of the cable guys" didn't, and even Verizon wasn't that big on it?

> Everybody comes into this on the assumption that "of course, industry drove this" ... what you really ought to ask is why, after industry called it quits, is this still on the top-five list of republican boogeymen? Why is it that in 2008, this shows up as a Democratic issue on the Democratic platform, and why is it that it shows up as a Republican issue on the 2012 Republican platform? What happened? And why, particularly in the Republican case, when all of the industry interest had gone away? It's not that the industry guys don't care, wouldn't be unhappy to see the rule go, but nobody in particular was very excited about it. ... If you ask that question, and don't treat the political outcome as a foregone conclusion, and instead ask why the issue is still around and work backwards from there, I think you come to some very interesting results. (Personal communication, September 27, 2012)

Feld puts his finger on what was so frustrating regarding the current "debates" swirling around this issue and how circular they became. Even as we witnessed a bifurcation between those who either approved of the idea (and actively pushed for it) or those opposed, there was a lack of any work that took a longer view. So much of the analysis examined the issue *as the issue itself,* taking one side or another. While seemingly a banal observation of little use, it turns out that this is significant. One reads the literature looking for surprises, and there are none to be found: immense as the literature is, if one decided to download the thousands of articles and decide to classify them, few wouldn't end up easily classifiable as "for" the issue and those "against." However, the partisan nature of the fight served to hide this ruse. The translation of this theoretical debate into one of party affiliation was a necessary and brilliant move to ensure that the mutually sustained trajectory of both sides remained obscured.

Reconsidering How We Tell the Story of Network Neutrality

Knowledge itself has become one of the chief pawns on the strategic board in politics: less in terms of determining truths than in determining whose views should be present when the major decisions are decided. The networks of economists who derided both open access and network neutrality policies may believe that they are influencing policy: yet one of the surprises of the network neutrality debate, and one of the things that it signals about our age, is that their "findings" hardly matter. It was merely these players' involvement in instilling a particular mode of processing the debate which mattered. These are two different things, and this one of the reasons it is so difficult to actually size up the quality or value of "contributions" to the network neutrality debate when one is taking in the long view.

The emergence and transformation of the open access debate into one exclusively about network neutrality is both a story of an emergent political ensemble as well as the fruits of a particular epistemic regime, materially sustained. A kind of reflection has commenced in the academy in exactly this regard. Streeter (2011) discerns in discourses surrounding the Internet and its development a persistent strain of romanticism of long vintage, and he offers a warning: "It is [a] habit of understanding freedom negatively, blindly, as freedom from government, freedom from dependency, freedom from others, that helps set the conditions for the popularity of the rights-based free market" (p. 13). His interest is not "What is the effect of the Internet on society?" but "How has the Internet been socially constructed and what role has that process of construction played in society?" Further, even more important sets of questions include (pp. 8-9), "How have various shared visions, even the inaccurate ones, shaped policymaking around the Internet? How have they shaped its construction and, therefore, its character, its role in social life? How have culture and policy interacted to make the Internet what it is?" In reality, his conception is not so far afield from Sum and Jessop's (2003) notion of "cultural political economy."

Streeter's emphasis is on the cultural meanings created by technology and how forces like the media reform movement have served to impact it: "The technology of the Internet is not inherently democratic, but interesting and rich experiments in how to do democracy have happened so frequently on the Internet that we have come to expect them there and have been building that expectation into its legal regulation and underlying code base to the extent that it is now a tradition" (pp. 186–187). Perhaps the most crucial element of Streeter's analysis for our purposes here is his concern that activism surrounding the Internet has been ensnared in exactly this mode of thinking. To diagnose the problem, he points directly to one of the most prominent voices on the subject of network neutrality and open access, Lawrence Lessig (see, e.g., Lessig, 2002), contrasting his thought with that of James Boyle:

> If Boyle was calling for his readers to abandon an obsession with the abstract free individual and start thinking more complexly about the social conditions that support innovation and culture, Lessig presented the choice as a simple, stark one: Lessig titled one essay, "An Information Society: Free or Feudal?" While standing alongside Boyle in attacking the libertarian notion that markets and private property are the sole guarantors of freedom, Lessig seemed to concede to the libertarians one thing that Boyle did not: the idea that freedom itself is a simple condition, an absence of constraint, the ability of individuals to do what they want, especially to express themselves, to engage their creativity. Boyle approached the romantic ideal of individualism skeptically. Lessig embraced it. (Streeter, 2011, pp. 163–164)

In his view, the likes of McChesney and Lessig (and the broader pro-network neutrality forces writ large) make appeals to a reification of a particular configuration of technology as "the way it should be" thanks to its inherent democratic possibility. For Streeter, this is flawed. The technological arguments lauding end-to-end network neutrality rest, he argues, on a "frail foundation"—that is, it reads "political morality tales" into technical successes, a reappearance of this "romanticism," that "as often as not have dissolved under the weight of experience" (Streeter, 2011, p. 184).

There is much to admire in Streeter's observations. This said, I do fear that he doesn't take the network neutrality debate seriously enough. Not because I believe he ignores the potential of particular formations of capital to constrain online activity, to restrict access to communications technologies, and to colonize whatever benefit users obtain from connectivity; rather, he leaves the story off where it needs to continue. Streeter's earlier assessment of the inside debates within Washington, DC, addressed via his discussions of interpretive communities with their own rules and interests in his *Selling the Air* (1996) perhaps come closer to the mark in regard to what is going on: the connection between the two arguments needs to be made. There, he powerfully lays out a concept of "corporate liberalism" which serves as the overriding policy prerogative throughout the creation of broadcast and cable policy, one that appears to apply in this instance. This represents a taken-for-granted notion that broadcasting—if not all media production—was *appropriately* commercial in nature. "Corporate liberalism," he argues,

> is ... in the first instance a set of values and forms of social life that helped resolve conflicts and knit together the diverse interests and points of view of the Progressive Era into a relatively stable social formation. As an underlying framework for understanding and legitimating the US political economy, corporate liberalism has persisted, with variations, for the rest of this century, providing a set of shared values and assumptions to the mainstreams of the business community and the Republican and Democratic parties. (Streeter, 1996, p. 41)

Throughout the twentieth century, this understanding never came under attack; in fact in the policymaking process itself, to question it is to render oneself "impractical" and thus outside the norms of respectable debate. "The point is not to criticize liberalism as a philosophy in the abstract but to show how the sheer fact of broadcasting simultaneously brings attention to liberalism's power as an imaginative system and to its contradictions" (Streeter, 1996, p. 11).

I argue that these discourse communities ride aboard an epistemic substratum which itself must be addressed in its own terms. While "corporate liberalism" might prove a useful construct to explain this, something more dynamic is going on, something captured better in the sense of a "thought collective." This substratum is hardly the driver of policy: but it slicks the way for policy to happen, often divorced of the content of this substratum entirely. One of the paradoxes of the network neutrality debate is that I fear it inscribed a particular "epistementality"—think, here, of Foucault's governmentality extended to a new register—all the more deeply upon the American psyche. When Streeter shunts aside McChesney and Lessig's concerns, he too shunts aside the case that this thing/event called "network neutrality"—as an ensemble, the arguments both for and against, and the manners in which they engaged—met the emergent needs of capital quite cleanly. That reason alone is reason to be concerned, one level removed from the arguments for or against its imposition. What Streeter does not address is the material-epistemic formation of this new controlling form of thought in the guise of what amounts to a platform for debate.

The struggle for network neutrality in the United States on the surface seemed to mesh well with the goals of a vibrant free press and diverse forms of expression and experimentation; at the same time, it fed in the material and cultural manner it was fought into the continued constitution of what autonomist theorists have termed the "social factory." This theoretical construct posits a world in which everyday efforts and activities are not so much colonized by capital interests than channeled to capital's benefit; despite this quandary, the network neutrality debates were both necessary and essential for the preservation of continued diverse expression aboard the newly dominant medium of our age, even as they inscribed more deeply a power structure that finds new ways to incorporate lived experience into profitable revenue streams. The Internet is one such vehicle; as Turow (2011) documents, actions aboard this vehicle are increasingly combined with those off of it, all put exactly to such channeling, sold into global capital flows in zero-sum games or into the machinery expanding the sales effort. As efforts contained in Fumagalli and Mezzandra (2010) and Negri (2008) make clear through concepts of the "communism of capital"—the channeling not only of individual neoliberal subjects' identities and actions but their savings as well, put to the use of broad financial interests to their own ends—entire ways of being, accumulating, and living have become fodder permitting capitalist systems to continue to grow or, at the very least, reproduce itself and stave off crisis. It makes perfect sense that one of Google's chief executives would travel to North Korea to press for "Internet freedom" there; the notion's complex history and the complications of operating within it are becoming clear (Connor, 2013; see also more broadly Powers & Jablonski, 2015).

In the global arena, pursuing "Internet freedom" ambivalently serves the coordinating needs of capital and finance as well as the desires of individuals to communicate and coordinate their own activities—the price of admission for new entrants amounts to the conscription of new populations' activities and identities to Google's data banks and beyond. Control in today's age, as scholarship increasingly is at pains to show, is less about overt constraint than it is about "nudging" and valuation of marketing targets (Cheney-Lippold, 2011, 2017; Pasquale, 2015; Turow, 2011). "Internet freedom" and, perhaps even more crucially, the simple notion of access which rose emergent from the network neutrality debates, themselves need to be viewed and reevaluated in this light: individual freedoms online exist uncomfortably next to the extant desires of capitalist expansion or, really, redistribution; and this is to put aside the material consequences of increased use of such technologies such as e-waste, the transformation of local economies by the building of server farms or warehousing, and beyond (Maxwell & Miller, 2012). In fact, media are themselves becoming enveloped as part and parcel of logistical chains which comprise what

Srnicek (2017) has termed "platform capitalism," one component—and an important one—in what Zuboff (2015, 2019) has termed the "Big Other."

The irony is that in the end, once the debates calcified around 2005 and 2006, it is quite possible that network neutrality as a debate turned out to be one of the chief wings of the social factory itself—one necessary to sustain, one necessary to fight, yet one that enabled in the background, behind our backs, for the overarching sales effort at its core to expand in new and dynamic ways—often antidemocratic. This bears reiteration. The efforts to "Save the Internet" went well beyond freedom of speech. It had become about the defense of a particular mode of life, and one rushes to note that this is not of a particularly romanticist notion. Hearn's (2008) description of the neoliberal self, and the observation of autonomist scholars who argue that today's forms of production and labor are "progressively 'articulated' in (and commanded by) valorization and accumulation processes of capital that function according to a logic that differs from 'industrial' logic" (Mezzandra, 2010, pp. 11–12), lead one to conclude that the urge to "Save the Internet" was as much about communities saving themselves as much as it was about any right to free expression. The irony may be that the mechanisms by which this activism was undergone may have served to entwine activists even more tightly into a set of systems against which they were struggling. As Streeter notes, big ideas, such as the perfection of markets "or an enthusiasm for digital democracy, are sometimes brought in to help individuals account for and connect their everyday experiences with machines to life as a whole rather than the other way around" (Streeter, 2011, p. 7).

This requires us to rethink the constitution of network neutrality itself, stepping back into debates long thought settled, over with, irrelevant. The unifying thread throughout our story is explored by Banet-Weiser (2012) in her identification of exactly this form of ambivalence in today's consumer capitalism, the necessity of the fight even as a necessary entwinement occurred. How Banet-Weiser handles the corporate power versus consumer power angle is productive: rather than seeing the struggle as one for or against capital, analysis should rather seek to explicate the ambiguities and ambivalences involved. "Concentrating on individual and corporate uses of power ... obscures the ways in which other entangled discourses in culture are deeply interrelated within it. ... [P]ower does not always work in a predictable, logical way, as something either corporations or individuals can possess and wield. Power is often exercised in contradictory ways, ... often holding possibility for individual resistance and corporate hegemony simultaneously" (Banet-Weiser, 2012, p. 12). A "nostalgia for authenticity" which posits cleaner struggles simply hides more than it reveals.

Knowledge, and Its Material Buttress

Knowledge itself has received renewed interest in the communications policy world, preceding the now-rampant discussions grappling with what appears a "post truth" era. Speaking during the years of the George W. Bush administration, Napoli and Seaton (2007) themselves noted what they saw as three trends at the time: "the growing importance of empirical research to public policymaking, the increased reliance of policymakers on externally conducted research, and the increased privatization of the key data utilized in policy analysis" that "contribute to a growing imbalance that can undermine effective and representative communications policymaking" (p. 330). In particular, their concern is the increased collection of data of public importance by private firms whose rates or practices render their information out of reach to many. Utilizing the FCC's 2003 loosening of media ownership rules as a case study, they take special note of the difficulty that public interest players faced in attempting to obtain access to proprietary data necessary to make their case. Ultimately, protection orders required researchers to use data on-site under time and other constraints. From this study and their overview, they make several recommendations. While laws as the Data Access Act and Data Quality Acts address publicly created data, the fact of the matter is that private sources are more important today: the FCC should actively collect data, in their view, perhaps even taking up the suggestion of the likes of Thomas Wolf's 1983 proposal to have a "data collection agency" to collect such information but not necessarily perform analysis on it. "Such an approach would be particularly desirable in that it would allow for a better tailoring of the data being gathered to the nature of the policy issues generally requiring attention. This would stand in stark contrast to the contemporary situation, in which data gathered to serve entirely different needs (i.e., the needs of communications firms, investors, and advertisers) are essentially 'repurposed' to address policy questions" (Napoli & Seaton, 2007, p. 323). By the same token, other researchers, such as Consumer Federation of America's Mark Cooper, were leery of any government agency being chiefly responsible for research or data collection, because once the findings were released, debate would end: the answer would be found, according to that agency's chiefs, with no further question necessary! Rather, what was truly lacking in all processes was adequate opportunity for cross examination (personal communication, September 21, 2012). In short, however, and providing a unifying thread, all desired data collection done free of market imperatives. Similar to a plea made by Napoli (2001) earlier in the decade, all here sought to involve more communications scholarship in the policymaking process. Free Press itself for a time attempted to create a short-lived "brain trust" of communications scholars, and several communications departments teamed up to send graduate students to Washington so as to encourage such engagement (Newman, 2009).

How quaint such questions have seemed to become as discerning the role and value of research in policymaking today has become quite murky. It surely proliferates, but is mobilized in different ways, to different ends across varying levels of our governmental infrastructure; but this is hardly also to argue that a great discontinuity has transpired. Rarely have scholars approached questions of policy, particularly a policy as critical as the operation of broadband networks, from the standpoint of the *historical and material constitution* of knowledge formations: a political economy of knowledge-formation, so to speak. Braman (2003) performed yeoman's work in assembling and synthesizing a broad set of articles regarding communications-oriented research in policymaking; therein, she notes a broad cycle which transpired through the twentieth century in relation to the roles knowledge production played, from bursts of enthusiasm for its inclusion in the mid-twentieth century to erosions of faith in it in the 1980s; she notes that in putting together the Telecommunications Act of 1996 that "there was very little influence on this rewrite of the Communications Act of 1934 from stakeholders other than large corporations and next to no research input" (Braman, 2003, p. 6). Streeter (1996, pp. 141–142) traces out the various strains of analysis vogue as well, from the heyday of positivist social science in the 1960s and 1970s before neoclassical methods supplanted them in the 1980s. Both Braman and Streeter note the challenges that scholars face in the policymaking realm in terms of making their work matter. A conference panel Streeter describes from the mid-1990s that featured policymakers speaking to the ways scholars could make their work more resonant (and the contradictions contained therein) have mirrored discussions since; *there* is a discussion that has moved nary an inch in decades. Communications scholarship in particular struggled in the 1990s for relevance, note Napoli and Friedland (2016)—both Braman (2003) and Streeter (1996) note the same—but express optimism in this shifting going forward. Lazarsfeld's (2004 [1941]) distinctions between "administrative" and "critical" research continue to resonate as categories, even as few would dispute that administrative research is, in many ways, critical in the same way that positive social science always contains normative elements. Structural features of the modern world have eroded the distinction; Braman (2004) similarly notes that to truly understand policymaking processes one must take into account seemingly "hidden" dimensions of policymaking—those moments when policy is indirectly affected, or made in realms other than in policymaking bodies, or when they "precess" across numerous dimensions, a notion that is distinct from a far simpler conception of path dependence. In considering factors which play no small role in agenda setting, Braman (2003) also performs the valuable labor of pointing to the material support that entities such as the Markle, Ford, Benton, Rockefeller, and Carnegie Foundations have provided in the creation of policy-oriented research. In terms of immediate pressures on continued production of academic knowledge and its access, while the Social Science Research Network has provided an independent and not-for-profit hub, as of mid-2016, it "joined" academic publisher Elsevier (Gordon, 2016), stoking fears that paywalls or other monetization practices were in the offing.

Yet stories of the generation of knowledge in the policymaking realm, even when such matters are considered, seem often to imply a quest for objective truth. Rather, seen as one process that feeds into broader processes proves a more revealing horizon: as part of a trajectory, of an initiative in play, at a distance removed from the topics of analysis. That is, the ontologies of approaches noted by Braman and Streeter were not created equal. This is a critical point because *taken as an artifact*, the *production* of the network neutrality debates themselves have much to tell us about challenges activists faced—why they faced such early disappointments in working with the Obama administration which purportedly shared their views; why even in subsequently winning strong antidiscrimination rules the neoliberal drive settled in more deeply; and why the Trump FCC's reversal of their gains represents continuity, not aberration. Policy and activist battles of the late 2000s and early 2010s are imbricated in the neoliberal project—and *project* is the correct term. In terms of a particular mode of governmentality in the abstract, Foucault's (2008) relatively recently published lectures from 1978 to 1979 provide initial insight. Foucault rightly recognized in the epistemic content of neoliberalism a constructed manageability out of chaos: the neoliberal "*Homo aeconomicus* is someone who is eminently governable," as compared to the *Homo aeconomicus* of classical liberalism which "basically functions as what could be called an intangible element with regard to the exercise of power" (p. 270).

Brown (2015) has powerfully built upon these lectures in recent work, expressing a worry that for the first time in Western history, we may have created a historical subjectivity which expressly, by its very nature, lacks a political side: when each of us has been recast *as* capitals in competition with each other, the embedded rationalities contained therein eliminate politics writ large. In her exploration of the concept and her call for a renewed democracy—importantly, one that needs to be struggled for, built, defended—she is perturbed at the growth of exactly these logics. While neoliberalism in itself, she notes, is often defined in terms of intensified inequality, rampant commercialization, increased intimacy between corporate and finance capital and the state, and their combined results—bubble bursts, austerity as a response (pp. 28–30)—she offers a useful corrective. "In contrast with an understanding of neoliberalism as a set of state policies, a phase of capitalism, or an ideology that set loose the market to restore profitability for a capitalist class," she writes, she conceives neoliberalism "as an order of normative reason that, when it becomes ascendant, takes shape as a governing rationality extending a specific formulation of economic values, practices, and metrics to every dimension of daily life" (p. 30). Such insight leads us away from the trap of confusing the *marketing* of the orthodoxies or the stances of powerful capitalist interests via think tanks and "bought research" for their *constitution*. Hers is a call to discover this rationality in its construction. The development of network neutrality was one channel among many aboard which these circuits were set and sometimes short-circuited. It serves to elucidate in concrete terms how this process works, how it plays out, how in both victory and defeat we find not a sudden break in favor of a revitalized or desiccated *demos* but instead a continuity playing out, one which constricts the terms of debate, renders them intractable; it is this very intractability which breeds new ground for argument which in fact renders a paradoxical stasis while simultaneously in motion. If Brown is arguing for a new, revitalized democracy, in concrete terms we might interpret this as the shattering of exactly this stasis. How it developed, how it is maintained, on whose terms—all of this must be explored in their materiality to understand our present age. In doing so, we realize how particular aspects of debate are rendered *erased* in the technopolitics of network neutrality in their transformation from "open access" debates into network neutrality debates—and then the debates that emerged transcendent from still those.

I am careful, yet, to heed the warnings here of Harvey (2005) that the broader regime that surfaces is *not* simply "an example of erroneous theory gone wild (*pace* the economist Stiglitz) or a case of senseless pursuit of a false utopia (*pace* the conservative political philosopher John Gray)" (p. 152). The development of the broader system's theoretical underpinnings matters and has its own materiality: network neutrality does not exist in a vacuum, a simple matter of corporate power versus the people. These undercurrents have *everything* to do with how its emergence and transformation out of open access took place, if indirectly yet effectively via the construction of a *platform* aboard which these debates would happen.

These currents' material origins have commenced being traced. Whereas Foucault (and, subsequently, Brown) spoke of the development of neoliberalism in the abstract and pointed toward many of the same roots—such as the postwar emergence in Germany of a particular brand of *Ordoliberalism* rightly seen as a fellow traveler to what would emerge in the United States—Dieter Plehwe (2009), joined by Philip Mirowski and numerous other collaborators, sought to shift understanding to the actual *production of knowledge* itself surrounding neoliberalism. Mirowski, an economic historian and a member of the diaspora of the now-disbanded heterodox program at the University of Notre Dame—this closure itself an indication of the times we occupy if there ever was one—has done work that fills a gaping hole in communications research; it begs to be built upon. "It is not enough to rest satisfied merely pointing at the seemingly potent generic political power of economic ideas, as did both John Maynard Keynes and Friedrich Hayek," he writes; one needs to "better understand the political and economic power of neoliberal ideas as they nave played out in philosophy, economics, law, political science, history, sociology, and many other disciplines" (Mirowski, 2009, p. 433). As opposed to defining neoliberalism as merely a concrete set of principles—or worse, conflating it merely with neoclassical economic theory itself—it needs to be viewed as a project of a loosely bound *thought collective* with a set of epistemic commitments rooted well beyond economics, reaching into politics and even science.[7]

As a means of providing one particular "nucleus," these authors use the emergence of the Mont Pèlerin Society (MPS) as one particular "Rosetta Stone" to translate the workings of the neoliberal project as it grew. They are not reductive when they do so; in more recent reflections, Mirowski is careful to note that observing the Mont Pèlerin Society alone is too narrow a focus—the full scope of this project needs to encompass Austrian schools surrounding Hayek, the Chicago School's progeny, more; the MPS is hardly the only site of construction—however, it proves an interesting and useful *rubric* for understanding the storms surrounding its creation. While institutions are important for the spread of ideas,

> Unlike previous histories of ideas, and taking a page from [Friedrich] Hayek's playbook, we have offered an account that strives to understand the fortification of the power of ideas through integration of highly dispersed knowledge capacities within a neoliberal international academy. Whereas leading neoliberals denied any possibility of mere mortals outcompeting the market as processors of highly dispersed knowledge, their own efforts succeeded in constructing and deploying elaborate social machinery designed to collect, create, debate, disseminate, and mobilize neoliberal ideas. By doing so, they greatly advanced the understanding of a modern reengineered division of intellectual labor with proper roles assigned to academic and other professionals, in what amounts to a new technology of persuasion. (Mirowski, 2009, p. 432)

The MPS was in fact an ingenious use of the style of "propaganda" espoused by the likes of Edward Bernays (2004 [1928]): a broad effort to shape the broader environment to create a reality that, naturally chosen by the populace, would create the new "good" society. In the same way that Schiller (2007b) notes that technological convergence was an agenda before it became a technological reality, the precepts of neoliberal thought were wide-ranging and a calculated response to trends that certain business interests found threatening.

While organized by capital concerns in consort with academic interests, this was no attempt to dogmatize academia: they saw mutual cause in the development of wide-ranging theory to confront, at a theoretical level, threats faced from both from left socialism and laissez-faire liberalism. "It was flexible in its intellectual commitments, oriented primarily toward forging some new doctrines that might capture the imaginations of future generations. At various junctures, this might involve unexpected feints to the left as well as to the right" (Plehwe, 2009, p. 14). The group was drawn from multinational sites of origin: any notion that neoliberalism was "made in the USA" is patently incorrect. The movement was hardly anti-union, at least at first; until the mid-1950s, a majority of the MPS considered arrangements between employers and trades beneficial: unionists should be educated as to the advantages of the "free society" being conjured. Only in the late 1950s would this start to change.

The development of the Chicago School of economics that would become so central to legal and antitrust thought over the coming decades was of a piece of the nurture of the MPS. The first meeting of the MPS, Mirowski and Plehwe note, was intimately connected to the development of the school. Friedrich Hayek "provided both the intellectual impetus and the organizational spadework for the Chicago School and the MPS" as corporate funds were raised in Europe by Albert Hunold while the Volker Fund played a similar role in the United States (Van Horn & Mirowski, 2009, pp. 158–159). The funders were very hands-on, leaning heavily on Hayek to keep the project moving (p. 157). Hayek and the Volker Fund recognized it was hardly enough to expect the field of economics to shift itself from within, turning to "professional problem-solvers" who were "scrupulously detached from active politics and from factional affiliations [who would] subtly and unobtrusively guide or arbitrate political debate by their own discussions." The aim was not to "revive a dormant classical liberalism" so much as it was to "forge a neoliberalism better suited to modern conditions" (p. 160). They sought, really, the production of an American version of Hayek's *The Road to Serfdom*. What they got was Milton Friedman's *Capitalism and Freedom*.

While viewed with interest and prodded on by these business interests, the ideas developed organically. The funders saw the development of a philosophy supporting their vision of a free market friendlier to this age's liberal context as an "elegant, sophisticated statement of their worldview" (Phillips-Fein, 2009a, p. 282). The relationship between funder and funded could be bumpy, of course—at times the MPS would be seen as insufficiently supportive—but they saw their mutual usefulness. It was an initiative wrought of a desire to draw in different approaches to the broader project, enabling cross-fertilization. The founding meeting was populated with professors, journalists from *Fortune* and *Newsweek*, foundations, think tank executives, business executives, and publishers of *Readers' Digest*. By 1981, political figures would be included as well (Plehwe, 2009, p. 22).

The loose collective that emerged harbored convergences of interest even as a plurality of opinions surrounding these points existed. Such diversity was actually their strength, however, in their propagation (Steiner, 2009, p. 196). The starting point of this emergent group is that the conditions of their vision for the "good society" would need to be "*constructed* and [would] not come about 'naturally' in the absence of concerted political effort and organization" (Mirowski, 2009, p. 434). This said, they did agree that "for purposes of public understanding and sloganeering, market society must be treated as a 'natural' and inexorable state of humankind. What this meant in practice is that natural science metaphors must be integrated into the neoliberal narrative. It is noteworthy that MPS members began to explore the portrayal of the market as an evolutionary phenomenon long before biology displaced physics as the premier science in the modern world-picture" (pp. 435–436). Because of the need to design this eventuality, the state must be redefined, not destroyed.

> Neoliberals thus maintain an uneasy and troubled alliance with their sometimes fellow travelers, the anarchists and libertarians. The contradiction that the neoliberals constantly struggle against is that a strong state can just as easily thwart their program as implement it; hence, they are inclined to explore new formats of techno-managerial governance that protect their ideal market from what they perceive as unwarranted political interference. (Mirowski, 2009, p. 436)

Democracy, then, needed be rendered "impotent." In lieu of direct input, "accountability" measures are preferred; the privatization of state services, even better. Mirowski is careful to note that none of this means an actual downsizing of the state; it likely only became more unwieldy (Mirowski, 2009, p. 436). (Harvey [2005] makes a similar point, and one need only look at the length of the Telecommunications Act or the Affordable Care Act to confirm). In lieu of democracy, markets are accepted instead to be "an information processor more powerful than any human brain, but essentially patterned on brain/computation metaphors.... [T]he market always surpasses the state's ability to process information, and this constitutes the kernel of the argument for necessary failure of socialism" (Mirowski, 2009,

p. 435; emphasis omitted). The veneer of democracy cannot yet be allowed to fade, however: it is needed to continue legitimating the neoliberal state. The contradiction is dealt with by treating politics as its own marketplace:

> In its most advanced manifestation, there is no separate content of the notion of citizenship other than as customer of state services. This supports the application of neoclassical economic models to previously political topics; but it also explains why the neoliberal movement must seek to consolidate political power by operating from within the state.... The spread of market relations is inevitably spearheaded by state actors.... The "night-watchman" version of the state is thus comprehensively repudiated. (Mirowski, 2009, p. 437)

What is curious is that, if we turn to the consumer society literature, when Ewen (1976) wrote of the changes in the social fabric sought by industrialists of the 1910s and 1920s and their propagandists as Bernays, they envisioned and championed a particular type of consumer society that expressed its choice in the marketplace as necessary for the continuation of a particular mode of capitalism. That is, it did not seek solutions to ills in the collective capabilities of organized people but rather in the large corporations that offered fixes purchasable over a counter. Here is a similar mind-trust operating in a wholly new register, seeking the construction of a particular understanding of society that could serve as a firm buttress for the continuance of a (neo)liberalism friendlier to capital.

Freedom was extolled over all other virtues; yet the notion is never clearly defined. "Freedom," Mirowski notes, "is not the realization of any political, human, or cultural telos, but rather is the positioning of autonomous self-governed individuals, all coming naturally equipped with a neoclassical version of rationality and motives of ineffable self-interest, striving to improve their lot in life by engaging in market exchange" (2009, p. 437). It would be Hayek that struck upon a "double truth" of the new regime; that is, while an "elite would be tutored to understand the deliciously transgressive Schmittian necessity of repressing democracy...the masses would be regaled with ripping tales of 'rolling back the nanny state' and being set 'free to choose'" (Mirowski, 2009, p. 445). The work to transform mere theory into a moral code (p. 440) involves what

> masquerades as a radically populist philosophy, which begins with a set of philosophical theses about knowledge and its relationship to society. It seems to be a radical, leveling philosophy, denigrating expertise and elite pretensions to hard-won knowledge, instead praising the "wisdom of crowds."...In Hayekian

> language, it elevates a "cosmos"—a supposed spontaneous order that no one has intentionally designed to achieve intentional ends. But the second, a linked lesson, is that neoliberals are simultaneously elitists: they do not in fact practice what they preach. When it comes to actually organizing something... suddenly the cosmos collapses to taxis. (Mirowski, 2009, pp. 425–426)

The notion of the "double truth" goes further. Later, in examining the 2008 economic crisis (and the curious survival of the theorizing to which blame might be laid), this extends to both an "exoteric" as well as "esoteric" discourse. "As a corollary of its developed understanding of politics, it would be necessary to maintain an exoteric version of its doctrine for the masses—because that would be safer for the world and more beneficial for ordinary society—but simultaneously hold fast to an esoteric doctrine for a small closed elite, envisioned as the keepers of the flame of the collective's wisdom" (Mirowski, 2013, p. 68). These two doctrines may well, and by necessity, contradict each other, a feature, rather than a bug. "It will be necessary to explore the possibility that these seeming contradictions are not *cynical* in the modality one often encounters in career politicians, but rather grow organically out of the structural positions that motivate the thought collective" (Mirowski, 2013, p. 68). Early studies from the Chicago School—the Chicago School of the likes of Henry Simons—were suspicious of the power of monopoly. By the 1950s this would shift as the Chicago law and economics movement, itself funded by the same benefactors as the MPS, spread to new theoretical treatments of innovation markets, ultimately beginning to argue that monopoly was not so harmful for the operation of the market, itself "an epiphenomenon attributable to the misguided activities of the state and interest groups" (Mirowski, 2009, p. 439; citations omitted). Indeed, "the market (suitably reengineered and promoted) can always provide solutions to problems seemingly caused by the market in the first place" (p. 439).

To emphasize, none of this, especially, is any conspiracy. Phillips-Fein is careful to note that those involved "are not the all-knowing, all-seeing caricatures of conspiracy theory; they were people who sought to build a political movement, who faced difficulties and setbacks, who often disagreed with each other about the right course of action, and who could not control the circumstances under which they worked" (2009b, p. xii). Nor is the attempt to tell a history of neoliberalism "simply economic history." Numerous others point to the confidential memo by Associate Justice

Lewis Powell to the U.S. Chamber of Commerce arguing at length that the Chamber should lead an "assault upon the major institutions—universities, schools, the media, publishing, the courts—in order to change how individuals think 'about the corporation, the law, culture, and the individual'" (noted in Harvey, 2005, p. 43). Powell was actually behind the times. This was no mere sales effort: it was a transformational movement that needed time and effort to attain the degree of coherence that it attained, a "long-term philosophical and political project" (Mirowski, 2009, p. 426).

This would be a reeducation effort for all elements of society—capital included, even if those elements of the MPS may not have completely agreed with that part of the program at all times: "The relationship between the neoliberals and capitalists was not merely that of passive apologists or corporate shills," although it certainly helped to have capital in your corner: "How much more powerful are ideas consciously forged with the vested interests kept firmly in mind" (Mirowski, 2009, p. 432). These vested interests enabled a wide-ranging "Russian doll" structure around these new ideas: academic settings at the center; foundations and philanthropic units one shell removed; think tanks who shelter neoliberals "who themselves might or might not also be members in good standing of various academic disciplines," with these groups begetting one more layer of instant-action groups (Mirowski, 2009, pp. 430–431). By the time one got to that outer layer, it would be challenging, if not impossible, to discern the myriad ties contained within. All the same, and as a bonus, and befitting the markets-as-massive-computers metaphor, it gave the appearance of orders emerging out of chaos, "although they were frequently nothing of the sort. Yet the loose coupling defeated most attempts to paint the thought collective as a strict conspiracy. In any event, it soon becomes too large to qualify" (Mirowski, 2009, p. 431).

This extended trip through such details serves several ends for my purposes here. One, it acts as foreshadowing: the moment that the "open access" movement unravels and "network neutrality" becomes the primary issue, the lessons learned from this decades-old experience will not be forgotten. Second, it is a warning: the growth of the ideas contained therein also become of surprising importance as they illuminate some core difficulties that activists fighting for "Internet freedom" face going into the future, including what they need to be conscious of when they look in the mirror. Third, the open access and eventually network neutrality debates served to point to this developed mode of thought's own contradictions, which, from an activist point of view, could well provide the seeds to its own demise.

The descendants of this "thought collective" were pivotal to communications policy processes within a few years. For one, Ronald Coase in 1950 addressed the Society on "Broadcasting in a Free Society" (Tribe, 2009, p. 87). For another which figured even more solidly in open access and network neutrality debates, De Sola Pool's "policies for freedom" contained in his classic *Technologies of Freedom* are derived quite distinctly from this thought collective's efforts (Pool, 1983, pp. 247–249). Summing his policy recommendations, First Amendment principles were to apply to all media, including electronic ones. "Anyone may publish at will." The "enforcement of the law must be after the fact, not by prior restraint." Regulation "is a last recourse.... If possible, treat a communications situation as free for all rather than as subject to property claims and a market." Further, "interconnection among common carriers may be required." This deserves further elaboration:

> Carriers may sometimes raise valid objections to interconnection. Some will wish to use novel technologies that are incompatible with generally accepted standards, claiming that they are thereby advancing the state of the art.... Such arguments are often valid, though they may also be used to lock a group of customers out of using the carrier.... An argument in favor of general connectivity is that it facilitates market entry by new or small carriers. It also makes universal service easier. (Pool, 1983, p. 247)

The "government and common carriers should be blind to circuit use. What the facility is used for is not their concern." Bottlenecks "should not be used to extend control." And lastly, "for electronic publishing, copyright enforcement must be adapted to the technology." Streeter (2011) accurately notes that this volume, and these ideas, largely sealed the deal for much of the thinking on the possibilities of communication technologies, equating as it did "free markets, corporate autonomy, and free speech in a common but slippery way, where in one breath the word freedom means, say, market competition for local phone service, the next it means abandoning antitrust regulation, and the next it means standing on a soap box in a park proclaiming ones' views" (p. 78).

Thus one lens via which to explore the struggle over network neutrality—to secure its existence in semantic, technical and existential terms—is of a movement utilizing neoliberalism's pet terms in a grand experiment to gain entrance to policymaking realms heretofore inaccessible to a bunch of scrappy outsiders; a movement that was about shifting the structures by which communication takes place, but with the contradiction that it was additionally the primary conduit by which commerce took place and was managed—not just online via retail, but in the transport of valuable information necessary for the management of transnational commercial operations and emergent modes of financial transactions. The quandary which obtains is that even as these movements seemed counterhegemonic to the dominant logics of neoliberal capitalism in a networked, financialized environment, they were largely moving the process along since the broader formation was never at issue. Yet the actions undertaken were the best options available: what capital formation won would matter in ongoing struggles for social and economic justice—certain configurations make the job easier or more difficult. Banet-Weiser's notion of ambivalence comes riding to the fore.

Network neutrality in these senses is thus arguably among the most neoliberal of debates. It was a struggle not against capital; rather, it was against a particular business model: private carriage as opposed to common carriage. It created an odd political brew. When Sandvig (2007) would intervene in the network neutrality debate himself, he would exclaim,

> de Sola Pool sought to advance a neo-liberal agenda of increased competition by warning against the menace of government intervention. In this, his agenda appears consistent with network neutrality critics like Yoo. However, the policy proposals he suggests are identical to those advanced by network neutrality advocates like Wu. One reason for this is that the regulatory context is so different now that de Sola Pool's proposals sounded like "hands off!" 23 years ago, and yet these same proposals are now the tools of interventionists, and sound like "hands on!" (p. 144)

What is surprising is that we as readers might even find this surprising. What he is essentially describing is not something new but something that was the product of an initiative commenced at the level of the epistemological decades previous, developing in loose fashion, into something that became the playing field for discussion out of necessity. Sandvig wasn't pointing to some odd twist in progressive/democratic politics. The neoliberal project was not a merely pro-corporate initiative: what the benefactors of that movement obtained for their funds was a set of theory which called for the all-encompassing system, capital included, to be transformed.

If anything, Sandvig's revelation is a mere recognition that capital would justifiably strike back against certain of the core tenets of this new system when it suited them. He points to the debate constrained, turned into "difference" from what had been heterogeneity on diverse fields of struggle, made understandable by given institutions, and thus decidable.

The Uses of Economic Theory

One additional danger is in reading this as some reductionist form of "economism." Concerns regarding the economism of political decision making and the antidemocratic potentials contained therein are relevant, as cities across Michigan fell into the hands of unelected managers (to disastrous effect, as felt in Flint) and as technocrats took over European governments for a time. Transitions to more right-wing authoritarian-friendly governments that swept across the West portend only an intensification of these logics, albeit for different reasons. The general concern, then, may be that a particular "economics" comes to rule. Blevins and Brown (2010) themselves examined the FCC's privileging of studies from orthodox economics perspectives in thinking through its media ownership rules between 2002 and 2007; studies from outside this closed universe were themselves buried by the commission. (Quite literally: a study that did not support further consolidation had to be leaked to see the light of day.) The authors ask, "What may the FCC overlook if it relies mostly on economics research in the formation of media ownership rules? And…if the FCC included research from a broader range of scholarly fields, might that research have suggested another course of action, rather than further relaxing media ownership rules?" (Blevins & Brown, 2010, p. 604).

However, our concern here is not the act of enacting a particular policy that stems directly from the machinations of a particular form of theory alone; rather, it is about the production of a particular form and content of debate to the ends of something else entirely—not theory, but a field of action via theory. That is, arguably, Blevins and Brown ask the wrong questions. A strongly economistic interpretation (in the narrow sense) of the modern landscape misreads the role that economic theorization seems to play in broader political realms. The one attempt, to my knowledge, to apply the historical material understanding of knowledge-processes to the formulation of communications policy aims directly at this notion. This was undertaken by Mirowski's student, Edward Nik-Khah (2005), as seen in his doctoral dissertation covering the fashioning of new spectrum auctions during the 1990s under the Reed Hundt FCC.

In examining the efforts of game theorists, experimental economists, and Walrasian microeconomists, Nik-Khah was first and foremost disturbed that when he evaluated the auctions in light of what Congress had represented as their goals, they were a disaster. Congress had mandated the "development and rapid deployment of new technologies, products, and services for the benefit of the public, including those residing in rural areas, without administrative or judicial delays"; it sought the "promot[ion of] economic opportunity and competition and ensuring that new and innovative technologies are readily accessible to the American people by avoiding excessive concentration of licenses and by disseminating licenses among a wide variety of applicants, including small businesses, rural telephone companies, and businesses owned by members of minority groups and women"; it desired "recovery for the public a portion of the value of the public spectrum made available for commercial use and avoidance of unjust enrichment through the methods employed to award uses of that resource"; and finally "efficient and intensive use of the electromagnetic spectrum" (quoted in Nik-Khah, 2005, p. 112).

Rather than reach these goals, the "consulting economists" proposed their own version of efficiency as the ultimate goal for the auctions—all, unfortunately, keeping their sights set on the maximization of revenue.

> The highest valued bidder criterion fails to consider structural aspects, which are the targets of public policy. But what makes it 'nonsense' is not merely that the criterion is inappropriate, but that it is not possible to determine whether it has been met. While offered as a way to promote all the public policy goals, the highest valued bidder criterion seems to entail replacement of relatively more concrete goals with relatively less concrete ones. (Nik-Khah, 2005, p. 129)

Game theorists offered not empirics but metaphor despite their "claim to designing the auctions" (Nik-Khah, 2005, p. 130). All concentrated on raising revenues while simultaneously "ignoring the things they did which likely decreased revenues" (pp. 130–131). For instance, due to what would be a lack of national licenses for biddees, MCI chose not to participate, removing competition for the spectrum. Further, these theorists were willing to take the additional step for their clients of "bull[ying] others on television, facilitating as well acts of collusion" (pp. 130–131). In the end, rules were gamed: large companies teamed with small to grab licenses intended for "small business" and other categories. What resulted was an eventual consolidation of licenses under large players.

Nik-Khah concludes that what shaped the auctions, then, had little to do with theory, even as it appeared to play a pivotal role. At issue was the "consulting engineer" model employed by the FCC. Powerful telecommunications operators knew how to play the system.

> [Pacific Bell Attorney James] Tuthill, who organized PacBell's lobbying before the FCC, knew it would be crucial to hire an expert who could figure out where, amid the highly technical details of the auction proposal, PacBell's interests lay.... He wanted someone who could speak plain English and come across to the FCC as more than just an opinion-for-hire. "If it's just another party coming up and telling our line, that isn't going to be effective."... During the summer before the FCC released its auction plan, Tuthill's staff drew up a list of games [*sic*] theorists.... By the time the FCC's plan was in the hands of PacBell's competitors, the company had signed a contract with Milgrom and Wilson. Although Wilson was a more senior professor, Milgrom was assigned the lead role because he was willing to lobby. (Nik-Khah, 2005, p. 91; citations omitted)

It is less the paymasters involved that resulted in shoddy outcomes than the "exigencies of the client-consultant relationship together with the enthusiasm of the Hundt FCC for solutions provided by economic theory" that "provided a golden opportunity for the large telecoms that were originally envisioned as targets of [spectrum] policy to tip the competitive balance and make them the beneficiaries of the policy" (Nik-Khah, 2005, pp. 135–136). The FCC's own effort to hire someone outside its purview to serve as an "objective" view on the matters—John McMillan of the University of California, San Diego—still, in the end analysis, did little good. In Nik-Khah's words, rather than an impartial judge, the FCC got in him "someone with an agenda to establish the practical relevance of game theory. This commitment led him to endorse an auction design broadly consistent with the wishes of the incumbent telecoms" given the models he favored (for, conceivably, broad institutional reasons) were theirs. In the end, "It should be clear that such claims as 'the auction design process was driven not by politics, but by economics' are misleading. Not only is it more correct to invert the claim to read, 'The auction design process was driven not by economics, but by politics,' one should conclude that the appropriateness of game theory to represent 'economics' was determined by politics as well" (Nik-Khah, 2005, pp. 96; citations omitted).

This is to say, critics charging the FCC with the "prevalence of an 'economist's view,' which stress[ed] the scarcity of spectrum" as the problem with these auctions missed the mark. There were economists who were far from oblivious to potential uses of spectrum that did not necessitate considering it scarce, such as Eli Noam. But "the important point to remember is that such views did not impact the policymaking process (and are still underrepresented) because they were of no use to the Baby Bells. FCC policy was forged in an environment of clashing business models, and while uses for spectrum might not naturally be mutually exclusive, the business models certainly were" (Nik-Khah, 2005, p. 139n185). Theory did not drive the decision-making process at the FCC. Material buttress of a bounded space of theory options ensured that "appropriate" theory won the day. Importantly, political economy does not disappear. With an availability not just of diverse theory (in Laclau and Mouffe's sense, importantly) but an undercurrent of *understanding that the use of such theory was the appropriate manner by which to run spectrum auctions,* the material resources to mobilize particular strains were brought to bear that resulted not in some economic system winning the day, but a business model that utilized the debate to that end.

These last points are crucial for what follows and, I believe, offer insight into the true roles that knowledge plays, in ambivalent ways, in our policymaking process. What Nik-Khah's story cannot account for, and the open access and network neutrality debacles present, is another form of natural experiment in which active, "ersatz" knowledge was brought into the FCC process. The consultant model that proved so effective during the spectrum auctions to gainsay the outcomes to prominent players' advantage would be combined with the background currents already set in motion decades ago: a move that, ironically, the emergence of network neutrality itself would only aid, not stifle.

It also speaks to why the "thought collective" is a more effective tool to utilize in analyzing the network neutrality debates than a notion of "interpretive communities" as employed by Streeter (1996). Hearkening here to the previous efforts of Fish (1982), in terms of reconstructing the corporate liberal "structure of feeling" (to borrow from Williams [1977]), Streeter suggests that analysis of its construction by policymakers can fruitfully be done

> as taking place within … a community of individuals that interact with one another in such a way as to generate a shared, relatively stable set of interpretations in the face of potentially unresolvable ambiguities. What makes a ruling

> appear practical, a legal decision seem sound, or a procedure appear fair, is the contingent, shared vision of the interpretive community itself, not simply rational policy analysis, legal reason, formal rules of process and procedure, or interest group pressures. (Streeter, 1996, p. 114)

He recognizes that such communities are not necessarily goal-oriented, nor predictable or clean in their operation (p. 116). The more indifference a particular interpretive community is able to show dissent, the more clearly the dominant framework demonstrates itself to be (pp. 117–118).

We might say that Streeter notes the apparatus by which such activities transpire, but his notion of the interpretive community seems to imply an insular mindset. This provides an interesting initial rubric for "reading" the debates to come but leaves aside several important facets. For one, the question of how "ersatz" knowledge invades policy process comes into question. The network neutrality debates provide one such opportunity to examine this. Streeter is also sensitive to the history of what forms of argument were acceptable at certain points in time in policy discourse, such as the shift to neoclassical economics in the 1980s. What is elided are the various ways that such debates followed a historical trajectory that did have a clear purpose applied in terms of reconceiving society as a whole: "corporate liberalism" is a static notion, and this new conception of the development of debate is a more dynamic approach. The moves Mirowski and Nik-Khah describe show how "corporate liberalism" may well be one instance of a broader class of neoliberalism. The notion of a "thought collective" renders something that possesses a seeming stasis as "corporate liberalism" (or an "interpretive community") more fluid, more adjustable to the times, even as it may appear the same on the surface.

Tim Wu's Contribution, Revisited

I return to Wu's *The Master Switch* briefly before beginning my story. Some challenges of his narrative now emerge. One, it is of a piece with the broader development of neoliberalism *as a project* itself. While advocates like the Consumer Federation of America, Consumers Union, and the Center for Media Education and the Media Access Project had been all along ambivalently using pieces of the neoliberal program as a weapon against itself, the emergence of the concept of network neutrality was less a weapon than a *shoehorn,* for reasons we will see. A second problem with Wu's account is its one-dimensionality: it doesn't allow for the mechanisms that rendered even the concepts of "open" and "closed" more or less stable. Wu, ironically, brought the debate to an *end* by changing the argument's position from one that effectively rendered consumer viewpoints *unfamiliar* next to the broader undercurrents rushing by to one that flowed *with* them all too well. This affected not just regulatory discourse but popular understanding. Wu's account, in other words, has nothing to say about the nature of the Web itself: how content should be subsidized and supported, to say nothing about the actual role of the public beyond their being innovators and contributors to some formation of commons, public or private. *That* would require an articulation of issues that effectively remained segmented in Washington, ensconced in their own silos.

This entire episode points to a new problematic regarding the function of activism itself, given the possibility that network neutrality debates themselves ambivalently served both social justice yet the emergent sales effort too. It served the needs of a newly revved-up commercial Web beautifully in a historical irony; the *manner* in which the fight was engaged performed a similar function. Going forward, activists will need to grapple with this, and it will necessarily be a long-term affair. The limitation of network neutrality was *due to the content of its theoretical construction*—it *could* have been justified differently, yet it was not—and this moved the entire debate onto the neoliberal platform long prepared by the neoliberal thought collective. A heterogeneous field was thus restricted to a diverse one, the players were categorized and catalogued, and new work served not to *expand* the debate but instead to shunt players to one side or another. Net neutrality both mattered and it differently did *not* matter. It was both a necessary debate and an opportunity to police knowledge. The role of research itself served an ambivalent role from this point forward—not moving debates, but instead aiding in determining whether a particular player was or was not a part of the "discursive community" in Washington. It determined who was allowed to sit at the table when policies were decided, not whether the policies should change. This differs from Thomas Streeter's formulation as he attempts to grapple with our collective "romanticism" surrounding the Web and new technologies in general. By 2018, the debate would perform even more spectacular (or horrific) labors, both culturally and materially; it would be harnessed to undo itself via the weaponization of the very means activists utilized to obtain it. Most remarkably, by the end of the story, the debates which circulated at the FCC only glancingly brush with the political economy of immanent trajectories of platform capitalism. The contradictions which emerge are frightening and portend a shift in how things like "media reform" and "media activism" are thought and practiced.

Perhaps what we discover in net neutrality *as a debate* is a way of processing the new inputs of the "ersatz" provided by the new opportunities on offer due to the emergence of the Internet, such that this input can be channeled in useful ways in the continued development of the network state—as a way of maintaining the production chain of capital across boundaries, or of maintaining a particular idea of "Internet freedom" that comes riding to the fore (Powers & Jablonski, 2015; Schiller, 2014). Perhaps "corporate liberalism" is but just one way among several that this is accomplished. The entry of the ersatz transformed the policy apparatus toward an interpretive, transformative mode that processed it and produced valuable cultural labor (Braman's [1995a] notion of the modern state as information processor comes explicitly to mind in a twisted way; see, too, Sassen [2006] and her discussion of "capabilities"). That network neutrality's underlying issues persist—now being argued in the courts, in state legislatures, and even nascently in attempts to rethink antitrust policy in light of emergent business practices—perhaps means that capital has moved on and figured out a way to process this in combination with the state. Such notions become especially in need of analysis when Ammori (2014) speaks of the new policy prerogatives emerging from the shops of online intermediaries and platform capitalists as Google and others, and these being among the most significant in years to come. When we ask questions of the need for ideological closure on the issue, it turns out that such closure ironically stems from its *lack* as the debate marches on. The neoliberal prerogative could hardly be better suited, the social factory grown to entirely new realms. Yet one cannot turn only to arguments; the core insight that Mirowski provides is the material nature of their firmament, and it is by seeking these connections that new theory can be drawn about the relationships between knowledge, the state, communications policy, and the issue of power itself and how it is exercised. To understand this process, we must start at the beginning, as consumer advocates sought to utilize neoliberal terms by hoisting them on their own petard, whether they realized they were doing so or not. It is to this story we now turn.

Let me be clear. None of this is to diminish the efforts of the advocates for network neutrality, nor is it to denigrate the role Tim Wu played. Similarly, capital did not drive the endgame of these debates: activists did. It is a falsehood to argue that activists were pawns in capital's game, that large firms or emergent startups were the true heroes of the story. Rather, a new dimension to media reform activism and research is making itself apparent. What I seek to accomplish is to look ahead to the future as we continue to seek ways to solve the problem of the digital divide, in Schiller's (2007b) sense: "The digital divide is, most profoundly, about the distribution of social power to make policy for the production and distribution of information resources. Unless that power is broadly shared, democracy itself is threatened" (p. 57). The remainder of this book is an effort to capture the nature of the efforts to reclaim just this.

2 Open Access: Nascent Moves to Counter Cable Giant Power in the Late 1990s

If "network neutrality" has a birth family, it is the twisted pair of AT&T and the cable industry who collectively fought so hard to retain what telecommunications players had lost: exclusive control to operate their systems under private carriage terms. Midwifed into the world by the term "open access," the fallout of the term and the actions taken in its defense put the lie to much scholarship that doom these debates to obscurity on the back of the seemingly plain-and-simple political economy of the shifting terrain of the late 1990s and early 2000s: no, advocates would be active shapers of what was to come.

Passage of the Telecommunications Act of 1996 set the terms for what was to come. The bill set up a complex game that, its authors hoped, would spawn new competition in conduit services. It sought to enable companies that provided exclusively long distance telephony (such as AT&T since its divestiture of the Baby Bells in the early 1980s and MCI) a way to potentially get into local telephony themselves. It created new openings for the Baby Bells to commence competing with each other and with new "competitive local exchange carriers" (CLECs) by purchasing 'unbundled' or leased services from the Baby Bells themselves (referred to as regional Bell exchange carriers, or RBOCs) which remained regional monopolies. Perhaps telecommunications and cable companies would come to compete with each other for the same services as well. Yet a difference between telephone and cable wires remained in statute: the impulse to liberalize telecommunications lines was not equally applied to cable wires. Set aside in their own Title (Title VI), cable wires were not subject to unbundling requirements or line sharing requirements for competitor access. Establishment of the details as to how these liberalizations would work and their tweaked to improve its own performance, it suffered from both speed and distance limitations cable did not face. Barring fiber upgrades, copper-wire-driven telecommunications companies would hardly be able to compete at the same level (Andrew Schwartzman, personal communication, March 12, 2019). Bills increasingly consisting of "line item" costs started to amount to "rate increases for monthly local phone service (which remains a monopoly)" (Cooper & Kimmelman, 1999, p. vii). The confluence of these factors meant that competition in these markets largely consisted of efforts to obtain high-volume and upper-end users. "Only big customers with big local bills are attractive to potential local market entrants" (p. vii).

This was the reality with which local governments were faced, and even as these difficulties made themselves known, so too were they imbricated in the discourse of the liberalization drive as a way to provide universal service to customers. This discourse provided the intuitive "solutions" to the problems faced in a seemingly tautological dance that would continue for the better part of decades to come. Reconciling the two is what drove the struggle that commenced a decades-long (and counting) battle over questions of what, somewhat hyperbolically, we might say is the soul of emerging two-way communications networks.

From Dial-Up to the Possibility of Cable Broadband

Greenstein's (2016) telling of the development of Internet service providers (ISPs) notes the differing aims of national and local services that enabled consumers and businesses to access the Internet. Indeed, in the dial-up universe—where the most competition could be found—old bulletin board services had expanded into the provision of Internet access, at least in urban and wealthy areas. While these may have seemed to magically appear across the landscape in the late 1990s, their emergence stemmed from specific circumstances that enabled these specialized services to become providers of connectivity to the Internet without too much difficulty, and this was even in advance of decisions to transfer control of the Internet backbone to commercial providers from the National Science Foundation (Greenstein, 2016, p. 135). These ISPs over telecommunications facilities were themselves continuing to experience protection from common carriage regulation themselves, seen as an access service to end users rather than as telecommunications carriers; the treatment of telecommunications services aboard which they operated as common carriers was pivotal for their existence. Accessible via a phone call and using a modem, telecommunications firms could not block users from using their services, even though these access companies likely competed with the phone company's own access service. This was only possible due to telecommuncations companies being governed by a "common carriage" regimen. Had a "private carriage" regime been in force, this would likely not have been the case. Some were national in scope, like those services run by AOL, AT&T, Microsoft, and CompuServe (later acquired by AOL). The most numerous and geographically dispersed category of provider were the emerging plethora of "specialized online service providers which largely provided support to clubs, games, news updates and email" (p. 144). These providers, in particular, were focused on ease of access for users, often with local focus, experimenters in terms of price. "Many were often content to supply service to a small town that would appear unprofitable to a major corporation. Many would focus on providing local news or specialized information that national outfits would otherwise ignore" (p. 145). A still larger category comprised pornography services that, due to their own revenue stream, were able to cross-subsidize development of other Internet-related functions as content providers and site hosting services. "Said another way, because of the pervasiveness of pornography BBSs [bulletin board services], every small town had at least one potential BBS that could convert to supply ISP service" (pp. 146–147). Indeed, the national firms did not have national *reach* as a core objective at all.

By 1996 virtually every major city had ISPs servicing them, but market share was skewed. In the late 1990s, a Federal Communications Commission (FCC) analysis noted that a "Big Four" comprising AOL, CompuServe, Microsoft, and Prodigy Inc. controlled 84 percent of the market; adding AT&T's WorldNet wrought a "Big Five" with 88 percent of the market (Esbin, 1998, p. 18). Greenstein's more recent survey concurred; while the majority of ISPs were small and regional, the majority of users utilized the national providers (Greenstein, 2016, p. 232). While dial-up ISP access was hardly deterred by major telephone companies initially, this was changing in the late 1990s.

In 1996, national firms found it made sense to offer service to areas with populations of 50,000 or more, utilizing 4,000 to 6,000 access numbers; in contrast, "For rural counties with a population under fifty thousand, services; add to this that it was "bleeding millions of dollars... rais[ing] $485 million in debt at the end of 1998 and... still struggling to resolve the technology issues that were plaguing the network," here was a step that would remove the company "from under the yoke of the cable guys" (p. 151). Recalled one insider who disagreed with the decision, "TJ [Thomas Jermoluk, CEO of @Home] wanted us to be another HBO," giving its cable company partners stakes in the new business and assuring @Home prime access status to households (p. 151). Malik is mystified by this: "What is hard to understand is why a company with a near-monopoly on the high-speed Internet access business would change its business model.... One thing that was going right for @Home was that its stock price was rising faster than mercury on a hot summer day in Manhattan" (p. 151). Before such content strategies were hatched, TCI decided to sell its infrastructural assets to AT&T in mid-1998, essentially flipping rotting infrastructure: TCI was sticking AT&T with the costs of upgrading, getting rich in the process. John Malone, chairman of TCI, was already legendary: business pages detailed his activities buying and selling cable systems, constantly buying low and selling high, and his influence cannot be underestimated in this environment. One advocate, long after the fact, offered that at one point he had been told that Malone complained that certain franchise operations were spending too much on customer service. Malone effectively ran his systems into the ground, extracting as much as he could from them, before dumping them on AT&T (Andrew Schwartzman, personal communication, March 12, 2019). With the pending sale, upgrades slowed to a crawl.

An additional wrinkle would be that AT&T would be required to seek express permission to take over ownership of what was still effectively monopoly infrastructure—locality by locality and cable franchise by cable franchise. This is a world apart from the requirements on the telecommunications side, governed by the provisions of Title II of the Telecommunications Act that sought to open telephone lines to rivals to create new markets for local telephone service. This was due to cable franchises being governed not by Title II but Title VI of the Telecommunications Act. As a result, such required negotiations with new owners give localities the opportunity to examine company financials (to some extent), to demand service upgrades, to request public buildings be wired, to negotiate a franchise fee to be regularly paid to the locality, and to request support for public, educational and governmental channels over the cable system. (Public access advocates often would complain that many locales were interested in the "governmental" channels for self-publicity but not so much the "public" channels, which could bring controversy.) These affairs were largely smooth sailing and out of public view, done with little fanfare nor controversy: perhaps with a public hearing or two, but without much genuine debate. The local franchise boards that drove the approval process (or provided merely advisory functions to city councils) were selected differently in most all locales, inevitably with varying interest and expertise in the matter.

The FCC Explores Its Options

The Federal Communications Commission was clearly grappling with how to think through broadband Internet access via cable in the wake of the Telecommunications Act of 1996. A white paper by Barbara Esbin, then–associate bureau chief of the Cable Service Bureau at the FCC, provided one insider's view of the landscape as far as cable was concerned.

The cable industry was deathly afraid of the potential to have to unbundle services on offer: the more it appeared to operate like a telecommunications service, the more stringently they would push back against such perceived commonality. This was because in U.S. law, while the Communications Act did separate facilities by technology, what distinguished them was their functionality, not the technology itself; the technology merely represented a convenient shorthand—one rapidly becoming less and less clear. Esbin notes that AT&T's announcement in June, 1998 added a wrinkle:

> AT&T's June, 1998 announcement that it would acquire the nations's [*sic*] second largest cable operator, TCI, has brought this issue into sharp relief. TCI owns 42% of @Home, which is reported to have exclusive contractual arrangements until 2002 to provide Internet access for TCI and its other cable affiliates, including Cox Communications, Inc., Comcast Corp., Cablevision Systems Corp., and Rogers Cablesystems Ltd. Although @Home presently has only 100,000 Internet access customers, these cable operators together serve more than 55 million cable customers. It is reported that @Home's contracts do not include rights to offer Internet-based telephone service, or full-motion video segments longer than 10 minutes; those services are reserved for the cable operators. (Esbin, 1998, p. 94)

The Telecommunications Act, while partitioning telecommunications firms and cable firms by technology into two separately and differently overseen services, potentially changed the landscape by the insertion of two words into one of the several definitions of cable service: "or use."

"Cable service" was now defined as "the one way transmission to subscribers of video programming or other programming service, and subscriber interaction, if any, which is required for the selection *or use* of such video programming or other programming service" (47 U.S.C. §522[6]; emphasis added). The introduction of "or use" was new and potentially consequential: could it mean that even the protocol conversions and data manipulations required simply to transmit a message were now no longer to be considered part of the common carriage portion of telecommunications services? Elsewhere, the act defines "information services" as "the offering of a capability for generating, acquiring, storing, transforming, processing, retrieving, utilizing, or making available information via telecommunications, and includes electronic publishing, but does not include any use of any such capability for the management, control, or operation of a telecommunications system or the management of a telecommunications service."[2] By the same token, the FCC had itself used a definition of "enhanced services" as "services, offered over common carrier transmission facilities used in interstate communications, which employ computer processing applications that act on the format, content, protocol or similar aspects of the subscriber's transmitted information; or involve subscriber interaction with stored information."[3]

Esbin notes that in the early 1970s, Congress established a dual regime in which states and localities issued franchises to suppliers of cable service while the FCC itself oversaw operations of those facilities. With the 1984 Cable Act, Congress recognized that cable could provide not just one-way communications but potentially two-way data transmission; all the same, it crafted the definition of cable service to avoid its being treated as a common carrier, thus maintaining a dual-tier regulatory framework (Esbin, 1998, p. 66). The 1984 act did, however, provide a firm distinction between cable services (one-way transmissions) and non-cable broadband services which would not fall within that definition of cable service. The excluded category "included two way communications services such as e-mail, facsimile transmissions and data processing, services which are identical to those long defined by the Commission as 'enhanced services' under the *Computer Inquiry* decisions, as well as basic telephone communications services" (Esbin, 1998, p. iv). This last notion is pivotal. Esbin notes that the Cable Act's legislative history "makes it clear" that these excluded services would not be considered part of the cable service's bundled content "insofar as they generally provide the subscriber with two-way capacity to engage in transactions, or to store, transform, manipulate, or otherwise process information or data" (Esbin, 1998, p. iv).

In the years leading up to the Telecommunications Act of 1996, the FCC had kept this distinction firmly in mind. The division of "basic" services (which would be treated as telecommunications providers and regulated as common carriers, subject to nondiscrimination rules, rate regulation, privacy restrictions, and more) from "enhanced" services (which utilized the transmission capabilities of common carriers and would not be regulated as such) established in the second FCC *Computer Inquiry* was carried over in part in its third *Inquiry*. The boundary between the categories of basic versus enhanced services remained challenging to draw as one bore into details. When was a particular "protocol conversion," in which one form of communication is transformed into another, something which could be considered enhanced and thus seen as in information service? Was *any* conversion sufficient to toss a service into the enhanced category? For instance, transforming an end user's input data and entering it into a proprietary database is obviously an enhanced service. But is transforming the voice transmission from an analog input into a digital one for transmission a protocol conversion which, even if necessary to transmit the call on modern technologies, takes the phone call out of the category of basic telecommunications service? Esbin notes,

> In *Computer III*, the Commission reaffirmed earlier decisions concluding that three types of protocol processing are not enhanced services within the meaning of the rules. First, the enhanced services definition applies only to end-to-end communications between or among subscribers. Thus, communications between a subscriber and the network itself (e.g., for call setup, call routing, and call cessation) are not considered enhanced services. Second, protocol conversions necessitated by the introduction of new technology (requiring protocol conversion to maintain compatibility with existing customer premises equipment) are also outside the ambit of the enhanced services definition. Third, inter-networking protocol conversions—those taking place solely within the network that result in no net conversion between users—are treated as basic services. (Esbin, 1998, p. 20)

In the mid-1990s, prior to passage of the Telecommunications Act in 1996, the FCC's *Frame Relay Order* affirmed such thinking, holding that processing undertaken by telecommunications companies, while utilizing protocol conversion, was part of providing the basic service and not an enhanced one free of scrutiny, as much as AT&T had pressed otherwise.

(p. 116). The challenge, at all turns, was "to examine the underlying purposes and policy goals behind existing regulatory categories, and to apply them only where those purposes and policy goals make sense. Any regulatory efforts in this arena should begin with an analysis of whether the operator in question exercises undue market power over an essential service or facility necessary to provide an essential service."

Ultimately, the conclusion of the paper rested on a foundation that cable did not represent a significant amount of market power at the time. There remained differing ways to access the Internet, with cable *one option among several*, even if only two wires (that of the phones or the cable wire) might pass a particular residence. However, the logic extended beyond access to the home: "There are multiple options for individuals to access the Internet, in addition to the commercial on-line services, including access through their schools and employers.... Many communities across the country have established 'free-nets' of community networks to provide their citizens with a local link to the Internet, and to provide local-oriented content and discussion groups" (Esbin, 1998, p. 20). Further, "individuals can also access the Internet using some (but not all) of the thousands of local dial-in computer services" (p. 20). In other words, the conclusions that were drawn by Esbin were *fully dependent* on the continuation of common carriage over telephone wires—something of which these companies were seeking to free themselves at local and national levels, as it required them to allow access to unaffiliated ISPs, even at turns via DSL.

A number of things stand out about Esbin's analysis. One is that there was an *overt acknowledgment* of the active role of government in shaping the development of the Internet and markets for connectivity. This is significant for what would follow. Second, the need for regulation was seen as something that needed to be stimulated by demonstrations of market power. How this power was to be construed was, however, contradictory. Under consideration in such calculations remained not the number of access "pipes" to a consumer's house but the number of providers one could obtain via that "pipe"; even as a maximum of two wires approached most homes, this fact was not considered (cellular service, even as it was then gaining a foothold, to this day remains a poor substitute for wired Internet service). Still, until cable became *the* principal carrier, a need to cast it as a telecommunications service was unnecessary. At the same time, cable was clearly seen as potentially superior to the telecommunications wire for the transmission of high-speed, two-way communications. One then needed to consider the state of play of the provision of Internet service itself in the form of the market for ISPs. "It is still possible," Esbin wrote, "to differentiate 'online service providers' from 'Internet service providers' or 'ISPs,' although the distinctions have blurred in practice. Online service providers, such as America Online, Inc., CompuServe, Inc., Netcom, EarthLink and the Microsoft Network generally combine content origination, computer database services and proprietary interfaces with IP [Internet protocol] access (a computer connection) to the Internet" (Esbin, 1998, p. 55).

The very month during which the Office of Plans and Policy released Esbin's paper, the agency released its *Advanced Services Order* (FCC, 1998a). If there was confusion over how cable facilities should be treated, there was no such confusion with the telecommunications side. At the state level as well as at the federal level, several of the regional Bell Operating Companies sought to offer high-speed Internet services, including DSL, "free from pricing, unbundling, and separations restrictions" (¶23). Ample evidence existed that telecommunications companies were making it challenging for competition to gain access to their wires (Ferranti, 1997; Taylor, 1997), and the *Advanced Services Order* clarified such issues in regard to DSL service. Significant for the story to come, US West was among the petitioners to the FCC seeking such freedom (¶25). The FCC—with no dissents by any commissioners—offered that "If all Americans are to have meaningful access to ... advanced services ... there must be a solution to the problem of the 'last mile.' No matter how fast the network is, if the connection between the network and the end-user is slow, then the end-user cannot take advantage of the network's high-speed capabilities" (¶8). Further, "[W]e first conclude that the pro-competitive provisions of the 1996 Act apply equally to advanced services and to circuit-switched voice services. Congress made clear that the 1996 Act is technologically neutral and is designed to ensure competition in all telecommunications markets" (¶11).

The FCC was similarly clear on what constituted telecommunications service. It was defined by statute as "the transmission, between or among points specified by the user, of information of the user's choosing, without change in the form or content of the information as sent and received."[4] As a result, in this Order, the FCC concluded that

> advanced services are telecommunications services. The commission has repeatedly held that specific packet-switched services are "basic services," that is to say, pure transmission services. xDSL and packet switching are simply transmission technologies. To the extent that an advanced service does no more than transport information of the user's choosing between or among user-specified points, without change in the form or content of the information as sent and received, it is "telecommunications," as defined by the Act. Moreover, to the extent that such a service is offered for a fee directly to the public, it is a "telecommunications service." (FCC, 1998a, p. ¶35)

Further, the FCC noted that none of the petitioners had disagreed with this assessment and allowed that "An end-user may utilize a telecommunications service together with an information service, as in the case of Internet access. In such a case, however, we treat the two services separately: the first service is a telecommunications service (e.g. the xDSL-enabled transmission path), and the second service is an information service, in this case Internet access" (FCC, 1998a, p. ¶36). The only quandary at issue at this time was whether incumbent operating companies would be allowed to set up a stand-alone unit to offer such advanced services alongside competitors utilizing their facilities and what kinds of protections competitors would require from a company favoring its own services over those of its competitor. The FCC specifically rebuffed entreaties by US West that its offering of DSL need not be shared with competitors.

The conclusions of the FCC were uncontroversial among the commissioners themselves, albeit each offered different reasons for supporting this logic. In separate statements, Commissioner Ness noted, "As I see it, the key issue we address today is whether advanced telecommunications capability is subject to the competitive framework so carefully established by Congress in Sections 251 and 271 of the Communications Act. The answer is yes. I don't believe that Congress wrote detailed amendments to the Communications Act only to address voice, but not data, services" (Ness, 1998, p. 2). Commissioner Michael Powell himself expressed enthusiasm at the pathway to incumbent entrance to this market, which did offer a glimpse at his future thinking on these issues; he emphasized the "deregulatory pathway" that ran through them as they provided the ability for incumbent Bell companies, "even incumbents that possess market power," to provide their own Internet services via a structurally separate affiliate—a cold comfort to upstart ISPs (Powell, 1998, p. 1). He acknowledged concerns that these powerful operators might use their already sizable advantage, but in his view, "incumbents that do not provide these services through separate affiliates will surely do so on a highly integrated basis"; enforcement of "interconnection, unbundling and other requirements with respect to advanced services will be as difficult and, I fear, as uphill a battle, as our enforcement of these requirements for traditional circuit-switched services" (p. 2). Summing, "the alternative may not put us in any better position to promote competition in advanced services" (Powell, 1998, p. 2).

Portland, Oregon: The "Mouse That Roared"

While the FCC clarified its approach to the telecommunications side of the equation, cable remained in a grey area, one regarding which localities grappling with AT&T and TCI's combination had little guidance. Additionally, much of the backroom thinking and dealing going on at TCI/AT&T/@Home was simply unknown to numerous local franchise authorities who gave AT&T their stamp of approval to go forward with the merger. Either due to historical exigency or mere chance, the situation would be quite different in the Portland and Multnomah County areas of Oregon. Overseeing cable operations on behalf of six local governments in this area was the Mt. Hood Cable Regulatory Commission (MHCRC). This commission consisted of appointed volunteers. Five cable franchises served these six local governments, all owned by the then–top two "multiple system operators" in the country: TCI served 31,000 customers between the two municipalities, and Time Warner, which possessed two systems held by a subsidiary called Paragon Cable in Multnomah County, served approximately 130,000 subscribers (MHCRC, 1999, p. 3). It was the responsibility of the MHCRC to put forward a recommendation to the Portland City Council and the Multnomah County Board of Commissioners whether to approve the transfer of TCI to AT&T; if so, they would also issue recommendations for conditions that would need to be fulfilled to allow the transfer to go through.

David Olson, director of the Mt. Hood Cable Regulatory Commission, was cut from different cloth than many other local regulators. He was a longtime local: a Reed graduate, a former cable company employee, and a former president of the National Association of Telecommunication Officers and Administrators; as of 1998, he had been serving as Portland's cable

combination; others simply demanded to know why Country Music Television had been removed from their cable service.

This would change at the following crowded meeting on November 16 (MHCRC, 1998b, 1999a). The minutes to this meeting reveal an MHCRC completely on its game on the nuances of technology law. All commissioners save one noted that they had been approached by representatives of the dominant local telephone company, US West, since the last meeting; the company sent Tim Sandos, director of public policy, to testify on their behalf. AT&T now knew better than to blow off the affair themselves. AT&T and TCI sent three representatives to testify: Debbie Luppold was present again, joined this time by Gloria Crayton, regional director for TCI, and Richard Thayer, who was chief commercial counsel for AT&T. Based on comments received in October and hence, MHCRC Director David Olson had prepared a resolution outlining proposed conditions for the transfer of the franchise to AT&T that would be forwarded to the Multnomah Board of County Commissioners and the Portland City Council for consideration. These conditions included the standard expectation that AT&T would adhere to the conditions of the former TCI agreements (which, given that TCI was allowing its infrastructure at this point to fester, likely would mean improvements, including a specific commitment to its "timely completion of the TCI upgrade in Portland and commencement of a comparable upgrade in Multnomah County").

Crucially, the resolution added nondiscriminatory access of ISP competitors to the cable platform to the list. The implications of this requirement were huge. Recall that telecommunications providers had been required by the Telecommunications Act to unbundle their services for lease to competitors (and also to offer their facilities to competitors at wholesale rates as another option). This requirement, while not nearly as stringent as the unbundling and resale requirements on their telecom siblings, remained in a legislative blind spot as yet unaddressed by either the FCC or Congress. In short, this seemingly insignificant request held potentially far-reaching consequences not just in Oregon but also *nationally.*

It would be understating things to say that AT&T and TCI representatives expressed their displeasure with such conditions. Luppold stressed that, first, this was something to be decided at the national level—at the FCC—and that, second, both companies believed that "the Commission does not have authority to determine this matter" (MHCRC, 1998b, p. 3). They asked that the issue be tabled for another meeting so as to hash out a compromise; best for this to simply go away behind closed doors before the next meeting.

When the floor was opened for comment, locals would not hear of any such delay. Not only were citizen commenters well read on the issue at hand, but the national significance of what was happening in the room was overtly realized. ORISPA, represented again by Richard Horswell and his counsel Stephen Kafoury, were joined by Steve Caldwell of Transport Logic and Susan Hamill of One World Internetworking. Kafoury noted that "The Commission is able to take a leadership position on this issue and hoped it would not delay its decision" (MHCRC, 1998b, p. 3). Horswell similarly supported the potential new precedent; he "asked the Commission to ensure that similar competitive promises extend to AT&T/TCI's provision of high speed Internet access to allow ISPs to buy access at a competitive price." Without the condition, consumers would be forced to purchase @ Home whether they desired it or not, meaning they would "pay for two ISP services to get the one they want[ed]." Further, the MHCRC's decision would "have a dramatic impact on consumer choice, competition in the market place and whether or not the community will have better Internet access. It [would] also set a benchmark for other regulatory bodies to take action to enhance the levels of Internet services and access throughout the nation" (MHCRC, 1998b, p. 3).

Hamill joined this argument to innovation in the operation of such networks. She stressed the importance of open platforms as opposed to closed, noting that on closed platforms businesses may not be able to use the latest services if the platform restricted them from doing so. "Some of the things that have made the Internet better are the open architecture, open standards and open competition. Consequently, consumers have an unprecedented number of opportunities for choice" (MHCRC, 1998b, p. 3). She emphasized "a community impact that may not be visible" in the form of "economic and social energy that goes into technology" (pp. 3–4). Presaging but not formalizing a principle that would come to play a central role in these debates a few years hence—the notion of the "internalization of complementary externalities"—Steve Caldwell testified that he was "surprised, shocked and disappointed that AT&T and TCI do not recognize other ISP's as a very strong, potential, additional revenue source" (p. 4).

Lest it appear that the lone voices of support were commercial interests merely defending their turf, unaffiliated residents showed up in greater numbers to this meeting than the last, all apparently well informed of the stakes involved. One who stated "he [was] not affiliated with any organization or consumer group" testified that "consumers are for competition" and that he was "in favor of the resolution with the open cable access provisions." He even "believed that AT&T and TCI would benefit from open competition" (MHCRC, 1998b, p. 4). Another Multnomah resident, who had previously worked with three cable companies, expressed his own concerns regarding digital inequality. He requested a review of records for the use of leased access aboard local franchises: by law, local cable franchises were supposed to offer up channel space for lease, a provision meant to increase viewpoint diversity. Such access, he noted, was exorbitantly priced and little used. Another unaffiliated Portland resident dug even more deeply into the weeds of telecommunications policy and inquired about the implications of TCI providing voice telephony over its Internet connection: would this then turn it into a common carrier subject to the full ledger of telecommunications regulations (p. 5)?

The policy director for US West also testified, couching his rhetoric in the parlance of fairness and playing to the need for a "level playing field to protect competition," in the face of a merger that would create a giant entity capable of "provid[ing] services to approximately 1/3 of the customers in America" and similarly able to "provide long distance services, manufacture equipment, enjoy pricing freedoms, and transmit data services, etc., and would be able to do so under a regulatory scheme that is far less stringent than that required of U.S. West or other telephone companies" (p. 4).

Commissioner Sue Diciple—herself the owner of a small consultancy and a former project manager for the Oregon Telecommunications Forum Council—saw directly through the disingenuousness of the comment, noting that US West had recently unsuccessfully lobbied at the Public Utility Commission to close their own platform to competitors. Not just in Oregon, but elsewhere, US West—as well as a coterie of other Baby Bells—was accused of playing favorites with its own in-house Internet provision service; competitors accused it of dragging its feet to provide interconnection facilities to competitors as well as practicing "slamming," where US West would "erroneously" set up Internet accounts through its own subsidiary even if the customer had requested a different provider's services (Ojeda-Zapata, 1998). In the meantime, Bell Atlantic Corporation had made specific entreaties to exempt new data networks from pricing and network-sharing aspects of the Telecommunications Act. US West and Ameritech Corp. had asked for similar provisions, even upping the ante by promising millions of dollars in future deployment investment. This investment, of course, was intended as a hostage they could sacrifice should regulators find against their requests (Krause, 1998). This said, the dynamic playing out between long distance providers (as AT&T) and the Baby Bells was instructive. Frank Simone, just months before this proceeding, was quoted as saying, "What this boils down to is whether you can make regulatory distinctions between data and voice services.... We would argue you can't, that it's all telecom networks, all (digital) bits being transferred over networks" (Krause, 1998). Commissioner Diciple arrived at her conclusion nonetheless: "Now ISPs have access to U.S. West's system. Similarly, ISPs should have fair access to cable" (MHCRC, 1998b, p. 5).

The only actors in the room disfavoring the open access provision appeared to be AT&T and TCI. The MHCRC passed the resolution containing the requirements they would recommend to Portland and Multnomah County in a 5–2 vote. The portion of the resolution focusing on "open access" read as follows:

> *Non-discriminatory access to cable modem platform.* Transferee shall provide, and cause TCI to provide, nondiscriminatory access to TCI's cable modem platform for providers of Internet and on-line services, whether or not such providers are affiliated with Transferee or TCI, unless otherwise required by applicable law. So long as cable modem services are deemed by law to be "cable services," as provided under Title VI of the Communications Act of 1934, as amended, Transferee and TCI agree to comply with all lawful requirements regarding such services, including, but not limited to, the inclusion of revenues from cable modem services and access within the gross revenues of TCI's cable franchises, and commercial leased access requirements. (MHCRC, 1999, p. 10)

Even those on the commission queasy about notions of increased regulation saw this as just and reasonable; Commissioner Robert Kreinberg, a vice president at Nike, would later comment to the *Wall Street Journal* that while he could "sympathize" with AT&T, that even as he was "not a big regulatory fan," he thought "there are some issues where regulation is needed to maintain a sense of competition and fair play. It's like if I owned all the airports in the world and I owned an airline and said only my airline could land there" (Gruley, 1999).

across jurisdictions. Somewhat jarringly, Olson noted that he had been prepared to simply file the compromise with Portland and Multnomah County as it stood. He had not done so because the city and county commissioners themselves wanted to see it adopted by the MHCRC first. Olson nonetheless concluded that they should pass the compromise.

The reason for hesitancy in enforcing the original conditions became clear later in the debate. In the course of negotiations regarding the compromise, AT&T's comments to the press had been gravely threatening. Commissioner Ruth Miles, a small business owner and former Multnomah Community Television board member, noted as such: "Thayer's remarks as relayed to the Commission…were, 'I hope you have a big budget'" (MHCRC, 1998a, p. 4). Debbie Luppold, who was once again representing AT&T and TCI, attempted to walk back the apparent flip remark, but failed: few things could have riled this commission more to action. In the days leading up to this meeting, one commissioner noted to reporters, "I know what it is to deal with a national company.… If you let them run over you without taking a stand, then they'll run over you." Commissioner Diciple told the *Oregonian*, "Local folks need to be the watchdog.… God knows, if you wait for the FCC, you'd really be in a bad way" (Yim, 1998b). Commissioner Miles piled on: "I have a deep suspicion of anything the two of them [AT&T and TCI] are going to do, separately or together" (Yim, 1998b).

Commissioners needled the now-hapless Luppold: they probed the legal definition of "cable services" and how the Internet service provided by AT&T's partner ISP figured in it. Luppold pointed toward Esbin's FCC white paper "characteriz[ing high-speed Internet services provided over cable] as similar to cable services. Until the FCC makes a ruling, TCI is deploying @Home as a cable service and paying franchise fees on it" (MHCRC, 1998a, p. 4). She noted that in testimony before the FCC earlier that day, another AT&T representative "testified that video services, telephone services and internet services were all cable services" (p. 4). Commissioners inquired as to what the regulatory categorization of online video and a proposed "@Work" service would be; Luppold "didn't know the answer" as to the classification of this enterprise service. This was less a lack of knowledge than a clash of worlds: it was a tacit acknowledgment of the bind into which her superiors were nestling her—one story was being delivered to Congress and the FCC and another to local commissions entirely. Ultimately, seemingly losing patience with the barrage of questions, Luppold informed the

MHCRC that "Under the Cable Act, communities have the right to approve a change in company control, by reviewing the technical, financial and legal capability of the new entity to uphold the terms of existing franchise; communities do not have the right to impose additional conditions. Therefore, it is a huge compromise for TCI/AT&T to agree to any additional terms and conditions as part of this transfer" (p. 5). Unintimidated, Commissioner Sue Diciple responded that "it was her understanding that the Act does not limit the Commission's ability to impose other kinds of conditions at the time of transfer" (p. 5).

ORISPA and US West's representatives brought a number of new details to the record while reiterating their old positions in defense of the original language. Kafoury of ORISPA decried the lack of consumer interest groups in the negotiations that Olson held with AT&T earlier in the month and noted a lack of faith in the FCC actually taking action on the open access issue in its AT&T/TCI proceeding. Horswell estimated that should the compromise language pass, "the estimated economic impact of broad band internet access being only available to TCI's @Home service would be $20 million revenue loss each year to the local economy from local internet providers; 500 jobs gone; 40 providers out of business because of @Home's monopoly; 100,000 internet subscribers left with no choice for high speed alternatives to their homes" (MHCRC, 1998a, p. 6). He also stressed the technical feasibility of an open access scheme and that "ORISPA is not seeking access to TCI's proprietary services; only to the last mile to the home. ORISPA is willing to pay for this access" (p. 6). To a question from Commissioner Miles regarding the relative costs a consumer would pay to use a competitive provider, "Horswell responded that ... diversity and competition drive prices down and innovators tend to charge less than a monopoly" (p. 6).

Tim Sandos of US West noted that the National League of Cities themselves now promoted "affordable access to all competitors and assert[] that local regulation is essential to prevent cable's misuse of a monopoly position and protect consumer interests and long range policy plans for telecommunication services." While acknowledging his rebuke during the last meeting, he still emphasized the importance of uniformity of regulation across providers. In response to a question as to whether TCI would be required to offer its @Home service wherever AT&T/TCI provided cable service, Sandos answered that "as a common carrier, U.S. West is required to offer services universally, but ISP's are not. Therefore, AT&T would be able made contact with Richard Horswell, the 27-year-old head of a Portland ISP and president of a trade group representing 40 Oregon ISPs" (all quotes here and below Gruley, 1999). Horswell noted to the *Journal* that speaking with Teplitz "really helped focus our strategy." AOL then hired a local lobbyist to work for ORISPA, also opening lines of communication with US West to coordinate. In arguing the case to the MHCRC commissioners, the ISPs were effective in part because "the small ISPs had been more diligent about getting service to rural areas where bigger providers wouldn't want to bother." The author of the *Journal* story was no fool, and (presciently) noted that "some observers believe that AOL, in particular, is using regulatory pressure to help it cut a deal with AT&T." AT&T argued to the *Journal* that "it shouldn't have to open its network to rivals that aren't taking the risk of buying and upgrading it. Such a burden would discourage other companies from investing in broadband technology too." AT&T's arguments deliberately directed attention to the potential competition they could provide to the Baby Bells while leaving issues of new technologies to the side (even though, recall, the argument they made to the MHCRC was that they would *not* in fact be providing any form of telecommunications service).

The untold story of this stage of the debate for the future of broadband was the extensive, if unheralded, involvement of a set of well-ensconced Beltway public interest organizations that provided the moral and thought leadership to the cause of "open access." The core of this ecosystem comprised four policy groups who had been active for years and had slowly built relationships with DC lawmakers and regulators—the Media Access Project (a long-standing, if small, public interest law firm), the Center for Media Education (an advocacy group soon to become the Center for Digital Democracy), Consumers Union, and finally, the Consumer Federation of America (a coalition of consumer groups from across the country). They were involved at the outset, working closely with ISPs AOL and MindSpring. On the corporate side, and with whom this crew interfaced, was the OpenNet coalition, a coalition of ISPs and other anti-cable forces including telecommunications operator GTE. The consumer advocates "had a coalition, a website, did outreach" with the ambitious goal of convincing the FCC to "define broadband as a telecommunications service" without regard to the technology which provided it. Doing so would hold tremendous implications: whether a cable company or a telephone company, providers would now be seen as common carriage providers of the service and would be forced to offer access to end users on such a basis (Andrew Schwartzman, personal communication, March 20, 2012).

In an early form of legislatively oriented Web activism, these groups collaborated to put together the website NoGatekeepers.org. While no vestige of its original form continues to exist, the Internet Archive contains several snapshots of its relatively brief run. This became a useful hub for all things open access—organizing press releases by partner organizations and trumpeting independent research of their own, that of other advocacy groups, and independent researchers, eventually publishing a short-lived electronic newsletter devoted to the cause of opening up cable lines by baby steps, starting with multiple ISP access. "This site," its home page announced, "is dedicated to educating the public, local, and federal policy makers, advocates, and the press about the importance of open broadband networks and the need to preserve competition in the Internet access market in order to protect consumer choice, privacy, and freedom of speech" (NoGatekeepers.org, 2000a). By the time the campaign had reached fever pitch, organizations adding their names to the effort included the Alliance for Community Media (which advocated on behalf of public access stations on cable networks), the Benton Foundation (which focused on the public interest obligations of broadcasters), the Civil Rights Forum on Communications Policy, Computer Professionals for Social Responsibility, the Consumer Project on Technology, the National Association of Counties, OMB Watch, and two utility-reform organizations, Toward Utility Rate Normalization and Utility Consumer Action Network (NoGatekeepers.org, 2000a).

When the *Wall Street Journal* wrote of the initial contact between AOL and US West's representatives, it hinted that such connections were newfound; perhaps some were, but as those who work on these issues well know, the universe simply isn't that big in this arena: "There weren't that many of us—a certain group that gets involved in arcane issues [as this]. It was more a soup, and you bumped into everyone else" (Donna Lampert, personal communication, September 6, 2017). AOL provided material resources to enable NoGatekeepers.org to function. "This site," the "About Us" page disclosed, "is maintained by Leslie Harris and Associates, a public interest government relations firm, and is supported in part by America Online. America Online does not exercise any editorial control over the content of this site" (NoGatekeepers.org, 2000a). It is significant that AOL had the resources and additional wherewithal to hire a lobbyist that paid attention to the Portland negotiations. Such strategic partnerships with sectors of capital itself would become a standard feature of such Washington-based organizing work, even as debates drifted further and further from the question of whether there were to be any particular *specific public purpose* to the emerging Internet.

The Washington, DC–based consumer groups had been constructing what became known as "open access" as a concept for many years. It was hardly new: it was simply an extension, a defense, of the notion of the common carrier applied to new technologies; more accurately, it applied conclusions wrought via the Computer Inquiries to the realm of everyday consumers. The early days of cable regulation featured active debates about making cable a common carrier as well, as noted by Pool (1983), which ebbed and flowed over the years leading to this point. As the Telecommunications Act of 1996 was being written, the Clinton administration themselves had proposed a new title (a separate category of service, with its own rules) under the act. As Eli Noam explained in 1994, "This new system would require interconnection, universal service, payments to local governments and 'open access,' a term not specified other than that it would apply to 'anyone, including end users and information service providers to transmit information, including voice, data and video programming, on a nondiscriminatory basis'" (Noam, 1994, p. 442). He noted that it is difficult to see why any provider of connectivity would willingly desire to see themselves categorized this way, something that was made all the clearer in the conflict surrounding the merger of AT&T with TCI. The fact that AOL was suggesting it at this stage only followed its own efforts to seek some arrangement with an emergent AT&T/TCI to purchase broadband connectivity at wholesale rates. AOL was hardly alone: Sprint (at this time primarily a long distance wireline company with a growing Internet backbone service with broader ambitions in wireless) sought access to cable wires as well. Both failed, with @Home reacting strongly against any notion. Increasingly, the last thing any provider wanted was to be a "dumb pipe" which carried other entities' content (Esbin, 1998, pp. 94–95). In the meantime, to the north, an example would soon be established: by late 1999, the Canadian Radio and Television Commission required that its largest cable companies open their wires to competitors for Internet access nationally ("Wholesale Broadband Access," 2005). In an irony, not only ISPs but giants like AT&T

desired such conditions so as to gain access to these networks themselves, even as they defended their ability to prevent competition aboard their own.

The consumer groups, in particular the CFA, felt the tensions between new technologies and this model at least as early as 1989, when the CFA published a report with the American Association of Retired Persons (AARP) entitled "Expanding the Information Age in the 1990s: A Pragmatic Consumer Analysis." In the years-long lead-up to the Telecommunications Act of 1996, telecommunications companies were seeking greater control over the operation of as well as the content that passed through their networks as a "quid pro quo for increasing investment." The CFA and AARP concluded that "such a union of conduit and content was antithetical to the consumer and public interest. Owners of wires should not be allowed to determine what services can use them. They should sell space on the wires and stay out of the programming business" (quoted in Consumer Federation of America, 1999b, p. 4). Their report discerned two competing models in play: a "decentralized and consumer based approach" versus a "centralized, network based" approach (with "network," in this sense, referring to the "telecommunications network," not some broader theoretical appeal to network action).

> Each of the models emphasized different characteristics of a telecommunications system and maximizes different goals. Decentralization emphasizes private and individual motivations. Risk and reward are borne by individuals and it is the willingness of individuals to incur costs in the hope of achieving benefits that dictates specific applications.... Centralization fosters larger decisions and commitments of resources which seek to enhance the social good by achieving economies of scale and scope. The telephone company makes larger, collective purchases and allocates costs to various services. Lowered costs and internal transfers between groups are intended to effectuate a [] more even spread of services. Costs are socialized and benefits allocated through centralized decision making of the franchise monopoly firm and regulatory bodies. (quoted in Consumer Federation of America, 1999b, pp. 5–6).

Even before the Mt. Hood Cable Regulatory Commission commenced its deliberations, the tug of war between these two models was rearing its head in consumer filings at the FCC as it considered how to wield its new "Section 706" authority given it by the Telecommunications Act. This section required them to encourage deployment of "advanced telecommunications," entailing the production of a regular report detailing whether

(Consumer Federation of America & Consumer @ction, 1999). With AT&T gobbling up cable systems with its exclusive ISP, should AT&T succeed in shutting down multiple ISP access over cable, "Two private toll lanes cannot replace an open superhighway" (Consumer Federation of America & Consumer @ction, 1999). While the FCC was still feeling its way with the broadband issue, it was clear that localities held the key to present pressure in favor of their position. "The fact that local authorities have a direct link to the open access debate makes it even more attractive as a point of leverage. The issue is removed from the backrooms of Washington and subject to much greater public scrutiny and more diverse input" (p. 11). The reasons were obvious to them:

> Department of Justice [DOJ] merger investigations are conducted with the utmost of secrecy. The DOJ asks questions in private and negotiates with parties, barely even acknowledging that an investigation is under way. The Federal Communications Commission typically takes written testimony and hears from a small number of experts, but does not allow discovery or cross-examination. Once the issue has moved to the front burner at the local level, it has resulted in an intense public information gathering process. (Consumer Federation of America & Consumer @ction, 1999, p. 12n35)

Finally, and crucially, "Outcomes that are truly in the public interest have a tendency to emerge when powerful commercial interests cancel each other out, as may happen in this case. Because the commercial interests may neutralize each other, it [is] possible to have two open networks [cable as well as DSL] to promote broadband Internet services" (pp. 11–12).

These consumer advocates were less "sandwiched" between the corporate factions involved than deliberately planting their flag on one side. They were forced by the circumstances to pick the side of the ISPs, with the top two in the country as ringleaders who possessed resources to advocate in their interests. As Chester would note later, "The OpenNET Coalition itself, of course, is not without its own brand of corporate self-interest. But as others without a vested interest in the outcome of the broadband battles have made clear, Main Street as well as Wall Street should have a say in this matter. An open, competitive, democratic broadband Internet is simply too important, not only for average Americans, but also for the educational, civic, social, and cultural organizations that serve them" (Center for Media Education, 1999, p. 6). GTE was similarly a member of this coalition, largely after efforts mirrored by other Baby Bells to operate a semi-closed network itself. Nonetheless, this unlikely combination of "open," "competitive," and "democratic" would govern exactly how they handled the issue of what open access *was*. It would end up being first and foremost a set of *principles for doing business that would be undertaken by private actors* and only second a set of principles for free speech. It was expected that the first would bring about the second, a quite striking equation of competition with democratic outcomes.

Consumer advocates for open access would be the first to admit that they—and frankly, numerous others involved in these debates—hardly had clear-eyed visions of how technology was going to evolve; and later, after the fact, they would note that nobody saw the explosion that was going to occur with online video and, eventually, social media. However, what these advocates agreed on was that dial-up, as a model, was competitive in the right way as far as they were concerned. Some ISPs accessible this way may have been tiny, run-out-of-a-garage affairs; others were regional companies; and others were national in scope. Cheaper services were available for plain-vanilla Internet access, whereas those with less technical knowledge could pay more for more hand holding by the likes of AOL. There was a great deal of differentiation of product, as well as price competition; for those who wished the more salacious sides of the Web to be filtered out, networks like Koshernet and Mayberry USA catered to Jewish and Christian customers respectively. It was this kind of price and product differentiation open access advocates sought for broadband on cable's superior technology: if multiple services would be able to ply their trade there, a similar ecosystem was expected to develop.

The utility of the small space into which these activists had inserted themselves revealed itself on numerous occasions. For one, at the *en banc* FCC hearing referenced during the pivotal December Mt. Hood Cable Regulatory Commission meeting, Gene Kimmelman used it to terrific effect. Upon US West's expression of desire of subjecting cable to a full unbundling regime—that would have required cable networks to break down their networks into their own "network elements" that competitors could purchase for access to end users using the cable company's own facilities—Kimmelman was able to respond, "I've been listening to my colleagues. I would like to associate myself with the thrust of much of what they are saying. It is one happy opportunity to say that I probably actually would encourage you to do a little less regulating than U.S. West [suggests] but

I think the general thrust of all the comments are right on point" (FCC, 1998b, p. 179).

Implementation of this objective was not something they were going to be able to leave in obscure FCC dockets. Working alongside their erstwhile corporate allies in the OpenNet Coalition, the group made strong use of NoGatekeepers.org and their own websites to broadcast their arguments and talking points. By teaming with AOL, these advocates were also indirectly allying themselves with the regional Bell companies that simultaneously were trying to free themselves of the regime that they themselves supported in 1996 while pushing cable into the regime that governed their own existence. This would be no grassroots-driven movement: this was a full-on effort to gain converts.

The issues debated at the local level, however, were much more pragmatic. Returning to the debate in Portland and Multnomah County, in a later interview, Erik Sten noted that in regard to the open access issue (to the extent it had that name at the time), his own first meeting on multiple ISP access to cable lines was with ORISPA. To arguments that such access to cable lines was not important, Sten's response was:

> There's been a lot of false statements put forward by the other side on this, saying that local governments that move forward on open access are tools of the companies opposed to cable. It couldn't be farther from the truth, at least in Portland. There are two points here. First, local ISPs add a lot to the life of the city. They are likely to have better targeted local content. For example, our biggest local ISP, Teleport, offers substantially discounted prices for websites to nonprofits that are based in Portland and they do that on purpose to build a niche, but it's also a wonderful service that's available.... The employees keep the money here, and the companies tend to be more civic oriented. But they also just have a local flavor, they're not national players. We have several hundred of them in Portland, if I recall correctly, and only five or six of them are very big. So almost all of those local companies are making a living based on some local niche, whether it's expertise on local nightlife or something else you'd never get from a big ISP. I think that's a very important piece. ("Interview with Erik Sten," 1999)

Summarizing his own experience with the fight, "If I understand the chronology right, we were early on, in the sense that the real fight started with our rule. But we were quite late in the hundreds of governments that approved this transfer, but I don't think that most of them really looked at this issue. Fortunately, we have a brilliant cable administrator in David

Olson. He's a public administrator and he's done this for his whole career, and he saw this coming. That worked well with our city council, which was willing to stand up for it" ("Interview with Erik Sten," 1999).

Much as the lawsuit threat from AT&T/TCI served as a galvanizing force which stirred the Mt. Hood Cable Regulatory Commission into action, the actual filing of the lawsuit in district court colored an *ex parte* submission Olson made to the FCC in late January 1999 as the agency was evaluating the merger itself. By this time, it was clear that they were networking with other municipalities, noting, "Many local franchising authorities and our local regulatory colleagues around the country have shared their concern with us regarding the likely negative impact on both consumers and the Internet of the cable industry as the bottleneck gatekeeper of broadband internet access" (MHCRC, 1999, p. 18). Further, they had "learned that just prior to the date of this filing the City Council of Los Angeles, California has expressed support for open access as a policy matter, and that the Executive of King County, Washington (comprising the suburbs of Seattle and including approximately 100,000 TCI cable subscribers) has recommended that the King County Council impose a similar 'open access' condition" (MHCRC, 1999, p. 6n14). The *Wall Street Journal*, in its extended piece about the Portland decision, noted that Los Angeles officials were flying Olson to town to discuss his commission's actions. Olson was not the only player on the move: with additional pressure evolving in other cities, AT&T dispatched its top counsel, James Cicconi, to meet with local governments in person (Gruley, 1999).

The MHCRC was at pains to tell the FCC that this transaction "was no ordinary cable transfer" in which cable companies sought to take advantage of economies of scale and scope through clustering of their franchises; rather, "the filing and the previous announcements from the parties described a transfer with national significance: a change in control of one of the largest cable operators in the nation to one of the largest telecommunications companies in the world" (MHCRC, 1999, pp. 12–13). They were mystified by the reaction of then–FCC chairman William Kennard to their actions: during an interview Kennard gave to Charlie Rose on PBS in mid-January, he made comments "to the effect 'we must be very careful in imposing regulations on nascent technology'" (MHCRC, 1999, p. 17n32). In strong terms, Olson responded,

Even as the Janus-faced AT&T made such arguments, ISPs looking to find their way onto their networks were too clever in their own right as their interests meshed against a common foe. Regarding their unusual "growing unanimity" on the issue, MindSpring's vice president of regulatory affairs told trade press, "We compete against each other every day for customers.... We want to keep competing" ("ISPs Band Together," 1999). This was not entirely true; they would surely prefer to wipe each other out—but it made for a good contrast with AT&T/TCI. One side could muddy the waters as well as the other. AOL's CEO, Stave Case, noted,

> We've never asked for cable to be a common carrier. We've asked that cable companies open up their network and provide it to others to resell in a non-discriminatory way, much as the cable industry now has certain non-discriminatory policies regarding how they pick programming.... I can say that versus six months ago... there's a growing recognition from a public-policy standpoint that stimulating competition in broad-band is important. (Buell et al., 1999)

The brushfire the Mt. Hood Cable Regulatory Commission sparked would erupt into a fierce blaze between cable conduits, the services which rode upon them, and the more cynical intentions of local Bell companies. Meanwhile, at a deeper level, a set of new struggles was being conjoined—one was foundational, the other was definitional. Given the types of fights involved, particular forms of activism were engaged which would set the tone for the next decade. A crucial assemblage was crafted that otherwise would have simply been trampled in Washington politics: one grown not from the grassroots up, but deliberately cultivated by seasoned players in national politics with a particular sense of the requirements of "the public interest" and who also possessed particular forms of knowledge and expertise in specific realms, realms which required no small amount of institutional memory to be effective. By the same token, such knowledge, and their choice to engage the debate in its particular terms and foundations, would mean that they were largely appropriating neoliberal imperatives to topple them under their own weight. In the process, they would receive little credit or notice in the long term.

A new, foundational front was opened in the policy debates surrounding the structure of the Internet as it emerged into the commercial realm and was moving into high-speed, one firmly ensconced in the unpredictable auspices of local officers, numerous volunteers with little financial or other stake in the outcomes in these debates—as opposed to the interests of the vested actors. At this level, localities were discovering that a particular "kink" in telecommunications law enabled them to render the politics of an entity largely without place ironically and absolutely place-bound. The local franchise board was suddenly a cable provider's worst nightmare: most worrisome for AT&T, these organizations were themselves networked. Each locale was unpredictable: some might easily grant AT&T its wishes with nary a fight; but then there were the places such as Portland and Multnomah County who might stir others to action. It did not help that cable was one of the least popular industries in the country due to their exploitative rate hikes to which consumers were particularly sensitive. Finally, they were willing to make their case national: in their ex parte comments to the FCC regarding the takeover of TCI by AT&T, they were not bashful in making their points. Thousands of new pressure points of activism were born, an outcome immediately seized by activists in Washington.

This first salvo in a post–Telecommunications Act consumer rebellion was an effort to push back against the worst of the neoliberal drive to increase the bounds of market authority via its own logic. It would come at a cost. In seeking to redefine ordinary users of advanced services away from their traditional roles of mere consumers (that were both payers into a cable system and a commodity to be traded to advertisers and to content partners), how resultant activism *could* be practiced was altered. If the market for liberalized networking services arose from the corporate sector, here was a desire to force the same in the residential one: this would need to be forcibly obtained. The MHCRC filing noted that, "In making its original recommendation to Portland and Multnomah County, the MHCRC consciously sought to carry out what the MHCRC and its staff sincerely understood to be a broad, federally-encouraged policy of providing for competition, deregulation, and an open and accessible marketplace in communications and Internet access" (MHCRC, 1999, pp. 6–7). It does not question the commercial imperative already at work upon the Internet universe at the time, still formative, something advocates, as we shall see, were well aware. With the question of a commercial or noncommercial Internet off the table at this point, even as noncommercial services were one of the aspects defended, the logics of this unfolding struggle only rang their death knell more loudly. The operative logics, those that shunted such worries aside in favor of arguments over competition and strains of antitrust law that would serve as their proxy, were *necessary* to continue to be invited to the table in Washington during this time.

one of the most significant episodes in the development of the commercial Internet—particularly since no other frame was on offer.

Such mobilization had significant material costs. One *New York Times* piece, often cited as showing the "odd bedfellows" contained in the coalitions that formed around the issue, does us an entirely different service, revealing the sheer cash resources necessary to be a part of this particular fight (Labaton, 1999). "While a precise figure on spending on the lawyers and lobbyists and for campaign contributions is not available, executives and lawyers involved in the case estimate that it is already in the tens of millions of dollars," the *Times* noted. The "revolving door" was a crucial factor in hiring decisions. The newspaper reported that AT&T and the cable industry had "retained many of Washington's lobbyists," including a former Republican representative from Minnesota and a lobbying firm started by a major Democratic fundraiser. James Cicconi, general counsel and head of government relations for AT&T, was a former aide to George H. W. Bush and had been active in fundraising for George W. Bush. George Vradenberg, the general counsel for AOL, was a top adviser and fundraiser for John McCain. Greg Simon, who headed up the OpenNet Coalition, had worked for Democratic vice president Al Gore; he was collaborating with Richard Bond, former chairman of the Republican National Committee. The regional Bell companies themselves had hired three well-connected advocates: Haley Barbour, former chairman of the Republican National Committee; Susan Molinari, former Republican congressman from Staten Island; and Michael McCurry, former Clinton press secretary. The campaign donations stemming from this inter- and intraindustry fight, the *Times* reported, would likely result in neither presidential candidate taking a stance, lest the money stop flowing from the losing side.

Perhaps more striking is an underexamined practice in Washington also revealed by the piece. AT&T had put numerous law firms on retainer—those, presumably, with expertise in telecom issues—simply to make it impossible for opponents to hire them due to conflicts of interest. Greg Simon of the OpenNet Coalition told the *Times*, "A lot of people have told me that they owe me thank-you notes.... They were retained just so I couldn't hire them. In Washington it took weeks to find somebody who was not lobbying for AT&T. I could not find three firms that had not been retained on the issue." To illustrate the point, later that year, advocates in the continuing Portland court case needed to file briefs with no less than fifteen law firms to serve all the parties involved (Citizens' Utility Board of Oregon et al., 1999, pp. 28–29). The *Times* further noted "Potemkin-like efforts at organizing" by "Astroturf campaigns, in contrast to grass-roots." The article called rallies in front of San Francisco City Hall "contrived," and "both" sides had "made extensive use of telephone banks to gin up support by asking loaded questions and making alarmist predictions" (Labaton, 1999).

The article is also instructive in that while it notes that "consumer groups and AT&T's rivals say the battle is as much over principle as it is over business," the go-to source for the consumer standpoint was Donna Lampert, who was now providing legal representation on behalf of AOL. While certainly an ally, not even a token advocate from the consumer groups was quoted at the time when this article was written. This, sadly, was exactly what the price consumer advocates' strategy would be. Up against such intractable odds, advocates played a skillful game of cat and mouse with all sides of the corporate sector and the Federal Communications Commission (FCC) itself, leveraging their connections in the states to bring more localities into the fold.

Consumer Advocates on the Move

As they seized on the Mt. Hood Cable Regulatory Commission's (MHCRC's) actions, consumer advocates continued to develop the policy innovation of open access itself. This was a crucial point in the concept's history. The notions that emerge are quite representative of the given neoliberal moment itself: a suspicion of markets is solved via yet more marketization, now put to the intent of preserving in certain instances *noncommercial* content. *Strong competition* would be turned into a weapon against the commodification of the consumer herself. Such understandings of commodification, looked through today's lens, are decidedly primitive; even at this moment new advertising networks were being established to track these individual users. The appropriate read of these events, seen from the vantage point of history, is a foundation-laying for exactly this type of tracked subject via a particularly truncated vision of freedom from commodification.

At the forefront of advocates' minds were the business models surrounding portals, the start pages users would encounter as they commenced their browsing: recall that these, rather than search engines, were seen as the pivotal point of contact. On January 27, 1999, the CFA, Consumers Union,

> and consumers. … Absent open access, AT&T would likely be able to force consumers to accept its closed system. (Citizens' Utility Board of Oregon et al., 1999, pp. 1–2)

"Openness" here is a defense of the free market itself. Access to the Internet is at once both an opportunity for free speech and access to a perceived genuinely free market. None of this is particularly theorized.

> Openness is a matter of design choice, not technological imperative. The Internet's signal characteristic has been open entry. That openness lowers entry barriers and facilitates instant market access. Entrepreneurs with a computer and an idea can start a business. Those seeking to disseminate messages can reach potential audiences far larger than any other mass medium can deliver. This network of networks also creates communities of common concern, locally and internationally. (Citizens' Utility Board of Oregon et al., 1999, p. 3)

While years later in the debate Sandvig (2007) would comment on the seeming irony that Ithiel de Sola Pool's "policies of freedom" were invoked in the network neutrality debate only indirectly, consumer advocates here in fact saw fit to make the connection *explicitly*: "There is simply no way to obtain the same level of freedom of expression and the same speed and quality of service in the closed model. Whatever the virtues of @Home's admittedly sophisticated technology, it is not being deployed as a 'technology of freedom.' See de Sola Pool, *Technologies of Freedom*" (Citizens' Utility Board of Oregon et al., 1999, p. 5).

The *manner* by which open access was to be implemented is, likewise, through private arrangement. When Schwartzman, writing Los Angeles cable authorities, tackled the issue of "what open access was" head on, it is explicitly a business arrangement and not a set of principles. Contrasting such an approach with direct content regulation to solve the problem of cable operator control, such as requiring an ISP to offer "balanced coverage to controversial issues" or "provid[ing] at least three sources for any consumer product that it includes," he proposes "adoption of content-neutral, structural, business-oriented safeguards to prevent providers from attaining and abusing a monopoly gatekeeper position." In more detail:

> No single, common definition of open access has yet been formulated. A number of regulatory models are available, ranging from traditional common carriage regulation to a more flexible "nondiscriminatory access" model. *We believe that a flexible policy of requiring nondiscriminatory access to all competitive service providers, coupled with strict enforcement of those requirements, allows for the best solution for competitive Internet service providers while imposing the least burden on cable*

providers. ... More precise regulations would need to be developed only if the cable industry is not responsive to a broader policy mandate. (Media Access Project et al., 1999; emphasis added)

In many ways, it is the willingness of these advocates to go along with the commercial imperative unfolding that is these advocates' continued ticket to policymaking settings in Washington. Given the term's flexibility, it is also what supplies continued entrée at the local level to credibly present its necessity. If it is merely a business arrangement, localities with less expertise than that of the likes of David Olson need not fear wading in and putting their foot down.

This said, did this make these advocates mere sycophants to the abstract form of competition to that was held in such high regard by the neoliberal thought collective? Absolutely not: the stance of these advocates is complex. To borrow Ruggie's (1982) conception, it contains a residual "embedded liberalism," which calls for the *competitive* part of their argument to be set within a broader *social* framework. Consumers Union and the CFA, in an early 1999 report, took stock of the different *levels* of communications-technology users by income (Cooper & Kimmelman, 1999). Their end recommendations were instructive, a combination of competition-driven policy *within* a framework of equity, forcing markets to do what they would normally resist. As inherently mistrustful of the desires of the conduits' owners they were, however, they also recognized the side benefits individual consumers had wrought from broader liberalization projects in the telecommunications sphere and sought to defend the strongest of these. Monopoly pricing practices needed to be addressed; where competition did not exist, continued price regulation should still be maintained; pricing protections for "low-volume, long distance users" would need to be established to "ensure that this segment of the market is not discriminated against with price increases that do not reflect real costs." They would actively *bolster* elements of the Telecommunications Act that enforced the opening of telephony markets to competition, since in many markets, local networks were expected to remain a bottleneck. Until competition developed "throughout the consumer market," local phone monopolies "must be required to allow potential competitors to connect to their networks at prices that facilitate competition and reflect only efficient costs for telecommunications equipment and services"; efforts to create loopholes in this regime "should be rebuffed" (Cooper & Kimmelman, 1999, pp. viii–ix).

of authorizations for international resale serves the public interest, convenience and necessity" (Furchtgott-Roth, 1999, p. 1). To draw attention to his point, he wrote,

> Beyond the threshold question of statutory authority to regulate mergers, I have concerns about the process employed in FCC merger reviews. The vast majority of license transfers ... even those that involve merging entities [] are not subject to the stringent review today imposed upon AT&T and TCI. For example, as I have observed, mergers of companies like Mobil and Exxon involve the transfer of a substantial number of radio licenses, many of the same kind of licenses as those at issue here, and yet we take no Commission level action on those transfer applications. (Furchtgott-Roth, 1999, p. 3)

Expanding Their Purview

In June 1999, the district court in Oregon found in the city of Portland and Multnomah County's favor against AT&T's lawsuit. It wasn't just a slight win: this was a decision in which District Judge Owen Panner was described by *Communications Daily* as "dismantling" AT&T's arguments in their entirety (AT&T Corp. v. City of Portland, 1999; "Court Says," 1999). AT&T claimed the locality had overreached its authority; the court disagreed, noting that Congress desired cable regulation to be at the local level. The court held that the locality could require open access since cable operated an "essential facility," something quite aside from regulating cable as a common carrier. To AT&T's complaint of a perceived mandate that it would have to install new equipment at its head ends, the court responded there was no such directive—it was up to AT&T to decide how to do this. To AT&T's complaint of its now being forced to carry certain speech, Panner responded this was not a speech regulation but an economic one. Supporters were ecstatic. On June 13, in an audacious move, the Center for Media Education, the Media Access Project, Computer Professionals for Social Responsibility, and the Oregon Consumers League placed an ad in the *Oregonian* celebrating Portland and Multnomah County's victory over AT&T in district court, hoping to call increased attention to the issue and to urge residents to contact Congress to make such access policies a national prerogative.[2] City Commissioner Erik Sten noted the spread of the idea to other locales, whose officials "stat[ed] that if any other city was victorious in applying open access, then those cities would revisit [the] issue." An

"MFN" or "most favored nation" provision was increasingly becoming the placeholder of choice for other locales while AT&T appealed the Portland District Court's decision to the Ninth Circuit. Itself a curious appropriation from international "free trade" discourse (at this time an especially hot subject of debate by activists, corporations, and governments alike), this meant that whatever elements of the condition survived in the courts would be what was required of a cable franchise under contention. Sten continued, "It's safe to say most of the city commissioners and mayors I've spoken with felt [open access] was the right requirement" ("Court Says," 1999).

There were few promising signals sent from the national level. It took two weeks for the FCC to respond to the district court decision; when it did, its reception was entirely negative. A *Television Digest* article described Kennard at the 1999 National Cable and Telecommunications Association conference as fearing the "chaos" of individual franchise authorities each setting technical standards. "We have to have a national standard in this area," he warned, and to applause of the cable executives present, "the market would be rocked with uncertainty [and] investment would be stymied" without such a national standard ("Kennard Hits Portland Ruling," 1999). In a speech entitled "The Road Not Taken: Building a Broadband Future for America," Kennard laid out his national broadband policy, a plan via no-plan:

> Here is my vision for broadband in America. Multiple broadband pipes serving America's homes. At least four or five facilities-based competitors. Digital Subscriber Line (DSL), cable modem, terrestrial wireless, and satellite. That's my vision for our broadband future. Because that is the best way to serve America's consumers. Multiple facilities-based carriers, competing robustly to bring all sorts of wonderful content to America's homes.... But how do we do it? We let the marketplace do it. (Quoted in Breckheimer & Taglang, 1999)

Kennard compared the power assumed by franchise authorities with a highway system "where every town could set parameters for the size of cars and the size of lanes.... We wouldn't be able to drive to the store, much less to another state." "Sometimes," he continued, "people talk about broadband as though it is a mature industry.... But the fact is that we don't have a duopoly in broadband. We don't have a monopoly in broadband. We have a no-opoly.... The broadband market is fertile, but still undeveloped." Kennard noted that the "best decision government ever made with respect to the Internet was the decision the FCC made years ago not to impose strategy document, the interests of warring corporate parties were seemingly canceling each other out.

AT&T Sets Its Sights on MediaOne

As Congress remained largely in stasis, in midsummer 1999, AT&T[3] filed its intent at the FCC to continue acquiring cable companies, this time setting its sights on MediaOne. As a result, a new wave of local action was set to commence as the giant would need to seek the permission of all of MediaOne's local franchise authorities to seal the deal. Advocates were determined to capitalize on this opportunity. At the same time, Excite@Home was diving more deeply into a premium-content model. By the time the MediaOne acquisition was announced, AT&T's single affiliated ISP had invested nearly $60 million in content startups, even as the company was strapped for cash (Malik, 2003, p. 154). The CEO blamed the cable conduits: "We are definitely supply-constrained right now. We know the demand is out there. The problem is the installers—there are only so many backhoes digging up the streets" (quoted in Malik, 2003, p. 154). Their foreseen business model, however, was clear. The company's president said outright that "The power has to be proprietary content.... People don't watch distribution" (quoted in Cooper, 2000a, p. 1043n83). This strategy was reinforced later in the year as Excite@Home bought online greeting-card upstart BlueMountain.com for $780 million, "reasoning that Blue Mountain Arts' traffic would add more oomph to Excite, which was falling behind Yahoo! by the month" (Malik, 2003, p. 155). When the *New York Times* gave public airing of the insider disagreements between Excite@Home and its conduit partners, it quoted Excite@Home's CEO: "We think that over time, the revenue from transporting data will continue to fall. That's why in our long-term business model, half our revenue comes from the media side," a comment that "pissed off" executives at Cox, Comcast, and AT&T (Malik, 2003, p. 152). While Malik attributes the lack of enthusiasm for the public sentiment to bad internal relations, he neglects to consider that the intense simmer of the ISP-access fight may have had just as much, if not more, to do with it.

When Erik Sten, in Portland, gave a *Washington Post* writer a tour of the city, the concerns became quite concrete. In an interview later in the year, he said,

> On the broader question of what happens if you don't have choice, I think it's chilling and obvious. We had a Washington Post reporter in town for the Court hearing a few weeks ago, and he just walked into Powell's Books, the largest independent bookstore in the country. He walks in and asks if they have an Internet department, since he wants to include this in his story. He went into their Internet department and asks the guy in the Internet department whether he supports Portland's decision on open access. And this guy says "yeah, and I'll show you why," and they call up the @Home Internet home page and he searches for books three different ways, and it all comes back Amazon.com—because Amazon bought that placement on the @Home service. So if you're searching for a book in Portland, Powell's, our number one tourist destination in the city and our biggest bookstore, a cultural icon that's incredibly important both socially and financially to the city of Portland, you can't even find Powell's through the @Home search engine. ("Interview with Erik Sten," 1999)

Concurrently, consumer advocates were growing in awareness of a potentially disturbing new market developing. As Excite@Home was increasingly becoming not just a *platform* but recrafting itself as a *content* provider, in late July, the CFA, Consumers Union, Media Access Project, and the Center for Media Education would note in a letter to FCC chairman Kennard that a cottage industry responding to cable's increasing demand for filtering technology was maturing. Large developers of routers, such as Cisco, were hardly being secretive in outlining the ways they could serve the interests of new broadband networks; it simply wasn't being reported in major press outlets. Advocates seized on these companies' marketing materials to drive their concerns home.

> Cisco Systems, for example, one of the leaders in providing sophisticated networking hardware and software to cable ISPs, is not reluctant to discuss the power of the new digital architecture, a power that translates directly into increased ISP profits and control. The new networking technology, Cisco promises the cable industry, gives "... you the information you need to offer advanced differentiated services at a profit.... [Y]ou can optimize service profits by marketing 'express' services to premium customers ready to pay for superior network performance." (Discussed in Center for Media Education, 1999, p. 7)

The openness with which such initiatives were (and would continue to be) discussed by router manufacturers was indicative of the known demand nascent broadband providers would provide for these tools. Met with FCC silence, action became increasingly intense outside the Beltway. In addition to those who had commenced taking action immediately after Portland

and Multnomah County made its own decision, others acting on their knowledge of the district court's decimation of AT&T's case advanced open access conditions on their own franchise transfers. Many would announce their intent to make final decisions later in the year as AT&T appealed the district court decision to the Ninth Circuit. San Francisco was one such locale, postponing a vote until December, but the city's board of supervisors made sure to point out that they "back[ed] Portland in its court battle with AT&T and declare San Francisco's general policy to be supportive of open access" ("Access Fight," 1999). Miami-Dade County set a hearing of October 19 on open access, even holding a late September workshop on the debate; at this point a "staffer for Commissioner Bruno Barreiro, [the] strongest open access advocate, said he saw 'very good likelihood' that [the] policy would pass." Los Angeles similarly scheduled a decision for the fall ("Access Fight," 1999).

Others chose to take action directly. Fairfax, Virginia, initially delayed a decision as to whether to mandate open access as Cox Communications took over a franchise from Media General—which, reflecting the exuberance only a bubble can provide, it was doing for the princely sum of $1.4 billion for a system of 260,000 subscribers at a rate of $5,385 per subscriber. It was also inheriting "local frustration at Media General's previous rate hikes and 'antiquated' system"; Media General had been promising upgrades but had allowed its systems to fester nonetheless ("Fairfax County Seeking Concessions," 1999). No matter: with the district court decision providing wind at their backs, Fairfax County instituted an open access condition on Cox. The trade rag *Warren's Cable Regulation Monitor,* catering to its core audience, could barely restrain hyperbole. "Behind closed doors in the dead of night and with no opportunity for public comment the City of Fairfax, VA, voted 4–2 to apply common carrier regulations to Cox and require it to unbundle its highspeed modem service in exchange for approving a franchise transfer from Media Gen[era]l" ("In the States," 1999b). The *Monitor* continued:

> "[The] vote underscores why 30K local franchising authorities across the US should not be making scatter-shot decisions about nat'l telecommunications policy," NCTA [the National Cable and Telecommunications Association] added. (Nice to see the NCTA getting a bit fired up, eh?). It appears not to be a coincidence that Fairfax Cty is home to many high-level AOL execs who certainly run into city councilors at the county's many golf courses, social events, and political

> fundraisers. Even a bunch of devo-land suburbanites, with more lawyers than raccoons, has to realize that this decision gets made by the Portland case. Why else wouldn't they insert a [most favored nation] clause, much like in San Fran, that reserves the right to revisit the issue once it is resolved by Congress, or more likely the 9th Circuit?

In July 1999, the Broward, Florida, Board of City Commissioners mandated that in transferring its franchise, it—and any other cable operator—would need to provide a similar standard of open access to competing ISPs ("In the States," 1999a). In response to Broward County's open access initiative, Comcast and Advanced Cable Systems sued, repeating most of AT&T's old points in Portland. The lawsuit was eventually thrown out due to the fact the company was not even supplying cable modem service yet but were told that once it upgraded their systems, it could try again ("AT&T Threatens," 1999). In early August AT&T filed a separate, second lawsuit in Broward County which stuck ("San Francisco Delays," 1999). Kennard and the FCC continued to press their case in the wake of Broward County's decision, arguing for "an intentional restraint born of humility" because "we can't predict where the market is going" ("Broadband Access Stays," 1999).

Municipal organizations took action as well. At their annual convention in St. Louis, the National Association of Counties (NAC) adopted a resolution that asserted local franchise authorities did have jurisdiction "to require MSOs [multiple system operators] to open their networks to all ISPs. [The r]esolution said that if Congress or FCC makes policy in that area, it should mandate open access to encourage competition among ISPs" ("Broadband Access Stays," 1999). It was largely alone in directly endorsing the policy among municipal groups, aside from the National League of Cities the previous year. The National Association of Telecommunications Officers and Advisors (NATOA) was mistrustful of the FCC's actions but not for the same reasons as the core advocates which operated NoGatekeepers.org; it was much more concerned about preemption of their authority. At a Strategic Research Institute conference in Washington, DC in late summer 1999, Jane Lawton, then-president of the organization, declared that it was "hard to trust a 'hands-off' policy." She noted the contradiction between what had been understood as "deregulatory" via the Telecommunications Act and what was emerging in FCC policy, as it was "'disingenuous of the FCC' to paint its own position as procompetitive and that of Portland and Broward County as 'regulatory'" (all quotes from "San Francisco Delays,"

1999). She said what was obvious to localities: that the differences in approach more accurately constituted "a couple competitive models," and that while at this time NATOA's position stood to protect localities' ability to demand open access provision but not to *favor the policy itself per se,* she believed that such a policy was "inevitable... that open access will become policy" due to its increasing popularity and the likely need for legislative response of the ilk already brewing ("San Francisco Delays," 1999).

AT&T and MediaOne, in addition to dispatching a legion of lawyers and lobbyists, launched a campaign that included "withholding investment in facilities, threats to drag localities into complex regulatory proceedings, and expensive TV advertising, not to mention heavy-handed threats to drag localities into costly law suits [*sic*]" (Cooper, 1999, p. 3). While cities were being given varying advice as to whether to pursue open access conditions with considerations colored by caution and the likely lawsuit, few were now *uninterested.* The OpenNet Coalition promised to be a powerful presence in any city negotiating its transfer of a MediaOne franchise to AT&T ("Cities Wary," 1999).

In response, in an effort to clear FCC rules limiting ownership of cable systems, AT&T was busy rearranging its own house so as to appear less powerful than it was by taking two tacks. One involved approaching the FCC to alter media ownership rules in their favor, engaging in an "intense lobbying campaign" that ultimately rendered only minor changes. A bigger victory for AT&T was simply delaying FCC decisions on horizontal cable ownership rules, providing time to "shift[] investments and consolidat[e] holdings in order to decrease their total ownership under the FCC's rules" ("AT&T/MediaOne Merger," 1999). The company created numerous "tracking stocks" to separate out amalgamated businesses under its purview while still retaining control of them. The net result was a tangled web of accounting prestidigitation that would make AT&T look less the behemoth it was and thus more palatable for anxious regulators to let be. "The new AT&T," a CFA report declared, "is now a jumble of management gimmicks intended to convince regulators that AT&T is not in charge—tracking stock for cable programming, tracking stock for wireless, tracking stock for Internet programming, a management committee for Time Warner Entertainment, and an independent operating agreement for Cablevision" (Consumer Federation of America, 1999b, p. 3).

In the face of such efforts, it is surprising how bold localities *were*. By the end of the year, Cambridge, Massachusetts, would require nondiscriminatory access, as did the Massachusetts towns of Somerville and Quincy ("Additional Open Access Victories," 1999; "News," 1999). They did this after requesting clarification from the FCC as to whether they had the right to do so; "the FCC never responded" ("Additional Open Access Victories," 1999). In Pittsburgh, ISPs lobbied the Pittsburgh City Council to require open access over cable plant during the city's franchise renegotiations. Pittsburgh, Pennsylvania, had considered the open access quandary in its own negotiations regarding AT&T and TCI earlier in the year, but dropped the issue in the face of a potential lawsuit by AT&T ("News," 1999). However, the process was renewed in the context of Portland's victory later in the year, and in late 1999 Pittsburgh regulators forced AT&T to provide open access should Portland prevail over AT&T's appeal in the Ninth Circuit. ISPs were ferocious in lobbying for their interests there in the months leading to this decision ("News," 2000a).

Consumer advocates, in conjunction with local affiliates, were actively pushing these debates along. In October, the Virginia Citizens Consumer Council (VCCC) teamed up with the CFA to urge the Virginia State Corporation Commission to make open access a condition of the AT&T-MediaOne merger, as had been done elsewhere in the state; they followed up with a letter to the Richmond city council the following day, submitting for the record the CFA's and Consumer @ction's report, *Transforming the Information Highway into a Private Toll Road*, which summarized in detail the means by which the emergent cable giants sought to prioritize profitable content surreptitiously (Consumer Federation of America & Virginia Citizens Consumer Council, 1999a, 1999c; the report is Consumer Federation of America and Consumer @ction, 1999). Advocates here turned the tables on the planned prioritization schemes made available by new routing capabilities: if these routers were good enough to *weed out* traffic, surely they could be useful to *direct flows* of traffic as well? "Alternatives for ensuring nondiscriminatory conditions of access have been identified in the months since Portland first ordered non-discriminatory access," they wrote. "Such alternatives include local peering, policy-based routing, and access to [the] cable modem transfer system" (Consumer Federation of America & Virginia Citizens Consumer Council, 1999d, p. 2).

("MediaOne Ads," 1999). As the new year turned, lobbying was intense at the statehouse by both sides, yet no bills were even on offer at that point. A staggering amount of money was being spent in the referendum struggle: advocates noted that cable interests had by that point spent more than $1.1 million trying to kill the referendum; Grace had spent $600,000 in support ("News," 2000).

The CFA and its affiliate organizations were active on multiple other fronts. The Vermont Public Interest Research Group and the CFA wrote to the Vermont Public Interest Board on the issue as it considered its own upcoming cable franchise renewals (Consumer Federation of America & Vermont Public Interest Group, 1999). In Miami-Dade, Florida, the CFA and the Florida Consumer Action Network urged the Miami-Dade Board of County Commissioners to impose its own open access requirement on its transfer of its MediaOne franchise to AT&T (Consumer Federation of America & Florida Consumer Action Network, 1999). Miami decided against requiring open access in the end, arguing that they believed it should be decided on a national level, "a belief that was no doubt helped by a visit from FCC chairman Bill Kennard, who reportedly advised local officials not to support Open Access" ("News," 1999). Working with Missouri Citizen Action, a similar request went to the St. Louis Board of Aldermen (Consumer Federation of America & Missouri Citizen Action, 1999). While earlier in February the King County, Washington, Council adopted a policy of nondiscriminatory access as part of its franchise renewal, it appointed an expert review panel to evaluate issues associated with implementing the policy. This panel would eventually split 4–4, producing no clear recommendation, and the CFA urged King County to proceed with its early recommendation of open access (Consumer Federation of America, 1999a). Addressing poor customer service, Fremont, California, took the step of requiring service standards over high-speed broadband provided by cable, demanding issues be handled "in a more prompt, efficient manner than had previously been the case" ("News," 1999).

The FCC Attempts to Thwart Local Efforts and Consumer Arguments

At all turns the FCC cast off indirect signals to stymie these efforts. A white paper by a staff economist entitled "The FCC and the Unregulation of the Internet" (Oxman, 1999) recalled many of the successes in actions preventing bottleneck controllers from controlling access to facilities but took away the opposite conclusions consumer advocates did. Oxman concluded that in "plotting a deregulatory course for the future," the lessons to take away would include not "automatically imposing legacy regulations on new technologies." Further, "when Internet-based services replace traditional legacy services, begin to deregulate the old instead of regulate the new"; the FCC should "maintain a watchful eye to ensure that anticompetitive behavior does not develop, [but] do not regulate based on the perception of potential future bottlenecks, and be careful that any regulatory responses are the minimum necessary and outweigh the costs of regulation" (Oxman, 1999, p. 3). In particular, regarding the last point, the author states,

> As the steward of the communications public interest, the Commission must ensure that all players in the communications marketplace, including owners and users of telephone networks and cable systems, have a fair opportunity to compete. That goal should, and very often can, be accomplished without governmental regulation, by permitting market forces to work and shape the competitive landscape. The Commission should, of course, avoid regulation based solely on speculation of a potential future problem. (Oxman, 1999, p. 25)

However, the FCC decided to intervene more boldly in local affairs later in October, publishing a staff report prepared by the Cable Services Bureau (and credited to its chief, Deborah Lathen) which sought to provide "guidance" to localities considering the question while defending a continued "watchful waiting" stance. The report was quietly authored based on closed-door meetings with various players in the broadband industry. Commencing cheekily with a rendition of the parable of the "Blind Men and the Elephant," it was seemingly blindly optimistic in its assessments of competition in the face of continued withering consumer critique:

> Far from finding harm, the Bureau's monitoring efforts have revealed a nascent residential broadband market containing a number of existing and potential competitors. Cable, telephone, wireless, and satellite companies are rushing to provide broadband services to the home.... Perhaps most importantly, government has provided the numerous incentives to broadband companies to invest in and deploy their technologies. By forbearing from imposing "open access" regulations on cable operators, the Commission has fostered an environment that encourages investment not only in cable, but also in the alternative broadband technologies, such as wireless, satellite, and DSL. (Lathen, 1999, p. 47)

As the FCC's mandate was to "allow market forces to flourish" only intervening "in the event of market failure," the Cable Services Bureau recommended that "the appropriate balance can be struck by monitoring the market and resisting the urge to fix a system that does not appear to be broken and shows early signs of healthy growth and competition" (Lathen, 1999, p. 41). Directly contradicting advocates' claims, and sending a direct (and intentional) signal to local authorities, it concluded that

> customer demand for choice ultimately will compel cable operators to open their systems to unaffiliated ISPs. If a cable operator opts for a closed, proprietary system in which consumers have no choice of ISPs or have to purchase unwanted services as a condition of subscribership, these companies will risk losing subscribers in favor of more open systems. These operators also would be susceptible to regulation intended to eliminate monopolistic and anticompetitive practices. We believe that market forces and our ongoing monitoring efforts will persuade cable companies to keep their networks open, even in the absence of regulation. (Lathen, 1999, p. 42)

The report hems and haws over what "open access" was, listing the varying ways players in the debate "defined" the term and finishes by throwing its hands up. "Despite a flurry of national and grassroots activity concerning 'open access,' our panelists—a collection of some of the nation's leading business, government, and public interest advocates on this issue—were not able to agree upon a single workable definition of the term, much less recommend an appropriate regulatory classification and enforcement mechanism" (Lathen, 1999, p. 38).

On the eve of this report's release, the core Washington, DC, advocacy groups behind NoGatekeepers responded with alarm. "We are distressed to hear that the Commission intends to release a staff report evidently intended to dissuade local franchising authorities from insisting that cable TV franchisees offer consumers the opportunity to choose among competing Internet service providers, and to grant citizens the right to transmit and receive Internet content without economic or content-based restraints," they wrote (Center for Media Education et al., 1999). Understanding full well the force such a report, even if nonbinding, would have in regulatory discourse across the country—particularly in the manner it would be mobilized by AT&T, MediaOne, and other cable companies with a vested interest in defending their nascent business models—they bemoaned:

> We believe that issuing of "guidance" or other recommendations, even camouflaged as policy analysis, would be incompatible with your expressed policy of "watchful waiting" on the open access issue. Most important, a "staff report" is susceptible to mischaracterization as an official policy statement. Even though publications issued without a vote of the FCC's members have no legal or

> precedential significance, cable industry lobbyists can misuse such documents in municipal and state legislative battles. The foundation of our democratic form of governance is open decision making.... Secrecy, on the other hand, engenders only suspicion and doubt. Secrecy also generates bad policy.... It is sadly ironic that the Commission should proceed in secret to prepare a document purporting to provide guidance on an issue of such national importance. As far as we are aware, public input on this report came from three invitation-only meetings with staff. (Center for Media Education et al., 1999)

Advocates pushed for what seemed common-sense proposals at this stage of the debate. Even if the FCC thought that it should not intervene in the opening of these networks at this time, they proposed that the FCC could "at least mandate that cable modems and cable modem termination systems have the capacity to provide multiple ISPs with non-discriminatory access" so as to prevent monopolistic lock-in of closed systems (Center for Media Education et al., 1999). No response was forthcoming.

Perhaps one of the more significant developments at this point was the *Broadband in the Public Interest* e-newsletter launched by NoGatekeepers in early October 1999. The significance of its brief run—released generally biweekly, its last update on behalf of the core groups speaking in a unified voice would be early February 2000—was collation of all of these significant happenings at the local, state, and national levels in Congress as well as at the FCC. It would touch on international affairs as well, given the United States appeared to be moving in the *opposite* direction as other nations when it came to broadband policy. *Broadband in the Public Interest* (*BPI*) would outline the victories and contradictions in official statements. They tracked developments and the intense lobbying which accompanied the AT&T-MediaOne transfer, collecting local reports and putting them in perspective. When it was discovered that the merger would violate ownership limits on cable, *BPI* broadcast the machinations inside the FCC to make this defensible ("AT&T/MediaOne Merger," 1999). The email blast was early to remind its readers that in Canada, open access was the law of the land, with "cable companies and ISPs... both working to implement Open Access. In fact, some cable companies in Canada have already implemented Open Access, such as Regional in Timmins, ONT" (Rogoway, 1999). Looking to Australia, they note "the initiative of the local power company, ACTEW, to build a broadband, multi-use network serving Canberra... [that will be] open to all comers—phone companies, cable companies, and ISPs" (Rogoway, 1999).

Bewildering to them were the motives attributed to efforts like the staff report just released. Perhaps the most challenging argument to counter, however, involved the repeated assertion at the FCC that any open access requirement would deter investment. Responding in force:

> When we went looking for the mythic Wall Street cabal standing with linked arms against Open Access (Hands across Wall Street) we couldn't find them. Consider the FCC Staff Report "Broadband Today," released earlier this month which states, "there was near unanimous agreement among the cable and investment panelists that government regulation of the terms and conditions of third party access would cast a cloud over investment in both cable and telephony applications." (The rest of us did not hear the panelist's testimony because it was received by the FCC in a closed proceeding last spring.) But when we turned to the footnote supporting that conclusion, we found only a citation to a Communications Daily article which cited unnamed Wall Street analysts for the proposition that the "uncertainty created by open access activity" had caused "cable stock prices to downturn in recent weeks." We emphatically agree with that conclusion. Uncertainty makes investors nervous. Ironically, the FCC's position of watchful waiting—also known as deciding by not deciding—is helping to fuel that uncertainty. But the question of how uncertainty affects the market is an entirely different question than whether requiring cable broadband operators to open their pipes to competition will chill investment.("Open Access: A Threat" 1999)

The advocates were incredulous that the FCC couldn't tell the difference between investor nervousness based on *uncertainty* versus the *open access policy itself.* They continued,

> On that question, the weight of the evidence clearly indicates that Open Access would encourage investment. In fact, at a recent KMB [Design Group] conference on telecommunications, two prominent Internet investors, Anna Maria Kovacs of Janney Montgomery Scott and Richard ("Ric") Prentiss of Raymond James & Associates stated that not only could the FCC eliminate the cloud of uncertainty by affirmatively resolving the issue, but that Open Access would actually speed market entry. ("Open Access: A Threat," 1999)

Sealing their case, the FCC's audacity and shortsightedness was confronted head-on. "FCC staff has recently said that they fear that conducting such an inquiry [into the possibility and technical aspects of open access] would have a negative impact on cable industry stocks. That is the worst, and most inappropriate, of all the reasons not to conduct an inquiry. Prompt completion of such a proceeding would substitute certainty and stability for confusion and rumors," they spat (Center for Media Education et al., 1999).

Cable and AT&T's collective response was increasingly hysterical in public even as they retained what appeared to be the backing of the FCC. *Communications Daily* reported on comments that crept out of the East Coast Cable 1999 conference, held in Baltimore. In the crosshairs were "aggressive municipal consultants" that were "forcing cable operators to fight off regulations and ordinances like never before." States and municipalities were "seeking to overlay blanket telecom ordinances on existing cable franchise agreements ... and operators need to stay alert in [the] face of Bells and ISPs." Cablevision Systems' vice president of cable policy noted: "We have to get [the rhetoric] taken away from the sound bites of 'open access' and 'don't pay twice.'" The "other side of this issue has the sound bites in their favor," said another executive. The emphasis was on increased efforts to "educate" local officials; the ISPs, in the form of OpenNet, "manufactured this issue," Cablevision's vice president of policy continued. Adelphia Deputy General Counsel Charles Stockdale was blunt: "Tell municipal officials there's no reason to jump into [open access] ... There's no reason to get out front and get sued." An emphasis on the plight of the smaller cable companies was mentioned, and Thomas Power, an aide to FCC chairman Kennard, was similarly supportive, noting the "surprising" result of lots of "competition" provided by small operators. (Again, at what particular *scale* this would be the case is not mentioned: it is clearly looking at the national market for cable, rather than what existed at the point of service, which often amounted to one provider at best!) Offering a bit of friendly advice, the article noted that "he recommended the best way to keep Congress from legislating cable's advanced services 'is to continue [rural] deployment.'" Noting that Canada had an open access requirement, Power "echoed other concerns about pricing regulation, noting Canada's experiment with [an] open access mandate. [Power] described how 3 years after passage Canada is wrestling with myriad tariffs, as well as questions such as what exactly is nondiscriminatory access, and can one provider be charged more than another" ("Cable Operators Believe," 1999).

In Mark Cooper's (of the CFA) comments to the November 1999 Consumer Conference sponsored by the VCCC, he laid out a continuing strategy going forward, emphasizing the ground game at the local and state level. It was as much a pep rally as a recruitment drive. Cooper trumpeted, "The advocates of non-discriminatory access have won the 'Battle of the Franchise Transfers' [for two reasons]. ... The moral and economic superiority of the 'open access' position—the fact that it promotes the public interest—has been demonstrated and endorsed by politicians, public interest groups, Wall Street, and local governments." Second, "The defenders of discriminatory access have expended immense political resources to just break even, using political tactics that have offended many, and their assets have been dramatically diminished" (Cooper, 1999, p. 1). The moral victory had been particularly important, and he took the opportunity to win more to its cause:

> The proposed AT&T/MediaOne merger galvanized the opposition to this [closed, proprietary model of Internet provision] for several reasons. Discriminatory access to communications infrastructure—roads, canals, railroads, highways, telecommunications networks—has never been tolerated in this country. Access to the highways of commerce and the marketplace of ideas has always been provided on a non-discriminatory basis to ensure the free flow of information.... Promises that there will be two competitors relatively evenly matched to provide broadband to residential ratepayers (e.g. telephone company DSL offerings are currently the next-best thing to broadband over cable) have failed to ease concerns about the public interest in access to communications.... Two is simply not enough to ensure a competitive market. Three or four produces only a highly concentrated market, which itself cannot be relied upon for vigorous competition. Three or four competing systems will not provide freedom of expression if they are all closed, and *all* closed is the inevitable outcome of allowing *one* to be closed. (Cooper, 1999, p. 2)

Localities that demand open access were portrayed as coming out ahead; their infrastructure would be "more hospitable to all independent ISPs" with "fewer exclusive business relationships" standing in the way. "The independent ISP community will have blossomed in these localities, since the creativity of the Internet is based on open access and, in many respects, the Internet's most vibrant attributes derive from local and regional content providers" (p. 4). Forebodingly, he intoned,

> As the war at the local level plays out, the AT&T/FCC cabal will seek to shift the issue to the federal level by having the broadband Internet declared a telecommunications service. The FCC will then assert jurisdiction and do nothing. The FCC's promise to act swiftly if it perceives market power are not convincing, especially in light of its failure to act in the past—when cable TV rates skyrocketed and mergers and acquisitions have moved forward in flagrant violation of FCC rules.... Whether the final decisions are made at the local or national level, the grassroots basis for open access will have been laid in the city-by-county fight.

> The more cities and counties that step up and take a pro open access position as the franchise renewal process begins, the bigger the base to ensure the ultimate victory. (Cooper, 1999, p. 4)

Advocates at an Apex

This moment, more than any other which would follow, is the closest the United States ever came to a regime whereby any mode of broadband provision, regardless of medium, would be required to provide anything approaching common carriage service. Taking advantage of legacy cable rules, advocates were able to advance their cause via their top-down network of consumer organizations across the country everyplace that possessed a cable franchise that AT&T desired to consume. The requirement that each locality had a say in how its infrastructure operated provided thousands of potential footholds from which to trumpet their case; and perhaps for this reason, in the years to come, this requirement would start finding itself winnowed or eliminated in state legislatures at the behest of broadband industry players.

These victories, however, would prove pyrrhic. This would be due to a number of factors of which broader systemic forces would be able to take advantage. The deliberate positioning of the consumer advocates *between capitals* provided both opportunity and peril. Even as they recognized the possibly duplicitous nature of their erstwhile strange-bedfellows, this provided them the needed legitimation to take part and be taken seriously in policy debates. The policy space they occupied was itself opened by the potential canceling out of corporate interests, a facet with which consumer advocates were well aware and playing to their advantage. To *retain* their position here as both an ally and a viable threat, they needed to hew their message to one strictly of competition. Other issues certainly lay in the recesses of their minds: a particular desire to preserve noncommercial activity online as well as noncommercial operators themselves, which they recognized served different constituencies and provided a needed corrective for the emergent commercial dominance of the medium. All the same, they did not take this critique to its logical end. Here was an opportunity to examine how, as Erik Sten was observing in learning about Powell's Books' predicament aboard online portals, a commercially driven semantic understanding of content aboard the Web might slant the availability not just of particular avenues of locally driven commerce but content crucial for democratic function as well at numerous levels. In lieu of such a direction, this was countered not with a questioning of the commercial drive but a suggestion to radically commercialize the Internet's operation by liberalizing it still further.

This, however, was not a choice that was possible for these advocates. They were as ensconced in the governmentality of the time in Washington as their corporate allies and enemies. Given the effort of the Hundt and Kennard FCCs to continue the liberalization drive online, such an argument was impossible if they expected to continue being called before local commissions and before national organs of governance such as the FCC and Congress. Such an epistemological foundation would prove both their strength and their Achilles' heel in this first phase of a struggle over the nature of the nascent public Web itself.

4 Knowing the Net, 2: The FCC Decides in Cable's Favor

Several events would bring an end to this phase of the struggle for the definition of open access in relation to the operation of quickly commercializing broadband networks. The first emerged from the fallout stemming from a small, quietly assembled working group that FCC chairman Kennard put together in the hopes that a deal could be hammered out on open access without official regulation. Meetings commenced in the late summer of 1999 among six parties—AT&T, Excite@Home, MindSpring (itself about to merge with EarthLink to create the second-largest ISP in the world at the time), Atlanta Mayor Bill Campbell, the FCC's Local and State Government Advisory Committee, and Andrew Schwartzman of the Media Access Project. These participants were hardly of like mind, and Schwartzman ceased his own involvement after it was clear discussions were fruitless from the perspective of open access advocates. All the same, the talks continued nonetheless, and they culminated in an early December announcement by AT&T that it would offer a "limited" opening of its network in 2002. The letter released on December 7 was signed by David Baker, vice president of legal and regulatory affairs for MindSpring; James Cicconi, general counsel and executive vice president of AT&T; and Kenneth Fullman, chairman of the FCC Local and State Government Advisory Committee (Baker, Cicconi, & Fellman, 1999).

To the uninitiated, this letter appeared to be a watershed moment in the overarching debate. The signing parties made a number of promises. One was that AT&T would provide its customers with "a choice of ISPs [Internet service providers]," giving users the ability to choose "without having to subscribe to any other ISP." AT&T would provide a range of speeds and prices "reasonable and appropriate" to those speeds. "Direct access to all content available" on the Web "without any AT&T-imposed charge to the consumer for such content" would be on offer. The emergent giant would guarantee that the "functionality of [a user's chosen] ISP" would be as good as that ISP's performance on other high-speed networks, "subject to any technical constraints particular to, or imposed upon, all ISPs using AT&T's cable system to deliver high-speed Internet access." AT&T would negotiate with ISPs seeking carriage aboard their network "upon the expiration of existing exclusive contractual arrangements"—that is, AT&T's own "obligation" to Excite@Home. In the course of these negotiations, the company promised newcomers "Internet transport services for high-speed Internet access at prices reasonable comparable to those offered by AT&T to any other ISP for similar services, subject to other terms negotiated between the parties on a commercial basis." Independent ISPs would be able to market their services using AT&T's network to those who had not elected an ISP; they could bill customers directly. AT&T would offer the ability to "differentiate services… such as enhanced customer care and advanced applications" and the opportunity to "maintain brand recognition." All of these facets were "subject to terms and conditions to be agreed upon… which will address, as appropriate, but not be limited to issues such as pricing, billing, customer relationship, design of start page, degree of customization, speed, system usage, caching services, co-branding, ancillary services, advertising and e-commerce revenues, and infrastructure costs" (all quotations Baker, Cicconi, and Fellman 1999).

The independent ISP community largely welcomed the development ("OpenNET Coalition Welcomes," 1999). However, in a supplemental letter to the FCC, one of the "grand bargain" signatories, MindSpring, confusingly walked back some of its perceived enthusiasm regarding the new deal. It expressed concerns about the extended period before such conditions would become a reality. While the principle established was positive, they wrote, it left AT&T maneuvering room to "impose constraints such as limitations on video streaming or IP [Internet protocol] telephony on all users of their system." Even as its signature on the AT&T letter sent a mixed signal, MindSpring looked to play both sides of the political fence, urging the adoption of a national policy on the matter:

> We hope that the Commission and other federal policy makers will grasp the opportunity that this initial agreement creates, because only clear and unambiguous federal policy can make the promise of this first step real, enforceable and timely. Otherwise today's agreement may not benefit consumers for years to

come. We again respectfully request that the FCC initiate a proceeding to address these issues on a comprehensive basis. In setting out public policy principles, the FCC would establish the "rules of the road" that would help ensure fair workable and enforceable agreements between parties. (Baker, 1999)

Public interest advocates smelled nothing but public relations gimmickry. Worse, it was via the trade press accounts of the agreement that news of Schwartzman's apparently under-the-radar involvement became known, causing no small amount of strife among the community of consumer advocates working on the issue. In his own response to the AT&T–MindSpring letter in an open letter to Kennard, Schwartzman wrote,

> In accepting your request to meet with AT&T and others, I placed at risk my relationships with my clients and my professional colleagues. I have had several very emotional conversations in the two days since word of my involvement was leaked to the press, and one client has directly accused me of a breach of trust.... I am confident that I will be able to convince my [colleagues] that I did the right thing. (Schwartzman, 1999)

Schwartzman, recall, had left the negotiations long before they came to a close; but he was hardly alone in having done so. Notably, Excite@Home had left the talks early as well, so AT&T may not even have been able to make good on its commitments expressed; this no doubt also informed Schwartzman's decision. With the letter's release, Schwartzman had several specific concerns, and these went to the heart of the manner in which AT&T was trying to stretch some notion of "open access" to the limit, serving both as a public relations move and further muddying the waters of "what open access was." AT&T was being disingenuous, claiming that it was waiting for its exclusive contracts with Excite@Home and RoadRunner to expire before committing to allowing rivals aboard—this despite having controlling stakes in the companies. AT&T remained unwilling to commit to its users in writing that they would not have to purchase a bundled "package" to obtain Internet access. Further, AT&T missed the point of "open access," which he stressed meant for consumer advocates that "cable operators provide competing ISP's with full access to their systems under the same terms and conditions, and at the same rates, that access is available to affiliated ISP's. An operator should not be able to restrict offerings to those which its affiliate chooses to provide" (all quotes from Schwartzman, 1999).

A crucial facet of AT&T's intentions was not readily apparent in their letter. *Where* ISPs could gain admittance to the last mile matters in Internet geography, and it was becoming apparent a simple requirement to "negotiate" with competitors was not going to be sufficient. From what Schwartzman could gather in his discussions behind the scenes, AT&T was forcing its ISP competitors to use AT&T's own transport from the cable headend (from which the wire goes straight to households) to the Internet backbone itself, thus allowing the company to still use its policy-based routing capabilities to potentially debilitate rival offerings. It would also result in additional revenue in AT&T's pocket, as ISPs would not only need to pay the company to access customers, but they would need to purchase "special access" to the Internet backbone; this would apparently be the case even if a rival ISP had already built a regional hub near the headend or even had constructed its own transport to the Internet backbone. AT&T's condition would render such investment redundant. Perhaps most offensive to Schwartzman was the duplicitousness with which AT&T handled the whole debate:

> Even as technologists at the highest levels of AT&T and Excite@Home were representing to me that there is no technological impediment to providing citizens with access to multiple ISPs, their lobbyists have continued to argue the contrary position before numerous state and local legislative and regulatory bodies. Indeed, a significant factor in my decision to withdraw from the talks you asked me to attend was the claim contained in an October 15, 1999 article by Excite@Home's General Counsel that "The technology simply does not yet exist to allow multiple ISPs to share a coaxial cable on a commercial basis." (Schwartzman, 1999)

He ultimately asked Kennard to "take a fresh look at the open access issue, realizing that AT&T's recent moves do not represent a solution to any of the serious public interest concerns voiced by consumer groups" (NoGatekeepers.org, 2000b).

The other core advocates were livid. Reacting to AT&T's announcement of an "agreement on principle" to open its network to rivals, the Consumer Federation of America (CFA), Consumers Union, and the Center for Media Education called AT&T on its half-baked compromise. Via press release, the groups announced that it

> fail[ed] to address the basic issues that surround the migration of the Internet into the high-speed cable environment. In particular, AT&T's new policy offers no assurances that it will treat all ISPs equitably, or that it will rescind the content restrictions that it currently imposes on its broadband Internet customers. And customers will have to wait two more years—an eon in Internet Time—for

even AT&T's meager concessions to take effect. (Consumer Federation of America, Consumers Union, & Center for Media Education, 1999)

The Center for Media Education's executive director, Jeffrey Chester, expressed his own dismay: "Unfortunately, AT&T's announcement has more to do with public relations than with the public interest.... It's not surprising that three of the six parties to the agreement refused to sign, which underscores the need for FCC action in this area." Gene Kimmelman of Consumers Union added, "Cutting preferential deals with affiliates and a few most-favored outsiders is no more likely to open high-speed broadband to more choice and lower prices than has occurred for cable television itself" (Consumer Federation of America, Consumers Union, & Center for Media Education, 1999). Mark Cooper of the CFA added,

> The real issue here concerns the basic architecture of the Internet... and how that architecture—traditionally open and nondiscriminatory—will be transformed in a closed cable environment. AT&T's announcement makes absolutely no concessions in the areas of differential service, discriminatory transport, and the ultimate control of customer accounts—all of the hallmarks of cable monopolies that we simply cannot allow to become the new standard of service for the Internet. (Consumer Federation of America, Consumers Union, & Center for Media Education, 1999)

Kennard's response was delivered in an address before the California Cable Television Association, responding only to the AT&T–MindSpring letter and leaving out any critique provided by public interest advocates:

> Some call it open access. Some call it forced access. Sometimes it's just a pain in the access.... Everyone I talk to about this issue—leaders in your industry, the ISP industry, franchising authorities—all embrace the concept of openness. Everyone seems to agree that openness and choice are what consumers want and will demand. This debate is really about how to get there. There are two choices: we can rely on the market to facilitate openness; or we can try to regulate our way there. For now, I'm putting my faith in the marketplace. Unless a compelling case can be made for government action—a failure of the market to maximize consumer welfare—then we should give the marketplace a chance to work.... Last summer, I encouraged some of the stakeholders in this debate to come together and really engage on the issue of how unaffiliated ISPs will get access to cable's broadband pipe. As a result, two weeks ago, these stakeholders, including AT&T and MindSpring/EarthLink [which had announced their merger three months before], announced an agreement-in-principle that will allow AT&T's cable customers access to the Internet through unaffiliated ISPs. This is a positive first step. It is just a blueprint, a plan-in-progress, but it is a start. I encouraged these

> discussions because all the stakeholders were telling me that they believed in openness, but the stakeholders weren't talking to each other. I wanted to facilitate a dialogue, a dialogue that could lead to marketplace solutions rather than government mandates. AT&T and MindSpring stepped up to the starting blocks. Now I urge them and I urge you today to be the first out of the starting blocks. I urge you to do this because this is what consumers want. (Kennard, 1999)

He further challenged the industry before him in the same talk to build with "openness" in mind—with one particular plank being "open boundaries," by which he meant, "interconnection is encouraged, and bottlenecks and content control are eliminated. The borders are porous, not closed or walled-off, and outside programming and services are allowed to enter the network and interact freely with consumers." But as long as his broadband vision was a plan by no-plan, the issue continued to fester.

From Vague Directive to the Core

DC-based consumer advocates and their allies in the states had long held nondiscriminatory open access not as a *technical* directive but rather as a business relationship that should be required of industry players; they left the details to the participants. Now, their arguments were increasingly forced into nascent networks' innards by AT&T's actions and the FCC's meandering. The FCC simply sat bewildered on the sidelines; meanwhile, AT&T used wordplay to force a technical definition. The core advocates in Washington increasingly drew on four papers to this end, with *Broadband in the Public Interest* and the NoGatekeepers.org website serving as their vehicle for mobilization. Two had been independently filed with the FCC as part of the AT&T–MediaOne docket proceeding, but they remained to be materially rendered relevant elsewhere: the DC-based advocates would do just this. One was a white paper written by University of Michigan economist Jeffrey K. MacKie-Mason (1999). MacKie-Mason provided a needed academic argument that open access requirements would not deter investment. Leading off with a quote from the Canadian Cable Television Association which defended Canada's open access policy, he presented evidence that not only would open access not "reduce the value of broadband last-mile transport infrastructure," it would render the companies who operated under open access quite profitable; looking to Canada as a comparison, arguments that the condition deterred investment were self-evidently false, as providers there were "investing in broadband facilities faster than the major U.S. cable operators" (p. 2). He summarized that broadband service profits would be "more than sufficient" to induce rapid investment; that cable broadband transport "profits will be higher," and "consumers will benefit tremendously from the greater quality and variety of ISP service," thus "increas[ing] penetration rates" (p. 3).

The remaining three papers provided extensive critique of the FCC's policy of waiting and watching as potentially causing great harm to the evolution and functioning of the Internet itself. These arguments informed Mark Cooper's reaction to the AT&T–MindSpring letter. While advocates had been arguing in the abstract in this matter all year, these papers provided explicit *technical* discussion of the ramifications involved. The first was a working paper for Berkeley's Roundtable on the International Economy by François Bar, Stephen Cohen, Peter Cowhey, Brad Delong, Michael Kleeman, and John Zyman entitled *Defending the Internet Revolution in the Broadband Era: When Doing Nothing Is Doing Harm* (1999). The second was a comment submitted into the FCC's docket regarding the AT&T–MediaOne merger by Mark Lemley and Lawrence Lessig (1999). Lessig had by this point been pounding home his message about the shifting nature of the Internet for going on three years (as he recalls in Lessig, 2000, p. 15); he certainly was prominent in other media and had to have been known by members of FCC staff throughout the agency (Streeter, 2011). Consumer advocates would take his involvement to an entirely new level and become *his* advocate. The last was a brief piece by the Massachusetts Institute of Technology's (MIT) Jerome Saltzer (1999), one of the original authors of the papers outlining "end-to-end" networking architecture.

Bar et al. sought to distill whether there was a pressing need for the FCC to "regulate" broadband over cable and, if so, what the least invasive form of such regulation may be. Theirs was no work of radicalism or even any attempt to bust up a potential trust forming: they offered no suggestion that AT&T should not be allowed to operate its own ISP or other "vertical" market services atop its network. They instead examined the various ways @Home thwarted innovation and freedom of use aboard its service. For instance, @Home limited downstream online video from other sources to "about ten minutes per day"; it limited upstream traffic, erected prohibitions against setting up a server over one's home connection, performed "technical biasing and limit[ed] … performance for non-partner content."

It enforced prohibitions against using @Home for "work-related activities, for which customers are expected to purchase the more expensive '@Work' service" (all quotations Bar et al., 1999, p. 25). They noted evidence from Excite@Home's annual report that @Home intended to explicitly privilege partners by steering users *unknowingly* to them, something quite simply done by ensuring that partner content would load faster than nonpartner content, among other options. Bar and his coauthors emphasized the location of innovators in networks: in present systems, these had productively existed at network edges rather than within the network itself; such activity stood to affect how the broader network itself would operate, and that, in their view, was the point. This would, of course, be the common refrain for years to come in these debates. They concluded that in regard to media that possess market power—with cable being a sure example—the FCC should look toward what its British counterparts had done in favoring *ex ante* openness principles to protect innovation.

> The policy stakes are much larger than the competitive fates of particular groups of ISPs. What is threatened, if open competition is not maintained, is the continuing evolution of the Internet, the innovation in and the evolution of electronic network-based business, and therefore the competitive development of the network economy as a whole.... We are not talking here about regulation of the Internet nor of dealings among the ISPs. Rather, we are talking about assuring competition for access to the Internet over local networks, broadband as well as narrowband. Open access should be guaranteed unless it can be definitely demonstrated that competition in access, and consequently throughout the Internet system, can be maintained. (Bar et al., 1999, p. 4)

Lemley and Lessig's comments were a far more scathing affair, but they are no radicals here either. They allow that the merger of AT&T and MediaOne could well open up a positive new competitor in telephone service; their concern was instead limiting end users access to a broad market of ISPs. Even more broadly, they expressed concern regarding AT&T control and its implications for the functioning of the Internet, particularly in maintaining the end-to-end principle which had been the basis for the Internet's robustness:

> By bundling ISP service with access, and by not permitting users to select another ISP, the architecture removes ISP competition within the residential broadband cable market. By removing this competition, the architecture removes an important threat to any strategic behavior that AT&T might engage in once a merger

> is complete. The architecture thus represents a significant change from the existing End-to-End design for a crucial segment of the residential Internet market. Further, there is in principle no limit to what AT&T could bundle into its control of the network. As ISPs expand beyond the functions they have traditionally performed, AT&T may be in a position to foreclose all competition in an increasing range of services provided over broadband lines. (Lemley & Lessig, 1999, p. 20)

Similar to the broad arguments presented by Bar et al. (1999) (who themselves reference an article Lessig had written over the summer), Lemley and Lessig provided additional technical detail and explicitly took the Cable Services Bureau's staff report *Broadband Today* to task. Their critique was a devastating, full-on shaming of the bureau. They were astonished at the FCC's "naïve assumption" that a monopoly would voluntarily open its market to competitors in the face of the rapid consolidation transpiring in the wake of the Telecommunications Act:

> The Bureau does not explain exactly what "market forces" will compel AT&T to open this market. How exactly will customers of a certified natural monopoly exercise the power to "vote with their wallets?"... [I]f the Bureau's hope is that AT&T will be forced into open access because consumers will delay their switch to broadband in boycott of its closed access policy, it is a supreme piece of irony to suggest that it is the threat of regulation that will delay the deployment of broadband technology. (Lemley & Lessig, 1999, p. 33)

With near ridicule, the authors noted that even if bottlenecks *should* develop, the FCC was unhinged if it thought it could put the genie back in the bottle once unleashed. The Cable Services Bureau was concerned that even the threat of regulation might be a barrier to investment in itself: the irony, Lemley and Lessig point out, is that if to hint at regulation presents a barrier to investment, the FCC is doing just this! The Cable Services Bureau's argument thus made no sense.

Perhaps most damningly, the bureau's difficulty in "defining open access" was lambasted in no uncertain terms. The bureau was creating confusion where none needed to exist to the seeming express end of being unable to craft policy:

> The Bureau maintains that there is neither agreement on how to implement "open access" nor agreement on what "open access" is. But this part of the report reads like a poor imitation of a Socratic dialogue. Obviously, if one gathers a collection of bright lawyers and technologists, each advancing different interests, one can create a cacophony of views about what "open access" is, just as a good

> law professor can create a cacophony of views about what "justice" is, or even what the "FCC" is. But a law professor can not deny that there is an "FCC" merely because no "agreement" in definition is found. (Lemley & Lessig, 1999, p. 30)

If Lemley and Lessig provided a devastating takedown compared to Bar et al.'s more toned offering, the last paper, by Jerome Saltzer, matter-of-factly emphasized the numerous ways that cable broadband providers were exercising gatekeeper control *already* (drawing on some of the same points that Bar et al. made and expanding on them). He foretold, "The argument between cable companies and municipal regulators that has been labeled 'Open Access' is actually just the first of a series of arguments destined to surface as it begins to dawn on customers that cable companies stand not only as access providers but also as gatekeepers to the Internet" (Saltzer, 1999).

Nearly all questioned AT&T's veracity as it pursued its interests in different regulatory settings. Lemley and Lessig noted that AT&T was deliberately speaking out of both sides of its mouth, pointing to reply comments the corporation filed in another proceeding requesting that dominant telephone companies open their networks to AT&T's services. Quoting directly, AT&T told the FCC that "the most important action the Commission can take to speed deployment of advanced telecommunications services is to vigorously implement and enforce the market-opening obligations that Section 251 [the unbundling and nondiscriminatory interconnection clause] imposes on incumbent LECs [local exchange carriers]" (Lemley & Lessig, 1999, p. 31n18). AT&T, of course, sought entry to local markets via open access conditions via telephone where it was dependent on someone else's wire; but where it was able to exercise control, it wanted to keep such control. Time and again this had been the case. MacKie-Mason was equally quick to point out that in Canada, AT&T had pushed for policies amounting to open access as well. Quoting AT&T directly in a filing to the Canadian regulator: "If the bottleneck nature of these services [cable broadband last-mile transport] is not recognized, the establishment of a competitive market may be jeopardized, and more significantly, *undermine the development of Canada's Information Highway*" (quoted in MacKie-Mason, 1999, p. 30n87; emphasis AT&T's).

These papers were increasingly cited in filings and reports produced by the four core consumer advocacy groups in presentations they gave to localities and state legislatures. All of these were easy to mobilize: their principal advantage in this regard was that none challenged a privately supplied and driven Internet. The significance of Bar et al.'s, Lemley & Lessig's, and Saltzer's contributions were less their novelty—the core advocacy groups in Washington, DC, were arguing many of their points but through an antitrust, consumer choice lens—than the opportunity to introduce a different version of Internet history, one that countered the FCC's own provided by Oxman's staff report: the FCC's "hands off" was never truly "hands off." In many ways, the *pedigrees* of these scholars mattered more than their arguments, even as their arguments were vital: the ability to broadcast research by unaffiliated scholars from Harvard (Lessig), the University of Michigan (MacKie-Mason), MIT (Saltzer), and Stanford and Berkeley (Bar et al.) and to name them as such commenced on a regular basis, particularly at the state and local levels. (The Berkman Klein Center at Harvard, it should be noted, was also providing assistance for localities fighting for open access.) Lessig's intervention cannot be underestimated here: it provided a new basis of analysis for Mark Cooper's own work in analyzing the state of affairs of the time, particularly through the model presented in Lessig's *Code and Other Laws of Cyberspace* (evident in Cooper, 2000a). As consumer advocates mobilized this work, open access shifted as a concept; it retained its connections to "open, competitive, democratic" networks but now also overflowed its semantic bounds into a vision of an expansive, "free" Internet (if not an expansive, "free" society itself). These seemingly complementary signifieds would actually find themselves in an ironic tension. Additionally, these arguments were released not just to supporters, but to more cynical corners on the corporate side of the debate. But even if the local Bells were putting the arguments to use, it was further circulating the arguments to places they may not have reached before; it was a win-win. Consumer advocates surely knew this.

Advocates faced increasingly daunting obstacles. Alongside the setback of MindSpring signing onto AT&T's raw deal for open access, cable interests continued an onslaught of political spending. On the telecommunications side, they lobbied aggressively to either eliminate unbundling and wholesaling rules on their own systems or force cable to open their own lines to these conditions. Nonetheless, advocates had managed to find a space to discuss something quite new in policy circles. They had reopened a discussion into the nature of how the Internet should operate, drawing implications for how *society* should operate, if indirectly. In late December, the

Center for Media Education, the CFA, and the Media Access Project sponsored a forum at the National Press Club (transcript at "Can We Preserve," 1999), the first of two which featured presentations from Lawrence Lessig (giving an early version of a talk that he would provide the next month in Germany); Ron Sims of the King County, Washington Executive Office; Erik Sten of Portland; and Mark Cooper. Moderating was Jamie Raskin, professor of law at American University's College of Law. Raskin implored, "The world of cable Internet offers none of the cornucopia-like choice that we have today for Internet service providers.... The new architectural infrastructure will thus give us a new and totalizing control to the cable ISP." He spoke of a growing movement:

> To a growing coalition of cities and counties, consumers, citizens and media access groups, the problems with this restrictive and closed-down Internet future are profound... but a clear solution may be at hand which is a requirement of open and equal access for all ISPs to the communications network on reasonable and nondiscriminatory terms. And it is important to note that a number of cities and counties have begun to become leaders in this movement. ("Can We Preserve," 1999)

Lessig would touch on points that within years would be on the lips of Web activists worldwide: he spoke of the importance of the free protocols that underlay the movement of data across the Web; the principle of "open code" that emphasized collaboration over proprietary cover; and finally, the principle of the end-to-end network. Years before Ed Whitacre muttered his famous threat against "freeloaders" that would touch off a second round of debates regarding the operation of broadband networks, Lessig called attention to AT&T Broadband and Internet Services CEO Daniel Sumners who, when asked barely a week previous if cable broadband would permit streamed video, responded, "No, it wouldn't be used to stream video, AT&T didn't spend $56 billion to get into the cable business, quote, to have the blood sucked out of our veins" (quoted in "Can We Preserve, 1999).

That this was spoken nearly a month *after* announcing their planned opening of their networks two years hence was an irony not lost on the crowd assembled. The moral high-ground had been reached with this gathering, and these advocates' worlds were about to be torn apart from within as a prominent ally would defect.

AOL Buys a Wire of Its Own

It had long been predictable that AOL would eventually peel off with some cable partner. In early January 2000, they announced their proposed takeover of Time Warner in the largest corporate merger ever as of that time. Even as the FCC continued to profess that, analytically, digital subscriber line (DSL) and cable belonged in the same market (even to the point of perhaps including dial-up Internet access as well in this mélange), the NoGatekeepers.org one-time ally knew as well as the consumer advocates did that cable was going to come to dominate broadband for the foreseeable future—for the reasons that they had helped to argue as part of the OpenNet Coalition. At a second briefing on these issues at the National Press Club—this time featuring the involvement of the American Civil Liberties Union (ACLU), although their worries centered around government filtering of the Internet—the CFA's Mark Cooper was justifiably unforgiving: "Two months ago, almost to the day, in this very room, I offered the observation that the large ISPs were probably off somewhere in their ski lodges in Aspen negotiating deals for commercial access. … I was, of course, far too limited in my vision," he intoned:

> The exotic location of the start of the negotiations was China, not a ski lodge in Aspen—even more difficult for the little guys to get there—and the outcome was even more dramatic. It wasn't a deal for commercial access; the largest narrowband ISP bought the second largest cable company. The message, however, is exactly the same, and quite clear: we cannot allow issues such as the freedom of speech, the free flow of ideas and the flow of commerce in our society to be decided by the whims of corporate interests which change with every merger. We must have a binding public policy obligation that provides open access to the thousands of little ISPs who seek to reach the public in an open and unhindered way. … Ironically, when the merger was announced, the two CEOs were proud to say that the first thing they did after they did their deal was call the CEO of AT&T and offer to cooperate. Now, from the view of a large cartel dividing up an industry, that's what you do. And from the point of a consumer advocate who wants competition, this is not comforting. ("The Future of the Internet," 2000)

AOL, in the meantime, sought to capitalize on its past affiliations with OpenNet and, indirectly, the NoGatekeepers coalition. Early on, the company announced that they were still committed to open access. CEO Steve Case told trade press that "now that No. 1 [multiple-system operator] AT&T and No. 2 AOL Time Warner are both on record supporting consumer choice," the issue would be resolved soon. Their vice president followed up that as a result, "government action is less and less needed," even though the company would remain "a dues-paying member of OpenNet" ("AOL–Time Warner Open Access," 2000). Large ISPs, such as MindSpring, expressed confidence in AOL; all the same, conflicting reports of members of the OpenNet group "seething" were indicative of the pressures smaller ISPs felt, now that their largest member may be partially responsible for their future viability.

Playing the bad cop to AOL's good, cable utilized front groups to argue their interests. The AT&T-born Hands Off the Internet introduced one of the tropes most useful in neutralizing the influence of the consumer actors—that consumer groups themselves had been serving as front groups or "astroturf" themselves for AOL (Jacobson, 1999). Its director, Peter Arnold—who had served in the 1980s as a speechwriter and congressional press secretary—said, "For a year now, AOL-backed groups have been active in pushing state and local access regulation in franchise transfers and renewals across the country. It will be interesting to see if they are as aggressive in promoting this regulation in the service territories for AOL–Time Warner" ("AOL Time Warner Latest," 2000). This was merely showboating for the press; the Center for Media Education, the CFA, Consumers Union, and Media Access Project issued a near-instantaneous statement that they did "not want to be beholden to a giant media-Internet dictatorship, even if it promises to be a benevolent one" ("AOL–Time Warner Open Access," 2000). However, with the profusion of front groups involved in the debate and the politics increasingly difficult to follow, merely the suggestion that they had ulterior motivations needed to persist to do damage.

An even more problematic message emerged, fomented by AOL's past push for open access and expressed best by the bipartisan pair of Senators DeWine (R-OH) and Kohl (D-WI) of the Senate Judiciary Antitrust Subcommittee: the deal "adds a new wrinkle to the broadband 'open access' debate by potentially resolving it through private negotiation rather than by government regulation" ("Few Regulatory Obstacles," 2000). National Cable and Telecommunications Association president Robert Sachs capitalized on exactly this message. "Cable systems and programming networks are being validated as key to any long-term business strategy for the Web.... It also removes any question that market transactions are far preferable to government regulation in sorting out the complex and promising destiny of the new economy" ("Few Regulatory Obstacles," 2000).

Action became intense once again at the local level. Given that this time AOL was purchasing cable franchises, the process of local negotiations were set to begin anew in each locality with a Time Warner system. Smart regulators attempted to topple AOL and AT&T's seeming benevolence under their own weight. Still awaiting an ultimate court ruling from the Ninth Circuit on his own case, David Olson wrote to franchise authorities, roaring that since AOL had been the biggest supporter of open access in the past, "it seems that no good-faith objection can or should be made by AOL under the circumstances" in all local franchise authority transfers of cable systems to the new corporate entity ("Decision Soon," 2000). In addition to being the first of a set of fraying relations with what had been a semi-unified front in the open access battle, the AT&T–MindSpring letter served its purpose to render the notion of "open access" deliberately less clear and more arcane—why ask us to do something that we're promising to do?—and put more of the onus on advocates to make the case that an officially mandated access policy remained relevant, necessary, and even understandable. *Broadband in the Public Interest* noted the developments regularly as the core group redoubled their efforts.

The new politics in play were apparent when a new front opened in Henrico County, Virginia, as the CFA and the Virginia Citizens Consumer Council (VCCC) urged authorities to require open access themselves. Advocates praised the initial expressed intention of doing so and sought to reassure them of their decision despite the AT&T–MindSpring letter, contesting any notion pushed by AT&T and their front groups that this settled matters. The CFA and VCCC emphasized that the FCC would most likely ignore MindSpring and their own requests to hold a rulemaking on open access. "Over a year ago, the FCC flatly denied our request to conduct just such a rulemaking. In the intervening months, the agency has aggressively sought to deny cities and counties the authority to take this issue up. The FCC also has reiterated its position that no open access policy is necessary" (Consumer Federation of America & Virginia Citizens Consumer Council, 1999b). Thus localities would need to drive the issue: "If, as we believe, open access is in the public interest, the only way it will happen is if local governments insist on it. All of our lives would be made much easier if the FCC acted responsibly in this matter. It has not, however, and we have no reason to believe it will do so any time soon" (Consumer Federation of America & Virginia Citizens Consumer Council, 1999b). They also pointed out the hypocrisy inherent in AT&T's approach, highlighting that AT&T itself "lobbied hard for conditions in the Telecommunications Act of 1996 that prevent the local phone companies, with whom it wishes to compete, from leveraging their monopoly control over the telephone network in exactly the way it is abusing its newly purchased market power in the cable TV industry" (Consumer Federation of America & Virginia Citizens Consumer Council, 1999b). AT&T long had "demand[ed] open access from telephone companies for DSL service, where it does not rely on its cable monopoly for access" and "has constantly litigated interconnection agreements to enforce open access conditions for local telephone service. ISPs have none of these rights under AT&T's proprietary, self-serving definition of open access" (Consumer Federation of America & Virginia Citizens Consumer Council, 1999b).

FCC inaction was in fact thick in irony. Whereas mass confusion and refusal to act at the agency seemed to reign on the cable side, in November 1999 via its *Line Sharing Order* it expressly commanded telecommunications firms to allow competing ISPs to have access to the high-frequency DSL portion of an incumbent's wire, effectively *easing* "open access" over telephony. Up to this point, should cable systems be required to provide the access to independent ISPs that consumer advocates sought, it would have been *easier* for an ISP to gain access to end users over cable systems than over a telecommunications company's DSL systems. (Specifically, before the *Line Sharing Order,* to gain access to end users of a telecommunications wire, an ISP would need to affiliate with a competitive provider of telecommunications service which had either leased the wire from the incumbent or leased "unbundled network elements" sufficient to reach the end user.) The decision was the result of a unanimous FCC vote. "Line-sharing provides more choice and flexibility for the consumer, ultimately, and of course more competition in the marketplace.... It's an important milestone," Kennard crowed to the *Washington Post.* The United States Telecom Association's reaction was grousier. "They're basically saying the competitors should be able to skim the cream," the *Post* reported (Goodman, 1999).

But no matter: vicious politicking erupted "with the now-typical television advertising, direct mail, and misleading print ads" ("News," 2000). Henrico County withstood the assault nonetheless and followed through with just such a requirement, lauded by the CFA. Such praise was necessary, as the AT&T–MindSpring letter easily could have flagged momentum on the issue:

> In what was to our knowledge the first opportunity by a local cable franchise authority to examine the open access debate since the AT&T–Mindspring plan was announced, open access was endorsed.... The Henrico decision in favor of open access was a victory for consumers. The Board of Supervisors, despite intense lobbying efforts by the proponents of closed access, stuck to its guns. They refused to buy the argument that private negotiations between two corporate entities, which produced negligible consumer benefit, can adequately replace a considered public policy. The lesson of Henrico is that this debate is far from over. Local authorities continue to have much to contribute to the development of a sound public policy on open access. (Consumer Federation of America, 1999c)

Henrico County was rewarded promptly for its efforts with a lawsuit by AT&T, but the company took its vengeance one step further, performing the kind of infrastructural blackmail Cooper had described earlier on: the MediaOne franchise's facilities would not be upgraded, it declared, until the lawsuit was settled ("News," 2000). AOL saw an opportunity in AT&T's arrogance to advance its own interests. *Warren's Cable Regulation Monitor* reported that OpenNet denounced the suit in a continuing corporate game of rhetorical subterfuge. AOL's parasitic perch within the organization gave it cover as ISPs condemned AT&T's actions as "completely contradicting [the company's] earlier pledge to embrace open access," and that consumers and regulators should pay attention not to what AT&T said but what it did. Cheekily, AOL averred, "monopoly is not just a board game—it is AT&T's business plan" ("State and Local Actions," 2000).

Los Angeles became hot again in early 2000 as its Culver City municipality approved an open access requirement; on its heels West Hollywood announced that, in its negotiations with Adelphia later in the year, open access would be "a top priority" ("News," 2000). San Francisco's Department of Telecommunications and Information Services recommended an open access mandate by the city council and board but not for three years ("News," 2000). Montgomery County, Maryland, close to Washington, held a hearing where "open access advocates squared off against Comcast. Other localities in the Washington area are also considering the issue as Comcast attempts to buy nearly every cable system from Northern Virginia to Philadelphia" ("News," 2000).

Significant pushback continued. Reports were emerging which noted AT&T's "carrot and stick" tactics—threatened lawsuits and withheld service for communities considering an open access policy while accelerating deployment in those that were not ("AT&T Threatens," 1999). As Portland's Erik Sten said in an interview,

> It looks to me like most city councils have come to the conclusion that open access is the right policy choice, but then they back off for pragmatic reasons. And that's a generalization that I'm making, but I have talked with a lot of city commissioners, and I'm following the media whenever another one gets reported, and I don't remember too many places where folks have come out and said that the right policy choice is closed access. So really it's a combination of heavy handed tactics that are pushing a lot of these mayors and commissioners, and that's unfortunate. ("Interview with Erik Sten," 1999)

Consumer advocates pinned their hopes on localities to increase pressure on the FCC to take more substantive positions ahead of upcoming elections; surely with a capital-D Democratic administration in place, they would gain more traction for consumer concerns than a potentially Republican one. For the time being, at the local level, they were holding their own in a number of key locales despite the challenges of AOL's defection from their coalition and AT&T's aggressive efforts. In Madera County, California, AT&T sent 45,000 prepaid postcards to residents that they could mail in to their local franchise authority that opposed open access provisions. Authorities nonetheless voted unanimously in favor of an open access provision despite the campaign ("Madera County," 1999). Once the expected lawsuit hit, the town folded and "reached a compromise" in early 2000 ("News," 2000). Richmond (Virginia), Seattle (Washington), and Plymouth Township (Michigan) decided against the policy—all cities in which advocates had submitted testimony—but Seattle and Richmond were likely to reexamine the issue in 2000 depending on the outcome of the city of Portland's lawsuit ("Open Access Setbacks," 1999). In St. Louis, Missouri, the board of aldermen and mayor in late 1999 voted in favor of open access, but in early 2000 cable interests—the principal provider for the city being Cox Communications, which was trying to collect clusters of cable franchises itself—launched an "astroturf" referendum campaign seeking to reverse the decision in the November election. Cox used its medium to its advantage, airing messages supportive of the campaign while denying NoGatekeepers and local allies' own paid advertisements ("News," 2000). In the meantime, cities that *were* already obtaining service via Excite@Home were feeling the tensions brewing within the company. Seattle was one: residents complained of blackouts, slow speeds, and poor customer service both via email and via telephone—hold times lasted forty minutes according to reports ("Customers in Seattle," 1999).

Advocate Frustration at the FCC

The culmination of this phase is summarized in a February 2000 public forum that the FCC held on the AT&T–MediaOne merger, presided over by Cable Services Bureau Chief Deborah Lathen. The escalating tensions between consumer advocates and the FCC were on full display, particularly when Andrew Schwartzman took the dais. "I'm afraid I'm not going to be the warm and fuzzy Andy Schwartzman today," he warned. "You've got the petulant, angry Andy Schwartzman here today, I'm afraid" (FCC, 2000c, p. 10). Noting the "curious neutrality" in favor of AT&T as exhibited by the FCC, Schwartzman was unremitting: his materials indicated that AT&T's approval was largely a foregone conclusion by all indications. As a result of past deals including the TCI merger, AT&T had been in violation of cable ownership rules for months, yet action at the FCC's Enforcement Bureau was nonexistent.

His testimony highlighted the challenges to being part of these debates at a national level. He was full of bombast, enraged at the FCC's seeming inability to keep tabs on its own rules, furious at the procedure that played to AT&T's advantage. The cable bureau, in particular, displayed a spectacular blind spot for the inequities provoked by their seemingly neutral actions:

> I have complained repeatedly that the Cable Services Bureau has given AT&T a platform to push its case by establishing a special web page which provide downloadable word processor files for all of AT&T's major filings. Only this week, in response to my repeated objections, has the staff added an explicit reference to the fact that other parties have filed pleadings in this case, and directions on how to find them in the Commission's ECFS [Electronic Comment Filing System]. A referral to the notoriously cumbersome and accident prone ECFS is hardly the same thing as prominent placement on the bureau's own website. Has anyone on the eighth floor tried to use the ECFS with a 28.8 modem, rather than their T-1 lines? Those who (unlike FCC staff) lack high speed connections and fast computers are unlikely to find our comments even if they go to look for them. (Schwartzman, 2000, p. 3)

He noted that the AT&T–MindSpring letter released in early December had been posted prominently on the page, whereas Schwartzman's extensive response was not—it wasn't *anywhere* on the FCC's website. "I take particular objection," he added, "to the staff's repeated expressions of belief that posting of documents on the Commission's web page or the impossibly cumbersome ECFS fulfills its outreach obligation. I represent those on the wrong side of the digital divide, many of whom have no Internet access, or are restricted to 28.8 baud or slower speed" (Schwartzman, 2000, p. 3n6). FCC officials and staff, by Schwartzman's count of *ex parte* filings, had *sixty-five* conversations with AT&T, "most of them involv[ing] upper level executives of the company." Adding to the challenge of public participation of any kind in these matters, such conversations by law needed to be memorialized in a public *ex parte* filing; these were often undertaken via unrevealingly "terse and artfully vague language." "There is little reason to seek meetings to reply when there is no way to know what was said," Schwartzman commented, providing a typical example: "The full text of the substantive 'notice' reads as follows: 'We discussed the need to conform the cable horizontal ownership and attribution rules to the programming concerns underlying the cable horizontal ownership statute. We also discussed the impact of the cable horizontal and attribution rules on the proposed merger of AT&T and MediaOne'" (Schwartzman, 2000, p. 5).

This was to say nothing of the resulting potentially problematic corporate entanglements consummation of the merger would create among the major cable companies, AT&T, and AOL. Schwartzman asked what the effect of the AOL–Time Warner transaction had on this affair, given that

> MediaOne and Time Warner are 50/50 partners in RoadRunner, the number two cable internet service provider. AT&T owns some 58% of Excite@Home, the number one cable Internet service provider. Consumers Union, et al. and other parties have complained that this combination will monopolize the market for delivery of Internet services, and inhibit free expression on the Internet. The possibility that AOL, by far the largest Internet service provider[,] will now share ownership of RoadRunner would give these companies even greater incentive to act in concert. (Schwartzman, 2000, p. 2)

Heather Barber, representing City Commissioner Erik Sten and the city of Portland, Oregon, offered a passionate plea for intervention. While Portland was at turns excited about the possibility of AT&T providing competitive local phone service and high-speed Internet, "both our citizens' commission and our elected officials came to the conclusion that we thought open access was necessary to provide the kind of Internet service that Portland has become accustomed to" (Barber, 2000, p. 1. Further:

> Portland believes in competition. Portland believes in choice. And from Portland citizens' point of view—and Commissioner Sten has talked to hundreds of citizens since this issue has been raging in Portland over the last year—the idea of having only one way to access the Internet over high-speed cable modems is not acceptable in Portland, Oregon. The city has gone through the problems associated with monopolies and simply believes that open access is the best approach. (Barber, 2000, p. 1)

Against claims that localities were seeking to simply "regulate the Internet":

> That couldn't be further from the truth. Portland has no interest in regulating the Internet, never has, never will. None of the city's regulations has anything to do with content.... [W]e do not favor different technical standards. FCC officials have made the argument—and it has been bandied about—that if local governments lake action on this issue, the country will end up with 30,000 technical standards. The city has not asked tor, nor has it regulated, any technical standard. (Barber, 2000, p. 2)

She finally appealed to the popular support for the actions of their regulators: "Whenever Commissioner Sten is stopped on the street or in the grocery store, the response is always, keep fighting for open access" (Barber, 2000, p. 2).

A representative of Seren Innovations (an overbuilder, started as a nonregulated subsidiary of Northern States Power Company, which was providing services in Minnesota and, imminently, California) offered, "The best evidence of AT&T's monopoly power is the fact that every time an overbuilder like Seren enters the market, AT&T responds by dropping its prices or adding new services at no charge" (Glass, 2000, p. 2). Khalil Munir, executive director of the Telecommunications Advocacy Project (TAP), testified to the uneven and hardly "colorblind" deployment schedule, calling into question the FCC's ambivalence at looking more deeply into deployment patterns in specific markets. He also testified to the difficulties in presenting evidence of any sort: "Due to the proprietary nature of much of the evidence, and TAP's inability to cross-examine MediaOne in a formal hearing process, TAP has been restrained in submitting further evidence to the FCC" (Munir, 2000, p. 6). Given the politically charged nature of calling out redlining, he was forced in open testimony to walk back some of his comments: structural inequality remained something nearly impossible to express in terms accessible to a proceeding such as this.

Some of the most revealing exchanges took place as a final case for open access was made to the FCC. Greg Simon, of the OpenNet Coalition, stressed the need for open access policy to enable a choice of varying ISP providers. This was a point made by consumer advocates all along, but Andrew Schwartzman expanded the horizon, a brief glimpse into what always lay behind the strategic choices they made both in coalition partners and in rhetorical strategy:

> Finally, this is not just about choosing your ISP, the formulation that we've heard repeatedly this morning. If you get to choose among a couple ISPs… but they all agree to limit uploading or to limit the size of video files because the terms and conditions offered don't give them that option. If they all agree that they're not going to permit certain kinds of filtering, [such as considerations as] parent[al] concern about how their children access the internet, it's not open access. Open access involves citizens, the customers who have a right to speak in an interactive medium and to receive information. It's not just their ability to have two or more ISPs to choose from as a customer. It's about their rights as citizens to use the internet as a medium of open expression. (FCC, 2000c, p. 49)

James Cicconi, representing AT&T, provided the common retort that would become rote when confronting the issue of opening its networks: that those who "took the risks" should reap monopoly rewards.

> Investors in this company, Excite@Home, which is not controlled by AT&T, but which TCI was an investor in, along with many others—and, in fact, there's a public component of it, as well as investment bankers and others, went out there and built a system when no one else would build it. They took the risks, they secured contracts from the cable companies who wanted to offer this service. And, in return, they were given a period of exclusivity within which to realize a return on the investment commitment they had made to build this system. (FCC, 2000c, p. 51)

OpenNet's members simply wanted to take advantage of this effort "for free. In essence, at wholesale. Deriving the benefit of somebody else's risk-taking. That isn't appropriate. It is not the business of the Government, and I think this agency has wisely concluded that it is not in the business of requiring the abrogation of contracts out there" (FCC, 2000c, p. 51). For another thing, GTE and other Bell members of OpenNet were hypocrites:

> The Bell companies themselves have absolutely no interest in open access, per se. They have no ISP benefit that they derive from it. Their sole interest in this issue is simply to bottleneck the realization of competition in their territories. GTE is

> particularly egregious.... They operate a cable system which itself is closed. The Worldwind system is actually advertised on the internet in a way at odds with the great principles of OpenNet. If you want a different ISP, you have to pay an additional charge. (FCC, 2000c, p. 51)

While Cicconi attempted to split the coalition this way, OpenNet's Greg Simon had a ready response. As time marched forward, it would prove a point on which advocates for openness would need to repeatedly waste breath to charges of freeloading off incumbent networks.

> Is access to the network under non-discriminatory terms, taking the network for free at wholesale? No. Is that what AT&T is asking when they go into the local loop, are they asking to ride for free? Because they want to get a discount?... We haven't even asked for a discount from what they charge their own affiliated ISP.... We have said treat people as you would treat your own affiliated provider. We have not even said you can't have discounts that are fair for different classes of customers. You just can't discriminate in favor of one customer or discriminate against one customer. (FCC, 2000c, p. 52)

Deborah Lathen, chief of the Cable Services Bureau, decided to test her conclusion from the staff report she had released the previous fall. In an environment in which multimodal competition in broadband had developed (far as it was from reality), she proposed, "Do you not believe that market forces would mandate that they would have to do that and the Government would not have to mandate it?" Simon responded, "When has a monopoly ever given up a monopoly without some help from the government?... AT&T says they'll give it up in two and a half years, but I've yet to see that they mean non-discriminatory open access as compared to deals. That is not open." (FCC, 2000c, p. 52).

It was the testimony of François Bar—who had written with his colleagues one of the papers that consumer advocates saw as crucial to mobilize—which brought order to the affair. He offered his critiques from the white paper he had coauthored; taking aim at Oxman's FCC working paper from the previous summer, he noted, "It was not the unregulation of the Internet, but active involvement by policy makers that guaranteed openness of the underlying infrastructure which was the telephone network, and made competition possible in order to spur the development of the Internet" (FCC, 2000c, pp. 66–67).

Offering the AT&T–Excite@Home combination as an example of what open access was *not,* he then offered his view of what it *was*. It would consist of two components. One was "transparency in the architecture. And here there's an interesting analogy which is that the power derived from control of the architecture in cable internet access is very similar to the kind of control the owner of an operating system on a computer derives from control over the APIs, the application programmer interface." Second, that "other ISPs should really have reasonable access to critical network features on a comparable basis." Action was appropriate because "what we have today is limited competition between the alternatives. Between cable broadband and a DSL. The footprints tend to not overlap" (FCC, 2000c, p. 68).

The FCC's chief economist at the time, Howard Shelanski, pressed Bar. Presented with the scenario of an "ideal world" in which numerous technologies exist to access broadband Internet in every home, Bar yet stressed that one would need to be sure that there was actual access to these technologies at the individual market level. To the question of whether open access would still be necessary in that instance, Bar responded,

> My preference, ultimately, would be to have a framework to deal with this issue which is not tied to individual technologies. Which is, I think, the reason why we're facing this problem today.... I think in the end, also, having an open framework that is cross platform, cross technology, has a sort of value.... [In sum,] it is not clear to me that in the end you want a system where you have to pick a whole package of underlying technology, network architecture, electronic commerce marketplace architecture and content provision.... My sense... is that the more cross pollination possibilities you make possible, the more experimentation you have. And the richer the environment will be. (FCC, 2000c, pp. 71–72)

Shelanski asked, what if there were thousands of ISPs, would open access still be desirable? Bar replied ideally it would, but the main point was that "if there are limits who gets to be let in should not be decided by the owner of the infrastructure. I mean, we have all kinds of mechanism[s]—auctions, licenses... that do not give the entire power to decide who gets programming or applications or ISP onto the infrastructure just because they own the infrastructure" (FCC, 2000c, p. 78). Bar noted that these issues were certainly complex and that he advocated debate on it—of the ilk consumer advocates had long desired, an honest inquiry into the challenges open access presents, not some exercise in handwaving. That was, "[one] that looks at the options. That looks at what exactly are the technical restrictions, not just what the owners of the infrastructure tells us are the restrictions.... An open debate about looking at alternative allocation mechanisms and consequences" (p. 79).

While the forum provided a consolidated version of debates that would stretch out another decade, it also revealed other more disturbing insights. Cable Services Bureau Chief Lathen, from the transcripts, occasionally revealed herself to be far less conversant on the broadband issue than one would expect of someone in her position. Several pages of the transcript are occupied with an exchange between AT&T's Cicconi and Lathen about the location of the ISP service itself. Cicconi spends no small amount of effort explaining to Lathen that the set-top box is not where Excite@Home or RoadRunner or the portal pages they offered were provisioned or stored (FCC, 2000c, pp. 45–46). This is intended less as slight to Lathen than an illustration of the newness of it all and the challenges of a regulator facing a new area; it also provides a degree of signal of what kinds of tacit knowledge underlay the debate there. Yet it is impossible to not come away from these proceedings without the impression that she seemed rather underprepared, far more comfortable (and generally far more interested) in issues of video service than this new emergent medium.

The fact that duplicitous testimony from large operators was taken for granted was also addressed when Schwartzman responded to Cicconi's attempt to hoodwink the panel into believing that cable's ability to corner the market on broadband was decreasing by the day, and so AT&T's power was less of a concern with new upstarts seemingly nipping at their heels.

> Maybe they don't win, but there's a lot of people out there who sure think that there's chokeholds.... Every now and then a CEO forgets that they're not sitting around [behind] closed doors... and they're at a convention and they speak truth that I'll be gosh darned if I'm going to let them get onto my cable, spend fifty billion dollars on it, then everybody says, oh, he didn't mean it. (FCC, 2000c, pp. 37–38)

That this went without comment from officials in the room spoke volumes more than the comment itself.

As the meeting wound to a close, Lathen's closing question set up what had been in many minds a foregone conclusion: "Do you think that the merger would give AT&T some kind of horizontal reach that would allow it to handicap or slow down the growth of competition from alternative broadband providers such as DSL or wireless, either by virtue of its being able to have first pick or exclusive arrangements with broadband content and application providers or through some other means?" (FCC, 2000c, pp. 111). The various participants largely offered variants of an either tentative or emphatic answer of no—with some, such as Bar, offering their caveats. All sought to add nuance to the semi-loaded, scope-constricted question. Nonetheless, this seemed to settle it: multimodal technologies would not be stymied, and one could predict that this was a done deal.

Wearing Down, Ramping Up

Even if the lawsuits were still to be decided, real chinks in the armor of local efforts to obtain open access conditions were appearing. The costs of litigation, for instance, were wearing down the will of localities to fight; Madison, Wisconsin, avoided the issue for this reason in late January ("State's Largest Car Dealer," 2000). By May, the Massachusetts Department of Telecommunications and Energy found that the local governments who had demanded open access had overreached their authority ("Comm Daily Notebook," 2000). The U.S. District Court in Richmond, Virginia, unlike their West Coast counterparts, upheld MediaOne's complaint (Kumar & Breznick, 2000). Hands Off the Internet, always at the ready to twist the knife, told trade press that the judgment "underscores the irrationality of having localities try to regulate high-speed Internet access systems, such as cable lines" ("Cable Notes," 2000).

Politics was intense as evidenced by moves in Congress. Pushed by cable players, a bipartisan group of legislators wrote FCC chairman Kennard to "move quickly to approve the AT&T–MediaOne merger"—without any "onerous regulatory penalties." Of course, the justification provided to congressional leaders had nothing to do with the Internet side of the equation: it had *everything* to do with the possibility of additional local telephone competition. The letter noted that the "only exception to new competition" wrought by the Telecommunications Act was "local residential telephone" where "facilities-based competition … has yet to become a reality on a broad scale" ("Microsoft," 2000). Other bipartisan pairings, such as Senator DeWine (R-OH) and Herb Kohl (D-WI), asked the Federal Trade Commission (FTC) to investigate the implications of "Internet routing and caching technology" whereby content providers could store information closer to end users, thus speeding up access to this information. Such practices raised "serious antitrust issues that should be investigated by the FCC and FTC"; and while allowing for the potential benefits of such technologies, they could also "give preferential treatment to content owned by affiliates"

("Microsoft," 2000). If it wasn't clear already that the largest players were feeling the strength of their positions, they expressed them outright at the National Cable and Television Association's Annual Convention in New Orleans. One report noted that executives from AOL, Excite@Home, and Microsoft—which itself was undertaking cable investments—all extolled privately driven partnerships with cable operators to "deliver services better and faster" all the while "downplay[ing] their influence as new-media conglomerates in [the] Internet economy." They emphasized that "speed to market" held precedence over scale: "Excite@Home CEO Geroge Bell said, 'it's victory to the fastest'" ("Microsoft," 2000).

In early June, the FCC followed through—not in investigating caching technologies, but in announcing its official approval of the AT&T–MediaOne merger. A remaining tension with this merger were continuing interests AT&T possessed in RoadRunner, a rival to its Excite@Home system (FCC, 2000b); these worries had been expressed by Schwartzman in the *en banc* hearing at the FCC. The Department of Justice required via a consent decree that AT&T divest of these interests. Ultimately, AT&T would not; and while consumer advocates would call the FCC on this malfeasance numerous times, the next chairman, Michael Powell, simply paid such concerns no heed. The consent decree also covered potential joint actions AT&T may wish to enter with the emerging AOL Time Warner. On the FCC side, in lieu of putting into place an open access regime, the FCC decided to go along with the voluntary (and to advocates, illusory) commitments AT&T made to provide nondiscriminatory access to broadband providers. Kennard was adamant. It was as if the hearing in February had never occurred.

> I believe that there are powerful marketplace incentives to ensure that consumers have such choices. Therefore, I have consistently advocated that we allow the nascent broadband marketplace a chance to develop before imposing a government-ordered regime.…I have been encouraged by voluntary commitments by AT&T and other cable operators to open their systems so as to accommodate consumer choice. AT&T has made these commitments to the FCC on the record in this proceeding, including the commitment that they will not restrict video streaming. (Kennard, 2000, p. 1)

What is truly remarkable about the order is what was *not* contained in any of the individual commissioners' statements: beyond Kennard's curt dismissal of advocate concerns for open access, putting his faith once again in the magic of market forces to stimulate multimodal competition (and whatever broadband universe that would bring), not one focused on broadband Internet access as an issue. Kennard focused on the procedural issues he followed in considering the merger; Furchtgott-Roth and Powell took issue with the seeming arbitrariness of these particular procedures described and were desirous of less emphasis on the "public interest" standard in decision making itself! Powell, in particular, disagreed with the notion taken by the chairman that even if an entity complied with "the rules specifically designed to address the harms at issue" yet "interfere[d] with the objectives of the Communications Act or other statutes," thus necessitating further requirements, these additional requirements "subsume[d] the rules and puts too much weight on our more ambiguous 'public interest' authority. That authority is meant to complement, not override, existing rules.... In circumstances where we have a rule that addresses issues raised by a merger, I would apply the rule and find that the public interest is satisfied" (M. K. Powell, 2000, p. 2).

Commissioner Tristani's objections (not to the point of dissent) focused on the delivery of television, mentioning broadband only in passing. "As with its approval of the CBS–Viacom merger, the Commission has once again failed to consider seriously the significant impact that an AT&T–MediaOne combination could have on the diversity of media voices. By focusing primarily on technical compliance with our rules, the Commission has not sufficiently analyzed whether the proposed transaction will undercut a fundamental purpose of the Communications Act—maintaining independent sources of news and information" (Tristani, 2000).

Localities Lose the Issue

Even as this merger was still under consideration, the oddball politicking surrounding the question of open access and the battling notions of what "deregulation" truly meant invaded state legislatures. Importantly, as in Congress, these initiatives remained as likely to be introduced by Republicans as Democrats. The CFA's Mark Cooper was continuing to be a presence across the country in statehouses thanks to the CFA's network of local affiliates.

In February, Cooper testified before the Maryland House of Delegates' Commerce and Governmental Matters Committee in support of the passage of the "Internet Consumers' Bill of Rights" that would "guarantee open access to the high-speed broadband Internet" (Cooper, 2000b). In Michigan, the message of pro-open access advocates was making it outside of legislative backrooms, as *Broadband in the Public Interest* reported that stories were appearing which highlighted "concerns many Detroit-area citizens have with the cable industry's plans to require consumers to purchase the cable monopoly's ISP" ("News," 2000b); but despite examination of the issue, no Detroit-area authorities had required open access. This was because, "according to one city councilwoman ... of AT&T and MediaOne's lawsuits against every locality supporting open access" ("News," 2000b). What wasn't happening at local levels *was* happening at the level of the state legislature: Mark Cooper appeared in early April before the Committee on Technology and Energy in Lansing, Michigan, to testify in favor of the "Internet Access Enhancement Act" which would do similarly to the bill proposed in Maryland (Cooper, 2000c). He prepared a statement for the Massachusetts Consumers' Coalition to promote open access via the proposed Massachusetts House Bill No. 5006, "An Act to Promote Competition in the Cable-Based Internet Access Market" (Consumer Federation of America, 2001). Further efforts saw letters to the San Francisco Board of Supervisors supportive of an open access ordinance (Consumer Federation of America, 2000a).

During these appearances, Cooper was able to turn AT&T and AOL's words to his own advantage; in late February, Consumers Union, the CFA, and the Media Access Project issued a report (2000) that analyzed AT&T and AOL's past stances in the United States and abroad; recall AT&T had *sought* open access principles elsewhere, as they had over DSL lines in the United States. For those *still* unable to accept a static definition of the concept of open access, they were able to identify key planks that *the companies themselves* had seen as necessary. Cooper distilled these planks into nine principles for broadband access going forward that would be advocated to state legislatures. These included:

"Comparably efficient interconnection, with the identification of several options for physical and virtual interconnection";

"Open standards with change management processes";

"ISP neutral network management";

"Minimum content and service restriction, consistent with neutral network management";

"Performance parameters, including a list of services to be made available and practices to be avoided";

"Confidentiality of competitively sensitive information and protection against abuse of such information by vertically integrated broadband service providers";

"A wholesale relationship between unaffiliated ISPs and vertically integrated service providers from whom the independents wish to purchase facilities";

"Rates for transport service that are subsidy free and not anticompetitive"; and

"Bundling and marketing provisions that prevent the abuse of leverage over monopoly services." (Consumers Union, Consumer Federation of America, & Media Access Project, 2000, p. iv)

Officials in Utah were grappling with their own quandary: its own 1995 Utah Telecommunications Act, approved by voters, apparently required its cable franchises to provide access to their systems, but the law's continued legality in light of possible preemption by the 1996 Telecommunications Act meant it remained contested ("Utah Law," 1999). In late 1999, Pennsylvania's state legislature was reportedly considering a bill that would force all cable operators to operate on open access terms. "After the bill gets out of Committee, [Rep. Ronald Raymond, the bill's sponsor] expects the Pennsylvania legislature to be 'flooded' by lobbyists from both ISPs and cable companies" ("News," 1999). One was introduced in early 2000 ("News," 2000a).

In Ohio, Republican Representative George Terwilleger introduced a pro-open access bill mid-February, which was greeted with a threat by the Ohio Cable Television Association to fight it ("News," 2000b). In Virginia, SB 707—proposed by Fairfax Republican Warren Barry—required all cable companies "to provide interconnection to ISPs on nondiscriminatory rates, terms and conditions at any technically feasible point (chosen by the ISP)"; further, it offered a "most favored nation" provision, providing that if another state offered more stringent requirements, those would apply in Virginia as well ("News," 2000b).

The news was hardly all rosy. Los Angeles's Information Technology Agency voted to approve the AOL–Time Warner franchise transfer with no binding access condition: rather, they accepted the companies' promises to maintain some form of open network. Gallingly, AOL even found this unpalatable despite past rhetoric, and commissioners chided representatives of the company for their duplicity ("Open Access Advocates Suffer," 2000). The city council would still need to approve the arrangement; Time Warner indicated it would fight even this weak provision. These were arrogant, heady moves considering its purportedly pro-open access position. Elsewhere, New Hampshire's House of Representatives' Science, Technology, and Energy Committee "killed a bill that would have required cable companies to open up the market if they had a 30% market share for Internet access" ("News," 2000b). In Vermont, then-Governor Howard Dean offered moderate support for a "leased access" provision of open access but shied away from anything else, supporting Kennard's cautious approach: "I commend your efforts to encourage cable companies to open their systems to ISPs voluntarily…this limited change in AT&T's policy [MindSpring deal] couldn't have taken place without the implicit threat of regulation that your efforts represented" (Ross, 1999).

By midyear, one count stood at fourteen state legislatures attempting to move on open access—all had been stymied (Kumar & Breznick, 2000). All the same, localities were reported to be thinking cleverly about ways to enhance their service; one report said, "Public-interest models are emerging in a number of other cities that are trying to gain concessions from the cable franchises. For example, some cities seek to retain 10 percent of the bandwidth for non-profit organizations. Others hoped to allocate 3 percent of cable fees to fund public-access channels or to get one-time grants to convert…libraries, community centers—to digital" (Hazen, 2000).

A Double-Edged Sword: The Ninth Circuit Decides

On June 20, the Ninth Circuit rendered its decision on the Portland appeal, fundamentally changing the political landscape well outside the bounds of the court's jurisdiction.[1] The most significant aspect of the decision was its effort to separate out a telecommunications service from the underlying cable service: by its read of the Telecommunications Act, Internet service was a *service that rode aboard this underlying network on a cable system* in the same manner that ISP service was provided over a telephone wire. A significant passage, cited by activists, read as follows:

> Among its broad reforms, the Telecommunications Act of 1996 enacted a competitive principle embodied by the dual duties of nondiscrimination and interconnection.... Together, these provisions mandate a network architecture that prioritizes consumer choice, demonstrated by vigorous competition among telecommunications carriers. As applied to the Internet, Portland calls it "open access," while AT&T dysphemizes it as "forced access." Under the Communications Act, this principle of telecommunications common carriage governs cable broadband as it does other means of Internet transmission such as telephone service and DSL, "regardless of the facilities used." The Internet's protocols themselves manifest a related principle called "end-to-end": control lies at the ends of the network where the users are, leaving a simple network that is neutral with respect to the data it transmits, like any common carrier. On this role of the Internet, the codes of the legislator and the programmer agree....
>
> ISPs are themselves users of telecommunications when they lease lines to transport data on their own networks and beyond on the Internet backbone. However, in relation to their subscribers, who are the "public" in terms of the statutory definition of telecommunications service, they provide "information services," and therefore are not subject to regulation as telecommunications carriers.... Like other ISPs, @Home consists of two elements: a pipeline (cable broadband instead of telephone lines), and the Internet service transmitted through that pipeline. However, unlike other ISPs, @Home controls all of the transmitted facilities between its subscribers and the Internet. To the extent @Home is a conventional ISP, its activities are one of an information service. However, to the extent that @Home provides its subscribers Internet transmission over its cable broadband facility, it is providing a telecommunications service as defined in the Communications Act. (Quoted in Consumer Federation of America, 2000b, pp. 1, 3–4)

All sides declared victory. Erik Sten offered a positive reaction and saw it as vindication: "We may have lost the battle but won the war," he commented (McCall, 2000). All the same, potentially dim realities were beginning to sink in nonetheless. *CableFax* ranted in a near-hysterical editorial, "I warned those regulators and their even more zealous supporters that local authorities might find that they had just stepped in 'Portland Cement' [a year ago]. The [Ninth] Circuit Court of Appeals just confirmed that prognostication." The publication crowed, "Local authorities have been told, at least in that Circuit, that they simply do not have legal jurisdiction over cable Internet access. Instead, the local authorities who had been collecting franchise fees from what they considered a 'cable service' now may find that their own overzealous efforts to regulate a nascent technology have resulted in them losing revenue operators were willingly giving them!" To those who would now point to the FCC and argue that they should finally see broadband provision over cable as a common carrier and start subjecting it to such terms, "Nonsense.... The FCC has the discretion to 'forebear' [*sic*] from regulating a telecommunications service as a common carrier, and [the court] also noted, right in the decision, that the FCC had already made a finding, in its AT&T–TCI merger approval, that the public interest did not require such regulation at this time" (all quotes from Effros, 2000).

Both sides were essentially correct. What the court had done was provide a bit of clarity to *definitions* contained within the Telecommunications Act, definitions with tremendously significant ramifications. A new tangle was appearing because Congress had decided that the appropriate way to break down regulation was by *technology* and not by function—yet the definitions they utilized for telecommunications networks (and their functions) embedded terms that increasingly applied to the functions of cable systems themselves. Had the court not found that telecommunications service was provided by cable systems in offering Internet access, one set of rules would have applied; however, with this finding, another set now did. The irony was that a finding of a *telecommunications* service riding on a cable service *removed* jurisdiction of this service from local purview: if the system was no longer under the rules of a cable system (rules that empowered local franchise authorities to negotiate with cable companies), then technically localities couldn't institute open access conditions. Cable companies were required to negotiate with local franchise authorities by law—but telecommunications companies faced no such obligation. Rather, these would be guaranteed by *federal* law under unbundling rules, to be rendered specific and clarified by FCC fiat via proceedings dedicated to the task. It also meant that the Internet service revenues that passed through these cable wires no longer were eligible to be considered in the calculation of franchise fees local cable franchises were required to pay to localities. In winning, local commissions found the rug swept out from underneath them: it would take a little time for them to realize this. In many regards, it was *too* much of a win for consumer advocates, given their strategy.

The CFA laid out a second "action plan" based on the decision (Consumer Federation of America, 2000b). The finding provided a wind at these advocates' backs to open a Pandora's box of full-fledged Title II treatment of cable broadband that would, if selectively applied as appropriate for the particularities of the technology, require cable companies to interconnect with other parties (eliminating the open access issue); provide robust consumer price, nondiscrimination and privacy protections; add accessibility rules for persons with disabilities; and even open the door to giving states a say in continuing to regulate the video provision side of cable services, "regardless of whether they are provided on a common carriage or private carriage basis" (p. 3). "In a sense," they argued, "the Ninth Circuit granted exactly what open access advocates were fighting for. ISPs possess the legal *right* to nondiscriminatory interconnection with cable modem networks, which they can exercise through private action. That right will be useless, however, unless government enforces nondiscriminatory access in meaningful fashion. This means open access advocates still have their work cut out for them" (p. 1).

The FCC's Kennard continued to vacillate on the issue. The strategy document the CFA prepared quoted him as reminding all that "the FCC has not determined whether high-speed Internet access over the cable plant is a 'telecommunications service'" and that "the categorization of 'telecommunications' service does not necessarily mean that service is subject to all of the common carrier regulations that apply to telephone companies" (Consumer Federation of America, 2000b, p. 2). Further, the CFA cited a press release from the chairman announcing the possibility of a proceeding to "establish a record on marketplace developments" which meant only that "the Chairman is talking about taking several months to start a proceeding that focuses on the wrong issues" (p. 2). The chairman was "already misconstruing the court's words"; advocates quote Kennard himself "claiming that this type of service is both a 'telecommunications' service and an 'information' service." They intone that he may well make moves to eliminate competition *even aboard telecommunications wires* in an effort to maintain regularity parity between the two technologies. "Given its track record on the issue, and the clear requirement that cable and DSL be treated in similar fashion, the FCC could decide that it no longer needs to require open access for any advanced telecommunications services" (pp. 4–5). In fact, the United States Telecom Association was using the decision to "renew its call to allow high speed Internet access over the telephone wires to be closed down and run on a proprietary basis" (p. 5).

Action thus needed to remain at the level of state and local levels despite ongoing ambiguity; the consequences of delay would be dire. The CFA called for localities outside the Ninth Circuit to "continue to press for open access in every manner possible, starting with the continuation of the effort to exercise cable franchise authority"; court cases elsewhere, such as the Fourth Circuit, should "be continued" to establish what would hopefully be further support for a similar position, given this would likely reach the Supreme Court at some point; at the least, differing rulings would force the FCC to take action. ISPs within the Ninth Circuit should "immediately seek agreements for nondiscriminatory access and interconnection with cable modem service providers," and failing this, they could now seek redress. Time was of the essence: "Delaying the process allows cable operators to embed discriminatory hardware and software more deeply into the network and impose discriminatory business practices on ISPs desperate for access" (Consumer Federation of America, 2000b, pp. 4–5). Given FCC "footdragging," "local governments have been the key counterbalance against the FCC's wrongheaded policy on open access. State public utility commissions are now another potential counterbalance, and their role should be defended" (p. 5).

If the FCC continued to have difficulty discerning how broadband should be viewed in the marketplace (in the same market as dial-up? In a different market?) the Department of Justice had no such confusion. Recall that it had, in its own analysis, determined that "narrowband" Internet service did not compete with broadband—which was the analysis that led them to (attempt to) force AT&T–MediaOne to divest of its holdings in RoadRunner to consummate their merger. Taking an opportunity to point out how the "public interest mandate" was lagging behind at the FCC, Cooper set the example in a filing with the agency shortly after the Ninth Circuit decision (Consumer Federation of America & Consumers Union, 2000), which supported Southwestern Bell Corporation (SBC), a regional Bell company in the southwest, in their request to be permitted to sell long distance service (and thus provide competition to AT&T). The Telecommunications Act had established in its Section 271 a list of requirements a regional Bell would need to fulfill to provide long distance service; prior to the act, regional Bells were to serve as regional local monopolies. These requirements involved efforts to offer interconnection, unbundling, and resale to other providers. A National Telecommunications and Information Administration (NTIA) explainer quotes a congressman summarizing the reasoning: "Once the [regional Bell operating company] open[s] the local exchange networks to competition, [they] are free to compete in the long distance and manufacturing markets."[2] While seemingly unrelated, this allowed Cooper to call on the FCC to force AT&T to file with the agency the "just, reasonable and nondiscriminatory" charges (in the language of the Telecommunications Act) it would necessarily offer for broadband interconnection—an action supportable particularly in the Ninth Circuit now that it was found to be operating a telecommunications service and thus subject to the same regulation as SBC. While outside the Ninth Circuit's jurisdiction, to twist the knife, he noted that AT&T had "complained bitterly that [SBC] was not providing nondiscriminatory access to DSL service" despite AT&T's continued operation of "millions of cable lines in Texas that it continues to operate on a closed, proprietary basis" (Consumer Federation of America & Consumers Union, 2000, p. 2). To go even a step further, the groups noted that Excite@Home—in which AT&T possessed a controlling interest—was itself "complain[ing] to the Federal Communications Commission that AOL must be required to open its instant message service" (p. 2). AT&T's hypocrisy could hardly be more glaring, nor the FCC's inaction more mystifying.

A strategy of boosting localities' own efforts while needling the FCC ran up against new realities. While the city of Portland decided against appealing the decision further, it now realized it would need to recalculate the franchise fees they collected from cable providers for cable services. As the *Cablefax* editorial foretold, public access facilities would be losing out due to the resultant revenue "hole"; one report noted that they had hoped to obtain a "slice of fees" from data services ("Portland Drafts Omnibus Franchise," 2000). To add insult to injury, despite Oregon's requiring a telecommunications franchise to provide telephony services, just one day after the Ninth Circuit decision was issued AT&T launched its @Home service in Portland, interpreting the circuit decision as removing local authority altogether. David Olson was incensed at the company he cast as possessing a "troubling history of taking the law into its own hands" (Estrella, 2000). All cities were being led to rethink their strategies for similar reasons. In the meantime, with another appeal pending in the Fourth Circuit of Appeals, the FCC submitted a brief expressing its desire that the court reach a less expansive conclusion—arguing that the only issue at hand was whether local authorities had statutory authority to order open access conditions on franchise transfers ("FCC Urges Court," 2000).

AOL Time Warner as Ambiguous Consolation Prize

As the year wound down, the effects of the rapidly deflating bubble and subsequent recession were being felt. The effects of this can hardly be overestimated, and they had a powerful influence on subsequent debates. Excite@Home went belly-up midyear, and with a new administration (and FCC) in the offing, the local fights for open access receded as efforts shifted to setting national policy. In Washington, DC, local efforts during a franchise transfer there were commenced to consider an access provision, but overall the sentiment was to wait for the FCC to render a policy itself (Stephens, 2000). In Minnesota, Governor Jesse Ventura did attempt to revive legislation requiring nondiscriminatory interconnection for both cable and telecom companies, shifting regulatory authority away from localities to the state public utility commission (Estrella & Haugsted, 2000). However, the overall feeling was that FCC action would be soon in coming. None of these efforts panned out.

While the AOL–Time Warner transaction was still under debate, the FCC maintained a noncommittal stance on the matter. The AOL–Time Warner merger was becoming a public issue, with articles appearing decrying the combination as media consolidation was coming into its own as an issue of public import. At an *en banc* hearing that took place shortly after the Ninth Circuit decision, Kennard remained bewildered at the notion of open access, even if he seemed more willing to explore it. Even after the intensity of the struggle of the previous two years, recalling the "Socratic" section of the Staff Report from nearly a year earlier, he said, "One of the frustrations I have with this debate is that there is not a baseline definition" (FCC, 2000d, p. 125). Mark Cooper, an invited panelist, responded that he had never directly advocated what the Ninth Circuit found, preferring "one sentence": "Unaffiliated Internet service providers shall be allowed to gain access to cable modem systems on 'rates, terms and conditions that are no less favorable than' affiliated ISPs" (p. 125). James Love of the Consumer Project on Technology, also a panelist, added regarding competing ISPs, "Give them the right [to access]. Tell them to arbitrate disputes so you don't have to try and write rules. We tried to get through this without writing rules by letting private parties have the private right of action" (p. 127).

As his tenure was coming to an end with the coming elections, Kennard finally issued a Notice of Inquiry (FCC, 2000a), essentially throwing the tough questions in the laps of the next set of commissioners. The exhaustive piece, asking how the FCC should classify cable services, *still* made such pronouncements as "What is 'open access'?" and "Is open access a desirable policy goal" (¶¶32–33)? It was clear that large cable interests' deliberate strategy of obfuscation, fear, uncertainty, and doubt had succeeded. "Industry participants have different conceptions of open access," the FCC declared (¶28), describing variants designed to render the subject as complex as possible and as far away from Cooper's one-sentence description as could be.

Shortly after the Notice of Inquiry was issued, in November 2000, a federal district court judge tossed out the Broward County, Florida, ordinance requiring open access, this time arguing that the locality violated AT&T's First Amendment rights. Advocates, in comments to the FCC in response to the Notice, took umbrage with the court's read of the situation. The National Association of Telecommunications Officers and Administrators were performing an about-face as well, telling *Multichannel News,* "We believe the FCC should decide this. And we're going to press our case that [Internet over cable is] a cable service, delivered over a cable platform." Such a "redefinition" would reinstitute the full boat of expanded franchise fees for localities and ensure broadest local authority (Hearn & Estrella, 2001).

It is in this context, with a decision about the AOL–Time Warner merger still in the making, that consumer advocates responded in December to the FCC's Inquiry. "This long-awaited *Inquiry* arrives during the throes of a debate that has proceeded much too long without active Commission involvement. A full rulemaking proceeding on open access is needed now" (Consumers Union et al., 2000, p. i). Consumer advocates' concerns, while couched in language of competition in the consumer market, had always been at base about the promotion and protection of marginalized and *noncommercial* content, and in the end stages of this initial battle, they were making this clear. At risk, should an open access policy not be instituted, were "hundreds of community 'Freenets'... [which] act as low-cost ISPs by purchasing connectivity from telephone companies and providing connections to individuals and social service groups for free or at cost, and maintain web pages for non-profits" (Consumers Union et al., 2000, p. 11). Further,

> Without open access policies, FreeNets are unlikely to obtain high speed connectivity because FreeNets provide services that the cable industry might well perceive as directly competitive. In addition, FreeNets are not likely to be replaced in the

> commercial marketplace. FreeNets often offer information services—particularly of local interest—without "banner advertising" and merchandising offerings. Just as many citizens, especially parents, may prefer non-commercial radio or television to commercial offerings, they may prefer to access—or have their children access—local information sources that do not come bundled with ads providing "click through" access. (Consumers Union et al., 2000, p. 11)

These advocates were watching the birth of a new, "channelized" Internet emerging before their eyes in its early stages. AT&T's ability, for example, to slow users' upload speeds to 128 kbps when once they had the ability to upload at 1 Mbps was worrisome. A network attuned to download-and-consume as opposed to create-and-upload signaled shifts to come.

> These technologies and features are not, of themselves, contrary to the public interest. They become so, however, when these choices inherent in those technologies are foisted upon users without options to go elsewhere. In such a case, the previously open, competitive, and diverse Internet becomes a limited-choice medium. Users become more like cable television viewers, hoping that their cable company will carry their favorite channel, despite the fact that without a financial link between their cable company and the content provider, such hope will likely remain futile. (Consumers Union et al., 2000, pp. 9–10)

They reminded the FCC that decisions it made, unlike in the restricted purviews of the Department of Justice and the FTC, "must include consideration of First Amendment values. Essential to the value of the Internet is the ability of citizens to speak to one another, to be publishers and broadcasters as well as readers and listeners" (Consumers Union et al., 2000, p. ii). Open access, as argued by these advocates, would "serve First Amendment values—fostering citizens' ability to speak and be heard—by preserving competition among independent content providers, including those providing and facilitating non-commercial and civic content"; it would "preserve the innovation that is the hallmark of the Internet and encourage competition among various providers of technical high speed services"; and "through competition among providers," it would "preserve consumer choice in areas such as niche marketing and filtering objectionable content," while "encourag[ing] deployment of competitive facilities to provide high speed Internet access" (pp. i–ii).

While these were reiterations of already long-expressed points, what was becoming apparent was a knowingly deliberate act of institutional amnesia on the part of the FCC. Foreshadowing developments to come, the FCC's Notice of Inquiry noted with little comment the recent "development of market-based access initiatives…there appears to be some movement toward allowing access to additional ISPs" (FCC, 2000a, ¶37). As evidence, the Commission pointed to the AT&T–MindSpring letter of the previous year. The Notice also pointed to a "Memorandum of Understanding" that AOL and Time Warner issued earlier in the year committing to opening ISP access aboard its combined cable platform. Time Warner in July had issued a news release as well that Juno Online Services would be the "first unaffiliated ISP to use Time Warner cable systems for the provision of high-speed Internet access" (FCC, 2000a, ¶37). The FCC cited this as evidence of a market "opening up" its architecture to competition absent the FCC's prerogatives.

Consumer commenters reacted with alarm. In the long view, they reminded the FCC that in light of the past Computer Inquiries proceedings, "the Commission's current inaction in the area of cable broadband open access is inconsistent with its historic decisions in the Computer Inquiry proceeding. While the FCC may believe such inaction simply continues its 'unregulation'of the Internet, we should be clear that non-intervention constitutes instead a fundamental policy reversal" (Consumers Union et al., 2000, p. iii). But even more of concern was the FCC's own recent actions being shunted down the memory hole. The consumer advocates were "compelled to point out that *none* of the initiatives mentioned are 'market based.' Each of these agreements was adopted specifically in response to a regulatory initiative or inquiry" (p. 22). Recall that the AT&T–MindSpring letter was the result of discussions initiated by Kennard himself; the AOL–Time Warner Memorandum of Understanding "was drafted in order to speed regulatory review of that merger at the FCC; and the recent spate of AOL negotiations are in response to the Federal Trade Commission's apparent position that it will not approve the AOL–Time Warner merger until such agreements, presumably with competition-enhancing terms, are achieved" (pp. 21–22).

Even these moves to "open" were flawed. These commenters had already long pointed out the contradictions contained in the AT&T–MindSpring promises; becoming more clear in the preceding months was that Time Warner's own offer, while superior to AT&T's, remained duplicitous. The AOL–Time Warner commitment had included providing a choice of ISPs and a promise to negotiate without prejudice with unaffiliated ISPs. Users would not be forced to purchase Internet access from AOL–Time Warner before purchasing access from another ISP; these ISPs would have direct access to their customers; and—unlike AT&T, consumer advocates note—these ISPs would be able to connect to the AOL–Time Warner network without purchasing "transport" from the conglomerate (summarized by Consumers Union et al., 2000, pp. 25–26). The advocates further noted that the company, in addition to promising nondiscrimination over its network with nonpartners, would not "prevent the provision of streaming video by unaffiliated ISPs" (p. 26). Consumer advocates even allowed that "AOL/Time Warner appears to recognize the legitimacy of civic discourse goals," committing to "partner[] to promote national, regional or local services in order to facilitate the ability of consumers to choose among ISPs of different size and scope" and "not allow[ing] selective service offering of service that 'redlines' a portion of an AOL/Time Warner cable system" (summarized by Consumers Union et al., 2000, p. 26).

Yet these turned out to be half-baked promises. AOL Time Warner insisted on calling these "voluntary" commitments, the details of implementation were not outlined, and there was no legal enforcement, thus "mak[ing] them untrustworthy" (Consumers Union et al., 2000, pp. 26–27). Worse, a detailed filing by ISP NorthNet had brought to light what awaited a provider of these services sitting down to undertake these "voluntary" negotiations (even if required by the FTC). NorthNet noted that the "term sheet" offered them by Time Warner offered usurious conditions to any ISP seeking access to their network, including "explicitly eschew[ing] any obligation to negotiate in good faith by Time Warner" (summarized by Consumers Union et al., 2000, p. 27; all citations below from same). An ISP would be required to disclose proprietary (and sensitive) data about their operations. They would need to give Time Warner a nonrefundable $50,000 deposit; all costs for connectivity would total $700,000. An ISP's portal (start) page was subject to Time Warner's approval; Time Warner also reserved the right to put its own content "above the fold" "without limitation as to content, applications, service or functionality" (p. 27). If privacy policies differed between the companies, they would need to be brought into alignment. The *price* of the offered ISP service needed mutual approval by Time Warner and the ISP. If the ISP sought to offer functionality that went beyond what Time Warner offered, then it required Time Warner's approval. Time Warner retained exclusive right to "bundle" its service, particularly video services, with others; additionally, Time Warner would "only optimize other ISP's services for personal computers, but not for other devices, such as set top boxes" (p. 28). Among these conditions, Time Warner required a stunning 75 percent of revenues gained by the ISP as well as 25 percent of all "ancillary revenues" generated by the ISP for "advertising, [other] transactions, premium services, e-commerce, web hosting, and other fees" (pp. 26–28). Press accounts of such challenging (if not impossible) negotiations were emerging, particularly regarding the 75 percent of revenues requirement—especially since earlier testimony revealed AT&T's arrangement with Excite@Home to be merely 66 percent (Estrella & Haugsted, 2000). Consumer advocates concluded, "Even under regulatory duress, cable operators have not demonstrated a willingness to negotiate agreements with unaffiliated ISPs that serve competitive and First Amendment goals" (Consumers Union et al., 2000, p. 28).

The disagreement of the federal district court that thwarted Broward County's open access requirement with the Ninth Circuit's own opinion—which gave the appearance of genuine ambiguity in the law—was the result of a botched understanding of how the Internet worked: it was clear that the newness of the technology and the ability to hide technological capabilities behind a particular business model that precluded such capabilities was working to incumbents' advantage. The mistakes that the court made, consumer advocates noted, were egregious. For one, the court assumed that the cable operators had the same First Amendment rights as newspapers, thus giving them a twisted form of "editorial control" over the content that passed through their wires. That *one* court could read past precedent this way was alarming enough but revealed that the argument still bore utility, and it would appear again and again in years to come in comments from conduit operators and their supporters. More embarrassing for the court was how it believed the technology itself operated:

> For example, the court asserted that users would attribute potentially offensive speech provided by an alternative ISP to the cable operator, and that all 5,000 ISPs in the country could potentially seek access to the cable operators system.... This miscomprehends how the Internet works or what the ordinance required. Internet Access is not like a cable channel: some affirmative action on the part of the user is required to obtain content, including offensive content.... Given that the Internet subscriber must affirmatively chose [*sic*] an alternate ISP, and affirmatively seek objectionable content, it surpasses belief that the subscriber would then attribute any offensive content to the cable system operator. Furthermore, the cable operators have consistently maintained that they exercise no editorial

> role in limiting a user's access to content; just the opposite, cable operators have pledged not to discriminate against any outside content.... Indeed, the only other district court to address the "forced speech" argument rejected it. (Consumers Union et al., 2000, pp. 7–8)

In January, the FCC issued its approval of the AOL–Time Warner merger. Following what had been the FTC's lead, the FCC did allow that it understood that negotiations with the cable giant for ISP access was proving challenging for several ISPs attempting to gain access (FCC, 2001, ¶126n357). The FTC required the combined entity to have access to at least one unaffiliated ISP within ninety days of the beginning of AOL's service and that "AOL Time Warner [was] not [to] interfere with content passed along the bandwidth contracted for by unaffiliated ISPs, or [to] discriminate on the basis of affiliation in the transmission of content that AOL Time Warner has contracted to deliver to subscribers over their cable systems" (¶47; footnotes omitted). Further, AOL Time Warner was required to supply its DSL service "at the same retail price" (¶47; footnotes omitted) in areas in which it faced competition as in those it did not. (With the ability to cross-subsidize its own markets, the ability to charge different rates would likely result in the provider simply underpricing competition to drive them out of business and then pump its prices back up once achieving monopoly status.) It should be noted that if the merger was almost a foregone conclusion at the FCC, it was actually quite contentious at the FTC: Commissioner Mozelle Thompson offered his own added statement that, while concurring with the agency's decision to allow the transaction to move forward, expressed his own concerns (Thompson, 2001).

The FCC added conditions that the emergent AOL Time Warner would not restrict the ability of ISPs or customers to reach each other. The newly combined entity was to allow these ISPs to have control over the "first screen" (i.e., the "portal" page a customer would first encounter) without some tithe to AOL Time Warner. These unaffiliated ISPs were to be allowed to bill customers directly; and "to the extent AOL Time Warner provides any Quality of Service mechanisms, caching services, technical support customers services, multicasting capabilities, address management and other technical functions of the cable system that affect customers' experience with their ISP," AOL would not provide differential access or service based on affiliation (FCC, 2001, ¶126). These ISPs would not be restricted from disclosing their contracts to the FCC. They established binding enforcement procedures via complaint. Even as the FCC made formal several of the conditions contained in the "Memorandum of Understanding," however, it is a far cry to call the conditions that it instituted "open access"; the FCC itself, with the cover of its Notice of Inquiry to shield it, pointedly declared (in a footnote) that "in particular, we decline to mandate 'open access' to AOL Time Warner's cable systems or to require that the merged firm divest itself of Road Runner, as requested by Consumers Union and other commenters" (¶126n363). Had full open access requirements applied, as opposed to the FCC's requirements of private negotiations with rival ISPs, AOL Time Warner would have provided "any requesting Internet Service Providers nondiscriminatory access to its broadband Internet transport services (unbundled from the provision of content) on rates, terms and conditions that are at least as favorable as those on which it provides access to itself, or its affiliates, or any other person," including support systems "and/or interfaces" to prevent AOL Time Warner's own Internet service be given favorable treatment (Consumers Union et al., 2000, p. 21). That is, open access in advocates' eyes involved ensuring that unaffiliated ISPs would be able to viably compete with AOL Time Warner's own Internet provider with ready access to numerous more elements of the provision service. The FCC's own conditions were a pale, watered-down version of this that left much room for unfair advantage by the incumbent. While Kennard offered in a separate statement platitudes about "long [being] concerned about bottlenecks… that could stifle competition and innovation" (Kennard, 2001, p. 1), controversy here surrounded whether any conditions should apply at all. Furchtgott-Roth reiterated his stance that the FCC should only be dealing with radio licenses (Furchtgott-Roth, 2001) and Powell bemoaned that the conditions "take excessive counsel of our fears, or, more accurately, the fears of AOL Time Warner's competitors" (Powell, 2001, p.1).

AOL Time Warner is certainly the go-to example for many writers for embarrassing deals run amok, with disastrous consequences, mistakes unseen. The FCC put off setting national policy as it concurred with the FTC conditions on AOL Time Warner as it formed. While this seems a reasonable test case and a victory of sorts for open access advocates, arguably the moment had been decided months before as the MediaOne transaction came to an end. A huge difference this time may have been that large content concerns as Disney (with its own portal to protect) expressed concerns about the combined entity, as Aufderheide (2002) notes. She similarly notes the emergence of a commons model that was finding its voice: the introduction of a victory for "commons" activists, however, was a subterfuge in a broader sense in two principal ways. For one, enforced was hardly open access in the sense intended by activists all along. For another, it ultimately would serve not to expand, but in a perverse way, *limit* the range of debate about the emergent dominant medium as it arose from the burst bubble anew.

The Powell FCC Takes Over

Following the election of George W. Bush in 2000, and with the sitting of a new FCC, Michael Powell ascended to become chairman of the Commission. National policy on open access was forced in midyear 2001 via a ruling in the Fourth Circuit that declared, against the Ninth Circuit's ruling, that federal law protected cable providers from having to offer a "telecommunications service" as part of their offering. With appellate circuit rulings that conflicted, at this time FCC chairman Michael Powell gave his staff the task of writing up a draft of what would become the Cable Modem Order the following year (Hearn & Estrella, 2001).

The resultant document was a *Declaratory Order and Notice of Proposed Rulemaking* (FCC, 2002b). In a brash political move, the Powell FCC skipped any rulemaking process (a "Notice of Proposed Rulemaking" on its own on which comment would be sought) and instead made a determination outright that a telecommunications service would not be "separated out" from cable facilities that would result in any open access claims. Yet the order went still further, pulling the rug out from under the entire debate itself. Up until this point, the open access debate had been two poles: at one pole was an argument that cable facilities, presently regulated as a "Title VI" service in their own "silo," possessed no requirement to open their wires to competition and should stay that way; at the other, the argument that given these wires' functionality now closely resembled telecommunications or "Title II" services, they should be reclassified and regulated as such, if with some modifications. Here, Powell opened up a third possibility that had never been on the table: cable modem service was now to be overseen as an *information service itself inseparable from the cable facilities themselves*. Neither a Title VI cable service nor a Title II telecommunications service, this would be governed under "Title I," which itself possessed no specific requirements

> as e-mail and web-hosting, but also equipment, network management, and in some cases billing and customer service functions that larger operators normally have self-provided. The ISP Channel and High Speed Access Corp., however, no longer provide turn key services, and the number of turn key providers is dwindling. Cable operators using independent ISPs to provide cable modem service have chosen in many cases to re-brand the service as their own or to co-brand the service. Charter Communications, for example, has contracted with EarthLink in several markets to provide cable modem service, and then rebranded the service as Charter Pipeline. (FCC, 2002b, ¶24; footnotes omitted)

The Notice notes that "Many of the business models described above are currently under transition," with "AOL Time Warner, Comcast, and AT&T [embarking] on a multiple-ISP approach to offering cable-modem service." In fact, "in accordance with conditions imposed on the merger by the FTC... as of January 2002 AOL Time Warner was offering cable modem service using both affiliated and unaffiliated ISPs on all systems in its 20 largest divisions with a choice of three national ISP services," with more markets offered shortly before the Notice was released. It pointed as well to the announcement by AT&T to "offer EarthLink high-speed cable Internet service to its customers in the greater Boston and Seattle markets" (FCC, 2002b, ¶26). Other operators

> have been conducting or have announced that they will conduct technical trials to determine how cable modem service can be offered using multiple ISPs, as AOL Time Warner is now doing, and AT&T and Comcast propose they will do. Cox and Charter both announced technical trials of multiple ISP service. While Cox began a technical trial of multiple ISP-service with AOL and EarthLink in the third quarter of 2001, Charter has since decided not to pursue a multiple ISP trial. (FCC, 2002b, ¶28; footnotes omitted)

All the same, a multiple ISP environment required

> a re-thinking of many technical, operational, and financial issues, including implementation of routing techniques to accommodate multiple ISPs, Quality of Service, and the compensation, billing, and customer service arrangements between the cable operator and the ISPs. While much more could be said regarding these issues, it is clear that they center around the difficulties of trying to modify a service designed to be provisioned by a single cable modem service provider to allow the provisioning of cable modem service by multiple service providers. (FCC, 2002b, ¶29; footnotes omitted)

Nonetheless, the *possibility* of providing the service was shown to be quite possible.

Beyond its ruminations regarding technology, however, the FCC's modus operandi in its overarching logic were clearly in view: in their narrative, activists would be removed from the story, subsumed in the decisions of *markets*. If this needed to be rendered even more clearly, later in the year, when the FCC gave its blessing (and to which Copps issued another scathing dissent, but not on open access grounds) to AT&T's purchase of Comcast and when advocates cited the conditions on AOL Time Warner as one of their reasons for demanding the institution of similar requirements on this new entity, the Powell FCC responded glibly,

> Commenters' reliance on the *AOL-Time Warner Order* as authority for the imposition of an ISP access condition is misplaced. We have never mandated, as a merger condition or in any other context, that any cable operator provide access to its systems to unaffiliated ISPs. In *AOL-Time Warner*, we supplemented an unaffiliated ISP access condition imposed by the FTC by requiring that, if AOL Time Warner provided such access voluntarily or otherwise, it must do so on nondiscriminatory terms. (FCC, 2002a, ¶135)

Conclusion

Between December 2000 and mid-February 2001, the NoGatekeepers.org site was effectively shut down, left with a message reading, "We have come a long way in educating policymakers and consumers about the importance of preserving the Internet's qualities of openness, diversity and consumer choice in the broadband world. But the need for continued vigilance to ensure open access remains. While this chapter has come to a close, we encourage you to stay involved." The page finished with links to the old supporting organizations.[3] AOL effectively defected from the coalition; given its previous connections to the site, the core organizations it supported had largely stopped adding material to it from early 2000 onward.

Often left as a side story or a curiosity, it is key to revisit this opening salvo, even as Lessig's protégé, Tim Wu, was waiting in the wings to spawn his new term, "network neutrality." True, open access *was* an internecine fight between well-heeled factions of capital, but it was crucially the terrain on which public-interest advocates—and a small number of them, to be sure—laid out the initial case not just for an open access regime but for a vision of what the emergent Web should look like and who it should serve. Their answers may give us pause. Working from a particularly guttural and deeply felt sense of transaction cost economics—it surely is easier to switch providers of ISP service without changing the *medium* through which one accessed the Internet—we end up with mixed outcomes: first is the vision of an "open, competitive, and democratic" space (as if this space has ever existed *anywhere*); second is an adjacent vision this one takes on as cargo—an even more sweeping vision of *freedom* in the Lessigian vein (Streeter, 2011).

We are left with an odd ambivalence. The placement of (weak) open access conditions on AOL Time Warner was surely a hard-fought victory for these players. All the same, it still did not amount to national policy. It may be tempting to point to AOL's defection as the last nail in a national policy's coffin, but this move was entirely expected by the ISP's activist colleagues. They treated this player with mistrust and not fealty. Instead, this was Kennard's doing. While much of the drive toward "multimodal competition" (via a plan-that-was-*no*-plan) has been of late pinned on Kennard's successor Michael Powell, the irony is that Powell would go far, far further than Kennard in enunciating a vision (even if not bearing the power of enforceability) for the Internet that laid a firmer groundwork on which new (and continuing) activists could act in terms of attempting to tame the worst impulses of the new medium's gatekeepers. This was via his "Four Freedoms" speech delivered a few years later (M. K. Powell, 2004). As far as activists working on structural reform of media are concerned—and these core groups in Washington certainly qualified throughout the row over open access—this would not be the last time that a Democratic administration snatched defeat from the jaws of victory, from its own allies at that. By mid-1999, open access seemed to be winning the war of ideas. At every step of the way, Kennard sabotaged the best-laid plans of these activists. Powell would close the bear trap on them permanently by introducing an option no one had yet considered, upending the debates that had come before. At the same time, while the FCC pleaded ignorance regarding open access over cable, it had no such difficulty commanding telecommunications providers to provide new pathways for competition over DSL, even if these pathways would themselves be fleeting.

One worry and several paradoxes emerge. Of worry was the use of the First Amendment on all sides. For advocates, the threat to the ability of end users to be able to speak aboard this new medium was a large concern: allowing broadband operators to operate as closed universes offering pride-of-place access to their own business partners (or those who elected to pay for play) was anathema to their own instincts. However, broadband operators had managed to convince a court that they had First Amendment rights as well to prevent them from *being forced to allow certain speech aboard their platforms*. For not the last time, the operators of communications conduits would claim that they had a right to see the Internet, provided via their own wires, as their own letter-to-the-editor page which need not include every one submitted.

Taking our view out still further, a first paradox obtains in that while they had been largely written out of the story, one is struck at the effectiveness of the consumer advocates. They were effective in keeping the debate moving forward and gathering new recruits, but they were called (and called themselves) "consumer" groups for a reason, even as the Center for Media Education cast wary eyes on the hypercommercialist imperatives unfolding online. In no way were any of them questioning the *commercial and private foundations of the Internet itself* as they developed, even as they extolled the virtues of noncommercial ISPs and services. This episode is an example of a pervasive continuance of dominant logics, as evidenced by their seemingly open invitation to FCC *en banc* and congressional hearings: even as egregious amounts of money were poured into these debates, their embedded liberalism clashed with the FCC's and certain others' newer neoliberal vision. In the FCC's case, could Kennard have described his vision as *laissez-faire?* Likely not: he would perhaps rather argue that leaving the Internet's development to the devices of protected new entrants was its own form of a self-organizing commons of the variety advocates (particularly in late 1999 and into 2000) were extolling. As far as the advocates went, to the extent they argued "competition," they were permitted to participate; localities similarly appreciated the message as at each level of the system, players saw markets as a solution to market problems; in Multnomah County, Commissioner Erik Sten pushed their liberal rhetoric even further. Advocates may have prevented one form of control from taking over, but the reality is that, in the end, one form of commodification was traded for another, one perhaps even more insidious.

In a time of tremendous uncertainty, given that no player that was involved at this level of the debate called for *a reversal of the commercial operation of the Internet conduit itself,* this episode serves as a clear snapshot in time of logics, justifications, and actions growing organically, with markets (spoken of as homogeneous, which is part of the problem) serving as handy ways to get out of having to plan. Schwartzman recalled that during this time, speaking for himself, he—and likely the activists pushing the issue as well—hardly possessed a clear-eyed vision of how the technology worked or would be upgraded, the explosion in use of streaming video, or the emergence of social media platforms (personal communication, March 12, 2019). A "commons" model may have been emerging, but "organization from chaos" was already alive and well in capitalist-regulatory discourse. We should see the invisibility in these debates of other actors who may have called for a different vision less as an indication of their passion, veracity, or ability than their understanding of the rules. For example, Om Malik, in an early account of these debates, described the scene at one of San Francisco's hearings on open access:

> The whole issue of open access was a political hairball. At a city hall meeting in San Francisco, Excite@Home folks were lobbying the city to help open the cable lines more quickly. One of the weirdest things about the meeting was that the AOL group brought in a bunch of elderly Chinese people wearing hats that said something about stopping discrimination, but it was really just a ploy to win support for their side. (Malik, 2003, pp. 153–154)

This could well be a gross misread of the event. "Astroturf" operations were surely in full swing in all corners, but the moral argument from which these sectors fed was unquestionably the province of the DC consumer advocates. With the dissemination of a particular *aspiration* even set aside from the *means to attain it*—an "open, competitive, democratic" communications system—fears of discrimination were real for those who caught the argument. Of course, this was the least of Excite@Home's problems: "At the meeting, groups of Excite@Home employees complained that they lived in San Francisco and couldn't get service from their own company yet" (Malik, 2003, p. 154). That Malik sees these two elements as incongruous is ironic: the fact he missed the *political* story points exactly to the chosen strategic imperatives of consumer advocates: this invisibility was the price they paid (if unintentionally) even as a particular vision of the Internet and its possibility seeped out. Perhaps as well, one of the most important outcomes of these debates were the "seeding" of a new activist ecosystem in Washington: staffers working for the core DC groups spun out into others. Numerous lawyers who would become prominent players emerged from their time at the Media Access Project under Schwartzman's tutelage and formed new groups like Public Knowledge in Washington, DC.

All the same, perhaps the biggest paradox is that these groups' success meant that, while they prevented one form of domination over new communications technologies, they did so by pushing the whole works further down the hole. Advocates were written out of the story, even as they were *integral* to it. From the start, consumer advocates engaged the FCC in a project of scale building and epistemic challenge: such are the tools available when the battle engaged is not one of class at all, even if the concept is invoked in advocacy—but often translated as "socioeconomic status," an entirely different and more static notion. Advocates' own arguments were hardly couched in any anticapital language: theirs was a form of "embedded liberalism," willing to go along with the infinite regress of marketization in new communications technologies as long as some escape hatch existed in case they didn't work. The former stance gained them entrance to the debates of the time and kept them from being disinvited to official gatherings. The latter created productive conflict: Kennard may have disagreed with it in principle, but it generated the lubricant to keep the machine humming, ironically enough. As in finance at the time, "modernization" was the catchphrase of choice. The FCC sought justification to protect what they saw as nascent industry, but did so by making deliberate misreads of their own institutional and regulatory history. They operated in a position of uncertainty reflecting the broader system in which these gatekeepers resided themselves. Industry argument that any form of requirement would result in less investment carried the day. These were untheorized maneuvers, an ongoing learning process by an FCC unwilling to go beyond asking a couple questions and throwing up its hands. No specific theory was operative: it was strictly a governmentality that was pervasive. In many regards, this was one of the last opportunities following the commercialization of the Internet to redefine what was fast becoming its core logic. The largest issue that remained unaddressed entirely was less *concerns over a particular set of entities' corporate control* than an issue of a *policy of corporate control of broadband,* an argument which mirrors that of Streeter's (1996) own telling of the story of the FCC's involvement in broadcasting, here in a new register.

5 Erasures and Emergences: Net Neutrality's Ambivalent Emergence

As the Michael Powell–led Federal Communications Commission (FCC) sought to pound a final nail in open access's coffin with his controversial Declaratory Order in 2002, his sidestep of attaching a *Notice of Proposed Rulemaking* would bring to light what was gestating below the surface all along. With the dot-com bubble still deflating and potential lost revenues stemming from a redefinition of cable service as telecommunications service, localities were no longer willing to put up a fight for the "future of the Internet." Independent Internet service providers (ISPs) would take the FCC to court over Powell's decision as their brethren began to be decimated by the new environment established under the Powell FCC. The Supreme Court would ultimately decide the issue in a rancorous decision in 2005, in which the majority found in favor of the FCC's policies (but not on their merits): at issue was the apparent ambiguity in the Telecommunications Act, which called for the agency's opinion to be granted deference (*National Cable & Telecommunications Assn. v. Brand X Internet Services*, 545 U.S. 967, 2005). This particular story has been well told by others. What has been less examined are the undercurrents swirling around this decision and their own internal politics; that is, how knowledge about the Web would be created and put to use. It is this task to which this chapter turns.

The creation of this issue of "network neutrality" was a fortuitous discovery that provided activists a handle that would simultaneously serve to erase open access struggles completely from the picture yet give broadband politics a crucial shot in the arm. A number of gears were moving at once: on the surface, they may appear to be at odds with each other, but beneath it, what transpired was a glorious instance of what Brown (2015) describes as governance of a particular neoliberal rationality. When we perform a deep study of the foundational writings in the concept's development, a common thread begins to emerge.

What we observe are several forms of erasure appearing at once: on the one hand, Powell in his actions sought to erase the actions of open access advocates from history; replacing them are the actions of markets, as we saw in chapter 4. The irony, however, is that advocacy for network neutrality and its growth stemmed from the very same erasures, albeit in particularized forms; advocates would need to treat the vehicle of these erasures as an empty signifier when pushing for policy change in public. Embedded in the ideas that gave birth to and that challenged the idea is an ironic unity, as all streams of argument were in fact fellow travelers on a road well paved.

Media Reform and Broadband Politics

"Media reform," which had a long pedigree leading up to these debates, found a new resurgence in the early 2000s in reaction to Powell's brash efforts in an adjacent policy area: he sought to brush aside media ownership rules for traditional media; this action would result in an even more heavily consolidated media landscape. The Telecommunications Act, which itself already gave major media companies the gift of loosened ownership rules, paved the way for a wave of consolidation in broadcast and print media even before the Powell FCC began its work. The new further loosened rules would permit, in major metropolitan areas, one entity to control the primary newspaper; the primary cable company; up to eight radio stations; and two, perhaps three, of the primary television broadcast outlets. The uproar stirred by MoveOn, Free Press, Common Cause, the Consumer Federation of America (CFA), Consumers Union, the Center for Digital Democracy, and the nascent Center for Media Justice and its member organizations merely highlighted issues that others across the country had been trumpeting for years, from groups and collectives like Fairness and Accuracy in Reporting, Reclaim the Media, Indymedia and beyond (for fuller examination, see González & Torres, 2011; McChesney, 2004, 2007; McChesney, Newman, & Scott, 2005; Wolfson, 2014). An early expression of a newfound energy in this arena could be found in the first National Conference for Media Reform held in Madison, Wisconsin, in late 2003. Dominated by concerns regarding the deficiencies of commercial journalism, an issue given added urgency with the Bush administration's moves to commence a series of wars, there was yet one panel devoted to questions of emergent broadband policy, where the topic of open access and network neutrality was broached. It was brand new at this point and only recently conceived by Tim Wu. The panel consisted of Michael Calabrese of the New America Foundation, Andy Schwartzman of the Media Access Project, Gigi Sohn of the upstart Public Knowledge, and Jeff Chester of the (now) Center for Digital Democracy.

As part of a volume that emerged from the conference, Chester and Larson (2005) addressed what amounted to a real point of convergence between the concerns surrounding the hypercommercialization of traditional media and those of open access activists. He was concerned at this juncture that the online universe "lack[ed] the set-asides and signposts that demarcate the nonprofit sector in the real world" and

> seemed scarcely to distinguish between for-profit and noncommercial.... We have yet to find a way to map these values onto the virtual world, where style often triumphs over substance and where marketing and cross-promotion often exert the same tyranny-of-the-majority pressure on new media that Nielsen ratings and box-office receipts exert on the old. (Chester and Larson, 2005, p. 186)

McChesney, taking in his own view of the landscape during the late 1990s, was already seeing the same media giants gaining similar prominence in the online world; in answer to the question, "Will the Internet set us free?" his answer was a resounding no—not unless action was taken (McChesney, 1999). Here were the same concerns, cast anew. "Especially as the Web grows increasingly commercialized (and increasingly becomes the domain of the media giants), the digital incarnation of the 'civic sector'—the loose collection of organizations and projects, online and off, that encompass democratic values, social services, educational opportunities, and cultural traditions—becomes all-the-more important" (Chester & Larson, 2005, p. 187). With the continued uptake of broadband, "there will be any number of efforts to exploit the commercial potential of the high-speed Internet. Our task is to ensure that broadband serves as effectively as it sells, fostering two-way, interactive applications" (p. 198). Crucially, this was not about simply making such tools available. "By working together at the local level, assessing the broadband infrastructure for its potential to serve the public interest, and building new alliances to ensure such service, we have the opportunity to develop the local online resources that will contribute to a larger information commons" (p. 198).

The crucial intervention Chester and Larson made is in asking us to think about the nature of commons-oriented resources online under development and the ends to which they would be put. Even if these resources were created to his satisfaction, he admits concern about finding them: "This is the crucial process of discovery that is likely to become even more perplexing in a highly commercialized broadband environment that favors big business over small, e-commerce over e-democracy, and public relations over public service" (Chester & Larson, 2005, p. 199). Would the answer to these concerns "be merely a collection of laudable URLs, or can it become something more dynamic and useful, drawing together the shared expertise of the nonprofit sector, while addressing local issues as well?" (p. 198). Can we "ensure, even as we make progress in bridging the Digital Divide that separates the haves from the have-nots, that we also overcome a new range of 'digital divisions' separating the haves from the have-mores, placing premium services (including such increasingly vital services as streaming media and video conferencing) beyond the means of community and other nonprofit organizations?" (pp. 198–199). Would the information commons "be truly inclusive, featuring not only the well recognized riches of nonprofit culture, but also information and services addressing the needs of those with low incomes, limited literacy or English skills, or one or more disabilities?" (p. 199). The answers to these questions required not just apt policy but "a more organized, coordinated movement, built around the theme of an electronic commons" (p. 199).

It is important to keep these views in mind as we move forward from Powell's commencement of the process of epistemological forgetting "open access" would undergo, a process he inherited from Kennard. The literature takes off in a small number of directions, hewing to particular arguments, playing a significant part in preparing the ground for the activism that would follow: if open access was the closest we have come in the United States (post–Telecommunications Act) to establishing a model of broadband as a full common carriage regime, for good or for ill, then the emergence of "network neutrality" would free up forces to utilize a new tack to quash any notion of common carriage, open access, or even some structural separation regime for good. This needed to be not just forgotten but stamped out in a particular set of terms, and a stream of thought of long vintage would provide the weapon: the development of the thought collective identified by Plehwe and Mirowski (2009) comes roaring back to the fore in unexpected ways. Now these efforts were about to pay off, big time: notably, less regarding specific arguments and more regarding the poisoning of the well for particular forms of argument—to lay claim to what was "reasoned" debate versus "unreasoned" debate. The appropriate frame would permit or prevent certain players from appearing at the bargaining table in Washington, DC, at a pivotal moment when broader public input and attention to issues surrounding the FCC was about to spike.

What followed was evidence not so much of malfeasance than it was the remarkable happenstance of a long-term effort bearing fruit yet somehow meeting its own crisis. Having already reshaped markets for spectrum in ways befitting the neoliberal imaginary, telecommunications and cable providers salivated at the opportunity to shape the future of the broadband Internet. Given increasing pressure and attention to the issue that Powell provoked via his brash moves, the strategies that had proven so successful in the past could now be called on again. Telecommunications companies, forever opportunistic and now seeing their cable brethren enjoying newfound control over their conduit, were able to concentrate their own efforts on closing down their own wires. Powell's definitive shutting down of local- and state-level debates meant, too, that these new efforts could be centralized in Washington, DC. Granted, dominant broadband interests would do their part in the states to prevent the emergence of publicly supplied counterparts (or even public-private partnerships) that might resuscitate the corpse of open access. This is an effort that continues. Lurking in the background were the interests of content providers (themselves, perhaps paradoxically, the preeminent entities Web users saw in the foreground) as well as of advertisers (and the emerging ecosystems online which supported them) that were seeking to shape the commercial Internet to their ends.

It is precisely this reason that the virtual open faucet of literature that would develop surrounding the issue of network neutrality cannot be viewed by any stretch as simply providing something akin to "objective knowledge" about the operation of broadband technology. There were certainly efforts to understand these new markets and networks, but this is to miss the broad labor the production of this knowledge performed. Read as event, the debate itself becomes about the instillation of a particular overarching frame. This is something quite aside from any form of conspiracy—this is the return of an overarching logic that for a brief time had managed to remain heterogeneous returned to a merely diverse field of action, in

Laclau's sense: in lieu of opening up the debate to new directions, it effectively served to constrict its bounds, and with them, the strategies available to activists. Tracing the foundations of this literature reveals a moment in which seemingly secondary resources become primary: it represents a crisis in the neoliberal field itself, one appearing as a clash of ideas even as the unity of their origins and their trajectory are obscured.

Setting the Tone: Developing on the "One Monopoly Profit" Principle

Perhaps one of the most important and most cited pieces to develop at this time is a theoretical piece by Joseph Farrell and Philip J. Weiser (2003) entitled "Modularity, Vertical Integration, and Open Access Policies: Towards a Convergence of Antitrust and Regulation in the Broadband Age." Farrell and Weiser performed invaluable labor for both Powell and for incumbents without even realizing it—they were the ones who could rightly boast that they were able to articulate the ad hoc arguments for open access presented by consumer advocates to the neoliberal thought collective for good. The challenge for regulators, as they framed it, "will be whether and how to integrate antitrust policy and telecommunications regulation into a coherent whole" (p. 86). In the process of threading this needle, a piece aimed at formulating a question would be turned into a full-fledged weapon in debates to come.

The article interrogates under what circumstances a regulator should worry when one service decides to move into and potentially monopolize a "vertical" service: in the case of broadband, when a conduit provider decides to supply the ISP service that rides on it or, even higher in the layer stack, the applications or content that utilize such services. The question ultimately posed is: when would it make sense for the operator of that line to foreclose or try to monopolize the services provided by those ISPs or by content providers that used their wires? "The question for regulators therefore is not whether modularity [structurally separating these goods or requiring open access] is good—it often is—but whether modularity is likely to be good even when it will not emerge (or survive) spontaneously, as it often will when it is most valuable to customers" (Farrell & Weiser, 2003, p. 97). Lurking in the background here is the ghost of Ronald Coase, whose theory of the firm augurs these later arguments. Farrell and Weiser commence their thinking with this:

> Analyzing a firm's choice of vertical structures is a focus of "new institutional economics" ("NIE"). Building on the insights of Nobel Laureate Ronald Coase, NIE "seeks to extend and enrich understanding of the microanalytic details of business behavior and the industry settings that shape firm conduct." Usefully, if tautologically, NIE suggests that firms will vertically integrate or depart from arm's-length market dealing when such arm's length dealing would be more costly. (Farrell & Weiser, 2003, pp. 99–100)

Farrell and Weiser introduce the notion of "internalization of complementary externalities" (ICE), which informs virtually every further effort from an antitrust perspective on the subject of open access or network neutrality:

> If a monopoly platform provider chooses to stick to its core platform business, it would prefer that applications—the complements to its product—be cheaply, innovatingly, and efficiently supplied. Thus, in choosing how to license interface information, certify complementors, and otherwise deal with developers, such a firm has a clear incentive to choose the pattern that will best provide it or its customers with applications. That is, a firm will internalize complementary efficiencies arising from applications created by others. (Farrell & Weiser, 2003, p. 101)

The principle maintains that in most situations, the owner of the platform is unable to increase their profits by monopolizing markets that need the platform—it is cheaper and likely more (economically) efficient to have those supplied by others. Farrell and Weiser hypothesize that "ICE claims that a platform monopolist has an incentive to innovate and push for improvements in its system—including better applications—in order to profit from a more valuable platform" (Farrell & Weiser, 2003, p. 103). This is but a stronger version of the "one monopoly profit" theory developed by Richard Posner and Robert Bork. That is, it should, in theory, make no sense for a network provider to wish to monopolize applications and content markets on the reasoning that a platform monopolist will protect an efficient market for the use of its services; it can extract no more monopoly profits by monopolizing such complementary markets than by charging more dearly for access to its platform alone. ICE goes further, however:

> [It stresses] the broader principle that the platform monopolist gains from an efficient applications market—whether that be unbridled competition, integration without independents, licensing of a limited set of independents, or some attempt to combine these or other structures. The "one monopoly profit" label fails to suggest this broader point. In sum, ICE better conveys the claim that the platform monopolist has an incentive to be a good steward of the applications

> sector for its platform and thus better captures the argument for laissez-faire vertical policies. (Farrell & Weiser, 2003, p. 104)

The authors are not unequivocal: this principle is particular, and they are able to concoct several exceptions to this seeming rule. For one, if the platform is subject to some form of price regulation but the applications market is not, there could be an incentive for the platform to discriminate, since it cannot maximize its profit from platform provision alone. For another, seeking gains via price discrimination might provoke a platform provider to discriminate. If a complementary service (say, voice over Internet protocol, or VoIP) threatens the primary monopoly (phone service), ICE may be broached. Independent innovators and gatekeepers may simply fail to reach agreement for access. "Incompetent incumbents" may not see their own interests reflected in maintenance of a vibrant complementary market and may need to be "educated." Fear of regulation might actually spook a platform provider into closing down its platform to complements for fear that the mere option of a "closed" strategy may be foreclosed once the results of an open platform are known. If a firm thinks that opening its platform "will increase its regulatory duties elsewhere," it would likely not open it; here the authors are thinking of video transmission over cable wires by independents that could potentially require it to open itself up to other video providers. If the complement can be valuable without the platform, then the platform may try to monopolize the complement: "In reality… an application for one platform—say, broadband transport—may also be useful for another—say, narrowband transport—and this may lead the broadband transport provider to try to control the applications market" (Farrell & Weiser, 2003, p. 119). In short, ICE as a normative principle needed to be tempered by real-world conditions.

Several implications followed for regulators. An authority would need to determine "whether an exception to ICE exists, and, if this seems likely, how well the regulator can address the competitive harms that might result" (Farrell & Weiser, 2003, p. 125). The regulator then needs to consider how easy or difficult it would be to diagnose an exception to ICE's occurrence. A regulator might assume that ICE holds in the abstract and that if a situation arises in which it does not, the regulator can assume it would be easy to recognize and diagnose. Alternatively, a regulator may be pessimistic that it would be so simple to diagnose and recognize an exception to the principle. Farrell and Weiser determine that this may be more often the case: "Such pessimism is hardly unreasonable, since some of the exceptions sketched above might be genuinely widespread, and yet might be colorably asserted even where they do not really arise" (p. 127).

One response to this mind-set would be to demand modularity or a structural separation regime outright as a result. An opposite response would be to assume simply that ICE always applies. "Some Chicago scholars," Farrell and Weiser note, "appear to trust ICE more than they trust imperfect regulators or courts to diagnose its exceptions. Open architecture advocates, such as Lawrence Lessig, appear to trust the history and future prospects of successful innovation through modularity more than they trust either ICE or regulators' ability to diagnose its exceptions" (Farrell & Weiser, 2003, p. 127). The authors' own take is more ambivalent:

> In developing its regulatory strategy for new environments such as broadband where price regulation is absent, the FCC should define more clearly when to restrict a firm's conduct—for instance, only after exclusionary conduct is demonstrated, where it seems probable, or where it would do the most harm.... [T]he FCC has an opportunity to adopt a coherent approach to information platform regulation that takes account of ICE and would facilitate convergence between antitrust and regulatory policy. (Farrell & Weiser, 2003, p. 134)

Farrell and Weiser themselves maintained this cautious stance going forward. In 2003, the Progress and Freedom Foundation held its own conference on the questions of network neutrality and open access. When the proceedings were updated and published in 2006, Farrell continued to urge caution, even as his was a voice lost in an increasing cacophony:

> Contrary to the claims of some opponents of open access regulation, I believe that broadband providers are likely to depart from modularity if allowed to do so. But this in itself does not show that regulation is desirable; such departures can have both good and bad consequences. Contrary to the tone of the debate (on both sides), the analytics are difficult and unsettled. Therefore I argue for treating this as a decision under severe uncertainty; but this does not simply mean a philosophical choice between presumptions or styles. (Farrell, 2006, pp. 195–196)

He retains his seeming caution in closing: "On this difficult subject, participants on both sides seem miraculously confident in their conflicting positions. I urge the FCC to shun such confidence; hence the conspicuously inconclusive tone of this paper. There are rational responses to uncertainty other than deciding based on philosophy or ideology. And ICE is too thin to rely on arguing simply that customers value modularity so firms will preserve it" (Farrell, 2006, p. 211).

This conference's attendees largely sang ICE applicability's high praises. The one voice of dissent was represented by that of Mark Cooper, but should the conveners' opinion be unclear, the editors lead off the volume as follows:

> With all due respect to the virtues of doubts, in our view, the arguments against a Net Neutrality mandate are substantially stronger than those on the other side.... [A]fter perusing the essays contained in this book, even if he or she still harbors some of the doubts that lead Joe Farrell to adopt a "consciously inconclusive tone," the reader surely will be in a much better position to make up his or her own mind in the important debate about Net Neutrality. (May & Lenard, 2006, p. xii)

As the literature trifurcated into directions in support of, against, or seeking "third ways" on the issue, Farrell's "be reasonable" stance itself possessed its own utility in the broader debate surrounding network neutrality: it served, at least at the outset, to define a "middle ground" that was, from the point of view of early 2003's media reformers, no middle ground at all. The game was commenced with the goalposts already shunted down the field apace: for the value to cable and telecom interests lie not in its "middle-of-the-roadness" but necessarily in its reasonableness as a frame through which to view the conflict at hand. Best of all, this perspective didn't cost them a dime. This was a victory in itself and would be the thing against which advocates for the public interest in this struggle would need to contend. Tim Wu would take up the invitation and run with it.

Wu Sketches Out Net Neutrality

Lessig protégé Tim Wu's (2003) sketch of "network neutrality" entered the debate at a pivotal moment, as FCC chairman Powell was setting to shut down the cable open access debate by fiat. Extensively debated and often referenced in oblique ways as if Wu's objectives and the citer's are shared, it is worth sketching out his broad premise, as it responds to and builds on the arguments of Farrell and Weiser and would have a radical effect on the broader debate. For all the hue and cry of it, this initial conception is not, by any stretch, an argument based on any theory of democracy or self-governance like what the consumer advocates who preceded him had on offer. It is its own form of forgetting of the open access debates, both a response to and a horizontal sidestep away from Farrell and Weiser's "internalization of complementary externalities" argument.

The basis of Wu's argument stemmed from the questions that regulators would be expected to face concerning the "conflicts between the private interests of broadband providers and the public's interest in a competitive innovation environment centered on the Internet" (Wu, 2003, p. 141). What is "attractive" about a neutral network—"that is, an Internet that does not favor one application (say, the world wide web), over others (say, email)"—must, in his terms, be understood as "a concrete expression of a system of belief about innovation, one that has gained significant popularity over [the] last two decades.... Here we can refer to it generally as the evolutionary model" (p. 145). Pointing to Lessig's previous accounts as a particular brand of example of this mode of thought, Wu argues that "adherents view the innovation process as a survival-of-the-fittest competition among developers of new technologies" (p. 146).

For Wu, network neutrality is not a policy; it is more accurately described as a state: "Network neutrality, as shorthand for a system of belief about innovation policy, is the end, while open access and broadband discrimination are the means.... A direct analysis premised to the normative principle of network neutrality may provide a better means to discuss the harm in question" (Wu, 2003, p. 144). This subtle distinction is important. In place of a multiple-ISP access regime (or the common carriage "lite" open regimes sought by advocates) is a new vocabulary based on long-defined, old terms. Wu desires to recast the debate through familiar concepts in telecommunications law, such as discrimination and common carriage, put to the normative end he seeks. In this, he is of a piece with Farrell and Weiser's mission.

The need for such a call is that Wu fears that the results sought by consumer advocates would not be wrought via open access regimes. "The preferable framework for ensuring network neutrality, I argue, forgoes structural remedies [that is, strict open access or multiple-ISP access regimes] for a direct scrutiny of broadband discrimination.... The basic principle behind a network anti-discrimination regime is to give users the right to use non-harmful network attachments or applications, and give innovators the corresponding freedom to supply them" (Wu, 2003, p. 143). Competition among ISPs themselves, he fears, "does not necessarily mean that broadband operators will simply retreat to acting as passive carriers in the last mile.... Hence, open-access does not end the debate over whether broadband operators are capable of engaging in undesirable behavior from the perspective of the public network" (p. 150). Thus, "we might do better to address questions of network neutrality directly, through the remedial concept 'broadband discrimination,' rather than through structural solutions like open-access" (p. 150), sussing out what forms of discrimination are desirable from those that are not. He accepts, like Farrell and Weiser and other partisans of the open access debates, that there likely are efficiencies to having the owner of a conduit also serve as the ISP for users; managing the network, dealing with congestion "and other legitimate goals, such as price discrimination" are reasonable. He also notes that given "best-efforts" service, in a bandwidth-scarce world, time-sensitive applications are impaired by virtue of this "best-efforts" regime, and thus there could be some desirable ways in which prioritization may be performed. What is feared is the manner in which such duties are undertaken: whether applications would be blocked or (de)prioritized in ways "which are likely to distort the market and the future of application development" (p. 143).

Advocates for network neutrality over the coming years would have their own internal disagreements over this last point, but this was not what stirred the intense debate. What gave this article such power was its concrete proposal, which Wu had submitted to the FCC in response to Powell's 2002 *Declaratory Order and Notice of Proposed Rulemaking* (Wu & Lessig, 2003). In lieu of simpler open access proposals, network neutrality as a principle "provide[s] a balance: to forbid broadband operators, absent a showing of harm, from restricting what users do with their Internet connection, while giving the operator general freedom to manage bandwidth consumption and other matters of local concern" (Wu, 2003, pp. 167–168). Operators should be permitted to police what they own, while end users should be able to select for themselves how and what to use on the Internet "in ways which are privately beneficial without being publicly detrimental," mirroring the words of Judge Bazelon's Hush-A-Phone ruling decades previous (*Hush-A-Phone Corp v. United States*, 238 F. 2d 266 [D.C. Cir. 1956]).

This was effectively accomplished by limiting the tools operators could use to manage their networks. One way for network operators to do so could have been to utilize tools operating at the "Internet protocol" (IP) layer. Operators manipulating this layer would be able to discriminate against intended destination of packets or packet contents while en route, allowing them to potentially select favored sites, applications, or protocols for privileged passage. In contrast to this, Wu instead proposed effectively limiting operators to tools available in "layer 2" of the layer stack, the "data link" layer. These manage local networks rather than *inter*networks: "In technical terms, this means imposing restrictions on the basis of... bandwidth, jitter, or other local Quality of Service indicia" (Wu, 2003, p. 171). This represents a far blunter instrument for control than the more powerful application-specific processes that could be discerned at the IP or Transmission Control Protocol (TCP) layers. "A carrier concerned about bandwidth consumption would need to invest in policing bandwidth usage, not blocking individual applications. Users interested in [for example] a better gaming experience would then need to buy more bandwidth—not permission to use a given application" (p. 171). This would amount to a difference in monitoring bandwidth usage as opposed to selecting particular applications. Had broadband providers been allowed to block gaming applications as opposed to simply monitoring bandwidth usage, "a market advantage [would be given] to competing applications that have not been blocked. But if broadband carriers only police bandwidth, the result is an even-playing field. It may be that the expense of more bandwidth leads people to choose different ways to spend their money. But if so, that represents a market choice, not a choice dictated by the filtering policy of the broadband carrier" (p. 172). Such a rule puts control of network use—in terms of what kinds of blocks might be desired by parents, for instance—in the hands of end users without the network operator having a veto. This is the principle as understood by activists in fights that would extend well into the second decade of the century.

However, as important as this principle is what Wu takes as his foundation and the *purpose to which a notion of network neutrality is to be put.* "The promotion of network neutrality," Wu says,

> is no different than the challenge of promoting fair evolutionary competition in any privately owned environment, whether a telephone network, operating system, or even a retail store. Government regulation in such contexts invariably tries to help ensure that the short-term interests of the owner do not prevent the best products or applications becoming available to end-users. The same interest animates the promotion of network neutrality: *preserving a Darwinian competition among every conceivable use of the Internet so that only the best survive.* (Wu, 2003, p. 142; emphasis added)

This view has great consequences for the epistemic battles that will unfold. It is one thing to call open access rules insufficient; it is another to do so on these terms. The romanticism expressed and critiqued by Streeter (2011) comes into full view, but in this instance, the language in which it is expressed was long a part of the neoliberal project, understood as the outgrowth of a dispersed thought collective. It is of a piece with the times, hardly counter to it. It is a vision of order emerging from chaos via the action of markets themselves as calculative engines of truth and efficiency (Mirowski, 2013).

This article and proposal sat at an in-between point amid the continued unfolding of a literature that was still grappling, on the one hand, with the concerns of open access advocates and, on the other, with that of others who dealt with the politics and economics of nondiscriminatory interconnection of telephony. In seemingly finding a niche that sat uncomfortably in between such discourses, it served a number of important functions, particularly as far as the longtime advocates of open access were concerned. On the one hand, it offered these advocates a new foothold in their continuing efforts to shape the future of rapidly converging broadband networks. Given that the FCC had skirted efforts to open networks to competing service providers (and was continuing to defend its prerogative to do so), and given, too, that the debates had effectively been removed from local and state levels, here was an opportunity to push a new agenda at the FCC and beyond on possibly more favorable ground. Such a vehicle was becoming of increasing importance as open access was looking like a regulatory dead end, particularly under the Powell FCC. It was a stopgap solution, in other words, even as Wu's concerns rang true to these advocates.

In its suppositions, however, Wu had effectively built a bridge between the arguments of consumer advocates and the long-standing descendants of the neoliberal project. The issue of network neutrality proposed by Wu was just the tip of the iceberg. It was because of the epistemological (yet material) freight that his proposal bore as its buttress that caused the debate to get out of hand. In lieu of any argument in favor of democracy or free speech, these concepts were considered subsumed in a theory of an evolutionary survival-of-the-fittest competition in the broadband sphere. Theories of democracy online—be they oriented toward a Habermasian deliberative democracy, a more commonly expressed "liberal" democracy, or one that theorizes the formation of counterpublics, or even theories of autonomous action—seek a mechanism for a profusion of viewpoints to find expression, not their decimation (see, for instance, Dahlberg, 2011). Yet, the notion of the Internet as a calculative engine that would enable markets to ferret out the best and eliminate the worst threw the debate into territory comfortably defended by microeconomists, by transaction costs theory, and by antitrust lawyers combining their trade with an orthodox, Chicago-led strain of economic theorizing. These quickly were established as the norm of debate, and for proponents to be taken seriously, it would need to be the language in which their support of the concept was spoken. While papers authored by proponents in the field of *communication* won accolades at its respective academic conferences, arguments from this corner of the academy played a diminutive role in the technocratic debates under way in Washington, DC. There, the game was expected to be entirely played in the realm of microeconomic theory of consumer surplus, producer surplus, deadweight loss, and these concepts' calculation. The broader field of action would need to shift at a fundamental level for proponents of other perspectives to possess any utility in influencing the outcomes of the debate.

As a result, in perverse ways, Wu's intervention also served the needs of telecommunications and cable opponents of open access regimes. For one, with the move away from any possibility of a common carriage or multiple-ISP access framework to one that necessitated a monitoring of discriminatory activity aboard every local network—something nearly impossible to obtain—they stood to gain much on a commercial level in keeping the debate from ever reapproaching the question of the separation of service from conduit. The now dominant Chicago School of antitrust had a long history of mistrust of regulators' abilities to monitor such a happenstance. The network neutrality debate opened the field to a new set of problematics on ironically friendlier ground for large broadband providers. Having learned the effectiveness of utilizing the ready expertise of economists enlisted as consultants to the FCC in the construction of spectrum markets (as detailed by Mirowski & Nik-Khah, 2007; Nik-Khah, 2005), this strategy would come back into force, in force. It had the added benefit that any move away from structural regulation suddenly looked like content regulation, something anathema to U.S. common sense.

The Trap, Tripped

On an epistemic level, among the most nuanced and substantive replies to Wu can be found in a series of three papers authored by Christopher Yoo (2004, 2005, 2006) that sought to challenge any need for either a structural separation regime or network neutrality regime at any level, drawing on multiple strains of microeconomic theory and antitrust analysis. Yoo is the perfect candidate to bring these viewpoints: he was self-selecting, already active in and an expert on antitrust issues and its history. He takes Wu's bait of an evolutionary foundation—recall, among the favorite metaphors of the neoliberal thought collective, order from chaos—and commenced creating terrific roadblocks in front of consumer advocates' designs, hoisting them on their own petard with their newfound epistemic connection. Wu had done the principal labor of creating the bridge.

The tack to recast the debate entirely as one of competition policy was the most obvious one to pursue. Yoo decides to write off any debate from the past that might construe otherwise. Ignoring anything outside the market relation, he notes, "Since network neutrality proponents defend their proposals almost exclusively in terms of the economic benefits of innovation, this Article discusses the issues solely in economic terms. I therefore set aside for another day any discussion of noneconomic issues, such as network neutrality's implications for democratic deliberation or the First Amendment" (Yoo, 2006, p. 1851). That day, to my knowledge, has not yet come. So right off he dives into redefining the issue for these advocates:

> The question posed by the debate over network neutrality is not whether consumers benefit from standardization; they clearly do. To the extent that is true, there is no need to mandate network neutrality, since the benefits to consumers from standardization should be reflected in market outcomes. The real issue posed by the network neutrality debate is whether regulators should step in and impose standardization in those situations where the market exhibits a preference for differentiation. The fact that the structure of the broadband industry makes it unlikely that any network owner will be able to use nonstandardization to harm competition indicates that such intervention is unwarranted. In addition, by preventing last-mile providers from tailoring their networks to pursue alternative strategies, barring network diversity threatens to make matters worse. (Yoo, 2004, p. 29)

Yoo is invoking Farrell and Weiser's ICE argument here but adds new layers of complication to it. Flowing through his articles is a nuanced opinion that runs as follows: he supports a policy of "network diversity," which might be seen as the opposite of network neutrality—but he insists it is not. "Network diversity is not the mirror image of network neutrality, in that it does not call for the imposition of any mandatory obligations. Rather, network diversity adopts the more modest position that regards regulatory forbearance as the appropriate course of action when confronted with ambiguity" (Yoo, 2005, p. 12). Shifting the debate away from concerns of hypercommercialism or democratic discourse, it becomes a story exclusively about rollout of broadband writ large.

The keystone to the consumer advocates' case regarding open access was that cable broadband providers were doing exactly the same thing as digital subscriber line (DSL) providers in simply moving information from "upstream" Internet providers to end users and vice versa; the case that cable companies were making, and that Powell made in the 2002 Declaratory Order and Notice of Proposed Rulemaking, was that cable Internet provision wrapped the two aspects of service so closely together that they were inseparable. The Supreme Court had agreed with the FCC, if not on the merits. But at the time of Yoo's initial forays, this was still in contention. In his own examination of cable broadband technology, Yoo notes that since providers maintain packet-switched networks themselves for traffic that is separated from other traffic, it is unsurprising that they would wish to operate and provide their own ISP service. Wu would certainly agree. Yoo looks at the manner in which AOL Time Warner was handling unaffiliated ISP traffic and finds that it

> exits the headend via AOL-Time Warner's backbone and is handed off to the unaffiliated ISP at some external location. It is hard to see how consumers benefit from such arrangements, given that they necessarily use the same equipment and thus provide the same speed, services, and access to content regardless of the identity of their nominal ISP. The fact that these unaffiliated ISPs have found it more economical to share AOL Time Warner's existing ISP facilities rather than build their own strongly suggests that integrating ISP and last-mile operations does in fact yield real efficiencies. (Yoo, 2004, p. 56; citations omitted)

Yoo is noting that under any "open access" regime, the common result appears that a bottleneck resource ends up being shared—and therefore activists were focusing their energies on the wrong policy concern. They were, for him, effectively only looking to buttress an already competitive market for content and applications.

> The central focus of broadband policy should be on how best to foster competition in the last mile.... Viewing the issues in this manner reveals how the major network neutrality proposals are focusing on the wrong policy problem. By

> directing their efforts towards encouraging and preserving competition among ISPs and content/application providers, they concentrate their attention on the segments of the industry that are already the most competitive and the least protected by entry barriers. (Yoo, 2004, p. 59)

What needed increased competition was not this but rather last-mile facilities themselves.

In making his case that consumer advocates were focusing on the wrong problem—that is, not addressing concentration of last-mile conduits—he invites his reader on a thought experiment. While at the point of purchase markets for broadband are heavily concentrated by Department of Justice Herfindahl-Hirschman Index guidelines, and he acknowledges this, he asks us to imagine that "every last-mile provider were required to sell their proprietary interests in ISPs, application providers, and content providers." Having done so, he argues, "Such a change would not affect the economic relationship between end users and last-mile providers; end users seeking to purchase last-mile services would still face a de facto duopoly [in terms of facilities] even if the broadband industry were completely vertically disintegrated" (p. 52). That means that the net effect of open access proposals is effectively in the "upstream market in which last-mile providers meet ISPs and providers of Internet content and applications that [must represent] the true target of network neutrality proposals." As such,

> This market is properly regarded as national in scope. Major web-based providers, such as Amazon.com or eBay, are focused more on the total customers they are able to reach nationwide than they are on their ability to reach customers located in any specific metropolitan area. Their inability to reach certain customers is of no greater concern, however, than the inability of manufacturers of particular brands of cars, shoes, or other conventional goods to gain access to all parts of the country. Being cut off from certain distribution channels should not cause economic problems, so long as those manufacturers are able to obtain access to a sufficient number of customers located elsewhere. The proper question is thus not whether the broadband transport provider wields oligopoly power over broadband users in any particular city, but rather whether that provider has market power in the national market for obtaining broadband content. (Yoo, 2004, p. 52)

The new emphasis is crucial. Yoo's shift to the national perspective enables him to suggest that users should not fear: they should expect to gain access to the commercial enclaves they desire, as some provider's policy to restrict access (or prioritize others) should not affect these services' ability to survive at the national level. Given concentration indices and market shares of broadband providers taken at a national level were nowhere near as concentrated as those at local levels, he believes that it would be impossible for the likes of, say, Netflix or other content providers to be forced out of business. Not everyone would necessarily *be able to access* to such content due to the decision of some broadband providers to block or slow it; but even if these content providers found themselves unavailable in some areas, given national reach overall, there was little to worry about in terms of their existence, if not survival.

Mandating open access or network neutrality, Yoo argues, would foreclose options for network operators to provide prioritization services that could, in theory, provide a different basis for a procompetitive outcome. Certain forms of content that needed and could take advantage of paid prioritization aboard broadband networks could foment new content and applications market entrants. In Yoo's vision, different last-mile technologies or overbuilders, driven by the possibility of supracompetitive profits to provide specific prioritization services (or other varieties of services yet unthought) would, also in theory, induce rollout of these new or overbuilt technologies. That is, he advocates waiting for "natural" market forces to take advantage of theoretically latent desires for differentiated services rather than mandating any kind of access regime to a plain-vanilla best-efforts service systemwide. Open access rules and network neutrality conditions would stymie such rollout in his view by decreasing incentives to invest. But should anyone worry about the market power of last-mile facilities at the time he was writing, such competition was right around the corner, if not ferocious already, according to FCC statistics (themselves, as we have seen, still collected in a loose manner when it come to access to such resources at the point of purchase as opposed to nationally). An emphasis on "network diversity" takes as given that new technologies, each supplying their own "pipe" to the end user, were already taking hold and pervasive. Thus, in reality, "network diversity" is at core little more than a continuation of Kennard's "do nothing" policy combined with support for Powell's grant of additional power to conduit owners.

Brandeisian Populism and Economic Efficiency

Yoo's second foray into the topic solidified the terms of debate. At this point he was now consulting on these issues for the National Cable and

Telecommunications Association (NCTA) and was forthright in noting their support for his work. The Supreme Court had supported the Powell position on open access, and thus the writing was on the wall for that issue while network neutrality remained a threat. He provides here a rebuttal to noneconomic justifications for network neutrality while sidestepping First Amendment and free expression concerns. Such justifications for him are hardly "incoherent," but "such a theory must provide a basis for quantifying the noneconomic benefits and for determining when those benefits justify the economic costs" (Yoo, 2005, p. 54). The "Populist" Brandeisian pluralist view of antitrust, he argues,

> embraced a noneconomic vision of competition policy that protected small players in order to promote democratic values associated with Brandeisian pluralism even when doing so was economically costly. Over time, courts and commentators began to recognize that because many industries are subject to economies of scale, preserving small producers has a price. The problem was that Populism failed to provide a basis for determining when the costs outweighed the benefits. By the 1980s, even those sympathetic to the Populist School were forced to concede that the economic approach to antitrust had prevailed. (Yoo, 2005, p. 55)

The net effect of this newfound ascendancy was to shift antitrust "from hostility toward vertical integration in order to protect small players for largely noneconomic reasons to a more nuanced, explicitly economic approach that recognized that vertical integration can yield substantial economic benefits" (Yoo, 2005, pp. 55–56). While populist principles could well provide clear directions and justifications for regulators, Yoo argues,

> no one has yet articulated such a theory with sufficient clarity to be coherent. That said, the populist vision rests in uneasy tension with the modern economy. Brandeisian populism aspires to the type of small scale economic activity typically associated with Jeffersonian democracy. It also tends to value economic stability for its own sake, since instability tends to break down the citizenry. As such, it does not seem well suited to industries like broadband, in which large scale, rapid, and often disruptive change are prominent features. (Yoo, 2005, pp. 56–57)

The problem of diversity arguments, Yoo claims, is that "arguments in favor of protecting small customers and speakers have historically failed to reflect any sense of optimality and have instead regarded additional diversity as an absolute good" (Yoo, 2005, p. 54). With the presence of scale economies, "promoting diversity exacts a cost that must be traded off against the benefits of additional producers" (p. 54). Quoting the D.C.

Circuit Court in 2001, which was then commenting on media ownership policy in a cable context, "Everything else being equal, each additional 'voice' may be said to enhance diversity.... But at some point, surely, the marginal value of such an increment in 'diversity' would not qualify as an 'important' governmental interest. Is moving from 100 possible combinations to 101 'important'?" (p. 54). Not "each and every incremental increase in the number of outlet owners can be justified as necessary in the public interest" and "there certainly are points of diminishing returns in incremental increases in diversity" (pp. 54–55). Since telecommunications networks are subject to economies of scale, "forcing communications enterprises to remain small can exact a price"—something, of course, no advocate was calling for. "At some point, the marginal benefit associated with protecting another small voice"—here, a small telcommunications company—"will fall short of the marginal costs of preventing network firms from realizing the available economies of scale" (p. 54). "As a result," Yoo continues, "those who take seriously the admonition that it takes a model to beat a model will be decidedly reluctant to embrace such an indeterminate [so far ad hoc] approach [to such issues]. The open-endedness of the approach and the lack of a clear notion of optimality leave it vulnerable to being redirected towards political purposes" (p. 55).

Yoo's attack is withering: preemptive rules like network neutrality were poorly suited to "context-dependent" settings; competition policy's response is "to place the burden on the opponents of the practice and to permit the practice to occur until opponents can demonstrate anticompetitive harm" (Yoo, 2005, p. 11). Implementation of network neutrality would be difficult: the necessary tools to maintain an interconnection regime, interface standardization, rate regulation, and to prevent nondiscrimination were both challenging to deploy and "unlikely to be effective in industries like broadband, where the services provided vary in quality and where technology is changing rapidly." Combined with "reduced investment incentives," network neutrality implies "regulation will continue indefinitely" whereas network diversity "is better at facilitating competitive entry. As such, it has the advantage of having embedded within it a built-in exit strategy." Until it is clear "complete interoperability" is the best course of action, regulators should allow all forms of architectures to go forward, lest "intervening... would have the inevitable effect of locking the existing interfaces into place and of foreclosing experimentation into new products and alternative organizational forms that transcend traditional firm boundaries" (all quotations Yoo, 2005, p. 11). Thus, letting "network diversity" take hold is not that it would make things better but rather that it would represent an exercise in "technological humility." Yoo is postmodern enough that to pose the need for a centralized authority to regulate network neutrality appeared antithetical to the "decentralization" desires of advocates, turning their true desires on their head.

When advocates spoke of the desirability of an innovation commons online, Yoo pokes fun at them, since the "accepted solution to the tragedy of the commons is the creation of well-defined property rights, which would be more consistent with network diversity than network neutrality" (Yoo, 2005, p. 74). Further, "The presence of innovation externalities more properly suggests the existence of an optimal size of a property right rather than a blanket presumption in favor of an innovation commons" (p. 74). A year later, he would make the claim that the optimal solution for achieving maximized social welfare in an online commons is to ensure that those who operate the commons are able to usurp such externalities—possible over an owned resource—which "effectively aligns social benefits with private benefits" (Yoo, 2006, p. 1891). In more depth:

> Direct network externalities do not represent an economic problem. Because they arise within a physical network that can be owned, the network owner is in an ideal position to solve the collective action problem by capturing the benefits created by increases in network size. Thus, even if end users are unable to appropriate all of the benefits associated with their adoption decisions, the network owner is in a position to internalize these benefits by charging prices that reflect the benefits new users confer on incumbents. Indeed, the owner of a physically interconnected network has every incentive to maximize the value of the network in this manner. The fact that the benefits resulting from any increase in the network's value would accrue directly to the network owner effectively aligns social benefits with private benefits. (Yoo, 2006, p. 1891; citations omitted)

If there is any doubt as to his sincerity regarding this interpretation—that the conduit provider's ability to capture what would ordinarily be a positive externality is a net benefit (allowing, of course, that in theory allowing a party to usurp additional surplus may be a tool to encourage entrants)—Yoo even goes as far as to make the argument, similar to the federal court that pushed back against Broward County's open access requirement, that platform operators rightly are seen to serve as "editors": "The fact that telecommunications networks now serve as the conduit for mass communications and not just person-to-person communications greatly expands the justification for allowing them to exercise editorial control over the information they convey" (Yoo, 2005, pp. 46–48).

The overarching point here, however, is that the bridge Wu built to the arguments of Farrell and Weiser created the necessary preconditions for exactly these arguments to appear. "Brandeisian" views also held another major disadvantage, in actuality. There were few monied interests like the NCTA who were willing to put up resources to ensure that the arguments were utilized, much less developed into the legal and theoretical framework Yoo argues was lacking.

If Yoo is measured in his thinking, J. Gregory Sidak (2006) provides a bombastic response often referenced as a second definitive argument against Wu. Which makes sense: as the head of Criterion Economics, Sidak had parlayed his past affiliations into economics for sale.[1] He had served as deputy general counsel of the FCC and as senior counsel and economist to the Council of Economic Advisers in the Executive Office of the President in the late 1980s. He had been involved in this realm for several years, already pushing similar opinions, either directly on behalf of the interests he favored or indirectly via such institutions as the American Enterprise Institute (Crandall & Sidak, 2002; Hausman & Sidak, 1999; Hausman, Sidak, & Singer, 2001). Sidak is spastic, throwing the Microeconomics 101 textbook at readers, with one section arguing in terms of overall surplus, the next in terms of transaction costs, the next shedding crocodile tears for the interests of those less well off, sacrifices offered to the gods of economic efficiency. One is quick to note: the tack Sidak (and his colleagues—even Yoo, if with less bombast and more nuance) takes, and the realm of theory from which he draws, is the accepted orthodoxy in FCC settings: the neoliberal thought collective, as has been noted, was instrumental in achieving this orthodoxy through decades of dedicated and organic effort. But it is an orthodoxy that eclipses much of reality. In what follows, it is at points useful to take its logic to its end.

Perhaps one of the more revealing moments of what is to come occurs as he quotes Lawrence Lessig's oft-repeated words from a *Foreign Policy* article in 2001: "The Internet revolution has ended just as surprisingly as it began. None expected the explosion of creativity that the network produced; few expected that explosion to collapse as quickly and profoundly as it has." In response, Sidak sneers:

> Lessig suggests no empirical methodology for measuring how much innovation in independent applications is occurring, let alone whether the level of innovation has changed over a period in which Lessig believes the Internet has lost its neutrality. In essence, Lessig is presenting a testable hypothesis, yet his argument is anecdotal and rhetorical rather than empirical.... To properly address Lessig's hypothesis that the "end of neutrality" stifled innovation among content providers, one would need to conduct an econometric exercise that controlled for other factors besides network neutrality. Is the decline of innovation in broadband applications that Lessig posits a phenomenon that, if it indeed exists, can be causally separated from the general collapse of the market capitalization of Internet startup companies that began in March 2000? In other words, the instances of broadband discrimination to which Lessig and Wu point all supposedly happened after the Internet bubble burst. So how can one distinguish between reduced investment in Internet applications that is "caused" by the prospect of broadband discrimination and reduced investment that is caused by reduced availability of capital for Internet ventures generally? (Sidak, 2006, pp. 407–408)

He contrasts Lessig's doomsaying with the vision expressed by John Battelle, cofounder of *Wired* magazine, of a "second coming" driven by the growth of the likes of Google, eBay, Amazon, Yahoo!, and Microsoft, with Google even making its first profits in the wake of the dot-com implosion. "Coincidentally," notes Sidak, "these same firms are the major proponents of network neutrality regulation," all—quoting Battelle—"in an all-out war for the market of the future, one where the spoils number in the hundreds of billions of dollars" (Sidak, 2006, p. 408). "Clearly," Sidak seems to cackle (p. 408), "Lessig and Battelle cannot both be correct. Morbidity and vitality cannot simultaneously describe the state of innovation at the edges of the Internet. One of these two Silicon Valley visionaries must be mistaken. Is it the columnist for *Wired* or the co-founder of *Wired?*"

While Sidak might not think so, it is, of course, a trick question: each simply envisions a potentially different Web. Even this choice harbors an erasure of the desires of former open access advocates; Lessig held "innovation" and a romantic notion of creation at pride of place—a lesson passed to his protégé—and Battelle held that the galloping presence of large commercial entities online constituted a resurgence of the Web's possibility. Neither vision includes a fuller discussion of the social purpose to which the technology should be put and how that might be attained. The blossoming of the Internet into a consumer paradise finds its champion in Sidak. Illustrating "how investment in Internet applications has thrived in the period of Internet deregulation," he points to the acquisition of Skype by eBay (Sidak, 2006, p. 402). Applications markets have blossomed, he extolls, particularly in the realm of video content.

> Apple offers television shows on its website from many networks, including NBC Universal, Comedy Central, the Sci-Fi Channel, USA Network, MTV, Disney, and ABC. These programs can be downloaded to a computer or an iPod in a high-quality H.264 QuickTime format that does not stutter, unlike streaming video. Apple currently offers episodes of many popular television shows, including Saturday Night Live, The Office, Monk, X-Games Highlights, Desperate Housewives, South Park, and Lost. Each video costs $1.99, and a given episode is available one day after it originally airs on network television. Because the videos can be synched with an iPod, consumers can watch the shows anytime, anywhere. (Sidak, 2006, p. 404)

In addition to this "success," he notes the booming business of the likes of Akamai's content delivery networks that situate this content closer to end users. "If one were to apply Google's business model to the network neutrality debate," he continues,

> a provider of DSL or cable modem service could subsidize the price of its broadband access to end-users through revenue earned from the sale of advertisements. This outcome would clearly be a Pareto improvement. It should be encouraged, not foreclosed by regulation. Likewise, allowing a network operator to subsidize the price of broadband access with revenue from a surcharge to content providers on the priority delivery of content would make possible a Pareto improvement and would allow potential end-users that are currently priced out of the market to enjoy broadband access. To deny broadband access to the marginal consumer—by prohibiting access tiering or vertical integration by network operators into Internet content and applications—is to pursue an anti-Pareto principle. Call it digital Schadenfreude. (Sidak, 2006, p. 464)

The increasingly commercialized nature of this second coming of the Web is trumpeted by Sidak in indelicate terms. "The debate over network neutrality regulation places subscriber-funded business models on a collision course with a newer generation of advertiser-funded business models" (Sidak, 2006, p. 427). The largest players are restructuring themselves

> through acquisitions, joint ventures, and new service offering—to dominate the market for search-related advertising. These efforts share the common strategy of aggregating different customer bases to offer a larger bundle of advertiser-funded

> services, much as television networks half a century earlier offered a blend of entertainment, news, sports, and other programming that all was advertiser-funded. … These efforts share the common strategy of aggregating different customer bases to offer a larger bundle of advertiser-funded services, much as television networks half a century earlier offered a blend of entertainment, news, sports, and other programming that all was advertiser-funded. (Sidak, 2006, p. 427)

As an example of the given orthodoxy in telecommunications thinking, it would be challenging to find something further from the democratic visions of the likes of Chester and Larson—if not their colleagues in the open access fights as well. Taking this logic to its conclusion, this consumer utopia is rather the antithesis of democracy—the scarcification of the Web at its most pernicious, the Internet as consumption machine. Further, Sidak proposes that net neutrality would potentially in fact *increase* the digital divide. Network providers permitted to charge content providers for speedier access would have an incentive to invest in continued networking, utilizing these funds, and perhaps even defraying the costs for consumers to access these new networks. Absent the ability to charge for priority, end users would end up paying for the entire cost of broadband rollout by network operators, increasing the costs to access high-speed networks and thus implicitly discriminating against those who could not afford these costs. "The natural question to ask is," he announces, "Why would it advance consumer welfare to exclude particular categories of firms from entering into transactions with third parties in a manner that would make broadband access available to the price-sensitive or income-sensitive consumers who currently forgo the service?" (Sidak, 2006, p. 352).

The framework within which to view questions of network neutrality has little to do with information or democracy; it is a paint-by-numbers total-economic-welfare calculation. Sidak (2006) lists five ways "banning access tiering" decreases social welfare. First, the "decrease [in] the quantity of prioritized delivery, given the differences in demand for priority among advertisers and end-users" is itself seen as problematic (p. 355). As a result, and representing his second concern, "upstart content providers" would be discouraged from "developing real-time applications" due to their inability to purchase priority (p. 355), which represents for him a key competitive strategy against large incumbent content or application concerns. Third, "contracting between end-users and access providers would generate greater transaction costs than would contracting between advertisers and access providers" (p. 355). Fourth, content providers themselves "are better positioned to price for priority according to application-specific price elasticities of demand, which is consistent with socially optimal pricing under Ramsey principles" (p. 355).[2] Finally, fifth, if even a "weak form" of a ban on "access tiering" were enacted (in which each type of content or application would be subject to uniform prioritization or discrimination), the resulting different "classes of customers across which differential pricing could be employed" would create significant "costs of administering the regulatory price-setting apparatus" (pp. 355–356).

Sidak then shifts concern from the provider with market power to the self-interest of those who use its services. From this vantage goint, network neutrality turns out to be an insidious plot by dominant online interests. "Despite having these net costs to social welfare, network neutrality regulation that prohibited access tiering would privately benefit incumbent providers of content or applications—which explains their support for it" (Sidak, 2006, p. 356). The reasoning for this is similar to the logic of cigarette makers who agreed in concert to a ban on advertising: the place of incumbents remains secure, but new entrants may find it difficult to reach potential customers with their offers. Similarly, by somehow allowing paid prioritization online, some new upstart (with, apparently, money to burn) could purchase prioritization over and above what the established players were obtaining for themselves, thus distinguishing itself.

In these early texts the emphasis is only in terms of prioritization as speeding up traffic, rather than holding back deprioritized traffic. This, of course, is simply a falsehood as to how this operates at the level of network management. The act of "privileging" certain traffic entails merely holding back deprioritized traffic flowing through a router; it is a zero-sum game (see, for instance, Lennett, 2009). Years later, as more became wise to the ruse, Sidak would hedge, "The FCC's focus should not be on whether permitting charging for optional [quality of service] enhancement is a 'zero-sum game' for content providers, but whether doing so is a 'positive-sum game' for social welfare" (Sidak & Teece, 2010, p. 48).

Avoiding any dwelling on the implications of handing network providers such power—particularly for the expression of noncommercial and political speech—Sidak shunts attention from the power he suggests be held by communications networks directly to advocacy groups and places them on a level equal with the likes of Google or Microsoft.

> I address the concerns that specialized regulatory rules are necessary to ensure that end-users have unfettered access to political websites and that political action groups, as diverse as MoveOn.org and the Swift Boat Veterans for Truth, are not relegated to the "slow lane" of the Internet, thus raising their cost of political advocacy. Although the portrayal of network neutrality as a competition issue concerning blockage of content may have visceral appeal to legislators and journalists, the true impetus to enact network neutrality regulation may relate more closely to the business models of advocacy groups that use the Internet to advance their political causes or to raise funding. (Sidak, 2006, p. 355)

When blocking is discovered, for Sidak, it is a misunderstanding—albeit one that seems to only afflict the left during this time. To cite one example, in 2005, "afterdowningstreet.org"—which had been responsible for exposing memos that revealed a long-standing interest by the Bush administration in invading Iraq—was attempting to organize protests and other happenings on the basis of these memos. Their plans were rendered difficult once it was discovered that the reason certain of their messages were not reaching their intended recipients was because anyone using Comcast's network could not receive emails with the name of the organization's website in the message body. Cofounder David Swanson (2005) wrote of the travails his organization experienced in attempting to resolve the issue. The cable company had not given any warning about the block, and it took days for the company to explain why a block had been put on in the first place. Comcast eventually told Swanson that their partner, Symantec, had blocked the messages and would not release the block because they "supposedly received 46,000 complaints about emails with our URL in them." Given the group had existed less than two months, this number was extraordinary. Comcast refused to show Swanson any of the complaints. A bit of activism apparently did the trick: a member of the group posted phone numbers at Symantec for protesters to call, and the company finally responded by clearing the block. For Swanson, the chief worrying message to take away from this episode was how easy it apparently was for political opponents to disrupt his group's communications and how difficult it was to track down and solve the problem.

Sidak preferred another interpretation entirely. What had occurred in his eyes was a practice that "appears to have been a content-neutral exercise of spam filtering," which proponents of network neutrality had considered a potentially desirable form of discrimination. Thus it was of little concern. This was actually neutrality-friendly in his view, since the farming out to a contractor of such duties "reduces the possibility that Comcast would make a blocking decision based on its own preferences." Additionally, it illustrated for him that "the market is capable of working efficiently to mediate disputes involving the legitimate concerns of both end-users who dislike spam and content providers who seek to express political speech to as wide an audience as possible" (Sidak, 2006, p. 438), thus undercutting the case for any network neutrality rules. He says this without irony. He does allow that "scenarios involving impaired delivery of political content, or blockage of access to political websites, do not fit neatly within the economic framework for evaluating the incentive and ability of a network operator to block or impair access to content or applications that in some manner compete against its own services" (p. 438), but that is the point of his intervention: this dimension should be considered irrelevant.

And frankly, should we even be concerned, Sidak asks, if political participation groups are unable to get their messages out online? After all,

> This concern about democratic participation through the Internet deserves serious consideration, unlike many of the economic arguments advanced in support of proposals for network neutrality regulation. However, neither MoveOn.org nor the Swift Boat Veterans for Truth provides a particularly compelling case in support of that concern. MoveOn.org received the financial support of a billionaire, George Soros. So it is debatable whether the group would lack the resources to pay for faster delivery of its packets over the Internet if access tiering were implemented. Similarly, the Swift Boat Veterans for Truth was partly (if not largely) a highly effective fund-raising organization that succeeded in raising millions of dollars within weeks. (Sidak, 2006, p. 436)

In Sidak's vision of online democracy, now that the debates had been rejoined to their old currents, one need not worry about having one's views heard: all one needed to ensure a view was heard online was to have sufficient capital.

Two Sides, One Coin

Even these concerns aside, perhaps of even greater significance is that the "legitimate" bounds of debate were often depicted as Wu pitted against Yoo during this time, represented well in a 2007 debate between the two (Wu & Yoo, 2007, p. 582). What is so revealing in this discussion is how little air there turned out to be between the two parties despite their disagreement on the issue at hand. Wu's perspective—presented as the public interest perspective in this fight, mind you—recalls the ambivalent line that advocates in this universe needed to walk. The issue was that this seeming ambivalence was anything but: it had joined the dominant current and strengthened it thanks to its underlying justifications for existence. For instance, Yoo's ability to take the argument once enunciated by Portland, Oregon, councilman Erik Sten during the early stages of the open access fights speaks to the shift, now that the sentiment had been "tamed" by Farrell, Weiser, and (paradoxically and certainly not intentionally) Wu:

> Competition in the last mile can achieve the same benefits while avoiding the problems associated with regulation. Once a sufficient number of last-mile options exists, it would matter little if one network chose to make Yahoo! its preferred search engine.... So I agree with Tim that we should place our faith in market entry. Where we differ is that I would focus on entry into the last mile, not entry into content and applications. (Wu & Yoo, 2007, pp. 584–585)

Wu adopts, with Yoo, a deployment frame, albeit in disagreement with Yoo's contention that the ability to charge prioritization or access fees will stimulate, not slow, investment in broadband networks (p. 584). Yoo puts his faith in the ability of last-mile competition to "emerge" out of seemingly nothing based on the decreasing costs of components of networks and the ability of new builders to potentially sell their wares to others if their efforts fail. Wu, who had spent time working in the telecommunications industry, countered with his knowledge of the enormity of the expenditures required to wire the last mile. Before any discussion of subsidization of any variety can transpire, however, Yoo quickly posits a particular version of history:

> In the vast majority of countries, telecommunications networks were government-created and -owned. The poor service quality, long waiting lists for installation, and slow development of new technologies in Britain and other government-owned telecommunications systems are legendary. The most eloquent proof is that essentially all of those countries are either in the process of privatizing their telecommunications networks or have already done so. Waiting for these new last-mile networks to emerge can be frustrating, and the lack of last-mile options may cause content and applications providers difficulty in the meantime. Before jumping in and regulating, policymakers should remind themselves of the inherent tendency to overvalue immediate harms and to undervalue future benefits. (Wu & Yoo, 2007, p. 589)

The new ground on which all here stand enabled Yoo to wave away the rationalities of the liberalization of networks on a global scale that, Schiller

(2000, 2007b, 2014) reminds us, did not emerge from the desires of individual residents and citizens but, rather, the global drive to network business operations. The lack of distinction between drivers of demand—business interests, financial interests and individual consumers are all conflated as one—represents one of the great erasures of the network neutrality debate on a large scale. For Yoo, privatization (as with technological convergence) elsewhere was not an agenda but rather a response to failed policy in the abstract. The latter may be true in any number of regards; but to ignore Schiller's distinction, and to be joined in ignoring it by Wu who was now standing in for the public interest on these affairs, is the height of the neoliberal drive dressed in new garb.

Similarly, in this debate between Yoo and Wu, the drive toward broadband rollout becomes a means to stamp out mechanisms that grant semi-democratic opportunities for meaningful participation aboard widely available media in the name of some *hope* for similar opportunities to emerge aboard new networks. We speak here of public access channels, media training centers, and other innovations wrought from local franchise negotiations with cable companies. Such franchise agreements were forms of local control over communication systems, if imperfect. Public access channels had become a main source of distribution of not just locally produced content but also programs like *Democracy Now*, one of the few news venues that would carry Wu's opinions on a regular basis. Such programs had cobbled together a "network" via community radio stations and public access facilities in an end run around an inability to gain carriage aboard NPR or PBS affiliates and the virtual lockdown on new channels cable companies maintained. Across the country telecommunications interests were attempting to unravel such agreements via state-level laws to consolidate such negotiations with blanket arrangements.[3] Yet here, Wu would intone,

> In telecom, the high upfront costs have sometimes but not always scared off private investments. They haven't scared off investment when the market entrant is offering a new and compelling service, like cable television in the 1970s, or at one point, telephone service between the 1890s and the 1920s. But when there's an incumbent in place, either its presence, or misguided regulation like franchising requirements, seems to have deterred market entry. (Wu & Yoo, 2007, p. 585)

It is a breathtaking sentiment: local franchise authorities were themselves the key to the entire open access debate—instigating it even. Some communities had even discovered that, through hard-won negotiations with cable companies, they could go beyond public, governmental, and educational stations or franchise fees or wiring of public buildings to subsidize entire media creation hubs that served as training centers for new local producers and creators. This friendly fire delivered by Wu only buffeted the attack of incumbent providers, stoking the flames of efforts to wrench away such gains by localities. In 2018 the FCC would put the final nail in their coffin, voting that local franchise authorities' purview did not include broadband and other "non-cable services" (Eggerton, 2018).

This is the way in which these debates were tangled and torn. The decades-long effort to establish a theoretical frame to evaluate all services and commodities, media included, as one and the same "widget" to be subjected to market forces as a means of locating truth and efficiency at once paid off in a big way: best of all, it managed to cut both to the (seeming) left as well as (seeming) right. The common ground shared gave Wu, standing in for advocates of the policy he concocted, a natural platform to agree that broadband rollout of any kind was desirable with nary a worry concerning what kind of Web one would obtain. Such a concern now fell outside the domain of debate.

Now, lest I be misconstrued: none of this should be read as an attack aimed at Wu and on advocates who struggled on this issue. However, because what kind of Web should be on offer was now taken off the table entirely in this debate, and because these desiccated terms would then constrain the nearly two decades of debate to come, this only meant that the commercial Web with its particular forms, logics and rationalities could spend that much longer cementing itself without broader discussion of the implications of its doing so. Such was the paradoxical "use" of the network neutrality debate. The themes of both "sides" included the abnegation of positive desires in favor of an evolutionary innovation model; regulations won to maintain accountability (such as the negotiations localities were entitled to with cable companies to win such resources as public access channels) were to be discarded in the name of competitive entry to a Web that was, barring a movement against it, providing wind at the backs of those who sought to eliminate such accountability mechanisms. The denizens of the Mont Pèlerin Society would be pleased: the debate now existed within a restricted range of theoretical options, helped by the appearance of this new form of ironically compliant resistance.

Conclusion

Yoo is not without his caveats regarding his vision. "I do not claim that every deviation from [network neutrality] will necessarily enhance economic welfare.... For my purposes, it is sufficient if some deviation from [network neutrality] may plausibly be motivated by legitimate concerns and it is hard to distinguish procompetitive and anticompetitive uses of such restrictions, as [network neutrality] proponents have conceded is often the case" (Yoo, 2006, p. 1855). Writing two years earlier, he reminds that

> These arguments should not be misconstrued as favoring noninteroperability as a general matter. On the contrary, I would expect most network owners to continue to adhere to a basic architecture based around TCP/IP. Maintaining interoperability provides consumers and network owners with such substantial financial advantages that most will adopt standardized protocols voluntarily. In most cases, then, mandating network neutrality would be superfluous. The only situations in which network neutrality has any purpose are those in which the market exhibits a preference for nonstandardization. My concern is that compelling interoperability under those circumstances runs the risk of reducing economic welfare, either by preventing the realization of efficiencies or by reinforcing the economies of scale that are the primary causes of potential market failure. (Yoo, 2004, pp. 54–55)

Such pronouncements increased his credibility, something that the NCTA certainly desired of their consultant; like the original sponsors of the Mont Pèlerin Society, the recognition is that the development of a system of *understanding* trumped bombast, although others would be able to provide that to fill out the tactical menu. Viewed less as a positive production of knowledge about broadband networks and networking, what we observe on full display is a vision of democracy of long vintage. It took the dance of Wu and Yoo to realize it. The discussions contained in these primary documents of the early network neutrality debate presented a potential new problematic on a grand scale with which media reform advocates would need to contend.

These arguments would be leavened by numerous others. The 2007 publication of a compendium of "significant" stances on the network neutrality debate by the *International Journal of Communication*, for instance, would provide the illusion of knowledge gained, understandings taken. The enactment of the debate itself was never about increasing the understanding of networks, although those directly involved in networking certainly found them helpful. Unwittingly, the academy had been drawn into a long-plotted project: tacking both right and left, the authors who were seen by the compendium's editors as constituting "serious" takes on the issue were being put to broader purpose: policing the boundaries of debates in official policy circles. The seeming "debate" yet concurrent closeness between the stances of Wu and Yoo leaves us nipping at the heels of rapidly supplied justificatory ammunition designed behind its own back to render a once heterogeneous debate now diverse, tractable, decidable, legitimatable. In short: they would serve as a vetting mechanism for those seeking to engage the debate with regulators; the irony would be that the final policies would largely ignore the actual content of these debates despite their profusion.

If there were any doubt as to how this happenstance shifted the ground, we need look no further than an award-winning comment from Barry (2008). Written then as a J.D. candidate, this piece won a "Second Prize in Comments" from the legal journal in which it was contained. While there had been several cases of discrimination online, activism to thwart such blocking was eliminated from the story: "So far, the few cases of network providers abusing their control of the network have been quickly remedied by complaints from consumers and application providers," he writes (Barry, 2008, p. 431). He casually hearkens back to Farrell and Weiser's ICE framework but is careful enough to note that there may be some exceptions to it, such as transaction costs for consumers to switch broadband providers—but this is of little concern. "Market demand has already had a considerable impact in safeguarding net neutrality in numerous instances," he writes; after all,

> AOL initially sought to offer its subscribers a "fenced-in" Internet of affiliated sites. This plan was quickly dropped, however, as the Internet grew and consumers demanded access to the whole Internet. A similar example of market demand safeguarding net neutrality involved network providers' early attempts at blocking or streaming video applications. Eventually, network providers gave in to consumer demands for unrestricted use of streaming video applications. (Barry, 2008, pp. 434–435)

Gone from the story were the efforts of consumer activists to ensure that these conditions existed; replaced are the power of market forces given a life of their own in an effort to square the dominant theory to the practices of the real world. Emerging naturally and without malice was yet another wild goose for consumer advocates to chase: they would need to continually remind all of the struggles past, that these desires were not made known simply by the forces of the market. They were forced to make these desires known in national venues and state and local venues in the form of policy debates that were now foreclosed. The market fought these developments tooth and nail until it was able to "cede" some ground to the consumer advocates who ironically were fomenting the growth of an increasingly commercial environment by keeping the wheels turning in this debate, even as the consequences of not doing so would likely be more dire.

Forgetting open access, crucially, was not about wiping out the possibility of activism alone. It was about forgetting the ad hoc articulations of new forms of knowledge that awkwardly attached themselves to a long-running frame that needed to incorporate them and yet had not found its way to do so. Farrell and Weiser provided one of the key ties; there surely were others. Wu, ironically, created the strongest tie and supplied the boundaries that commenced to be filled: the horizon suddenly became viewable. Other activists working on the issue would do similarly, such as when Marvin Ammori in an interview would emphasize, "Because innovators did not need to seek the permission of a centralized bureaucracy at an ISP (let alone dozens of ISPs), [they] faced low economic barriers to entry and could reap the rewards of innovation, successful innovators were able to create technology like Google, eBay, and Twitter, none of which kept its initial business model nor was envisioned by an ISP [*sic*]" (Picot & Krcmar, 2011, p. 329). As Streeter (2011) reminds, often forgotten are the financiers, the material supports necessary to push an "invention" and model out of the garage. This had been, at least in the background, one of the concerns of open access, now buried and rarely discussed.

What FCC chairman Powell did was give the process a shove toward its own realization. Activists (and his own colleagues) accused him of brash political maneuvers with his 2002 proposals and declaration; here was politics in another register. The Wu-ian intervention mattered because of the foundation on which it rested. Unlike the ad hoc nature of the consumer advocates' arguments that predated it, here was the application of descendant thought of the thought collective of years past in new clothes: it wrenched back and forth to the seeming "left" and "right" at once. It reigned supreme. Wu was the product of it: the debate itself was now necessary for the broader system's survival. As such it fit into already-occurring debates regarding antitrust and the calculation of surplus, the new Theory of Everything. Yoo's response meant that this theory could now firmly be applied, with network neutrality advocates' blessing, to this new realm. The urge to shape an emergent market could not be resisted.

We end with a truly ambivalent stance on the contribution of Wu. He saved consumer advocates from oblivion by providing a new opening for debate as Powell was shutting down another. Simultaneously, Wu served to transform the battle by unwittingly taking away one of the best tools advocates had due to the foundation from which he chose to draw his arguments; these tapped into a long-simmering current that now could pick up steam like a hurricane gaining power after happening across warmer waters. Worse, the debate had wealthy benefactors to keep the winds churning. In the process, for advocates to retain legitimacy in Washington, they would be set chasing their tails answering the new charges and arguments tossed out—and then doing so again and again as the same arguments seemed to spring like weeds from the newly fertilized soil—no conspiracy necessary.

6 Advocates, Regulators, and the Ersatz: Defeat Snatched from the Jaws of Victory

Ben Scott, policy director of Free Press until 2011, would at times note that in Washington politics, in order for one to succeed, one needed two of the following three things: money, constituency, or expertise. In the open access debates of the late 1990s and early 2000s, the players involved—seasoned Washington players all—supplied the latter two. The growth of new groups of the early 2000s like Free Press, and the emergence of others who took advantage of the Internet as a new organizing platform, supplied the same. However, in the course of the network neutrality debates proper, the dynamic was entirely different than in the open access struggle, with Wu's intervention firmly linking this policy debate to streams of the thought collective of old. Particular terms would be sought "inside the Beltway." Wu, while saving the issue for further debate, cemented the terms of contest to obtain legitimacy in any office. Constituents with limited knowledge of such terms themselves could express popular support but little else: the function of constituency had been turned on its head. Constituency could accomplish a small number of things: for one, it presented pressure on legislators to themselves put pressure on regulators; on regulators, however, constituency's influence would be minimal. With the terms of debate firmly cemented inside the Federal Communications Commission (FCC) (and, for that matter, in other institutions as the Federal Trade Commission [FTC] and the Department of Justice [DOJ]), their knowledge would be considered, at best, a form of ersatz understanding of it, in McCloskey's sense (Amariglio & Ruccio, 1999; McCloskey, 1999).

Engagement of any stripe with these undercurrents needed to be blessed, and usually a firm "marker" of legitimacy is being called before some congressional committee or official FCC *en banc* hearing (something quite removed from offering comment with the rabble at the informal "town meetings" the FCC was holding, either of their own volition or sponsored by others). Free Press, for instance, was granted access with the help of the Consumer Federation of America (CFA) and Consumers Union's willingness to pass on an invitation to appear before a congressional committee to debate universal service policies—something with which the organization had not engaged nor had accumulated much expertise at the time. Nonetheless, with this performance, its reputation was secured (Free Press, 2006). As Gene Kimmelman—of Consumers Union, but later the Department of Justice under Obama and then Public Knowledge—would reflect later,

> You want to be a witness, but you don't even have to be the witness. During hearings, there are recesses, people are going off to vote, and you can grab them and actually engage. And then there are enormous feedback loops that come once you're out there and you're known. If you have the credibility, you're called back. If the press sees that you're taken seriously by members of Congress, they call you. Or you're in The New York Times and the Wall Street Journal, or you're online, on social media, and people are coming to you and taking to your way of presenting thinking... you're more likely to be invited in by the policymakers. It means you're easily identifiable, and you're influential. And then you start getting calls from editorial writers, and you build those relationships. (Quoted in Holt, 2016, pp. 5797–5798)

Free Press' presence was buttressed by the production not necessarily so much of useful materials but of materials that represented an involvement with the key movers of debate. Given that so many of those economists that attacked pro-network neutrality positions made such grand motions toward always-already-there vibrant competition (based on FCC data), one of Free Press's most effective forays in this regard was the production of two *Broadband Reality Check* reports calling into question the FCC's methodologies for collecting data (for example, Turner. 2006). White papers were issued and submitted; one learned the ins and outs of submitting comments into proceedings; in short, one became ensconced within the discourse community of Washington.

Significantly as well, there were efforts across the country in state legislatures to decrease the influence of local cable franchise authorities. This was a bipartisan activity: Democrats in California rolled out their own plan to deregulate cable access in the state by fashioning a press conference in a mock living room set-dressed to the hilt in 1970s décor (Denina, 2006), seeking to craft the ever-present message that regulations (of the ilk which sparked the open access debates themselves and, indirectly, the network neutrality debates of the 2000s) were themselves outdated. The Alliance for Community Media, which worked with local cable access stations across the country, sought to push back against these. Free Press ran its own campaign to track such legislation and to aid local forces push back against it via their "Defend Local Access" effort which mirrored its similarly styled "Save Community Internet" that tracked statewide efforts to ban local municipal networks at the behest of powerful incumbents.

All of this is to say that network neutrality was never something that was fought alone, on its own terms: rather, it was part of a panoply of communication policy related efforts that circulated around several components. Network neutrality mattered to the extent that long-standing concerns about press freedom, freedom of expression, implications for independent media, access to communication, and implications for civil rights were affected. It fit neatly in a broad portfolio of concerns stemming from media consolidation to defending local franchising authorities' ability to negotiate for supplied services by cable operators and seeking to expand these. If there *was* a shift from the early days of the organization, however, it was that gaining entrance to the regulatory realm as a player meant shedding a critique that was of pivotal importance at the beginning of the organization's history: critiques of "hypercommercialism." These critiques were never wholly jettisoned, but they took a backseat in favor of overarching strategies of obtaining basic access to means of communications itself rather than the nature of the networks on offer. This is hardly to say that such concerns were absent; but these were unable to find expression inside the FCC and Congress, and this was the fault not just of adversaries but because of governmental *allies* as well.

The effectiveness of activists in inserting themselves in these debates is not disputable. The emergent SavetheInternet.com campaign brought together an odd bedfellows coalition of "small businesses, consumer advocates, librarians, civil libertarians, journalists, bloggers, YouTubers and others joined together ... to demand a more open, neutral, and affordable Internet for everyone" (Karr, 2007)—a wide, bipartisan, growing, and ongoing coalition focused on Internet nondiscrimination whose roster grew to enormous size.[1] It performed the function of slowing congressional debates on the issue and applying pressure on an administrative agency unused to such interventions. When Alaska Republican Ted Stevens attempted to revise the Telecommunications Act in the middle of the decade, network neutrality became a key issue that portended the effort's failure (a clip of Stevens referring to the Internet as "not a truck" and "a series of tubes" evinced massive public ridicule to boot).[2] This was the moment network neutrality became a grassroots issue and it became of interest outside of the Beltway—and make no mistake, this was to take everyone by surprise. As an illustration of how surprising this coalition was, a hearing before the House Judiciary's Task Force on Competition Policy and Antitrust Laws featured the odd combination of Damian Kulash, lead singer of the popular band OK Go; Michele Combs, vice president of the Christian Coalition; Caroline Fredrickson, director of the Washington Legislative Office of the American Civil Liberties Union; and Susan Crawford, then of Yale Law School, all speaking in favor of legislation that would protect net neutrality (for a fuller telling of some aspects of this time period, see McChesney, 2013; *Net Neutrality and Free Speech*, 2008).

Activity was frenzied as in the wake of the *Brand X* decision, the now–Kevin Martin–led FCC took the step of reclassifying all modes of broadband delivery as Title I services, albeit with an adjoining "Internet Policy Statement" that at least elevated former chairman Powell's "four freedoms" to unenforceable policy goals (FCC, 2005). Gone were any of the protections that telecommunications rules provided. Even so, activists were able to expand their purview in 2007. The release of the iPhone—and the limited number of providers able to offer the phone—saw Tim Wu release another paper entitled "Wireless Carterfone" (2007) which advocates used to bring academic heft to their cause. While not directly about network neutrality per se, it made having a choice of device to use aboard one's wireless platform an intrinsic part of the debate itself: the principle of maintaining innovation at network edges represented the common thread. There was significant pushback against efforts to block or lock access to numerous capabilities on these devices:

> The hallmarks of the software development environment for personal computers and Web applications are (1) permissionless market entry, (2) relatively low costs of market entry, and (3) open development standards that make it possible to write to many platforms.... Many application developers believe that the mobile applications market is stalled, or much less active than it might be. Developers describe many reasons, though three are dominant: (1) access to phone capabilities, (2) extensive qualification and approval procedures, and (3) pervasive lack of standards in many areas. (Wu, 2007, pp. 408–409)

Even more significant, if obscure to general consciousness, was the unfolding of debates surrounding what was to be done with spectrum that would be vacated by television broadcasters following the transition to digital broadcasting. The proceedings surrounding the auction of these airwaves showed advocates near the peak of their influence. Seeing opportunity, and much as open access advocates did with significant academic work that helped the cause, advocates mobilized Wu's paper to drive the issue home, connecting it to the larger network neutrality debate—now inexorably linked to oligopolistic control over networks by the largest incumbents that were only consolidating further. The Martin FCC, in lieu of a regulatory proceeding, instead used the upcoming auctions for mobile wireless spectrum to nudge providers to open their networks to other equipment. The result was the creation of a block of spectrum that would be subject to "net neutrality lite" conditions that required them to "publish a suitable air interface so any equipment manufacturer could make devices that could connect to the network" (Feld, 2018a). Verizon complained, but ultimately won the auction for access to this spectrum. "How much of this would have happened without any sort of regulatory nudge, and whether we would have avoided a duopoly on mobile phones if the FCC had adopted a real open device rule in 2007, is something we can debate" (Feld, 2018a). This was an extraordinary breakthrough nonetheless, as was an undersung proceeding initiated by Martin and unanimously approved by the FCC—a Notice of Inquiry on Broadband Practices that included a statement that the FCC had "the ability to adopt and enforce the net neutrality principles it announced in the Internet Policy Statement" (FCC, 2007; Feld, 2018a).

Institution Building and Expansion

The expressions of desire by the multitudinous members of the ersatz were adjoined by a second strategy emergent activists could utilize. That was to recognize—and to recall the experience of the former FCC staffer in the introduction—that, to maintain a seat at the policymaking table when both the rhetorical and literal whiteboards were drawn up, this now-diverse range of thought needed to be engaged with, at least in public, even if the decisions at the whiteboards had little or nothing to do with the ontic content of their arguments. Marvin Ammori, who would play a key role in the Open

Internet debates to come, noted at the outset of the Obama administration, "Though ideas alone are often not enough in 'politics,' they do matter in policy debates. The incumbent telephone and cable industries succeeded in winning the war of ideas, largely because they were able to fund an army of lobbyists, as well as scholars at universities and think tanks, many of whom published books and articles in the most cited law and economics journals supporting their cases" (Ammori, 2009, p. 91). Some efforts to expand the debate, to render it (like the consumer advocates of the late 1990s) heterogeneous, emerged from within the Washington discursive community itself as advocates pushing for network neutrality sought to legitimize new and expanded foundations for the concept, to "transcend" it (Meinrath & Pickard, 2008; Meinrath et al., 2010). All this said, today's happenstance is of a quite different piece than other eras, when the likes of James Q. Wilson made the charge that the use of research in policymaking—constrained by time and funding—was, at best, "ad hoc, improvised, quick-and-dirty." That is,

> A key official, needing to take a position, respond to a crisis, or support a view that is under challenge, will ask an assistant to "get me some facts." The assistant will rummage about among persons who are reputed to be expert, who are perceived to be politically sympathetic, and who are available at the moment. The process may take a few weeks, it may be done in a few hours. Social science is used as ammunition, not as a method, and the official's opponents will also use similar ammunition. (J. Q. Wilson, 1978, p. 92)

Adversaries to network neutrality already possessed a neoliberal, Russian-doll style of discourse production which could feed into both the old methods and what was emerging as the new. Hands Off the Internet, now with ex-Clinton spokesman Michael McCurry at the helm to provide cover for wavering Democrats and to lend a bipartisan flavor to the initiative, set up a particularly (and transparently) "astroturf-y" website mimicking the activist websites but with little information to be found regarding their sponsorship. This front group masked the real intellectual labor being performed by others. The Progress and Freedom Foundation (PFF), started in the early 1990s, was a primarily conservative think tank that provided early pushback against network neutrality. The environment shifted before the 2010s began, and this organization folded. The more neoliberal Information Technology and Innovation Foundation (ITIF), started by Robert Atkinson, took a leading role in its stead; as one activist put it, "It was clear no one in a Democratic administration cared what [PFF] said; ITIF has much more of a reputation for 'reasonableness' and was much more open, and benefitted from that enormously" (Harold Feld, personal communication, September 27, 2012). The Phoenix Center and the Free State Foundation provided additional support to incumbent interests. The Mercatus Center at George Mason University—with the accompanying legitimacy a university pseudo-affiliation can provide—took in some of the PFF membership and became more active in these areas itself. The term "pseudo-affiliation" is appropriate; in a recent report, while using the university's letterhead, the institution would suddenly claim "independent!" when subject to basic Freedom of Information requests, revealing its affiliation as primarily a convenient way to launder its efforts: "Freedom of information experts briefed on the matter said the Mercatus Center was trying to have it both ways, benefiting from being associated with an academic institution while shirking the responsibilities of that institution" (Dayen, 2018).

The Web was thick with interrelationships among the Russian doll structures supportive of cable and telecommunications interests. The New Millennium Research Council (a project of Issue Dynamics Inc., a public relations firm) itself served to provide overarching umbrella access to a number of experts affiliated with still other organizations such as the American Enterprise Institute (AEI), the Brookings Institution (and AEI-Brookings Joint Center for Regulatory Studies), the Manhattan Institute for Policy Research, the Analysis Group (featuring Verizon-hired Coleman Bazelon and Thomas Hazlett, who was also a fellow at the Manhattan Institute for Policy Research and held a post at the University of Pennsylvania's Wharton School), the Beacon Hill Institute, the Cato Institute, the Competitive Enterprise Institute, Criterion Economics (a consulting firm for telecommunications companies, featuring Robert Crandall, Hal Singer, J. Gregory Sidak, Jeffrey West, and Jeffrey Eisenach—himself cofounder of the PFF), the Heartland Institute, the Heritage Foundation, the Institute for Policy Innovation, the Pacific Research Institute, the PFF, the Progressive Policy Institute, TeleNomic Research, and the U.S. Internet Industry Association.[3] What united all these groups were present or past funding from large telecommunications operators. Their strength came from both the fact that they hardly stood unified on all issues, and, true to the form of the Russian doll structure, their interrelationships were rendered challenging to parse, much less to track. Vigorous debate was always far more effective than unified stances, even as these organizations' positions on issues as net neutrality were predictable. What would differ, however, were their *justifications,* and this is what mattered. Such institutions, long a product of the neoliberal thought collective's funding centers (now telecommunications firms were direct sponsors), provided the fodder for discourse and took part in the workshops sponsored by the FCC and beyond.

FCC chairman Powell's brash moves in the early 2000s to loosen media ownership rules had the effect that left-leaning funding sources—foundations and individuals alike—took notice of media policy and were beginning to help feed the growing infrastructure of organizations both on the ground in Washington and outside to create a space for this discussion. Efforts to continue growing this sector continued through the Obama administration. Free Press itself, brand new as of 2003, grew to nearly forty people in a relatively brief time; Public Knowledge experienced a similar spurt in growth. The Center for Media Justice in the early 2000s was a loose group of a small number of people and affiliates and itself had grown tremendously during those years, forming the Media Action Grassroots Network (MAG-Net) in 2008 with support from the Media Democracy Fund. The group now is able to boast nearly 100 member groups.[4] The New America Foundation, which already possessed a "Wireless Future" division to focus on spectrum policy, sprouted a new division, the Open Technology Institute, which focused on questions of broadband policy, "Internet freedom," and eventually surveillance circumvention projects; with the election of President Obama, the division experienced its own spurt of growth, utilizing grants from the U.S. State Department, among other donors. Alongside this was the growth of M-Lab, a "consortium of research, industry and public interest partners" focused on producing "an open, verifiable measurement platform for global network performance, ... hosting the largest open Internet performance dataset on the planet," and "creating visualizations and tools to help people make sense of Internet performance."[5] This was a collaboration between the New America Foundation, Google, and a number of universities, including Princeton and Northwestern. There was regular communication as well between these initiatives and the likes of Common Cause, Consumers Union, the CFA, the Media Mobilizing Project, the Center for Media Justice, MAG-Net, and more. The formation of the Media and Democracy Coalition provided a venue for all these groups to share notes on all aspects of media reform, a stab at partial operationalization and facilitation of alliances between the Washington-based players and advocacy organizations outside Washington.

Advocates as well were playing the same justification game as the industry players, as they realized that their work carried much more weight once it was presented at academic conferences (such as that of the International Communication Association's annual gathering) and published in academic and law journals. In short, they were learning how to legitimize their efforts. These organizations did what they could to mobilize such research, but all the same, the surprise had left it: the research could be effectively categorized rather than articulated in surprising ways to the undercurrents now flowing hard. Such is the nature of a debate that may at one point have been heterogeneous, but had been rendered merely diverse.

Strikingly, it also led to organizations like Free Press to foment a new, neoliberal-appropriate style of organization that itself mirrored the thinking of Hayek in the old thought collective. I think here of the essence of the "double truth": the constitution of an elite discourse that moves the works forward while maintaining a populist-appearing foundation that leads people to believe that they are participating in meaningful ways. I do not denigrate it: the paradox is that the populist portion was meaningful even as it could never drive the policy debate in official settings. When the populist base got too ornery, they would seemingly need to be apologized for in Washington with policymakers for unreasonableness. Taking in lessons from their experience, Free Press president Craig Aaron and senior director of strategy and communications Tim Karr advise, "The key is establishing symbiosis. The insiders need the threat of a public outcry to get a seat at the table. But hundreds of thousands of calls and letters to Congress and the FCC are worthless without the inside knowledge to target the right decision-makers at the right time. You need to strike a balance between the credibility of the policy experts and the creativity of the field" (Aaron & Karr, 2016, p. 103).

Successful politicking in Washington meant refashioning oneself as a moderate and reasonable expert, which similarly requires radicalism in the field to sometimes be apologized for or downplayed in private. Free Press, for instance, learned this as it put on the first National Conference for Media Reform, navigating the divide between the policy realm and the activist realm. Low-power FM enthusiasts (of which Free Press counted itself one) desired to set up unlicensed radio transmitters; the organizers were forced to shut down the idea as legislators from Congress, and FCC officials even, were going to be in attendance! Free Press in fact found itself *protested* by those it saw as erstwhile allies, such as various Indymedia collectives and others seeking revolutionary change—or by those who observed ugly forms of power and privilege reproduced inside. These internal negotiations and protestations represented a compounded challenge to that of negotiating with Congress and regulators themselves. It created numerous contradictions that required address, and such address necessarily requires long periods of hard effort.

There are numerous ways of "eliminating the ersatz" from consideration in Washington in any proceeding. Often, the majority FCC members simply stopped attending even their own "official" town meetings when it was realized ordinary people would actually show up (for a recent example, among several, see Consumers Union [2014]). Submission of comments to the FCC via their online webform is incredibly intimidating for newcomers: in older proceedings, the preponderance of filers tended to be lawyers representing industry groups or state/local governments, the occasional public interest group, and perhaps representatives of the FCC itself. Once Free Press compiled an algorithm that allowed the easy filing of comments to the system, the FCC installed a feature on the search page, at the bottom, that one could check to "Eliminate brief text comments." As it became regular practice to encourage their email lists to file comments in controversial proceedings, this button became a permanent feature, conceivably to quickly discern the "important" or "substantive" comments. With Obama's ascendancy, an additional button was added to provide *exclusively* these comments, adding a veneer of inclusion.[6]

Activist groups sought all manner of options to include the ersatz in policy proceedings: this had been one of the original goals of Free Press at its inception—to bring the public's voices more firmly into this arena. Perhaps never before had such a wide-ranging set of perspectives and groups banded together on a tech policy issue. The ersatz understanding made appearances in town hall meetings that the FCC held as well as those held by independent groups with the presence of certain of the commissioners (generally, Commissioner Michael Copps or Commissioner Jonathan Adelstein). (For more details of these initial hearings, see McChesney et al. [2005] and Pickard & Popiel [2018].) It made its appearance in numerous dockets. Several subsequent landmark National Conferences for Media

Reform were held and attended by thousands. Following the departure of Michael Powell from the FCC, media ownership continued to play large in these debates as the Kevin Martin FCC pushed to loosen these rules as well; numerous times advocates turned on the "noise machine" to push back, and lawsuits were filed when Martin attempted to overturn most.

The "double truth" was especially apparent in how network neutrality was reframed. The concept needed to be disattached from the ontic content of its moorings by flipping Wu's contention around, taking the effect (or the state) of network neutrality as, now, a policy to be invoked: so done, the empty signifier was then set adrift, ready to find itself articulated to new foundations and justifications that were not always mobilized in its proponents' favor. The effect of this was that while the issue became increasingly tractable with the broader public (in a certain sense), the "ersatz" understandings would nonetheless be prevented entrance to the official debates due to this detachment from its original foundation in theory. Nonetheless, the ability to extend beyond the "grasstops" efforts of the earlier consumer advocates in Washington during the open access debates proper would be crucial. Thanks to Wu's rendering of a once heterogeneous realm now *diverse* (in Laclau's sense), and Powell's snapping shut the interloping open access concerns that could have possibly reversed the process, either another round of additional knowledge of an ad hoc variety would need to be found to make the boundaries recede once again into shadow, or something else would need to perform that function indirectly.

This is also not to misunderstand what was going on outside the Beltway: these logics for network neutrality may have been unmoored from their particular theoretical roots which had been laid in elite Washington legitimation discourse, but they were quickly being retrofitted to other logics entirely—just different ones, ones unrecognizable to the conceptual apparatus now firmly constructed in Washington. The efforts outside the Beltway were also no naïve moves: like the consumer advocates of the late 1990s and early 2000s, ordinary people had discovered for themselves the ways in which their lives had improved thanks to the introduction of broadband technologies and were seeking to defend their own ways of life in the face of its shifting under their feet. Activists' concerns were rendered quite real when then–Southwestern Bell Corporation (SBC) head Ed Whitacre told Businessweek regarding upstarts like Vonage, "How do you think they're going to get to customers? Through a broadband pipe. Cable companies have them. We have them. Now what they would like to do is use my pipes free, but I ain't going to let them do that because we have spent this capital and we have to have a return on it" (O'Connell, 2005). Romantic conceptions of how the Internet worked (Streeter, 2011) resulted in continued efforts not against capital but between capitals: an ambivalent space. This might appear to be similar to what was undertaken during the open access debates of the late 1990s and early 2000s, but it is not, as network neutrality was becoming about free speech and freedom itself, disconnected from its origins in evolutionary economics. This mattered: a heterogeneity machine was under (re)construction, but on different terms than during the open access debates of the late 1990s. Whereas in open access debates the concept's advocates had a large role in defining the issue on their terms, with network neutrality they did not: it was predefined in a manner only half-suited to activist organization at its root. Organize they would, but the weapon that could be used against them was simple incommensurability as well as the heft that decades of construction work of the Chicago variety could bring to the table. Given this stream, even if confronted head on, it possessed such lineage with support networks constructed to support it that it would be an uphill battle the whole way. The Mirowskian Russian doll stood at the ready after decades of institutionalization and support to be activated once again.

To a degree, the tactics worked, precisely because it took so long for the whiteboard to ever get fashioned as a result. Massive, unexpected public involvement did render the field heterogeneous for a time. It is incredibly revealing, for instance, that FCC Commissioner Jonathan Adelstein in 2003 called network neutrality a "solution awaiting a problem," and longtime "net diversity" supporter Christopher Yoo trots him out as a weapon in a footnote to his arguments in 2006—years after Adelstein had met some of the ersatz public in settings outside of Washington and had become one of network neutrality's stalwart defenders (Yoo, 2006, p. 1856n33). The massive outcry by ordinary people with varying degrees of understandings of the issue did stall a process that, for all intents and purposes, should have barreled forth full steam.

Meeting the Ersatz

The operationalization of this strategy was effectively a massive *channeling* of citizen voices in needed directions. While this was necessary as part of what advocates described as the "noise machine," particularly during the

Bush years, a crucial sidecar strategy was, in a sense, the *elimination* of the ersatz when it proved inconvenient. This was hardly so different during the Obama years—in fact, during the latter, the challenges would be even more vexing as the "allied" administration found ways of disadmitting views even more effectively than the previous Republican administration. The ersatz expressing its views on its own was generally less than helpful: channeled to diverse causes (to declare a side or not, seen in Laclau's sense) so as to legitimate a particular policy actor was when these voices were more welcome. Official Washington, on the other hand, would selectively bask in their contact with the ersatz.

Efforts to include solicited public opinion, for instance, were easily subverted—even if unintentionally. It was often established systems themselves that performed the task: the structure of politicking and the resultant internal pressures were sufficient to do the job. An instance of such a clash between the ersatz—even a highly informed set of it—and the legislative realm was Senator Richard Durbin's "Legislation 2.0" initiative, now largely lost to history and the challenges of archiving online events on platforms that are server-driven. During the summer of 2007, the senator, seeking to make good on a campaign promise to be active in a rewrite of the Telecommunications Act of 1996 himself, held a series of live-blogging events over the course of the week that were intended to provide public input.[7] This input would ultimately be used in the fashioning of a bill. Matt Stoller, who at the time had started a new blog, OpenLeft.com, agreed to host the session, necessary to negotiate the challenges at the time of what was permissible over "official" lawmaker websites; it was simpler to go elsewhere. Stoller, while writing for the prominent blog MyDD.com, had followed the network neutrality issue more closely than many other bloggers.

Four nights of "live blogging" were be wide ranging, covering network neutrality, privacy, public provision of broadband, and spectrum policy—an issue that was front and center at the FCC at the time as plans were being laid to auction bands that broadcasters would soon vacate as part of the transition to digital broadcasting. The cast of characters spoke to the kind of coalition-building achieved by activists. Included were San Francisco advocate and radio personality Davey D (who has repeatedly spoken out on issues of media justice), members of the Communications Workers of America, and Kent Nichols of "Ask a Ninja" fame (who had dedicated a much-watched online video to the cause of network neutrality). Ben Scott of Free Press and Eric Rotenberg of the Electronic Privacy Information Center focused on network neutrality and privacy. Discussion of spectrum policy included former FCC chief economist (and oftentimes advocate for the privatization of spectrum) Gerald Faulhaber, Harold Feld (of the Media Access Project), Wally Bowen (who ran an independent wireless service operation in North Carolina), and Sascha Meinrath of the New America Foundation (who had been a leader in setting up the Champaign-Urbana Community Wireless Network and was instrumental in pushing the development of wireless, scalable "mesh" networking over unlicensed airwaves). Universal service policy reform was discussed by Paul Morris of the Utah Telecommunication Open Infrastructure Agency (UTOPIA) project (a municipal fiber-broadband initiative advocates held up as a possible model), Jim Baller of the Baller-Herbst Law Group (who advocated for municipal broadband networks), John Windhausen (a longtime Hill and FCC advisor on telecommunications issues), Waldo McMillan of the nonprofit OneEconomy, and Andrew McNeill of ConnectKentucky (which was already controversial in its practices of "measuring broadband access" while essentially delivering customers to the major telecommunications providers).

No telecommunications firm invited would agree to allow any representatives to participate, leaving that task instead to surrogates from the telecommunications incumbent-funded group Hands Off the Internet, who appeared unannounced once blogging began. This was also an indication of how seriously these players were taking the initiative. A brazen voice mail from a Verizon representative left to those organizing the affair made this even more clear. In so many words, he intoned that they were mystified at what was slated to happen, they really *didn't* want this "net neutrality" topic to receive more attention, and they would prefer to defer and not participate.

The resulting challenges were on multiple levels. For one, the platform itself was not altogether intuitive to use, resulting in the ruin of what was by all accounts going to be one of the most interesting debates of the week. During the third night, even as Harold Feld chomped at the bit—"Finally, an honest debate!" he wrote—Gerald Faulhaber could not find the correct "spot" on the site to engage. Initially believing Faulhaber had forgotten about the correct time to appear, repeated instant messages were sent to him with the appropriate link and inquiring to his whereabouts. To these, he responded with a bewildered, "I'm typing as fast as I can!" It turned out he had clicked on the link to his own commentary earlier in the day and had been busily engaging a couple anonymous stragglers in discussion entirely in the wrong locale all along. The irony of this influential-in-policy-circles expert on broadband issues not being able to find the right thread (and not switching over to it once informed of his mistake) was not lost on his would-be sparrers.

As for the senator's staff, each live blog was exhausting—but anticlimactic: computers lined the wall outside Durbin's main office in the Capitol, and staff as well as the senator would arrive in a blaze of energy to find themselves relentlessly scanning threads for points demanding response in near silence. The senator *still* had not come down on a particular side of the network neutrality issue, remaining ambiguous in any comment on the matter. Make no mistake: after the first night, this was a chore for some staffers. It wasn't the first time that Durbin and his staff had done something like this: following one of President Bush's State of the Union addresses, they had spent an evening eviscerating him, and the staff had fond memories of it. This time, it wasn't *fun*. Here, respondents were angry, "outwonking" staff (not always a positive thing), and some were seen as crazy, hysterical. It was clear that much of the way opinion was expressed in the comments was not going to be legislatively useful; its benefit was largely in the publicity that it was bringing to the senator.

Even more revealing was that a staffer whose task was to call their own contacts at telecommunications companies to invite them to take part never fulfilled their promise. The official word was that no telecommunications providers had agreed to participate; the statement was thus *literally* true, if not in a bit of a deceptive spirit; it was almost a relief that the incumbents' front group showed. This was a calculated move by the staffer: all telecommunications and cable providers *would* demur to his request, but he would face some indignity in even asking, given the senator had remained ambiguous on network neutrality quite on purpose up to this point. Why would the office even bring it up, then? Better, if this position needed to be maintained, for a front group to show up and shape the debate into a rehash of the same arguments that had been circulating for, at this point, three years. Little chance of new confrontations to make headlines; no advancement of the debate. (This said, in private, advocates expressed their own confidence that if pressed on an actual vote, he would have voted in favor even at that time.) The telcos had clearly won this night, even as the arguments advanced by their surrogates were skewered by advocate and anonymous commenters alike in the broad light of day for the umpteenth time. A "see, it all worked out" attitude prevailed. Surely it did. Real arguments, *legislatively useful arguments,* would continue behind the scenes and out of view. With Faulhaber unintentionally dodging his own debate, in many ways, one could consider most of the week a bust.[8] Some deliberate if politically useful (and, for his own job, perhaps necessary) subterfuge by staff (intentional or not), and the honest mistake of a former FCC chief economist, resulted in no new vocabulary, semantics, or meaning being introduced, so one cannot even say that at least new attention was drawn to the issues at hand. The news-hook novelty remained largely that a senator initiated a live discussion with the broader public.

Activist groups were energized afterward, and the Sunlight Foundation offered to house the content so as to try and push the initiative to next steps. But with the 2008 election on the horizon, and new legislative priorities (not to mention that Durbin didn't exactly have direct jurisdiction over this issue), the initiative largely festered. (One blogger, in a post that is often cited regarding the effort, says outright, "Remember two years ago when Senator Richard Durbin took the blogosphere and specifically MyDD .com [*sic*] and RedState.com for a series of open thread discussions about shaping a broadband bill? 'Legislation 2.0' got some attention at the time, but then the Durbin staffer who was responsible for shepherding the process reportedly went back to graduate school, and little more was heard of the notion.")[9]

This was a perfect illustration of how, when faced with threats, such new input which potentially heterogenized the field of action needed to be reined in, classified, revealing the field every bit as diverse as it had been rendered with the elimination of the open access debates from consideration. The continued and loud protests of the ersatz drove those economists long affiliated with telecommunications policy debates nuts. Bruce Owen, for instance, would exclaim in 2007,

> Net neutrality debate has taken place in the rhetorical equivalent of the fog of war. The originators of the debate chose to invent new language to describe both a familiar economic problem and a familiar legal and regulatory solution to that problem. Much of the popular writing by pro-neutrality advocates is maddeningly vague and heavy with sloganeering. Their argument seems tailored chiefly for political effect rather than analytical rigor. It has taken several years for scholars on both sides to penetrate the fog. (Owen, 2007, pp. 15–16)

Back to basics: "Translated into the language used by economists, the debate is about preventing bad (anticompetitive) behavior by vertically integrated firms that enjoy market power at one stage or another of the vertical chain of production" (Owen, 2007, p. 16), to be "implemented through detailed price regulation, an approach that has generally failed, in the past, to improve consumer welfare relative to what might have been expected under an unregulated monopoly" (p. 14). Following in the footsteps of others, Owen reminds that the boundaries to this realm of knowledge are well policed: "The consensus view nowadays is that vertical integration is simply an instance of the determination of the scope of firms, as distinct from markets" (p. 16). Letters signed by numerous economists—some directly compensated for their efforts, some indirectly, some not at all—appeared making virtually the same points (Baumol et al., 2007).

Engagement with this set, too, hardly meant that such engagement was effective, even if it countered arguments expertly. Such research certainly emerged: Frischmann (2005) presented a theory of infrastructure to counter the dominant frame that was highly relevant. He emphasized a need to account for the positive externalities which accrue to a network maintained as neutral, externalities that the orthodoxies of the concept's opponents refused to consider—or if they did, they discounted them, preferring to emphasize the benefits of granting broadband providers the ability to consume all potential consumer surplus. Frischmann and van Schewick (2007), in the heat of the debates, struck at Yoo's contributions point by point in exactly his terms at the same time Bruce Owen was complaining that advocates of network neutrality just wouldn't speak the language. The problem was that these viewpoints simply didn't have the material buttress at that time to give them perceived pride of place: their potential sponsors in their realm didn't yet see the value in supporting such work. Google and other online giants did not see the need to lobby so aggressively since the broader environment was commercializing nicely already; the company was a latecomer, and an inept one to hear the consumer advocates tell it, when it finally did engage. (One advocate noted on background, "If Google had spent some money and time [during these years] we may have gotten net neutrality in a bill.") The effort by the National Cable and Telecommunications Association (NCTA) to buttress the work of legal scholars as Christopher Yoo throughout these years paid off in spades as the FTC leaned heavily on his research in their own take—which amount to a punt—on the issue in 2007, as Frischmann and van Schewick note. In the report, Yoo is cited no less than twenty times, nearly twice as many times as Wu (FTC, 2007).

Pro-neutrality advocates' neoliberal form of organization, importantly, worked in that it successfully gained entree to the realm of regulators and the congressional sphere. This was hardly intended: the original goal of Free Press, of course, had been to agitate from the outside, but as they gained new competencies, the value of an inside-outside strategy became very apparent—but a particular emphasis on the "inside" took precedence given the seeming successes advocates were experiencing. They were internalizing the lessons long ago expressed by Thomas Streeter in his description of the environment as an "interpretive community," among the most important being that the worst threat to a potentially destabilizing discourse was its being ignored (and *ignorable*), the greatest tactic in an interpretive framework's arsenal of defense (Streeter, 1996, pp. 117–118). Remaining unignorable was, at this stage, what was sought; and this involved maintaining a commitment to particular terms of debate, even as these risked angering the activists they were seeking to mobilize. Free Press spent these years gaining competencies on what were certainly considered the more under-the-radar components of media policy, wading into intercarrier compensation issues and special access; but acquiring such expertise was necessary, for it granted one access—even aside from the fact that these sleeper issues were of pivotal importance in their own right. While being crusaders for transparency and *ex parte* filings, advocates noted after the fact on background that they found themselves inadvertently violating the rules on occasion, but this was only because it was how all sides operated. As one advocate would confide on background, "If you [actually] filed some shit you said on the eighth floor [of the FCC building], you'd never get invited back."

The events of the years preceding the initial 2010 Open Internet proceedings only reinforced such thinking. For instance, the inclusion of a net neutrality policy statement in mergers of the mid-2000s stemmed from the entrance advocates gained via the sheer noise and political action driven by Congress. When two massive mergers were announced, the shape of telecommunications itself was transformed with the final reversal of the early 1980s separation between long distance and regional networks: Verizon was to merge with MCI; SBC, in turn, was absorbing its onetime parent, then turning around to rebrand *itself* as the "new" AT&T. With network neutrality having become a significant issue, there was active coordination between Google and groups like Free Press, who had obtained terrific access to (at least Democratic) Commissioners Michael Copps and Jonathan Adelstein. This had been built via years of active engagement with them at Free Press's National Conferences for Media Reform as well as the town halls which were held with them in cities across the country as an organizing tool. Copps in particular found himself a willing participant in many of these gatherings offered up by numerous national and regional activist groups. It was for these reasons that when these tremendous mergers went through, temporary network neutrality requirements were placed upon the new monoliths as a condition of their merger. Remarkable public involvement made Copps and Adelstein righteous defenders against further media consolidation; and to make no mistake, they took hits from congressional *Democrats* as well, getting raked over the coals at congressional oversight hearings at turns. The reason was obvious: standing up to powerful players as the largest media companies as well as powerful telecommunications operators was itself politically damaging for a legislator concerned about campaign contributions and the kind of support for a challenge these deep-pocketed entities could provide. Even at the local level, officials recognized how the discursive games needed to be played. In 2004, local organizers of a "Town Meeting on the Future of Media" in Portland, Oregon, asked that the Backbone Campaign, which sought to present an award to then-Commissioner Michael Copps, do it in private as opposed to during the meeting proper. The award was hardly controversial, nor was the group bestowing it, but the organizer feared *any* kind of connotation that might besmirch their continued involvement in local politics. The award was bestowed backstage after the proceedings had ended.[10]

The peak of pro-network neutrality influence, however, was only to come with Comcast's blocking of the BitTorrent protocol in 2007. The story is now legend: Comcast made a blunt-force decision to actually *break* ordinary networking protocols to identify and thwart BitTorrent packets. After months of prevaricating, the Associated Press subsidized network scientists to figure out what was going on, catching Comcast red-handed at blocking these packets. Yet they continued to lie about it (McChesney, 2013; McCullagh, 2007). Free Press mounted a formal complaint against Comcast with this evidence at the FCC, and in one of the most surreal episodes of the network neutrality debate, advocates would find an ally in the Republican, then–FCC chairman Kevin Martin—who was trying to push through a new loosening of media ownership rules and apparently sought to reduce some political heat for doing so.

Ben Scott, at this time policy director for Free Press, noted the remarkable happenstance which followed. He and Marvin Ammori, counsel for Free Press, were called into meetings with Martin and his chief of staff. "He said, remember where you hammered me on media ownership? What if I were to be on your side on Comcast-BitTorrent and you were in support of me?" (Ben Scott, personal communication, March 5, 2012). It was "not so much a vendetta with cable, but Kevin genuinely thought we were right on the policy." While not willing to pursue an overarching blanket order of nondiscrimination, he remained "irate that Comcast was lying to him about what they were doing. At one point, he even gave Comcast the opportunity to come clean in exchange for taking the boot off their throat, and they still said their lie." So followed a series of public hearings on the affair, with cooperation from the chairman but with advocates picking the panels. At Harvard's Kennedy School, overflow rooms were packed after Comcast was caught once again being deceptive, paying attendees off the street to take up the seats so as to prevent protesters from gaining access to the hearing itself. Activists photographed these paid attendees with their giveaway fluorescent lapel clips sleeping during the proceedings, posted later to the SavetheInternet.com blog. "All those public hearings on Comcast, we were in total cohoots with him the whole time. He let us pick the panel. Marvin and I sat with his general counsel and he couldn't believe he was made to talk to us. Later he ran for Republican congressman in the Virginia primary and lost as the far-right candidate. Marvin gave him a $50 contribution out of solidarity" (Ben Scott, personal communication, March 5, 2012). Martin was politically savvy and "didn't lose sleep at us calling him a sellout, he didn't care. But he said these guys, I can use them" (Derek Turner, personal communication, September 20, 2012).

For advocates, the Comcast-BitTorrent complaint represented a win-win. When the FCC issued its *Comcast* order that required Comcast to find a content-agnostic way to handle congestion instead of utilizing a protocol as proxy for undesirable traffic (FCC, 2008), it importantly kept broadband communication firmly within the category of a Title I "information service." This Order was very effectively testing the limits of that authority, rather than pushing for a full reclassification to a Title II telecommunications service. Barring reclassification, this was the desired outcome of activists pressing their complaint against the cable giant: the hope *was* that Comcast would test the FCC's mettle in court and that perhaps Obama, if elected, would defend it. First, it would be demonstrated that such traffic management could be done. Secondly, "We would either get backup for the approach of Title I, or the court would eviscerate the Title I justification, in which case the only option would be to go Title II. That was the whole game" (Ben Scott, personal communication, March 5, 2012). As for the public hearings, advocates full well recognized the game being played: the real action was occurring on the upper stories of the FCC building behind closed doors; in paying "fake protesters" to take up seats at the hearing, Comcast had played directly into their hands.

Playing this inside game is not inexpensive. Scott estimated that the whole Comcast complaint process and adjoining activism easily took up nearly half of Free Press's budget. "This notion that the system will produce the right outcome irrespective of resources is absurd. Even though we had the advantages we did, we almost lost" (Ben Scott, personal communication, March 5, 2012). Lest one forget, personalities abound at federal agencies: according to one account on background, the usual stalwart ally of net neutrality advocates, Jonathan Adelstein, almost voted against the *Comcast Order* out of his distaste for the idea that it would be *Martin* that cowed Comcast; it didn't help that Commissioner Robert McDowell, who was guaranteed to dissent, was whispering in his ear that the FCC's Order would get thrown out anyway by the courts.

In short, Comcast was, if temporarily, held to account—and a giant test case of Title I authority put at the ready—because Kevin Martin broke rank with the other Republicans on the FCC and worked with advocates. To someone outside Washington, this is likely difficult to square, especially since Martin's reputation at the FCC was that of a rather vengeful leader. In fact, a report documenting his "abuses of power" was released by Congress even without hearings (albeit just a month before Martin was slated to leave the agency), given that "due to the climate of fear that pervades the FCC … we found that key witnesses were unwilling to testify or even to have their names become known" (quoted in Masnick, 2008).

Shifting Terrain

As advocates gained steam and proved adept at finally harnessing the FCC's levers to achieve parts of their aims—with a *Republican* chairman, no less—and inspiring in Congress a succession of multiple Internet Freedom Preservation Acts in 2006 and 2007, even forcing presidential candidates to make public stances on the issue in the 2008 presidential election, production of knowledge by the Russian doll turned to performing two sets of tasks. One was to provide additional buttress to the idea that network neutrality was hardly necessary, or, if a solution *was* warranted, that "third ways" could be found. Another tack that emerged with force was work arguing that the FCC may not be the correct place to even consider such issues; that this was, plainly and simply, a problem of vertical combinations that antitrust was the optimal frame to utilize.

Nuechterlein (2009), for instance, revived thought, hardly new, that the FTC was the appropriate venue. Such argument was of long standing, extending to the 1990s, if not further: Peter Huber (at this time part of the Manhattan Institute for Policy Research, funded by "almost all of the phone companies since the 1990s"[11]) had made a case for eliminating the FCC itself (Huber, 1997) and is cited in Nuechterlein's thinking. Nuechterlein's solution: "Under the arrangement proposed here, competition issues would be addressed by one of the two antitrust agencies (DoJ [Department of Justice] or the FTC); consumer-protection issues would be addressed by the FTC's Bureau of Consumer Protection; and the FCC would maintain jurisdiction over residual, non-competition-related issues within its peculiar expertise" (Nuechterlein, 2009, p. 22). This would be for the reason that since

> these agencies regulate the economy at large rather than a single industry, they are less vulnerable than the FCC to capture by industry or interest-group factions; they are less likely to develop industry-specific bureaucracies with incentives to keep themselves relevant through over-regulation; and, because of their firm grounding in antitrust enforcement, they are more likely to resolve competition-oriented disputes dispassionately and on their economic merits. I would thus revive in this context the competition-policy model that prevailed for much of the final quarter of the last century: a regime in which antitrust authorities, rather than industry-specific regulators, take the lead in addressing vertical-leveraging claims against providers of telecommunications transmission platforms. (Nuechterlein, 2009, p. 21)

The benefit of the FTC and the DOJ was *precisely* their generalist orientation—and the fact that they were held to strict standards in the form of merger guidelines.

> [The] DoJ and the FTC have gained invaluable perspective on competition disputes by exercising, between them, oversight of the entire American economy. That perspective allows them to keep their eyes on dispassionate analysis and diminishes the significance of lobbyists for particular interest groups.... When confronted with a dispute about whether a large firm's business practices are "fair," their first response tends to be: "what type of competition dispute is presented here, and how does antitrust law frame the analysis for such disputes?" Obviously, in answering that question, the FTC and DoJ may be subject to any number of biases, but they are at least asking the right question. (Nuechterlein, 2009, pp. 58–59)

In contrast, the FCC, he posits, "too often asks, 'what do we need to do in order to remain important players in the telecommunications industry?'" (Nuechterlein, 2009, p. 60).

To make such claims requires several erasures. The common tack is to erase all activism as having had any influence over the direction of rollout of broadband telecommunications or its operation. Nuechterlein erases the late 1990s and early 2000s activism from the story. The open access debate is described as related but "antiquated"; "That debate had focused on the rights of independent ISPs such as AOL and EarthLink. It had become clear by the early 2000s, however, that broadband technology made such ISPs, if not irrelevant, at least much less central to a user's Internet experience" (Nuechterlein, 2009, p. 25). But this, again, was not a natural progression; as we saw, this was only because deliberate policy choices had been made. It is equally possible to establish networks that served as conduits for various types of ISPs. In fact, the whole problem with the *present* debate is that the riffraff simply wouldn't behave. Cited in this paper is former FTC chairman Timothy Muris, echoing economist Bruce Owen: "net neutrality has become an epithet devoid of any analytical content" (p. 26). "As a glance at SavetheInternet.com makes clear," Nuechterlein spits, advocates "portray[] the issues as a war of good (edge providers) against evil (access providers), with barely a nod to the complex economic trade-offs at stake. That advocacy is often uncritically accepted by the popular media, and it has surfaced, largely unfiltered by economic nuance, into popular political discourse" (p. 56). He continues later: "Today's net neutrality debate is a study in rhetorical ugliness. What it badly needs, if it is to be resolved properly, is a referee inclined towards calm objectivity and a rigorous adherence to economic principle.... And the FCC is less equipped to deliver on those aspirations than either of the two antitrust agencies" (p. 58).

In an interesting footnote, Nuechterlein reads the *Comcast* cease-and-desist order as resistant to emergent stands of antitrust economics which are untroubled by vertical integrations:

> In the *Comcast Order*, the Commission noted that it did "not decide today whether other actual or potential conduct, such as giving real-time communications packets (e.g., VoIP [voice over Internet protocol]) higher priority than other packets or giving higher priority to packets of a particular, unaffiliated content provider pursuant to an arms-length agreement, would violate federal policy." ... Although this passage should be taken at face value—the Commission did not address the issue because it had not thought it through—the modifier "unaffiliated" before "content provider" may reveal the reflexive mistrust of non-antitrust-oriented policymakers for vertical integration. (Nuechterlein, 2009, pp. 33–34n32; citations omitted)

Indeed, there was a "proper" conception of network neutrality:

> No matter how one comes out on these various subdebates within the net neutrality discussion, the following generalization seems valid: Proposals for net neutrality rules could have merit only if (i) the broadband Internet access market is inadequately competitive and will remain so indefinitely; (ii) such market concentration will give incumbent broadband providers both the incentive and the ability to discriminate against specific applications providers; (iii) such discrimination would harm *consumers* and not just particular *providers*; and (iv) any such consumer harm would exceed the costs of regulatory intervention. (Nuechterlein, 2009, p. 43)

Thus the debate boiled down to three "core antitrust concepts: about market power, market failures, market definition, and the costs and benefits of government intervention in a rapidly evolving, high-technology market" (p. 43).

For good measure Nuechterlein recalls some of the adjoining favorite arguments against any notion that nondiscrimination principles were necessary at all. The Internet has never really been a neutral platform, and net neutrality rules would hardly render it so (Nuechterlein, 2009, p. 36). Content delivery network services which put content closer to end users are themselves unfair mechanisms (pp. 37–38)—although making such arguments is to leave aside the issue was always in relation to network providers' power. But he adds his own flavor of breathtaking philosophy: "The American marketplace of ideas has prospered for centuries even though the government has rarely given anyone an enforceable right to speak as loudly as anyone else or through exactly the same channels of expression," then comparing requiring ISPs to carry content to forcing newspapers to carry content (p. 38), a regurgitation of the application of First Amendment arguments to allow providers to *deny* speech. Further, "there is a radical mismatch between the speculative free-expression concerns raised by net neutrality advocates and the ambitiously interventionist 'solutions' they would impose today. So far, no one has identified a concrete 'problem' to be fixed in the marketplace of ideas" (p. 38). Even more stunning, perhaps, he waves away concerns that Comcast *was* blocking BitTorrent traffic with the logic that

> even if the FCC's criticisms of Comcast's treatment of the BitTorrent peer-to-peer technology were valid on the merits, Comcast's actions still would have been completely content-neutral: Comcast would not have "discriminated" against *viewpoints* at all, much less in ways that could threaten the marketplace of ideas, and much less in ways that could justify government intervention to protect that marketplace. If a discernible problem does arise, there will be time enough to contemplate appropriately tailored solutions to it. And even then, such problems, whatever they may be, would be exceedingly unlikely by themselves to support the full-blown scheme of economic regulation proposed by net neutrality advocates. (Nuechterlein, 2009, pp. 38–39)

Indeed, production in this vein was pervasive, and the authors were sure to reinforce the message by referencing each other. Yoo (2007) made similar points and is cited by Nuechterlein alongside Yoo's other efforts; the PFF compiled a book-length treatment as well that touches on similar arguments, arguing that their favored framework involved "a continuing level of administrative regulation to be carried out predominantly through adjudication in complaint proceedings, albeit under a competition-based antitrust-like statutory standard that will constrain the agency in a way that the agency's broad public interest authority generally did not" (Progress and Freedom Foundation, 2006, p. 42). This framework had been developed by their own "Digital Age Communications Act Project," whose working groups offered a veritable who's who of the neoliberal Russian doll that enveloped not just political conservatives and their advocacy arms but also more moderate comers from think tanks and the academy; all were welcome—as the point was always the continued constitution of debate: not its resolution, but certainly a maintenance of a *trajectory*. We find representatives of the predictable corporate think tanks—the Free State Foundation (Randolph May), the Competitive Enterprise Institute (Braden Cox), the Heritage Foundation (James Gattuso, also representing the Roe Institute for Economic Policy Studies), the PFF (Adam Thierer, Raymond Gifford, Kyle Dixon), the Progressive Policy Institute (Robert "Rob" D. Atkinson), the Mercatus Center (Jerry Ellig), the Manhattan Institute (Thomas Hazlett), and the Heartland Institute (Steven Titch). Brookings is also present, represented by Robert Crandall. Alongside these are representatives of the academy: Northwestern University School of Law (James Speta), University of California, Berkeley (Howard Shelanski, Michael Katz and Philip Weiser), University of Colorado (Douglas Sicker and Dale Hatfield), Kansas State University (Dennis Weisman), New York University's Stern School of Business (Lawrence J. White), Duke University School of Law (Stuart Benjamin), Wharton School of Business at the University of Pennsylvania (Gerald Faulhaber), Stanford Institute for Economic Policy Research (Gregory Rosston), George Washington University (John Duffy), Columbia University (Michael Riordan), the Columbia Institute for Tele-Information (Robert "Bob" C. Atkinson), and the California Institute of Technology (Simon Wilkie). Rounding out those represented was the nascent right-wing political action group FreedomWorks (by Wayne Brough).

Van Schewick (2010, 2015) would later directly engage such thinking. Drawing on the efforts of conservatives and neoliberals alike to point to antitrust as a panacea in this conflict, she draws distinct differences between the views of antitrust enthusiasts and both longtime and emergent defenders of net neutrality. Antitrusters "interpret concerns about blocking, discrimination, or other practices as concerns about anticompetitive vertical leveraging or vertical foreclosure and apply an antitrust framework to evaluate and address these concerns"; in contrast, "most network neutrality proponents base their calls for regulation on a theoretical framework that considers a wider range of economic and noneconomic harms.... Due to these differences, proponents of an antitrust framework and proponents of a broader framework will reach differing conclusions when evaluating proposals" (van Schewick, 2015, pp. 16–17). Network neutrality, of course, was always about a series of trade-offs (as any policy decision is):

> According to this broader theoretical framework, network neutrality regulation serves three major goals. Most generally, network neutrality rules are intended to preserve the Internet's ability to serve as an open, general-purpose infrastructure that provides value to society over time in various economic and noneconomic ways. More specifically, network neutrality rules aim, first, to foster innovation in applications. Fostering application innovation not only is critical for economic growth, but also increases the Internet's potential to create value in the social, cultural, and political domains. Second, network neutrality rules are designed to protect users' ability to choose how they want to use the network, without interference from network providers. This ability to choose is fundamental if the Internet is to create maximum value for users and for society. Third, network neutrality rules aim to preserve the Internet's ability to improve democratic discourse, facilitate political organization and action, and provide a decentralized environment for social, cultural, and political interaction in which anybody can participate. (van Schewick, 2015, pp. 17–18)

She outlines four precepts a nondiscrimination rule should fulfill: innovation without permission, user choice, application-agnosticism, and low costs of application innovation (van Schewick, 2015, pp. 21–22). Alongside these, "a nondiscrimination rule should not constrain the evolution of the network more than is necessary to reach the goals of network neutrality regulation and should not impose other unnecessary social costs" (p. 23). Lastly, "the rule should make it easy to determine which behavior is and is not allowed in order to provide certainty for industry participants" (p. 23). The trade-offs of such concerns include limitation of development of the "core" of networks—limiting providers' ability to "realize all potential efficiency gains or optimize the network in favor of the applications of the day"—and a possible reduction in profits (p. 18). There may be regulatory costs, as in any regulatory regimen, which "burden providers, users, and society as a whole" (p. 18). However, "As Tim Wu put it, [forgoing the social benefits] is like selling the painting to get a better frame. Based on this reasoning, proponents of network neutrality resolve the trade-off in favor of the social benefits" (p. 19).

Van Schewick's outline of the problematics that accrue to applying antitrust analysis to the problem of online discrimination is important. For her, antitrust is wholly insufficient for addressing the harms network neutrality advocates are concerned about. One issue is the frame: casting the concerns of network neutrality proponents as concerns about "anticompetitive vertical leveraging" misses much of what they are trying to prevent. "The term 'vertical foreclosure' applies to situations in which a monopolist in a primary market—that is, a provider of Internet access service—uses its market power in the first market to deny firms in a second, vertically related market—that is, the market for a specific application—access to that second market" (van Schewick, 2015, p. 55). However, "over the years, the views of U.S. antitrust scholars and courts toward these practices have evolved considerably. Today, U.S. antitrust law condemns vertical leveraging or vertical foreclosure only if the exclusionary conduct meets the criteria of section 2 of the Sherman Act, which prohibits monopolization or attempts to monopolize" (p. 55).

This holds several important ramifications. First, a provider's discrimination against content or applications would trigger antitrust concerns only to the extent that *it participates in the marketplace for that kind of content or application itself* (van Schewick, 2015, p. 56). But network neutrality advocates were concerned about *any* kind of discrimination: there are countless instances in which a network provider might block an application of a variety it might not supply itself. Even if the reasons were hardly political in intent, doing so for network management reasons themselves remains a concern that similarly isn't touched by antitrust law. Second, antitrust law is only invoked if the network provider "in the market for a specific application must be reasonably capable of creating, increasing, or maintaining monopoly power in the market for that application or in the market for Internet access services" (p. 58). Again, advocates would find such conduct harmful even if the provider were *not* necessarily capable of such control. Third, in this vein, "U.S. antitrust law generally only condemns exclusionary conduct if there is a reasonable likelihood that the behavior will harm competition, not just competitors, by worsening the structure or performance of the affected market" (p. 58). Antitrust enthusiasts had long argued that the case against net neutrality was that policy should protect *competition,* not *competitors,* as if this were a gold standard. This is, however, antitrust law to the letter: "A firm's exclusionary behavior that just harms one or more competitors (e.g., by enlarging that firm's market share at the expense of its competitors) without creating or sufficiently threatening the higher prices or lower output or quality associated with monopoly is outside the scope of section 2 of the Sherman Act" (p. 58).

Further, what is considered socially harmful conduct represents an incredibly high standard. "A network provider's discriminatory conduct in the market for a specific application would have to drive affected applications from the market for that application, prevent new entry into an application market that the network provider has already monopolized, or impair the application provider's ability to compete effectively by forcing it to operate at a less efficient scale" (van Schewick, 2015, p. 58). As Yoo argued in his earlier work (to soothe fears, not to critique the antitrust regimen), many times these applications or content (like Netflix, for instance) are national in scope, meaning they might be available via some provider in one locale but not in another. But due to its availability *somewhere*, antitrust would not consider this a harm, even if users of the network excluding the content had no other options to obtain it. Of course, proponents *would* find the inability of an audience in, say, Sandusky, Ohio, from seeing particular content as in itself socially harmful by their standard. Network neutrality proponents would find it problematic for anyone, served even by a tiny provider, to be denied access to content or applications of their choice. Worse, "In the Internet context, discrimination will often be profitable even if it does not monopolize the market for the application in question. While the resulting harm may be irrelevant for antitrust law, network neutrality proposals are driven by concerns about a broader range of harms than the specific type of 'harm to competition' that antitrust law is concerned with" (p. 60). She points to a reduction of incentives to innovate if one was unsure anyone could access their new application; thus, discrimination does not just deprive some users of a new development, it deprives all when new innovations are not developed. Finally, the damage to democratic discourse is another harm. "All of these harms arise even if the behavior is unlikely to monopolize the market for the application in question" (p. 60).

Pro-neutrality proponents are left with the apparent paradox that those of the antitrust-only set believed that "conduct that is designed to increase the network provider's private efficiency should not be considered socially harmful" (van Schewick, 2015, p. 61); in fact, "*discriminatory* conduct that is justified by a legitimate business purpose would be classified as socially beneficial" (p. 61; emphasis added). For antagonists of network neutrality, discrimination to manage congestion is always procompetitive and socially beneficial discrimination. If this was put to the end of recovering fixed costs, costs of upgrades or network innovation (itself "often mentioned as another example of a business justification that may legitimize discriminatory conduct"), "the efficiencies created by the conduct do not need to outweigh any harm to competition. Nor does it matter whether there is a less restrictive alternative that might reach the same goal with less harm to competition" (p. 62). *But this is exactly the point to advocates:* "Network neutrality proponents evaluate nondiscriminatory conduct based on its social costs and benefits"; in contrast, "network providers make decisions based on the conduct's private costs and benefits," and "these decisions often diverge" (p. 62). For proponents, network neutrality was necessary "precisely because what is privately efficient for network providers is not necessarily socially efficient. Under these circumstances, the fact that certain behavior is privately efficient for the network provider cannot automatically excuse the behavior" (p. 62). For proponents, "network neutrality rules are based on the assessment that the social benefits associated with network neutrality rules are more important than the social costs, including the loss of short-term efficiencies" (p. 63).

Framed this way, the core problem for van Schewick is a perpetual incommensurability between network neutrality proponents and skeptics. Adding to the difficulty, she notes that network neutrality proponents had started to incorporate antitrust language loosely into their pleadings. Unfortunately for them, while unmooring network neutrality from its ontic moorings carried few costs, the (mis)use of antitrust terminology was set to backfire, being met with derision by the law and economics set. There was a "correct" way to think through these issues that worked to advocates' disadvantage, even as what they argued was not *technically* incorrect outside the realm of antitrust and its minutiae:

> For proponents of a narrow scope of network neutrality rules, terms like "anticompetitive" or "harm to competition" are meant to evoke the standards used in antitrust analysis, where behavior is only anticompetitive if it harms competition, not just a competitor.... By contrast, proponents of network neutrality use terms like "anticompetitive" or "harm to competition" in a looser sense that is not tied to antitrust law. To them, any discriminatory behavior that singles out specific applications or classes of applications for differential treatment distorts competition among applications or classes of applications. This harms the competitive process, and thereby competition, by making it impossible for all applications to compete on a level playing field, without interference from network providers. (van Schewick, 2015, p. 65)

Van Schewick performs a terrific service in clearly delineating these myriad approaches to the topic, applying herself a frame stemming from her own background in both engineering and economic theory. All the same, the value of undertaking this task may give one pause when the broader labor wrought of its efforts is considered. Critics such as Candeub (2012) look at both the likes of Yoo and van Schewick and make the blanket statement that both scholars' treatments of the issue "reflect[] a disturbing, perhaps endemic trend in communications legal scholarship—on both the right and left—to latch on to some model, treat it as truth, and avoid critically engaging its limitations and assumptions" (p. 673). Such a critique might match the concerns of critical scholars of communication—that these debates are all problematic in and of themselves in that the language of markets is itself the frame that unites all these perspectives, and it is this frame that requires change (see, for instance, Blevins & Brown, 2010; Day, 2017). However, to leave the debate there is to miss the actual historical trajectory of these arguments themselves. Van Schewick herself may well be contributing not just to a discourse that privileges markets but also one that performs in exactly the way that the neoliberal thought collective desired: poking at the core concepts of antitrust analysis itself is something that *helps* the broader cause rather than hurts it; neoliberalism is itself built of ambivalence, after all, not through definitive answers. That is: van Schewick was hardly adding *heterogeneity* to this debate; she was rendering it still more diverse, drawing lines in the sand that would be useful for the categorization of future offerings.

Calling for a discourse that floats above markets—to call for a desire to remove markets from the picture and offer a social-democratic view of broadband operation and communications, perhaps—misses the true lesson of this time period. The long game is to tilt the *entire playing field itself,* even to accommodate those miscreants who might desire to remove markets from the picture. As part of the same paper, van Schewick very astutely outlines the myriad forms of network neutrality (or its lack) proposed by scholars, think tanks, activists, and industry players; but the very description of the varying stances that van Schewick offers is less an outline of a substantive argument than it is *an epistemic game playing out.* The public was quite clear on what they wanted defended; by the same token, keeping this *production* in motion restrained the discussions that took place at a formal level.

For it is production that matters in this instance; and the players may *believe* that they are contributing to the broader issues of the day (and they may well be incorporated into the Orders and reports and notices of proposed rulemakings) and point to this as evidence of same; and perhaps at one point this may have been true, but it now operates in a different register. This similarly goes beyond notions of corruption and paymasters on the parts of those offering these takes. Nuechterlein offers this disclosure in his article: "Although I have represented broadband companies on net neutrality issues, the views expressed here are my own" (2009, p. 19). But the potential influence of the paymaster is moot: the reason he represented these companies is precisely because they value his views as is; the opinions, tacks, and output of these individuals would hardly be swayed by corporate largesse. It would not; it was not necessary. Such support merely kept the process moving and enabled the production of discourse, which was what was sufficient, because whether these economists believed that their studies were being used or not, the tenor of our times is such that these economists themselves were being used. It worked marvelously, at least until the narrative consumed and repeated by the ersatz, through time and action, were able to secure the message to such a strong *intuitive* current it could not be ignored.

I can assure as well that the civil servants I met at the FCC and beyond sincerely believed that these contributions added to the debate, and they were sincere in actually seeking broad input on these initiatives. One staffer, still speaking on background, wondered to me why the throngs who would occasionally protest FCC actions outside the building just didn't come in to express their grievances in a sit-down setting. Yet even such discussions in today's world amount to a channeling of effort into activity which both helps and hurts their cause. Helps: they may well get taken seriously. Hurts: their engagement might hint that their activities, once viewed as mysterious, threatening, or just annoying (and which could push the horizon further away), can be categorized among the available options presented by the logics pervading an actually diverse epistemic setting and thus have sense made of them—they become one more voice in the pot which, when the whiteboard is sketched, doesn't matter anyway. Diverse settings are far more comfortable than the terror rendered by a horizon one cannot see.

Wrenching Defeat from the Jaws of Victory

With President Obama elected in 2008, and with advocates having had the opportunity to be part of the tech policy transition team, this push toward insider access appeared ready to pay off. The FCC, under Julius

Genachowski, represented all the hallmarks of openness. Activists who were privy to conversations with the transition team on tech and media policy issues (and, in fact, advised the team) noted that Genachowski was "the guy that signed off on the platform" that included such policies as network neutrality. Additionally, providing what advocates interpreted as wind in their sails, fellow advocates were being siphoned up into the Obama administration in key advisory positions or even as decision makers themselves; for but a couple prominent instances, Consumers Union's Gene Kimmelman would go to the Department of Justice; Free Press's Ben Scott would move to Department of State; and Susan Crawford became President Obama's Special Assistant for Science, Technology, and Innovation and Policy. There was such a draw up into the administration from the ranks of the nonprofits that one person recalled concern that the infrastructure's institutional memory was being hollowed out. The FCC launched a series of websites, such as Broadband.gov, and other blogs where individuals could "upvote" commentaries left by others. It all *felt* very open and transparent. A *National Broadband Plan*—the first of its kind and hardly uncontroversial in itself—was issued. Genachowski finally announced a Notice of Proposed Rulemaking (NPRM) in 2009 to institute "Open Internet" rules, following on the heels of and applying the approach of the Comcast Order of 2008.

This moment would be considered the high point for activists of the Genachowski FCC. The original proposal sought to codify Powell's "four freedoms" and build on them with strict nondiscrimination and transparency rules. These, however, would avoid any effort to shift the works into the sturdier foundation of Title II: rather, they would remain justified using an argument couched in the FCC's Title I authority (FCC, 2009a), just as Chairman Martin had done with *Comcast*. This was a dicey move given the courts might well find against their actions against Comcast. (Advocates, after the fact and on background, confided that the lawyers at the commission were well aware of the need to "go hard" in this NPRM just in case the FCC lost in court—"This was not a case of them not understanding what was necessary or misreading the law; they knew"—but Genachowski would not do it, keeping any discussion of "reclassification" of broadband to a Title II service out.)

The debates that transpired on release of the proposed rules had every appearance of ferocity. Once the NPRM (FCC, 2009a) was released, in late 2009, early 2010, and mid-2010, the FCC held a series of workshops inside and outside of Washington on debates long played out. On December 8, 2009, one such event was held that covered "Technical Advisory Process Workshop on Broadband Network Management" (FCC, 2009b); on December 15, 2009, "Speech, Democratic Engagement, and the Open Internet" (FCC, 2009c); on January 13, 2010, "Innovation, Investment, and the Open Internet" (FCC, 2010e); on January 19, 2010, "Consumers, Transparency, and the Open Internet" (FCC, 2010c); and finally, on April 28, 2010, "Approaches to Preserving the Open Internet" (FCC, 2010b). President Obama himself extolled the concept at least eighty-three times across various addresses, blog posts, and beyond and in a positive light.[12]

Yet at one and the same time these performed the function of revealing once again the boundary-policing functions that the gatekeepers can wield once the issue has been rendered diverse. Following the NPRM's release, instead of acting quickly, the chairman let the proceeding drag and allowed industry opposition to truly mobilize. Mobilize they did: telecommunications and cable lobbies are among the most powerful in Washington, and they succeeded in convincing seventy-two Democrats in October 2009 to send a letter to Genachowski cautioning against strong net neutrality rules. This was perhaps predictable, given that many of these legislators had received not insignificant funding from incumbent operators themselves. Advocates on background shared with me stories of Obama himself, pressured by the telecom and cable lobbies (and even perhaps on the advice of advisors such as Lawrence Summers, who saw other matters as higher priority), now himself pressuring Genachowski against strong action; Democratic donors similarly sounded concerned in all of the wrong ways.

Shortly after the release of a *National Broadband Plan,* the D.C. Circuit provided the kind of clarity that advocates sought during the *Comcast* ordeal. The D.C. Circuit slapped down the FCC's *Comcast Order* in its entirety but not on its merits: the question was entirely over the legal framework utilized—the attempt to use the spare tools of Title I to effectively treat operators as if they were subject to a Title II regime. As Marvin Ammori put it in the wake of the case, the "worst-case scenario for us was that we would get an unclear answer on jurisdiction" (Ammori, 2010). Given this Order was *intended* by advocates to either prevail or leave no option for the FCC *but* to adopt a Title II framework to accomplish its goals,

> The last thing we wanted was for the DC Circuit to avoid the key question of the test case on appeal—does the FCC have jurisdiction to protect consumers,

> preserve the open Internet, encourage deployment of new technologies.... We were given the guidance we wanted, although the answer we didn't.... This clarity derives partly from our case before the FCC, where we urged the FCC to adopt every single possible basis of jurisdiction under Title I, so that a reviewing court could either reject them all or sustain one. (Ammori, 2010)

In the end, the answer of the court was unequivocal. Ammori summed it this way:

> The court decision is a stunning, sweeping defeat for the FCC and for its ability to protect consumers, foster competition and innovation, and preserve the Internet's role as an engine of free speech and democratic discourse. It means, essentially, that the largest phone and cable companies can secretly block dozens of technologies used by large corporations, nonprofits, and individuals to speak and organize, and the FCC can do nothing to protect us. (The subject of the Free Press-Comcast case, which this decision vacated, was precisely this factual scenario.) Tuesday's decision also means the FCC cannot implement many aspects of its recently-issued *National Broadband Plan*, and the US will continue to fall behind the rest of the world with far slower, more expensive, and less innovative broadband service, strangling our economy and harming our democracy.... Really. At least, that's the effect if the Obama FCC continues to follow the legal framework adopted under the Bush administration—a framework that requires the FCC to play football with a tennis racket, a framework for authority that the DC Circuit just beat to death, shot, and then drowned. (Ammori, 2010)

The court decision provided the opening that advocates had long sought from the open access debates onward: finally, presenting itself was the opportunity to right what they saw as a wrong. In their view, the FCC now definitively seemed to have no other recourse but to reclassify the provision of Internet service to Title II of the Telecommunications Act if it sought to do what it claimed to want to do. They pushed hard for this. Free Press continued to produce reports to inform the proceeding, with one in particular calling attention to the use of deep packet inspection, which would hand broadband providers the tools they needed to determine what content was passing through their wires for purposes of discrimination (Riley & Scott, 2009). Recall, these concerns had been raised by the Center for Digital Democracy almost ten years previous! They broadcast the results far and wide, returning to them again and again. Yet, in the end, none of these debates seemed to have moved the FCC one way or another.

What followed the D.C. Circuit's decision was months of frustration and struggle. The FCC floated its own "third way" that amounted to a "Title II lite" approach that advocates favored (Genachowski, 2010). This approach would have treated "the transmission component of broadband access service—and only this component—as a telecommunications service," applying "only a handful of provisions of Title II ... that, prior to the *Comcast* decision, were widely believed to be within the Commission's purview for broadband" (Genachowski, 2010, p. 5). The FCC would then forbear from "application of the many sections of the Communications Act that are unnecessary and inappropriate for broadband access service" and "place up-front forbearance and meaningful boundaries to guard against regulatory overreach" (p. 5). Advocates mobilized to support this position, producing such publications for the press and public consumption entitled "The truth about the third way" to counter industry talking points that were now circulating (Sridhar, 2010). But the sole lesson that the telecommunications companies took was that if they roared, Genachowski could be cowed. The Title II–lite approach went nowhere, and the FCC returned to the same strategy that Martin had taken with Comcast, even despite the court decision: that is, the chosen tack was going to be "play football with a tennis racket, a framework for authority that the DC Circuit just beat to death, shot, and then drowned" (Ammori, 2010).

If the Save the Internet Coalition represented nonprofits, individual creators, small business interests and others pushing for a level playing field, the larger corporate equivalent—which did allow DC-based advocates to join in—was the Open Internet Coalition. This entity became more of the "center of gravity" as the year wore on. This was the umbrella organization for tech operations that had started to establish their own DC presence. A more corporate-centric gathering, it described itself as a coalition of "consumers, grassroots organizations, and technology and Internet companies," including Amazon.com, the American Civil Liberties Union, the Computer and Communications Industry Association, Consumers Union, Data Foundry, DISH Network, EarthLink, eBay, Entertainment Consumers Association, Evite, Free Press, Google, IAC [InterActiveCorp], Internet2, Media Access Project, Mozilla, Netflix, New America Foundation, PayPal, Public Knowledge, Skype, Sony Electronics, Ticketmaster, TiVo, Twitter, U.S. PIRG [Public Interest Research Group], and YouTube (Open Internet Coalition, 2010). Thus there was overlap between the two groups in the form of the DC-based advocacy organizations, but the interests contained in both diverged in numerous ways as to how far they were willing to compromise. The political economy of these struggles was also shifting: while Google in the early fights had been at least an (underinvolved) ally, now it was starting to become a provider of access services themselves with the resultant shift in interest in the issue.

The summer saw the fracturing of longtime alliances on the issue, a wound inflicted by the slow-pedaling of the FCC. The agency commenced increased discussions that advocates revealed were geared toward compromise between the Internet companies as well as the conduit companies. If the energy in the 2006–2007 fights lay with activists, the companies' coalition now held sway. One advocate noted on background something quite telling—that once Genachowski steered away from reclassification to Title II, his senior team all left. The advocate moaned, "the worst thing about it is what AT&T learned was that all they needed to do was rough up Julius and he would bend. Anytime he got in a scrap they would punch him in the nose and he would back off." As far as activist groups were concerned, the opportunity provided by the demise of the *Comcast* order was being lost: the whole objective, recall, was to either bless or eviscerate a non–Title II approach to the question of net neutrality. The courts had delivered a very clear answer. Yet here was Genachowski, who had expressed the right sentiments during Obama's election campaign, who had blessed all of these plans, now deciding to try the same quixotic approach likely to get knocked down in the courts once again.

Over the summer of 2010 advocates noted that Google was drifting closer to the phone companies; they took note of the increasing meetings happening behind closed doors, and advocates began to sound their former allies out. "You had a lot of public interest groups gravitating toward a company-run table. Some like ourselves, New America, Public Knowledge sat at it, but didn't feel this Open Internet Coalition was speaking for us; we didn't feel represented" (Craig Aaron, personal communication, September 9, 2012). Representative Henry Waxman attempted to broker a compromise, and this created friction among the various DC-based institutional players on the public interest side. Some groups favored a compromise, while others, such as Free Press, felt they had already compromised enough; the organization leaked the bill surreptitiously but were discovered when they hadn't covered their tracks well enough in the metadata of the file. But even as the Waxman bill divided allies who were pushing for network neutrality, it ultimately was done in by yet another surprise: the issue had become partisan. Organizations like FreedomWorks stoked the flames of the Tea Party movement, projecting "government takeovers" of health care and now the Internet, backed by the largesse of the telecommunications and cable lobbies.

> The Tea Party would not allow the Republicans to sign off on it. The bill was brokered by Waxman, it was approved by AT&T and Verizon and the NCTA; Representative Barton [R-TX], who was then chair of the [House Energy and Commerce] Committee, was initially favorably inclined. Then Marsha Blackburn, a Tea Party favorite on the committee, [announced] network neutrality is regulation of the Internet, it's bad bad bad. That marked when net neutrality became not just a superpartisan issue, but actually got out of control from the companies [themselves]. (Harold Feld, personal communication, September 27, 2012)

This was no accident, of course. Whereas for years the national gun lobby stood side by side with MoveOn, "By the end of 2010 it was clear that if you were a Republican you were now supposed to hate net neutrality, the same way you hate Obamacare, and you hate the law of the sea treaty, and you hate cap and trade—on the list of things you now have to hate, unless you want a primary challenge, is net neutrality, and that substantially changes it" (Harold Feld, personal communication, September 27, 2012).

Advocates faced the added challenge that numerous long-standing civil rights organizations, joined by the Minority Media and Telecommunications Council (now the Multicultural Media and Telecommunications Council—MMTC) expressed concerns that strong network neutrality rules would stymie deployment of broadband services, with an assist from their long-standing partners in the telecommunications and cable industries from whom they received support (McMurria, 2016). While the concerns were real, advocates and these groups found themselves at loggerheads. In 2013, the Center for Public Integrity published a story outlining the strong ties the MMTC possessed to the telecommunications and cable industry, hinting strongly that there was a virtual quid pro quo on offer (McLure, 2013), the intonations of which put on full display the distrust of the media reform advocacy groups and the counterstance provided by these organizations. There are several ways of reading this; while the inclination of some advocates may have been to assume that these organizations were "captured" by the largesse of their donors, McMurria leads one to believe what might well be operative is clashing theories of change. As González and Torres (2011) describe in their own history of media activism, and to which McMurria (2016) also alludes, one of the chief strategies of the post–civil rights era was to try and work with corporations to change from within, sometimes working in cooperation with them. There were, of course, moments where quid pro quo at least seemed to be *exactly* what was going on: in a legendary example, it was revealed that Representative Bobby Rush (a Democrat from Illinois), who did not favor net neutrality, was found to have received a $1 million grant from SBC/AT&T for a local community center; *Black Commentator* called him "AT&T's Million Dollar Man" (Stills, 2006). Newer civil rights groups, like Color of Change, would join pro-neutrality advocates and rebut the claims of the older institutions. Color of Change was among those 2010 groups who pushed back against Rush's near-ascension to ranking member of the House Subcommittee on Communications, Technology, and the Internet, pointing to sizable donations from cable and telecommunications interests as well as his past stance on the issue (Gustin, 2010). Only the advocates from the MMTC and the older civil rights groups know if corporate largesse affected their opinions on the issue. Nonetheless, likely what we observe here is clashes in paradigms of change, combined with gestures by the telecommunications companies and cable companies toward some of their concerns; the cooperative approach to achieving change was something that the telecommunications and cable companies could exploit in the new environment. Nonetheless, real rifts developed between the legacy organizations and DC-based media reform advocates, and these rifts were also easily exploitable by dominant broadband conduit interests.

On June 23, Free Press and SavetheInternet.com ran a full-page ad in the *Washington Post* "to express our outrage that the Federal Communications Commission held closed-door meetings with industry representatives and lobbyists about important Internet policies" (Tady, 2010). Free Press president Josh Silver called the meetings "inexcusable.... After the financial crisis and the oil spill, you would think the Obama administration would have learned a lesson. But we won't stand by and watch the Internet go the way of Wall Street and the Gulf of Mexico" (Tady, 2010); responding to Genachowski's chief of staff, Ed Lazarus, who sought haplessly to explain the meetings on the FCC blog, Silver called it a "fig leaf attempting to cover for what appears to be secret negotiations to sell out the future of the Internet. It's a preposterous assumption that inviting comments from the public carries the same weight as a face-to-face meeting with some of the most powerful industry leadership and lobbyists in Washington" (Tady, 2010). The text of the ad read:

> Big oil, big banks, big phone, big cable, same $ellout. FCC Chairman Julius Genachowski's top deputies are meeting behind closed doors with industry lobbyists to cut a deal that would effectively hand over control of the Internet to Verizon, Comcast and AT&T.... President Obama, you promised to take a "back seat to no one" in protecting Net Neutrality and free speech online. Don't let our Internet go the way of Wall Street and the Gulf of Mexico. Insist that the Federal Communications Commission protect the future of communications in America. Stand up to Big Phone and Big Cable. Save the Internet.[13]

The harder advocates pushed for their position, the more they were marginalized by Genachowski himself. One of the favorite ways to silence the input of organizations like Free Press in 2010 was red-baiting, a strategy engaged by both conservative commentator Glenn Beck on television and Julius Genachowski himself. When Google destroyed the trust of its own coalition by teaming with Verizon to suggest their own negotiated compromise, which allowed for forms of "reasonable network management" permitting the kind of wiggle room advocates were dead set against, advocates cried foul. Genachowski saw fit to position himself between these two opposing sides, characterizing his onetime champions Free Press and the Save the Internet coalition as somehow extremists: "I reject extremism on both sides" (Zapler, 2010). The red-baiting attacks took their toll. As per one example, when the Prometheus Radio Project—whose founders had started in pirate radio—was set to present an award to a congressional representative, the representative's office informed Free Press that it was not welcome at the ceremony. Remarkably, Free Press was now seen as too radical to be associated with, a message reinforced by the FCC chairman himself.

Come December, after a disastrous election for Democrats that saw them lose control of Congress, Genachowski issued his final rules as the holidays hit (FCC, 2010a). Advocates were incensed at their weakness. They treated wireline and wireless networks differently: wired networks were not permitted to block disfavored content or applications; they were also subject to a "no unreasonable discrimination" rule. Alongside these prohibitions were requirements to disclose network management practices, details of performance characteristics, and their terms and conditions of service. In contrast, wireless networks were spared from the "no unreasonable discrimination" rule while still subject to the others.

These rules were hardly uncontroversial within the Democratic majority at the commission itself. Commissioner Michael Copps did consider voting no on the rules, seeking instead "plain and simple Title II reclassification through a declaratory ruling and limited, targeted forbearance—wiping the slate clean of all question marks" (quoted in Pickard & Popiel, 2018, p. 37). However, seeing the proceeding as at least a move forward toward this ultimate goal, he compromised for pragmatic reasons nonetheless, concurring with the decision.

Advocates were livid. Craig Aaron would note:

> So many failures by the FCC.... If you're going to make weak net neutrality rules, why not make them at a moment where Congress couldn't overturn them? Why didn't you do this while Democrats were in control of Congress?... Such bad strategy. Compromise on compromise, not only based on legal arguments that were questionable based on the *Comcast* decision... but they did it too at a time when a "resolution of disapproval" was a possibility. (Personal communication, September 24, 2012)

A "resolution of disapproval" is a special congressional move that, within sixty legislative days of the publication of an agency regulation in the Federal Register, allows Congress to overturn the new rule and, at the same time, eliminate the issuing agency the ability to revisit it in substantially the same way. Illustrative of the tenor of the times, Republicans attempted this maneuver shortly after the FCC passed these rules, but activists mobilized to prevent its passage and succeeded. The rules would stand, but only to face further challenge from a lawsuit brought by Verizon.

An FCC staffer, who insisted on speaking on background, revealed striking information about the formulation of the Open Internet Order of 2010. This staffer noted that ordinarily an "encyclopedia" of the comments is prepared with a common summary. This time, that summary was not on offer. Rather, staffers received an outline of what was to be said with the expectation that the blanks would get filled in. Worse, the numerous new ways that the FCC sought to reach out to the public similarly had a less benevolent function: users who submitted to the FCC blog as opposed to the official comment engine did not contribute to the end decisions at all. In supplying more ways to facilitate public input, the agency had instead found a way to channel all of this effort straight into a wall. It was a cynical move in effect, if not intent.

The Perils of Access

Concurrent with the 2010 proceeding, and adding insult to injury for net neutrality advocates, was the Genachowski FCC's approval of the merger of Comcast and NBCUniversal. While temporary network neutrality conditions were placed on the merger, these expired in 2018. Even in failing to stop this merger, the sheer effectiveness of the machine that advocates had constructed was fully on display. The submissions supporting the merger that would be required of Comcast and NBCUniversal would be voluminous by the very nature of the size of the firms, but this also was an advantage for the companies: any potential public interest worries could be buried in mountains of paperwork and may never even be noticed. Perhaps the companies themselves were unaware of such potential problem points themselves. Unfortunately for them, Adam Lynn—who had started as an intern at Free Press in its early days, and who now was employed full-time in Washington, DC, as a policy coordinator—had initially been granted access to sensitive, confidential files put into the record. (In such proceedings, advocates may view confidential and market-sensitive information but under strict rules, and any filings containing snippets from these files would be redacted in the public record.)

Comcast protested Lynn's access, delivering to Free Press (and Lynn) a letter from the company's legal team that was filed in the relevant docket as well, requesting that he be removed from access to such files (Hammer, 2010, April 5). Their logic went as follows: while Comcast had no quarrel with Free Press's gaining access to confidential files, the terms of the Protective Orders signed by the organization (and Lynn) stipulated that confidential documents may be "reviewed by Counsel, and *Counsel may disclose* Stamped Confidential Documents and other Confidential Information to ... outside consultants or experts retained for the purpose of assisting Counsel in this proceeding" (Hammer, 2010a, p. 2). The Protective Order also limited such materials to "Outside Counsel of Record, their employees, and *Outside Consultants and experts whom they retain to assist them in this proceeding*" (p. 2). Lynn was not a lawyer, and Comcast wanted to tar him at this point as not sufficiently "expert" enough to be used as such an "expert" despite his nearly six years of on-the-ground experience with the organization:

> While Free Press appears to be a non-commercial party, it makes no showing that Mr. Lynn is an "expert," or that he is working under the supervision of counsel. From the job description that is available online, Mr. Lynn is described as "conduct[ing] research on issues related to media ownership, public media and the future of the Internet." It is not clear that Mr. Lynn has the type of advanced or specialized training, or has demonstrated expertise, that this Commission has typically associated with being an "expert." (Hammer, 2010a, p. 3)

Their fears were warranted. Lynn was remarkably tenacious and passionate about perusing the documents and, on doing so, unearthed a number of concerns that were there for the finding but buried in the stack of documentation filed. Lynn teamed with Mark Cooper of the CFA to present their findings. Comcast was forced to respond to any number of concerns that arose from these confidential documents. The work that Lynn and Cooper put into their perusal of these materials stimulated a series of objections from EarthLink as well which Comcast found itself needing to address (Hammer, 2010b). This is to say, one of the most significant elements of the expansion of Free Press (and groups like it which were similarly growing) was that the institutional strength to devote staffers to issues such as this was a powerful force to contend with. It was the efforts of Lynn, to boot, that revealed the existence in the public record of the Open Internet proceeding's numerous fake letters from dubious organizations concocted just to comment in the proceeding, such as that from the "Arkansas Retired Seniors Coalition" expressing their concern that "the elderly community here is concerned about the proposed rulemaking on net neutrality" (p. 1). What gave this particular group away was the sentence that followed: "XYZ organization shares this concern." Whoever concocted the group neglected to take out the placeholder. Comparable "astroturf" was discovered on the letterhead of Northrup Grumman's letter expressing similar concerns to the elusive retired Arkansans. The letter was revealed to be a form letter: its creator had forgotten to remove the reference header reading "Governor/PUC letters to FCC on net neutrality" (p. 1). It took institutional resources and staff to obtain and dig through the myriad trade brochures offering ISPs access to deep packet inspection technologies, such as that tendered by Allot Communications that offered ISPs the ability to "improve the performance of applications with positive influence on revenues (e.g. churn reduction)" while also allowing them to "reduce the performance of applications with negative influence on revenues (e.g. competitive VoIP services)" (Riley & Scott, 2009).

In fact, the FCC staff itself appreciated the efforts of groups like Free Press for discovering elements of filings that they either might not or did not have time to dig for themselves. The dockets at the FCC were, with the necessary staff, a treasure trove of evidence if one had the time and tenacity to look. This was tremendously costly work. In describing the failed AT&T–T-Mobile combination, Ben Scott of Free Press noted, "Part of that combination being shot down was the audacity to buy local groups that [would] weigh in, but they had been doing it for years, and it was Adam [Lynn] that called them out. It was only later that people came to the evidence of wrongdoing" (personal communication, September 20, 2012). In the meantime, working in coalition, these groups were able to submit nearly two million legitimate comments into the *Open Internet* proceeding: even despite the disappointing outcome, this represented a new kind of mobilization that could not be ignored. Even more importantly, the material in the dockets is what is allowed in litigation: planning the next legal battle and arranging for appropriate comments to find their way into the docket is crucial. Advocates had learned how to engage the FCC, and the form this engagement took was neoliberal to its core. Given the disappointing result, this form would start to come under question during a period of institutional soul-searching.

The 2010 proceeding had one additional, fateful detail which would also prove significant in the years to come. Derek Turner, research director of Free Press, told me in the aftermath of these fights regarding the early days of cooperation with the Genachowski FCC, "The first thing the commission asked me to do was to frame our comments in terms of jobs, even if he liked our perspective. How does this impact investment? Jobs? We say, your product is only as valuable as the stuff that runs on top of it, [which] bring value to your product" (personal communication, September 20, 2012). This approach would find its way into the eventual Order that Genachowski would offer. Even if on the extremely tenuous footing of Title I, the theory that the Genachowski FCC turned to was that of the "virtuous circle" of access net neutrality offered to justify rules of any stripe. After listing a litany of uses to which the Internet, as a general purpose technology, had been put—from receiving content of one's choosing without being blocked, to the development of new technologies as the World Wide Web without permission, to the benefit to startups and small businesses, to being able to "contribute to the economy through e-commerce and online advertising" (FCC, 2010a, ¶13)—the FCC notes,

> The Internet's openness is critical to these outcomes, because it enables a virtuous circle of innovation in which new uses of the network—including new content, applications, services, and devices—lead to increased end-user demand for broadband, which drives network improvements, which in turn lead to further innovative network uses. Novel, improved, or lower-cost offerings introduced by

> content, application, service, and device providers spur end-user demand and encourage broadband providers to expand their networks and invest in new broadband technologies.... These network improvements generate new opportunities for edge providers, spurring them to innovate further. Each round of innovation increases the value of the Internet for broadband providers, edge providers, online businesses, and consumers. Continued operation of this virtuous circle, however, depends upon low barriers to innovation and entry by edge providers, which drive end-user demand. Restricting edge providers' ability to reach end users, and limiting end users' ability to choose which edge providers to patronize, would reduce the rate of innovation at the edge and, in turn, the likely rate of improvements to network infrastructure. Similarly, restricting the ability of broadband providers to put the network to innovative uses may reduce the rate of improvements to network architecture. (FCC, 2010a, ¶14)

The "virtuous circle" is mentioned in this Order five times (and elsewhere occasionally referred to as the "virtuous cycle"); it undergirds the entire justification for the new rules. This would prove fateful in the years to come.

Conclusion

In the aftermath of open access debates themselves transforming into net neutrality debates, utilizing the new tools the Internet offered, activists were able to construct an oddly (yet necessarily) neoliberal organizational form of activism that mirrored the "double truth" apparent in the thought collective examined by Mirowski and his colleagues. Such an organizational form (which advocates described as an "inside-outside" strategy) was absolutely necessary given the debate's new terms and the challenges they presented: true to the form of the neoliberal thought collective now transposed to a new plane, this required an esoteric discourse for policymakers and an exoteric discourse for the throngs comprising the noise machine (Mirowski, 2013). While network neutrality as a concept offered a lifeline to the cause despite Powell's 2002 attempt to end debates about competition aboard broadband wires, it simultaneously hobbled one of the core elements of nascent organizations such as Free Press's original sources of concern: hypercommercialization. It similarly buried the implications on and for class politics in relation to the governance of media systems themselves. These facets needed to be jettisoned for more favorable terminology and specialization to remain relevant and legitimate, yet even in the process of acceding to such language, they experienced attack after attack, not only from forces on the right (publicly so, via Glenn Beck's television program) but also from seeming allies on the purported left as Chairman Genachowski himself as he hobbled along indecisively. This form of neoliberal activist organization was effective—if not in actually obtaining policy goals of activists, then in at least gaining them a seat at the table. In an environment in which new technologies offered new opportunities for massive input from "ersatz" forms of understanding, activist groups needed to "manage" this knowledge in sometimes discomforting ways.

Similarly, the issue needed to be transformed. The fact that network neutrality had become about *free speech and freedom* disconnected it from its theoretical origins in evolutionary and antitrust economics. This mattered: a heterogeneity machine was under (re)construction but on different terms than during the open access debates of the late 1990s. The differences which appeared here were that whereas in open access, its advocates had a large role in defining the issue on their own terms. With network neutrality, they did not: it was predefined in a manner only half suited to activist organization at its root. Organize they would, but the weapon that could be used against them was their campaign's incommensurability with the heft of decades of construction work the Chicago School and its kin brought to the table. Even if confronted head on, it possessed such pedigree with its own support networks constituted to support it that it would be an uphill battle the whole way. Which isn't to say that successes were absent: using what tools they possessed at their disposal, advocates prolonged a debate that, in any other circumstance, would have been ended with *Brand X* and the subsequent decisions by the Martin FCC to remove any ISP competition from all means of broadband transmission. This was no small feat.

The descendants of the neoliberal thought collective called for the ouster of these miscreants on their home turf; for this old order's calls were effective, and their past struggles for legitimacy—long sought, earned over time through organization and Russian doll models of engagement—all ensconced it firmly in both institutional and ideological firmament. They were aided, of course, by the awakening of a Tea Party movement that provided helpful pushback against government involvement in any number of sectors. Net neutrality became one of those areas, a happenstance illustrative of how effective pro-neutrality advocates had become at gaining seats at important tables, but by the same token, this ended any bipartisan consensus on the issue.

Advocates were hardly united in approach to the issue. Activism that commenced in one economic era had bridged another: the 2007–2008 commencement of economic crisis had very real material effects on the debate. General understandings of network neutrality and the function of the Internet itself continued in the public mind (and that of the concept's advocates) to hew to classical liberal terms of free speech and enterprise, even as the capitalist economy was shifting in important ways that would affect debates to come. This found expression in the arguments that the economists who opposed them made: not so much made-to-order or even bought by telecommunications and cable interests: rather, this would be more subtle, calls to effectively remove the FCC from its perch, the beginnings of arguments to jettison "public interest, convenience, and necessity" oversight in favor of straight antitrust. It would be a push for a strict definition of the issue of net neutrality as an instance of a set of possible vertical transactions, extensions of firm activity themselves. This served a number of purposes. For one, expressed in its own language, it made a modicum of sense, and these practitioners had long made livings out of such an application of Chicago-style antitrust thinking. Rebutting these arguments would be important.

However, by the same token, continued *knowledge production* on network neutrality was important in and of itself. Such production was emphasized on all sides by emergent platform players and telecommunications companies alike. With or without their knowledge, the ground on which all of these players were operating was itself shifting as capitalist logics in communication shunted, stemming from the economic crisis, among other commercial pressures. Along with the economy, the approach to information production itself shifted—it, too, needed to assume a neoliberal *modus operandi* as the institutions that provided productive capacity moved from centers of conservatism (the PFF) to those more attuned to neoliberal frameworks of combined left-and-right reconciliation (ITIF). The institutionalization of new bulwarks to counter them (such as the Open Technology Institute) illustrated a new layer of production which could be utilized against incumbents, even as the ground continued to move beneath their collective feet. Production, in lieu of moving debates, provided stasis in a period of transition: to follow this debate alone, absent the shift to an intensified platform-driven capitalism, might make it seem like this was simply a matter of powerful interests battling powerful interests, the insertion of activists between commercial opponents, the same strategy which was employed—explicitly—during the open access debates. However, something very different was happening: platform capitalism (Srnicek, 2017) or, as some have posited, surveillance capitalism (Zuboff, 2019) was itself blossoming before our very eyes—an event we will return to later.

One of the chief ironies of this period would be that FCC chairman Martin—lambasted in congressional reports as running the agency with an iron fist, hiding information, shunting viewpoints with which he disagreed out of view via the banishment of economists or employees who disagreed to institutional Siberia—turned out to be easier to work with than Obama's first appointee, Julius Genachowski. Eliminating the nonpartisan nature of the debate held a number of advantages as well for incumbents: Craig Aaron noted to me in 2012 that, if *Kevin Martin* had issued the 2010 weak net neutrality rules, Democrats would have been livid; that a *Democrat* had done so meant on the whole prominent party members remained silent on the matter, even as groups such as Free Press were demonized.

Due exactly to the foundations available in elite discourse in Washington and the need to stay relevant to maintain one's place at the table, such organizations offering what one activist called "retail politics" (as opposed to the "grasstops" efforts of the late 1990s and early 2000s consumer advocates) needed to maintain the populist grandeur with the outside world while operating an entirely different discourse inside policy circles. What the populist side did accomplish was hardly meaningless: it supplied, in lieu of money, the legitimacy of those chasing the breadcrumbs left by those descendants of the thought collective of old, all in the hopes that when it came time to make decisions, that group's politics might have a say, no matter what they were arguing.

7 The Shifting Political Economics of Net Neutrality: A Continuum, Not a Break

Following Genachowski's outmaneuvering of his own initial champions, advocates spent the aftermath of the 2010 Order reassessing their approach to these issues and their supposed "champions" in particular. If there was one lesson that they learned, it was that they had skipped much of the movement-building process in favor of playing the "inside game" harder. The head of one advocacy group lamented that even if colleagues had been pulled into the administration, it was still no guarantee that they would push back against structural imperatives or incumbent pressure. "It's not enough if Democrats won't criticize Democrats." This advocate similarly emphasized was that there were limits to the inside game; it was time for a flip from an inside-outside to an *outside-inside* strategy. The legacy civil rights groups which served as allies to telecommunications and cable interests during that battle did great damage to the cause in providing cover for Genachowski to continue ceding ground to powerful incumbents. "A close fight with guys who know what they're doing like AT&T lobbyists" was not where activists could shine; rather, "we benefit from these things being fought in the light of day." There was similarly a realization that a move to consider these questions *internationally* was emerging: "What we've learned is that we made a decision a number of years ago there was enough here [in the United States]. That's not a luxury anymore… we need to recognize that the companies are working internationally. There's policy laundering. If you can't get it locally, get it internationally, and vice versa." Free Press, for instance, worked with others to generate a proactive declaration for demands online via the Declaration of Internet Freedom.[1]

Another advocate, speaking off-record, told of renewed efforts to be far more aggressive in the aftermath. The Obama administration's seeming effort to grant access to these groups turned out, intended or not, to form a powerful ruse. "[We said,] 'all we need to do is get access, be a part of these things.'... That, it turns out, has no effect on policymaking. It's access without power. And people are very enamored by access." At one point, this advocate had effectively been banned from Chairman Genachowski's office. "The worst thing the chairman's office could think to do to me personally was say, 'We will no longer meet with you.'... Reality is, that has no detrimental impact on the ability to get things done." The lesson was that humiliation was the strategy that wrought any results. "The mechanism to get things done with Genachowski, and the Obama administration, [was] negative public relations. You can come with infinite facts, [but] that [didn't] matter. But you blast them publicly with 'We have this mountain of verifiable facts and they're still not moving,' then they move. The lesson is clear. You [have to] beat them up a bit and then they move." Thus, with the election of Obama, perhaps there were improved communications and access for outside the Beltway organizations, but access was not power; rather, it was the siphoning away of energy into task forces and working groups and more. "It's possible that we [had] *less* power... because of our energy going into these timesinks of endless processes than when we were building a more critical analysis when we didn't have access. It's a powerful jiu-jitsu move" (personal communication, on file with author).

While advocates in public defended the new Federal Communications Commission (FCC) rules from challenges both in Congress and the courts to maintain the foothold that they *had* obtained, in private, numerous activists were frankly chomping at the bit for the 2010 rules to be vacated by the D.C. Circuit, which would simultaneously be exciting yet terrifying. The result would be a great indeterminacy, a period of no rules at all. At the same time, production continued on intellectual discourse, as by this time several points were rising to the surface. One was a matter of jurisdiction: who should oversee broadband networks after all? What would the standards be? The even partial success of advocates set the Russian doll to ferocious labor. New directions for pushback against network neutrality needed crafting; yet even more importantly, the FCC's own role in overseeing questions of Internet discrimination would come under sustained attack.

The Engines of Production Rev Again

In the wake of the 2010 Order, Hazlett and Wright (2011; later revised and published as Hazlett & Wright, 2012) were absolutely outraged at the FCC's flimsy defense undergirding the commission's worry that conduits might favor some content over other. They offer a sustained attack principally on the "no blocking" and "no unreasonable discrimination" rules: the anecdotal evidence brought by activists, and used by the FCC as justification for what weak rules there were, are brushed aside as irrelevant to a more "correct" analysis; a lone paper referenced by the FCC as economic evidence outside of anecdote is borrowed from a separate proceeding altogether, the media ownership proceeding, and even then related to cable programming, not broadband nor network neutrality in particular—certainly evidence of more hamfistness by the Genachowski FCC on this issue. But this, as they say, is primarily just (extended and lengthy) commentary. The real objective is revealed when Hazlett and Wright taunt policy activists who sought to question antitrust as a basis for production of a democratic public sphere. "The FCC and net neutrality proponents often argue that that [*sic*] the fact that antitrust analysis might not prohibit all use of vertical contracts is a bug rather than a feature of that regime.... However, that antitrust is not a 'slam dunk' can be a feature as well as a bug" (p. 39). Antitrust would require "the Commission to establish a real theory, garner actual evidence, and convince judges who do not depend on the regulated industry for future employment. The rule of reason, as applied to vertical contractual arrangements, represents a century-old attempt to develop a legal rule aimed at reliably distinguishing procompetitive from anticompetitive arrangements" (p. 40). To those who might argue that antitrust was "too restrictive" and overlooks certain forms of discrimination, "This description of the rule of reason is correct; but these features of the rule of reason are consumer protections that stem from an incremental evolution now over a century old and are based upon increasing economic knowledge and evidence. These features are precisely why it has garnered so much support from scholars and commentators" (p. 40).

Indeed, the effort was now shifting: arguments about net neutrality itself had generally reached a (useful) impasse, and those who had been connected to the interests of the incumbents at some point in the past turned their attacks toward the FCC's own role. It was clear that even as advocates themselves were chomping at the bit for the courts to strike down the weak rules as their foundation itself had been weak, those on the other side were similarly concerned about the eventuality that the courts would explicitly push a Title II solution to the conundrum. In preparation for the task, new realms of theory would need to be developed.

One never knows the order of events when scholars are publishing their work (we all dust off old drafts once we realize their utility or a sudden reinterest), but it is telling that around this time classic detractors of network neutrality found a number of strategies to get around the seeming stasis of argument. As the Genachowski rules faced their court challenge brought by Verizon, and with supporters and detractors both largely expecting the rules to be struck down by the D.C. Circuit, even the idea of common carriage—the idea that Title II, as opposed to Title I, should apply to broadband communication of all stripes—itself needed to be deposed. Eli Noam's (1994) prediction of the death of common carriage in favor of private carriage was predicated on the logical summation of market forces, but it was also something he *lamented:*

> Common carriage will erode in time, and … a hybrid coexistence [with private carriage, or "contract" carriage] will not be stable. This is not to say that the common carriers qua carriers will become extinct; many of them will remain significant players, but they will conduct their business as contract carriers. Common carriage as such will disappear. This will not happen overnight, of course. Intermediate arrangements can buy several decades of transition time. But the basic dynamics will eventually assert themselves. … This conclusion is reached with much regret, because the socially positive aspects of common carriage are strong, and because the absence to common carriage often means gatekeeper power. But we should not let preferences obscure the clarity of analysis. (Noam, 1994, p. 450)

What he listed as an inevitable outcome was now itself a *program* that neoliberals saw fit to push. Importantly, it was entirely an epistemic battle, something that van Schewick misses in her critique of any notion that antitrust authority was sufficient to rein in the worst excesses of broadband providers.

To take but one example of this stream, Christopher Yoo continued his prodigious production by attempting to lay a foundation for a future FCC to reject common carriage regulation of broadband. The moves made at this point by Yoo are seemingly trifling but become much more significant in time. His 2013 article asks, "Is There a Role for Common Carriage in an

Internet-Based World?" Seeking to preempt renewed calls for broadband to be regulated as a common carrier of any stripe—as the so-called third way proposal by the Genachowski FCC briefly threatened—Yoo seeks to argue via an extended discurcus on what seem to be interminable challenges of common carriage regulation. For example, one such move is simply to throw sand in the gears: this is fodder from the old neoliberal playbook. He offers a vast literature review of challenges facing common carriage regulation, each study in themselves inconclusive; but the point was hardly to show any guarantee of deleterious effects of common carriage policy—it was always instead to show how *hard* it is to implement. The best plan is thus to leave all of these details to the players to work out among themselves in the way they find most efficient. Most of these facets come down to the challenges facing rate regulation, which had been a feature of *telephony,* but in 2010, neither the FCC nor were activists on the ground entertaining any notions of applying rate regulation to broadband providers in the same sense. (The economists who side with Yoo would argue that when it came to the pricing of *privileged access,* rate regulation was being stringently applied, effectively setting a price for priority at zero by fiat—but this is not the nature of the challenge Yoo describes here.) Yoo, and those with the material support to write these white papers, were effectively making mountains out of molehills. Should broadband operators be reclassified as common carriers, Yoo makes the assumption that *all* Title II provisions would need to be implemented, including even those that were inapplicable to broadband services; thus none should be implemented. This, of course, was something never proposed by pro-neutrality proponents. However, going even further, tautology is offered as insight. When describing the impact of regulation of virtually any stripe on rate of return, for instance, he notes, "Whatever the precise impact of the effect, it does underscore that introducing regulation would distort decisions away from those that marketplace participants would make in the absence of regulation" (Yoo, 2013, p. 592).

But the confusion hardly ends there: in his earlier work the idea was to stimulate an environment of several intermodal forms of competition. Accepting that none has yet appeared, he now provides apologia for monopoly and oligopoly instead. "Although competition policy would ideally hope for even more competitors, the high fixed cost nature of this industry makes such entry unlikely" (Yoo, 2013, p. 562), then ironically footnoting *this* pronouncement with his original article, "Beyond Network

Neutrality"—in which he predicted that a policy of not instituting a network neutrality regime "has the potential to mitigate the supply-side and demand-side scale economies that concentrate telecommunications markets and make it easier for multiple networks to coexist" (Yoo, 2005, p. 77). Back to 2013: "Fortunately," he continues, "empirical studies indicate that markets with three firms are workably competitive, with most of the competitive benefit occurring with the entry of the second or third firm and minimal benefits resulting from entry in markets that already have three to five firms" (Yoo, 2013, p. 562).

Significantly, he reintroduces an argument that would prove important in time. For Yoo, if any manipulation of traffic occured between sender and recipient, the service involved cannot be telecommunications and thus *must* be categorized under Title I by a future FCC. "Firms that offer pure, transparent transmission capability to the public between points chosen by the end user with no computer processing or storage are common carriers. Firms that instead offer a service that combines transmission with additional functions, such as computer processing or storage, provide an information service that is not subject to common carriage" (Yoo, 2013, p. 564). He points his gaze at the Domain Name System (DNS), which translates natural language website addresses (such as www.mit.edu) into an Internet protocol address of strings of numbers.

> When an end user accesses content that is stored in multiple locations across the Internet, it is DNS—and not the end user—that decides which of the many content storage locations is the closest and least congested and routes the request to that location. The fact that DNS determines from which of the multiple available endpoints a particular query will be served makes it hard to characterize Internet communications as being between "points specified by the user" as required by the definition of telecommunications service. (Yoo, 2013, p. 567)

At this point one wonders if even analog, switched telephone service is a telecommunications service, since we are not selecting the particular circuit pathway that will ultimately be used to complete a call. The conclusion is surprising, given Yoo's exposure and familiarity with much of the computer science literature, which he and his cohorts seem to read selectively.

A curious similar move made by Yoo is to make the seemingly innocuous claim that broadband markets—again, themselves self-forming affairs and not the result of human endeavor or policy—are themselves unique, while repeatedly pointing in his work to how microeconomic calculations of utility and surplus apply to *all* markets. He cannot have it both ways. He points to a "recent survey of the empirical literature indicat[ing] that, aside from a few isolated studies, the weight of the evidence indicates that 'under most circumstances, profit-maximizing vertical-integration decisions are efficient, not just from firms' but also from the consumers' point of view,' a conclusion that the researchers did not have in mind when they began their review of the evidence and which they found somewhat surprising" (Yoo, 2013, p. 601). The study to which he refers—Lafontaine and Slade's "Vertical integration and firm boundaries: The evidence" (2007) never even mentions telecommunications networks.

In the end, however, given the heterogeneous nature of demands put on broadband networks, the sheer complexity of it all leads him to the conclusion that no regulation is necessary. Yoo points to challenges in regulating factors other than price: "Interconnection," for one example, "becomes considerably harder to police when the product varies in quality and the interface is complex. When that is the case, providers who are reluctant to provide service have access to a nearly endless source of nonprice ways in which they can defeat access" (Yoo, 2013, p. 600). That this is a reason to have no cop on the beat at all is quite remarkable.

If trying to preempt common carriage options by throwing sand in the gears isn't enough, there is an effort to move the theoretical foundations of the network neutrality argument to a new realm, one that finds its way into future writing in bits and pieces. While van Schewick accepts that net neutrality is about trade-offs and net neutrality advocates find in favor of the edges, Yoo assiduously now provides the mirror image. Turning to modularity theory (in which modularity stands in for innovation at the edges with architectures that permit standardized inputs and outputs—not unlike the layer stack of the Internet), he argues that modular architectures might stimulate changes at the edges, but core architectures, once established, are themselves challenging and slow to alter. Thus modular architectures, where power resides at the edges, are not necessarily always the optimal design choice. "Although flexibility is generally regarded as one of the advantages of modular systems, closer inspection reveals that modular structures facilitate only certain types of innovation while impeding others. Specifically, modular systems are very good at promoting improvements and replacements of individual modules, which require little coordination with other modules. They are less accommodating to systemic innovations that reorganize the ways that modules interact with one another" (Yoo, 2014, p. 38). Further: "Modularity is not a natural construct. Indeed, modularity theorists expect the design to change as the architects gain a better understanding of the underlying interdependencies. Technological and economic changes can create pressure for high-tech industries to evolve toward a fundamentally different architecture" (p. 44). Providing the opening to consider giving incumbent telecom and cable operators more control over how the Internet works, he argues, "Attempts to evolve away from existing modular architecture may thus represent nothing more than the natural response to changes in the economic and technological environment. Indeed, experimentation in new standards and competition between standards are properly regarded as a sign of innovative health" (p. 45).

The game played here is fairly consistent: everywhere Yoo looks, he sees suboptimal investment; he sets whatever realm of theory is on hand to the task of offering the case that the world is better if one entity centrally controls more and more of the core of a system in the name of maximizing producer surplus. Similarly, it is not choice, but *consumer* choice that is to find expression in this optimal universe. It is creatively treading new ground yet contributing the same analysis each time, and it always points to the incumbents, always to centralization (with the obligatory nod to "but maybe not sometimes" to stay safe), always away from independent creators unless well resourced. It is a parlor trick that eliminates class structures from appearing in the analysis, keeps broader political economic forces from wrecking the view, and shoves aside activist history aboard networks as these and the public desires of how these networks should work in favor of "innovating." If all markets exist in a reified plane, self-congealing computational engines of efficiency, then there is no need for an FCC or a notion of the "public interest" at all; it will naturally fall out of market outcomes. That this is an agenda to push, with arguments marshaled to generate this outcome, reveals Mirowski's (2013) irony roaring back to the fore, the necessity of the neoliberal "double truth": these calculative engines require the assistance of enlightened actors to sandwich society into them.

Yet by the same token it is somewhat beside the point to dive deeply into the arguments themselves and to treat them as true or false. That was never the point. The point, of course, was always the mere fact of *production,* of generating a discourse (in fact, Yoo's job, and mine, requires it of us). When I interviewed two research directors of prominent public interest groups in these debates about the value of research in the wake of the 2010 debacle, I received two striking responses. One person had gotten wise to the whole game and told me that he had stopped bothering to go to the Telecommunications Policy Research Conference, perhaps the most renowned of the communications policy conferences. The other told me that it was becoming difficult to tell the real research from the fake. What they were sensing is that the game had shifted. In one sense, it has changed in that the ontic matter of research has ceased to matter in our age, even as the knowledge produced by our efforts remains vital. The production of knowledge now ceased to be about technology and its operation. It was about the removal of these discussions to questions of antitrust authority and its operation; and even beyond this, it was about preparing the parameters such that no matter which direction the debate headed, a debate which appeared intractable reared its head and could be constitutive of the next fight. It was the mere fact of continued *production* that was significant: in the process of laying in wait, justification for particular moves needed to be at the ready.

The thought collective valued the input of longtime combatants-in-arms; close-knit frenemies such as Mark Cooper provided useful fodder for continued production even in sticking fiercely to his principles. In 2014, for instance, Cooper neatly summed his (longtime) position in a presentation entitled "The Digital Past as Prologue," delivered at an American Enterprise Institute and University of Nebraska Forum entitled "Regulating the Evolving Broadband Ecosystem" (Cooper, 2014). He argues that the political right "is correct to trumpet the important role of entrepreneurship, innovation and private investment in driving the digital revolution, but is dead wrong in denying the critically important role that active public policy played in creating the environment for success and the vital need for active policy to preserve and protect that environment." Similarly, the political left "is correct to trumpet the important role of active policy; but it is dead wrong to deny the critically important role that the private sector played in creating the digital revolution and must play in continuing to innovate and expand the digital space" (p. 1). "Progressive capitalism," Cooper writes, "reduced market imperfections and barriers to make markets work better, improving productivity and expanding output."

This sounds like neoliberal theorizing but is not; look into Cooper's own works and up pops Scherer and Ross's *Industrial Market Structure and Economic Performance* again and again. Industrial policy is anathema to the thought collective; nonetheless, Cooper is close enough to the ground that he gets invited to their gatherings. Cooper, in Laclau's sense, is a source of terrific heterogeneity in the open access debates, working in concert with the other public interest groups. His arguments and activist method don't fit neatly in the growing, emerging strains of theory that Mirowski describes. What we saw leading up to Wu's contribution was a messy, ad hoc approach that Michael Powell had to forcefully shut down with his 2002 declaration; Cooper was a major part of that ad hoc approach. Wu effectively "cleaned up" the debates for what was to follow. Cooper's own evolving stance on network neutrality and how to achieve it, particularly after 2010, was contentious within the community of groups pushing for strong network neutrality rules. Cooper's strategy all along was to exploit neoliberal discourse to turn its agents against each other. This was an old tactic, however, and one that emergent activist groups were not seeing as nearly sufficient. In fact, such engagement on the new terrain had lost its rebellious force: it had become just another part of a stream of productivity that *constituted* a broader, more threatening project; it had become incorporated into that which it believed it fought. Sensing such things, the old strategy that Free Press had sought to bring to the field in the early days of its existence was about to come roaring back to the fore.

Shifting Dynamics of Resistance

In 2014, the D.C. Circuit Court struck down Genachowski's Open Internet Rules in favor of the complaint brought by Verizon, as advocates feared would happen—or perhaps even wished would happen. It was not on their merits, however. This was predictable: given that the Genachowski FCC was trying to tie a shoe with an eggbeater by keeping the rules within a Title I framework, the merits remained to be determined. The court essentially ruled, to advocates' ears, what was plainly obvious: if the FCC desired to regulate broadband providers as telecommunications services that were not permitted to discriminate, then they would need to reclassify them as such and be done with it. By the same token, the court expanded the FCC's "Section 706" authority: if the FCC were to find that broadband deployment was not reasonable or timely, it confirmed that it was permitted to take steps to rectify the situation. Only the transparency rules were permitted to stand (*Verizon v. FCC*, 2014). Shortly after the court case, to no advocate's surprise, Julius Genachowski left the FCC to join the Carlyle Group, a hedge fund, to become "Director and partner in the U.S. Buyout team," focusing "on investments in global technology, media and telecom, including Internet and mobile" (Carlyle Group, 2014, p. 1). Free Press's Craig Aaron duly noted that "The revolving door never seems to stop spinning at the Federal Communications Commission" (Lazare, 2014).

Public interest groups in Washington found themselves at loggerheads in determining how to react to President Obama's newly selected FCC chairman, Thomas Wheeler, an ex-lobbyist for the cable and telecommunications industries. With Wheeler's ascension, however, to advocates' horror, in lieu of seeing the D.C. Circuit's decision as exactly the excuse to reclassify broadband service as a telecommunications service, Wheeler sought to intensify the mistakes made by his predecessor. In the first set of open Internet rules the new chairman proposed, rather than make any such move to reclassify, he instead chose the opposite route—to propose rules that would allow for Internet service providers (ISPs) to explicitly discriminate (FCC, 2014). Despite a court decision that advocates saw as virtually screaming for a reclassification of broadband provision to Title II, the notice frustratingly still sought to explore options under Title I that had now already been struck down twice (while opening the door just a little to exploring reclassification options; see ¶4). It sought to broaden the transparency rules established in 2010, but when grappling with the question of blocking by providers, retained a no-blocking rule similar to that passed in 2010 but rendered weaker, driven by a "commercially reasonable" legal standard of action aboard networks maintaining some baseline level of service. Efforts were painstakingly made to avoid common carriage designations. "While maintaining [the 2010] rule text, we propose to make clear that the no-blocking rule would allow individualized bargaining above a minimum level of access to a broadband provider's subscribers ... but, also consistent with the court's analysis, separately subject such practices to scrutiny under the commercially reasonable practices rule (or its equivalent)" (¶95). As far as what was "commercially unreasonable," the FCC clarifies,

> It would prohibit ... those broadband providers' practices that, based on the totality of the circumstances, threaten to harm Internet openness and all that it protects. At the same time, it could permit broadband providers to serve customers and carry traffic on an individually negotiated basis, "without having to hold themselves out to serve all comers indiscriminately on the same or standardized

terms," so long as as such conduct is commercially reasonable. (¶116, quoting the court's decision)

The move had the effect of fomenting a series of stunning actions undertaken by a core group of activists both inside and outside Washington, DC—what Craig Aaron described as "a new generation of Internet activists combined with really interesting grassroots activism, an emerging group of civil rights organizations countering where the traditional civil rights groups had been on this issue. It was not a legion of white geeks" (personal communication, February 20, 2015). A heterogeneity machine wrought of a decade of organizing sprung into action and with renewed attention turned to the ersatz as a source of strength. Flying under the banner the Battle for the Net, at the core were groups like Free Press and Public Knowledge that provided the institutional expertise of bureaucratic Washington; these served to "funnel" the viewpoints of the myriad Americans who contributed to the new proceeding's docket to where they might have an impact, be it at the FCC or in the offices of particular congressional lawmakers. In a concentric ring around these groups were a new breed of civil rights groups like Color Of Change and the National Hispanic Media Coalition. Also taking part were the Electronic Frontier Foundation, Avaaz, the American Civil Liberties Union, and numerous others. Creative actions were undertaken by groups like Fight for the Future (FFTF) and Demand Progress, all of which had cut their teeth on pushback against the Stop Online Privacy Act (SOPA) and Protect Intellectual Property Act (PIPA) several years earlier (Dunham, 2016), which were attempts by large content giants to ensure even those who merely *linked* to copyrighted content without permission would face draconian penalties, threatening to break the way the Internet functioned at base. These groups were relatively new, riding firmly on liberal prerogatives of transparency and "good government." Their outlandish and highly visible activities gave new meaning to the network neutrality debate; Evan Greer, in explaining to journalists why their efforts were successful, explained, "We used the Internet to save the Internet." Splinter groups from the Occupy protests of a few years before were similarly active. All of these participants were on multiple listservs with regularly coordinated phone calls. This was a well-oiled heterogeneity machine in action. Funders similarly took notice, and the Democracy Fund played an active role in supplying funds as needed as quickly as needed to support the cause (Lentz, 2016).

There was hardly unity in tactics or strategy. While groups like Free Press pushed hard for reclassification of broadband to Title II, other longtime inside players urged caution. Speaking after this fight was through, Gene Kimmelman would note regarding the prospect of Title II that it was not in fact as strong as some believed it appeared: "There was never in U.S. law a flat ban on discrimination under Title II"; rather, Title II augurs no *unreasonable* discrimination (quoted in Holt, 2016, p. 5803). Kimmelman continued:

> There [were] a lot of people posturing that way—that anything different from Title II would be a sham. That might be great rhetoric if you are trying to pressure policymakers or galvanize the grassroots, but if people had actually followed through on the threat to oppose anything short of "full Title II," I think it would have been calamitous because we never were going to get a "Title II regulation" that absolutely bans all forms of discrimination. It's never been the law, and it can't be the law under Title II. It's a misreading of the law. (Holt, 2016, p. 5803)

Such a sentiment spoke once again of the esoteric and exoteric discourses that circulated, even as a shift in strategy was in the offing. Craig Aaron, now president of Free Press, described that the lesson advocates took from the 2010 proceeding's disappointing results was that an emphasis on almost exclusively "inside-ball" strategy was a loser; a renewed focus on direct activism was warranted. The organization certainly "worked…the 'inside' people [staff] to death" in their Washington office, although Aaron recounted that he had never spent so much time outside the FCC with a bullhorn before. *Outside* Washington, the events of 2014 were remarkable: a message from Holmes Wilson of FFTF outlined the ways that the ersatz were massively mobilized, pointing to the myriad fronts of the network neutrality war—not just at the FCC, but directed at the president, Congress, and even the major tech companies largely sitting out the fight.

> We've been part of an awesome coalition of DC groups, grassroots groups, not-so-small startups like Tumblr & Etsy, and lone gunmen like Marvin Ammori (who is really at the top of his game now). Coordination between groups has been the best we've seen, ever. The work has been pretty well funded too, with support from foundations like Voqal and MDF [the Media Democracy Fund]. I think the organization Free Press deserves a huge amount of credit for the coalition and the support behind it. Their work made net neutrality a key plank in a progressive media agenda, and that seems to be paying off right now, big time. (Wilson, 2014)

He then proceeded to outline the myriad tactics they utilized, truly stunning in their scope: joining with thousands of websites for an "Internet slowdown" late in the year, sites across the web displayed the common "buffering" symbol to illustrate the possible cost of net neutrality remaining unreinstated. The group pointed to pages featuring updates that kept interested comers informed on the positions of lawmakers and goings-on in Washington. A large video billboard was placed outside the FCC, playing homemade clips, produced by users, of what network neutrality meant to them. Physical protests and "dance parties" were held outside the FCC itself, forcing the agency's rank and file to further engage with the ersatz, indirectly, if not directly. A novel new tool, callthefcc.org, was developed to drive calls from net neutrality supporters to some staffer at the FCC; this tool offered a "daily caller" option which called the supporter and connected them directly to a staffer every day. A similar tool was developed to call White House staffers.

Ten years of aggressive activism were bearing fruit outside Washington as a new generation of advocates were springing up, a generation that recognized the value and risk to the Internet the debate represented. Many of these emerging activists had been involved in the SOPA and PIPA fights of just a few years earlier. The old myths that telecommunications and cable companies would never discriminate were easily debunked, as activists kept ready lists of malpractice going back years. Activists pointed to North Carolina's Madison River Communications in 2005 blocking Vonage's voice over Internet protocol (VoIP) service; they pointed to Comcast's blocking of peer-to-peer technologies; they pointed to the Canadian giant Telus blocking access to a server hosting a website supporting a strike against the company (which, in ham-fisted fashion, ended up blocking nearly 766 other sites too); they pointed to AT&T's demand that iPhones block Skype and other competing voice services, as well as Google Voice; they pointed to Windstream Communications (a digital subscriber line provider) hijacking user-search queries to siphon them to its own search portal; they pointed to MetroPCS's blocking of streaming video over its 4G services, with the exception of YouTube; they pointed to the actions of several small ISPs to redirect search queries intended for Bing and Yahoo! to vendor Paxfire, which in turn would allow these ISPs to collect referral fees; they pointed to AT&T's, Sprint's, and Verizon's 2011–2013 blocking of Google Wallet on mobile phones, which might have competed with Isis, a program being developed by the three carriers; they pointed to a 2012 Body of European Regulators for Electronic Communications report that found one in five users were subject to network neutrality violations as VoIP services, peer-to-peer protocols, gaming, and email services were affected; they pointed to Verizon Wireless's 2012 blocking of tethering applications on their cell phones, requesting Android remove eleven free tethering applications from their marketplace; they pointed to AT&T's 2012 disabling of FaceTime video on iPhones, barring subscription to a more expensive text-and-voice plan (all examples found at Karr, 2017). An issue that had lain dormant and given barely a glimpse by the FCC—that being issues of peering and interconnection between broadband networks—reared its head as well, as the Open Technology Institute and M-Lab released a study revealing that the underperformance of sites like Netflix or video conferencing sites aboard AT&T, Time Warner Cable, and Verizon was caused by these networks deliberately "fail[ing] to provide enough capacity for this traffic to make it on to their networks in the first place. In other words, the problem was not congestion on the broadband lines coming into homes and businesses, but at the 'interconnection' point where the traffic users' request from other parts of the internet first comes into the ISPs' networks" (Karr, 2017; see also Open Technology Institute, 2014).

Perhaps most damning was what Verizon's own lawyers emphasized in oral arguments while fighting the FCC's 2010 Open Internet rules in court. Despite a promise in 2011 to not "unduly discriminate against any lawful Internet content, application or service," when asked whether they planned to prioritize certain content, one of Verizon's lawyers responded in chilling fashion, "I'm authorized to state…that but for these rules we would be exploring those types of arrangements." In describing the confession later, advocates pressed, "[Verizon's] admission might have gone unnoticed had she not repeated it at least five times during oral arguments." Taking it one step further, advocates reported, "In response to Judge Laurence Silberman's line of questioning about whether Verizon should be able to block any website or service that doesn't pay the company's proposed tolls, [Verizon's representation] said, 'I think we should be able to; in the world I'm positing, you would be able to'" (all quotations Karr, 2013).

Through the summer, the FCC, stunned by the strong public show of force—as the nearly two million comments filed in the 2010 proceeding were dwarfed by the four million that appeared this time—offered a series of weak half-measures, so-called hybrid plans, some proposed by the agency and others by providers themselves; the Mozilla Foundation proposed its own. By November, however, the tide clearly turned, as President Obama issued a direct statement to the nation—and, implicitly, the FCC—favoring strong network neutrality protections, including even the massive step of full reclassification of broadband networks as telecommunications services, reversing over a decade's worth of policy at the agency (Wyatt, 2014). Holmes Wilson of FFTF noted to supporters that

> Our coalition created the circumstances in which they could move. FFTF was a key part of that. From the "buffering" gag at the beginning to the emphasis on "cable companies" (not telcos, or ISPs) Obama's video statement was built from our memes and framing. In the emails they sent to the Organizing for America list, they cribbed exact phrasing from FFTF emails. Our stuff was both resonating with them, and showing them the political path forward. And it mattered: Obama's statement has very much changed the balance of power on this issue, especially because it means he'll likely veto any action by Congress against a good FCC rule. (Wilson, 2014)

His comment on what was deemed effective is notable: "Through this process we continue to be shocked by how influential creative, targeted pressure can be, relative to massive protests like the Slowdown." He noted the effectiveness of calling office lines in particular, and some of the ironies involved:

> I think callthefcc.org has done much more to make the FCC itself feel public pressure, even though it drove far fewer calls than the Slowdown. It's disturbing to think that our & Namecheap's video billboard at the FCC (which was almost zero effort for us) may have generated more conversation within the FCC than the Slowdown—an event that was absolutely tremendous amount of work [*sic*] for ourselves and others. But according to some sources who are closer than us to the FCC, it's not impossible. (Wilson, 2014)

Right-wing opponents of network neutrality smelled conspiracy, claiming the White House was busy constructing a "parallel FCC." "The Obama White House has worked directly with online activists to pressure the Federal Communications Commission to regulate the internet," the online *Daily Caller* proclaimed (Picket, 2015). The *Caller* examined White House visitor logs from September 2014 onward, attempting to make the case that the FCC was not nearly as independent as it seemed, that it was in fact following directives from the White House. This article, and another which appeared in the *Wall Street Journal* in February 2015 which explicitly cited a "parallel FCC" in the White House, noted the possibly dozens of meetings between activists and White House staff (Nagesh & Mullins, 2015).

The *Caller* fixed particularly on an email from Evan Greer of FFTF to the organization's members:

> We've been hearing for weeks from our allies in DC that the only thing that could stop FCC Chairman Tom Wheeler from moving ahead with his sham proposal to gut net neutrality was if we could get the President to step in. So we did everything in our power to make that happen. We took the gloves off and played hard, and now we get to celebrate a sweet victory. (Picket, 2015)

Further, Greer wrote,

> If you watch the Obama statement closely, you'll see many moments where he incorporates the memes and talking points we've built, together, as part of battleforthenet.com campaign [*sic*], from the "buffering" joke at the beginning to the way he talks about this as cable companies vs. the public.…Obama's statement has this movement's fingerprints all over it, and it wouldn't have happened without our work together. We're proud. You should be too. (Picket, 2015)

In February 2015, the Wheeler FCC followed through, issuing what were rightly seen as historic rules (FCC, 2015). This was far and beyond anything that activists had imagined a year earlier. Wheeler instituted three bright line rules for broadband providers of all stripes, wired or wireless: no blocking, no throttling, and no paid prioritization. Additionally, for the first time, responding to the interconnection disputes experienced by users in 2013 and 2014, the FCC would begin examining interconnection peering agreements among backbones, middle-mile companies, and last-mile providers. Perhaps most significantly, as these issues were left to be handled on a case-by-case basis, a "general conduct rule" was left in place which would guide FCC action going forward:

> Any person engaged in the provision of broadband Internet access service, insofar as such person is so engaged, shall not unreasonably interfere with or unreasonably disadvantage (i) end users' ability to select, access, and use broadband Internet access service or the lawful Internet content, applications, services, or devices of their choice, or (ii) edge providers' ability to make lawful content, applications, services, or devices available to end users. Reasonable network management shall not be considered a violation of this rule. (FCC, 2015, ¶21)

By the same token, the justification for the rules retained the notion of the virtuous cycle (revised from 2010's "circle") no less than fifty times in its own verbiage, aside from the myriad times the concept appears in the footnotes. The Verizon court had blessed the conception, so this is no surprise, but it remains significant regarding the overall rationality of the rules, which would be fateful. The FCC's reach extended beyond the outermost layers, acknowledging that all parts of the network were ancillary to services. Similarly, recalling FCC findings of the late 1990s that found that any of the "processing" necessary to successfully transmit information may be considered part of the telecommunications component of the service, Yoo's contention that content management services and DNS lookups constituted material "processing" to render all broadband provision an information service is repudiated in the footnotes as almost silly, not once but several times. This logic would not fly.

Activism Led, Capital Followed: The Cultural Labor of Network Neutrality

Despite the *Daily Caller*'s entreaties, however, this was as far from the result of a conspiracy as one can imagine. No activist who had been working on this issue would ever argue Obama had been fully vested in it from the beginning. Emerging in 2015 with stronger open Internet rules than advocates ever believed possible with a complete reclassification of broadband networks as Title II telecommunications services, it might appear that we have witnessed nothing short of a stunning reversal. To the contrary, the victory by advocates in 2014 in obtaining strong net neutrality protections represents not a *divergence* from the neoliberal drive but rather a *continuum*.

Obama's announcement in November 2014 was seen as a tremendous turning point. A number of historical accidents were necessary for this to have happened, and a *Wall Street Journal* account from Feburary 2015 mirrored stories activists told (Nagesh & Mullins, 2015). The disastrous midterm elections left Obama's staff hunting for legacy-oriented issues, and network neutrality was testing well according to opinion research. Similarly, a changeover of staff from the more unconcerned Lawrence Summers to younger staff—who, given the debate's longevity, were more aligned with proponents' sense of alarm—created an opening. The *Wall Street Journal* notes the chance meeting at a fund-raiser between Obama and Tumblr's CEO, David Karp, who relayed his own concerns regarding Wheeler's original approach.

A shifting political economy played a significant role in the outcome. Advocates like Free Press were hardly the only players today concerned about the growing power of broadband incumbents. While large online companies like Amazon, Cogent, Dropbox, Google, Microsoft, LinkedIn,

Lyft, Yahoo!, and dozens more were often framed in press accounts as the protagonists in this fight versus the telecommunications and cable companies, a letter they sent to the FCC in May 2014 would be the first and largely last public show of their support for "a free and open Internet"—but not necessarily for reclassification.[2] At around the same time, over fifty large venture capitalists wrote the FCC, including representatives of SV Angel, Andreessen Horowitz, Greylock Partners, and Foundry Group; "If established companies are able to pay for better access speeds or lower latency, the Internet will no longer be a level playing field," they argued (Selyukh, 2014). Union Square Ventures, in its own meeting with the FCC, themselves expressed concern about the practice of "zero rating" itself, in which incumbents would set data limits and only count unaffiliated content toward them. They emphasized the concerns of startups that had also raised their voices, noting that one of Verizon's reasons for challenging the 2010 Order was expressly to gain the ability to zero rate:

> Union Square Ventures takes this opportunity to re-emphasize the need for the Commission to apply bright line bans against the most egregious forms of "zero rating." We agree with Verizon that the 2010 Order banned such practices; the Commission should not step back from the 2010 Order. Seven nations have concluded that zero rating is a violation of net neutrality; if we have the "strongest possible net neutrality rules" they should not be the eighth best. As has been frequently noted in the record, the importance of the open Internet has only grown since the Commission's previous attempt to protect it. (Grossman, 2015, p. 1)

In contrast to the big Internet companies, the "Ad Hoc Telecommunications Users Committee," a long-standing organization representing a group of powerful business interests including United Parcel Service (UPS), Bank of America, Visa, and Ford that have commented for years on numerous FCC proceedings, took particular note of this one. *Bloomberg* noted, "A corporate alliance with subtle interests in this fight has been quietly pushing the Federal Communications Commission for strict broadband rules" (Brustein, 2014). While in the press representatives did not emphasize Title II as an objective—representatives were very coy with reporters about their aims, emphasizing not net neutrality but "terminating access monopolies," for fear of damaging their dealings with a prime input into their operations—their filings were far stronger. The difference in their stance between 2010 and 2014 bears noting. In 2010, they expressed strong reservations about network power, seeking oversight of peering processes then as well as pointing to the concentrated nature of networks themselves (Ad Hoc Telecommunications Users Committee, 2010). Their concerns only grew in the present proceeding, noting in their comments that:

> Every major corporation in America, including the members of Ad Hoc, is an "edge provider" of Internet content who depends upon Internet openness to do business. Every retailer with an online catalogue, every manufacturer with online product specifications, every insurance company with online claims processing, every bank offering online account management, every company with a web site—every business in America interacting with its customers online is dependent upon an open Internet. (Ad Hoc Telecommunications Users Committee, 2014, July 18)

While leaving it alone in 2010, they pressed for a full reclassification as well as oversight of the peering regime in 2014. "As a result of changes in the engineering and deployment of network and Internet technologies, the Commission's classification of Internet service ... as an unregulated 'information service' is simply out of step with reality," they noted (p. 1).

Yet in digging more deeply into the *ex parte* notices required of lobbyist visits to the FCC in the midst of a proceeding, what starts to emerge are concerning signals involving the apparent *cultural labor* performed by the network neutrality fight. The *form* these rules would take was up to the actors legitimated by the outpouring of support of the ersatz. Network neutrality's proponents recognized that to win in the regulatory sphere, an alignment with a particular sector of capital—the new startups—would be increasingly necessary; public interest actors, and even numerous commenters, emphasized free speech, but behind the scenes were alliances of convenience that served to instill more deeply a particular nascent form of labor, one of our neoliberal times. What we truly see in full force is the neoliberal style of activism necessary today once again. Such alliances are hardly extraordinary; this said, the emergence of this sector as a new force capable of swaying both the president and the FCC does serve as a significant data point in diagnosing broader developments.

The strategic ties between developing sectors of capital and the longtime advocates becomes apparent when examining who was present during crucial meetings. According to documents obtained by the *Daily Caller,* those present at the September meeting at the White House included former Free Press staff attorney Marvin Ammori, who was there representing the New America Foundation; at the same time, he was also serving as a consultant for new tech startups on First Amendment issues, and he had built a practice around this. Others present included grassroots civil rights activists from the Center for Media Justice, representatives from Consumers Union and the Future of Music Coalition, Common Cause, and the National Hispanic Media Coalition—all of whom were active in the early 2000s when the FCC attempted to loosen media ownership rules as well as in the 2010 Open Internet proceeding. Alongside them were Free Press, FFTF, Demand Progress, the Electronic Frontier Foundation, the ACLU, A Learned Hand (a consultancy run by Cheryl Leanza, who herself had been deputy director of the Media Access Project and had represented the United Church of Christ Office of Communications media advocacy arm), independent strategists, and directors of conferences such as "Museums & the Web" and the "Personal Democracy Forum." Representatives of Reddit and the left-leaning blog Daily Kos were in attendance, as was public relations firm Spitfire Strategies. The international community was represented by Joshua Tabish of OpenMedia.ca, an open Internet advocacy group based in Canada. The presence of this widely varied group represented the labor of a decade of coalition building by activists as well as their professionalization and organizational prowess, learned through time and experience.[3]

A coalition of new Internet startups—as well as realtors!—formed their own alliance under the banner of the Internet Freedom Business Alliance (IFBA), geared toward finally breaking conservative resistance to network neutrality (Romm, 2015). Behind the scenes as well were independent advocates who had been involved in past debates and who spoke on background about digging through the FCC comments as they came in, identifying businesses that were submitting comments and crafting summaries about them for activists to distribute to relevant representatives of Congress. Efforts were also made to get representatives or owners of these businesses to take a more active role by addressing their congressional representatives themselves. At several meetings at the FCC, Ammori represented their interests. The day that President Obama made his public pronouncement asking the FCC to reclassify broadband as a telecommunications service, a meeting transpired at the FCC featuring the chairman and staff as well as representatives from AOL, the Computer and Communications Industry Association, DISH, Engine, Etsy, Facebook, Google, the Internet Freedom Business Alliance, the Internet Association, Microsoft, Tumblr, Yahoo!, Demand Progress, and MoveOn (Ammori, 2014, November 12,

p. 1). At this meeting, a survey commissioned by the IFBA was delivered; it had found that "support for net neutrality is broad and consistent across demographics. When confronted with some of the implications of ending net neutrality such as ISPs having the power to charge tolls, give different access speeds to a variety of providers and limit freedom to access content, conservatives were as concerned or more concerned than liberals" (Internet Freedom Business Alliance, 2014, p. 2). Another meeting in February 2015 included public interest actors Free Press, New America's Open Technology Institute, the IFBA, and even the Ad Hoc Telecommunications Users Committee, Level 3, Cogent, Netflix, and Comptel; the purpose of the meeting was to express support for reclassification and for the FCC's asserting jurisdiction over issues of interconnection (Kronenberg, 2015, p. 1).

This signals several possibly worrisome things. First and foremost, the fight over network neutrality was never anti-capital. It was a struggle against a *business model*. Network neutrality is, at base, capital struggling over the neoliberal environment itself, a victim of its own successes. But let us be clear: *activists outside industry led this fight from the start*. Without them, there would have been no hope of the outcome that resulted. The *Wall Street Journal* and activists alike noted that an active and arduous process to *convince* startups to become active in policy circles was necessary when it was found that the tech giants were riding this fight out aside from beyond submitting a letter in late Spring 2014 to the FCC. Indeed, in the end stages, the *Wall Street Journal* account notes that Google recommended to the president that he *not* push for reclassification after all (Nagesh & Mullins, 2015). The inside game was driven by now-professional advisors—like Ammori—to startups, advocacy organizations like Engine ("the voice of startups in Washington"),[4] and assists by operatives in network neutrality like the Open Technology Institute at the New America Foundation working in concert to place needed messages where they would have the most impact. Or, rather, the converse was equally true: one needed to bring to the table those voices that would *matter* in a neoliberal environment.

A second-order problem becomes increasingly apparent as well. Network neutrality in practice, as discourse, reconstructed a particular form of labor and at one and the same time instilled this labor *as* freedom. This second-order problem was called back into relief with the tremendous service the Sunlight Foundation performed in parsing hundreds of thousands of comments submitted in 2014 (Lannon & Pendleton, 2014). The transparency group determined, using natural language processing algorithms, that of the initial batch, less than 1 percent of the initial comments opposed network neutrality. Given the sample size of over 800,000 comments at this time, at one level, this is useful information: the ersatz were quite effectively mobilized. Yet this is actually a perfect illustration of the dead, diverse politics Laclau abhors.

What the Sunlight Foundation did not observe was the debate, in its unity, effectively pushing the problem of a broader intensification of particular developments within capitalism further down the hole. They do provide initial parsing: one might reasonably see in the fights that raged through 2014 an instillation of a neoliberal dystopia, particularly in reading through comments by those largely barred from the rooms in which whiteboards fashioned futures. More than half the comments noted Internet access "as an essential freedom," with other key themes being small businesses, innovation, consumer choice, consumer fees, and competition. Among the voluminous comments collected by Free Press (Aaron, 2014), it takes little time to find similar, familiar frames. One: "As a citizen, computer professional, researcher, and small business owner, net neutrality is crucial to my success and functioning. I need access on a level playing field to the entire Web; I need my site's visibility on a level playing field.... These goals can only be achieved by declaring the Net a common carrier utility and enforcing net neutrality" (p. 7). Another: "What happened to letting the market decide? Haha, what a sham, the 'free' market. Say no to this monopolistic outline these rules propose for yet another of our media, perhaps the most important" (p. 15). Another: "No less than our freedom and democracy are at stake. Net neutrality protects us from a form of capitalist totalitarianism" (p. 23). The refocus, years in the making—by necessity—away from hypercommercialism and toward the more ambivalent project of deployment had done its work. The role of capital as a whole is rarely critiqued; given this lack, one might argue that "capitalist totalitarianism" may have already arrived. Rather, it is the role of a particular sector that is vilified, and not necessarily for bad reason.

Crucially, however, these commenters are hardly dupes: network neutrality has become about survival, as numerous civil rights groups were quick to comment, particularly in terms of expanding entrepreneurial opportunities for people of color alongside supporting free expression and facilitation of civic engagement. It provided "new ways to access capital, such as crowdfunding" (Internet Freedom Supporters, 2014, p. 9). The importance of the Internet in "applying for work, doing schoolwork, finding a home, and running a business" is pervasively expressed (ColorOfChange.org, 2014, p. 2). The urge to "save the Internet" was as much about communities saving *themselves* as much as it was about any right to free expression; and this was against the backdrop of a historically unique circumstance still evolving, enveloping them ever more snugly.

The irony may be that the mechanisms by which this activism was undertaken may have served to entwine activists even more tightly into the systems against which they were struggling. Recall that when FFTF, one of the most prominent players in the latest round of debate, sent out a celebratory email on the heels of President Obama announcing his support for strong rules in November 2014, a discussion of the strategies which had been employed noted they had always pushed against cable companies, "not telcos, or ISPs" (Wilson, 2014). This was not only partially smart messaging (cable companies were perennially among the most freakishly unpopular in the United States), but also it was something revealing of our time, of what is necessary in this arena of struggle to remain legitimate in the corridors of power. It certainly wasn't the activists targeted by this email that wrote the new rules.

Network neutrality in practice, as discourse, reconstructed a particular form of labor and instilled this form *as* freedom. Etsy, taking part in meetings with the FCC, emphasized in its materials new forms of flexible labor of which it was a part. However, they went further in acknowledging the political economy surrounding neoliberal subjects while offering continuing justification of these new forms of labor. In a section called "Shaping the New Economy," the authors of this study note that "Etsy sellers personify larger shifts in the economy, most notably the recent dramatic increase in flexible forms of work, the rise of Internet-enabled, peer-to-peer businesses, and declining economic security within the middle class" (Etsy, 2013, p. 8). Noting secular increases in self-employment and nontraditional contract work, Etsy sellers were found to be cobbling together income from several sources. "Those who combined income sources demonstrated higher personal earnings and were more likely to move out of poverty than those who pursued employment or self-employment exclusively. The Etsy community reflects this trend towards diversifying income to bolster economic security and resilience. 58% of all Etsy sellers work other jobs in addition to managing their creative businesses" (Etsy, 2013, p. 9; footnote omitted). Citing the Aspen Institute Field Trendline Series for such info, it is hard to imagine many "lifting themselves from poverty" with Etsy, given that access to the kinds of time, materials, and technology to run these businesses would not be present: rather, this represents a reification of a particular new flexible form of labor put to any number of particular arguments.

The report similarly allows the experiences of a select number of individual participants to serve as proxies for a system that was increasingly being gamed in favor of larger commercial enterprises. Almost a third of Airbnb revenues in the top twenty-five markets came from commercial listings, not individual households; Lyft and Uber offered car leasing programs (Lee, 2017). The myth, however, needed to be sustained. "Etsy sellers also represent a successful model of the emerging peer economy, where people use technology to trade, sell, rent and share with each other. Online platforms like Etsy, Airbnb (short-term home rental), and Lyft (ride sharing) have enabled individuals to conduct these transactions with relative strangers at scale, creating huge opportunities for new income streams and enabling both personal connections and more efficient uses of scarce resources" (Etsy, 2013, p. 9). This section was particularly striking:

> The potential for the peer economy to supplement income is particularly heartening in light of increasing struggles within the middle class. In September 2012, the U.S. Census reported that the American middle class had shrunk to an all-time low. Unemployment remains stubbornly high, pay rates have decreased, number of hours worked has dropped, and home prices have yet to stabilize. Middle class workers face increasing job insecurity and depressed wages. Many Americans are fearful that they may be unable to maintain their standard of living. Faced with ever-diminishing prospects for long-term job security and economic stability, middle-class workers have been forced to recalibrate both their skill sets and strategies for building financial security. Etsy sellers represent a particularly encouraging response to these trends. They invest personal time and resources to build businesses that diversify their household income streams and build financial resilience in the face of broader insecurity. (Etsy, 2013, p. 9)

The moves that are made here are revealing: desperation and insecurity serve as recurrent themes, alongside the hope and possibility of lifting oneself from poverty—by one's own bootstraps, no less. Of course, this is only available to particularly classed entrepreneurs, of course; the neoliberal form of self-care that scholars of neoliberalism expound—with its own vicious tendencies—is here raised as reason for optimism requiring a shift in how basic services might be met. Nonetheless Etsy's existential fears were certainly well founded: such platforms overall struggled for profitability; any tithe to the largest communications companies, robbing it of surplus-value, represented a mortal threat (Srnicek, 2017). By the same token, it was a company that was well aware of the structural conditions facing workers. In a section on public policy implications, Etsy recommends "updat[ing] social protections to include and accommodate this sector of the economy. Flexible forms of work lack many of the social protections we have traditionally associated with a full-time job, including health insurance, retirement security, and unemployment protection. Policy makers should develop new policies to bolster financial security in the new economy" (Etsy, 2013, p. 11).

Etsy also expounded on the growing nature of its sector. "Etsy sellers represent a growing sector of the U.S. economy: independent, flexible solo-entrepreneurs who are taking their economic and social well-being into their own hands. Together, they offer a new way forward—a path that relies not on the actions of a few big businesses, but on the proliferation of many small ones to build capacity and resilience of the U.S. economy" (Etsy, 2013, p. 11). It should be noted that the part of the economy Etsy represents is small compared to the claims made: "Nearly all of the estimates suggest that around 1 per cent of the US labour force is involved in the online sharing economy formed by lean platforms [like Etsy]" (Srnicek, 2017, p. 80)—generally thrown into precarious employment stimulated by the 2008 crisis and its aftermath. Another critic notes that the notion of the "sharing economy" transforming modern capitalism is certainly overblown, contrary to the seeming breathlessness of its champions: "[A] lot of the future growth on these platforms is likely to be driven by professionals, because at this point most of the people with idle cars or rooms to rent out are already doing it" (Lee, 2017). The same critic notes that, egalitarian and democratizing rhetoric aside, on lending platforms, banks, hedge funds, and other institutions remain the bulk of the lenders (Lee, 2017). Thus Etsy making its argument represents less the structural *importance* of this sector; it remains rather small. Rather, it is about selling the *dream* of this particular form of capitalism, of individual *survival,* of freeing oneself from oppressive capital formations. Or perhaps it is delusion as, increasingly, some authors such as Srnicek (2017) argue. Nonetheless, the continued neoliberalization of a precariat remained attractive enough to the likes of President Obama to push his FCC chairman for reclassification so as to stoke the flames.

When sites as Etsy or Tumblr turned to their users to defend net neutrality, it was a brilliant double move. On the one hand, these sites were clearly important to their users. By the same token, having users defend Etsy or Tumblr from the vicissitudes of the largest cable and telecom incumbents stood *as defense of a particular sector of platform capitalists under construction*, even alongside an emergent core logic of contemporary capitalism overall. One user of Etsy made the case perfectly. This user was well versed in aspects of the policies under discussion: "These principles of fairness and openness should not only apply to the so-called last-mile network, but also at points of interconnection to the broadband access provider's network. Likewise, strong net neutrality rules must apply regardless of whether users access the Internet on fixed or mobile connections" (Hurtado, 2014, p. 1). However, the focus of her concern is key; it is one of survival, clearly economic.

> The FCC's proposed rules would be a significant departure from how the Internet currently works, limiting the economic and expressive opportunity it provides. Investors, entrepreneurs and employees have invested in businesses based on the certainty of a level playing field and equal-opportunity marketplace. The proposal would threaten those investments and undermine the necessary certainty that businesses and investors need going forward. The current proposed rules, albeit well-meaning, would be far-reaching. Erecting new barriers to entry would result in fewer innovative startups, fewer micro-entrepreneurs, and fewer diverse voices in the public square. *The FCC should abandon its current proposal and adopt a simple rule that reflects the essential values of our free markets, our participatory democracy, and our communications laws.* (Hurtado, 2014, p. 1; emphasis added)

The neoliberal thought collective would be very proud at this self-adopted equation of free markets and participatory democracy.

Continuity across Seeming Transformations

Wheeler emerged from these debates effusively celebratory; there is an iconic image of him holding hands with his fellow Democratic commissioners high after they cast their votes, and he lauded the change, thanking the millions of commenters who had piled their submissions into the docket. All the same, while these were significant, they did not nearly perform the function that he claims; their arguments were hardly commensurate with the ones that won the day on the inside. All had much to celebrate, even in expectation of the court challenges already mounting—but the FCC's logics were justified differently.

The arguments of the ersatz themselves were reflective of the prevailing logics and imaginaries of capitalism flowing ever stronger at the time—in fact, they may have even reinforced them. In a paradoxical sense, as they pushed back against the power of broadband incumbents—network neutrality was itself now a fully fledged battle over not just the First Amendment or concerns about innovators, but *civil rights*—their desires were antithetical to broader systemic imperatives and incentives that played such a significant role in the rooms where decision makers decided the policy's fate. That is, rather than attacking systems, they attacked business models—business models that were stacked against them, while aligning with others that sounded as if they were not due to liberal ideals having found their environment transformed but not acknowledging the fact, as we will see.

There were multiple purposes to which the generation of knowledge was put in the network neutrality proceeding. A crucial concern that motivated Free Press at its inception was the very hypercommercialist nature of media and its attendant effects that skewed the nature of media production (and, in particular concern, news production) such that it reliably favored corporate power; now that people were making their own media via commercial platforms, this particular facet went by the wayside as advocates learned to live with the contradiction. The very reasons to support network neutrality involved invoking the myth of the entrepreneur that only further ensconced a neoliberal governmentality and adjoining political economy more deeply: pointing to Google and other behemoths as go-to models of the realm of possibilities an open Internet provided (the argument is not for a less commercial environment but for an environment that is competitive and providing equal opportunity for all comers), the paradox makes itself even more apparent. Seen through this lens, are network neutrality requirements that trumpet individualism or consumerism (alongside facets of nonprofit media on occasion) incongruent with similar calls for equal access to broadband networks—itself vital for us to explore next? On second glance, the network neutrality argument is all about dragging the unconnected, kicking and screaming, into a neoliberal governmentality, even as it will feel like their choice to do so. The net effect of both of these would be to eliminate from the table discussions of what kind of web was on offer.

The victory by advocates in 2015 in obtaining strong net neutrality protections represents not a *divergence* from past streams of history but rather a *continuum*. The involvements of the startups were crucial—albeit not sufficient—for getting the new rules to pass; but they were also constitutive of a particular future that is increasingly facing its own crossroads. When Ammori (2014) would argue that the platform startups were a "new speech vanguard" (p. 2265) and that "lawyers at leading technology companies are on the front line of battles for, and over, freedom of expression.... The companies they represent have pro-speech incentives—incentives no weaker than those felt by great newspapers" (p. 2294), it was a matter of fact. Undoubtedly, "lawyers at [these] private technology companies have an enormous impact on free expression globally through the policies they adopt for their millions of users—most significantly, terms of use" (p. 2263). However, it also signaled more than their elevation as examples of innovation that activists trumpeted as one possibility of the maintenance of net neutrality on the Internet. It was pointing to the growing influence of a segment of capital that found itself on the rise—if especially in the regulatory imagination—given the particular alignment of policy at that time. It signaled a shift in the political economy of the broader environment to which we need to shift our attention. It signaled, in short, a real break in what access to the Internet was increasingly being made to *mean;* the network neutrality debate, as a whole, had served as one form of its buttress.

Conclusion

By the time the FCC's initial rulemaking was turned back by the courts, the universe had shifted. Verizon admitted, full on, that it saw the Internet as its own "letters to the editor" page to censor at will, even as deep packet inspection had become quite common knowledge. During these years there were basic economic transformations afoot that were rendering what some termed "platform capitalism" ascendant as a prevailing logic, particularly following the crash of 2008. With the rules pushed back, the installation of a new FCC chairman in Wheeler, and groups such as Free Press working in consort with alliances and coalitions long under construction, now thinking about how to attack this in new terms, a renewed emphasis on "outside-in" efforts while continuing to push its "inside" connections any way possible fomented an uprising that drew from the same well of concern and strategy used to thwart laws such as SOPA and PIPA. Even those earlier efforts were the result of tactics learned and tools constructed through many more years of active engagement and development: there would have been no successful SOPA and PIPA struggle, much less a victory for network neutrality advocates, absent the growth of a new wave of media reform efforts that sprouted with passage of the Telecommunications Act in relation to *traditional* media.

When sociologist Yochai Benkler joined colleagues Robert Faris, Hal Roberts, Bruce Etling, and Dalia Othman to analyze the role of public activism in the proceeding in its aftermath, they noted, "The sole significant new factor in the political economy of net neutrality that unfolded over the five months between May and November 2014 was mass mobilization in the networked public sphere. On the background of this history, and the dramatic change in the FCC's ultimate stance from its initial position in May, it seems warranted to believe that networked mobilization and communication were decisive in tipping the political scales" (Faris et al., 2016, pp. 5858–5859). However, what these authors mistake for the power of the public sphere to motivate political actors is more accurately the public sphere itself legitimating particular voices in settings where they could matter (which, themselves, required this outside contingent for said legitimation). Inside actors who spoke the esoteric discourse, like Ammori, were pivotal; by the same token, the political economy of the Internet—its logic of surveillance at its heart for commercial ends—similarly played a role, with emergent actors that utilized such logics to their advantage finding sympathetic political actors for their cause. The authors of this study make one more mistake. In concluding that "Given the current political environment, it is notable to see such broad support for a policy that provides the government with greater latitude to intervene in private markets" (Faris, 2016, p. 5860), they neglect to consider that the very root of neoliberalism was precisely its willingness to extend the role of government so as to pull more elements of life into the market relation. The details were always where questions lay: not all sectors of capital might gain equally depending on how this was done.

The outcome remains truly remarkable—particularly as the old corporate allies like Google were largely sitting the battles out this time. It is crucial to understand: even if reading press accounts of this era might leave one with the impression that corporate tech giants took the lead on this matter and had the most to lose, that it was behemoth versus behemoth with the public merely playing an ancillary role, interviews with key actors show that activism was what truly stoked the fires of rebellion. Business certainly played a role: the emergence of the IFBA—driven in part by pressure by activists—represented two things. For one, it activated sectors of capital that had not seen policy development as a necessary activity to undertake in the Internet economy or did not recognize their own stakes in the outcome. Other edge (if older, more established, and pre-commercial Internet) companies were coming to recognize the risk to their own operations and profit margins (likely thinner than they liked, as evidenced by investor capital increasingly seeking its margins in the newer technology firms). Any effort by telecommunications operators to steal away surplus from them would be life threatening. But at the same time, what we witnessed was, once again, a battle of business models in a shifting capitalist environment. Activists scoured the comments submitted to the FCC for the presence of local businesses expressing their own concerns—itself a time-consuming and arduous task, given the volume of comments—and mobilized these comments still further (if not the businesses themselves) to push legislators to supply further pressure on the FCC in favor of strong rules. Even this effort, however, wrought meager results: so strong was both the neoliberal drive and the power of the broadband lobby that at no point did more than twenty senators support a reclassification of Internet services to Title II! (Holt, 2016). Historical accidents play numerous roles in any decision; a disastrous election for Democrats in 2014 clearly saw an administration looking for wins and a legacy. Net neutrality, it turns out, tested well.

The 2015 victory was hard-won by Internet activists. It was over a decade and a half in the making. Activists *indisputably* led the charge, as much as the general representation in major media was a battle of Internet giants versus conduit giants or even Internet startups versus the conduit giants. Yet we might be concerned that the victory carried its own cost: in the end, the thought collective of old saw its greatest victory in what was now being cast as freedom online. Increasingly prevalent, long-developing modes of tracking and newfound uses for increased precarity all won the day. On the one hand, these sites were clearly important to their users. By the same token, having users defend Etsy or Tumblr from the vicissitudes of the largest cable and telecom giants stood *as defense of a particular form of platform capitalism under construction*. Still further, an analysis of the supportive comments submitted appears to show that network neutrality in practice—importantly, as discourse—seems to reify a particular form of labor, instilling this form *as* freedom. Key actors defending particular modes of "Internet freedom" overall leaves an ambiguous sense as liberal ideals were ill-fitted for the development of an immanent logic of capitalism writ large. Paying attention to the political economic aspects of this universe is important, but the *cultural labor* performed by this debate is every bit as important as well, particularly as the imaginaries provided both within and outside of the debate a very specific future, one that was experiencing its own growth and accelerating beneath the feet of all involved. It is to this we now turn.

8 Knowledge, Access, and the Currents Flowing Beneath

Taking advantage of the authority it now possessed, the Federal Communications Commission (FCC) moved to operationalize its Title II authority in a number of realms. It sought to make the long-standing Lifeline program—which offered subsidies for rural and underserved areas for telephony—apply to broadband for the first time. Following on the heels of the General Conduct Standard, it opened inquiries into practices as "zero rating" by wireless providers, in which these networks would not count certain affiliated content or applications against monthly data limits, thus driving traffic to these preferred providers.

In perhaps one of its most significant moves, the FCC explored the possibility of instituting strong privacy safeguards that would apply to broadband operators, and did so after rancorous debate (FCC, 2016). These rules carried new transparency requirements on broadband providers as to how they used potentially sensitive customer data. The FCC considered the collection of personally identifying information off limits (such as browsing history, app usage history, the content of communications, information about children, health information, geolocation information, financial information, and more) without explicit opt-in consent by users. This was a momentous shift in a universe that, to this point, had acted with an opposite logic: the default, both on online conduits as well as on online platforms, was to assume that it was fine to collect all information barring a user's opting out of such collection—if they could even figure out the appropriate avenues for doing so. Other forms of information that were less sensitive (the examples the FCC gives are email addresses and service tiers) could be collected, but users needed to be permitted to opt out of such collection. Broadband providers would no longer be able to offer "take it or leave it" offerings that hamstrung users regarding their privacy.

All of these questions stemmed from overriding tensions related to the quandary of access to communications overall, a signal element in struggles of intersecting dimensions of class, race, gender, sexuality, and other dimensions of power and privilege. Amid these fights, the events in Ferguson, Missouri, that led to widespread Black Lives Matter protests made this incredibly clear. It revealed the inability of large journalistic organizations to pay due deference to concerns from long-repressed groups—the most effective record of police brutality came from social media and was only later reported on by larger organizations. Net neutrality was increasingly a civil rights issue. Access to broadband was little different.

Universal service, however, once defined simply as access to a telephone, has become complex indeed. Debates surrounding access to communication have remained rather static, almost removed from the broader political economy unfolding as the Web has continued to modify its circuits to suit newer, deeper modes of not just commodification but the service of grander logics entirely. The 2015 settlement on network neutrality did not change this fact; it merely shunted power from one set of corporate concerns to others and instilled particular incentives to drive in some directions and not others by all players involved. But with the shunt to Title II after decades of debate, new dimensions to the question of access and what notions of "Internet freedom" truly meant came into view. In short, the *historical subject* that was assumed during the network neutrality debates of the first decade of the new millennium, as well as those that led to the Wheeler rules in 2015, was itself under transformation and yet did not recognize itself as such. The Internet that was the object of debate during this time period was perhaps operationally not so different to users, but the logics undergirding it were themselves transforming beneath everyone's feet, and these logics meant that even as net neutrality debates themselves remained familiar in *terminology and intent,* the actual intersection of their operation with new commercial impetus was not.

What we observed in the last two chapters was that, as far as both the Genachowski FCC and Wheeler FCC were concerned, of pivotal importance to justifying an Open Internet regime of any stripe was the issue in relation to access to broadband. The term "virtuous cycle," birthed in the first Open Internet order of 2010, makes its appearance, as we saw, at least fifty times in the 2015 order. An open Internet, according to this logic, was necessary to stimulate further rollout of broadband itself via the stimulation of demand for it wrought by the emergence of new and desirable services that would traverse its circuits. The D.C. Circuit Court, even in striking down the 2010 order, supported this logic in their finding. Universal service of broadband in a neoliberal register, however, is hardly an innocent concept. The significance of this is that while struggles over network neutrality were about myriad overarching issues of free speech, innovation, and even civil rights, it was now *oddly reducible* to the issue of access as far as regulators were concerned. All other benefits were sidecars. This odd reduction carried as much freight as the transformation of open access debates into network neutrality debates because it considered access a static concept—when in fact what is necessary is a more dynamic one. The Web has not stayed constant, nor has the historical subject utilizing it. A theorization of what exactly access, privacy, and "media reform" means is necessary—one that encompasses both the successes and failures of consumer movements. This chapter will explore the shifting nature of the value-subject amid these debates. It will examine the implications of the evolving Internet and its structure and what theorists have termed "platform capitalism" or "surveillance capitalism." It will examine the intersections and implications of the network neutrality debate with the question of access—and the contradictions that obtain. Finally, it explores the contradictions that reign in activist discourse surrounding the issue.

The Issue of Universal Service

The issue of universal service may have experienced its own critical juncture. For years, the assessment made by the FCC as to whether broadband was being deployed in a reasonable and timely manner (as required by law) was a bone of contention to activists. The development of this very assessment was an object of controversy; the Republican FCC under Powell (and later Martin) looked at the U.S. broadband universe and saw only a plethora of competition, even despite its lack locally where consumers chose their providers. To the FCC, speeds were quick, competition was bountiful, and the status quo ruled; the continual wistful hope—as emphasized by the likes of Yoo—was that multimodal competition was developing even as this phantasm's shadow touched few outside the most concentrated urban centers. A possible turning point in this debate came after years of political action by advocates, when the Obama FCC under Genachowski found, for the first time, that deployment was *not* competitive, nor reasonable, nor timely. This move represented several significant steps in the development of broadband and, more broadly, neoliberalism.

For years, advocates had struggled against the FCC's measurement of broadband deployment. Advocates bemoaned that the frustration surrounding these debates revolved around how the issue was framed, rather than the technology itself (Derek Turner, personal communication, September 20, 2012). The goalposts were always moving: for years, in perennial *Broadband Reality Check* documents and beyond, Free Press protested that the FCC was producing data that made it *appear* as if there were plenty of competition. Such competition would, conceivably, be resulting in lower and lower prices, but the FCC never saw fit to indicate what prices were charged. And worse, even if additional information that might be useful to consider was being collected elsewhere by the government or other private sources, the FCC did not seek it out; and once it *had* commenced collecting useful data, it restricted the horizons of its own analysis:

> The Commission wasn't gathering the basic kind of data it needed to do classic antitrust analysis. So they made changes, made promises to make more, and we beat on them…and got Congress to do a National Broadband Plan. In the end they're gathering this great data and not doing anything with it. They have very granular data that would allow them to do granular data analysis, combine with private databases, but don't. They ignore our suggestion to do it. (Derek Turner, personal communication, September 20, 2012)

Pushing the FCC to recognize what was plain to most Americans—a lack of real competition for broadband access, with adjoining high prices, as reflected in international rankings—was itself *part and parcel* of the network neutrality debates. In an effort to exhaust all options, this was a response to losing the *Comcast* suit, stirring the FCC to do *something* regarding an "open Internet" that used the authority it appeared to have in Section 706 of the Telecommunications Act. The finding *might* supply the justification for the FCC to use this clause to act on network neutrality without having to reclassify broadband as a Title II service, even as for advocates, the latter was always the gold standard. The strategy for them was always clear: put forward in *Comcast* the strongest possible justification for Section 706 authority to box the chairman into having no option *but* to reclassify broadband. Genachowski did not bite; he did not have the fortitude or stomach to do it, resulting in the tremendous disappointments for advocates in the wake of his tenure.

Nonetheless, when the Genachowski FCC issued its 2010 *Sixth Broadband Deployment Report* (FCC, 2010d), it did mark a radical shift: in contrast to the previous reports, and building on the *National Broadband Plan*, which preceded it, the 2010 report finally increased the necessary speed to be considered "broadband" from 200 kilobits per second to 4 megabits per second download and 1 megabit per second upload. The fact that the FCC for years had considered 200 kilobits per second to serve as the benchmark broadband speed allowed it to effectively continue manufacturing competition for it where none existed. Former FCC reports considered a county "served" by a broadband provider if just one household had access to the service, which similarly inflated industry performance; in contrast, with this report, to be considered served one *percent* of households would need to have access going forward (¶21). Additionally, the FCC announced, "for the first time, we also used Census Bureau data to help us understand how broadband availability varies by particular demographics, such as income level and population density" (¶16). They came to the conclusion, following their first Broadband Consumer Survey, that those without broadband were

> disproportionately lower-income Americans and Americans who live in rural areas. The goal of the statute, and the standard against which we measure our progress, is universal broadband availability. We have not achieved this goal today, nor does it appear that we will achieve success without changes to present policies. The evidence further indicates that market forces alone are unlikely to ensure that the unserved minority of Americans will be able to obtain the benefits of broadband anytime in the near future. Therefore, if we remain on our current course, a large number of Americans likely will remain excluded from the significant benefits of broadband that most other Americans can access today. Given the ever-growing importance of broadband to our society, we are unable to conclude that broadband is being reasonably and timely deployed to all Americans in this situation. (FCC, 2010d, ¶28)

Of course, in true Genachowskian fashion, the FCC did not wish to offend. Offered in a footnote, the FCC adds, "We emphasize that our conclusion in this report in no way diminishes the progress broadband providers have made to expand broadband deployment throughout America.... Nor should our conclusion be taken as evidence that we are questioning the adequacy of the Commission's prior efforts to increase broadband deployment"—although perhaps longtime activists might beg to differ in their assessment (FCC, 2010d, ¶28n122).

In the years hence, up until 2018's rendition, the FCC continued to find that deployment of broadband services was not reasonable nor timely, which continued to provide wind at the back of Section 706 authority granting the FCC to take proactive steps to rectify the situation. As Republican Commissioner McDowell put it the first time that the FCC made this finding, "Instead of focusing on the great strides that America has made in broadband *deployment*, as the Act requires, this Report emphasizes subscribership" (McDowell, 2010, p. 1). Access for its own sake, and not for poor reason, was the rallying cry of advocates throughout the early 2000s, with numerous studies of areas which did not have access to it—Free Press, in fact, dispatched organizers to see for themselves the state of broadband access and take-up in Appalachia; continued analysis into strategies for take-up have proliferated (for example, the series of studies in Rhinesmith, 2017). During these years, advocates similarly offered support for local municipal efforts (and public-private partnerships) to launch their own broadband services to break the stranglehold of cable and telecommunications duopolies, mobilizing against well-funded efforts to pass state and local laws that would render illegal any efforts that proliferated in their wake. Unable at the state level to turn back a plethora of laws making public broadband provision illegal, advocates did manage to convince the FCC to override such legislation—until the courts struck down the action as an overreach by the FCC.

Yet even with these victories, the *terms* within which access were considered rarely wavered from the conception of proximity or purchase of access as itself sufficient focus; for as the times dictated, the ability to connect was absolutely determinative of future success. The digital divide continues to be a real problem in the United States, with cost of access being one of the greatest impediments, something that has been a constant of debate; reformers even in the middle of the first decade of the twenty-first century were emphasizing that broadband access in the United States was expensive and slow compared to that of other countries; think tanks affiliated with the neoliberal Russian doll dutifully attacked the data itself and provided excuses for the status quo. It is stunning that reformers were forced to continue to state the obvious a decade later in 2016 in *still* attempting to get the FCC to consider broadband as part of Lifeline access programs (see, for instance, Turner, 2016).

Recent work on universal service seems to continue to emphasize such a brute-force approach, as if access to broadband is not so different from access to a telephone. The logics undergirding the universal connection to broadband *are distinctly different from that of the telephone,* however. The functions a connection to broadband serves rev up entirely different engines. When the FCC moved to make it more challenging for Verizon to compile and sell the same kinds of personal information to which Google or Facebook might have access (more, even), it touched not just Verizon's desire to become a data-sales and data-processing giant on a plane with the tech giants, but its core incentives to roll out broadband itself. Here, scholarly histories of telecommunications rollout throughout the twentieth century provide some parallel insights upon which to draw (such as Mueller, 1997). Horwitz (1989) usefully makes clear that activism had a great deal to do with the rollout of telephony and with managing the prices that households would pay. These moves, particularly at the level of state public utility commissions, often set up future fights in the national arena by challenging profit models of the dominant telecommunications providers of the time. Horwitz's history of access emphasizes costs, consumers, legal battles, and other conundra in the liberalization of telecommunications. The present conjuncture finds these issues compounded with complex additional calculations that remained absent from debates about network neutrality.

Newly Emergent Value Subjects: An Industry View

The importance of broadband and its function were clearly laid out by advocates when AT&T, before the FCC declared broadband a Title II service, announced to the agency that it desired to be exempted from Title II regulation altogether. Phone companies had been ceding control of wired communications to cable companies for years, and they were making every effort to get out from under even state-level regulatory authority for their wired connections, arguing that telephony had itself undergone a switch to Internet protocol in its transmission (Crawford, 2013). Harold Feld, now of Public Knowledge, outlined what he saw as essential protections that would be required of the unified telephony-broadband pipe if the FCC were to allow this: "service to all Americans," "competition and interconnection," "consumer protection," "network reliability," and "public safety" (Griffin & Feld, 2013).

In contrast to such a call, shifts in political economic function were apparent when one takes into account the advice that was being bestowed on information technology departments and more by consultancies such as Gartner. This consultancy took it upon itself to garner its own governing philosophy, which they called "digital connectivism," that offered a contrast to the hopes of the likes of Public Knowledge in thinking through the transition to Internet protocol telephony. It represents a guide to an inaugural, perhaps even normative notion of citizenship which Gartner's analyst believed would be necessary, one increasingly shared by the likes of their clients.

Taking a surreal postmodern turn, the analyst writes, "We are creating a digital society in which the virtual world and the physical world merge, and in which everyone and everything is connected" (Buytendijk, 2016b, p. 1). Gartner crafts its own notion of the digital divide: given that the "digital society, like any society, is characterized by persistent social interactions, and through patterns of relationships between members of a group that are associated by common interests"—and that these relationships are increasingly through technology ("We talk to things, and things talk back"), the analyst concludes,

> This lifts the idea of the "digital divide" to new levels. The term is not new. It once meant the divide between people that could use the internet, and those that couldn't. But this was really a virtual divide only seen in the virtual world. Life as we know it continues outside Second Life, and believe it or not, it also continues without Facebook. What's next is the *real* digital divide, as "digital" is about the physical and virtual world merging. (Buytendijk, 2016b, p. 2)

Confirming what activists have long argued (and continue to do so), "People that don't have the skills to interact with digital technology, or simply have no access, are shut out of more than being online. They're shut out of life.... Nonparticipants in the digital world will have trouble sustaining jobs, friendships and even a place to live" (Buytendijk, 2016b, p. 2).

The increased interactions between humans and machines which might render life more "machine-like" and machines more "human" (Buytendijk, 2016b, p. 4) required a "new philosophy": "For a society to work, we need to find a shared way of interacting, and standards of behavior. This applies to people as much as things. The term we are proposing for this is 'digital *dasein.*' Dasein is a German word best translated as 'being there,' or perhaps a combination of 'being' and 'doing'" (p. 5). "Digital connectivism," as Gartner defines the term, "describes how people and things exist and interact in the global ecosystem of digital connections, and how this shapes a digital society" (p. 5). It possessed its own five tenets: "We all have a digital identity"; "We need to be connected in order to exist"; "We value connections through context"; "We do not differentiate between people and things"; and "We treat our connections with care" (p. 6).

It is in how these tenets are operationalized which draw the most reason for pause. Analysts such as Cheney-Lippold (2011, 2017) point to the overriding importance in today's environment of one's algorithmic identities: it is the selective measurement of the traces we leave behind that feed into far-reaching models that determine whether we are offered a mortgage on favorable terms or not, whether our communities receive incongruous police scrutiny, whether we are offered a digital coupon—or if we are considered "waste" to commercial concerns (see also Gangadharan, 2012; Greenfield, 2017; Pasquale, 2015). At first, Buytendijk mirrors these concerns in describing how ordinary subjects may misapprehend their digital profiles: "we often dismiss our online profiles as 'not real.' These profiles are not created based on who we are, but on an algorithmic interpretation of our online behavior. These profiles exist separate from us, and—if we could see and examine them—are completely divorced from our real identities." Buytendijk urges that this understanding is false, pushing well past the apprehensions of the critical scholars into a full-on acceptance of a merger of material and digital. "This is misguided … we increasingly cannot distinguish between our physical and virtual identities. A virtual identity is as real and impactful as a physical identity, and merging the two creates something else: a digital identity" (Buytendijk, 2016a, p. 6). We should be, in this analyst's view, preparing ourselves for the coming "distributed self":

> Many assets already have a "digital twin"—a dynamic software model of a physical thing or system that relies on sensor data to understand its state, respond to changes, improve operations and add value. Through receiving sensor data, the digital twin mirrors the functions of the real asset. Digital twins are proxies for the combination of skilled individuals (technicians) and traditional monitoring devices and controls (for example, pressure gauges, light sensors and accelerometers). … For human beings, digital citizens should ready themselves for a "distributed self" where things become part of our digital identity. Algorithms can already take mundane tasks out of our hands, and algorithms can represent us

> in daily communications and help us display desired behaviors. In all of these cases—tasks, communication and behaviors—technology takes over a certain type of responsibility, or even a "moral agency." (Buytendijk, 2016a, p. 7)

In fact, the analyst circles back and applies a neoliberal notion of self-care and obligation to the finding. "Manage your digital identity carefully. It is as real as your physical identity. In fact, your digital identity allows you to live skillfully and comfortably in the digital world, and it is the core of your digital dasein" (Buytendijk, 2016a, p. 7).

All relationships are contextual, but the "distributed citizen" would need to be forgiving of the environment's digital designers:

> Increasingly, algorithms are trained through machine learning. The decisions come from data inferences, and, given the large volume of data and the number of combinations, these decisions are hard or even impossible to predict. How can the designer be held responsible?... [Distributed citizens should] exercise patience and tolerance. It will take a long time before digital technologies based on machine learning will "get it" in their interactions. Don't be insulted if an algorithm gets it wrong. (Buytendijk, 2016a, p. 11)

Similarly, "Don't immediately blame the designer when the technology gets it wrong. Through machine learning, digital technologies quickly depart from their original programming, sometimes with unintended consequences.... Demand that designers of digital technology closely monitor how their 'creations' learn, and encourage them to build in ways to correct dysfunctional learning" (Buytendijk, 2016a, pp. 11–12). All of us, the analyst continues, collectively bear the responsibility of "build[ing], car[ing] for, and sustain[ing] this world and make sure the digital society is fair and just" (p. 12).

With this in mind, the new distributed subject "should not see 'your' digital technologies as your possessions. Instead, you should see purchasing digital technologies as an admission fee to the digital society, to participate in a specific ecosystem" (Buytendijk, 2016a, p. 13). Perhaps horrifyingly, the author argues one should "be helpful to digital technologies that base their interactions on machine learning. As a digital citizen, you carry a responsibility to set the right example, as you would with children" (p. 13). Thus nascent technologies and business models are portrayed as simple interventions into the world which require tutelage so as to become actants in a new universality; the author is agnostic as to who will benefit, merely outlining a philosophical offering and letting the cards remain where they lay.

Now, this hardly means that this report is a representation of truth; it is, rather, an interpretation of our universe. As Mosco (2014) reminds us, Gartner is playing its part in boosting such technologies as cloud computing, artificial intelligence, machine learning, and more, which comprise important parts of the political economy of this sector. However, given the privileged place of such consultancies in today's economy in advising businesses new and old, it is much more: presented *as* research, it is less this than a clear statement of neoliberal governmentality crystallized in brief form, feeding back to enterprises what they already knew: the deployment of a particular imaginary for the consultancy's customers. All the same, if the article is Gartner's trip to graduate school, they fail the qualifying exam: in a quick rundown of the author's sources, one learns that the philosophy was gleaned by looking at the Wikipedia pages (exclusively) of "sociomateriality," "sociotechnical system," "ontology," "ontology (information science)," "connectivism," "Heideggerian terminology," "Actor-network theory," "communitarianism," "utilitarianism," "classical liberalism," "posthumanism," "agency (philosophy)," and three other overview articles on connectivism and posthumanism. It is a perfectly neoliberal philosophy down to its source: Jimmy Wales, founder of the platform, noted in an interview, "One can't understand my ideas about Wikipedia without understanding Hayek" (Dahlberg, 2010, p. 352n313). Perhaps this node of research, one that fetches an undoubtedly high price, is perfectly representative of its time, a second-order distillation of exactly this tendency. In short, whereas in activism and in policymaking the question of the double truth arises, here it is constructed in how the political economy of technological concerns should operate.

When the author finally turns to address the audience for which this article was intended—the business executives paying for these insights—the moves presage what is to come, extending the notion of digital citizens to the enterprise itself. "Every business has a digital identity, whether it has its own digital presence or digital strategy or not" (Buytendijk, 2016b, p. 13). But the implications are far greater. "Every business will be an ecosystem business," the analyst notes; "Digital technologies, often based on machine learning, require a different type of R&D [research and development] and product management. Products are not launched when ready; instead, their launch marks the beginning of their development"; and "the profitability of new and digital business models is often based on maximizing the life span of the product or service, rather than designing it for periodical replacement" (p. 13). If the analyst here has taken a deep dive into Wikipedia to assemble a tautological set of insights to reflect the executive back to herself, then it is worth a brief excursion to the development of responses to these moves and their development to understand the contradictions that result between the network neutrality debates and this environment—and how the notion of access, to which network neutrality had been reduced, only intensifies them.

Shifts in the Political Economy of Access

Simultaneously present yet absent in advocate discourse is the political economy underlying the development of capitalism itself in the wake of what Schiller terms the post-2008 "digital depression" (Schiller, 2014). It produced any number of effects, but one of the most important feature was that the Web was, through it all, a site of continued growth. If Greenstein (2016) recalled developments leading up to the late 1990s as a process of "capital deepening"—that is, the creation of a market for middlemen actors that enabled existing enterprises to lower their own costs and enabling the growth of economies of scale or scope—what we observe here is something quite different, driven more by the quest for yield. Srnicek (2017) summarizes that this was for several reasons. Fear of the effects of steep government indebtedness, preparations for future crisis, and the continued bipartisan privatization drive across much of the field drove pushes to austerity, an environment of low interest rates, and for the government's taking active stakes in bonds, a step termed "quantitative easing." The net effect of these moves was the creation of an environment of easy money coupled with lower yields on myriad assets: left with few options to make larger returns, "investors seeking yields have had to turn to increasingly risky assets—by investing in unprofitable and unproven tech companies, for instance" (p. 30). As Schiller would note, "As network services and applications developed, scrambles to occupy what were seen as newly strategic, high-profit boxes became recurrent, inducing dizzying changes in communications commodity chains" (Schiller, 2014, p. 91).

This was coupled with the buildup of enormous cash hoards, part of a larger trend already but itself accelerated in this climate as corporate profits started to accumulate in the wake of the crisis. Much of these earnings were stashed overseas in a calculated move to avoid owing taxes. This was particularly prevalent among tech companies; repatriating these revenues, and paying the taxes on them, was more costly than taking on new debt (Schiller, 2014; Srnicek, 2017, pp. 30–31). "In their SEC [Securities and Exchange Commission] filings tax avoidance is explicitly given as a reason for holding such high levels of offshore reserves" (Srnicek, 2017, p. 32). The combination of a glut of cash for investment in corporate cash hoards and the ease with which one could avoid taxes put pressure on government revenues, thus resulting in "exacerbated austerity. The vast amount of tax money that goes missing in tax havens must be made up elsewhere. The result is further limitations on fiscal stimulus and a greater need for unorthodox monetary policies. Tax evasion, austerity, and extraordinary monetary policies are all mutually reinforcing" (pp. 32–33). As more countries were increasingly integrated into the market relation due to formerly communist countries joining global economic currents, the reserve army of labor was increased with adjoining pressure on those already employed, a pressure multiplied when unemployment surged in the wake of the 2008 crisis (Schiller, 2014; Srnicek, 2017).

The present online environment cannot be understood outside of these developments, with online platforms taking advantage of the increased overall precaritization of labor. By the same token, with such pressures on labor, an adjoining potentiality for broadened economic crisis made itself apparent as the purchasing power of these laborers took a similar hit: "The digital depression intensified [the need of advertisers to have access to buyers] by jeopardizing capital's ability to dispose profitably of mountains of accumulating merchandise" (Schiller, 2014, p. 125). As Baran and Sweezy (1966) posited decades ago, advertising served the function of attempting to increase aggregate effective demand in an environment in which corporate entities, increasingly oligopolistic, preferred not to compete on price. With the development of capabilities of such new tools as cookies that were developed during the dot-com boom, the sales effort (that is, not just advertising, but all processes geared toward clearing markets, including marketing and research and development) only intensified its attempts to reach potential desirable buyers for commodities that continued to be produced in an environment of overcapacity and overproduction. The ingredients for immediate, structural, and possibly fatal crisis lurked at every stage of the production chain.

These moves meant that the subject generated by access to these networks was itself only becoming more valuable and sought after—unevenly so across the social landscape. Stoked by the emergence of phones which possessed the ability to track their users ever more effectively, the amplification of online surveillance became pervasive across the field (Turow, 2011, 2017; Turow, McGuigan, & Maris, 2015). As the sales effort only heightened—and proved its usefulness beyond clearance of markets, extending its techniques into the realms of government surveillance, financial ratings, and more (McChesney, 2013; Pasquale, 2015)—the collective leap of faith in "predictive analytics" as a powerful new mode of governance (broadly construed) took hold across myriad operative logics. As Andrejevic noted in 2012 (only to have Gartner reify the concept four years later as "digital connectivism"):

> We are increasingly coming to rely on services and communication infrastructure that rely on the effectiveness of targeting marketing, data mining, and predictive analytics.... The wager that data-driven marketing will be profitable enough to offset the costs of data collection, storage, and sorting, may, in the end, turn out to be a losing one, but if it is, we should understand that we are staking the future of one of the most important communication media of our era upon it. (Andrejevic, 2012, pp. 74–75)

His concerns extended to the implications of the value-producing subject itself: "There is more at stake in such forms of surveillance than profit: specifically the prospect that consumers will be put to work marketing to themselves, and, through this extra work, generate a customized product for which they are required to pay a premium" (Andrejevic, 2012, p. 73). That is, the *presumption* that predictive analytics would be the panacea for salvation from imminent crisis meant technologies would continue to be turned to the sales effort, a point expressed eloquently by Schiller nearly half a decade previously: "The circuits of daily life are being set at the service of the sales function so that virtually any area of cultural practice can be reorganized to suit the demands of its underwriters. Captured by proprietary interests, the culture skis and slides away from democratic development" (Schiller, 2007b, p. 161).

Concerns about algorithmic discrimination have abounded, and they grip the popular imagination in such books as the popular *Weapons of Math Destruction* (O'Neil, 2016) and in academic work emphasizing the reinscription of offline inequality, racism, gender disparities, and other intersecting axes of power in algorithms (Gangadharan, 2012). Entire courses are now being taught, under the rubric of ethics, regarding these concerns.[1] Reports have appeared revealing the numerous ways, both accessible to present-day subjects and not, that we are scored and thus find ourselves at the mercy of our online algorithmic identities for future life options (Dixon & Gellman, 2014), a darker version of the story than anything the analyst at Gartner was concerned about and one closer to the concerns of Cheney-Lippold (2017). The logics of the sales appeal away from "demographics" to desired individuals has resulted in a growth industry in tracking technologies, or "marketing tech," all seeking to connect our online behaviors to offline activities (for earlier thinking in this realm, a seminal work is Gandy, 1993; Turow, 2011, 2017). Others have focused on the invisible "black boxes" comprising search, algorithmic sorting, and new symbioses between governmental and commercial surveillance, both working hand in glove with each other (Pasquale, 2015). So-called smart cities at various stages of development are sites of expansion themselves, undergirded by a large market of corporate facilitators (Greenfield, 2013; Sadowski & Pasquale, 2015). In addition, the creation of "fusion centers" where governments can obtain data about individuals it might not lawfully be able to collect itself—with a reciprocal arrangement for corporate partners—represents yet another site of expansion (Pasquale, 2015).

However, too much discussion of things as "privacy" are relegated to silos (consumerism; discrimination), all negative categories. These authors generally have sought reform of a system that allows such tracking, not necessarily questioning capitalism in and of itself in instigating and fomenting these new abilities. Andrejevic (2012) points to exactly the problem in terms of predictive analytics systems, although the sentiment could easily be expanded: "Privacy-based critiques do not quite capture the element of productive power and control at work in the promise of monitoring-based marketing.... Critical approaches, however, locate coercion not solely at the level of discrete individual decisions, but also in the social relations that structure them" (p. 86).

The notion of *systemic* coercion—wrought in this context from the privatization of Internet infrastructure and available tools—"provides those who own these productive resources with control over the terms of access" (Andrejevic, 2012, p. 86). The evaluation of the place of the individual subject has become of increasing concern analytically and politically. A classic insight of communications theory of decades' vintage is experiencing a resurgence of interest in this environment: the "audience commodity" (Smythe, 2014). This was a complex entity, however, not just a commodity sold to advertisers but a performer of labor itself in the process of viewing broadcast media. This notion has seen itself in ascendance in an era of increased cognizance of pervasive tracking online, both by advertisers as well as government interests (a full revisit, with responses both classic and updated, can be found in McGuigan & Manzerolle, 2014).

Yet the notion of commodification is similarly insufficient to grasp widespread cultural shifts. Taking the necessary step beyond commodification to encompass the wider environment within which such commodification might occur, the autonomists in the late 1990s, investigating nascent forms of immaterial labor often done for free (and even for pleasure: posting to social media provides a modern example), devised the concept of "free labor" (Terranova 2000 [2012 offers updates and a new conclusion]). This was a step beyond commodification, an effort to deal with one of the theoretical ambivalences of the time: that arguments which theorized the Internet as both a potential tool of democratization and liberation coexisted with arguments that it represented the best tool for control and exploitation yet devised. "Free labor" brought both arguments under a single umbrella: the point was that this conflict was itself *constitutive* of the moment. The emphasis was that our efforts were themselves channeled to the ends of capital: the unemployed were often only so in name only, Terranova notes; and borrowing from the powerful vision of the "social factory"—in which productive capacity has left the factory and in fact comes to encompass everyday activities—our immaterial labor was done not just aboard electronic circuits but offline via the affective labors we performed, knowingly or not. All could be channeled to the profit-seeking ends of capital. It encompassed the idea that, while labor was certainly being appropriated and channeled to capital's ends, "The relation between culture, the cultural industry, and labor in these movements is much more complex than the notion of incorporation suggests. In this sense, the digital economy is not a new phenomenon but simply a new phase of this longer history of experimentation." Crucially, free labor was "a desire of labor immanent to late capitalism, and late capitalism is the field that both sustains free labor and exhausts it" (Terranova, 2012, p. 50). This is a powerful rubric for the evaluation of the value-producing subject settling in.

In seeking to give the notion greater analytical purchase, Fast, Örnebring, and Karlsson (2016) sought to compile a typology of free labor practices in an attempt to gain more precision in the concept. While such breakdowns can be useful, Zuboff (2019) offers perhaps an overly totalizing conception of what has emerged. Her project is to outline the contours of a new phase of capitalism that she terms "surveillance capitalism." As an overall logic, she eschews descriptions of companies like Google as multiple-sided markets, favoring instead a focus on what it produces, which she terms "surveillance assets": "These assets are critical raw materials in the pursuit of surveillance revenues and their translation into surveillance capital. The entire logic of this capital accumulation is most accurately understood as surveillance capitalism, which is the foundational framework for a surveillance-based economic order: a surveillance economy" (p. 94). These surveillance assets, or "behavioral surplus," are transformed by continually updated modes of "machine intelligence" to render "prediction products" for sale to "behavioral futures markets" (p. 96). Importantly, while advertising is the obvious initial customer to such commodities, "any actor with an interest in purchasing probabilistic information about our behavior and/or influencing future behavior can pay to play in markets where the behavioral fortunes of individuals, groups, bodies, and things are told and sold" (p. 96). As the autonomists and theorists of audience labor commodities noted, "we are the objects from which raw materials are extracted and expropriated for Google's prediction factories" (p. 94). Importantly, the overarching purpose of these logics and protocols is "to influence and modify human behavior at scale as the means of production is subordinated to a new and more complex means of *behavior modification*" (p. 19).

Perhaps confusingly, Zuboff distinguishes between "capitalists" and "surveillance capitalists," the former being those firms that "collect[] behavioral data with permission and solely as a means to product or service improvement" (p. 22) as opposed to processing it for sale. Such moves have drawn reasonable detractors. Morozov (2019), reviewing her work, makes the observation that this overarching emphasis on behavioral surplus as *the* central facet of our age is itself not historicized nor contextually situated enough; her treatment of Google as the origin-point of this epoch "hides the geopolitical formations that made that foray possible" (n.p.). Further: "What Zuboff doesn't offer is an account of how value—all of it, not just those parts accruing to behavioral surplus—is produced in the digital economy" (n.p.).

Even more bewilderingly, Zuboff appears to cast aside all other value-production logics and structuring mechanisms entirely, tossing the baby out with the bath water to declare a new capitalism (and Morozov quotes this passage as well in his review): "The struggle for power and control in society is no longer associated with the hidden facts of class and its relationship to production but rather by the hidden facts of automated engineered behavioral modification" (Zuboff, 2019, p. 309). Further, "False consciousness is no longer produced by the hidden facts of class and their relation to production but rather by the hidden facts of instrumentarian power's command over the division of learning in society… Who knows? Who decides who decides? Power was once identified with the ownership of the means of production, but it is now identified with ownership of the means of behavioral modification" (p. 379). Such sentiments serve to obfuscate more than they reveal about the interrelations of systems both new and old: in lieu of declaring new ages, one is wiser to appreciate that even in times of change, new logics intermix with and render more complex their relationships with older ones, rather than displacing them altogether.

There is much to still appreciate in Zuboff's analysis, but one might suggest that the notion of "heteromation," coined by Ekbia and Nardi (2014, 2017), may prove to offer tools for capturing in more granular fashion systems of value production (or cost savings, depending on one's theoretical commitments) without being as all-totalizing. They define the term as a new division of labor in which humans are increasingly inserted into technological systems so as to *aid machines,* contrary to the usual assumption that automation will inevitably replace human labor, even as it certainly does in certain instances (Ekbia & Nardi, 2014). Any idea that distribution of labor is technologically determined—that is, "machines do this well" and "humans do this well"—has been countered by history. Rather, it is social and economic systems that determine the mix. The costs of innovation have increased, meaning that, when it comes to computationally complex tasks, it makes more short-term cost-benefit sense to have humans do it, even if in the long term it might be beneficial to replace them altogether. "Labor supplied by human workers is cheaper than comparable automated systems. Certain tasks that humans can perform are not impossible for computers, but would require expensive research and programming labor to be realized. In the long run, it might be more cost-effective for enterprises to automate labor performed by human workers in heteromated systems, but capitalists are driven by near-term profits" (Ekbia & Nardi, 2014, p. 6). Of more value today are built-in holes (filled by users, such as on Facebook and Google, or via Google's now-ubiquitous CAPTCHAs, which both confirms a user's "humanity" and also provides semantic interpretations of Google-housed images by humans—for free, of course). "With fiendish ingenuity, heteromated systems are designed so as to *subsume* earlier mechanisms of automation and augmentation in complex and composite assemblages. Augmented by the new layers of information provided through electronic gadgets…and supported by a fast global communication infrastructure, heteromated labor can be made available 24/7 at almost any point on the globe" (p. 9).

Heteromation can be rendered quite complex. As opposed to the generic classification of all interactions in this realm as "free labor," more usefully we should be examining the various "moments" in the production chain: we are heteromatons, dwelling not just in the realm of labor but also of circulation. "Data exhaust," produced by the activities spanning all daily life by both humans and machines, Srnicek notes, "have come to serve a number of key capitalist functions: they educate and give competitive advantage to algorithms; they enable the coordination and outsourcing of workers; they allow for the optimisation and flexibility of productive processes; they make possible the transformation of low-margin goods into high-margin services; and data analysis is itself generative of data, in a virtuous cycle" (Srnicek, 2017, pp. 41–42). Zuboff makes a similar point, speaking to the perils of this practice of extraction and processing and offering the rubrics of "behavioral surplus" being provided to "prediction products," producing "markets for future behavior" (Zuboff, 2015, 2016). This is hardly limited to tech firms; nontech firms have similar interests as it represents "a key method of building a monopolistic platform and of siphoning off revenue from advertisers" (Srnicek, 2017, p. 58; compare with Zuboff, 2015). Market forces only propel these tendencies ever further. As Pasquale (2015) makes clear, "In an era where Big Data is the key to maximizing profit, *every* business has an incentive to be nosy. What the search industry blandly calls 'competition' for users and 'consent' to data collection looks increasingly like monopoly and coercion" (p. 81).

The approach of the likes of Schiller (2014), Caraway (2016), and Srnicek (2017) provide the necessary vantage point from which to most soundly observe the implications of the twin conundra of net neutrality and its adjoining issue of access, to which the issue had been reduced in the regulatory sense, even if advocates utilized the argument primarily—and exclusively—as a means to an end. These authors, as Schiller expresses it, focus on "the pressures, the drives, the incentives, the limits, and the conforming tendencies of an environing political economy" (Schiller, 2014, p. 82). Perhaps "free labor" or "behavioral surplus" (Zuboff, 2019) may be a useful way to conceptualize the cultural development of the present conjuncture, but to examine shifting production of *value* itself, other analytics seem necessary. Schiller's approach to the examination of commodity chains themselves provides such a lens, particularly given that personal data itself has entered them—the primary function of which is an effort to keep capital in circulation. Efforts of advertisers to reach their perfect marks, Schiller notes, are "grounded in capital's need to realize the sale of commodities already produced in order to resume the cycle by producing and selling once again. A break in this process of commodity circulation—whether local to a specific company or industry, or sweepingly widespread—is a desideratum of crisis" (Schiller, 2014, p. 125). Arguments do abound as to how to conceive of the labor that obtains in the social factory; does it allow for infinite exploitation, tossing untold new value into capitalists' laps (Fuchs, 2012a, 2012b)? Or is this more accurately a cost savings, the mere facilitation of new labor processes where value is *actually* created (Caraway, 2016)? Srnicek similarly questions the utility of considering what has been termed "data exhaust" a site of unlimited exploitation, itself productive of value:

> If our online interactions are free labour, then these companies must be a significant boon to capitalism overall—a whole new landscape of exploited labour has been opened up. On the other hand, if this is not free labour, then these firms are parasitical on other value-producing industries and global capitalism is in a more dire state. A quick glance at the stagnating global economy suggests that the latter is more likely. (Srnicek, 2017, p. 56)

Such critiques of the notion are struggles surrounding the fundamental tension between capturing the *cultural* moment versus instituting a way to provide a more exacting *accounting* of it in analysis. How one theorizes the production of value in this environment *matters*.

Considering Platforms

What does unify these approaches overall, however, is the idea that the sales effort needs and appropriates data as raw material "that can be refined and used in a variety of ways by platforms" (Srnicek, 2017, p. 56). This is something quite aside from worries of manipulation alone. It is these collective characteristics, and the (perceived or actual) competitive advantages accruing to those who make the wager on increased accumulation of data, that have given rise to what Srnicek has termed "platform capitalism": "Platforms, in sum, are a new type of firm; they are characterised by providing the infrastructure to intermediate between different user groups, by displaying monopoly tendencies driven by network effects, by employing cross-subsidization to draw in different user groups, and by having a designed core architecture that governs the interaction possibilities.... They are an extractive apparatus for data" (Srnicek, 2017, p. 48). Importantly, Srnicek (making a similar point to Andrejevic, Fuchs, and Zuboff) properly theorizes what too many others have left hanging: "The important element is that the capitalist class owns the platform, not necessarily that it produces a physical product" (p. 49).

Srnicek identifies four types of platforms: advertising (such as Facebook and Google), cloud services (Amazon Web Services [AWS], Salesforce); industrial platforms (with top positions occupied by General Electric [GE] and Siemens), and what he terms "lean" platforms such as Uber and Airbnb, where capital is effectively supplied by a private user-owner and the platform simply facilitates transactions. What unifies these platforms is their emphasis on open interfaces for clients from which user data is extracted, channeled, and combined with strategies of lock in.

The place where Srnicek may misstep is in underplaying the strength of conduit operators as telecommunications and cable companies:

> While we might think that being lower in the stack is correlated with greater power, this is not necessarily the case. Perhaps surprisingly, network providers (i.e. those that provide the basic telecommunications infrastructure) are in a low margin position in the ecosystem around platforms—a position that has compelled them to push for discriminatory pricing in moving data around (the end of "net neutrality") as a way to generate more revenues. *The strategic importance of a position has much more to do with controlling data from businesses and customers than with just being lower in the stack.* (Srnicek, 2017, pp. 106–107; emphasis added)

However, being a conduit gives one potentially limitless power and advantage, depending on the policy frameworks under which it operates; the specifics of the conduit's operation similarly matter. Its function as connection and interface for the broader universe within which platforms operate cannot be discounted. As more transactions once beholden to the conduit provider's circuits move to "over the top" services, network operators have learned the lesson that being a "dumb pipe" means to forego significant potential revenue streams. In the United States, investment in carriers earned significantly lower earnings than investment in services: thus operators desired to jump into these vertical markets but were constrained from doing so by such regulation as potential network neutrality rules alongside "chronic pressure on [generating increasing] average revenue per user, and intense competition from both smartphone suppliers and ... destabilizing Web applications" (Schiller, 2014, p. 91). While the cost of text messaging for a carrier is low, servicing the onslaught of data is expensive, even as broadband remains in and of itself a high-margin industry; thus incumbents turned to providing service bundles, diversifying services vertically and attempting to restructure their relationships with those services that depended upon them (p. 92). As a *Business Insider* analyst wrote in 2015, "Dumb pipe strategies can lead to limited opportunities and increased regulation. Offering applications allows more flexible pricing models, greater aggregate pricing power, and higher optionality from future profit pools that could be created. The other key reason to avoid becoming a dumb pipe is that a dumb pipe looks more like a utility business model, and utilities are usually heavily regulated, including price regulation" (Bryan, 2015).

Two platforms in particular—advertising platforms and the lean platforms in which user-owned resources are leveraged by online applications—have received the lion's share of attention. Lean platforms are post-2008 entities; venture capital deals for lean platforms have tripled since 2009 (Srnicek, 2017). In terms of maintaining this sector, Srnicek notes that it is primarily and almost exclusively the effect of the hunt for yield: "Rather than a finance boom or a housing boom, surplus capital today appears to be building a technology boom. Such is the level of compulsion that even non-traditional funding from hedge funds, mutual funds, and investment banks is playing a major role in the tech boom. In fact, in the technology start-up sector, most investment financing comes from hedge funds and mutual funds" (p. 86). Companies such as Google and DHL hardly have sat this out, with Google investing in (the unsuccessful) Homejoy and DHL creating MyWays, an on-demand service; Intel and Google have also purchased equity in neonatal startups (p. 86). This growth in lean platforms reflects faith, as of the late 1990s, in future profits; until then, "their profitability appears to be generated solely by the removal of costs and the lowering of wages and not by anything substantial" (p. 87).

Advertising platforms were hardly new phenomena (Turow [2011] offers a history extending to the late twentieth century), but alongside the disclosures of Edward Snowden in 2013, these have come under increasing (relative) scrutiny by the general public. The 2016 privacy proceeding at the FCC, of course, had everything to do with the nation's broadband operators' attempts below the radar to become some of the largest players in this arena as platforms and as sellers of user data. For years it has been known that broadband operators were interested in taking charge of and selling data about the activities of their customers, with some designing plans for which privacy cost extra; these drew much attention and ire of activists, but the drive absolutely remains (Auerbach, 2015). In early 2016, the Center for Digital Democracy (CDD) compiled a report listing the efforts of telecommunications and cable companies' efforts to become pivotal platforms themselves to the sales effort. "As consumers have grown to rely on many screens to view digital content, Verizon, Comcast, Google, AT&T, Time Warner, and others have incorporated powerful layers of data collection and digital marketing technologies to better target individuals," the report notes (Center for Digital Democracy, 2016, p. 1). With an eye toward reaching users across their screens, for but one example, AT&T has grown its own division, "AT&T Adworks," to allow advertisers to perform targeting. This was a major feature of the AT&T–Time Warner merger, consummated in 2018. The report similarly notes that Comcast can "harvest 'terabytes of unstructured data' from the set top boxes it controls, including homes that have them in 'multiple rooms'" (p. 5). The CDD notes the interrelationships among these providers and router manufacturers like Cisco and data brokers as Acxiom to connect users' online and offline behavior (p. 2).

Verizon has been on a revealing tear over the last few years. When Turow (2011) compiled a list of the top advertising networks (which track users across websites) and advertising exchanges (which supply platforms for the offer and sale of data or ad placement at auction), the top slots across each category comprised Google, Yahoo, Microsoft, and AOL. By 2016, Verizon entered the top ranks via its purchase of both AOL and Yahoo, which it folded into a subsidiary it called Oath, later renamed Verizon Media (Macmillan, 2016; McCormick, 2015). On the strength of "native advertising" divisions birthed by the likes of the *New York Times*, Verizon expanded its foray into content itself, teaming up with Hearst to purchase Complex Media, which specialized in branded content (Knutson, Hagey, & Alpert, 2016). In

2019, it trumpeted its application distribution network (and its ownership of some of the most "well known and loved names in media and tech").[2] Its DNS Search solution "can offer users a page of sponsored and algo[rithmic] listings to help them find what they are looking for," performing its own keyword search on queries that ordinarily might reach a "Page Not Found" message; this tactic is "often leveraged by Internet Service Providers (ISP's) and toolbar Partners to monetize" such traffic, creating a "win-win—you're assisting your users, while creating a new revenue stream for yourself."[3]

Access to user email is a tremendous perceived advantage. The general trend had started shifting away from reading and analyzing user emails to mine for data useful for advertisers—at least in public. Google claimed that it had ceased the practice, saying it knew enough about its users based on search data; Microsoft claimed it had never employed the practice (MacMillan, Krouse, & Hagey, 2018). All the same, a *Wall Street Journal* investigation revealed that Gmail continued to allow third-party developers to "scan the inboxes of millions of Gmail users who signed up for email-based services offering shopping price comparisons, automated travel-itinerary planners or other tools." Google "does little to police these developers, who train their computers—and, in some cases, employees—to read their users' emails" (MacMillan, 2018).

Verizon was loath to lose out on this gravy train, and to push it still farther, pitched Yahoo's 200 million inboxes to advertisers (MacMillan, Krouse, & Hagey, 2018). The practice extended to AOL Mail (to which Verizon had pushed its customers as it retired its own Verizon-branded email service). The *Wall Street Journal* remarked, "They constitute the only major U.S. email provider that scans user inboxes for marketing purposes"; email scanning had "become one of the company's most effective methods for improving ad targeting" (MacMillan, Krouse, & Hagey, 2018). An executive claimed that the scanning only applied to commercial emails and that users could opt out (if they even realized this was happening). Opting out was hardly obvious; in communications to their users advising them of these practices, Yahoo "gave two options—'I Accept,' or 'I'll do this later'" (MacMillan, Krouse, & Hagey, 2018). The system analyzed receipts, travel itineraries, and promotions that were delivered to users. Another executive said, "Email is an expensive system.... I think it's reasonable and ethical to expect the value exchange, if you've got this email service and there is advertising going on," even if Verizon pushed a paying customer to the service, it appears (MacMillan, Krouse, & Hagey, 2018). Never mind, of course, that Verizon customers were already paying for the service themselves. Verizon divided users into "interest profiles" based on their email and used this garnered information to "target them elsewhere on the web," grouping users who are similar "as an 'audience' to which marketers can target ads," further bolstered by cookies left on user machines by (then) Oath to identify to which audience a user belonged (MacMillan, Krouse, & Hagey, 2018). Oath's new privacy policy similarly "prevent[ed] users from filing class-action suits and instead requires them to pursue their grievances through arbitration or small-claims court" (MacMillan, Krouse, & Hagey, 2018). This email-scanning practice was a reason Amazon started to shy away from sending fully itemized receipts in 2015, as the company hardly wanted to allow Yahoo and the like to use that data for their own purposes.

AT&T was following a similar trajectory. Alongside its purchase of Time Warner, in 2018 it entered into a $1.6 billion deal to acquire AppNexus. "While some ad tech firms work only for publishers, helping them manage ad space on their sites, or ad buyers, helping agencies purchase ads, AppNexus is in both lines of business," noted the *Wall Street Journal*. Illustrating the dense ties across tech, conduit, and advertising giants themselves, AppNexus itself was already backed by investments from giant advertising umbrella company WPP, TCV (an investment firm), and News Corporation (Mullin, 2018). With more than 170 million "direct-to-consumer relationships across its TV, video streaming, mobile and broadband services in the U.S., mobile in Mexico and TV in Latin America," with its Time Warner purchase and with "digital properties including HBO Now, Boomerang, FilmStruck and the upcoming DC Universe streaming service… All of that data—including email addresses, IP addresses and device IDs" will be at their disposal across its properties (Munson, 2018). *FierceCable* projected that with its AppNexus purchase, AT&T was two years from "build[ing] out its real-time ad exchange… so it no longer has to sell its ad inventory using 'brute force'" (Munson, 2018). Later in the year it held a gathering of three hundred media, advertising and entertainment executives to discuss how it was transforming into "what it calls a modern media company, a stack of content, data, ad tech and distribution tuned to maximize their tandem value" ("AT&T and Verizon," 2018).

One is reminded that this is a process of experimentation, not the absolute and imminent establishment of monoliths. By the end of 2018 and early 2019, Verizon's plans and fortunes were shifting; to the same gathering of executives, Verizon announced that it wanted "nothing to do with owning more content shops"; instead, "it now plans to remain in a position where it can partner with as many different content providers as possible, and sees managing another big media company as a potential albatross in that pursuit" ("AT&T and Verizon," 2018). Its media unit was "focused on just four core verticals: sports, finance, entertainment and news" ("AT&T and Verizon," 2018). The *Wall Street Journal* would report late in the year of the two divergent strategies by the broadband giants: "AT&T is diving headfirst into entertainment and advertising, spending tens of billions of dollars to control in-demand programming like HBO's 'Game of Thrones' and live National Basketball Association games on TNT that it can distribute throughout its wireless, satellite and fiber-optic networks;" in the meanwhile, "Verizon ... is doubling down on wireless-network upgrades to enable the commercial use of 5G technology, counting on industrial and consumer uses beyond smartphones to deliver a fresh wave of revenue" (FitzGerald & Krouse, 2018). After shuttering its Go90 app, instead of creating a new platform of "third-party content pay-TV channels," it would "help market third-part[y] over-the-top video services similar to what Amazon Channels does" ("Verizon looking to bundle," 2018).

Of concern to observers, Verizon's advertising share in fact shrunk, earning 3.3 percent of United States digital ad revenue, down from 4.1 percent the previous year (Krouse, 2018). The company was described as exploring subscription models to its content properties, including HuffPost and Yahoo Sports. Comparisons to AOL-Time Warner's disastrous marriage started to rear their head, as the *Wall Street Journal* reported, "Integrating AOL's and Yahoo's advertising-technology platforms took longer than anticipated and still isn't complete.... Verizon was unwilling to share some data on its wireless subscribers that would have helped its media operations create more sophisticated ad targeting" (Krouse, 2018). Blame seemed to lay at the feet of AOL and Yahoo themselves being more focused on the desktop space rather than mobile. Analysts appeared to push Verizon to become more exploitative of its users' data: Verizon planned to marry digital ad inventory with wireless subscriber data to increase the ability to target, but the *Journal* reports an analyst arguing they "never fully followed through on that plan due to user privacy concerns" (Krouse 2018). Layoffs followed at the Oath unit, now renamed Verizon Media ("Verizon layoffs indicate,"

2019). Whether the capabilities rest in-house or not, the role of the conduits as intermediary is emphasized in their relationships. For instance, Verizon expanded its global partnership with Microsoft, in which Verizon Media was set to "open[] up 20% more native advertising inventory on Microsoft News through its Oath Ad Platform. Additionally, both companies have extended their existing relationship, allowing advertisers access to brand safe video, display and content marketing solutions across Microsofts global properties. Advertisers can continue to partner directly with the Verizon Media [*sic*] ... to access these ad opportunities across devices" ("Verizon Media and Microsoft," 2019). AT&T's own initiatives to "revolutionize TV advertising" were less than smooth sailing as it integrated its own operations with its ad-tech partners (Toonkel, 2019).

Such stories merely scratch the surface of experimentation afoot; when the CDD examined the full panoply of AT&T, Comcast, Cablevision, Charter, Cox, Verizon, Dish, Time Warner Cable, Viacom, Google, News Corporation, Turner Broadcasting, and Disney, across the board, the model of accumulating and selling data about consumers had long been experiencing a huge push. Telecommunications firms collaborated with data collection, data analysis, and onboarding (that is, connecting offline behavior to online) firms such as Acxiom and its various affiliates, as well as affiliating with or operating alongside data management platforms like Oracle (Center for Digital Democracy, 2016). Their cable siblings were little different: Comcast collaborates with Rubicon's Advertising Automation Cloud to offer individuals to marketers (p. 5). In fact, in 2017, under the rubric of "fin-tech meets ad-tech," a collaboration of efforts by expats from AOL, Microsoft, Dow Jones, Reed Elsevier, and Mojiva Inc., the New York Interactive Advertising Exchange offered advertisers and marketers "a trading platform that brings Wall Street to Madison Avenue through a Nasdaq-powered, seamless global exchange that allows publishers and advertisers to buy, sell and re-trade premium advertising inventory as guaranteed contracts" (Nasdaq, 2017). The announcement of the initiative continues, "Trading, a vital part of other market sectors, has now come to media. With the ability to trade guaranteed media contracts, advertisers and publishers can now be efficient and rid themselves of unnecessary costs and risks" (Nasdaq, 2017).

Many of the telecommunications operators and their service-side counterparts have become virtual hedge funds themselves. Comcast operates Comcast Ventures.[4] AT&T in 2017 invested $200 million in collaboration with Coral Group, which specializes in "telecom systems integration, internet-based consumer and enterprise-facing applications and services," to start up its own venture capital fund (AT&T, 2017). Google set up its own fund, committing both money and engineers, to foment the growth of artificial intelligence startups (Novet, 2017). Whereas venture capital overall has had every interest in the network neutrality and open access debates—its investments depend on these conduits for safe passage, of course—when the conduits become the suppliers of capital themselves for such new enterprises, they have every interest in assuring the success of their own investments against the initiatives of competitors.

The nature of competition is also difficult to discern in this environment. While various cable companies may seem to compete with each other, National Cable Communication (NCC) Media—originally started decades ago under different auspices but now jointly owned by Comcast, Cox, and Spectrum (and listing affiliations as diverse as DirecTV, AT&T's U-Verse, Sling, Google Fiber, CenturyLink, and numerous more)[5]—sells itself as "an advertising sales, marketing, and technology company that harnesses the enormous reach and consumer power of cable television programming, new interactive technologies, and online products in every US market. We work on behalf of virtually all of America's leading regional and national advertisers. NCC is headquartered in The Chrysler Building in New York City with over 450 employees across 17 offices nationwide."[6] With the inclusion here of CenturyLink, which purchased Level 3 Communications (Oyedele, 2016), numerous middle-mile and long-haul networks are involved, not just consumer-facing companies. Verizon's own development of over the top capabilities, as with AT&T, is only partially about customer retention in an environment of online video; it is about data collection, the same side-objective Amazon had in purchasing Whole Foods (Turner, 2017). Alongside these moves, we should not forget the efforts of the world's largest advertising and marketing agencies—at present, WPP, Publicis, InterPublic Group, Omnicom, and next top-tier players Havas and Dentsu—to themselves create relationships and initiatives with players like Twitter, Apple, and more (Schiller, 2014). Facing pressure from tech giants and conduit giants themselves, these entities are accumulating their own massive data troves and the ability to analyze them. In late 2018, for instance, InterPublic Group, in what was termed by one account the "deal of the year," purchased Acxiom Marketing Solutions (Adams, 2018). In 2019, fellow advertising giant Publicis looked to acquire Epsilon and Conversant (units of Alliance Data) for $4.4 billion. This deal would give its myriad agencies "access to Epsilon's database of 250 million U.S. customers," alongside mechanisms to manage "first-party data like CRM [customer relations management] stats pulled from email and loyalty programs"; further, "the firm also layers third-party data like transactional and behavioral stats on top of first-party data to create audience segments, and the company's ad-tech arm Conversant takes the data to run ads" (Johnson, 2019). This purchase also represents a bit of consolidation of major players. "With Acxiom and Epsilon off the table, there are less independent data firms for marketers to work with or acquire," *Business Insider* wrote; left were firms like the credit reporting agencies Experian, Equifax, TransUnion, and even the large broadband companies such as AT&T, Verizon, and Comcast "as being sources of data for marketers" (Johnson, 2019).

The popular, cluttered LUMAScapes[7] and other similar charts put together by *Venture Beat* (and the genre these have sparked in other realms; for instance, on blockchain applications, see Lange [2017])[8] depicting various sectors and players of marketing and sales tech might appear to provide clear condensations of the political economy of this sector, but they do more to muddy the issue than to enlighten. They are hardly focused on the value generation process: rather, they revel in the spectacle of the rapid growth of this sector, sure to continue along the path of consolidation as conduits or online giants snap up capabilities and as winning providers develop economies of scale against which newcomers cannot compete.

Conduit operators have similarly been experimenting with cloud platforms, either by directly providing them or by facilitating them. Mosco (2014) outlines several varieties, and more have grown since: this is the realm of infrastructure as a service, platform as a service, and software as a service provided via a client interface. These are stored on private, public, hybrid, or community clouds. While the field is increasingly dominated by Amazon, Apple, Google, Facebook, and Microsoft, Mosco notes, "It is important to understand that these businesses, especially large companies like AT&T and Verizon, are not just conduits for other firms' data. Through their subsidiaries, they are well integrated into the entire digital economy, including content provision" (Mosco, 2014, p. 65). Verizon has employed a "strategy that has been used over and over again in the industry's history: when the next new thing comes along, buy it" (Mosco, 2014, p. 65).

In 2011, it purchased cloud companies Terremark (for $1.4 billion) and Cloudswitch (the terms of which were undisclosed). Since such purchases, Verizon has been halting in figuring out how to integrate these services into its other offerings. In the lead-up to 2014, Mosco argued, "For Verizon, the cloud is a key component of a media, telecommunication, and information convergence strategy that will allow the company to control practically all key nodes in the networks that produce, store, process, and distribute services to individual and organizational customers. Moreover, Terremark gives Verizon a significant international presence, something that the company has lacked, particularly in Latin America" (Mosco, 2014, pp. 65–66). By 2017, however, both Verizon and AT&T had left the public cloud business while maintaining enterprise and governmental cloud operations. Verizon sold its cloud and hosting services to IBM, ceding the public cloud space to the likes of Amazon and Microsoft, shifting from a "cloud provider to a cloud enabler" to focus more on the Internet of things (IoT), "hybrid enablement, and digital advertising"; additionally, it sold twenty-four data centers to Equinix (Meyer, 2017). At around the same time, AT&T made side arrangements with Oracle (Meyer, 2017). As one analyst put it, "There are 523 cloud providers left in the world, and it's an economy of scale business.... Everyone has problems keeping pace with AWS on pricing, even Google. It just made sense for the telecom guys to get out of it" (Meyer, 2017). Illustrating how economies of scale are increasingly determinative of victors in this realm, resulting in competitors using competitors' services, it was recently revealed that Apple's iCloud was actually housed by its competitor, Google Cloud (Liao, 2018) as well as AWS (and other smaller cloud services), even as Apple was cutting back on use of the latter while simultaneously building its own infrastructure (Novet, 2019). Mosco also notes that China was expected to lead the world in cloud computing by 2016—faced with little competition from U.S.-based providers, Alibaba Group, Baidu, Tencent, Huawei, and MeePo only provide pressure on U.S. providers to push ever onward (Mosco, 2014, p. 72). There, the development of "cloud cities" in partnership with international partners are part of this supremacy.

The pressures inherent to the Chinese drive only maintain pressure on U.S. and other competitors, baking in the logics of these platforms ever more fully. This is significant: in his investigation of early cloud computing networks—for example, the Cybersyn project of Chile under Allende with the objective of institutionalizing workplace digital democracy and economic planning—he finds Amazon's AWS, for but one instance, offers stark counterpoint, even as (illustratively?) it "powered Obama's candidacy": "What is striking... is how little this has to do with practicing democracy, with civic participation, or with activism at any level. In place of democracy, including anything envisioned in the Cybersyn project, we have population management and control" (Mosco, 2014, p. 28). Chinese firms pushing new boundaries, such as the gargantuan application WeChat—which provides enough connections to services that one rarely even needs to leave the application for virtually any service, including banking and more—leaves American firms salivating about the possibilities (Mosco, 2017).[9]

The fourth platform, and the one perhaps most underappreciated by scholarship related to communications policymaking, is the "industrial Internet." The sector is predicted to be worth $225 billion by 2020 (Srnicek, 2017, p. 70). The industrial giants who dominate at the moment maintain the familiar platform model: provide open platforms aboard which clients can store data and build applications while making it difficult to transport their efforts to other platforms. GE and Siemens dominate, as well as tech giants such as Intel and Microsoft, in developing such platforms; Siemens has sunk €4 billion to acquire smart manufacturing capabilities to construct its MindSphere; GE worked to develop its own Predix platform (p. 67). The establishment of a particular platform that can interoperate across myriad varieties of industries—from raw materials extraction to different factory setups to trucking and more—adjoins a strategy of locking in those who partake of it by becoming an industrial standard which won't necessarily translate to competitors' systems (pp. 66–67). All the same, and illustrative of the centralization of resources in this realm, GE uses AWS (p. 70). Perhaps most profoundly, the "industrial Internet" promises even more dramatic shifts, and the move toward maximized data extraction makes its presence felt here in sweeping ways. "The industrial internet promises, in effect, to make the production process more efficient, primarily by doing what competitive manufacturing has been doing for some time now: reducing costs and downtime" (p. 66). Further, "it also aims to link the production process more closely to the realisation process. Rather than relying on focus groups or surveys, manufacturers are hoping to develop new products and design new features on the basis of usage data drawn from existing products (even by using online methodologies like A/B testing to do so). The industrial internet also enables mass customization" (p. 66). As Verizon notes in its *2017 State of the Market: Internet of Things 2017* report, it broadcasts its goal to enable enterprise to "ascend[] the data value chain" (Verizon, 2017, p. 7); as Srnicek notes, "In one factory from BASF SE, the largest chemicals producer in the world, the assembly line is capable of individually customising every unit that comes down the line" (Srnicek, 2017, p. 66).

Competition is ultimately over "the ability to build the monopolistic platform for manufacturing" (Srnicek, 2017, p. 68), both to collect data as well as to analyze it.

> In competition with more generic platforms as like AWS, industrial platforms promote themselves as having insider knowledge of manufacturing and the security necessary to run such a system.... By positioning themselves as the intermediary between factories, consumers, and app developers, these platforms are ideally placed to monitor much of how global manufacturing operates, from the smallest actuator to the largest factory, and they draw upon these data to further solidify their monopoly position. (Srnicek, 2017, pp. 69–70)

Telecommunications operators are an integral part of the construction of these platforms. *Fierce Wireless* reported in 2014 that Verizon, as well as Intel and Cisco, teamed with GE "to add connectivity and transform a wide range of M2M [machine-to-machine] vertical markets, including rail, aviation, energy and healthcare" utilizing GE's Predix platform. "Intel's gateway productions for the IoT markets will be combined with Predix to add in features like integrated security... GE also said it will integrate Predix software on Cisco's next generation of ruggedized networking products for harsh environments such as oil and gas exploration" (Goldstein, 2014). Verizon's information collection capabilities, such as via its Verizon Share platform with both its corporate- and consumer-facing operations, lead it to offer itself as a core all-purpose logistics manager itself connecting across these universes: "Industry watchers also predict ongoing consolidation in the IoT market space, as larger providers continue to acquire start-up and specialty IoT firms. The goal for providers and enterprises alike is a seamlessly aligned ecosystem" (Verizon, 2017, p. 15). The *Wall Street Journal* more recently reported that Amazon's Alexa voice system is "going to work in the warehouse" via Amazon's integration with e-commerce technology firm ShippingEasy, which enables the voice system to "manage orders, print labels, check postage rates and handle other order-fulfillment tasks hands-free.... Supply chain and logistics operators say the use of familiar technology has grown as high shipping demand has put more stress on distribution networks and the available labor supply has tightened" (Phillips, 2018).

The categories of logistical possibility are only proliferating; and while some emerge only to be reabsorbed into other categories, experimentation along a singular, discernable trajectory is clear. Gartner's bevy of reports allows one to collate lists. While the common entries such as "data management platforms," "data classification engines," and "tag management" will ring familiar to many who study the growth of marketing technologies online, new terms enabling algorithmic hyper-Taylorism are apparent—moves from "enterprise resource planning" to "postmodern enterprise resource planning" (piecing together the components of numerous services to plan production chain activities), "predictive B2B [business-to-business] marketing analytics," "price optimization and management for B2B," and "product portfolio and program management" all hint at the myriad ways that such technology is only partly about managing consumer interests and advertising, extending these logics to optimization of production chains themselves in an environment of overproduction and a need to trim costs (see, for instance, Casper, 2017; Davis & Herschel, 2016).

Consultancies emphasize that "postproduct development activities that focus on demand generation, advertising, promotion and sales" can be "applied further upstream to product development, dynamic pricing and distribution ... where speed is used to improve business advantage" (Davis & Herschel, 2016, p. 10). Another analyst found that "top internal IoT initiatives addressed operational optimizations, such as work flow management, supply chain and inventory management. The top external IoT initiatives focused on creating connected products that allow customer data to be collected by the enterprise" (Hung et al., 2017, p. 2). A category called "voice of the consumer" illustrates how access to both individual and industrial consumers can prove useful, described by one analyst as the combination of "multiple, traditionally siloed technologies associated with the capture, storage and analysis of direct, indirect and inferred customer feedback. Technologies such as social media monitoring, enterprise feedback management, speech analytics, text mining and web analytics are integrated to provide a holistic view of the customer's voice. The resultant customer insights are acted on by disseminating relevant information to the right employee at the right time on the right channel" (Davis & Herschel, 2016, p. 24). The innovation is to combine myriad channels into one stream for analysis so as to direct action not to consumers, but to divisions of corporate marketing activity; there is no reason why this could not be directed into research and development or other nodes of the production chain upstream. Using wireless signals to determine, passively, the emotional state of individuals is already being tested (Hotz, 2016); and while coverage has focused on medical uses, one also imagines that these would be useful for workplace workforce surveillance and management. A report by another consultancy noted that augmented reality products would primarily be a boon to the enterprise sector, dwarfing the consumer sector (Juniper Research, 2016). Mosco similarly describes General Electric's dreams of the "Brilliant Factory," which maps onto all of these initiatives (Mosco, 2017).

The overlap with cloud services here is strong; and while numerous software-as-a-service vendors continue to jockey for position on this playing field, conduit giants continue to occupy catbird seats to the entire game, holding themselves out to enterprise users as soup-to-nuts managers of industrial logistics, generally by forming partnerships with others, as AT&T did in teaming with Cisco, GE, IBM, and Intel to form the Industrial Internet Consortium in 2014 (AT&T, 2014). Verizon holds itself out as a partner in as diversified a set of industries as construction, education, energy, manufacturing, automotive, government, retail, media, and more.[10] Comcast in 2017 announced the expanded rollout of its MachineQ enterprise IoT service: "As a part of the machineQ service, Comcast is working with its commercial partners to enable businesses and cities to gather, transmit, and analyze data about the operation of connected devices distributed throughout their locations. Using the service, organizations are empowered to use data collected from their IoT devices, learn from it, and make better-informed, data-based decisions to improve how they serve customers, tenants, and citizens" (Comcast, 2017).

In sum, any effort to downplay the ability to face both individuals and corporate businesses alike via the *facilitation* of such activities—in partnership with industrial platform providers—seems a grave mistake to make. Conduits' structural importance and advantage becomes even more crucial to consider, given that how competition works in this environment becomes quite complex. The problems facing advocates in such an environment multiply and require new forms of analysis.

Emergent Trends

Srnicek outlines several important trends from his investigation of platform capitalists. For one, he notes what is already obvious: the drive toward data extraction is only expanding and intensifying. Mergers involving data doubled between 2008 and 2013 (Srnicek, 2017, p. 99). This trend is continuing. In marketing technology alone, for instance, there were nearly twice as many mergers in the four quarters of 2017 than 2013 (Results International, n.d.). With growing data stores, and the challenge contained in making sense of it, centralization is further incentivized (Srnicek, 2017, p. 102). Gartner's conjurer of a new, globally unifying "digital connectivism" to which all would be subject recognized the double nature of large brands making claims on their privacy policy pages that they will keep consumer data "safe." While *intended* as reassurance, the analyst recognizes it in the true sense: "Organizations in the information business should be much more careful with the information they are selling. It's not just information, but it is part of a customer's identity" (Buytendijk, 2016a, p. 7)). What he leaves out is the double meaning behind their assurances. Users are told that their data is valuable and protected—as in a vault. If others were to gain hold of it, it would be less exploitable and its value would drop. The development of analytical abilities to process this data and the race to develop them has led to heavy investment in artificial intelligence and machine learning by online giants (Apple, Google, Facebook, Amazon, and Microsoft, not to leave out their Chinese compatriots Alibaba, Baidu, and Tencent/WeChat), telecommunications and cable companies, and software companies that seek to be contenders (Greenfield, 2017; Mosco, 2017; Srnicek, 2017, pp. 102–103). Firms also have incentives to "develop the entire stack," self-designing hardware as well as software (Schiller, 2014; Srnicek, 2017, p. 103).

Given these dynamics, an imperative for these companies is to jockey for strategic placement in a particular core business segment via mergers "more like rhizomatic connections driven by a permanent effort to place themselves in key platform positions," something different from vertical and horizontal combinations of yore (Srnicek, 2017, pp. 103–104) as dominance of particular *interfaces* becomes the rule. Google works with Omnicom to make purchases of display ads easier; Omnicom made similar arrangements with AOL, Yahoo!, and Microsoft. Rivals WPP and Publicis did comparably. WPP partners with Twitter for integration into their analyses; an older Twitter prospectus revealed that five "data partners" "accounted for three-quarters of its data-licensing revenue" (Schiller, 2014, pp. 133–134). In fact, Twitter's "Find a Partner" page is now swimming in ad tech firms and data management partners to aid prospective clients in "monitoring social trends," "listening to consumer insights," "measuring social efforts," "managing customer care," "managing my social presence," "campaign management," "targeting management," and "creative management."[11] Facebook's new Portal smart-home system utilizes Amazon's Alexa technology (Seetharaman, 2018), and Alexa is similarly baked into next-generation Sonos wi-fi speaker systems.

As capabilities grow, all sectors necessitate the consumption of new raw materials, leading Srnicek to posit a possible *convergence* across perhaps surprising gulfs: intensified is "the tendency for different platform companies to become increasingly similar as they encroach upon the same market and data areas" (Srnicek, 2017, p. 107). There is a question of the form such convergence will take—will they "converge into an ur-platform model? Or will they diverge and maintain competitiveness through specialisation? . . . This means that, despite their differences, companies like Facebook, Google, Microsoft, Amazon, Alibaba, Uber, and General Electric (GE) are also direct competitors" (p. 108). Srnicek offers several examples: IBM, as it moves into the platform business, bought Softlayer for its cloud services and BlueMix to aid in its software development. Similarly, Google is lobbying with Uber on self-driving cars. Amazon and Microsoft were discussing partnerships with German automakers on the cloud platform needed by self-driving cars. Alibaba and Apple have investment in Didi, with iPhones a "major interface to taxi services" (p. 108). Medical platforms are also being developed by virtually all comers (p. 108). Amazon's own interests and incentives are shifting, as its advertising business is projected to overtake its AWS service earnings by the early 2020s (O'Rielly & Stevens, 2018). International competition is similarly the order of the day. Mosco is careful to note that even if the European Union's own privacy initiatives might result in a check on this system, nationalist movements which are moving to break up this alliance could render it far less effective, creating a potential bipolar universe between the twin drives of development in China and the United States (Mosco, 2017). In sum, "Ultimately, we see convergence—and therefore competition—across the field: smartphones, e-book readers, consumer IoT, cloud platforms, videochat services, payment services, driverless cars, drones, virtual

with the already combined Comcast—NBCUniversal to thwart new "over the top" video services, and concerns that the pay-TV channel HBO won't be available to other conduit providers to draw new customers. This case was utterly destroyed by the presiding judge, and the Department of Justice did appeal, only to give up; but it was illustrative of the weakness of classic antitrust analysis in such cases, a step beyond van Schewick's concerns. Even a revamped consideration of multiple-sided platforms put to the end of improving antitrust *qua* antitrust might find its limit. "These mergers consist not so much in the vertical integration of classic Fordist firms or in the lean competencies of the post-Fordist era; they are more like rhizomatic connections driven by a permanent effort to place themselves in key platform positions" (Srnicek, 2017, p. 104). It is unclear at this time what the implications for any network neutrality policy will be in such an environment. But we return to such concerns shortly.

One is wise to remember that it is less what all these platforms (and artificial intelligence and machine learning built in) can do and do well than what we believe they can do; the stories that are told about these technologies, as Greenfield notes, "saturate popular culture, leavened significantly by commercial hype—our estimates of machinic competence can grow to the point that they become dangerous" (Greenfield, 2017, p. 254). Further: "The lesson for all of us is clear: beliefs about the shape of the future can be invoked, leveraged, even weaponized, to drive change in the present. Even in advance of its realization, automation based on machine learning and the algorithmic analysis of data serves some interests and not others, advances some agendas and not others" (p. 257). But even to state such worries this way is to evade particular questions of political economy. Algorithms will be put to further commercial imperatives to satisfy effective demand for the visions they carry as freight, creating a reflexive feedback loop across the lived environment, which both reshapes this environment and provides its own feedback into these processes; and for the time being, such changes only demand more and more data be consumed by these processes as work life and nonwork life alike is both commodified and put to new labors (Mosco, 2017). As advocates have long recognized, these futures are hardly preordained: they are not technology-driven affairs, but rather socioeconomic ones in determining what the competitive environment looks like going forward.

It is for this reason that the focus of advocates so far in this realm should give us cause for alarm.

The Dimensions Missed on All Sides

When Srnicek sums up his observations, he notes that no platform innovation actually addresses the core structural challenges twenty-first century capitalism faces. The ongoing crisis of secular overproduction continues; yet bets made regarding the industrial Internet do not address these dynamics. "Rather than improving productivity or developing new markets, the industrial internet appears to drive prices still further down and to increase the competition for market share, thereby exacerbating one of the main impediments to global growth" (Srnicek, 2017, p. 116). "Lean" platforms remain reliant on continued investment and generosity of surplus capital for their survival. Perhaps tax cuts to the investor class that were passed in the United States in 2017 might provide a shot in the arm for them; but, this is continued borrowed time once the bills come due in the future, as public debt skyrockets and as calls for austerity by Republicans in the United States might yet well come to pass with some pliant Democrats in tow. When Uber released its prospectus in the leadup to its initial public offering, for instance, one critic upon reading the document declared, "So the company is losing billions, has essentially no underlying value, and its business could be hammered overnight.... After reading this, who would buy Uber stock?" (Henwood 2019). The same critic quotes Sarah Lacy, a journalist who had been critically covering Uber, "The thing that's gonna kill Uber is when Uber finally has to charge what it costs to get a car to you." Many of these lean platforms will likely go out of business; perhaps many will adjust to serving wealthy customers via luxury services: "Whereas the tech boom of the 1990s at least left us with the basis for the internet, the tech boom of the 2010s looks as though it will simply leave us with premium services for the rich" (Srnicek, 2017, p. 121). Advertising platforms remain among the most important as far as capitalism is concerned in oligopolistic environments: it can aid in redistributing demand among firms or across markets and increase aggregate demand overall, all in lieu of competing on price (Baran & Sweezy, 1966; Caraway, 2016). But they are hardly immune from structural forces; as scholars of communication have long known, advertising itself is hardly a counter to economic trends: rather, it magnifies both booms as well as busts (Leiss et al., 2013).

Advertising platforms today face special challenges. Facebook and Google are particularly dependent on advertising dollars, and the majority of these come from the financial sector, and even Google's Hal Varian noted that ad growth was down and a pay-per-view business model of sorts might be in the offing (Srnicek, 2017, pp. 122–124). Besides these risks, there is a continuing war with users who utilize adblockers, virtual private networks, TOR browsers, and numerous other means to avoid the sales effort. Caraway (2016, p. 72) offers a litany of these and asks, "How and when do these individual pockets of disruption constitute a genuine crisis in the circuits of production?" Of course, this remains another reason that broadband providers—increasingly advertising platforms and brokers of data themselves—are so keen on eliminating network neutrality: doing so enables them to exert pressure on users to avoid such technologies by throttling traffic that is encrypted or identified with some privacy-enhancing protocols or software. One could also envision an intensification of the sale of personal data toward perhaps other ends or to new vectors of the sales effort—an effort, if history is any guide, that is only growing as advertising represents a shrinking proportion of it (Foster & McChesney, 2014). *Should* some external shock occur, however, Srnicek (2017, p. 124) hypothesizes that the likely result will be a move to only increase enclosure online: ad blockers don't work inside proprietary apps (yet); moves to direct payments, subscription models, incessant micropayments or other fees can certainly be imagined.

When the FCC's 2016 privacy proceeding was under debate, however, activists focused their sights almost exclusively on consumer-side advertising platforms. They were fully aware, in the wake of the Snowden disclosures of 2013, of the intermeshed nature of the online tech giants, telecommunications and cable giants, and government surveillance. They were suspicious principally about data collection and its sale, not broader structural forces. Free Press, in their comments submitted as part of the FCC's privacy proceeding docket, wrote, "Essentially, subject to well-established carve-outs for reasonable network management, what it's carrying for you is not your carrier's business. Just as it shouldn't charge more based on the content of the message or the identity of the sender, a telecommunications carrier shouldn't peek at the message's content and address to sell you unrelated products either" (Free Press, 2016, p. 3). Further: "As our lives have moved online, these ISPs [Internet service providers] have gained more access to our most sensitive personal information. Advanced technologies allow companies to track their customers invisibly, collecting and selling data on nearly every detail of who we talk to, what we do and say online and, with location tracking, where we do it" (Free Press, 2016, p. 4). For the Center for Digital Democracy, the primary concerns were the acquisition of "powerful new data technology assets"; the "unchecked expansion of commercial data collection by ISPs and others to identify, reach, and try to influence consumers regardless of where they are"; ISP collaboration with "data management platforms that help collect and make 'actionable' data on consumers that are gathered across their devices and interactions and can be used for ad targeting"; the "use of new cross-device measurement and attribution techniques"; and disingenuous claims that these distributors and conduits were "privacy compliant" via anonymous and aggregate data collection practices. "ISPs and others tell policymakers that data targeting isn't personal—but make it clear when discussing their capabilities to clients and others that they are engaged in various ways to target individuals" (Center for Digital Democracy, 2016, pp. 8–13). Most offensive is that those affected had no say in their fates at the hands of these efforts. The myriad petitions which were circulated illustrated similar concerns, largely stemming from the "creep factor" associated with the increasingly obvious efforts at near-constant data extraction. The Electronic Frontier Foundation themselves documented "Five Creepy Things Your ISP Could Do if Congress Repeals the FCC's Privacy Protections," and this was widely circulated (Gillula, 2017).

When the FCC *did* step in, proposing rules that required for the first time that users be explicitly asked by their broadband providers whether several categories of "personally identifying information" could be collected and utilized to mysterious ends, the Republican dissents were quite revealing. Commissioner Pai exclaimed that unless the same rules applied to the online giants as well as broadband incumbents, no rules should apply:

> Slanted regulation is bad enough. Illogically slanted regulation is worse. Here's the reality: There is no good reason to single out ISPs—new entrants in the online advertising space—for disparate treatment.... It's clear that online companies now have greater access to consumer data than ever before—and that the success of their business models depends on their ability to use it. Ironically, selectively burdening ISPs, their nascent competitors in online advertising, confers a windfall to those who are already winning. (Pai, 2016a)

Commissioner O'Rielly exclaimed that consumer choice had in fact been desiccated in even proposing the rules: "Unlike governmental entities using the information to potentially threaten and undo the freedom of individuals, the high crime and misdemeanor at issue here is the ultimate desire of some to want to market a commercial product to others. Simply put, they may want to try to sell you something that you would actually enjoy purchasing. It is as if we all forgot how the Internet economy actually works today" (O'Rielly, 2016a, p. 5). When the Order establishing such rules was issued, he added,

> I was appalled to see a case-by-case approach imported to review mislabeled "pay for privacy" offers. These are consumer incentives offered every day in the real world and now ISPs will need to obtain a blessing from an agency that has no privacy experience. The result is that broadband providers will be reluctant to extend, and may even forgo, valuable offers and discounts that consumers would want for fear that they will fall into another zero-rating style abyss [of continued FCC attention]. (O'Rielly, 2016b, p. 7)

Pai joined him once again in dissenting, simultaneously acknowledging how much consumer information was known by edge providers (like Google) as well as broadband providers, but he seems less concerned about that than that the agency had "adopted one-sided rules that will cement edge providers' dominance in the online advertising market and lead to consumer confusion about which online companies can and cannot use their data" (Pai, 2016b, p. 3).

The focus remains exclusively on consumer-facing and advertising- or marketing-driven communications; there is mention that perhaps something deeper would be explored—O'Rielly mentions that the FCC would be considering the IoT, but his sentiments remain at that level of abstraction. The fact that all concerned constrain their observations to the consumer arena to the detriment of others carries terrific costs. The collective response to the privacy proceeding is illustrative of numerous quandaries with which media reform, going forward, will need to engage. Inasmuch as the Republican commissioners generally screamed that the rules set up "unfair playing fields" and eliminated options by telecom operators to offer service at lower cost (itself a disingenuous ploy), they also vastly preferred the environment of the Federal Trade Commission (FTC) as the "rightful" site of these debates. In perhaps one sense, the Republican commissioners were more honest, if callous, in their opinions: they recognized that increased FCC authority in this area represented a gigantic wrench stuck in the gears of modern business models. It was one more in a line of policy interventions even previous to this effort that performed similar labors. Schiller (2014) notes actions at the FTC, the National Telecommunications and Information Administration, the Department of Commerce (via its "Internet Policy Task Force"), and Congress that provided significant input from various industry players. Obama proposed at the end of his first term (2011 into 2012) a Privacy Bill of Rights, while in the meantime industry players sought to cement the status quo in place. In effect, "innovation" is really doublespeak for profitmaking (Schiller, 2014), and these furtive, perhaps even unironic efforts left individuals rather naked in the face of the onslaught of these new platform logics. The notion of access is inherently wrapped up in this, rendering it far more complex a question than when the question was applied to telephones.

In regards to the privacy rules being considered by the FCC, taken on their face and with their base assumptions kept intact, these are certainly reasonable first steps in giving users control over their own information, into their own inputs into widespread systems. Activists, on their release, saw them as still not strong enough; by the same token, the telecom companies and cable companies and wireless companies ("broadband Internet access service" [BIAS] providers in new FCC parlance since the 2015 Open Internet Order) who were likely to be subject to the rules found themselves removed from value chains they were very much gunning to join. The utility of possessing an advertising network is more in the ways that this data can be put to myriad uses elsewhere in places still to be determined—not just in the realm of advertising but also in law enforcement, future surveillance technologies, the industrial Internet, and more. A threat to one was a threat to all: it is no wonder that when California tried to pass its own strict privacy regimen that would satisfy Pai's concerns by applying the rules to both broadband providers as well as the online companies, Google and others banded with cable and telecommunications companies to kill it (Bode, 2017). The following year a second swing at the legislation featuring fierce activism on all sides led to successful passage of the California Consumer Privacy Act despite strong opposition from telephone and tech companies again (Coldewey, 2018a). The bill was still accused of not going far enough, and while the intent to strengthen it in the coming year was in the offing, by mid-2019, efforts to do so were withdrawn and amendments designed by telecom and tech interests to weaken it were the only ones being considered—changes designed to weaken it (Corbett, 2019).

Activists focused on consumer privacy protections, in other words, don't look widely enough at the phenomenon; neither do the theorists of free labor. What they face are the strains placed upon modern liberal subjectivity itself (as Couldry, 2012 reminds us), one set among others we soon explore. "Were surveillance capitalists to abandon their contested practices according to the demands of aggrieved parties, the very logic of accumulation responsible for their rapid rise to immense wealth and historic concentrations of power would be undermined," Zuboff reminds us; lawsuits and other challenges to these practices serve to "establish new precedents" (Zuboff, 2015, p. 86). We are commodified in this environment; but we are heteromated subjects as well. The former has received the lions' share of attention; the latter requires a far vaster scan of the horizon, and the terms of debate have not changed to reflect this. Concerns about inequality of access similarly miss the dynamism of this process. It is a positive step that analysis is looking more deeply at the notion of "free labor" and contesting its terms; as is becoming clear in incipient research, and to use old terms to new effect, we are no longer just free variable capital but dead labor too in the form of constant capital, circulating in abstract form through numerous steps of varied production chains—and not just ones related to media. In fact, media itself is likely increasingly in and of itself a site of mere *activity* for the generation of data about present-day subjectivity; in accumulating and distributing the abstract dead labor we create, in fact, media reform is effectively required to vacillate between the notion of media as communication and media as logistical force (or worse, combine both at once), itself feeding into other logistical forces. A necessary move needs to be made from a theory of control and of privacy to one in which we are talking about holding back vital ingredients for which the infrastructure has long been designed over the last decade.

Access to broadband is now less about its necessity to participate in modern life (even as this dimension remains true); it is about the decision, by necessity and quite contrary to O'Rielly's odd notions of coercion-as-consumer-choice, to provide raw ingredients into lengthy and invisible production chains. This is hardly a novel argument—but these battles are being settled piecemeal as Internet provision, as net neutrality, as privacy, when they need to be considered under one and the same rubric: *logistics*. Schiller (2014) counters the expectations of critical theorists who, through the 1990s and early 2000s, expected global conglomerate power only to grow: the surprise was actually that online players upended many industries. But this signaled less a stall in a grand drive to commodify information and communications; far from it. It merely meant new vectors of commodification would appear. Capitalism is not just new opportunities for monopoly but new forms of competition as well. Analysis of this field, however, has become increasingly complex. If van Schewick noted the challenges of the utilization of antitrust analysis to address the concerns regarding the *content and use* of broadband networks raised by network neutrality activists, here even the entire edifice of antitrust analysis itself becomes untenable for the analysis of firms increasingly scrambling to be platforms with the intent of extraction of data. In those times in which one cannot control a particular platform, the idea shifts to *become* the platform oneself; such is the worry and strategy of the American auto industry as the *Wall Street Journal* (Colias & Higgins, 2018) asked, "Can Detroit Become a Software Business?"

We might reframe the notion here: a second-order relation is what is reconstituted, this being the operating logic of capitalism itself—the constantly shifting ambivalence of neoliberalism—(re)produced not by any discursive or political economic closure but by its lack. Couldry (2012) once described the "drive to discourse" impressed on the users of platforms such as Facebook by both the site's mechanics as well as pressure to self-brand; here, a push and "drive to access" means an even deeper hole, a reinforcement of the neoliberal drive itself in all its logics. Barring addressing that—something impossible unless one wanted to be cast out of official circles—the problem will only recirculate, grow, and gather force. This is the lesson of the network neutrality debates for universal service policy, all reinforced by these debates over what has been known as privacy. Neoliberal drives require ambivalence to be sustained.

Given the raw materials (and the interrelations by necessity) of the various platforms, what we see emerging is more akin less to typical oligopolies of years past than a possible germinal oligopoly in *logistical processes themselves,* taking Srnicek's worry of newformed fragmentation to an entirely new level. The sense that I mean here goes beyond what others like Greenfield (2017) have termed "Stacks." In this conception, one looks at an enterprise like Amazon that, as a self-contained unit, is refashioning logistical processes itself on a grand scale, reconfiguring distribution mechanisms across (and up) its production chain, looking for any opportunity to absorb some new startup that might offer it a possible advantage or skill it lacks or has not yet explored. Many decentralized producers eagerly supply proofs-of-concept to Stacks in the hope of being bought, an environment that incentivizes a drive to monetize new areas of life in novel ways (pp. 273–302). This said, a focus on any single company as comprising a concerning Stack may miss the evolving, equally decentralized logics undergirding the development and control over the interstices of logistical processes themselves. The interstices are where logics are established, as are standards of interconnection that might be shared by numerous such Stacks. Perhaps in lieu of Stacks, we should be watchful for crystallizing "Processes" that may or may not be enveloped by the bounds of a singular firm. The movement, storage, and algorithmic (or even brute-force) analysis of data becomes simultaneously its own end, gestating chains of activity that themselves represent a new kind of oligopolistic (for lack of a better expression) composition of pattern, relation, and interrelation that is potentially (even) messier than the workings of one particular enterprise but potentially dominating nonetheless.[12]

In an infrastructure or *logistics* context, when does this data become not just "personally identifiable" but itself a "trade secret?" Arun Sundararajan, a prominent enthusiast of the "sharing economy"—itself comprised of "lean" platforms here—expressed his admiration for a nearly completely automated process once perhaps unthinkable: the automation of higher corporate executive function. Upstart iCEO automated the production of reports via its algorithmically driven use of the resources offered by oDesk, Elance, and Amazon Mechanical Turk, as humans were contracted by machines to write pieces of and assemble these finished projects—heteromated, if you will (Sundararajan, 2016). He notes at one point, "The emergence of ways in which the consumer voice can be rapidly aggregated and harnessed as a force in a regulatory debate ... seems like a good development in general, since, in a sense, it gives consumers a seat at the regulatory table alongside the corporate lobbyists, government officials, and labor collectives" (p. 136)—striking for its "carving out" of labor from the consumer category, a confusing breakdown indeed. His enthusiasm on this front—away from any style of class politics—is remarkably revealing, no less so than the viewpoints and world-building efforts of the consultancies themselves.

The notion of access, then, is something quite aside from its common connotations, yet liberal notions of access proliferate; and privacy rules, alongside drives to supply access to networks, are about more than consumerism (as the Republican commissioners are careful not to hint). It is about the collection of trade secrets, packaged for use in production chains, that are vital ingredients to budding tech industries on which governments increasingly depend; in turn, the regime is solidified and defended under the rubric of "security." The situation becomes all the worse, however, when we realize that, as Andrejevic has argued, all of this amounts to a *wager:* a wager that the development of these platforms will render success, will overcome structural dangers to global capitalism's reproduction—even as it appears many of these efforts seem more a way of staving off an impending disaster as opposed to addressing systemic core maladies. The drive to control the use of these platforms via proprietary mechanisms means intensification is inevitable. The circuits of not just media but of the design of new commodities itself are set to those that benefit from the raw materials comprising the wager, and in turn, to effects that researchers increasingly realize are every bit as discriminatory as their complements in the offline world; and, in a further turn, algorithms and decisions about these digital profiles materially affect one's offline existence. As media increasingly become more than vehicles for information in a classical liberal sense, interactions with this media become the privileged commodity produced, at as low a cost as possible (if not free), put to the service, once processed, of the production of cost savings or surplus value; and the *expectation* that we will participate (lest the social costs of not doing so punish us) means that there is a cultural dimension as well with which engagement will be necessary.

Whereas the analyst for Gartner looks at the present conjuncture perhaps less with enthusiasm than an ambivalent understanding of the system's logics, the activists who look on it with a critical eye may also seem to be undertheorizing their object; or, rather, they define it as something which must be dealt with via forms of negative power dynamics or, at best, propose a positive political project that might constitute a commons. While laudable, their political projects are doomed to failure if they do not tackle the underlying systemic dynamic that pushes us ever further from a goal of a commons-operated architecture. When activists focused on the quandary of zero-rating as part of their struggle for net neutrality, again, they focused on access. When they utilized the language of antitrust, even vaguely, they performed several functions that would serve only to doom them: even as antitrust was entirely insufficient to handle their primary concerns, it faced the added obstacle of being unable to even comprehend the new environment in which merger activity encompassed entirely new realms of possibility related less to the *direct* market served by a particular company than the raw materials provided by the users of these services *indirectly*. Media reformers, in short, are moving into an era that will require them to concern themselves as much with the classically liberal functions of media (particularly as purveyors of fabricated news turn systemic logics of commercial platforms against themselves—but oddly still to the benefit of these platforms at one and the same time) as with such media serving as an intermediary between "distributed selves" at all stages of platform capitalism in logistical chains. That is, every choice subjects make are themselves mere indications that feed into varying stages of production processes—these choices all now "ascending the value chain," as Verizon says.

The fact of the matter is that framed as *consumer choice* is the incorporation of all of us into the coproduction of neoliberalism—and again, the notion of ambivalence comes back, racing to the fore, as access to broadband *is* increasingly necessary, *is* vital for the continuation of one's career, *is* increasingly vital in finding a job, *is* increasingly a key part of one's education. Our actions online are attuned toward the aims of distribution and redistribution of resources in a time of great economic uncertainty. Any step in this chain that is rendered weakened for whatever reason threatens crisis, and this is the threat privacy rules possess on a large scale. What a theorization that speaks to the *positive constitution of power* long unmoored from media reformers' liberal ideals is necessary: we have so long been imbricated in such discourses that the notion of our activities not as mere information but as *logistical inputs*, "data exhaust," has been left behind in all of their implications.

Conclusion

While winning on the network neutrality front, advocates set the stage for a pivotal, pitched move on the part of platform capitalists. It was less network neutrality that threatened these companies—even as the policy *did* impinge on the ambitions of would-be telecommunications and cable company rivals—than the more expansive "public interest standard" that governs the FCC's activities. Whereas the Department of Justice and the Federal Trade Commission worked within stricter antitrust standards and could only act after harm has been done (selectively defined), the FCC could be far more freewheeling in proactively adopting preemptive policies. It was the newfound authority that the FCC possessed after reclassifying broadband as a telecommunications service that created threats to gestatory capitalist modes. While efforts to enhance access would certainly be welcome (to an extent: those who were worse off were not necessarily of that much interest to advertising and marketing platforms, of course), efforts to preclude telecommunications operators from the bonanza were not. Learning more about the habits of users was a *feature* of now being an access network as these networks were clumsily making their way into content production as well. For other platform giants as Google, Facebook, Amazon, and certainly others, a threat to one advertising giant was a threat to all data collectors. It was *this* threat that needed to be stopped.

The digital divide is a static concept; something more dynamic is now necessary. Media reformers were dealing with a potentially new historical subjectivity but had not yet hatched the vocabulary or conceptual grounds to handle it. This stemmed not from any lack of ability on their part—increasingly the stakes are understood by people outside policy circles—but stemmed from the ad hoc and generally short-horizon nature of the regulatory institutions with which they were forced to engage. In fact, this sets the stage for the death knell of media reform activism in its old form. Media consolidation's own forms have shifted. Universal service has been rendered exceedingly complicated as user interactions with their media, in all forms, have become themselves activities from which data can be drawn as a chief part of their business model. There is a complete relation-shift of citizens to citizenship now that they are nestled in activity-sensing apparatus writ large, a realm nearly beyond escape. The consequences for those lacking citizenship are magnified exponentially. The citizen-subject was being dramatically transformed, and network neutrality itself was starting to play a very large role in changing this environment less through its own imposition, hardly painful for the providers themselves, than the threat represented by newly reinstituted Title II authority. And if media reform *were* to comprehensively retackle the implications of the role played by media in increasingly oligopolistic logistical production chains, old notions of antitrust would be insufficient to address changes afoot: however, an agency with expansive, flexible authority would be. The FCC had obtained such authority and was willing to commence exercising it. For platform capitalists of all stripes, it would need to be dealt with.

If the network neutrality debate served to push the neoliberal conundrum further down the hole even in victory, the adjoining push for access operated as a fellow traveler to the cause. Here the contradictions became even more glaring. As seemingly ensconced in political economic analysis as activism was on network neutrality, it ironically still manages to not take into account widespread systemic imperatives and their fast-developing logics. In fact, the network neutrality debates served to legitimate exactly their construction. Part of this was due to the activists' own disowning of anticapitalist discourse, in public at least: they needed the startups. By the same token it was structurally driven: the FCC allowed only certain debates for discussion. Holding an enthusiastic line for a vanguard of startups still sounded good, much like supporting the dot-coms and the broader liberalization drive of the late 1990s seemed to make intuitive sense.

9 Net Neutrality as Wrecking Ball

If network neutrality itself had been unmoored from its origins—even in the sense of the "exoteric" and "esoteric" doctrines the debate extolled—now long-standing debates over the role of the Federal Communications Commission (FCC) would be themselves removed from their context in their entirety. Net neutrality was primed to serve as a vehicle for the elimination of the FCC's authority itself. What transpired was surreal: a truly postmodern debate not rooted in facts or modern liberal discourse even while referring to their existence and terms; the long-constructed supportive institutions of liberalism itself were turned against themselves with a ferocity that took even the most world-weary observers by surprise.

The 2017 battles over communication policy in general represent the culmination of the triple move encompassing network neutrality. First was the transformation of open access into network neutrality debates, which rendered a heterogeneous debate diverse; it nurtured a universe of production surrounding the issue. As new work was produced, it was easily categorizable, slotted into existing silos, and rendered a dead politics. *Yet, activists had no better options but to contribute to this growing corpus.* Second was the effective reduction of network neutrality to issues of access and the deployment of broadband facilities, and this similarly wrought a substantial body of work, ongoing, proffered by both adjuncts and residents of the neoliberal thought collective and activists as well. This was asked of activists by the FCC itself, and then in their own reports they buffered this notion dutifully. *But again, they had no other option.* Network neutrality, for activists, was always about the function to which the Web would be put, not about access to it. But reduced to the latter, when what the Internet permitted was only partly about connecting individuals to their desires, even enabling them a platform for their own creation, it was about hooking these same subjects into broader systems under construction that were only minimally facing critique. If open-access advocates in the late 1990s expressed fleeting—but sincere!—concerns about access to noncommercial media and to uncommodified access to the Internet (which was increasingly impossible in practice, of course, but the desire was at least spoken), these were entirely lost in the wake of Comcast's malfeasance, the 2010 Order, and the 2015 Order. All discussion turned to "innovation," among the most neoliberal tropes to be found.

The third transformation extended to the very purpose of the FCC: mobilization of network neutrality as a debate would now provide the impetus to shunt oversight of broadband networks from an agency around which activists had constructed an effective infrastructure of influence to one in which they did not, nor could they—that is, the Federal Trade Commission (FTC). The FCC would itself be rendered reduplicative and unnecessary, a move away from public-interest regulation to an effort to bring broadband into the universal market subject only to the oversight of antitrust. In fact, the mere threat to emergent platform capitalism of an agency that activists could possibly activate, and which took a wide-ranging and more unpredictable authority stemming from its legislative charge in the Communications Act of 1934 to promote "the public interest, convenience and necessity," rendered this last move essential to capital's dominant logics as they developed.

The election of Donald Trump presented this possibility, perhaps even more appropriately in that it was without the popular vote. With his ascension, ex-Verizon counsel Ajit Pai—a stalwart opponent of network neutrality, privacy rules, media ownership rules, controls on usurious prison phone prices, the Lifeline program—was handed the chairmanship of the FCC. Yet it is important to remember that he was not originally appointed by Trump. As activists gnashed in private, it was Barack Obama who had given him the seat on the commission; with Obama's appointment of his colleague Michael O'Rielly, the former president had *purposely* allowed two ideologues to be installed at the FCC.

Pai's justification for launching his new rollback of network neutrality itself rested on three pillars: first, a claim that broadband deployment had slowed since the Open Internet Order of 2015; second, that somehow "economic analysis" needed to be restored at the FCC; and third, that FCC authority over broadband wires should itself be put to contest, that is, that the only regulation necessary for broadband is to be placed under the bailiwick of antitrust. Each of these pillars reflected a stance against the strengths of the institutions that advocates in favor of network neutrality had built. For one, they had built the infrastructure to promulgate tremendous numbers of comments into FCC dockets; they were similarly networked and learning how to leverage local concerns into targeted congressional advocacy. Advocates had learned how to gain access and, after finding their initial efforts rebuffed by former FCC chair Julius Genachowski, turned to more outside-in tactics in an effort to undergird future challenges. However, in all instances, they were forced to align with dominant or ascendant new platform partners to close the deal. They had learned the points of pressure to gain influence in policy debates and had run a hugely effective education campaign nationwide. These were all about to come under attack. The irony would be that the liberal ideals espoused by many of these advocates, which were baked into such modern institutions as administrative law, could themselves be turned around and used against them via a weaponized liberalism, one that Pai wielded masterfully.

A Suggestion, and a Warning, Is Offered

Four days after Thomas Wheeler moved from serving as FCC chairman to life as a private citizen, and the day that Ajit Pai was announced as the next chairman by Donald Trump, Wheeler held a discussion at Harvard Law School with Susan Crawford. She had witnessed the early years of the Obama administration herself from her perch as the former president's special assistant for science, technology, and innovation policy.[1] The discussion was broad-ranging: Wheeler, recalling his moments as a lobbyist in former days, noted the oft-repeated plea of the largest telecommunications providers that any regulation would stymie deployment (an argument, too, that had been advanced by such advocates as Christopher Yoo, J. Gregory Sidak, and a bevy of others). He recalled that his "lowest" regulatory moment was when he argued these very terms on behalf of the wireless industry against the ability for customers to take their phone number with them when they switch carriers (called "number portability"):

> I regret that activity, but I'm guilty of this. "It is going to slow down our incentive to invest" is kind of the first line of defense of everybody and it's balderdash.... The reason that you invest is to get a return. You don't say, "Well, I'm not gonna invest because I might trigger some regulations." The question is: Am I going to make a return off of this? Broadband is a high-margin operation. You can make a return off of it. The facts speak for themselves. Since the open Internet rule went in place, broadband investment is up, fiber connections are up, usage of broadband is up, investment in companies that use broadband is up, and get ready for it, revenues in the broadband providers are up because people are using it more. The reason why you invest is for this reason, to generate more revenues and a good return on those revenues. The oh-my-goodness-it's-gonna-be-a-terrible-thing-for-investment is just the first refuge that everybody makes, and you have to look past that. (Bavitz, 2017)

The former chairman offered a concerning response when an audience member asked how to protect network neutrality. Wheeler replied that there was a need to be heard, but a "need to be heard in different ways than before." When 3.7 million emails and comments hit the FCC under his watch, they "were pushing on a door that was already open." The door was now "locked, latched, bolted, and welded." The strategy he offered as purportedly new was in fact the selfsame strategy that advocates used to steer Obama toward taking his stance in favor of strong network neutrality rules in 2014:

> Madison had this great line in Federalist 10 where he said that ambition must be made to counteract ambition. This was the whole concept of how the government was set up. Economic ambition is what is driving this handful of companies. There must be economic ambition that counters them.... [W]e need to hear the voices of those that'll be affected. Yes, the small startups but also the big companies.... Artificial intelligence and machine learning, what is it? It is the connectivity of all kinds of database resources. If that connectivity has to worry about gatekeepers, what happens to AI, the Internet of Things? The Internet of Things is going to change the whole economics of the Internet I believe from a push environment to a pull economics.... Who will be deciding which things get connected and on which terms? (Bavitz, 2017)

The ones to deliver the message to Congress thus needed to be "the companies that are affected... because I think that's what the Congress would be most responsive to."

Such suggestions were eagerly received by the audience, but the bitter irony is that this was exactly how *every* fight in this realm had been fought since the late 1990s, and it would likely be activists themselves who would deliver these companies again and again while the overall trajectory of history continued unchanged. If we instead recenter capitalism, activists are faced with a nightmare scenario: "free speech" arguments will no longer be the driving factor (if they ever were when the whiteboards were drawn up); capital would be, wholly and exclusively. Throughout telecommunications history, universal access to telephony was a side effect of a true emphasis on the business-to-business dynamics within the industry; presumably the ability to create, to be politically active, to utilize broadband networks for the breaching of numerous divides would be a similar sidecar to the continued commercial engulfment of all in the platforms of tomorrow.

Even if he didn't recognize that he was describing business as usual, Wheeler similarly attacked the legislation that he had seen that would restructure or "modernize" the FCC (importantly, by hamstringing it) as "fraud." A sign of advocate success in the early 2000s, indeed, was the increasing calls for FCC "reform." As advocates became more successful at the agency, even as a number of congressional players offered legislation to strengthen network neutrality, there was always a fresh batch of legislation to define network neutrality weakly, to thwart the FCC in its efforts, or to remove the FCC from the purview of those it was tasked with regulating. For instance, in 2017 Republican representative Marsha Blackburn offered an "Internet Freedom Act" that would overturn open Internet protections; she had also been a sponsor in the House (with Jeff Flake in the Senate) of the resolution of disapproval that eliminated the privacy protections the FCC instituted in 2016. Other bills in the past sought to institute new requirements the FCC would need to complete before acting, such as onerous new "cost and benefits" analyses that were designed not toward any better regulations but toward paralyzing the agency, preventing proactive steps in virtually any circumstance (Floberg, 2017a).

The prospect of removing authority from the FCC stunned Wheeler. The reasons numerous advocates on all sides had desired reform of the agency could not be more divergent, yet all sides were nonetheless active in bringing us to this point. He recounted a September 13 article in the *Washington Post* that spoke about how the FCC could be defanged: the familiar cry of relocating regulatory activity in communications to the purview of the FTC, something he noted, without surprise, that the Trump transition team desired. While the FCC has *rulemaking* authority, the FTC served only an *enforcement* function. They could step in only if a practice was "unfair or deceptive." Similarly, he reminded all that the FCC specialized in communications, whereas the FTC was a "morass" that covered a wide swath of diverse areas. He was unsurprised that the Trump transition team, drawn from the American Enterprise Institute who were longtime promoters of the concept, would absolutely desire that their interests get lost in the morass of the FTC's breadth.

The story only became more surreal. In a court case brought by AT&T Mobility against the FTC in the Ninth Circuit, AT&T emerged victorious. The court determined that, based on its interpretation of the law governing the FTC, the commission had no authority over not just a common carrier business, but *any part of any business that happened to possess a common carrier business as one of its activities*. That is, because AT&T provided telephony (still defined as a common carrier), *all* other aspects of the business were potentially untouchable by the FTC. Wheeler intoned:

> The court said, "Yes, you are right. And not only are you right about the FTC not having jurisdiction over common carriers, the FTC doesn't have jurisdiction over the non-common carrier activities of common carriers." Now, we have a situation where the carriers and their supporters at the AEI [American Enterprise Institute] and inside the commission are saying, "We should transfer everything to the FTC," which is a result of a Ninth Circuit decision on a case brought by the same people that are arguing it should be moved, doesn't have authority. Go figure. (Bavitz, 2017)

In early 2018, this decision was turned back (*FTC v. AT&T Mobility*, 2018), yet the context, and the willingness of these players to make these calls even if the court had ended up deciding otherwise, is illustrative. How the tables had turned: if Weiser (2009), among numerous others, points to Lawrence Lessig in the early 2000s calling for the abolishment of the FCC, shortly after the election the notion would come from quite different quarters and for equally divergent reasons. Mark Jamison, then one of two members of Trump's technology policy transition team, announced in a blog post (alongside Jeffrey Eisenach of Verizon, a long-standing member of the numerous arms of the Russian doll; they would be joined soon by American Enterprise Institute fellow Rosslyn Layton), "Most of the original motivations for having an FCC have gone away.... Telecommunications network providers and ISPs [Internet service providers] are rarely, if ever, monopolies" (Fung, 2016). Multichannel News noted that Jamison similarly believed that since Internet content was a "competitor" with broadcast, FCC oversight of the latter was similarly unnecessary (Eggerton, 2016). In true neoliberal form, however, a strong state was necessary to enforce such stances: "Strong leadership at the FCC is needed regardless of the new administration's regulatory agenda.... If the FCC's work remains largely unchanged, the rebuilding is needed to ensure that the agency is strong enough to provide substantive decision-making and to withstand future politically-oriented chairmen. If the administration follows the other extreme and moves to largely disband the agency, effecting the change will require strong leadership" (Eggerton, 2016). The original post from which much of Jamison's thinking was drawn has seemingly been scrubbed from the American Enterprise Institute website—the double-truth does need maintaining, after all. The Business Roundtable similarly had numerous designs on the new administration along the same lines (Floberg & González, 2017).

Dismantling the Administrative State

Activists expressed alarm as the Trump FCC barely wasted any time in dismantling several of the former administration's achievements (Floberg, 2017b). Dubbed the "Friday Night Massacre" by advocates, Pai utilized "delegated authority" (meaning a full Commission vote would be unnecessary to make a decision—ironically, Free Press noted, a practice that Pai had excoriated his predecessors for using in other matters) to close an emergent inquiry into zero-rating launched by Wheeler—even as Canada was taking action against zero-rating practices, declaring them against Canada's own network neutrality rules (if with loopholes that left it to individuals or groups to detect the practice and make a formal complaint, while simultaneously not addressing so-called managed services like providers' own Internet protocol (IP)-driven television offerings) (Khoo, 2017). He stopped nine companies from offering Lifeline-discounted service and commenced the march to effectively close down the program; he reopened loopholes that might allow increased broadcast consolidation in the form of the long technologically obsolete "UHF discount"; he shuttered an inquiry into spectrum sharing; he made it more challenging for the FCC to enforce rules requiring broadcasters to maintain particular records and make them publicly available; and he eliminated a requirement that noncommercial stations would be required to file ownership diversity data. Alongside these directives, he quashed several inquiries intended to inform future rulemaking: he stifled an uncontroversial report by the Office of Science and Technology Policy regarding the country's digital infrastructure, a move that would be significant in the proceedings to come: to advocates, he was simply "trying to cover up facts that he doesn't like," that is, those that revealed just how uncompetitive such infrastructure was in the United States. He similarly rescinded an educational access e-rate progress report, another item that had been seen as uncontroversial, as well as a white paper in progress by the FCC's Homeland Security Bureau on cybersecurity. It would also not be long before the FCC's privacy rules would be set aside by the new chairman, ultimately to be undone permanently by Congress in a brazen move, speeding two bills through the two houses and signed by Trump on a Friday evening before widespread protest could mount even more fully than it already had. Fight For the Future responded to the actions by purchasing billboard space in the districts and states of legislators who voted to undo the privacy protections to chastise the lawmakers who voted for it, in the hopes that perhaps voters would remember the transgression in the 2018 midterm elections (Floberg, 2017b). To depressingly little avail: Marsha Blackburn, one of the original authors of these bills while in the House of Representatives, was elevated to the Senate by Tennessee voters and would be given a seat on the Committee on Commerce, Science and Transportation's Subcommittee of Communications, Technology, Innovation and the Internet.

In May 2017, Pai announced his effort to completely overturn the strong net neutrality rules passed by his predecessor. Assisted by the American Enterprise Institute and unironically held at the Newseum in Washington, DC, he announced his proposed rulemaking, named, in Orwellian enough fashion, *Restoring Internet Freedom*. To this end, he sought to reverse not just the results of the previous proceeding but also to effectively eliminate the FCC's jurisdiction over broadband communications in a purported effort to stimulate broadband infrastructure investment. The notice (FCC, 2017b) revealed an FCC seeking to read the Telecommunications Act narrowly enough to define broadband service out of FCC purview altogether; it similarly questioned the need for *any* antidiscrimination rules at all. In fact, we find ourselves here where we began: the document asks virtually the same questions that Barbara Esbin, and her later colleague Deborah Lathen, had asked—here a repeat performance of the latter, a sophistic throwing-up of hands, the sheer disingenuous wonderment accompanying how-does-the-Internet-work-anyway questions.

The FCC knew full well how the Internet worked, but the document was designed by a lawyer, not a technocrat, with designs on grappling with a key problem: despite a lawsuit by telecommunications and cable interests, the D.C. Circuit that had struck down the FCC in regard to its Comcast and 2010 Open Internet Orders offered a lengthy, full-throated defense of all aspects of the 2015 rules (*United States Telecom Association v. Federal Communications Commission,* 2016). They accepted wholesale the "virtuous cycle" justification; even more significantly, they accepted that reclassification of broadband to Title II authority addressed the court's past concerns. In 2015, Christopher Yoo made the claim that since users typed web addresses instead of typing full IP addresses into their browsers, "processing" was necessarily being done that transformed the broadband service into an information service, as defined by the Telecommunications Act. Here, the court cast aside any such notion. Returning to FCC understandings of law in the late 1990s, the court found that DNS services and content delivery networks and more operated as *part of the telecommunications service itself* and not as some additional "processing" services that would suddenly trigger a definition that rendered their operation an information service. They left unaddressed claims that operators were having their First Amendment rights infringed by being "forced" to carry all content and not possessing an ability to be selective about it. (There was one dissent, and the judge that wrote it could have well outsourced the entire thing to Yoo or any member of the neoliberal thought collective's extended Russian doll—it reified markets as calculative devices as well as, or better than, any of the law review articles we have encountered so far; this also points to the importance of judge appointments in these affairs.)

Upon appeal, telecommunications companies lost yet again—albeit with the full-throated dissents of two judges, which would remain historical sidenotes if one of these judges had not ended up being nominated by President Trump to the Supreme Court: Judge Brett Kavanaugh. Kavanaugh's dissent rode on two factors: for one, he did not believe Congress "clearly authorize[d] the FCC to issue the net neutrality rule" (Kavanaugh, 2017, p. 1). His second reason was more concerning.

> Second … the net neutrality rule violates the First Amendment to the U.S. Constitution.… [T]he First Amendment bars the Government from restricting the editorial discretion of Internet service providers, absent a showing that an Internet service provider possesses market power in a relevant geographic market. Here,

> however, the FCC has not even tried to make a market power showing. Therefore, under the Supreme Court's precedents applying the First Amendment, the net neutrality rule violates the First Amendment. (Kavanaugh, 2017, p. 2)

The majority found that both lines of argument were "misconceived" (*United States Telecom Association v. Federal Communications Commission,* 2017, p. 1). Other commentators were less forgiving, such as one who subtitled his summary, "To Err Is Human, But Come On": "Two judges had dissenting opinions to bruit, and so the court published them alongside the denial—though unfortunately for them [Judge] Srinivasan used the same opportunity to demolish their arguments. It would have been better for them, in retrospect, if they had remained silent, rather than raising their profound ignorance like a dirty flag to be mocked and pointed at forever—as we do here today" (Coldewey, 2018). Nonetheless, the 2015 rules had successfully passed court muster, even if they now would hang by a thread.

While broadband incumbents sought to take the case to the Supreme Court, the Pai FCC set to accomplishing the task of dismantling the justification that the D.C. Circuit had blessed. Having lost the public opinion battle itself, the Pai FCC was dead set on dismantling every foothold that public interest advocates had constructed for themselves over the past two decades. The FCC itself, as an institution, now represented such a foothold. The blunt instrument put to this purpose would be the question of broadband rollout itself: it needed to counter any notion that the "virtuous cycle" of nondiscrimination enforced by a general conduct rule had any positive impact on investment. This strategy was hardly going to be a surprise and was widely realized: at a hearing of the Congressional Internet Caucus,[2] Wheeler's former counsel Gigi Sohn was pitted against Berin Szoka of advocacy group TechFreedom (one of the activist arms of the broader neoliberal think tank infrastructure). Among all participants there was agreement that this time the proceeding would center on the issue of access and perhaps a "return of economics" to the FCC. The fact that this most recent fight would be fought on *that* ground missed that the true battle was over the question of FCC oversight in the first place, albeit of a sort: similar to the views of Jamison, Szoka at one point in the proceedings noted that he did believe there needed to be a "cop on the beat." But this was, in Szoka's view, not a cop that was amenable to the influx of concerns outside the realm of antitrust; it was a cop that would maintain an overarching environment of "competition," which really translated to the subjection of this realm to a generic notion of markets as themselves self-forming and reified affairs. Advocates working on behalf of the telecommunications companies (either directly or indirectly) now pined for the 2010 compromised rules. As Szoka intoned, "We're better dealing with competition issues via laws of general applicability, we deal with lack of expertise by building up that expertise. We can transfer folks from FCC there. We can empower that agency to be the regulator here. This is the Waxman bill 2010, the Verizon/Google framework, read those documents yourself, study the history of these bills."[3]

Perhaps most disturbing was the chumminess of those present despite the quite divergent takes on policy and the stakes involved. Lives were at stake here, but one would never know it from the demeanor of the actors performing their drama for the Congressional Internet Caucus; overall the tone was subdued, tired; perhaps even the caucus knew that it was simply going through the motions here on this issue. These would-be sparrers had spent plenty of time together honing their dance in the years leading up to this point. The direction was preordained.

In reaction to the claims of the likes of Pai that broadband deployment had somehow declined, a thoroughly documented study titled "It's Working" was released by Free Press's Derek Turner (2017) that laid waste to the agency's arguments. Turner notes several pivotal developments in the access market. Legacy incumbents who in the past were full-throatedly unsupportive of network neutrality rules were themselves taking advantage of neutral pathways to prepare for or offer their own over-the-top services. Owners of pay-TV channels, such as Viacom, Discovery, and AMC, were rumored to be considering offering a bundle of channels that did not include sports networks, which in other bundle packages drove up prices (p. 61). Other wired providers, such as CenturyLink, toyed with over-the-top offerings themselves, as did such giants as Apple and Amazon (p. 61). Traditional "linear" channels increasingly offered their own streaming services (p. 62). Noting the myriad deals that Comcast was making to prepare the ground for its own content to be offered by other carriers' virtual service provider's over-the-top facilities, Turner notes,

> Without the certainty against unreasonable discrimination offered by Title II and the Open Internet rules, it would be impossible to imagine a world in which an MSO [multiple-system operator] offers its pay-TV services to customers of other MSOs' via those competing MSOs' distribution facilities. But now we have two

> of the nation's four largest pay-TV providers (AT&T/DTV and DISH) doing just that, and Comcast seemingly preparing to. These positive, pro-competitive marketplace developments are precisely what we'd expect (and what we predicted) when internet users and content producers have access to nondiscriminatory, high-capacity telecom services. (Turner, 2017, p. 60)

Turner argued that Verizon's (now defunct) go90 initiative might receive a renewed boost with the purchase of Yahoo!; Verizon was trying to leverage AOL's assets and cash in on advertising to millennials (Turner, 2017, p. 63). But regardless, the point for Turner was that "this is the outcome the Open Internet decision's framework helped to create: incentivizing ISPs to innovate and invest in all parts of the internet ecosystem, instead of chasing rents that could in theory be earned from using their gatekeeper power to discriminate against the successful innovations of edge companies and users" (p. 63). Nonetheless, it is striking that the evidence being marshaled to the end of pushing back against the elimination of the Wheeler rules involved mobilizing the intensification of platform logics and processes themselves as positive ends.

There was no evidence of a slowdown in deployment: "The broadband industry's pre-2015 trajectory was not in any way, shape, or form harmed by the Open Internet Order, and in fact there was an acceleration in capacity-enhancing deployments in response to greater demand for streaming video-capable connections" (Free Press, 2017, p. 32). Most damning, however, the report documented in painstaking detail the myriad communications that the broadband providers had had with their investors. To every single question posed by an investor or reporter to the firms asking what the influence of the 2015 proceeding had been, none expressed worry or offered any inkling that it was causing the industry to stumble. They were being patently dishonest either to investors or to the FCC itself.

Of course, production was ramped up in all sectors. The *Review of Industrial Organization* in 2017 published a special issue reflecting on the aftermath of the Wheeler FCC's actions. The issue is full of what Philip Mirowski (2013) terms "tinker-toy" models and arguments castigating the rules. They featured many of the usual players, pushing back on any notion that service providers should be precluded from offering paid prioritization arrangements to customers who had already paid for access to their networks. Other arguments stressed the value of zero-rating arrangements abhorred by advocates. Tim Brennan, famously quoted for saying the FCC had been an "economics-free zone," castigated the arguments of the ersatz while putting on blinders and covering his ears: "As an economist, I am continually struck by how little reassurance non-economists take from an observation that profit maximization removes incentives for a large firm to act nefariously," particularly "despite the paucity of incidents so far" (Brennan, 2017, p. 482). Yoo (2017) adapts comments he submitted to India's Telecommunications Regulatory Authority with Facebook's support to defend zero-rating as a practice that provides a dimension of competition involving something other than price: "Restricting producers to competing solely on price naturally gives the largest players a decisive advantage. Permitting producers to compete along dimensions other than price enables smaller players to survive despite having lower sales volumes and higher unit costs (and thus charging higher prices) by tailoring their products for subsegments of the market that place a particularly high value on different product attributes" (p. 514). For a provider like T-Mobile, being allowed to offer users unlimited access to Netflix might be attractive to potential users of that provider. Enabling noncommercial or marginalized voices' content to reach an audience remains left out of the story.

The purpose of the special issue, however, was something quite aside from presenting new arguments, for these arguments were hardly new. It was, of course, obligatory *production* for production's sake, the necessary grist for a millstone long rubbed bald.

Hearkening Back to the Future

Free Press expressed the exasperation likely evident in all advocates who had fought these fights for more than a decade—and some, decades more. They noted that there was no controversy about these rules outside Washington itself, and one can sense the tiresome nature of reiterating the same arguments over and over:

> We once again explain the history of the Communications Act and of Net Neutrality protections that fostered innovation and investment throughout the twenty years—both before and after they were put on the right legal footing in the 2015 order. We once again address disingenuous broadband provider arguments that their separate offer of information services, or even their use of some information processing capabilities (such as DNS or caching), transforms broadband internet access from a telecom service into an information service. We also reply

> once again to the similarly ill-founded yet even more absurd claim that because [broadband Internet access service] provides access to other entities' information services, like email or search, the underlying transmission service likewise is transmogrified into an information service. (Free Press, 2017, p. 8)

Advocates recognized the near futility of their struggle but used the docket to prepare for the legal challenges ahead, putting the entirety of their "It's Working" report into the docket alongside a thorough debunking of the FCC process and the logics of the Notice of Proposed Rulemaking. The fact that twenty years later they are required to readdress the 1998 *Advanced Services Order* reflects the stretched rationalizations of broadband interests in this latest proceeding (Free Press, 2017). They point out that AT&T, in its own filings, offered an "unwelcome invitation to misread decisions made in the 1980s and 1990s and misapply them to today's broadband marketplace" (as the FCC would do); assured that the D.C. Circuit hardly misread *Brand X* in its support of the Wheeler FCC's reclassification of broadband services; and noted that none of the industry commenters had challenged the statements of their executives that Title II categorization had not affected investment strategies nor profitability. Given that part of the notice (FCC, 2017b, ¶¶97–98) stated that the public had not benefited from the Open Internet Order, they contended that more than 47,000 informal complaints—themselves facilitated by provisions of the 2015 rules—had been ignored and were still awaiting investigation. These might provide clues to the extent to which rules were in fact necessary. All the same, the FCC had dragged its feet in letting the public evaluate these:

> Although the Commission was slow to begin releasing these complaints in response to a Freedom of Information Act request, it has finally begun to do so. But it still must explain how its erroneous assertions (about lack of public interaction with the rules, and with the Commission's consumer assistance and enforcement mechanisms) can be trusted as a basis for the proposals made in the *Notice*. That is, unless the Commission is so hell-bent on repealing the *Open Internet Order* that it intends to ignore the fact that such complaints' existence directly contradicts a number of conclusions the *Notice* posited. (Free Press, 2017, p. 4)

The Pai FCC's questions regarding how the Internet operated and its relation to the Telecommunications Act were so concerning that hundreds of high-profile technologists offered their own submission reminding the FCC of how the Internet actually functioned:

> Based on certain questions the FCC asks in the Notice of Proposed Rulemaking (NPRM), we are concerned that the FCC (or at least Chairman Pai and the authors

> of the NPRM) appears to lack a fundamental understanding of what the Internet's technology promises to provide, how the Internet actually works, which entities in the Internet ecosystem provide which services, and what the similarities and differences are between the Internet and other telecommunications systems the FCC regulates as telecommunications services. Due to this fundamental misunderstanding of how the technology underlying the Internet works, we believe that if the FCC were to move forward with its NPRM as proposed, the results could be disastrous: the FCC would be making a major regulatory decision based on plainly incorrect assumptions about the underlying technology and Internet ecosystem. (Internet Engineers, Pioneers, and Technologists, 2017, p. 1)

Mirroring the lead-up to the 2015 proceeding, in the docket we find myriad startups; we find broad coalitions of new civil rights groups; we find the Ad Hoc Telecommunications Users Committee once again expressing its concern that the marketplace had not changed since 2015, "nor have the essential technical and physical characteristics of Internet access changed since Ad Hoc's earlier filing.... The Commission properly updated its initial classification in 2015 and should now leave that classification unchanged" (Ad Hoc Telecommunications Users Committee, 2017, p. i). The committee added: "Marketplace competition cannot protect customers and the public interest where it does not exist, of course.... [T]he subscriber's ISP has a monopoly on access to that subscriber by any business trying to communicate with that subscriber over the Internet" (p. ii). Recognizing the problem of the ISP as terminating access monopoly regarding reaching users, the committee wrote: "The Commission must retain the rule that prohibits ISPs from exploiting their terminating monopoly by blocking or throttling traffic or demanding any payments from non-subscribers for access to subscribers, including 'pay-for-priority' arrangements" (p. ii).

Epistemic Battles, Redux

Indeed, the old strategies were pointless. The epistemic warfare of a metaphysical sort that this proceeding represented (if not virtually all of the actions taken by the Pai FCC) was perfectly summed up by a controversy involving a former FCC chief economist. During 2016, Gerald Faulhaber (who served in the role from 2000 to 2001) and Hal Singer (one of the go-to economists the Pai FCC would turn to justify its findings in the "Restoring Internet Freedom" docket) submitted to the FCC's docket proposing consumer privacy protections a sponsored study that would later be laundered through the prestigious *International Journal of Communication.* Their study had been funded by the advocacy group CALInnovates,[4] "a non-partisan coalition of tech companies, founders, funders and non-profits determined to make the new economy a reality," which stood against the privacy rules under consideration; the white paper in its original form was titled "The Curious Absence of Economic Analysis at the Federal Communications Commission: An Agency in Search of a Mission" (Faulhaber & Singer, 2016). Extending over sixty pages (common in law review articles, less so in social science academic journals), the authors bemoaned the entire state of policymaking at the FCC as an "economics-free zone" in the wake of the 2015 Title II proceeding. Faulhaber and Singer offer a history of the FCC parallel to that supplied by Wu (2011b) but take away quite different lessons.

Focusing on the liberalization of long distance markets, attachments, and more, they emphasize "court-assisted liberalizations" that "had the effect of pushing the FCC towards using economic theory as a principal [*sic*] of regulation" (Faulhaber & Singer, 2016, p. 13).

> What were the effects of these three decisions on the FCC's economic leanings? Prior to *Hush-a-Phone*, the FCC effectively functioned as a monopoly-sanctioning agency rather than a regulator of free commerce, working hand-in-hand with incumbents to support the industry standard. The court-mandated liberalization of the FCC's rigid monopoly polices forced the Commission to acknowledge that a moderate deregulation of control could lead to positive consumer benefits. (Faulhaber & Singer, 2016, pp. 16–17)

In their view, that state has now changed irrevocably: "We hypothesize that the waning influence of economic analysis is correlated to the politicization of the agency and its search for a new mandate. If true, this insight offers crisp policy prescriptions to reinsert dispassionate economic analysis into decision-making at the FCC" (Faulhaber & Singer, 2016, p. 6).

The Computer Inquiries represented a step in the right direction for these authors: gone from their analysis, of course, are broader moves and incentives within capitalism itself—business users demanding lower rates, consumer activism at the level of the states, and public interest activism at the federal level (Horwitz, 1989; Schiller, 2000)—in lieu of simply a turn to a generic notion of "economics" as the motor of history. As for the FCC's recent moves, they hypothesize that if "economics" were the primary motivator for policy, the agency would find itself lost at sea with nothing to do, since no oversight was necessary of the Internet. Net neutrality has served, then, a truly insidious purpose: "Net neutrality has given [the FCC] a mandate to extend its regulation to the Internet, where it will no doubt have a full and busy life" (Faulhaber & Singer, 2016, p. 57). Further:

> How does this hypothesis explain the FCC abandonment of economics? Now that the Commission has found a new mandate to regulate the Internet, it certainly does not want to minimize that mandate by re-adopting economic analysis, which would argue that virtually no regulation is needed for the Internet, which has progressed amazingly well without regulatory intervention. As more advocates and interest groups ask for more regulation to meet their organizational objectives, however, the FCC appears happy to oblige, in effect keeping itself in the regulatory business into the far indefinite future. (Faulhaber & Singer, 2016, p. 57)

Indeed, the consequences of this "lack of economics" at the FCC had been severe. "It should be no surprise that when serious economic analysis is shown the backdoor, special interests and advocacy groups gain power" (p. 58). The notion that *no* regulation would be necessary is in fact a misnomer; what they are really saying is that broadband networks needed to be *reregulated* by market forces alone, reifying their favorite construct. The only time external political economy is consulted is in refuting the "casual empiricism of an advocacy group that operates outside of the constraints of academic reputations" (Faulhaber & Singer, 2016, pp. 33), unwilling to spit the name of Free Press into the body of the text. The result would be the sins contained in the 2015 order: now-barred paid prioritization agreements are equated with an inability to obtain quality of service necessary for such developments as "telemedicine and HD voice."[5] It might prevent "innovative offerings" like the zero-rating plans activists abhorred, or AT&T-initiated more-privacy-for-pricier-subscription plans:

> Because sponsored-data plans by wireless carriers (including zero-rating plans) may run afoul of [the FCC] "general conduct" standard, the *2015 OIO* [Open Internet Order] could discourage innovative offerings that would subsidize Internet access for low income Americans. By discouraging ISPs and content providers from pursuing different ways to subsidize Internet access for consumers—another form of collaboration—the *2015 OIO* could deny the poorest Americans hundreds of millions in benefits annually. There are millions of Americans for whom (wireless) broadband is just out of reach and who would otherwise be eligible for a subsidy in the form of a sponsored-data plan. (Faulhaber & Singer, 2016, p. 59)

Faulhaber and Singer lament that the privacy rules on ISPs would unfairly tilt the market away from their own nascent growth of advertising platforms (among others) in favor of online giants like Google and

Facebook. But they take the concern one step further: that perhaps these platform giants will be restrained in how "innovative" they might be with our digital identities. I know of one Gartner analyst who would be quite pleased indeed with their conception:

> This is a classic example of asymmetric regulation on only one set of market participants (ISPs), while specifically exempting or ignoring direct competitors (edge providers) in the market for online ads. As explained above, if adopted in its current form, the Privacy NPRM will put upward pressure on broadband access prices and immunize edge providers from competition in online advertising markets, while reducing consumer welfare in various ways, including preventing consumers from receiving promotional information about service bundles and price discounts for home security or energy efficiency services. This reduction in competition will likely lead to less innovation by incumbent content providers that dominate online advertising, and by discouraging ISPs to innovate, as doing so could run afoul of the FCC's new privacy rules. (Faulhaber & Singer, 2016, p. 60)

Rote to the core, the function of advertising is seen as providing information to consumers, once again leaving aside its political economic function, that of increasingly becoming one of several arenas in which our actions are taken and commodified out of our control, even sent "up the value chain" to the development of new potentially oligopolistic production processes and chains themselves unamenable to antitrust analysis in its current form.

The way forward, then, was to "reinsert economic analysis into FCC decision-making," the lack of which has apparently allowed interlopers to get in the way of the will of emergent commercial logics whether desired by the public or not. "The waning influence of economic analysis seems to be connected to the politicization of the agency and its search for a new mandate. Based on that diagnosis, policymakers should shield the technocrats at the FCC from political pressure of the kind we observed in net neutrality and set-top-box proceedings" (Faulhaber & Singer, 2016, p. 60). The authors correctly assume that the DC Circuit would accept the rules as written, and looks then to Congress. Their suggestion is that Congress should "clarify its intent in the 1996 Telecom Act to keep the Internet, including fixed and mobile broadband access, free from common-carrier regulation" (p. 60). It should "give the FCC authority to regulate ISPs precisely along the lines dictated by the FCC's 2010 [Open Internet Order]. This could be achieved by either expanding the agency's authority under section 706, or by issuing a new grant of authority" (p. 60). Third, "Congress should require that the

FCC perform rigorous cost-benefit analysis before promulgating any new rules" (p. 61).

To serve maximal utility, such articles need the legitimation of an institutional home beyond appearing—in sponsored form, no less—attached to an interested party's pleading. Off to the *International Journal of Communication* it went in revised and shortened form, where it managed to wriggle its way through the review process.

What proceeded next was nothing short of extraordinary. Dwayne Winseck of Carleton University and Jeffrey Pooley of Muhlenberg College discovered the earlier paper submitted in the privacy docket and its updated version, which, they noticed, contained no mention of the source of the paper's original support. In social science journals such as the *International Journal of Communication,* this could easily be seen as a cardinal sin. Winseck and Pooley published their own response in short order (Winseck & Pooley, 2017). They called out the article's source: "CALinnovates submitted a lengthy white paper, commissioned from the Washington-based economics consulting firm NERA, to the FCC's official docket" (p. 2706). In fact, CALinnovates had itself been the subject of a ProPublica investigation when it appeared an odd group to lack support for the FCC's move to Title II (p. 2706). Winseck and Pooley hit back at any notion that somehow the FCC just made its decision willy-nilly, absent the input of economics advice, listing the establishment by the FCC of an Open Internet Advisory Committee (OIAC), a "half dozen roundtables designed to examine net neutrality" (p. 2712); they noted the pedigree of the chair of the OIAC, Harvard law professor Jonathan Zittrain (p. 2712); they pointed similarly to reports the FCC produced on data caps and Internet access pricing (p. 2712); and perhaps most damning, they noted that "Singer and Faulhaber were party to many of these events, which they do not mention" (p. 2712). Further:

> [The OIAC's annual report of 2013] brought together a who's who list of industry, think tanks, and academia representatives with well-known—and cross-cutting—views on the topic. The FCC's top brass, including Robert Cannon, whose authoritative account of the FCC's trilogy of Computer Inquiries helps us grasp how we got from the first melding of computing and telecommunications in the 1950s to the broadband Internet of the 21st century, were there, too. All of this is conspicuously absent from the *IJoC* paper. (Winseck & Pooley, 2017, p. 2712; citations omitted)

Winseck and Pooley pointed to the words of a previous FCC chief economist, Jonathan Baker:

> At the roundtable, Baker stressed that he was not working for clients or otherwise involved in the Open Internet proceeding. He also argued that strong ex ante net neutrality rules were needed and (unlike Singer and Faulhaber) that antitrust law and economic approaches cannot adequately address the issues.... He was also clear that the "costs of FCC rules are likely to be small." This was because the cut and thrust of such an approach had already been in effect due to the earlier Open Internet principles and the conditions placed on Comcast in return for the FCC's blessing of the cable/ISP giant's NBC Universal acquisition. "Sketch the benefits and costs," Baker said, "and I conclude that the rules... would pass any sensible cost-benefit test even with concerns about mobile data and interconnection." ... Baker's points are widely known and contradict the *IJoC* authors' central claim about cost-benefit analyses at the FCC. (Winseck & Pooley, 2017, p. 2713)

One would accurately surmise that any claim that economics had not been present—much less notions of cost-benefit analysis—while making these decisions is pure hokum. Further: "That Baker also sees common carrier regulation along the lines that the FCC ultimately adopted as the right tool for the job... also clashes with the authors' indictment of the 'irrationality' of common carriage/net neutrality regulations" (p. 2713). Winseck and Pooley then drove their point home:

> Nothing riles the friends of industry more than this run of events, and they have done everything they can to discredit anyone with the temerity to stand up against incumbent industry players. This, we suspect, is what's really behind the Faulhaber, Singer, and Urschel criticisms. And having lost their battles before regulators, the courts, and the public, they are now trying to fight back and win the day, resorting to unsubstantiated charges of economic illiteracy. (Winseck & Pooley, 2017, p. 2719)[6]

Winseck would exclaim on his blog:

> [The paper's] undisclosed origins as a commissioned piece of policy advocacy runs afoul of scholarly publishing norms and ethics. Indeed, the paper is a model of information laundering... with *no* acknowledgement of these origins,... finally recycled back into the policy process on several occasions by Pai to justify his sprint to reverse many of the signature accomplishments of his predecessor—all with the telcos, consultants, industry-friendly think tanks such as the American Enterprise Institute, etc., cheering him on from the sidelines, both within the US and beyond. (Winseck, 2017)

Even more striking than the damning critique they offer is what transpired as the rejoinder was under review and set to be published. The funders of the original purchased paper initially sought to sue the *International Journal for Communication* for even considering the publication of Winseck and Pooley's rejoinder. The journal, to its credit—now ten years after it initially waded into network neutrality's waters—published their rejoinder anyway. Winseck illustrated how Faulhaber and crew, after being publicly chastised on Twitter by Winseck himself, commenced modifying their disclosure statement from nothing at all to "The authors would like to thank CALinnovates for funding," to the fuller (but to Winseck "still inadequate") "The authors would like to thank CALinnovates for funding the basic research for this paper. A much longer (and rather different) paper by the authors was submitted by CALinnovates to the FCC in WC Docket No. 16-106 (July 21, 2016) and WC Docket No. 16-243 (August 21, 2016) and appears on CALinnovates website" (Dwayne Winseck, personal communication, April 29, 2019). The full story of the crescendo of legal challenges to the publication of Winseck and Pooley's "bias-motivated hit-piece" bears reading aboard his blog, and certainly casts the former chief economist in a rather compromised and unsavory light (Winseck, 2017). Thus is the double-truth of the neoliberal thought collective operationalized.

To the best I have found, the only place that this episode received any coverage was at *Inside Higher Ed* (Flaherty, 2017) and the *Register* (McCarthy, 2017). Even as ordinary Americans may have never heard of the entire affair at the *International Journal of Communication* (or even of the journal itself), in numerous senses, that was beside the point. The point was never the logics of these arguments at all, even as in certain circles Winseck and Pooley were academic heroes of a sort in doing something about the hidden origins of the article. Examining the privacy proceeding from a structural standpoint, the threat that was made to the emergent form of platform capitalism as it developed was that the FCC's broad authority itself could crimp immanent logics in inconvenient ways; it *did* create an uneven playing field against the other platform capitalists that sought to operate in converged market spaces.

However, as heroic as Winseck and Pooley's actions were, they were engaging a foe on one plane when the real action was on another. The battles that transpired were never about their *content*; they were about *production*, and they were about turning usual arguments of the advocates for network neutrality against themselves in terms of form as well as function. Which is to say, even in this episode I fear Winseck and Pooley still misread the significance of this episode in other subtle ways. They announce in their rejoinder,

> We also sense that they are unsettled by the decline of the Chicago School of Economics, which has come under growing strain after a 40-year reign of orthodoxy in telecommunications economics and regulatory circles. The fact is that long-standing debates in modern economic thought between rule-of-law approaches to market power and the rule-of-reason alternative are once again cresting. This battle of ideas, stretching back to the late 19th century, is buried in the authors' frequent appeals to a singular "economics" perspective. (Winseck & Pooley, 2017, p. 2719)

For them, this was a battle of wills between the twin forces of bought research and the standing of a particular strain of that research that had served those interests well for years. However, the point was less the content of the knowledge; for the purpose of the Pai FCC, its content mattered less than its existence, bought as it may be, although it is handier in legitimated form after its purchase. The Chicago economists had long articulated themselves to these telecommunications debates, a trap into which advocates, starting with Wu, found themselves enmeshed. But now the struggle had moved to what even the *existence* of these battles meant, and that they themselves existed was what Pai needed to move forward.

In this environment, exposés that might have been incendiary in the past were now rote exercises. In the lead-up to Trump's election, the *New York Times* crafted a perennial mockup of the revolving door between corporate advocacy firms, think tanks, and the inner sanctum of government, laying out the cozy relationships between corporate-dominated think tanks and regulators. Amongst its myriad examples was an email from Jeffrey Eisenach of Verizon to FCC commissioner Michael O'Rielly regarding the use of an American Enterprise Institute event to lay out the case against net neutrality. All the same, the longer historical trajectory of the *institutionalization* of the interrelationships themselves was left behind in favor of a story of almost dull cynicism, as if the phenomenon wasn't terribly new but not terribly structurally significant either (Lipton, Confessore, & Williams, 2016). Winseck himself notes that within mere days of Faulhaber and crew's article appearing in the *International Journal of Communication,* Pai was using the freshly laundered article as justification for the creation of a new Office of Economics and Analytics at the FCC. This office was established in early 2018 in one fell swoop on the back of a thin report and over the objections of the two Democrats on the commission (FCC, 2018b). The proposal was, of course, received with acclaim from predictable corners of the thought collective as the American Enterprise Institute, the Competitive Enterprise Institute, the Hudson Institute, and the Mercatus Center, with quotes that seemed to wonder how the FCC ever managed to get by without thinking about economics or data (FCC, 2018c).

Given the chance to respond to Winseck and Pooley, the various players replied with nonreplies. However, as proceedings continued, it became newly fashionable to pay attention to the myriad and often obscure, indirect connections between (net neutrality friendly, but hardly passionate) Google and scholars writing about network neutrality and other issues of interest to the giant. For instance, a report issued midyear by the Google Transparency Project (2017) traced Google subsidies to university scholars, think tanks, and more received a great deal of attention, including in the *Wall Street Journal* (Mullins & Nicas, 2017). This report and Google received significant attention (for Google, fleetingly unflattering in nature) because of the novelty of the tech giant starting to wade into the waters long occupied by the telecom companies, oil companies, and other legacy enterprises. By the same token, however, it did indeed find undisclosed direct subsidies for the research the company might find useful in policy dealings, some quite troubling. Numerous other connections, however, were themselves almost filler: tenuous five-degrees-removed relations seemingly drummed up for numbers among the genuinely worrisome ones. All the same, this approach does attest to the institutional learning that the online platform giants are beginning to wield as they study their longer-standing siblings. It raised complicated questions at institutions generally associated with the center-left, like the New America Foundation, when close ties to Google appeared to hamstring the efforts of their division working on antitrust policy (Vogel, 2017), which was creating output not favorable to this benefactor. In contrast, the essence of why the "Google study" controversy stuck and similar efforts by broadband conduit giants flew below the radar was likely because Google was mobilizing for its own defense, not the defense and maintenance of a broader, systemic imperative that had rooted itself so deeply for years that it had become part of the background noise of politics and news.

Pai himself mobilized an emergent ire against Google and the other online platform giants as themselves being restrictive of "free speech" stemming from their efforts to tackle (in ham-fisted fashion) the problem of deliberately false information flowing through their networks; combined with increased concerns of the mounting boldness of a latent racist, misogynist, and xenophobic undercurrent in the United States given new confidence by the tacit and direct support of the new administration, inevitably right-wing players were ensnared in the fray. (Accusing the tech companies of bias against conservatives has become a regular part of the Republican playbook, it seems; see Brustein, 2018). The tactic was in full force to cast aspersion on the large tech companies and away from the conduit firms, and Pai fanned the flames.

Perhaps all the players in this episode continue to believe that in this context the core function of the production of knowledge was to produce truth, even Winseck and Pooley; how disappointed all sides will be (particularly the Faulhabers of the world) when they discover in time that their job was simply to *produce*. The sheer effort Faulhaber and Singer put into their piece in the first place on the surface seems to hint at significant epistemological battles underway, but such battles are phantasms. Full-throated defenses of their brand of economics in regulation are almost like Coke and Pepsi continuing to spend fantastic sums of money on advertising and marketing not due to any worry that someone, anyone is unaware of their existence, but instead due to pressures to compete on anything but price and perhaps the need to stoke additional aggregate demand for their product.

Activism in a Void

In such an environment, what does it even mean to perform network neutrality activism? The FCC was unmoored from any argument about the actual function of the Internet itself; it was in fact uninterested in holding any public hearings whatsoever. Whatever one thought of Pai's leadership, perhaps there was an honesty in holding no hearings, an overt acknowledgment that everything that needed to be said had been said, and that what remained was only raw power in place of any aspirations to liberal rationality, even nobility.

Activism did erupt accordingly—those involved in Washington circles knew that the FCC could potentially be pressured by congressional forces, and all forms of surprise can occur; thus tactics were fierce, even transformative. Years of activism resulted in broad-based coalitions unlike anything we had seen before; the newly emergent Voices for Internet Freedom,[7] a nationwide coalition of a new generation of civil rights groups that had possessed a large presence in 2014 and 2015 but now resounded with renewed force, was a seemingly ubiquitous presence. Throughout the year, activists held nationwide open phone calls with activists hosted by a rotating crew of media policy and civil rights groups, organizing a nationwide crack team of activists dubbed "Team Internet" that exchanged information, coordinated congressional office visits locally, and organized other actions across the country. The largest Internet giants this time out did join in calling attention to the issue, but it would be largely public relations. They would win no matter whose voices prevailed. Activists remembered all too well that Google was more than happy to compromise with the likes of Verizon (as we saw in 2010), and even Netflix in 2017 was willing to admit that, come or go, net neutrality really didn't matter all that much to it.

A large part of this effort involved preparing for the inevitable legal challenges to come: no one was under any illusion that the Pai FCC would relent. As courts would only admit in future proceedings the materials submitted into the docket as evidence, activists urged network neutrality supporters across the country to not file form letters—rather, they should speak directly to their expectations of how Internet services operated. As Gigi Sohn advised in a widely circulated post, "Write about what you understand you are buying when you purchase broadband Internet access. For the FCC to reverse its 2015 determination that broadband ISPs are 'telecommunications services' subject to greater oversight under Title II, it must show that ISPs are offering, and you understand that you are buying, not just a fast on-ramp to the Internet, but a bundle of 'information services,' like email, cloud storage and other proprietary over-the-top services" (Sohn, 2017). In 2015, Sohn noted that when the FCC looked at the market for broadband Internet access, "What they found was that overwhelmingly, consumers were looking to buy a fast pathway to the Internet." This seemingly obvious observation was incredibly important: if users were merely seeking a fast means to information, services, and communication with others, broadband service was, almost to the legal definition, a telecommunications service, not an information service—quite counter to the on-their-face asinine claims made by the *Restoring Internet Freedom* notice of proposed rulemaking regarding how the FCC now believed the Internet worked.

However, activists went so much further. Central to the far-flung campaign to save the 2015 rules was framing network neutrality specifically as a civil rights issue. Activism occurred along numerous fronts. What unified them were efforts by longtime media reform activists to act in solidarity with those involved in efforts for addressing intersectional power dynamics along a broad spectrum. The worst tendencies of the Trump administration galvanized such efforts with its inherent racism, Islamophobia, the unleashing of Immigration and Customs Enforcement agents, and general lawlessness. Commissioner Mignon Clyburn, hosted by Voices for Internet Freedom, traveled to Los Angeles to listen to perspectives from the area known as Skid Row (Torres, 2017). Speaking at the event were professors from the University of Southern California; representatives of 18 Million Rising, the Black Alliance for Just Immigration, and Common Cause; and Denise Cortes, who earned a living via her website Pearmama.com, which featured brief personal articles alongside sponsored content that she produced in collaboration with brands. (One might note neoliberalism's ambivalences rising again to the fore: here, the practice of the production of branded content—which would be anathema to the critiques of journalism produced by Free Press, among other critics—is mobilized in the defense of another policy altogether.) The overarching sentiment was twofold. For one, broadband adoption by people of color was lagging behind that of white populations primarily because of cost, itself due to a lack of competition in the broadband market. For the other, the now oft-repeated mantra that network neutrality was itself a civil rights issue was reinforced by all, as movements neglected by dominant media sources were able to make their views heard aboard an unrestricted Internet. A message returned to time and again in activist gatherings, virtual or offline, was the sentiment of Patrisse Cullors, one of the founders of Black Lives Matter, that "it is because of net neutrality rules that the internet is the only communication channel left where Black voices can speak and be heard, produce and consume, on our own terms" (quoted in Torres & Cyril, 2017). This particular theme—especially in the wake of such powerful movements as Black Lives Matter, which reached mass consciousness first because of live reporting via live stream on social media—served as a centerpiece of the activist case as they sought to grow public support for the issue.

Early on, groups initiated a fight with social media and tech companies to disavow any possible effort to produce a registry of Muslims in the United States, recognizing how easy this would be for those who possessed so much data about their users (Cuthbert, 2016). These rode alongside concerns about facial recognition technologies, highlighting a report that the FBI now maintained a biometric database constructed of mug shots and drivers' license photographs:

> It's the first time our nation's history that the FBI has maintained a biometric database made up primarily of innocent people.... [Additionally,] several of the leading algorithms were 5–10 percent less accurate when used to identify Black people.... One of the algorithms failed to identify white people accurately 11 percent of the time, but that failure rate jumped to 19 percent when the subject was Black. (Fulton, 2016)

Then-senator Al Franken stoked such fears when he revealed that the FBI had used facial recognition technologies at both Hillary Clinton and Bernie Sanders rallies; equally ominous, "the FBI itself released 18 hours of spy-plane footage it had taken at Black Lives Matter protests in Baltimore in spring 2015" (Fulton, 2016).

In March, activists attempted to maintain the tactics they employed in 2015, standing up during an open FCC meeting to reveal t-shirts asking the FCC to "protect net neutrality"—but they were forced out and required to remove the shirts (Kroin, 2017b). A similar protest in April, a joint effort of Free Press, Fight For the Future, Demand Progress, the Free Software Foundation, and Popular Resistance resulted in several being outright banned from the FCC building ("FCC Chairman Ajit Pai," 2017). In May, Pai was picketed at the Washington Peace Center (Forester, 2017). At another FCC meeting in May, a reporter for *Roll Call*, attempting to pose a question to commissioner Michael O'Rielly, instead found himself pinned to a wall by security as the commissioner passed by: "What is the culture of the FCC that says this is ok?" the reporter later asked (Mele, 2017). On May 8, John Oliver stepped into the fray once again and once again overtaxed the FCC web servers as comments poured in; however, this time, much controversy would swirl around mysterious "denial-of-service attacks" that prevented commenters from achieving their purpose. The Pai FCC's claim that these attacks were the cause of outages was proven to be a fabrication a year later, to no consequence.

Activists had managed to mobilize a segment of the Senate yet again, securing two letters from a quarter of the body calling against the gutting of network neutrality rules.[8] As the FCC vote neared, recalling chairman Ajit Pai's past history as counsel for Verizon, protests outside Verizon stores across the country grew and were simultaneously held in all fifty states.

Nonetheless, it bears repeating that the arguments outside the FCC versus those inside were completely at odds. The concerns expressed at these protests were not even the terms of debate in which the issue was being argued. They were legislatively useless—but politically powerful nonetheless in growing coalitions for long-term action to uncertain ends, something all sides understood was necessary.

If 2015 witnessed the construction of a terrific heterogeneity machine, the Trump FCC rediscovered how to make such tactics disperse into mere diversity once again, taking away the ability to even get the machine moving of its own accord. Weaponizing liberalism against itself proved hugely effective: that is, finding ways to deliberately render the machinery of classical liberalism (or, at least, its ideals: its purported basis in rationality, the institutions established toward discernment of this rationality) itself illegitimate or tainted, unworthy of support or trust. If in 2010 we saw the FCC send user comments on its blog straight into a wall, then this time the objective would be to delegitimize the entirety of the public comment system itself. Administrative procedures themselves could be subverted if an exploit could be found. When right-wing provocateurs/racists/white supremacists/trolls Milo Yiannopolous and Richard Spencer sought to travel the country speaking at universities, for instance, the objective was less to get across a point of view and more to generate enough pushback against their presence that the *institution* of the university itself might be rendered illegitimate as a site of open discourse, and thus perhaps unworthy of continued support in itself. Thus there was an incentive to even broadcast an 'edgier' persona, all to generate the greater resistance; and Donald Trump would play along in 2019, signing an executive order "protecting free speech" on college campuses (Svrluga, 2019).

One way to accomplish this was to attempt to co-opt the protests themselves that were occurring. In May, for instance, activists protested outside the FCC building. Having already accrued more than one million comments into the "Restoring Internet Freedom" proceeding, Senators Ed Markey and Ron Wyden and Representatives Barbara Lee and Jared Polis spoke against the Pai FCC's drive to undo the 2015 rules. They were joined by representatives of the ACLU, the Center for Media Justice, CREDO Action, Color of Change, Common Cause, Demand Progress, the Electronic Frontier Foundation, Faithful Internet, the Free Press Action Fund, the National Hispanic Media Coalition, Popular Resistance, Public Knowledge, Fight For the Future, *Daily Kos*, the *Nation*, and the Women's Institute for Freedom of the Press (Kroin, 2017a). At the same rally, a number of masked protesters showed up with signs deliberately misstating what network neutrality was fighting for: on their signs (and with a cameraman from the right-wing outlets *Rebel Media* and the *Daily Caller* in tow to ensure coverage for later dissemination) were protests that what protecting net neutrality meant was actually a desire to shut down numerous right-wing media outlets. These protesters were called out by Harold Feld from the podium, and efforts by onlookers to discern who the interlopers were behind their masks proved unsuccessful. But in today's barrage of shared content via platforms that weaponize homophily, the distinction between the genuine and the cloying may or may not have been clear, as multiple universes of "truth" proliferate (for a terrific discussion, see Vaidhyanathan, 2018). All the same, those who were affiliated with the side of the cloying could point to the video as an illustration that net neutrality supporters apparently supported censorship, and thus sides could again be taken; diverse debates reign supreme, even once debates leave the realm of the grounded and enter that of the apocryphal.

Perhaps more concerning was the pollution of the FCC docket itself. Activists discovered during the comment period that millions of comments were being filed under people's names without their consent, amounting to massive identity theft on a broad scale. Activists set up websites that enabled visitors to check whether a comment had been filed under their name without their knowledge. As state attorneys general started sounding the alarm—alongside Democratic commissioners Jessica Rosenworcel and Mignon Clyburn—the FCC was deliberately unhelpful in investigating these fake comments and showed no interest in figuring out whether or not millions of comments were legitimate: the proceeding would move forward regardless (Rosenberg, 2017). The strategy of dark groups leveraging data breaches to obtain stolen lists of names and home and email addresses to sully and delegitimate other public commenting mechanisms was activated outside the FCC at the Consumer Financial Protection Bureau as well (Grimaldi & Overberg, 2017). The FCC would dissemble when its server went down due to what it claimed was a denial-of-service attack. Such strategies assured that analyses of the breakdown of comments for and against network neutrality like that undertaken in 2014 by the Sunlight Foundation—or even the more recent 2018 breakdown revealing that most non-form-letter contributions favored net neutrality (Singel, 2018)—would in this context be rendered almost meaningless.

A virtual echo chamber of right-wing media concerns stood at the ready to "debunk" activists in formats easily shareable via social media. Numerous increasingly well-known right-wing has-explanation-for-everything pundits and provocateurs, such as Ben Shapiro and a host of others, were welcomed as new layers of the Russian doll; better yet, Ajit Pai was willing to speak with them.[9] Their tremendous utility was that of tossing scurrilous arguments into the air that advocates would be forced to field. The universe was once again separated into pro-net neutrality and anti-net neutrality camps, even as the old issues of the implications of the ability to discriminate *were not even the core considerations* being mobilized via the *Restoring Internet Freedom* proceeding inside the FCC. The technique of *rendering diverse* what was a potentially heterogeneous argument was employed once again, even in a sphere that would ultimately carry no influence within the FCC itself but might serve to confuse any other decision makers' thinking on the issue. The surreality of it, and Pai's complicity, was something to behold: here was a commissioner willing to stoke phantasmagoric illusions of debate outside the FCC, knowing full well that they would have no effect in drawing up the Order; the sole purpose of the proceeding was to remove a government institution that had become cathected to a machine constructed painstakingly by activists—materially, epistemically, and even affectively—from their ambit.

Even commissioners long departed the agency played along. In April 2017, Pai gave a speech at the Hudson Institute on "the importance of economic analysis at the FCC," opening his comments with, "What an honor it is to be introduced by Harold Furchtgott-Roth for a speech about economic analysis at the FCC! A Stanford Ph.D. in economics and the only economist to ever serve as a Commissioner at the FCC? This is like Bruce Springsteen bringing a garage band onstage to cover 'Born to Run'" (Pai, 2017a). Furchtgott-Roth, now with the Washington Legal Foundation, did submit a comment in the *Restoring Internet Freedom* proceeding (Furchtgott-Roth & Washington Legal Foundation, 2017). The commissioner's academic pedigree was largely sidelined as he argued the old chestnut that broadband providers had First Amendment rights that prevented them being forced to carry speech against their wishes:

> By forcing broadband Internet service providers (ISPs) to carry, transmit, and deliver all Internet content—even that with which the provider disagrees—the [2015] Order impermissibly compels speech and deprives ISPs of their editorial discretion under the First Amendment. Moreover, by singling out for burdensome regulation the dissemination of information by ISPs—without imposing similar restrictions on other Internet entities that also disseminate information—the Order constitutes a content- and speaker-based restriction that discriminates against ISPs in violation of the First Amendment. (Furchtgott-Roth & Washington Legal Foundation, 2017, p. 2)

Mansions of glory in suicide machines! Economics indeed![10]

The Order

The Order itself, once it emerged, was devastating to supporters of network neutrality. Despite the approach of the 2015 FCC being twice court approved, it rereclassified broadband as an information service, Mobile broadband service was similarly relegated back to the category of "private mobile service," performing the same task for Internet provided wirelessly. All blocking, throttling, and unreasonable discrimination rules were similarly removed from these media, leaving behind only a transparency rule that ISPs would be required to disclose any planned discriminatory activities to their users (presumably in the fine print of the service contract) and to the FCC. Oversight would be removed to the FTC, which is able to adjudicate only "unfair, deceptive, and anticompetitive practices" (as strictly defined by antitrust law, not in the colloquial sense)—which would in turn mean that, once such practices were disclosed, they would essentially be legal. The "general conduct standard" instituted by the Wheeler FCC was rescinded. To boot, despite the Republican commissioners' abhorrence to efforts in previous proceedings to override state or local laws—recall that the Wheeler FCC sought to override such laws that made it difficult or impossible for localities to supply public broadband services—the newly empowered majority promptly preempted any state and local efforts to establish their own network neutrality rules, or anything that smacked of network neutrality rules.

The FCC was effectively eliminating all foundations of its ability to have any say at all over the activities of broadband providers, salting the earth behind them. Contrary to the DC Circuit that understood that the DNS architecture was part and parcel of the telecommunications service provided by a broadband provider, here Pai turns this logic on its head, favoring the view held by Christopher Yoo (recall, which was tossed aside as outlandish in the 2015 Open Internet Order): because *some* processing of any kind transpired behind the scenes, this meant that, by definition, presto!—what is being provided was an information service. The Order returns to the *Stevens Report* of the late 1990s for inspiration. The Republicans on the commission cast aside the technologists who wrote en masse to remind them how the Internet worked in twelve footnotes, favoring instead a read so literal of the Telecommunications Act that the only assumption one can draw is that they presume the intent of Congress was that they would brook no change at all in how communications media worked going forward from 1996. The *intent* of the law, in the commonsense view, was cast aside for the *literal words* of the law, and the Order strains to prove that the law's words described how the Internet worked today. The FCC is so literal in its interpretation of the definitions of "information services" and "telecommunications services" that it is questionable if even a telephone service remained a telecommunications service, given that no telephone user, even of a landline phone connected to analog switches, saw fit to request *which* switches through which to direct a circuit. The FCC offers a brief paragraph to explain that, no, telephones just transmit, so they stay telecommunications services, but until we all learn to refer to websites by their IP addresses, the Internet *processes* the information (FCC, 2017a, ¶56). The FCC painfully splits hairs to derive the result it desires, extending for pages.

Users of the Internet that expect that their Internet connection's function is to transmit content they request will find the FCC wholeheartedly disagrees with their commonsense evaluation. In fact, the only times that any of the millions of comments filed by the public (genuinely) appear is when the Pai FCC desires to browbeat them: to anyone who expressed that this is how they expected the Internet to work, their words are twisted back on them, thrown in their face: "Indeed, record evidence confirms that consumers highly value the capabilities their ISPs offer to acquire information from websites, utilize information on the Internet, retrieve such information, and otherwise process such information" (FCC, 2017a, ¶46). Users will also be surprised to learn that this FCC believed that when they were on the market for a new smartphone, they were shopping for phone service *or* data services, not both (¶85).

Of course, the strain is hardly indicative of how Pai and his colleagues genuinely saw the Internet. They were fully aware that they were using the strategy of the advocates in their complaint against Comcast's blocking of BitTorrent: every possible tack was being taken to release the FCC of any responsibility whatsoever for overseeing communications, realizing the dreams of the thought collective that had sought this all along. The Order itself rests entirely on a sloppy reread of the FCC's own data so as to apply a reinterpretation of years previous: reading competition into statistics that render none, it performs the old perennial parlor trick of taking national markets as indicative of what is available at the point of sale (FCC, 2017a, ¶132). But this should be no surprise: we have seen how, since the very beginnings of the network neutrality debate, the ontic content of knowledge hardly matters anymore, and this Order is no exception. Given that this FCC held no hearings on the issue before plowing ahead, the Order instead finds a single legitimation, "economics," but of a particular vintage, to fulfill its aims; it has a choice and it picks a closely interconnected school, one given sustenance and support for decades, even as it has pulled those who purport to argue with it right into its orbit.

The thought collective's work is duly rewarded, particularly since the collective force of the debates of the last fifteen years had led to the buttress of any notion of net neutrality not being the overall social function of the Internet but instead a "virtuous circle" (in 2010) and "virtuous cycle" (in 2015). The evidence offered is almost arbitrary; the fact that Hal Singer and the Phoenix Center (Ford, 2017) provided a counterpoint of any variety against Free Press's evaluation of the broadband ecosystem allows him to cast aside the latter and pay attention to headcounts so favored by incumbents, despite the words to investors; the debate rendered diverse, as opposed to heterogeneous, provides him the necessary interpretive opening: "The balance of the evidence in the record suggests that Title II classification has reduced ISP investment in the network, as well as hampered innovation, because of regulatory uncertainty. The record also demonstrates that small ISPs, many of which serve rural consumers, have been particularly harmed by Title II"—a claim easily debunked by advocates (for example, Turner, 2019)—"and there is no convincing evidence of increased investment in the edge that would compensate for the reduction in network investment" (FCC, 2017a, ¶88). The FCC leans on Graeme Guthrie's 2006 "Regulating Infrastructure: The Impact on Risk and Investment," "a survey of the economic literature on the ways regulation can affect investment" (referenced at ¶89). Guthrie would likely to be pleasantly surprised that twelve years later he could exert such sway. The Pai FCC dutifully recites its favorite analyses of the neoliberal collective (Thomas Hazlett and Joshua Wright appear at ¶94, continuing their insistence that take-up of DSL was influenced more by its being closed to competition than by cultural factors rendering access to faster Internet connections increasingly necessary). It also cites American Enterprise Institute presentations to reiterate the neoliberal trope that "public interest" regulation can be used by regulators as a form of capture by those regulated (even as the example used had nothing to do with network neutrality, deriding "radio spectrum awarded on basis of public interest, prior to the advent of auctions, and broadcasters using the Commission to fight the development of cable television"; see ¶100n368). This argument, of course, is similar to that provided by the litigious Gerald Faulhaber and his writing partners; it is the same argument advanced by Christopher Yoo and his colleagues in their critique of Tim Wu's *The Master Switch* (Decherney, Ensmenger, & Yoo, 2011).

The Pai FCC is similarly disconcerned with the litany of examples of discrimination marshaled by advocates—much less those international examples described by Marsden (2017). In describing Comcast's blocking of BitTorrent over ten years before, the problem was apparently very simple and seemingly cost-free if one lets the historical distance of the events allow them to fade into the mists of time: "After receiving a formal complaint about the practice, the Commission found 'that Comcast's conduct poses a substantial threat to both the open character and efficient operation of the Internet, and is not reasonable,' and ordered Comcast to cease the interference" (FCC, 2017a, ¶111). Perhaps the courts did overturn this action, not on the merits but on its legal foundation—to which the Pai FCC was now returning, yet taking the further step of abandoning the commission's interest in overseeing broadband entirely—but no matter. The favorite neoliberal trope of seeing such things as seemingly minor problems solved with a complaint that results in publicity that in turn foments a market reaction, correcting course—and not the action of hundreds of thousands of individuals and millions of dollars in legal fees—can always be depended on to make an appearance. Out of disorder, order; no effort necessary—it will solve itself, being the vast calculative engine markets represent. After all, as the Pai FCC notes, "ISPs have strong incentives to preserve Internet openness, and these interests typically outweigh any countervailing incentives an ISP might have" (¶117), recalling an unceasing faith in the hypothesis of internalization of complementary externalities (ICE) nearly a decade and a half after its inception. To take its content for truth is one thing, but it is important to recall that the true labor of ICE, now on full display, was less its insight (with no insult intended to its philosophers, who offered their own warnings of accepting it wholesale) than the creation of a connection of this debate to the neoliberal stream.

Those who join Barbara van Schewick in her concern about the assumption in antitrust law that an increase in efficiency can salve an arrangement from scrutiny will find little succor. The Pai FCC is not just open to such arrangements; it is absolutely enthusiastic about them. It trumpets, "As the economic literature teaches that vertical integration generally increases efficiency, the antitrust laws will permit greater innovation in vertical agreements than the tightly regulated confines of the Title II Order" (FCC, 2017a, ¶148n532). (The quote here is contained in the public draft. It is noteworthy that in the final version of the rules, the FCC hedges its bets: "As the economic literature teaches that vertical integration *may* increase efficiency" [FCC, 2018a, ¶148n532; emphasis added].) As van Schewick screamed into the academic aether, net neutrality advocates were less concerned with efficiencies obtained by corporate entities than implications for their own free speech, civil rights, and more; the FCC proceeds to offer a litany of examples—from their favored economists—of the benefits of vertical integration (FCC, 2017a, ¶148n532).

It is all so tiresome; it is so rote; it is so predictable; it is so *uninteresting;* it is so disconnected from any actually relevant notion to what was on issue—but this was precisely the point, and objective, of the thought collective. Activists did what they needed to, but this beast was feasting on their efforts as it grew; it was well maintained by the collective works, given vaccination by the Russian doll and sustenance by the advocates, even as they had little to no other option and could make no different decisions. Here seems a real bookend to Tim Wu's history of technology as following an arc of his concept of "The Cycle" (2011), the seeming inexorable progression of new technologies from operating in open fashion to closed, now applied to the dominant medium of the next generation or more. Yoo, joined by others, at one point critiqued this historical account (Decherney, Ensmenger, & Yoo, 2011), arguing that it lacked sufficient detail, that it sought too earnestly to fit communication history into his concept of "The Cycle." The critique may bear some credence. Yet, by the same token, the efforts to render *present-day* episodes in greater detail—to examine the role activism played in the generation of regulation or in the operation of firms in markets—will never be explored by the thought collective or its extended family; there is simply a rote faith that *antitrust protects free speech,* and the Pai FCC recites the catechism faithfully:

> The market competition that antitrust law preserves will protect values such as free expression, to the extent that consumers value free expression as a service attribute and are aware of how their ISPs' actions affect free expression. The lack of evidence of harms to free expression on the Internet also bolsters our belief that Title II is unnecessary to protect social values that are not the focus of antitrust. The anecdotes of harms to Internet openness cited by supporters of the *Title II Order* almost exclusively concern business decisions regarding network management, rather than being aimed at or impacting political expression. In any case, the transparency rule and the ISP commitments backed up by FTC enforcement focus are targeted to preserving free expression, particularly the no-blocking commitment. (FCC, 2017a, p. ¶153)

Jonathan Nuechterlein's goal, expressed a decade prior, of removing the FCC entirely from the picture was now realized—and conveniently so, as in this proceeding he was representing AT&T (see FCC, 2017a, ¶128n465). As the FCC declared, "Finally, applying antitrust principles to ISP conduct is consistent with longstanding economic and legal principles that cover all sectors of the economy, including the entire Internet ecosystem. Applying the same body of law to ISPs, edge providers, and all Internet actors avoids the regulatory distortions of Title II" (¶154). All markets is markets indeed.

Hypercharged Neoliberalism

In an interview, in answer to the question of whether Pai had a governing philosophy, former FCC commissioner Michael Copps offered:

> Yes, I think he believes this stuff, I think he's a true believer. He was in the Office of General Counsel when I was in there—very articulate, very bright, very pleasant. He is an attractive personality, but he has this *Weltanschauung* or whatever you want to call it that is so out of step with modern politics and where we should be in the history of this country that it's potentially extremely destructive. And Michael O'Rielly, the other Republican commissioner, is about the same. He's an ideologue, too.... It's all about the ideology, the world of big money, the access

> that the big guys have and continue to have. It's not that the FCC outright refuses to let public interest groups through the door or anything like that; it's just the lack of resources citizens and public interest groups have compared to what the big guys have. The public interest groups don't have much of a chance, but I think they've done a pretty good job given the lack of resources. (Winship, 2017)

Pai's weltanschauung was made clear when, in a poke in the eye of activists, he starred in a video produced by the *Daily Caller* titled "Seven Things You Can Still Do on the Internet after Net Neutrality."[11] He lampoons his critics by describing "things you'll still be able to do on the Internet after these Obama-era regulations are repealed." The viewer is invited to "[Insta]gram their food," to post photos of animals, to shop for fidget spinners and eclipse glasses, to watch *Game of Thrones* (dragon wings are made to deliberately resemble horns on the chairman's head), to stay in fan communities. He finishes with an invitation to "drive memes right into the ground" and is joined in a rendition of a suitably cringeworthy Harlem shake paroxysm. Alongside Pai in his gyrations is Martina Markota, one of the promulgators of the long-debunked Pizzagate controversy of 2016 and now part of *The Rebel* conservative network; this alone provided some possible support, yet not proof, of some advocates' contentions that when fake protesters showed up outside the FCC to recast net neutrality as an effort to censor political right-leaning websites, Pai may well have called them in himself. (On YouTube, Markota posted the video featuring her discussing Pizzagate and commented below it, "The media decided that slandering me as a conspiracy theorist was somehow an argument against the repeal of net neutrality.... I did not realize I [was] not allowed to utter the words [*sic*] pizzagate since everyone else was, and I was just a performer making a silly video to upload to youtube.... I had nothing to do with net neutrality or the ajit pai video. I was a new hire and was asked to dance in a video."[12] Yet one might read this less as exoneration than as a marker of the increasing *professionalism* of the weaponization of liberalism itself, as well as markers of the kindred spirits who gravitate to its infrastructure.) Pai intones at the end, "And everything else you ever did, all of it." Yet it is clear the kind of Internet he envisions. The Internet, in his view, is clearly not for creation, for political expression, for activism and protest; it is a vast consumption engine, realizing the dreams of Procter & Gamble executives in the early 1990s, as Turow (2011) documents. Some of the comments on the video similarly revealed the cultural labors of the net neutrality debate bearing fruit, even in their protest: from Raptor302, "And they know the answer is: 'No, you will not be able to stream your favorite shows if your service provider throttles the bandwidth of Netflix and HBO down to a trickle to promote their own video service.' Fuck you, Ajit Pai."

Pai's vision of the Internet is concerning, but perhaps still more significant is the manner in which knowledge itself was mobilized, something that is revealing of Pai's own past disingenuousness. When Chairman Wheeler issued the 2014 notice that would have permitted discrimination to occur online, Pai had issued a scathing dissent. He wrote regarding his dissatisfaction with the process that would follow:

> So what is the way forward? Here's one suggestion. Just as we commissioned a series of economic studies in past media-ownership proceedings, we should ask ten distinguished economists from across the country to study the impact of our proposed regulations and alternative approaches on the Internet ecosystem. To ensure that we obtain a wide range of perspectives, let each Commissioner pick two authors. To ensure accuracy, each study should be peer reviewed. And to ensure public oversight, we should host a series of hearings where Commissioners could question the authors of the studies and the authors of those studies could discuss their differences. Surely the future of the Internet is no less important than media ownership.... But we should not limit ourselves to economic studies. We should also engage computer scientists, technologists, and other technical experts to tell us how they see the Internet's infrastructure and consumers' online experience evolving. Their studies too should be subject to peer review and public hearings. (Pai, 2014, p. 5)

The function to which said research would be put is now apparent, and in fact it was wholly unnecessary to go get it. I have noted throughout this book that the *ontic content* of knowledge barely mattered anymore; and here this was the case, as Pai the economics fan rewarded the objects of his awe with footnote after footnote not as actual legitimate buttress of the agency's findings but as simple legitimation, as the actualization of "economics," whatever this might be, and to rest all of his decisions on this. How the Web worked was insignificant; instead, only the logic of rollout mattered, itself instituted by the previous Democratic FCC chairs, bolstered by the cooperation of advocates by necessity.

Pai is a neoliberal subject through and through. He is a fan of economics as the topic, not its contents; the utility of the economists, in this instance, was that they simply *produced,* serving wittingly or not to render another debate diverse rather than heterogeneous. Yet their labors were largely wasted anyway; they were hardly necessary, but appearances needed to be maintained. The true issue under contention had little to do with their content: that is, the real question was simply whether or not to relegate the FCC to obscurity, a level wholly removed from the question of how it should oversee communications infrastructure itself, or if it should be overseen at all. To add insult to injury, the perverse outcome of the weaponization of liberal comment-gathering instruments was that an entirely chimerical debate, as diverse as can be despite advocates' best efforts to use the strategies they had learned in the mid-2010s to render it otherwise, circulated through the public sphere with phantoms to chase, misinformation to rebut, and effort to waste—all as earthquakes shook unnoticed underfoot, completely unaddressed entirely by all levels of action.

This renders a rather uncomfortable conclusion to the role of activist academics as well as academics writ large, particularly since the questions that were debated in 2017 were so removed from the actual trajectories of the emergent business models that drove contemporary capitalism itself. What happens when both the advocates and the agency tasked with answering these questions operate in zones that have nothing to do with the overarching structures underneath? Not only have the debates left the sources of their meaning, but now we are in a postmodern space where we intersect with broader political economy only at glances. It is rendered all the more uncomfortable when even posing the question of its trajectory is politically deadly. When Pai announced his Restoring Internet Freedom proceeding at the Newseum in Washington, DC (weaponizing liberalism once again), he focused his ire at Free Press in a calculated move to perhaps inoculate against such a possibility (even though it really wasn't necessary to do so), referring to a number of articles written by the organization's founder, Robert McChesney:

> Consider, for example, the leading special interest in favor of Title II: a spectacularly misnamed Beltway lobbying group called Free Press. Its cofounder and current board member makes no effort to hide the group's true agenda. While he says "we're not at th[e] point yet" where we can "completely eliminate the telephone and cable companies," he admits that "the ultimate goal is to get rid of the media capitalists in the phone and cable companies and to divest them from control." And who would assume control of the Internet? The government, of course. The overall goal is to "remove brick by brick the capitalist system itself, rebuilding the entire society on socialist principles." And what would the government do once it is in control? Certainly not protect free speech as we know it here in the

> United States. For example, he has said that "[w]e need to do whatever we can to limit capitalist propaganda, regulate it, minimize it, and perhaps even eliminate it." And this "Free Press" founder takes his inspiration from Venezuela. No, really!…To be sure, it is tempting to dismiss these statements as isolated rants. But unfortunately, it is all too typical of a larger movement in our country today that is fundamentally hostile to free speech. (Pai, 2017b)

It was a tack taken to ensure the organization would be forced to disavow any such statements. Free Press's Craig Aaron made the necessary response: "The facts about Net Neutrality aren't what Pai wants to debate. Despite the voluminous public record of where we stand and what we want, Pai would have you believe we're secretly being guided by some offhand comments to an obscure Canadian socialist academic website by Robert McChesney, a professor who co-founded Free Press in 2003" (Aaron, 2017). Time to perform some damage control: "McChesney is now an emeritus member of our board and isn't involved in our day-to-day decisions or operations.…Pai was also worked up about an Op-Ed McChesney co-wrote about U.S. coverage of the Venezuelan media a decade ago. Neither of these articles involved Free Press staff, and they weren't published on our website" (Aaron, 2017). This apologia was not optional: this was the stuff that would get one tossed from congressional offices, maybe even those of allies at the FCC still, even in the wake of the wildly (and, for some, surprisingly) successful 2016 run at the presidency of a self-avowed democratic socialist, Bernie Sanders; perhaps even *because* of it.

Such a defense performs any number of functions. For one, it reasserts the diversity of the state of debate in lieu of further heterogenizing it. For another, even as Free Press would continue to stand for particular forms of systemic change, it would emphasize that other forms of systemic change were out of bounds, even as those forms might come closer to addressing the earthquakes occurring underfoot and unimpeded as these debates continued to play out.

Conclusion

Interregnum

At the time of writing (early 2019), the rules of the Ajit Pai Federal Communications Commission (FCC) were being actively resisted. Longtime network neutrality advocacy organizations Free Press, the Open Technology Institute, and Public Knowledge launched a lawsuit to overturn the rules, as did Mozilla and multiple attorneys general (Bode, 2018). In October 2018, New York's attorney general, Barbara Underwood, was deepening an investigation into identity fraud in the FCC docket (Confessore, 2018); by early 2019, Gizmodo reported that this effort continued and was inquiring into a troubling network of Trump and Republican Party–connected operatives (Cameron, 2019a). Oral arguments commenced on February 1, 2019, as Mozilla Corporation, Etsy, Free Press, Public Knowledge, the National Hispanic Media Coalition, the Open Technology Institute, the Center for Democracy and Technology, twenty-two states, and the District of Columbia faced off against the FCC (Cameron, 2019b; for further write-ups, Feld, 2019b and Johnson, 2019 provide detail). Numerous states have proposed or are proposing laws (contravening the FCC order) to force broadband providers to obey varying degrees of network neutrality rules; California's 2018 success at passing what was the nation's most stringent such law—going as far as even clamping down on zero-rating practices—was immediately met with a Department of Justice lawsuit, one filed the moment Governor Jerry Brown signed the bill. Industry groups also promised a lawsuit (Brodkin, 2018). Activists as well launched an effort to convince the Senate and House to pass a Resolution of Disapproval of the FCC's actions; while, remarkably, the Senate passed it, the House allowed it to fester, with even congressional Democrats not standing in unison on the issue. No matter: if the bill made it to Trump's desk, the chances were infinitesimal that he would sign it, much less with the same enthusiasm he signed away the public's hard-won privacy rights. After the 2018 elections, and with a newly Democratic-controlled House, even with several FCC-weakening "fake net neutrality" bills wafting through the halls of Congress, activists succeeded in passing the Save the Internet Act, which would undo the FCC's actions; this time it would be the Senate that provided the likely roadblock to further passage; even with success there, a presidential veto is almost certain (Coldewey, 2019).

Given the courts will likely be where this is settled, a process likely to be extracted, network neutrality looks set to continue its float, to continue performing its labor, to continue serving as a potential platform for the next sets of moves to come. As I have described in this book, the present conjuncture is hardly some piecemeal initiative of recent vintage; the institutions to support it have been constructed, slowly, over decades. So it remains somewhat uncanny and odd to hear FCC commissioner Jessica Rosenworcel—who, with commissioner Mignon Clyburn, dissented from the *Restoring Internet Freedom* order—and other advocates in the wake of the decision recast the events of the last decade plus:

> So it was twelve years ago—when President George W. Bush was in the White House—that this agency put its first net neutrality policies on paper. In the decade that followed, the FCC revamped and revised its net neutrality rules, seeking to keep them current and find them a stable home in the law. In its 2015 order the FCC succeeded—because in the following year, in a 184-page opinion the agency's net neutrality rules were fully and completely upheld. (Rosenworcel, 2017, p. 1)

Make no mistake: Rosenworcel and Clyburn should be remembered as heroic figures in this fight as more histories are written about this whole affair. Both commissioners' names should be remembered for their continued fight on this matter, as well as others. But the sentiment above is wishful thinking—little more than words of encouragement. The FCC did not "revamp[] and revise[] its net neutrality rules, seeking to keep them current" (Rosenworcel, 2017, p. 1). The FCC fought these rules tooth and nail. They did so partially because the interests against which activists were arrayed themselves possessed history, power, wealth, lobbyists, and relationships. Activists were able to mobilize a particular form of advocacy that was effective, bit by bit, playing smart strategy, building coalitions, learning as they went. They made the choices that they had to make at the times they had to make them.

They did so at a cost. The paradox here is that the *very manner* in which the network neutrality issue was fought was part and parcel of the environment that resulted in a Pai FCC burning the field to the ground and salting the earth behind it. Network neutrality initially served the function of linking a heterogeneous debate to a stream of thinking of long vintage, thus rendering it diverse, tractable, and in many ways *static*. It then found itself transformed in the manner it was fought: once Open Internet rules were obtained, the concept had actually been reduced to a sidecar to the notion of broadband access and rollout. With the success of advocates in securing strong protections in 2015, it again switched purpose, now a platform and an opportunity to reevaluate the very standing of the FCC itself and its involvement in such issues, using access as a cudgel in the process. The irony throughout was that the broader political economy aboard which these debates rode was itself transforming around shifting logics to which these debates even possibly contributed; the debates that *seemed* central to all these processes only touched upon them at glances.

Ambivalence in Teleology

We are left in a true place of ambivalence: a term, and a tone, that must be taken as the overarching theme of this book and its object. As a debate, this affair was anything but radical except in the manner it was fought; but these were struggles of great consequence even though they were channeled aboard a particular platform to other ends entirely. Telling its story can be seen as an effort to recover two things: first, the possibilities made apparent in turning neoliberalism's own contradictions back on itself; and second, the limits of this as a strategy, something of great relevance to those who continue to fight these fights today. What one observes is the reconstitution of the neoliberal drive from below. From a commission in Oregon itself intertwined with players fluent in the discursive language of Washington, a unique form of resistance regarding a foundational new communications medium took shape, a struggle that was crucial, even as the basic questions that needed to be asked never found address. When the *Oregonian* announced David Olson's retirement in 2012, it eulogized,

"Olson fought cable operators in court to force them to open their cable networks, sought to persuade Portland to build a rival fiber-optic network, and summoned fresh outrage every year to rail against the industry's regular rate hikes." However, he was generally being forced out, as the mayor was moving the Office for Community Technology "under the auspices of the Revenue Bureau.…The consolidation, which the city says will cut costs and expedite franchise renewals, closes a chapter in Portland history." Indeed, "his exit suggests that the city is adjusting to new fiscal and regulatory realities—and that the time for crusading has passed" (Rogoway, 2012). Passed it was; the burial of the questions this extraordinary regulator raised represented a true victory for capital. Via the transformation of open access to network neutrality as a conceptual foundation and all it entailed, here we see in passing how something quite ordinary for its time in its operative logic—the solution to the problem of markets via markets—was seen as extraordinary, even dangerous.

From Portland to Washington, the strategy was to position oneself between warring factions of capital so as to gain concessions. This can appear to a critic as entirely conciliatory, but without examining the logics of the resulting arguments more closely, we miss important elements worthy of recovery and the warnings they offer. Understanding what transpired—neoliberalism confronting its own success and finding its own best arguments turned against itself—requires us to understand this period and this debate as an ambivalent ensemble: it contained *radical moves* that are recoverable, even though they don't appear as such. There was a great need to argue in the terms on offer; what was lacking was not some radical current but a lack of acknowledgment of the *multiple levels* upon which these debates were being conducted. It is striking that public interest advocates in Portland and Washington alike suggested what amounted to a continued liberalization of the Web as a solution to problems stemming from its original liberalization. The outcome was less that neoliberalism won the day than that it required a solution counter to its own rhetoric (if not its actual operation) to stabilize the neoliberal drive itself, if only to open itself to further contradictions. FCC chairman Powell's decision to reclassify Internet provision over cable as an information service in 2002 performed this function.

No player involved in these debates called for a reversal of the commercial operation of the Internet itself, even as the desires of these players would for all intents and purposes require it. However, during the open access argument, these tensions were what provided apparent success in keeping the issue alive; its numerous contradictory elements provided the needed related *epistemic* dysfunction that kept these battles heterogeneous rather than diverse. At the same time, their input was useful to such key corporate players as AOL, at least until the connection was no longer needed. A prominent feature of this landscape was that all were arguing speculatively about an Internet for which no one save the largest industry players had real data. Operating as they were under great uncertainty, their tactics made sense. They were able to secure relatively small (if temporary) victories by poking holes in the seeming self-assuredness of the neoliberal drive; the dominant narratives of the neoliberal thought collective were kept in battle with themselves—or, at the very least, unable to maintain comfortable footing on its most friendly terrain. The irony of network neutrality as a concept (as it was conceived) would be that it settled these internal disagreements more cleanly than could FCC chairmen William Kennard and Michael Powell, creating opportunities for the erasure of those incongruities and their exploit in favor of a unified narrative that provided for what looked like a disagreement, yet was not: the field of argument had been transformed into a diverse one where sides could be discerned and thus contained, channeled toward a unified purpose.

Tim Wu (2011b, p. 130) has argued regarding the use of knowledge in lobbying,

> The government can act only on the basis of what it understands to be established fact. Much of what is called lobbying must actually be recognized as a campaign to establish, as conventional wisdom, the "right" facts, whether pertaining to climate change, the advantages of charter schools, or the ideal technology for broadcasting. Much of the work of Washington lobbyists is simply an effort to control the conversation surrounding an issue, and new technologies are no exception.

This conception is only partially true. Also only partially true is an increasingly popular notion of corruption, one only stoked by the naked openness of the Trump administration in its own. Clearly stated, "In really existing capitalism, the kind Americans actually experience, wealthy individuals and large corporations have immense political power that undermines the principles of democracy. Nowhere is this truer than in communication policy making" (McChesney, 2013, p. 217). Big money rules the day, not just at the FCC but in Congress and even stretching into the judiciary. Recent documentaries such as *Dark Money,* aired by PBS in 2018, have put forward this message as well.

In addition to the material imbalances that have reshaped the processes by which policy is drawn, however, another bias needs to be countered at another level entirely. At the moment when perhaps a different formulation of a "network neutrality" argument might have transformed the entire trajectory of these debates and admitted an altogether new constituency to envision and enact a fresh vision for communication politics on a broad scale, instead an old set of epistemic commitments of long lineage greased the tracks for the entire works to move in another direction that cast such input aside. This constituency's *existence* mattered, but only in the same way that the *production of debate* regarding network neutrality mattered: as an ambivalently both crucial and banal affair working from a long-established (yet immanently flexible) teleology. That popular participation in these matters is necessary is undeniable, yet here the debate arguably was over before it began, at least in the dimensions where it mattered, in dimensions that could have provided a stronger discussion regarding the purpose to which the Internet and networking technologies should be put. Perhaps there is a way to unlock such debates again. While numerous advocates expressed frustration at then–FCC commissioner Michael Copps's concurrence with the weak 2010 Open Internet Order (as opposed to a dissent that would have sent it back to the drawing board), his legacy will be that he managed to keep the issue alive to revisit. Indeed, this turned out to be the gift he left behind, and it ended up offering the chance of renewal in 2015.

The same renewal that brought about the 2015 rules may have been one of the key ingredients of the morass that followed. Each phase of activist activity between 2005 and 2010, then between 2010 and 2015, and the struggles that have ensued since consumed the efforts and labors of an untold number of people. This mobilization was tremendously materially expensive, yet it served broader imperatives perfectly, their expenditures proving more contribution than subterfuge. This is something quite different from some claims that these were not progressive or radical in inclination: they were drives of necessity; their moves were largely predetermined and surprising at one and the same time. To describe what advocates were doing in Washington as merely pupating or perpetuating an "informationist" guise is to miss the real story. They did what was necessary to gain entrance to those places where the ontic content of arguments could be set aside and real bargaining might commence; hewing to such a mission served to neuter the influence of the desires of the broad base of support these groups helped to stimulate among the public. This is precisely because multiple debates were happening at once, each in their spheres, and this was something quite aside from contentions that the levers of policy have been taken over by monied interests, even as they have, and this dimension is both separate from yet entangled with the one I seek to outline here.

Neoliberal Sincerity

In my process of hunting down old comments from old proceedings for this project, it was disheartening, if amusing, to come across numerous offerings of earnest citizens seeking to file a complaint on a new issue in an old docket that seems to be relevant but has long been gathering electronic dust waiting to be canned-air-blown away in a server farm somewhere. The increased ability to access government has not rendered more effective communications with it. It may have arguably become more difficult, with the discursive communities surrounding so many issues closing ranks all the more tightly—ironically, by expanding debates in diverse ways.

What we are witnessing is less some form of "capture," although it certainly exists, than a broader systemic imperative with which media reform (any form of reform, actually: platform capitalism presents new opportunities for convergence and competition, after all) will need to grapple. Interviewed in *Jacobin* magazine, Victor Pickard elucidated a notion of "corporate libertarianism": "An ideological project that has origins at a core moment in the 1940s. It sees corporations as having individual freedoms, like those in the First Amendment, which they can use to shield themselves from public interest oversight and regulation. It's also been connected to this assumption that the government should never intervene in markets, and media markets in particular" (Day, 2017). Elsewhere he defines this as "an ideology that conflates corporate privilege with First Amendment freedoms and is girded by a logic that advances individualistic negative liberties at the expense of the collective positive liberties that are central to a social democratic vision of media" (Pickard, 2014, p. 190).

The notion of "corporate libertarianism" performs the same function as the calls for "free labor" considerations. The concept is certainly an accurate *description* of the present circumstance, but it does not drill deeply enough into the specifics of what is occurring to render it an *explanation*. Rather, a more dynamic concept can be found by examining the production chains of modern capitalism, which require the inputs of the ersatz and the manufacturing facilities alike, to which media reformers will need to attend. Media reform, as it was, is now quaint, one component of a broader problem that will need to be solved. Part of this dilemma is in limiting the power of the thought collective that has wound its way not just into the battle of network neutrality but into other areas as well.

The answer takes us beyond notions of bought science or "merchants of doubt" (Oreskes & Conway, 2010). The practice certainly exists, and surely some merchants are happy to trade their integrity for a price. Yet the gift, the bribe as theorized in capture theory, is often not the reason for continued productivity in a particular vein. It is a negative conception of power; it says, *you wouldn't have done it were it not for the bribe.* Such pronouncements have a degree of power, much like Pai's boxing of Free Press into an unnecessary corner regarding their Apparently Evil Socialist Founder. A positive conception, on the other hand, assumes the bribe is not a bribe; this conception assumes that a specific historical structure, constructed over time, presented an opportunity available for the right comer. Institutions may have started partially or even wholly as producers of "bought" research, but as the collective grows and becomes background noise and engagement starts to occur in surprising ways, it offers obvious points of contact that become attractive for the correct soul, even perhaps a goal to shoot for, something with its historical origins scrubbed or beyond mattering. Neoliberalism, as thought collective, turns out to be about *belonging,* an ironic turn on the equally neoliberal notion of self-care. And it is a belonging that carries significant benefits, to be sure: to be a part of it means one gains easy exposure via the various organs of its institutional apparatus long under continued and even internally conflicting (re)construction. Receiving such support naturally leads one to believe that one has revealed a deep truth and maybe, just maybe, one's view of the world *does* turn out to be how logics really operate. It means that one gets to join the revolving door of players with influence; that, when the right administration is in charge (and even when the wrong one is, at times), one gets to leave the everyday existence of the think tank's cubicles or the academic offices with their (sometimes) teaching responsibilities to *work for the greater good*; and that, when that administration ends, one finds oneself even more valuable to academic markets, or consultancies, or hedge funds. It is its own parachute and rocket launcher mixed into one. It can be a thrilling existence. It is a neoliberal politics of self-care rendered libertarian in the extreme but with people there to always pat you on the back. And it barely costs anything, because self-rationalization and rationalizing is self-taught: it represents a payoff of systemic investment of years past.

The best thing about institutions that have been built over time is that, like the fast work the Pai FCC is attempting to do to itself, they can be dismantled, and history remains the guide to doing so. This is why present debates, and the directions toward which they are turning, are treading on hazardous, if simultaneously necessary, ground.

Rational Responses as Traps

Media reform (and media justice) frameworks, it turns out, are central not just to the liberal ends of democracy (the old refrain "whatever your first issue is, make media reform your second" comes back to mind). It is potentially central to the very construction of platform capitalism, surveillance capitalism, platform-infused capitalism, whatever one calls it. The FCC's privacy rules represented a deep wound and were thus dealt with quickly, but they remain a spectre that haunts capital nonetheless. This, however, points to the most challenging debates ahead for those who grapple with communication policy and media politics at all levels, and turning neoliberal logics against themselves may not be of as much assistance as they once were in this regard. Mass consumer access to telecommunications was always incidental to capital's imperatives; now, free speech and ordinary creation are themselves incidental to industrial logics, permutations that are still experimental. These logics required the heterogeneous potential of a newly empowered FCC out of the way to determine their optimal configurations. All indications are that these permutations (which themselves might drift toward a small number of dominant models aboard proprietary logistical platforms and chains) are not generative of free speech, or of trust, or of democratic governance. *These* are political projects to be obtained only by a program that both solves the problem of the neoliberal institutionalization of belonging and involves itself more deeply with the logics of the capitalist forms under construction. Just as the logistical chains under construction will start to form discernable patterns, one must remember that the neoliberal project was itself extensive across multiple sciences and fields: moments like this reveal that their interactivity is necessary.

The broader lesson of years of neoliberal epistemological institution building (and simultaneously of *material* institution building) is that Pai-in-the-abstract had been under construction for decades. It made perfect sense for him to thumb his nose via a snotty video at net neutrality supporters in the wake of its elimination. These are not the moves of someone who was working for a payday; this was not someone who was acting because he is corrupted by his past affiliations with Verizon, although it helped in bolstering his own understanding of the issues he faces. Advocate Harold Feld, in a Wired profile of Pai, would remark (Rice, 2018), "Why was my area of policy the one that got the guy who actually knows what he's doing?" Rather, these were the actions of someone who was perfectly sincere in his beliefs—a "true believer," in Copps's words. And it is absolutely of a piece with the logics of the corporate partners brought onboard to defend network neutrality since Obama became president. The fight was hardly over social subjectivity; it was about business models.

And yet it seems that potentially the wrong lessons are being learned from this whole sordid affair. Instead of leaving the treadmill, advocates risk doubling down, and for the same reasons they did during the network neutrality debates: there seems little choice but to do so. A story in the *New York Times* finds the whole process revving up once again, even contributing to it in its framing, with advocates falling squarely into the trap (Streitfeld, 2018). Lina Khan, a law student whose influential "Amazon's Antitrust Paradox" appeared in the *Yale Law Review*, suddenly found herself flung into the midst of numerous debates, with hundreds of thousands of downloads of her paper. "Ms. Khan…was refining an argument about monopoly power that takes aim at one of the most admired, secretive and feared companies of our era: Amazon," the *New York Times* reports. "Her argument went against a consensus in antitrust circles that dates back to the 1970s—the moment when regulation was redefined to focus on consumer welfare, which is to say price. Since Amazon is renowned for its cut-rate deals, it would seem safe from federal intervention."

Khan's argument is a withering, full-frontal assault on Chicago School antitrust doctrine as itself inapplicable to an age of such multiple-sided markets as platforms. "My argument is that gauging real competition in the twenty-first century marketplace—especially in the case of online platforms—requires analyzing the underlying structure and dynamics of markets.... Animating this framework is the idea that a company's power and the potential anticompetitive nature of that power cannot be fully understood without looking to the structure of a business and the structural role it plays in markets" (Khan, 2017, p. 717). Supplementing Barbara van Schewick's (2015) own critiques of antitrust in a network neutrality context, given the current orthodoxy's emphasis on results of a particular sort—consumer surplus—versus market structure itself, "The current framework in antitrust fails to register certain forms of anticompetitive harm and therefore is unequipped to promote real competition—a shortcoming that is illuminated and amplified in the context of online platforms and data-driven markets. This failure stems both from assumptions embedded in the Chicago School framework and from the way this framework assesses competition" (p. 737). Whereas predatory pricing and vertical integration were at one point items of concern (and continued to be so for consumer advocates), present-day antitrust considered such concerns as either problems that did not exist or were irrational (predatory pricing) or as generally beneficial to consumers (vertical integration). However, Khan argues—sounding like a network neutrality advocate—the approach of such network neutrality detractors as Christopher Yoo, Gerald Faulhaber, and their kin

> fails even if one believes that antitrust should promote only consumer interests. Critically, consumer interests include not only cost but also product quality, variety, and innovation. Protecting these long-term interests requires a much thicker conception of "consumer welfare" than what guides the current approach. But more importantly, the undue focus on consumer welfare is misguided. It betrays legislative history, which reveals that Congress passed antitrust laws to promote a host of political economic ends—including our interests as workers, producers, entrepreneurs, and citizens. It also mistakenly supplants a concern about process and structure (i.e., whether power is sufficiently distributed to keep markets competitive) with a calculation regarding outcome (i.e. whether consumers are materially better off). (p. 737)

In contrast, Khan proposes "focusing on competitive process and market structure" (p. 745) with a particular emphasis on barriers to entry, conflicts of interest, tracking gatekeepers and bottlenecks, the uses and control of data, and the bargaining power of emergent entities—Amazon, for example, had been able to leverage its heavy use of delivery services to obtain cheaper rates, which were made up by these same distribution services by charging independent shippers still more (p. 746). "A focus on process assigns government the task of creating background conditions, rather than intervening to manufacture or interfere with outcomes" (2017, pp. 745–746). Mirroring the concerns of Adam Greenfield in thinking through Amazon as a "Stack" (2017),

> On the Chicago School's account, Amazon's vertical integration would only be harmful if and when it chooses to use its dominance in delivery and retail to hike fees to consumers. Amazon has already raised Prime prices. But antitrust enforcers should be equally concerned about the fact that Amazon increasingly controls the infrastructure of online commerce—and the ways in which it is harnessing this dominance to expand and advantage its new business ventures. (Khan, 2017, p. 780)

In a supreme irony, investors in Amazon (and even venture capitalists with a stake in Uber, and perhaps its new shareholders when its public offering is through) "have unambiguously endorsed and funded online platforms' quest to bleed money in their race to draw users, [but] antitrust doctrine fails to acknowledge this strategy.... Strikingly, the market is reflecting a reality that our current laws are unable to detect" (Khan, 2017, p. 788). Contrary to antitrust dicta, for an entity like Amazon (or, for that matter, Verizon, AT&T, Comcast, or Time Warner Cable), "antitrust should reckon with the fact that pursuing growth at the expense of returns is—contra to current doctrine—highly rational" (Khan, 2017, p. 790).

For the *Times* reporter, Khan emphasized that with Amazon's tremendous data troves, "it is so willing to forego profits, it is so aggressive and has so many advantages from its shipping and warehouse infrastructure that it exerts an influence much broader than its market share," making it more akin to the "all-powerful railroads of the Progressive Era" (Streitfeld, 2018). Mirroring Stucke and Grunes (2016), she argues, "[A] company like Amazon—one that sells things, competes against others selling things, and owns the platform where the deals are done—has an inherent advantage that undermines fair competition" (Streitfeld, 2018).

The expansion of antitrust, or boosting antitrust authority, is now a popular topic. Tim Wu and Zephyr Teachout, in their failed but surprisingly strong primary run against New York governor Andrew Cuomo and Kathy Hochul in 2014, themselves trumpeted the argument that antitrust should be strengthened or revived (or, frankly, resuscitated) as a primary plank in their platform (Zhou, 2014). But it is painfully clear that the solutions to our present conundrum are a continuance of solving the problems of markets with markets. The infinite regress continues: make the markets fair, open to everyone. Popular books like Robert Reich's *Saving Capitalism: For the Many, Not the Few* are screaming such arguments, even in their titles.[1] Senators Bernie Sanders's and Elizabeth Warren's vocal calls against the dismantling of the Consumer Financial Protection Bureau and to break up the tech giants ring just as familiar today, even with the addition of the democratic socialist tag attached in Sanders's case.

When Stucke and Grunes (2016) completed their magisterial study of data-extractive industries, they drew similar conclusions to Khan (and she cites them): antitrust has been misapplied—competition policy has ignored the role of big data and its extraction and analysis. Even the European Union, with its more stringent rules, has missed any number of theories of harm, the kind that Khan is trying to elucidate. Markets, Stucke and Grunes conclude, have not wrought "appropriate levels of privacy" not because it is not demanded but because privacy-centric options are not even available; in a marketplace one cannot choose options not offered. Antitrust law *could* approach these issues more effectively, taking into account the numerous ways data represents potential advantage to an enterprise in constructing a "moat" around itself—Stucke and Grunes consider the variety of data an organization possesses, its volume, its velocity, and its own value—that is always contextual. What is their solution? A perfectly rational response: they suggest past mergers be evaluated to draw out how data issues *should* have been considered (one could start, for example, with the failure of the Department of Justice's case against the AT&T–Time Warner merger of 2018).

Khan's solutions are similarly seemingly rational. "If it is true that the economics of platform markets may encourage anticompetitive market structures, there are at least two approaches we can make. Key is deciding whether we want to govern online platform markets through competition, or want to accept that they are inherently monopolistic or oligopolistic and regulate them instead," she intones (Khan, 2017, p. 790). She then rushes headlong into the home turf of the neoliberal thought collective; indeed, she had been on it from the very beginning, now offering further nuances of predatory pricing and vertical integration, then to a discussion of the backstory of common carriage and public utility policy, comparing the features of the Amazon platform to past such entities and opening the door to considering their application there.

It is the sheer rationality of these responses that are likely their own undoing. Returning to the *New York Times* account of Khan's sudden celebrity in policy circles, "She has her own critics now: Several leading scholars have found fault with Ms. Khan's proposals to revive and expand antitrust, and some have tried to dismiss her paper with the mocking label 'Hipster Antitrust'" (Streitfeld, 2018). It will, at this point, come as no surprise that, "in think tanks and universities, the battle has been joined." Among the critics is a familiar name, Jonathan Nuechterlein, who (writing with Timothy Muris, former chairman of the Federal Trade Commission [FTC]) argued in a recent white paper, "Don't let the government pursue Amazon the way it pursued [retailer] A&P" (Muris & Nuechterlein, 2018, p. i). The *New York Times* quotes the pair: Amazon "added hundreds of billions of dollars of value to the U.S. economy.... It is a brilliant innovator" (Streitfeld, 2018). In their paper proper, Muris and Nuechterlein argue, "Critics from both the right and the left claim that modern antitrust doctrine, rooted in consumer welfare, is inadequate to handle the challenges of the twenty-first century economy. They express nostalgia for 1960s antitrust, when the field had no clear objectives and cases were decided on impressionistic notions of "fairness" and good corporate citizenship" (Muris & Nuechterlein, 2018, p. i). Their paper "exposes the intellectual void at the heart of this new populist movement.... Antitrust doctrine does not need an overhaul. It is shaped by many economic perspectives, follows no one 'School,' and is flexible enough to address any monopoly abuses in today's economy. It is also well-calibrated to serve its central function: promoting consumer welfare" (p. i). This is, of course, the perfect description of how the neoliberal thought collective conceived itself and operated, growing to such size, spreading to so many corners of the academy and even life.

Even at a level removed, a note of disclosure on the first page of the paper itself revealed that the thought collective's appropriately entrepreneurial spirit lived on, unabated, seeking new partners: "Our knowledge of the A&P story began when one of us was an FTC representative on a Justice Department task force to study the Robinson-Patman Act in the mid-1970s. In 2017, we approached Amazon Inc. for funding to tell the story, and we gratefully acknowledge its support.... All views expressed here are our own" (Muris & Nuechterlein, 2018, p. 1). Free markets for knowledge indeed! But the views *are* their own; Amazon did not purchase it; it merely subsidized it. This, similarly, is the whole point: it too has become part of an organic movement walking on its own legs. Amazon did not seek out its sages. The sages came with an investment opportunity.

Antitrust's new apparent epistemic fluidity is not a sign of hope; it is the gears winding up again on familiar terrain. FTC hearings in September 2018 regarding "Competition and Consumer Protection in the 21st Century" featured several of the same players as the network neutrality debates, even as they hardly offer unified, homogeneous views (FTC, 2018). It will be necessary to respond—think tanks (and Amazon) could not let this law student's article fly without response, and handily enough, she was building a bridge right back to their most comfortable turf even as, to outside observers, it appears to be a frontal attack. Her arguments are altogether reasonable, and when advocates use them to try to rein in platform giants, to try to obtain net neutrality via other means, or even to wrest back some semblance of humanity from the apparatuses of abstract extraction that now are both firmly embedded in and surrounding our lives (and, if ingested or implanted so as to transform our bodies into authentication devices themselves, *inside* our very beings), they will be presented as rational responses to corporate challenge. Legislators and regulators will find themselves listed on activist websites as receiving donations from these companies, which will serve as ready explanation for why a particular legislator voted against the public interest and in favor of Google, Facebook, Verizon, and Amazon (who all now, of course, increasingly find themselves in competition, barring the influx of Chinese firms gaining a foothold—or perhaps these votes will enable our home-grown extractors to become every bit as invasive as WeChat, to whatever end). Activists will perhaps scream of bought votes, but they will fight these fights on a field long prepared for them and in a language long under construction. They may even find themselves welcomed there.

However, this does not counter what has grown for decades—it feeds it. What reformers (and, arguably, revolutionaries) of communications policy are fighting now is not a rational debate even as it clothes itself in its garb: they are battling an institutionalized understanding that possesses strong material support networks. There will always be a ready response, and perhaps to realize media reformers' worst fears, they will come to understand that the arguments they face are not insincere at all. They are facing not just neoliberal argumentation as a struggle that moves history itself; they are facing *neoliberal sincerity* and its representatives who are the new true believers, who are equally comfortable speaking the esoteric discourse out of one side of their mouth and the exoteric one on the other, for together, and only together, do they make perfect sense. It is a message of innovation and convenience for the masses, a more formalized understanding behind the scenes, one that thrives on its own internal disagreements rather than cohesion. Bring on the hipsters.

For this was Pai's strength, the reason he was happy to twist the knife at every opportunity, giving himself demon horns, provoking with jokes about serving as a "Manchurian candidate" for Verizon, all moves extraordinary for an FCC chairman to make (particularly as these efforts were hardly his own, but produced by entities like the *Daily Caller*). Perhaps the process was completely corrupted: perhaps millions of fake comments entered the docket and remained uninvestigated. What matters is the end, and the desired end is deeply seen, *felt*, as the correct end nonetheless. I suspect that Pai knows something that the objects of his trolling may not. None of this ever had anything to do with any payoff or bribe; it had everything to do with being comfortable in one's own skin. It is *sincerity*.

Three Questions

I pose three questions that likely frame the next-generation challenge for those thinking through communications policy and its reform. A common fixture in this discourse is Metcalfe's Law: the notion that a network's value grows exponentially with each additional node. Turning the notion on its head, scholars have increasingly realized that the costs of being excluded from networks are similarly exponential in nature (Tongia & Wilson, 2011). Which leads to a first question: what happens when basic survival and the rising costs of exclusion from emergent networks actually intensify the neoliberalization process and its attendant logics? Second, what does it portend when the strategy of exploiting struggles between sectors of capital is at one and the same time also an ingredient of the deepening of this drive? Third, what institutions will activists need to defend, even contradictorily so, that are receptive to their incorporation into the institutions constructed by activist networks themselves?

We are commodified, but we are also heteromated in this environment on a massive scale. If activism, particularly regarding access, sticks to concerns about inequality, we miss the dynamism of the process unfolding. We are not just "free labor"; through our communicative labors we produce "dead labor" too or, to use old Marxist frameworks' bailiwick, "constant capital." Given this is the case, media reform is effectively becoming simultaneously about liberal ideals of democratic governance and information provision, as well as the broader problem of societal logistics. To tackle one will require tackling the other. If concerns about platform giants are met with an attempt to reinvigorate antitrust as its sole hope, the process will continue, even intensify, because this has always been the playing field where diversity, not heterogeneity, reigns: it is the thought collective's specialty.

Perhaps there is hope on the horizon, as some veterans of these fights attempt to build new thinking about platforms as entities in themselves from the ground up based on fresh first principles, hardly casting aside topics that represent the home turf of the neoliberal thought collective but not taking the bait of assuming their justifications and rationalizations (for example, Feld, 2018b, 2018c, 2018d, 2019a). However, any such conceptualizations are incomplete absent the construction of a much larger structural, material apparatus whose function is to propagate, develop, critique, and defend not just the conception but its justifications—even to ensure outright disagreements regarding the latter. By the same token, adopting the same form that the neoliberal thought collective took is likely not to be effective against it; new imaginaries must be dreamt. Even these visions may be insufficient to address the forms of interstitial power conduits might possess in the fast-developing environment, as perhaps new conundrums lie not just in the power of platform considered singly (or even as a "stack," taken as one entity that has managed to craft and manage multiple platforms to form its own logistical supply chain). Rather, I refer to those forces that incentivize and provide the imaginaries for the possibilities of logistical chains implied in their interstices that may well lead to entire *processes* not so cleanly delineated that are absolutely untouchable by even renewed antitrust thinking or a novel archetype of platforms or stacks, but become the key drivers of material and existential futures nonetheless.

The producers of knowledge, even (perhaps especially) the neoliberals, are so ensconced in their long-running discursive stream, comfortably placed in institutions of higher learning, themselves seeking to appear "relevant" to policy debates by hiring and promoting those who appear to be making quite the splash in policy matters, FCC dockets, and beyond, supported by interests that see value in their continued production of theory—how surprised they will be when it becomes clear that they no longer matter in the way they once did to broader systems that continue to expand. Their function is no longer to churn out truth (even as I am sure they seek to do so); it is to churn out *understanding* to bolster a broader mode of being. They will deny it, and their denials will ring true as they will continue to be treated as if their contributions matter beyond the material fact of their production. But am I remiss in seeing some degree of desperation in their efforts? Were Winseck and Pooley on to something when they sensed worry in Faulhaber and Singer's work, that perhaps their strain's purchase at places like the FCC was loosening? Was Faulhaber and Singer's effort one of continued diversity maintenance, knowingly or not—or a cheap shot in the face of a feared defeat on a broad scale? Is the sheer drama of the drastic moves of the Pai FCC similarly indicative of the same?

The largest paradox of all, and the problematic with which activists will need to contend as the next round of debates surrounding our communications media (and beyond) commence, goes well beyond concerns like that of Bruno Latour (2004), that the critique of science may have sown incredulity to it (while certain interests certainly gain from such new skepticism and support this outcome), well beyond that all matters in official policy up to and including knowledge have become up for sale, corrupted (even as they have). It is a far greater challenge: in consumer society, one had the *illusion* of choice, yet the choice one made mattered; in the present day, perhaps, one has the *illusion* of debate even as the debates matter. What happens when policy debates become productive platforms in and of themselves for the kind of production necessary to neutralize threats to emergent logics?

The Mont Pèlerin Society and its fellow travelers' end goal was achieved. The system worked. Materially buttressed research in the quest for a discourse wins the day, and the researchers themselves are permitted to believe that they had an actual role in the process. They did, just not the one they expected, and should they decide to matter more fully, to reconstruct a fresh vision of freedom that is more just than the one solidifying today, they will need to rebuild anew, materially, theoretically, across disciplines and interests, a blueprint for a new paradigm, materially buttressed, from the ground up, with strategies that build upon yet supersede those of the thought collective of old.

Notes

Introduction

1. See Gizmodo, "Leaked Video of FCC Chairman Ajit Pai's 'Funny' Skit," YouTube, December 11, 2017, https://www.youtube.com/watch?v=DzHleu03fxY.

2. A running timeline that mirrors this story can be found at https://whatisnetneutrality.tumblr.com/timeline (accessed April 27, 2019). New histories have started to touch on this era at glances. Harold Feld, in telling his own condensed rendition of the early years of this fight, does acknowledge what came before as important, but for practical reasons sets it aside: "As I say, I've been participating in what is now known as 'net neutrality' and what used to be known as 'open access' since 1998. This included the back and fourth between the Ninth Circuit in a now forgotten case called AT&T v. City of Portland. Wetmachine didn't start until the end of 2003, so for Wetmachine-based flashbacks, we begin in 2004" (Feld, 2018a). Similarly, Pickard & Berman (2019) offer perspective on happenings of the late 1990s into the 2000s.

3. Informed readers will complain that this statement doth protest a touch too much, and a clarification is certainly worthwhile. While absolutely true of dial-up access, access to competitive DSL-supplied ISP provision varied throughout the late 1990s in terms of challenge to accessing the wire. Before late 1999, any access by an ISP seeking to provide Internet connectivity via DSL needed to partner (or be) a "competitive local exhange carrier" (CLEC) that was taking advantage of unbundling to gain access to the whole loop, not just the high-frequency DSL portion. In late 1999, the FCC made just the DSL high freqency portion available to services seeking to provide DSL service; but with the turn of the century, courts reversed this decision. Nuechterlein and Weiser (2005) emphasize this not-insignificant point.

4. There exists a discrepancy between this notion as sold and as expressed in the technical literature. A significant element of van Schewick's work (2010) is that there have effectively been not one but two "end-to-end" principles. They are not antidiscrimination principles in themselves but, rather, particular design architectures for programmers which apply certain conditions to the functionalities of one layer versus another. In the process of the debates that ensued over the last decade, both versions

have been misinterpreted or misused. "Nondiscrimination" is an effect of following a particular version of the end-to-end principle rather than an overt objective of the principle itself, as van Schewick is at pains to point out. Breach of the "end to end principle" in its broadest form is a design decision—importantly, one not necessarily designed to promote discrimination, although it can be put to such a purpose.

5. I am careful to note that Benkler is hardly naïve on these matters, expressing numerous caveats and limits to his conclusions. He lays out policy prescriptions with which pro-network neutrality advocates largely agreed.

6. The field of "anthropology of policy," still growing, differs from such an approach. Wedel et al. (2005) note that as a field,

> the anthropology of public policy takes public policy itself as an object of analysis, rather than as the unquestioned premise of a research agenda. Anthropology is well suited to explore the cultural and philosophical underpinnings of policy—its enabling discourses, mobilizing metaphors, and underlying ideologies and uses. Anthropologists can explain how taken-for-granted assumptions channel policy debates in certain directions, inform the dominant ways policy problems are identified, enable particular classifications of target groups, and legitimize certain policy solutions while marginalizing others. (p. 34)

The difference between this approach and my own is that the object of my analysis is less *policy* than the *epistemic undercurrent* of this specific policy. Shore (2012), alongside a tremendously useful literature review, speaks to the development of the field in the 1990s which drew from governmentality studies that observed how policy creates new subjectivities (citizens, criminals, and so on) as well as naturalizes its own arbitrariness, thereby providing the opportunity to observe how power operates or to see the hidden forces underneath. Shore also notes that the field has moved on from governmentality since then; my approach hardly discards governmentality, but the focus on "thought collectives" and their material foundations takes such studies to a register that I find promising.

7. This is a slightly different move from other frame analysis approaches; for instance, that of Schön and Rein (1994).

1 Knowledge and the Neoliberal Thought Collective

1. Starr (2004) and Wu (2011b) speak to events and controversies surrounding the early monopoly days of AT&T, including the dual service era when rural cooperatives were involved and the resultant feuds leading to the Kingsbury Commitment and congressional action to bless the AT&T monopoly in the 1920s. Mueller (2013) provides additional detail and in senses a different interpretation of what resulted. Horwitz (1989) and Wu explore the liberalization drive well; Decherney, Ensmenger, & Yoo (2011) provide interesting counterpoint and detail.

2. The history of the Internet and computing in general has its own expansive literature. Abbate (2000) is almost always mentioned; Mueller (2002, 2010) speaks to the

politics behind Internet addressing and governance; Castells (2001) speaks to economic and political implications as well as history; recent efforts such as Greenstein (2016) provide backstory on the events surrounding privatization of the Internet in the 1990s and are more friendly to it than the likes of Schiller (2000) or contemporary reports as Hauben & Hauben (1997). There are volumes and volumes more.

3. The act, of course, took on any number of areas in traditional media, where it was largely seen (accurately) as a cave-in to powerful traditional media interests which sought loosened media ownership rules. The act encoded in law a presumption that the FCC would periodically examine its media ownership rules with the intent to progressively eliminate them (M. Cooper, 2003; McChesney, 1999, 2004).

4. To obtain this number, the following Google search was performed, which yielded the result on August 23, 2013: "'network neutrality' OR 'net neutrality' site:whitehouse .gov."

5. Go have a look! FCC, "Welcome to the FCC's Electronic Comment Filing System," https://www.fcc.gov/ecfs/.

6. Speaking the parlance necessitates speaking in letters. Hopefully this sentence offers good practice.

7. Mirowski is certainly but one (albeit a leading light) of a recent crop of historians who have traced numerous aspects of the development of the neoliberal thought collective. Other works that have provided deep treatments on either the epistemological or political development of this movement include MacLean (2017), Peck (2010), and Phillips-Fein (2009).

2 Open Access

1. This is hardly the only solution to such a problem, as Sandvig (2006) and van Schewick (2010) note; "multicast" technologies, never utilized, are one such possibility.

2. 47 U.S.C. §153(20).

3. 47 CFR §64.702(a).

4. 47 U.S.C. §153(43).

3 Knowing the Net, 1

1. Note that should some form of "open access" condition—still vague in the FCC Order—be placed on cable providers, it would have given ISPs *better* access over high-speed lines at this time than they were able to receive over DSL. Until late in 1999, in order for a competitor ISP to provide service over an incumbent local exchange carrier's (ILEC's) local loop, it needed to be either a lessor of that entire loop *or* have

an arrangement with a competitive LEC that was. It could not deal directly with the ILEC to use only the high-frequency portion of the loop.

2. The ad can be found at NoGatekeepers.org, "Thank You, Portland," *Internet Archive*, August 16, 2000, http://web.archive.org/web/20000816033956/http://www.nogatekeepers.org/archive/06131999.oregonian.ad.pdf.

3. Recall that at this time AT&T was primarily a long distance telephony company; while AT&T Wireless at the time did provide cellular service, it operated separately (and was in fact rendered completely independent of AT&T in 2000). At the time these events take place, the story is about a major telecommunications company purchasing a cable company.

4 Knowing the Net, 2

1. It is useful to remind the reader that circuit decisions only apply to the region in the appellate court's jurisdiction.

2. See National Telecommunications and Information Administration, "Executive Summary," Section 271 of the Communications Act, n.d., https://www.ntia.doc.gov/legacy/ntiahome/staffpapers/section271/summary.htm (accessed May 15, 2019).

3. NoGatekeepers.org, website, *Internet Archive*, April 29, 1999; retrieved from http://web.archive.org/web/20010224141604/http://www.nogatekeepers.org/.

5 Erasures and Emergences

1. Sidak's website, Criterion Economics, is at http://www.criterioneconomics.com/.

2. Ramsey pricing refers to a means of pricing by a provider of differentiated services that, in theory, maximizes welfare. One prices those services in an inverse relationship to the price elasticity of demand for each service. That is, a higher price elasticity of demand means a small shift in price causes a greater shift in demand. Services with lower elasticities of demand would then receive greater markups in a Ramsey scheme.

3. A list of such state regulations as of 2014 was maintained at National Conference of State Legislatures, "Statewide Video Franchising Statutes," November 2014, http://www.ncsl.org/research/telecommunications-and-information-technology/statewide-video-franchising-statutes.aspx.

6 Advocates, Regulators, and the Ersatz

1. See SavetheInternet.com, "Members," June 15, 2006, https://web.archive.org/web/20070819081620/http://www.savetheinternet.com:80/=members.

2. See bluefalcon561, "Series of Tubes (Senator Ted Stevens talking about the Net Neutrality Bill," July 17, 2006, https://www.youtube.com/watch?v=f99PcP0aFNE.

3. Bruce Kushnik, of TeleTruth, followed the development of these webs closely. See TeleTruth.org, "New Millennium Research Council Experts and Their Corporate Affiliations," n.d., http://www.teletruth.org/NMRC.htm.

4. See Center for Media Justice (MAG-Net), "About," n.d., https://mag-net.org/about/.

5. See M-Lab, "What Is Measurement Lab?," n.d., https://www.measurementlab.net/about/.

6. This version of the form, with both the "exclude" and newer "only [brief comments]" button, is available in archived form at FCC, "Electronic Comment Filing System," *Internet Archive*, October 14, 2011, https://web.archive.org/web/20111014235836/http://fjallfoss.fcc.gov/ecfs/comment_search/input?z=866ku.

7. This section stems from firsthand knowledge of the event. I was a COMPASS telecommunications fellow in his office at the time and was largely responsible for organizing this event.

8. Off the Hill, an old colleague informed me that once the senator had announced this initiative, few in the public interest community believed that advocates stood a chance of being taken seriously during the discussion—or if they were, they were merely serving to provide cover for the senator to vote in ways antithetical to their interests. Of course, once the initiative was over, it could be taken in any direction by the remaining staff.

9. The link is at http://techpresident.com/blog-entry/legislation-202-starting-gain-momentum.

10. At the time I was an organizer for Free Press and had assisted in setting up this Town Meeting. This particular happenstance I had to negotiate myself with the Backbone Campaign to continue securing the local convener's continued cooperation.

11. See compiled sources at TeleTruth.org, "New Millennium Research Council Experts and Their Corporate Affiliations," n.d., http://www.teletruth.org/NMRC.htm.

12. The following Google search was performed, yielding the result on August 23, 2013: "'network neutrality' OR 'net neutrality' site:whitehouse.gov."

13. The ad is available at https://web.archive.org/web/20150301204058/https://www.freepress.net/sites/default/files/fp-legacy/same-sellout.pdf.

7 The Shifting Political Economics of Net Neutrality

1. See Free Press, "Declaration of Internet Freedom," n.d., https://act.freepress.net/sign/internetdeclaration (accessed May 15, 2019).

2. The letter is available at Amazon et al., "Letter to the Federal Communications Commission," May 7, 2014, https://cdn1.vox-cdn.com/assets/4422119/letter_to_FCC.pdf.

3. The list remains in the Internet Archive's Wayback Machine at https://web.archive.org/web/20151025130240/https://dailycaller.com/wp-content/uploads/2015/02/list_WH_NN.pdf.

4. See Engine's website at http://www.engine.is/.

8 Knowledge, Access, and the Currents Flowing Beneath

1. At Cornell, for instance, there is INFO 4270: Ethics and Policy in Data Science; see the course syllabus at https://docs.google.com/document/d/1GV97qqvjQNvyM2I01vuRaAwHe9pQAZ9pbP7KkKveg1o/edit (accessed April 21, 2019).

2. https://www.oath.com/partners/ (accessed April 28, 2019).

3. https://www.oath.com/partners/dns-search/ (accessed April 28, 2019).

4. http://www.verizonventures.com/ (accessed April 28, 2019).

5. NCC Media, "Overview," https://web.archive.org/web/20180606052053/https://nccmedia.com/about/owners-affiliates/ (accessed April 21, 2019). The Center for Digital Democracy blog at www.democraticmedia.org pays close attention to such initiatives as this one.

6. See Advertising Week, "Advertising Week New York 2017: Partners—NCC Media," *AdvertisingWeek.com*, n.d., http://www.advertisingweek.com/events/ny/2017/partners/-ncc-media (accessed April 21, 2019).

7. See LUMA, "Content: Rich and Valued," *LumaPartners.com*, n.d., https://www.lumapartners.com/luma-content/ (accessed April 21, 2019).

8. See also J. Desjardins, "Comparing Bitcoin, Ethereum, and Other Cryptos," *Visual Capitalist*, September 13, 2017, https://www.visualcapitalist.com/comparing-bitcoin-ethereum-cryptos/ (accessed April 21, 2019).

9. A striking, if at times offensively Amerocentric, illustration of WeChat's capabilities is shown in "How China Is Changing Your Internet," YouTube, August 9, 2016, https://www.youtube.com/watch?v=VAesMQ6VtK8.

10. See Verizon, "Solutions to Transform Your Business," n.d., https://enterprise.verizon.com/solutions/industry/ (accessed April 21, 2019).

11. Twitter's matchmaking page is located at https://partners.twitter.com/en/find-a-partner.html?section=des-services (accessed April 29, 2019).

12. Rossiter (2016) offers a number of tools useful for the analysis of such resultant structures via what he terms "logistical media theory," which stresses the

infrastructural features of media. "Infrastructure provides an underlying system of elements, categories, standards, protocols, and operations that, as many note, are only revealed in its moment of failure and breakdown" (p. 5). In particular, it posses-ses a focus on an analysis "of how labor is organized and governed through software interfaces and media technologies that manage what Anna Tsing identifies as 'supply chain capitalism'" (pp. 5–6).

9 Net Neutrality as Wrecking Ball

1. A transcript of the event can be found at Bavitz, 2017.

2. A record of this hearing can be found at https://www.netcaucus.org/12149-2/.

3. See video at https://www.netcaucus.org/12149-2.

4. See http://calinnovates.org.

5. One might usefully compare here the manner in which these authors describe quality of service (QoS) arrangements with that of Barbara van Schewick (2015). For Faulhaber and Singer, such arrangements are made with those who provide services. For van Schewick, it is users that request it; see p. 133 onward in van Schewick (2015).

6. While the original paper was written by Gerald Faulhaber and Hal Singer, on the revised version, published in the *International Journal of Communication*, Augustus H. Urschel—with Singer, a fellow representative of Economists Incorporated (see https://ei.com/)—is credited as third author.

7. See https://www.internetvoices.org/voices-home.

8. See https://www.hassan.senate.gov/imo/media/doc/170508.Pai_.NetNeutrality.Ltr_.pdf and, from Senator Markey's office, https://www.markey.senate.gov/imo/media/doc/2017-05-08-NetNeutralityLetter.pdf.

9. See https://www.youtube.com/watch?v=z0F9bUbVhAQ.

10. With apologies to Springsteen—he's innocent of all this.

11. Available at https://www.youtube.com/watch?v=LFhT6H6pRWg.

12. "My Notorious Pizzagate Video," posted at https://www.youtube.com/watch?v=KFx34mEnOig (accessed April 30, 2019).

Conclusion

1. I thank an anonymous reviewer for planting the suggestion to explore these examples.

References

Aaron, C. (2012, December 13). What's so funny about the FCC's failures? *Huffington Post.* Retrieved from http://www.huffingtonpost.com/craig-aaron/whats-so-funny-about-the_b_2289958.html.

Aaron, C. (2014, July 15). *Re: GN Docket No. 14-28, Protecting and promoting the open Internet.* Retrieved from http://apps.fcc.gov/ecfs/comment/view?id=6018234827.

Aaron, C. (2017). *FCC chairman's attacks on Free Press don't change the facts. FreePress.net.* Retrieved from https://www.freepress.net/our-response/expert-analysis/explainers/fcc-chairmans-attacks-free-press-dont-change-facts.

Aaron, C., & Karr, T. (2016). Internet freedom from the outside in. In D. Freedman, J. A. Obar, C. Martens, & R. W. McChesney (Eds.), *Strategies for media reform: International perspectives* (pp. 100–106). New York: Fordham University Press.

Abbate, J. (2000). *Inventing the Internet.* Cambridge, MA: MIT Press.

Access fight stage set. (1999, August 2). *Television Digest.*

Adams, P. (2018). Deal of the year: IPG buys Acxiom Marketing Solutions. *MarketingDive.com.* Retrieved from https://www.marketingdive.com/news/deal-of-the-year-ipg-buys-acxiom-marketing-solutions/541307/.

Additional open access victories: Somerville, MA and Quincy, MA. (1999, November 19). *Broadband in the Public Interest, 1*(4). Retrieved from http://web.archive.org/web/20000816033633/http://www.nogatekeepers.org/newsletter/943041241.shtml.

Ad Hoc Telecommunications Users Committee. (2010, January 14). *Comments of the Ad Hoc Telecommunications Users Committee in the Matter of Preserving the Open Internet, GN Docket No. 09-191, and Broadband Industry Practices, WC Docket No. 07-52.* ECFS FCC filing. Retrieved from https://ecfsapi.fcc.gov/file/10717937608186/COM%20FINAL.pdf.

Ad Hoc Telecommunications Users Committee. (2014, July 18). *Comments of the Ad Hoc Telecommunications Users Committee in the Matter of Promoting and Protecting *the Open Internet, FCC GN Docket No. 14-28*. Retrieved from http://apps.fcc.gov/ecfs/comment/view?id=6018211153.

Ad Hoc Telecommunications Users Committee. (2017). *Comments of the Ad Hoc Telecom Users Committee in the Matter of Restoring Internet Freedom, FCC WC Docket No. 17-108.*

Amariglio, J., & Ruccio, D. F. (1999). The transgressive knowledge of "ersatz" economics. In R. F. J. Garnett (Ed.), *What do economists know? New economics of knowledge* (pp. 19–36). New York: Routledge.

Ammori, M. (2009). Competition and investment in wireline broadband. In A. M. Schejter (Ed.), *…And communications for all: A policy agenda for a new administration* (pp. 81–108). New York: Lexington Books.

Ammori, M. (2010, April 7). How I lost the big one, bigtime [Blog post]. *Balkanization*. Retrieved from https://balkin.blogspot.com/2010/04/how-i-lost-big-one-bigtime.html.

Ammori, M. (2014). The "New" *New York Times*: Free speech lawyering in the age of Google and Twitter. *Harvard Law Review, 127*(8), 2259.

Ammori, M. (2014, November 12). *Notice of ex parte presentation, GN Docket No. 14-28, Protecting and Promoting the Open Internet*. Retrieved from http://apps.fcc.gov/ecfs/comment/view?id=60000978244.

Andrejevic, M. (2012). Exploitation in the data mine. In C. Fuchs, K. Boersma, A. Alberchtslund, & M. Sandoval (Eds.), *Internet and surveillance: The challenges of Web 2.0 and social media* (pp. 71–88). New York: Routledge.

AOL Time Warner latest problem for local franchise authorities. (2000, January 17). *Warren's Cable Regulation Monitor.*

AOL–Time Warner open access commitment questioned. (2000, January 17). *Television Digest.*

Assange, J. (2014). *When Google met Wikileaks*. New York: OR Books.

AT&T. (2014, March 27). AT&T, Cisco, GE, IBM and Intel form Industrial Internet Consortium to improve integration of the physical and digital worlds [press release]. Retrieved from http://about.att.com/story/att_cisco_ge_ibm_intel_industrial_internet_consortium.html.

AT&T. (2017, July 6). AT&T investing up to $200 million in venture capital fund [press release]. Retrieved from http://about.att.com/story/investing_venture_capital_fund.html.

AT&T and Verizon are making very different bets on what 5G will mean for consumers and content. (2018, September 5). *ICT Monitor Worldwide.*

AT&T Corp. v. City of Portland, 43 1146 (United States District Court, D. Oregon 1999).

AT&T/MediaOne merger update. (1999, October 7). *Broadband in the Public Interest, 1*(1). Retrieved from http://web.archive.org/web/20000816033652/http://www.nogatekeepers.org/newsletter/939324790.shtml.

AT&T threatens, rewards local officials. (1999, December 13). *Broadband in the Public Interest, 1*(5). Retrieved from http://web.archive.org/web/20000816033628/http://www.nogatekeepers.org/newsletter/945143812.shtml.

Atkinson, R. D. (2011). Economic doctrines and network policy. *Telecommunications Policy, 35*, 413–425.

Atkinson, R. D., & Weiser, P. J. (2006). *A "Third Way" on network neutrality.* Unpublished white paper. Retrieved from http://www.itif.org/files/netneutrality.pdf.

Auerbach, D. (2015, March 31). Privacy is becoming a premium service. *Slate.com.* Retrieved from http://www.slate.com/articles/technology/bitwise/2015/03/at_t_gigapower_the_company_wants_you_to_pay_it_not_to_sell_your_data.html.

Aufderheide, P. (2002). Competition and commons: The public interest in and after the AOL–Time Warner merger. *Journal of Broadcasting & Electronic Media, 46*(4), 515–531.

Baker, D. (1999). *Supplemental letter to Chairman William E. Kennard, Federal Communications Commission, December 6, 1999.* Retrieved from http://web.archive.org/web/200012171546/http://www.opennetcoalition.org/news/12061999/mspringlttr.shtml.

Baker, D. N., Cicconi, J. W., & Fellman, K. S. E. (1999). *Letter from AT&T, MindSpring, and the Chairman, FCC Local & State Government Advisory Committee to Chairman Kennard.* Retrieved from http://transition.fcc.gov/mb/attmindspringletter.txt.

Banet-Weiser, S. (2012). *AuthenticTM: The politics of ambivalence in a brand culture.* New York: New York University Press.

Bangeman, E. (2008, February 26). Comcast denies crowd shaping, crowd delaying at FCC hearing. *Ars Technica.* Retrieved from http://arstechnica.com/uncategorized/2008/02/comcast-denies-crowd-shaping-crowd-delaying-at-fcc-hearing.

Bar, F., Cohen, S., Cowhey, P., DeLong, B., Kleeman, M., & Zysman, J. (1999). *Defending the Internet revolution in the broadband era: When doing nothing is doing harm.* E-conomy Project Working Paper 12, Berkeley Roundtable on the International Economy. Retrieved from https://brie.berkeley.edu/sites/default/files/wp137.pdf.

Baran, P. A., & Sweezy, P. (1966). *Monpoly capital.* New York: Monthly Review Press.

Barber, H. (2000). *Statement of City of Portland to FCC, Public Forum on MediaOne Transfer to AT&T, February 4, 2000.* Washington, DC.

Barry, D. G. (2008). The effect of video franchising reform on net neutrality: Does the beginning of IP convergence mean that it is time for net neutrality regulation? *Santa Clara Computer & High Tech Law Journal, 24,* 421.

Bauer, J. M. (2007). Dynamic effects of network neutrality. *International Journal of Communication, 1.* Retrieved from http://ijoc.org/ojs/index.php/ijoc/article/view/156.

Bauman, Z., Bigo, D., Esteves, P., Guild, E., Jabri, V., Lyon, D., & Walker, R. (2014). After Snowden: Rethinking the impact of surveillance. *International Political Sociology, 8*(2), 121–144.

Baumol, W. J., Cave, M., Cramton, P., Hahn, R., Hazlett, T. W., Joskow, P. L., Kahn, A. E., Mayo, J. W., Messerlin, P. A., Owen, B. M., Pindyck, R. S. Smith, V. L., Wallsten, S., Waverman, L., White, L. J., and Savage, S. (2007). *Economists' statement on network neutrality policy* (AEI-Brookings Joint Center for Regulatory Studies Working Paper No. RP07-08). Retrieved from https://papers.ssrn.com/sol3/papers.cfm?abstract_id=976889.

Bavitz, C. (2017). Transcript: US Communications at a Crossroads: Featuring Chairman of the Federal Communications Commission, Tom Wheeler, in Conversation with Harvard Law School Professor Susan Crawford. *Berkman Klein Center.* Retrieved from https://cyber.harvard.edu/events/luncheons/2017/01/Wheeler.

Belli, L., & De Felippi, P. (Eds.). (2016). *Net neutrality compendium: Human rights, free competition and the future of the Internet.* New York: Springer International.

Benkler, Y. (2006). *The wealth of networks: How social production transforms markets and freedom.* New Haven, CT: Yale University Press.

Bernays, E. (2004 [1928]). *Propaganda.* New York: Ig Publishing.

Blevins, J. L., & Brown, D. H. (2010). Concerns about disproportionate use of economic research in the FCC's media ownership studies from 2002–2007. *Journal of Broadcasting & Electronic Media, 54*(4), 603–620.

Bode, K. (2017, October 24). Google worked with Comcast to kill California privacy bill. Retrieved from https://www.dslreports.com/shownews/Google-Worked-With-Comcast-to-Kill-California-Privacy-Bill-140581.

Bode, K. (2018, January 17). Mozilla, consumer groups sue the FCC for its attack on net neutrality. *TechDirt.com.* Retrieved from https://www.techdirt.com/articles/20180117/10282539021/mozilla-consumer-groups-sue-fcc-attack-net-neutrality.shtml.

Braman, S. (1995a). Horizons of the state: Information policy and power. *Journal of Communication, 45*(4), 4–24.

Braman, S. (1995b). Policy for the Net and the Internet. *Annual Review of Information Science and Technology, 30,* 5–75.

Braman, S. (Ed.). (2003). *Communication researchers and policy-making*. Cambridge, MA: MIT Press.

Braman, S. (2004). Where has media policy gone? Defining the field in the twenty-first century. *Communication Law and Policy, 9*(2), 153–182.

Braman, S. (2009). *Change of state*. Cambridge, MA: MIT Press.

Breckheimer, V. L., & Taglang, K. (1999). Broadband and the future of the Internet. *The Digital Beat, 1*(14). Retrieved from http://web.archive.org/web/20010223100829/http://www.consumerfed.org/internetaccess/bentondigitalbeat200899.html.

Brennan, T. (2017). The post–Internet Order broadband sector: Lessons from the pre–Open Internet order experience. *Review of Industrial Organization, 50*, 469–486.

Brenner, R. (2006). *The economics of global turbulence*. New York: Verso.

Broadband access stays hot. (1999, July 26). *Television Digest*.

Brodkin, J. (2018). Calif. enacts net neutrality law—US gov't immediately sues to block it [Updated]. *Ars Technica*. Retrieved from https://arstechnica.com/tech-policy/2018/09/california-governor-signs-net-neutrality-rules-into-law.

Brown, W. (2015). *Undoing the demos: Neoliberalism's stealth revolution*. Cambridge, MA: MIT Press.

Brustein, J. (2014, November 17). Behind closed doors, Ford, UPS, and Visa push for net neutrality. *Bloomberg Businessweek*. Retrieved from https://finance.yahoo.com/news/behind-closed-doors--ford--ups--and-visa-push-for-net-neutrality-172203230.html.

Brustein, J. (2018, March 8). This Peter Thiel–backed Senate candidate has it in for Google. *Bloomberg Businessweek*. Retrieved from https://www.bloomberg.com/news/articles/2018-03-08/josh-hawley-s-missouri-senate-bid-could-be-a-problem-for-google.

Bryan, B. (2015). Cord-cutting doesn't spell doom for cable companies. *Business Insider*, July 15. Retrieved from https://www.businessinsider.com/cord-cutting-doesnt-spell-doom-for-cable-companies-2015-7.

Buel, S., Gillmor, D., Helft, M., Keith, R., & Kong, D. (1999, January 25). Interactive services for the mainstream. *San Jose Mercury News*, p. 1E.

Burger King. (2018, January 24). *Whopper neutrality*. Retrieved from https://www.youtube.com/watch?v=ltzy5vRmN8Q.

Buytendijk, F. (2016a). *Digital connectivism: Appendix*. Retrieved from the Gartner database at https://www.gartner.com/document/code/296955?ref=grbody&refval=3499717.

Buytendijk, F. (2016b). *Introducing digital connectivism: A new philosophy for the digital society*. Retrieved from the Gartner database at https://www.gartner.com/document/3499717?ref=solrAll&refval=221655033&qid=ebd893cdb0ccfb4a5dc4fb4.

Cable notes. (2000, May 15). *Warren's Cable Regulation Monitor.*

Cable operators believe regulatory threat is growing. (1999, October 14). *Communications Daily.*

Cameron, D. (2019a). Fake FCC comments linked to ex-Trump campaign director's org, boosted by Roger Stone. *Gizmodo.* Retrieved from https://gizmodo.com/fake-fcc-comments-linked-to-ex-trump-campaign-directors-1832233664.

Cameron, D. (2019b). FCC faces off in net neutrality lawsuit against consumer advocates and Internet giants. *Gizmodo.* Retrieved from https://gizmodo.com/fcc-faces-off-in-net-neutrality-lawsuit-against-consume-1832269448.

Cammaerts, B. (2008). Critiques on the participatory potentials of Web 2.0. *Communication, Culture and Critique, 1,* 358–377.

Candeub, A. (2012). An end to end-to-end? A review essay of Barbara van Schewick's *Internet Architecture and Innovation. Federal Communications Law Journal, 64,* 661–674.

Candeub, A. (2015). Is there anything new to say about network neutrality? *Michigan State Law Review,* 455–463.

Cannon, R. (2003). The legacy of the Federal Communications Commission Computer Inquiries. *Federal Communications Law Journal, 55,* 167–206.

Can we preserve the Internet as we know it? Challenges to online access, innovation, freedom, and diversity in the broadband era: Special forum at the National Press Club, December 20, 1999 [Transcript]. (1999, March 15). Retrieved from http://web.archive.org/web/20000816034211/http://www.nogatekeepers.org/cybercast/testimony.shtml.

Caraway, B. (2016). Crisis of command: Theorizing value in new media. *Communication Theory, 26,* 64–81.

Carlyle Group. (2014). *The Carlyle Group names Julius Genachowski Managing Director in U.S. Buyout Team* [press release]. Retrieved from https://www.carlyle.com/media-room/news-release-archive/carlyle-group-names-julius-genachowski-managing-director-us-buyout.

Casper, C. (2017). Hype cycle for privacy, 2016. Retrieved from the Gartner database at https://www.gartner.com/document/3380737?ref=solrAll&refval=221655610&qid=8be7d6ead4b8bcfe6884f2.

Castells, M. (2000). *End of millennium.* Oxford: Blackwell.

Castells, M. (2001). *The Internet galaxy.* Oxford: Oxford University Press.

Castells, M. (2004). Informationalism, networks, and the network society: A theoretical blueprint. In M. Castells (Ed.), *The network society: A cross-cultural perspective.* Northampton, UK: Edward Elgar.

Castells, M. (2009). *Communication power*. New York: Oxford University Press.

Center for Digital Democracy. (2016). *Big data is watching: Growing digital data surveillance of consumers by ISPs and other leading video providers*. White paper. Retrieved from https://www.democraticmedia.org/sites/default/files/field/public-files/2016/ispbigdatamarch2016.pdf.

Center for Media Education. (1999). *Song of the open road: Building a broadband network for the 21st century*. White paper. Retrieved from http://www.edis.sk/ekes/cme_openroad.pdf.

Center for Media Education, Consumer Federation of America, Consumers Union, Media Access Project, & OMB Watch. (1999). *Letter to Chairman William Kennard, Federal Communications Commission, October 13, 1999*. Retrieved from http://web.archive.org/web/20010502071014/http://www.consumerfed.org/internetaccess/Kennard131099.htm.

Center for Media Education et al. (1998a). *Comments of Center for Media Education, Office of Communication, Inc., United Church of Christ, Minority Media and Telecommunications Council, the Civil Rights Forum, and Consumer Federation of America In the Matter of Inquiry Concerning the Deployment of Advanced Telecommunications Capacity to All Americans in a Reasonable and Timely Fashion, and Possible Steps to Accelerate Such Deployment Pursuant to Section 706 of the Telecommunications Act of 1996, FCC CC Docket 98-146 (September 17, 1998).*

Center for Media Education et al. (1998b). *Reply comments of Center for Media Education, Office of Communication, Inc., United Church of Christ, Minority Media and Telecommunications Council, the Civil Rights Forum, and Consumer Federation of America In the Matter of Inquiry Concerning the Deployment of Advanced Telecommunications Capacity to All Americans in a Reasonable and Timely Fashion, and Possible Steps to Accelerate Such Deployment Pursuant to Section 706 of the Telecommunications Act of 1996, FCC CC Docket 98-146.*

Cheney-Lippold, J. (2011). A new algorithmic identity: Soft biopolitics and the modulation of control. *Theory, Culture & Society, 28*, 164.

Cheney-Lippold, J. (2017). *We are data*. New York: New York University Press.

Cherry, B. A. (2007). Analyzing the Net Neutrality Debate through Awareness of Agenda Denial. *International Journal of Communication, 1*. Retrieved from http://ijoc.org/ojs/index.php/ijoc/article/view/155.

Chester, J., Cooper, M., Kimmelman, G., Namioka, A., & Schwartzman, A. (1999). *Consumer and Media Advocates Ask FCC to Require Open Access to High-Speed Cable Internet Networks, Letter to FCC Chairman William Kennard, Commissioner Harold Furchtgott-Roth, Commissioner Susan Ness, Commissioner Michael Powell, and Commissioner Gloria Tristani, 27 January 1999*. Retrieved from https://web.archive.org/web/20000816034024/http://www.nogatekeepers.org/archive/19990127-3.pdf.

Chester, J., & Larson, G. O. (2005). Sharing the wealth: An online commons for the nonprofit sector. In R. McChesney, R. A. Newman, & B. Scott (Eds.), *The future of media: Resistance and reform in the 21st century* (pp. 185–206). New York: New Press.

Chynoweth, D., Frogozo, C., Setteducato, M., Haigh, M., Pacheco, B., & Karr, T. (2015, February 26). *Civil rights leaders applaud the FCC's vote to protect the open Internet* [press release]. Retrieved from http://www.freepress.net/press-release/106828/civil-rights-leaders-applaud-fccs-vote-protect-open-internet.

Cities wary of prolonged FCC battle for AT&T-MediaOne approval. (1999, September 6). *Warren's Cable Regulation Monitor.*

Citizens' Utility Board of Oregon, Consumer Action, Consumer Federation of America, The Utility Reform Network (TURN), & Network, U. C. A. (1999). *Amicus Curiae brief of Citizens' Utility Board of Oregon, Consumer Action, Consumer Federation of America, The Utility Reform Network (TURN), Utility Consumers' Action Network In the United States Court of Appeals for the Ninth Circuit, No. 99-35609, AT&T Corporation et al., Appellants, v. City of Portland et al., Appellees.* Retrieved from http://web.archive.org/web/20000824073411/http://www.consumerfed.org/internetaccess/portlnd.pdf.

Clark, D. D. (2007). Network neutrality: Words of power and 800-pound gorillas. *International Journal of Communication, 1*(1), 701–708. Retrieved from http://ijoc.org/ojs/index.php/ijoc/article/view/158/83.

Coldewey, D. (2018a). California passes landmark data privacy bill. *TechCrunch.com.* Retrieved from https://techcrunch.com/2018/06/28/landmark-california-privacy-bill-heads-to-governors-desk/?sr_share=twitter&utm_source=tctwreshare.

Coldewey, D. (2018b). Supreme Court nominee Brett Kavanaugh's brutal education in net neutrality: To err is human, but come on. *TechCrunch.com.* Retrieved from https://techcrunch.com/2018/07/11/supreme-court-nominee-brett-kavanaughs-brutal-education-in-net-neutrality/.

Coldewey, D. (2019). Net neutrality restoring Save the Internet Act passes House, moving on to Senate. *TechCrunch.com.* Retrieved from https://techcrunch.com/2019/04/10/net-neutrality-restoring-save-the-internet-act-passes-house-moving-on-to-senate/.

Colias, M., & Higgins, T. (2018, October 20–21). Can Detroit become a software business? *Wall Street Journal.* Retrieved from https://www.wsj.com/articles/can-detroit-become-a-software-business-1540008107.

ColorOfChange.org. (2014). *Comments of ColorOfChange.org in the Matter of Protecting and Promoting the Open Internet, GN Docket No. 14-28, and Framework for Broadband Internet Service, GN Docket No. 10-127.* Retrieved from http://apps.fcc.gov/ecfs/comment/view?id=6018214475.

Comcast. (2017). *MachineQ, Comcast's enterprise Internet of Things service, expanding to 12 major U.S. markets* [press release]. Retrieved from https://corporate.comcast.com

/news-information/news-feed/machineq-comcasts-enterprise-internet-of-things-service-expanding-to-12-major-us-markets.

Comm Daily notebook. (2000, May 2). *Communications Daily*.

Confessore, N. (2018, October 16). New York Attorney General expands inquiry into net neutrality comments. *New York Times*. Retrieved from https://www.nytimes.com/2018/10/16/technology/net-neutrality-inquiry-comments.html?utm_campaign=Newsletters&utm_source=sendgrid&utm_medium=email.

Connor, N. (2013, January 10). Google's Schmidt urges N. Korea Internet freedom. *AFP*.

Consumer Federation of America. (1999a). *Comments on the report of the expert review panel to the Budget and Fiscal Management Committee, Metropolitan King County Council, October 25, 1999*. Retrieved from http://web.archive.org/web/20001028112050/http://www.consumerfed.org/internetaccess/wa251099.pdf.

Consumer Federation of America. (1999b). *Keeping the information superhighway open for the 21st century*. Washington, DC. Retrieved from https://web.archive.org/web/20000824073252/http://www.consumerfed.org/internetaccess/keeping1299.pdf.

Consumer Federation of America. (1999c). *Press backgrounder: Broadband open access debate far from over*. Retrieved from http://web.archive.org/web/20010304062740/http://www.consumerfed.org/internetaccess/backgrounder171299.htm.

Consumer Federation of America. (2000a). *Letter to Supervisor Tom Ammiano, Chair; Supervisor Alicia Beceril; Supervisor Leland Yee, San Francisco Board of Supervisors Re: Statement in support of open access, May 23, 2000*. Retrieved from http://web.archive.org/web/20001101235939/http://www.consumerfed.org/internetaccess/sanfranletter_230500.pdf.

Consumer Federation of America. (2000b). *Open access: Phase II action plan—opportunities to press for nondiscriminatory access to the broadband Internet after the Portland case*. Retrieved from http://web.archive.org/web/20000815095619/http://www.consumerfed.org/internetaccess/phaseII_0700.pdf.

Consumer Federation of America (Producer). (2001). *Consumer documents on the "broadband" debate*. Retrieved from http://web.archive.org/web/20010303055953/http://www.consumerfed.org/internetaccess/documents.htm.

Consumer Federation of America & Consumer @ction. (1999). Transforming the Information Highway into a Private Toll Road: The Case against Closed Access Broadband Internet Systems. Retrieved from https://consumerfed.org/pdfs/bbreport.pdf.

Consumer Federation of America & Consumers Union. (2000). *Ex Parte submission Re: Application by SBC Communications Inc. et al. pursuant to Section 271 of the Telecommunications Act of 1996 to provide in-region, interLATA service in Texas, FCC CC Docket No. 0065*. Retrieved from http://web.archive.org/web/20010612092233/http://www.consumerfed.org/internetaccess/fcc_exparte_270600.pdf.

Consumer Federation of America & Florida Consumer Action Network. (1999). *Letter to the Hon. Gwen Margolis, Chairperson, Board of County Commissioners, Miami, Florida, October 15, 1999*. Retrieved from http://web.archive.org/web/20001027232801/http://www.consumerfed.org/internetaccess/fl151099.pdf.

Consumer Federation of America & Missouri Citizen Action. (1999). *Letter to the Hon. Francis G. Slay, President, Board of Aldermen, St. Louis, MO, October 21, 1999*. Retrieved from http://web.archive.org/web/20001028060854/http://www.consumerfed.org/internetaccess/mo211099.pdf.

Consumer Federation of America & Vermont Public Interest Group. (1999). *Letter to the Hon. Michael H. Dworkin, Chair, Vermont Public Service Board Re: Docket 6101, "Adelphia Cable Litigation," October 11, 1999*. Retrieved from https://web.archive.org/web/20000824073338/http://www.consumerfed.org/internetaccess/vtpsb111099.PDF.

Consumer Federation of America & Virginia Citizens Consumer Council. (1999a). *Letter to Joel H. Peck, Clerk, State Corporation Commission, Richmond, VA, October 5, 1999*. Retrieved from http://web.archive.org/web/20010303055953/http://www.consumerfed.org/internetaccess/vscc051099.PDF.

Consumer Federation of America & Virginia Citizens Consumer Council. (1999b). *Letter to the Hon. Patricia S. O'Bannon, Chairman, County of Henrico Board of Supervisors, December 10, 1999*. Retrieved from http://web.archive.org/web/20001027235325/http://www.consumerfed.org/internetaccess/henrico1299.pdf.

Consumer Federation of America & Virginia Citizens Consumer Council. (1999c). *Letter to the Hon. Timothy M. Kaine, Mayor of Richmond, October 4, 1999*. Retrieved from http://web.archive.org/web/20000824073352/http://www.consumerfed.org/internetaccess/041099.pdf.

Consumer Federation of America & Virginia Citizens Consumer Council. (1999d). *Letter to the Hon. Timothy M. Kaine, Mayor of Richmond, November 8, 1999*. Retrieved from http://web.archive.org/web/20001028094409/http://www.consumerfed.org/internetaccess/va081199.pdf.

Consumer Federation of America, Consumers Union, & Center for Media Education. (1999). *Public-interest advocates reject AT&T's empty promise, call for FCC policy*. Retrieved from http://web.archive.org/web/20000815223843/http://www.consumersunion.org/other/0817pressdc899.htm.

Consumers Union. (2014, October 28). Despite an FCC no-show, New Yorkers speak out for the open Internet. Retrieved from http://consumersunion.org/news/despite-an-fcc-no-show-new-yorkers-speak-out-for-the-open-internet/.

Consumers Union, Consumer Federation of America, & Media Access Project. (2000). *Who do you trust? AOL and AT&T… When they challenge the cable monopoly? Or AOL and AT&T…When they become the cable monopoly?* Retrieved from http://web.archive.org/web/20010604230626/http://www.consumerfed.org/internetaccess/trust.pdf.

Consumers Union, Consumer Federation of America, Center for Media Education, & Media Access Project. (2000). *Comments of Consumers Union, Consumer Federation of America, Center for Media Education and Media Access Project In the Matter of Inquiry Concerning High-Speed Access to the Internet Over Cable and Other Facilities, GEN Docket No. 00-185.*

Cooper, M. .(1999, November 16). *Open access to broadband internet service: The right public policy prevails against the political odds, Statement of Dr. Mark N. Cooper, Director of Research, Consumer Federation of America to the 99 Consumer Conference.* Paper presented at the Virginia Citizens Consumer Council '99 Consumer Conference, Richmond, VA.

Cooper, M. (2000a). Open access to the broadband Internet: Technical and economic discrimination in closed, proprietary networks. *University of Colorado Law Review, 71*, 1011.

Cooper, M. (2000b). *Prepared statement of Dr. Mark N. Cooper, Director of Research, Before the Commerce and Governmental Matters Committee, House of Representatives, Annapolis, MD.* Retrieved from http://web.archive.org/web/20000929225731/http://www.consumerfed.org/internetaccess/md290200.pdf.

Cooper, M. (2000c). *Prepared statement of Dr. Mark N. Cooper, Director of Research, Before the Committee on Technology and Energy, Lansing, Michigan, April 5, 2000.* Retrieved from http://web.archive.org/web/20010303055953/http://www.consumerfed.org/internetaccess/lansing_statement_050400.pdf.

Cooper, M. (2003). *Media Ownership and Democracy in the Digital Information Age.* Washington, DC: Center for Internet & Society, Stanford Law School.

Cooper, M. (Ed.). (2004). *Open architecture as communications policy.* Stanford, CA: Center for Law and Society, Stanford Law School.

Cooper, M. (2014). *The digital past as prologue: How a combination of active public policy and private investment produced the crowning achievement (to date) of progressive (American) capitalism.* Presentation to AEI/University of Nebraska Forum on Reguating the Evolving Broadband Ecosystem, September 10. Retrieved from https://perma.cc/4YZ8-X267.

Cooper, M., & Kimmelman, G. (1999). *The digital divide confronts the Telecommunications Act of 1996: Economic reality versus public policy.* Washington, DC: Consumer Federation of America & Consumers Union.

Copps, M. (2002). *Dissenting Statement of Commissioner Michael J. Copps In the Matter of Inquiry Concerning High-Speed Access to the Internet Over Cable and Other Facilities, Internet Over Cable Declaratory Ruling, Appropriate Regulatory Treatment for Broadband Access to the Internet Over Cable Facilities, Declaratory Ruling and Notice of Proposed*

Rulemaking, GN Docket No. 00-185, CS Docket No. 02-52. Washington, DC: Federal Communications Commission.

Corbett, J. (2019). Digital rights defenders sound alarm over Big Tech's efforts to 'erode' California's landmark privacy law. *CommonDreams.org*. Retrieved from https://www.commondreams.org/news/2019/04/23/digital-rights-defenders-sound-alarm-over-big-techs-efforts-erode-californias.

Couldry, N. (2012). *Media, society, world: Social theory and digital media practice*. Malden, MA: Polity Press.

Court says Portland can impose access requirement on AT&T. (1999, June 7). *Communications Daily*.

Crain, M. (2014). Financial markets and online advertising: Reevaluating the dotcom investment bubble. *Information, Communication & Society*. doi: 10.1080/1369118X.2013.869615.

Crandall, R. W., & Sidak, J. G. (2002). Is structural separation of incumbent local exchange carriers necessary for competition? *Yale Journal on Regulation, 19*, 335.

Crawford, S. (2013). *Captive audience: The telecom industry and monopoly power in the new Gilded Age*. New Haven, CT: Yale University Press.

Crawford, S. (2016). The limits of net neutrality. *Backchannel*. Retrieved from https://www.wired.com/2016/08/net-neutrality-is-only-a-start/.

Crovitz, L. G. (2015, February 1). "Economics-free" Obamanet. *Wall Street Journal*, p. A11. Retrieved from https://www.wsj.com/articles/economics-free-obamanet-1454282427.

Crowcroft, J. (2007). Net Neutrality: The technical side of the debate—A white paper. *International Journal of Communication, 1*(1). Retrieved from http://ijoc.org/ojs/index.php/ijoc/article/view/159.

Customers in Seattle unhappy with @Home. (1999, November 19). *Broadband in the Public Interest, 1*(4). Retrieved from http://web.archive.org/web/20000816033633/http://www.nogatekeepers.org/newsletter/943041241.shtml.

Cuthbert, C. (2016, December 21). This is what resisting looks like. *FreePress.net*. Retrieved from https://www.freepress.net/blog/2016/12/21/what-resisting-looks-like.

Dahlberg, L. (2010). Cyber-libertarianism 2.0: A discourse theory/critical political economy examination. *Cultural Politics, 6*(3), 331–356.

Dahlberg, L. (2011). Re-constructing digital democracy: An outline of four "positions." *New Media & Society, 13*, 855–872.

Davis, M., & Herschel, G. (2016). Hype cycle for customer analytic applications, 2016. Retrieved from Gartner database at https://www.gartner.com/document/3388328?ref=solrResearch&refval=222397425&qid=.

Day, M. (2017). Net neutrality is just the beginning: An interview with Victor Pickard. *Jacobin*. Retrieved from https://jacobinmag.com/2017/11/net-neutrality-fcc-ajit-pai-monopoly.

Dayen, D. (2018). Koch-funded think tank linked to George Mason University is now pretending it's not part of George Mason University. *The Intercept*. Retrieved from https://theintercept.com/2018/09/19/the-mercatus-center-is-a-part-of-george-mason-university-until-its-not.

Dean, J. (2009). *Democracy and other neoliberal fantasies: Communicative capitalism and left politics*. Durham, NC: Duke University Press.

Decherney, P., Ensmenger, N., & Yoo, C. S. (2011). Are those who ignore history doomed to repeat it? *University of Chicago Law Review, 78*, 1627–1685.

Decision soon on whether justice or FTC handles AOL Time Warner. (2000, January 24). *Communications Daily*.

Denina, C. G. (2006, June 13). Cable TV switch may cost city a bundle. *Vallejo Times Herald*.

Diddlebock, B. (1999, January 8). Portland denies TCI, AT&T system transfer. *Denver Post*, p. C2.

Diffie, W., & Landau, S. E. (2010). *Privacy on the line: The politics of wiretapping and encryption*. Cambridge, MA: MIT Press.

Dixon, P., & Gellman, R. (2014). *The scoring of America: How secret consumer scores threaten your privacy and your future*. Retrieved from http://www.worldprivacyforum.org/wp-content/uploads/2014/04/WPF_Scoring_of_America_April2014_fs.pdf.

Dolber, B. (2013). Informationism as ideology: Technological myths in the network neutrality debate. In Z. Stiegler (Ed.), *Regulating the Web: Network neutrality and the fate of the open Internet* (pp. 143–163). Lanham, MD: Lexington Books.

Drake, W. J., & Wilson, E. J. I. (Eds.). (2008). *Governing global electronic networks: International perspectives on policy and power*. Cambridge, MA: MIT Press.

Dunham, I. (2016). Fight for the Future and net neutrality: A case study in the origins, evolution, and activities of a digital-age media advocacy organization. *International Journal of Communication, 10*, 5826–5838.

Effros, S. (2000, June 29). Think about that for a minute… *Cablefax*.

Eggerton, J. (2016, November 22). FCC vetter Jamison: Do we need an FCC? *Multichannel News*. Retrieved from http://www.multichannel.com/news/content/fcc-vetter-jamison-do-we-need-fcc/409255.

Eggerton, J. (2018, September 25). FCC: Local franchise authorities can't regulate broadband. *Broadcasting and Cable*.

Einstein, M. (2016). *Black ops advertising*. New York: OR Books.

Ekbia, H., & Nardi, B. (2014). Heteromation and its (dis)contents: The invisible division between humans and machines. *First Monday, 19*(6).

Ekbia, H. R., & Nardi, B. A. (2017). *Heteromation, and other stories of computing and capitalism*. Cambridge, MA: MIT Press.

Esbin, B. (1998). *Internet over cable: Defining the future in terms of the past* (FCC OPP Working Paper no. 30). Washington, DC: Federal Communications Commission.

Estrella, J. (2000, July 3). Portland is latest @Home market. *Multichannel News*, p. 2.

Estrella, J., & Haugsted, L. (2000, December 4). Access still tops cable's legislative agenda. *Multichannel News*, p. 18.

Etsy. (2013). *Redefining entrepreneurship: Etsy sellers' economic impact* (GfK, Custom Research, LLC report). Retrieved from https://blog.etsy.com/news/files/2013/11/Etsy_Redefining-Entrepreneurship_November-2013.pdf.

Ewen, S. (1976). *Captains of consciousness: Advertising and the roots of the consumer culture*. New York: McGraw-Hill.

Fairfax County seeking concessions from Cox in transfer. (1999, August 9). *Warren's Cable Regulation Monitor*.

Faris, R., Roberts, H., Etling, B., Othman, D., & Benkler, Y. (2016). The role of the networked public sphere in the U.S. net neutrality policy debate. *International Journal of Communication, 10*, 5839–5864.

Farrell, J. (2006). Open access arguments: Why confidence is misplaced. In R. J. May & T. M. Lenard (Eds.), *Net neutrality or net neutering: Should broadband Internet services be regulated?* (pp. 195–214). New York: Springer.

Farrell, J., & Weiser, P. J. (2003). Modularity, vertical integration, and open access policies: Towards a convergence of antitrust and regulation in the Internet age. *Harvard Journal of Law & Technology, 17*(1), 85–134.

Fast, K., Örnebring, H., & Karlsson, M. (2016). Metaphors of free labor: A typology of unpaid work in the media sector. *Media, Culture & Society, 38*(7), 963–978.

Faulhaber, G. R. (2007). Network neutrality: The debate evolves. *International Journal of Communication, 1*(1). Retrieved from http://ijoc.org/ojs/index.php/ijoc/article/view/151.

Faulhaber, G. R., & Singer, H. J. (2016). The curious absence of economic analysis at the Federal Communications Commission: An agency in search of a mission [white paper submitted as part of CallInnovates' comments in WC Docket 16-106]. Retrieved from https://ecfsapi.fcc.gov/file/10711657902329/FaulhaberSinger_FINAL%20TO%20FILE.pdf.

FCC. (1997). *Report to Congress In the Matter of Federal-State Joint Board on Universal Service, CC Docket No. 96-45*. Washington, DC: Federal Communications Commission. Retrieved from https://transition.fcc.gov/Bureaus/Common_Carrier/Reports/fcc 98067.pdf.

FCC. (1998a). *Memorandum Opinion and Order and Notice of Proposed Rulemaking in the matters of deployment of wireline services offering advanced telecommunications capability (CC Docket No. 98-147), Petitions of Bell Atlantic Corporation, US West, and Ameritech for relief from barriers to deployment of advanced telecommunications services (CC Docket 98-11, CC Docket 98-26, CC Docket 98-32), Petition of the Alliance for Public Technology requesting issuance of notice of inquiry and notice of proposed rulemaking to implement Section 706 of the Telecommunications Act (CCB/CPD No. 98015 RM 9244), Petition of the Association for Local Telecommunications Services (ALTS) for a declaratory ruling establishing conditions necessary to promote deployment of advanced telecommunications capability under Section 706 of the Telecommunications Act of 1996 (CC Docket No. 98-78), Southwestern Bell Telephone Company, Pacific Bell, and Nevada Bell petition for relief from fregulation pursuant to Section 706 of the Telecommunications Act of 1996 and 47 U.S.C. § 160 for ADSL infrastructure and service (CC Docket No. 98-81)*. Washington, DC: Federal Communications Commission.

FCC. (1998b). *Transcript of en banc hearing in regards to ILEC Mergers, December 14, 1998*. Washington, DC: Federal Communications Commission.

FCC. (1999a). *Connecting the globe: A regulator's guide to building a global information community*. Washington, DC: Federal Communications Commission.

FCC. (1999b). *In the Matter of Applications for the Consent to the Transfer of Control of Licenses and Section 214 Authorizations from Tele-Communications, Inc., Transferor To AT&T Corp., Transferee, Memorandum Opinion and Order, CS Docket No. 98-178*. Washington, DC: Federal Communications Commission.

FCC. (1999c). *Report, In the Matter of Inquiry Concerning the Deployment of Advanced Telecommunications Capability to All Americans in a Reasonable and Timely Fashion, and Possible Steps to Accelerate Such Deployment Pursuant to Section 706 of the Telecommunications Act of 1996, CC Docket No. 98-146*. Washington, DC: Federal Communications Commission.

FCC. (2000a). *Notice of Inquiry in the Matter of Inquiry Concerning High-Speed Access to the Internet Over Cable and Other Facilities, GN Docket No. 00-185*. Washington, DC: Federal Communications Commission.

FCC. (2000b). *Memorandum Opinion and Order In the Matter of Applications for Consent to the Transfer of Control of Licenses and Section 214 Authorizations from MediaOne Group, Inc., Transferor To AT&T Corp., Transferee, CS Docket No. 99-251*. Washington, DC: Federal Communications Commission.

FCC. (2000c). *Transcript: Before the Federal Communications Commission In Re Applications of: Cable Service Bureau, AT&T-MediaOne Public Forum, MM CS Docket No. 99-251, February 4, 2000*. Washington, DC: Federal Communications Commission.

FCC. (2000d). *Transcript of en banc hearing on America Online, Inc., and Time Warner, Inc. Applications for Transfer of Control, CS Docket No. 00-30, July 27, 2000*. Washington, DC: Federal Communications Commission.

FCC. (2001). *Memorandum Opinion and Order in the Matter of Applications for Consent to the Transfer of Control of Licenses and Section 214 Authorizations by Time Warner Inc. and America Online, Inc., Transferors, to AOL Time Warner Inc., Transferee, CS Docket No. 00-30*. Washington, DC: Federal Communications Commission.

FCC. (2002a). *Applications for Consent to the Transfer of Control of Licenses from Comcast Corporation and AT&T Corp., Transferors, to AT&T Comcast Corporation, Transferee, MB Docket No. 02-70, Memorandum Opinion and Order*. Washington, DC: Federal Communications Commission.

FCC. (2002b). *Declaratory Ruling and Notice of Proposed Rulemaking in the Matter of Inquiry Concerning High-Speed Access to the Internet Over Cable and Other Facilities, Internet Over Cable Declaratory Ruling, Appropriate Regulatory Treatment for Broadband Access to the Internet Over Cable Facilities, GN Docket No. 00-185, CS Docket No. 02-52*. Washington, DC: Federal Communications Commission.

FCC. (2005). *Report and Order and Notice of Proposed Rulemaking in the Matters of Appropriate Framework for Broadband Access to the Internet over Wireline Facilities (CC Docket No. 02-33); Universal Service Obligations of Broadband Providers (CC Docket No. 01-337); Review of Regulatory Requirements for Incumbent LEC Broadband Telecommunications Services; Computer III Further Remand Proceedings: Bell Operating Company Provision of Enhanced Services; 1998 Biennial Regulatory Review—Review of Computer III and ONA Safeguards and Requirements (CC Docket Nos. 95-20, 98-10); Conditional Petition of the Verizon Telephone Companies for Forbearance Under 47 U.S.C. at 160(c) with Regard to Broadband Services Provided Via Fiber to the Premises; Petition of Verizon Telephone Companies for Declaratory Ruling or, Alternatively, for Interim Waiver with Regard to Broadband Services Provided Via Fiber to the Premises (WC Docket No. 04-242)*. Washington, DC: Federal Communications Commission.

FCC. (2007). *Notice of Inquiry in the Matter of Broadband Industry Practices (WC Docket No. 07-52)*. Washington, DC: Federal Communications Commission.

FCC. (2008). *Memorandum Opinion and Order in the Matters of Formal Complaint of Free Press and Public Knowledge Against Comcast Corporation for Secretly Degrading Peer-to-Peer Applications (File No. EB-08-IH-1518); Broadband Industry Practices, Petition of Free Press et al. for Declaratory Ruling that Degrading an Internet Application Violates the FCC's Internet Policy Statement and Does Not Meet an Exception for "Reasonable Network Management" (WC Docket No. 07-52)*. Washington, DC: Federal Communications Commission.

FCC. (2009a). *Notice of Proposed Rulemaking, GN Docket No. 09-191 on Preserving the Open Internet, WC Docket No. 07-52 on Broadband Industry Practices*. Washington, DC: Federal Communications Commission.

FCC. (2009b). *Open Internet workshops: Technical advisory process workshop on broadband network management*. OpenInternet.gov. Retrieved from OpenInternet.gov website, http://www.openinternet.gov/workshops/technical-advisory-process-workshop-on-broadband-network-management.html.

FCC. (2009c). *Panelists announced for Dec. 15 workshop on speech, democracy and the open Internet*. Washington, DC: Federal Communications Commission.

FCC. (2010a). *Report and Order in the Matter of Preserving the Open Internet, GN Docket No. 09-191, and Broadband Industry Practices, WC Docket No. 07-52*. Washington, DC: Federal Communications Commission.

FCC. (2010b). *Open Internet workshops: Approaches to preserving the open Internet*. Washington, DC: Federal Communications Commission. Retrieved from http://www.openinternet.gov/workshops/approaches-to-preserving-the-open-internet.html.

FCC. (2010c). *Open Internet workshops: Consumers, transparency and the open Internet*. Washington, DC: Federal Communications Commission. Retrieved from http://www.openinternet.gov/workshops/consumers-transparency-and-the-open-internet.html.

FCC. (2010d). *Sixth broadband deployment report*. Washington, DC: Federal Communications Commission.

FCC. (2010e). *Workshop: Innovation, investment, and the open Internet*. Washington, DC: Federal Communications Commission. Retrieved from http://www.openinternet.gov/workshops/innovation-investment-and-the-open-internet.html.

FCC. (2014). *Notice of Proposed Rulemaking In the Matter of Protecting and Promoting the Open Internet, GN Docket No. 14-28*. Washington, DC: Federal Communications Commission.

FCC. (2015). *Report and Order on Remand, Declaratory Ruling, and Order In the Matter of Protecting and Promoting the Open Internet, GN Docket No. 14-28*. Washington, DC: Federal Communications Commission.

FCC. (2016). *Report and Order in the matter of Protecting the Privacy of Customers of Broadband and Other Telecommunications Services, WC Docket No. 16-106*. Washington, DC: Federal Communications Commission.

FCC. (2017a). *Declaratory Ruling, Report and Order, and Order, WC Docket 17-108, In the Matter of Restoring Internet Freedom [public draft]*. Washington, DC: Federal Communications Commission. Retrieved from https://apps.fcc.gov/edocs_public/attachmatch/DOC-347927A1.pdf.

FCC. (2017b). *Notice of Proposed Rulemaking In the Matter of Restoring Internet Freedom, WC Docket 17-108*. Washington, DC: Federal Communications Commission.

FCC. (2018a). *Declaratory Ruling, Report and Order, and Order, WC Docket 17-108, In the Matter of Restoring Internet Freedom [Final order].* Washington, DC: Federal Communications Commission.

FCC. (2018b). *Order In the Matter of Establishment of the Office of Economics and Analytics, MD Docket No. 18-3.* Washington, DC: Federal Communications Commission. Retrieved from https://apps.fcc.gov/edocs_public/attachmatch/FCC-18-7A1.pdf.

FCC. (2018c). *What they're saying about Chairman Pai's proposal to create an Office of Economics and Analytics.* Washington, DC: Federal Communications Commission. Retrieved from https://apps.fcc.gov/edocs_public/attachmatch/DOC-348913A1.pdf.

FCC Chairman Ajit Pai got rickrolled by net neutrality activists. (2017, April 21). *FreePress.net.* Retrieved from https://www.freepress.net/blog/2017/04/21/fcc-chairman-ajit-pai-got-rickrolled-net-neutrality-activists.

FCC urges court to avoid open access. (2000, August 14). *Television Digest.*

Feld, H. (2018a). The history of net neutrality in 13 years of Tales of the Sausage Factory (with a few additions). Part I. *Wetmachine.com.* Retrieved from https://wetmachine.com/tales-of-the-sausage-factory/the-history-of-net-neutrality-in-13-years-of-tales-of-the-sausage-factory-with-a-few-additions-part-i/.

Feld, H. (2018b). So what the heck *is* a digital platform? *Wetmachine.com.* Retrieved from https://wetmachine.com/tales-of-the-sausage-factory/so-what-the-heck-is-a-digital-platform/.

Feld, H. (2018c). Using the cost of exclusion to measure the dominance of digital platforms. *Wetmachine.com.* Retrieved from https://wetmachine.com/tales-of-the-sausage-factory/using-the-cost-of-exclusion-to-measure-the-dominance-of-digital-platforms/.

Feld, H. (2018d). Why platform regulation is both necessary and hard. *Wetmachine.com.* Retrieved from https://wetmachine.com/tales-of-the-sausage-factory/why-platform-regulation-is-both-necessary-and-hard/.

Feld, H. (2019a). *The case for the Digital Platform Act: Market structure and regulation of digital platforms.* White paper, Roosevelt Institute and Public Knowledge. Retrieved from https://www.publicknowledge.org/assets/uploads/documents/Case_for_the_Digital_Platform_Act_Harold_Feld_2019.pdf.

Feld, H. (2019b). Net neutrality oral argument highlights problem for Pai: You can't hide the policy implications of your actions from judges. *Wetmachine.com.* Retrieved from https://wetmachine.com/tales-of-the-sausage-factory/net-neutrality-oral-argument-highlights-problem-for-pai-you-cant-hide-the-policy-implications-of-your-actions-from-judges/.

Ferguson, C. H. (2004). *The broadband problem: Anatomy of a market failure and a policy dilemma.* Washington, DC: Brookings Institution Press.

Ferranti, M. (1997, December 8). Stall tactics. *Network World.*

Few regulatory obstacles seen for AOL Time Warner merger. (2000, January 17). *Warren's Cable Regulation Monitor.*

Fish, S. (1982). *Is there a text in this class? The authority of interpretive communities.* Cambridge, MA: Harvard University Press.

FitzGerald, D., & Krouse, S. (2018, November 13). AT&T and Verizon once marched in lockstep. Not any longer: The two biggest U.S. phone companies have chosen two very different strategies into the media future. *Wall Street Journal.*

Flaherty, C. (2017, July 7). Net neutrality battle. *Inside Higher Ed.* Retrieved from https://www.insidehighered.com/news/2017/07/07/questions-funding-and-disclosure-surround-article-advocating-more-economic-analysis.

Floberg, D. (2017a). Internet users beware: Marsha Blackburn—a diehard net neutrality foe—is now in charge of a powerful house subcommittee. Retrieved from http://conference.freepress.net/blog/2017/01/10/internet-users-beware-of-marsha-blackburn.

Floberg, D. (2017b). New FCC chairman Ajit Pai is off to an Orwellian start. *FreePress.net.* Retrieved from https://www.freepress.net/our-response/expert-analysis/explainers/new-fcc-chairman-ajit-pai-orwellian-start.

Floberg, D., & González, J. J. (2017, March 2). Will Donald Trump allow wealthy elites to call the shots? *The Hill.* Retrieved from http://thehill.com/blogs/congress-blog/politics/321982-will-donald-trump-allow-wealthy-elites-to-call-the-shots.

Ford, G. S. (2017). *Below the belt: A review of Free Press and the Internet Association's investment claims.* White paper. Phoenix Center for Advanced Legal & Economic Public Policy Studies. Retrieved from http://www.phoenix-center.org/perspectives/Perspective17-06Final.pdf.

Forester, B. (2017, May 9). Net neutrality activists picket Pai. *FreePress.net.* Retrieved from https://www.freepress.net/our-response/advocacy-organizing/stories-field/net-neutrality-activists-picket-pai.

Foster, J. B., & McChesney, R. W. (2011). The Internet's unholy marriage to capitalism. *Monthly Review, 62*(10), 1–30.

Foster, J. B., & McChesney, R. W. (2014). Surveillance capitalism: Monopoly-finance capital, the military-industrial compex, and the digital age. *Monthly Review, 66*(3), 1–31.

Foucault, M. (2008). *The birth of biopolitics: Lectures at the College de France 1978–1979.* New York: Palgrave Macmillan.

Freedman, D. (2012). Outsourcing internet regulation. In J. Curran, N. Fenton, & D. Freedman (Eds.), *Misunderstanding the Internet* (pp. 95–120). New York: Routledge.

Free Press. (2006, March 2). *Congress should expand universal service funding to broadband networks* [press release]. Retrieved from http://www.savetheinternet.com/release/118.

Free Press. (2016). *Comments of Free Press In the Matter of Protecting the Privacy of Customers of Broadband and Other Telecommunications Services, WC Docket No. 16-106.* Retrieved from https://ecfsapi.fcc.gov/file/60002079232.pdf.

Free Press. (2017). *Reply comments of Free Press in the Matter of Restoring Internet Freedom, WC Docket No. 17-108.* Retrieved from https://ecfsapi.fcc.gov/file/10831280772298/Free%20Press%2017-108%20Reply%20Comments.pdf.

Frieden, R. M. (2007). Internet 3.0: Identifying problems and solutions to the network neutrality debate. *International Journal of Communication, 1.* Retrieved from http://ijoc.org/ojs/index.php/ijoc/article/view/160.

Frischmann, B. M. (2005). An economic theory of infrastructure commons management. *Minnesota Law Review, 89*, 917–1030.

Frischmann, B. M., & van Schewick, B. (2007). Network neutrality and the economics of an information superhighway: A reply to professor Yoo. *Jurimetrics, 47* (Summer), 383.

FTC. (2007). *Broadband connectivity and competition policy, FTC staff report.* Retrieved from http://www.ftc.gov/reports/broadband/v070000report.pdf.

FTC. (2018, September 13). *FTC Hearing #1: The Current Landscape of Competition and Privacy Law and Policy; Hearings on Competition and Consumer Protection in the 21st Century.* Retrieved from https://www.ftc.gov/news-events/events-calendar/2018/09/ftc-hearing-1-competition-consumer-protection-21st-century.

FTC v. AT&T Mobility (9th Circuit 2018).

Fuchs, C. (2012a). Critique of the political economy of Web 2.0 surveillance. In C. Fuchs, K. Boersma, A. Alberchtslund, & M. Sandoval (Eds.), *Internet and surveillance: The challenges of Web 2.0 and social media.* New York: Routledge.

Fuchs, C. (2012b). Dallas Smythe today—The audience commodity, the digital labour debate, Marxist political economy and critical theory. Prolegomena to a digital labour theory of value. *TripleC (Cognition, Communication, Co-Operation): Open Access Journal for a Global Sustainable Information Society, 10*(2), 692–740.

Fulton, S. (2016, December 21). Facial-recognition technology is racially biased. *FreePress.net.* Retrieved from https://www.freepress.net/our-response/expert-analysis/explainers/facial-recognition-technology-racially-biased.

Fumagalli, A., & Mezzandra, S. (Eds.). (2010). *Crisis in the global economy: Financial markets, social struggles, and new political scenarios.* Los Angeles: Semiotext(e).

Fung, B. (2016, November 22). "We don't need the FCC": A Trump adviser's proposal to dissolve America's telecom watchdog. *Washington Post.* Retrieved from https://www.washingtonpost.com/news/the-switch/wp/2016/11/22/we-dont-need-the-fcc-a-trump-advisers-proposal-to-dissolve-americas-telecom-watchdog.

Furchtgott-Roth, H. (1999). *Concurring Statement of Commissioner Harold Furchtgott-Roth, In the Matter of Applications for the Consent to the Transfer of Control of Licenses and Section 214 Authorizations from Tele-Communications, Inc., Transferor To AT&T Corp., Transferee, Memorandum Opinion and Order, CS Docket No. 98-178.* Washington, DC: Federal Communications Commission.

Furchtgott-Roth, H. (2001). *Furchtgott-Roth supports merger, but decries review process as "broken": Statement of FCC Commissioner Harold W. Furchtgott-Roth, concurring in part and dissenting in part in the matter of applications for consent to the transfer of control of licenses and Section 214 authorizations by Time Warner Inc. and America Online, Inc., transferors, to AOL Time Warner Inc., transferee, CS Docket No. 00-30.* Washington, DC: Federal Communications Commission.

Furchtgott-Roth, H., & Washington Legal Foundation. (2017). *Comments of Harold Furchtgott-Roth and Washington Legal Foundation to the Federal Communications Commission in the matter of Restoring Internet Freedom (June 2, 2017).*

The Future of the Internet: Special Forum at the National Press Club. (2000). Retrieved from http://web.archive.org/web/20000816034200/http://www.nogatekeepers.org/cybercast/02232000testimony.shtml.

Gandy, O. H. (1993). *The panoptic sort: Political economy of personal information.* Boulder, CO: Westview Press.

Gangadharan, S. P. (2012). Digital inclusion and data profiling. *First Monday, 17*(5). https://doi.org/10.5210/fm.v17i5.3821.

Genachowski, J. (2010, May 6). *The third way: A narrowly tailored broadband framework.* Washington, DC: Federal Communications Commission. Retrieved from https://apps.fcc.gov/edocs_public/attachmatch/DOC-297944A1.pdf.

Gillula, J. (2017, March 19). Five creepy things your ISP could do if Congress repeals the FCC's privacy protections. *Electronic Frontier Foundation.* Retrieved from https://www.eff.org/deeplinks/2017/03/five-creepy-things-your-isp-could-do-if-congress-repeals-fccs-privacy-protections.

Glass, P. M. (2000). *Vice President and General Counsel, Seren Innovatins, Inc. Before the Federal Communications Commission Cble Services Bureau Forum on AT&T/MediaOne Merger Application, February 4, 2000.* Washington, DC.

Goldstein, F. R. (2005). *The great telecom meltdown.* Norwood, MA: Artech House.

Goldstein, P. (2014). Verizon teams with GE and Predix platform to connect Internet-enabled industrial machines. *Fierce Wireless.* Retrieved from https://www.fiercewireless.com/wireless/verizon-teams-ge-and-predix-platform-to-connect-internet-enabled-industrial-machines.

González, J., & Torres, J. (2011). *News for all the people: The epic story of race and the American media*. New York: Verso.

Goodman, P. S. (1999, November 18). FCC adopts line-sharing rules. *Washington Post*. Retrieved from https://www.washingtonpost.com/wp-srv/pmextra/nov99/18/fcc.htm?noredirect=on.

Google Transparency Project (2017, July 11). *Google Academics Inc.* Retrieved from http://googletransparencyproject.org/articles/google-academics-inc.

Gordon, G. (2016). *SSRN—the leading social science and humanities repository and online community—joins Elsevier*. Retrieved from https://www.elsevier.com/connect/ssrn-the-leading-social-science-and-humanities-repository-and-online-community-joins-elsevier.

Greenfield, A. (2013). *Against the smart city* [e-book]: New York: Do Projects.

Greenfield, A. (2017). *Radical technologies: The design of everyday life*. New York: Verso.

Greenstein, S. (2016). *How the Internet became commercial: Innovation, privatization, and the birth of a new network*. Princeton, NJ: Princeton University Press.

Griffin, J., & Feld, H. (2013). *Five fundamentals for the phone network transition*. White paper. Retrieved from https://www.publicknowledge.org/files/PKThinks5Fundamentals.pdf.

Grimaldi, J. V., & Overberg, P. (2017, December 12). Millions of people post comments on federal regulations. Many are fake. *Wall Street Journal*. Retrieved from https://www.wsj.com/articles/millions-of-people-post-comments-on-federal-regulations-many-are-fake-1513099188.

Grossman, N. (2015, February 18). *Ex Parte of Union Square Ventures Re: Protecting and Promoting the Open Internet; Framework for Broadband Internet Services; GN Docket No. 14-28; GN Docket No. 10-127*. Retrieved from https://ecfsapi.fcc.gov/file/60001030760.pdf.

Gruley, B. (1999, January 15). Must AT&T give Internet rivals access to TCI's network? *Wall Street Journal*, p. A1. Retrieved from https://www.wsj.com/articles/SB916293316764717500.

Gustin, S. (2010). Net neutrality group slaps back at AT&T-funded lawmaker. *Wired*. Retrieved from https://www.wired.com/2010/11/color-of-change-bobby-rush.

Hahn, R. W., & Litan, R. E. (2007). The myth of network neutrality and what we should do about it. *International Journal of Communication, 1*. Retrieved from http://ijoc.org/ojs/index.php/ijoc/article/view/161/87.

Hammer, M. H. (2010a, April 5). *Letter in the Matter of Applications for Comcast Corporation, General Electric Company and NBC Universal, Inc. for Consent to Assign Licenses or Transfer Control of Licensees, MB Docket No. 10-56*. Retrieved from https://ecfsapi.fcc.gov/file/7020408590.pdf.

Hammer, M. H. (2010b, November 23). *Letter in the Matter of Applications for Comcast Corporation, General Electric Company and NBC Universal, Inc. for Consent to Assign Licenses or Transfer Control of Licensees, MB Docket No. 10-56, Redacted for public inspection*. Retrieved from https://ecfsapi.fcc.gov/file/7020921770.pdf.

Handley, J. (2005). *Telebomb*. New York: Amacom.

Hart, J. A. (2011). The net neutrality debate in the United States. *Journal of Information Technology & Politics, 8*(4), 418–443.

Harvey, D. (2005). *A brief history of neoliberalism*. New York: Verso.

Hauben, M., & Hauben, R. (1997). *Netizens*. Los Alamitos, CA: IEEE Computer Society Press.

Hausman, J. A., & Sidak, J. G. (1999). A consumer-welfare approach to the mandatory unbundling of telecommunciations networks. *Yale Law Journal, 109*, 417.

Hausman, J. A., Sidak, J. G., & Singer, H. J. (2001). Residential demand for broadband telecommunications and consumer access to unaffiliated Internet content providers. *Yale Journal on Regulation, 18*, 129.

Hazen, D. (2000, April 26). Consumers likely on the short end as AOL gobbles up Time Warner in world's biggest merger… so far. *Alternet.org*. On file with author.

Hazlett, T. W., & Wright, J. D. (2011). *The law and economics of network neutrality* (George Mason Law & Economics Research Paper No. 11-36). Retrieved from http://papers.ssrn.com/sol3/papers.cfm?abstract_id=1917587.

Hazlett, T. W., & Wright, J. D. (2012). The law and economics of network neutrality. *Indiana Law Review, 45*, 767–840.

Hearn, A. (2008). "Meat, mask, burden": Probing the contours of the branded "self." *Journal of Consumer Culture, 8*(2), 197–217.

Hearn, T., & Estrella, J. (2001, July 16). AT&T wins open-access case in Virginia. *Multichannel News*, p. 1. Retrieved from https://www.multichannel.com/news/att-wins-open-access-case-virginia-131789.

Henwood, D. (2019). Uber nichts. *LBO News from Doug Henwood*. Retrieved from https://lbo-news.com/2019/04/12/uber-nichts/?utm_source=feedburner&utm_medium=email&utm_campaign=Feed%3A+LboNewsFromDougHenwood+%28LBO+News+from+Doug+Henwood%29.

Herman, B. D. (2006). Opening bottlenecks: On behalf of mandated network neutrality. *Federal Communications Law Journal, 59*(1), 107.

Hindman, M. (2008). *The myth of digital democracy*. Princeton, NJ: Princeton University Press.

Holt, J. (2016). Net neutrality and the public interest: An interview with Gene Kimmelman, President and CEO of Public Knowledge. *International Journal of Communication, 10*, 5795–5810.

Hope, W. (2006). Global capitalism and the critique of real time. *Time & Society, 15*(2/3), 275–302.

Hope, W. (2009). Conflicting temporalities: State, nation, economy and democracy under global capitalism. *Time & Society, 18*(1), 62–85.

Horwitz, R. B. (1989). *The irony of regulatory reform: The deregulation of American telecommunications*. New York: Oxford University Press.

Hotz, R. L. (2016, September 20). Researchers use wireless signals to recognize emotions. *Wall Street Journal*.

Huber, P. (1997). *Law and disorder in cyberspace: abolish the FCC and let common law rule the telecosm. New York: Oxford University Press*. New York: Oxford University Press.

Hundt, R. (2010, April 7). *Future of (international) broadband and practically everything else*. Paper presented at the USC Annenberg Research Network on International Communication Seminar, University of Southern California.

Hung, M., Friedman, T., Ganguli, S., Heidt, E. T., Liu, V. K., & Tsai, T. (2017). Internet of things primer for 2017. Retrieved from https://www.gartner.com/document/3579717?ref=solrAll&refval=221660081&qid=efffde7f7f49ff6ef288efc6.

Hurtado, A. (2014, September 11). Comment from Andrea Hurtado, Patsy Texas Rose Etsy Shop, FCC Proceeding 14-28. Retrieved from http://apps.fcc.gov/ecfs/comment/view?id=60000794327.

Hush-A-Phone Corp v. United States, 238 F. 2d 266 (DC Cir. 1956).

Internet Engineers, Pioneers, and Technologists. (2017). *Joint Comments of Internet Engineers, Pioneers, and Technologists on the Technical Flaws in the FCC's Notice of Proposed Rule-making and the Need for the Light-Touch, Bright-Line Rules from the Open Internet Order, offered In the Matter of Restoring Internet Freedom, WC Docket 17-108*. Retrieved from https://ecfsapi.fcc.gov/file/1071761547058/Dkt.%2017-108%20Joint%20Comments%20of%20Internet%20Engineers%2C%20Pioneers%2C%20and%20Technologists%202017.07.17.pdf.

Internet Freedom Business Alliance. (2014, November 12). *Notice of Ex Parte Communication, GN Docket No. 14-28, Protecting and Promoting the Open Internet, GN Docket No. 10-127, Framework for Broadband Internet Service*. Retrieved from https://ecfsapi.fcc.gov/file/60000982626.pdf.

Internet Freedom Supporters. (2014). *Comments of Internet Freedom Supporters [Voices for Internet Freedom; Center for Media Justice; ColorOfChange et al.] in the Matter of Protecting and Promoting the Open Internet, FCC GN Docket No. 14-28, and Framework for Broadband Internet Service, GN Docket No. 10-127*. Retrieved from http://apps.fcc.gov/ecfs/comment/view?id=6018204313.

Interview with Erik Sten: The Portland commissioner who helped to start the open access issue. (1999, November 19). *Broadband in the Public Interest, 1*(4). Retrieved from http://web.archive.org/web/20000816033633/http://www.nogatekeepers.org/newsletter/943041241.shtml.

In the states. (1999a, July 14). *Cablefax*.

In the states: City of Fairfax, VA pulls fast one on Cox in access debate. (1999b, October 1). *Cablefax*.

ISPs band together as cable access war moves to Dallas, Denver. (1999, January 11). *Warren's Cable Regulation Monitor*.

Jacobson, B. (1999). *Broadband cable: The open-access debate*. White paper. Retrieved from http://www.netaction.org/broadband/cable.

Johnson, L. (2019). "This is a bit of a Swiss Army Knife": Ad giant Publicis is buying Epsilon for $4.4 billion as it looks to get ahead of its rivals in the data wars. *Business Insider*. Retrieved from https://www.businessinsider.com/publicis-acquires-epsilon-for-44-billion-but-marketers-say-combining-forces-will-be-a-challenge-2019-4.

Johnson, T. (2019). Net neutrality back in court: Takeaways from marathon oral arguments. *Variety*. Retrieved from https://variety.com/2019/politics/news/net-neutrality-marathon-oral-arguments-1203126249/.

Jordan, S. (2007). A layered network approach to net neutrality. *International Journal of Communication, 1*. Retrieved from http://ijoc.org/ojs/index.php/ijoc/article/view/168.

Juniper Research. (2016). *Augmented reality: Not just fun and games* [white paper]. On file with author.

Karr, T. (2007). *Testimony of Timothy P. Karr, Campaign Director, Free Press Before the New York State Assembly Regarding Network Neutrality and Wireless Freedom*. Retrieved from https://www.savetheinternet.com/sites/default/files/resources/tim_karr_nys-testimony.pdf.

Karr, T. (2013). Verizon's plan to break the Internet. *Savetheinternet.com*. Retrieved from https://www.savetheinternet.com/blog/2013/09/18/verizons-plan-break-internet.

Karr, T. (2015, February 26). Historic win for Internet users [press release]. *FreePress.net*. Retrieved from http://www.freepress.net/press-release/106826/historic-win-internet-users.

Karr, T. (2017, April 25). Net neutrality violations: A brief history. *FreePress.net*. Retrieved from https://www.freepress.net/blog/2017/04/25/net-neutrality-violations-brief-history.

Kavanaugh, B. (2017). *Dissenting statement of Judge Kavanaugh, United States Telecom Association v. Federal Communications Commission and United States of America, On Petitions for Rehearing En Banc*. Retrieved from https://www.cadc.uscourts.gov/internet/opinions.nsf/06F8BFD079A89E13852581130053C3F8/$file/15-1063-1673357.pdf.

Kende, M. (2000). *The digital handshake: Connecting Internet backbones*. Federal Communications Commission Office of Plans and Policy, Working Paper No. 32.

Kennard, W. E. (1999, December 16). *Broadband cable: Next steps*. Paper presented at the Western Show, California Cable Television Association, Los Angeles. Retrieved from https://transition.fcc.gov/Speeches/Kennard/spwek944.html.

Kennard, W. E. (2000). *Statement of Chairman William E. Kennard In the Matter of Applications for Consent to the Transfer of Control of Licenses and Section 214 Authorizations from MediaOne Group, Inc., Transferor To AT&T Corp., Transferee, CS Docket No. 99-251*. Washington, DC: Federal Communications Commission.

Kennard, W. E. (2001). *Statement of FCC Chairman William E. Kennard on conditioned approval of AOL Time Warner merger, in the matter of applications for consent to the transfer of control of licenses and Section 214 authorizations by Time Warner Inc. and America Online, Inc., transferors, to AOL Time Warner Inc., transferee, CS Docket No. 00-30*. Washington, DC: Federal Communications Commission.

Kennard hits Portland ruling. (1999, June 21). *Television Digest*.

Kennard, Powell stake federal claim for open access jurisdiction. (1999, June 21). *Warren's Cable Regulation Monitor*.

Khoo, C. (2017). How public participation saved Canada's Internet (Or: What happens when decision-makers actually listen). *FreePress.net*. Retrieved from https://www.freepress.net/blog/2017/05/05/how-public-participation-saved-canadas-internet.

Knorr Cetina, K. (1999). *Epistemic cultures*. Cambridge, MA: Harvard University Press.

Knutson, R., Hagey, K., & Alpert, L. L. (2016, April 18). Verizon, Hearst agree to buy Complex Media. *Wall Street Journal*.

Krause, R. (1998, July 22). Will regulators' wrangle impede telecom reform? *Investor's Business Daily*.

Kroin, A. (2017a, May 18). Net neutrality activists rally against Trump FCC. *FreePress.net*. Retrieved from https://www.freepress.net/our-response/advocacy-organizing/stories-field/net-neutrality-activists-rally-against-trump-fcc.

Kroin, A. (2017b, March 23). Net neutrality protesters face FCC chairman Ajit Pai. *FreePress.net*. Retrieved from https://www.freepress.net/our-response/advocacy-organizing/stories-field/net-neutrality-protesters-face-fcc-chairman-ajit-pai.

Kronenberg, A. (2015, February 12). *Notice of Ex Parte, FCC GN Docket No. 14-28, Protecting and Promoting the Open Internet*. Retrieved from http://apps.fcc.gov/ecfs/comment/view?id=60001016425.

Krouse, S. (2018, December 3). Verizon shifts its business beyond advertising. *Wall Street Journal*.

Kumar, D., & Breznick, A. (2000, May 4). U.S. Dist. Court rules for AT&T in VA. open access case. *Communications Daily*.

Labaton, S. (1999, August 13). Fight for Internet access creates unusual alliances. *New York Times*. Retrieved from https://www.nytimes.com/1999/08/13/us/fight-for-internet-access-creates-unusual-alliances.html.

Laclau, E. (2005). *On populist reason*. New York: Verso.

Laclau, E., & Mouffe, C. (2001). *Hegemony and socialist strategy* (2nd ed.). New York: Verso.

Lafontaine, F., & Slade, M. (2007). Vertical integration and firm boundaries: The evidence. *Journal of Economic Literature, 45*, 629–685.

Lange, A. (2017). Mapping the decentralized world of tomorrow. *Medium.com*. Retrieved from https://medium.com/birds-view/mapping-the-decentralized-world-of-tomorrow-5bf36b973203.

Lannon, B., & Pendleton, A. (2014, September 2). *What can we learn from 800,000 public comments on the FCC's net neutrality plan? (Sunlight Foundation report)*. Retrieved from http://www.sunlightfoundation.com/blog/2014/09/02/what-can-we-learn-from-800000-public-comments-on-the-fccs-net-neutrality-plan.

Lathen, D. A. (1999). *Broadband Today: A Staff Report to William Kennard, Chairman, Federal Communications Commission*. Washington, DC.

Latour, B. (2004). Why has critique run out of steam? From matters of fact to matters of concern. *Critical Inquiry, 30* (Winter), 225–248.

Lazare, S. (2014). 'Revolving door keeps spinning': Former FCC head hired by Carlyle Group. *CommonDreams.org*. Retrieved from https://www.commondreams.org/news/2014/01/07/revolving-door-keeps-spinning-former-fcc-head-hired-carlyle-group.

Lazarsfeld, P. (2004 [1941]). Administrative and critical communciations research. In J. D. Peters & P. Simonson (Eds.), *Mass communication and American social thought: Key texts, 1919–1968*. Oxford: Rowman & Littlefield.

Lee, T. B. (2017). Uber and Airbnb are not the future of capitalism. *Vox*. Retrieved from https://www.vox.com/new-money/2017/3/6/14563112/sharing-economy-not-a-thing.

Lehr, W. H., Sirbu, M. A., Gillett, S. E., & Peha, J. M. (2007). Scenarios for the network neutrality arms race. *International Journal of Communication, 1*(1), 607–643. Retrieved from http://ijoc.org/ojs/index.php/ijoc/article/view/164.

Leiss, W., Kline, S., Jhally, S., & Botterill, J. (2013). *Social communication in advertising: Consumption in the mediated marketplace*. New York: Routledge.

Lemley, M., & Lessig, L. (1999). *Written Ex Parte of Professor Mark A. Lemley and Professor Lawrence Lessig In the Matter of Application for Consent to the Transfer of Control of Licenses, MediaOne Group, Inc. to AT&T Corp., CS Docket No. 99-251*. Retrieved at https://ecfsapi.fcc.gov/file/6009850927.pdf.

Lennett, B. (2009). Dis-empowering users vs. maintaining Internet freedom: Network management and quality of service (QoS). *CommLaw Conspectus, 18*, 97–147.

Lentz, B. (2016). Funding net neutrality advocacy: An interview with the founder and director of the Media Democracy Fund. *International Journal of Communication, 10*, 5811–5825.

Lessig, L. (2000, February 10). *Cyberspace's constitution*. Paper presented at the American Academy, Berlin, Germany.

Lessig, L. (2002). *The Future of Ideas*. New York: Random House.

Lessig, L. (2007). In support of network neutrality. *I/S Journal of Law and Policy, 3*, 185.

Liao, S. (2018, February 26). Apple confirms it now uses Google Cloud for iCloud services. *The Verge*. Retrieved from https://www.theverge.com/2018/2/26/17053496/apple-google-cloud-platform-icloud-confirmation.

Lipton, E., Confessore, N., & Williams, B. (2016, August 8). Think tank scholar or corporate consultant? It depends on the day. *New York Times*. Retrieved from https://www.nytimes.com/2016/08/09/us/politics/think-tank-scholars-corporate-consultants.html.

Lomas, N. (2016, February 7). Verizon accused of net neutrality foul by zero-rating its Go90 mobile video service. *TechCrunch.com*. Retrieved from http://techcrunch.com/2016/02/07/verizon-accused-of-net-neutrality-foul-by-zero-rating-its-go90-mobile-video-service.

MacKie-Mason, J. K. (1999). *Investment in cable broadband infrastructure: Open access is not an obstacle*. School of Information, the Department of Economics, and the School of Public Policy at the University of Michigan white paper. Retrieved from http://www.applecon.com/images/uploads/whitepaper.pdf.

MacLean, N. (2017). *Democracy in chains: The deep history of the radical right's stealth plan for America*. New York: Penguin.

MacMillan, D. (2016, April 17). Verizon tops pack of suitors chasing Yahoo. *Wall Street Journal*.

MacMillan, D. (2018, July 3). App developers gain access to millions of Gmail inboxes—Google and others enable scanning of emails by data miners. *Wall Street Journal*.

MacMillan, D., Krouse, S., & Hagey, K. (2018, August 29). Yahoo, bucking industry, scans emails for data to sell—Web giant pushes harder to analyze inboxes for advertisers. *Wall Street Journal*.

Madera County, CA approves open access, braces for lawsuit. (1999, November 19). *Broadband in the Public Interest, 1*(4). Retrieved from http://web.archive.org/web/20000816033633/http://www.nogatekeepers.org/newsletter/943041241.shtml.

Maher, M. (1999). Cable Internet unbundling: Local leadership in the deployment high speed access. *Federal Communications Law Journal, 52*, 211–238.

Malik, O. (2003). *Broadbandits*. Hoboken, NJ: John Wiley & Sons.

Marsden, C. T. (2017). *Network neutrality: From policy to law to regulation*. Manchester: Manchester University Press.

Marx, K. (1990). *Capital*, vol. 1. New York: Penguin Books.

Masnick, M. (2008). Congress slams Kevin Martin for abuse of power. *TechDirt.com*. Retrieved from https://www.techdirt.com/articles/20081209/1223123065.shtml.

Massachusetts Consumers' Coalition. (1999). *Letter to Keith Mitchell, Chairman, North Andover Board of Selectmen, October 22, 1999*. Retrieved from http://web.archive.org/web/20001028041919/http://www.consumerfed.org/internetaccess/ma221099.pdf.

Massachusetts Consumers' Coalition & Consumer Federation of America. (1999). *Letter on Open Access to Massachusetts Department of Telecommunications and Energy, September 9, 1999*. Retrieved from http://web.archive.org/web/20000824073424/http://www.consumerfed.org/internetaccess/mcc-cfaletter_0999.pdf.

Maxwell, R., & Miller, T. (2012). *Greening the media*. New York: Oxford University Press.

May, R. J., & Lenard, T. M. (2006). Foreword. In R. J. May & T. M. Lenard (Eds.), *Net neutrality or net neutering: Should broadband Internet services be regulated?* (pp. vii–xii). New York: Springer.

McCall, W. (2000, June 23). AT&T wins access case; Portland had tried to force it to loosen control of Internet access on cable systems, but ruling's long-term impact is unclear. *Contra Costa Times*, p. B01.

McCarthy, K. (2017, July 3). America's net neutrality rage hits academia: Corporate shill allegations spark furious response. *The Register.* Retrieved from https://www.theregister.co.uk/2017/07/03/net_neutrality_rage_hits_academia.

McChesney, R. W. (1993). *Telecommunications, mass media and democracy.* Oxford: Oxford University Press.

McChesney, R. W. (1999). *Rich media, poor democracy.* New York: New Press.

McChesney, R. W. (2004). *The problem of the media.* New York: Monthly Review.

McChesney, R. W. (2007). *Communication revolution.* New York: New Press.

McChesney, R. W. (2013). *Digital disconnect.* New York: New Press.

McChesney, R. W., Foster, J. B., Stole, I. L., & Holleman, H. (2009). The sales effort and monopoly capital. *Monthly Review, 60*(11), 1.

McChesney, R. W., Newman, R., & Scott, B. (Eds.). (2005). *The future of media: Resistance and reform in the 21st century.* New York: Seven Stories Press.

McChesney, R. W., & Nichols, J. (2013). *Dollarocracy: How the money and media election complex is destroying America.* New York: Nation Books.

McChesney, R. W., & Schiller, D. (2003). *The political economy of international communications: Foundations for the emerging global debate about media ownership and regulation.* Retrieved from http://www.unrisd.org/80256B3C005BCCF9/(httpAuxPages)/C9DCBA6C7DB78C2AC1256BDF0049A774/$file/mcchesne.pdf.

McCloskey, D. (1999). Jack, David, and Judith looking at me looking at them. In R. F. J. Garnett (Ed.), *What do economists know? New economics of knowledge* (pp. 60–64). New York: Routledge.

McConville, J. (1999, February 22). Big pipe dreams for AT&T-TCI: Merger approval spawns a giant. *Electronic Media.*

McCormick, R. (2015). Verizon will share your browsing habits with AOL's massive ad network. *The Verge.* Retrieved from https://www.theverge.com/2015/10/6/9468025/verizon-will-share-your-browsing-habits-with-aols-massive-ad-network.

McCullagh, D. (2007). Comcast really does block BitTorrent traffic after all. *CNet.com.* Retrieved from https://www.cnet.com/news/comcast-really-does-block-bittorrent-traffic-after-all.

McDowell, R. (2010). *Dissenting Statement of Commissioner Robert McDowell, Sixth Broadband Deployment Report.* Washington, DC: Federal Communications Commission.

McGuigan, L., & Manzerolle, V. (Eds.). (2014). *The audience commodity in a digital age: Revisiting a critical theory of commercial media.* New York: Peter Lang.

McLure, J. (2013, June 6). Civil rights group's FCC positions reflect industry funding, critics say. *Center for Public Integrity*. Retrieved from https://www.publicintegrity.org/2013/06/06/12769/civil-rights-groups-fcc-positions-reflect-industry-funding-critics-say.

McMurria, J. (2016). From net neutrality to net equality. *International Journal of Communication, 10*, 5931–5948.

McRobbie, A. (2004). Notes on postfeminism and popular culture: Bridget Jones and the new gender regime. In A. Harris (Ed.), *All About the Girl: Culture, Power, and Identity* (pp. 3–14). New York: Routledge.

McTaggert, C. (2006). *Was the Internet ever neutral?* Paper presented at the 34th Research Conference on Communication, Information and Internet Policy, George Mason University School of Law, Arlington, VA.

Media Access Project et al. (1999). *Comments of Media Access Project, Center for Media Education, and Civil Rights Telecommunications Forum, filed March 19, 1999 before the Los Angeles City Council*. Retrieved from http://web.archive.org/web/20010304062726/http://www.consumerfed.org/internetaccess/commentstolacitycouncil190399.html.

MediaOne ads in MA. (1999, November 19). *Broadband in the public interest, 1*(4). Retrieved from http://web.archive.org/web/20000816033633/http://www.nogatekeepers.org/newsletter/943041241.shtml.

Meinrath, S. D., Losey, J. W., & Pickard, V. W. (2010). Digital feudalism: Enclosures and erasures from digital rights management to the digital divide. *CommLaw Conspectus, 19*, 423.

Meinrath, S. D., & Pickard, V. W. (2008). Transcending net neutrality: Ten steps toward an open Internet. *Journal of Internet Law, 12*(6), 1, 12–21.

Mele, C. (2017, May 19). Roll Call reporter says FCC security pinned him to a wall. *New York Times*.

Meyer, D. (2017, May 5). Verizon and AT&T exit from cloud business applauded by analysts. *SDX Central*. Retrieved from https://www.sdxcentral.com/articles/news/verizon-and-att-exit-from-cloud-business-applauded-by-analysts/2017/05.

Mezzandra, S. (2010). Introduction. In A. Fumagalli & S. Mezzandra (Eds.), *Crisis in the global economy: Financial markets, social struggles, and new political scenarios* (pp. 7–16). Los Angeles: Semiotext(e).

MHCRC. (1998a). *Meeting minutes of Mt. Hood Cable Regulatory Commission meeting, 14 December*. Portland, OR: Mt. Hood Cable Regulatory Commission. On file with author.

MHCRC. (1998b). *Meeting minutes of Mt. Hood Cable Regulatory Commission meeting, November 14, 1998, approved as corrected*. Portland, OR: Mt. Hood Cable Regulatory Commission. On file with author.

MHCRC. (1998c). *Minutes for public hearing regarding proposed TCI ownership transfer to AT&T, October 19, 1998*. Portland, OR: Mt. Hood Cable Regulatory Commission. On file with author.

MHCRC. (1999). *Ex Parte Comments of Mt. Hood Cable Regulatory Commission In the Matter of Joint Application of AT&T Corporation and Tele-Communicaitions, Inc. For Approval of Transfer of Control of Commission Licenses and Authorizations, Federal Communications Commission CS Docket 98-178*. Retrieved from https://ecfsapi.fcc.gov/file/6006241703.pdf.

Microsoft, AOL pitch cable. (2000, May 15). *Television Digest*.

Mirowski, P. (1989). *More heat than light: Economics as social physics, physics as nature's economics*. New York: Cambridge University Press.

Mirowski, P. (2004). *The effortless economy of science?* Durham, NC: Duke University Press.

Mirowski, P. (2009). Postface: Defining neoliberalism. In P. Mirowski & D. Plehwe (Eds.), *The road from Mont Pèlerin: The making of the neoliberal thought collective* (pp. 417–455). Cambridge, MA: Harvard University Press.

Mirowski, P. (2013). *Never let a serious crisis go to waste: How neoliberalism survived the financial meltdown*. New York: Verso.

Mirowski, P., & Nik-Khah, E. (2007). Markets made flesh: Performativity, and a problem in science studies,augmented with consideration of the FCC auctions. In D. MacKenzie, F. Muniesa, & L. Siu (Eds.), *Do economists make markets? On the performativity of economics* (pp. 1–19). Princeton, NJ: Princeton University Press.

Mirowski, P., & Plehwe, D. (Eds.). (2009). *The road from Mont Pèlerin: The making of the neoliberal thought collective*. Cambridge, MA: Harvard University Press.

Mirowski, P., & Sent, E.-M. (2002). Introduction. In P. Mirowski & E.-M. Sent (Eds.), *Science bought and sold: Essays in the economics of science* (pp. 1–68). Chicago: University of Chicago Press.

Morozov, E. (2019). Capitalism's new clothes. *The Baffler*. Retrieved from https://thebaffler.com/latest/capitalisms-new-clothes-morozov.

Mosco, V. (2014). *To the cloud: Big data in a turbulent world*. Boulder, CO: Paradigm Publishers.

Mosco, V. (2017). *Becoming digital: Toward a post-Internet society*. Bingley, UK: Emerald Publishing.

Mueller, M. (1997). Telecommunications access in the age of electronic commerce: Toward a third-generation universal service policy. *Federal Communications Law Journal, 49*(3), 655–673.

Mueller, M. (1999). Universal service policies as wealth redistribution. *Government Information Quarterly, 16*(4), 353.

Mueller, M. (2002). *Ruling the root: Internet governance and the taming of cyberspace.* Cambridge, MA: MIT Press.

Mueller, M. (2010). *Networks and states: The global politics of Internet governance.* Cambridge, MA: MIT Press.

Mueller, M., Jr. (1997). *Universal service: Competition, interconnection and monopoly in the making of the American telephone system.* Cambridge, MA: MIT Press.

Mullin, B. (2018). AT&T in talks for digital ad firm—Telecom giant is expected to pay about $1.6 billion to acquire AppNexus. *Wall Street Journal.*

Mullins, B., & Nicas, J. (2017, July 14). Paying professors: Inside Google's academic influence campaign. *Wall Street Journal.* Retrieved from https://www.wsj.com/articles/paying-professors-inside-googles-academic-influence-campaign-1499785286.

Munir, K. (2000). *Written statement of Khalil Munir, Executive Director of the Telecommunications Advocacy Project before the Federal Communications Commission Public Forum on AT&T/MediaOne Proposed Merger (CS Docket 99-251), February 4, 2000.* Washington, DC. Retrieved from https://ecfsapi.fcc.gov/file/6010953519.pdf.

Munson, B. (2018, July 9). AT&T's advertising behemoth is coming for Facebook and Google. *FierceCable.*

Muris, T. J., & Nuechterlein, J. E. (2018). *Antitrust in the Internet era: The legacy of United States v. A&P.* George Mason Law & Economics Research Paper No. 18-15. Retrieved from https://papers.ssrn.com/sol3/papers.cfm?abstract_id=3186569.

Nagesh, G., & Mullins, B. (2015, February 5). Blindsided: How White House thwarted FCC chief on net rules. *Wall Street Journal,* p. A1. Retrieved from https://www.wsj.com/articles/how-white-house-thwarted-fcc-chief-on-internet-rules-1423097522.

Napoli, P., & Seaton, M. (2007). Necessary knowledge for communications policy: Information asymmetries and commercial data access and usage in the policymaking process. *Federal Communications Law Journal, 59*(2), 295–330.

Napoli, P. M. (2001). *Foundations of communications policy: Principles and process in the regulation of electronic media.* Cresskill, NJ: Hampton Press.

Napoli, P. M., & Friedland, L. (2016). US communications policy research and the integration of the administrative and critical communication research traditions. *Journal of Information Policy, 6,* 41–65.

Nasdaq. (2017, March 14). *Announcing NYIAX, the world's first advertising contract exchange* [press release]. Retrieved from http://ir.nasdaq.com/releasedetail.cfm?releaseid=1017259.

National Cable & Telecommunications Assn. v. Brand X Internet Services, 545 U.S. 967 (2005).

Negri, A. (2008). *Goodbye, Mr. Socialism.* New York: Seven Stories Press.

Ness, S. (1998). *In the matters of deployment of wireline services offering advanced telecommunications capability (CC Docket No. 98-147), Petitions of Bell Atlantic Corporation, US West, and Ameritech for relief from barriers to deployment of advanced telecommunications services (CC Docket 98-11, CC Docket 98-26, CC Docket 98-32), Petition of the Alliance for Public Technology requesting issuance of notice of inquiry and notice of proposed rulemaking to implement Section 706 of the Telecommunications Act (CCB/CPD No. 98015 RM 9244), Petition of the Association for Local Telecommunications Services (ALTS) for a declaratory ruling establishing conditions necessary to promote deployment of advanced telecommunications capability under Section 706 of the Telecommunications Act of 1996 (CC Docket No. 98-78), Southwestern Bell Telephone Company, Pacific Bell, and Nevada Bell petition for relief from fregulation pursuant to Section 706 of the Telecommunications Act of 1996 and 47 U.S.C. § 160 for ADSL infrastructure and service (CC Docket No. 98-81).* Washington, DC: Federal Communications Commission.

Net neutrality and free speech on the Internet. (2008). House of Representatives Committee on the Judiciary Task force on Competition Policy and Antitrust Laws, 110th Congress, 2nd Sess.

Neubauer, R. (2011). Neoliberalism in the information age, or vice versa? Global citizenship, technology and hegemonic ideology. *tripleC, 9*(2), 196–230.

Newman, L. H. (2018). Australia's encryption-busting law could impact global privacy. *Wired.* Retrieved from https://www.wired.com/story/australia-encryption-law-global-impact/.

Newman, R. (2009). *COMPASS: An Assessment.* Evaluation for the Ford Foundation. Washington, DC.

News. (1999, October 22). *Broadband in the Public Interest, 1*(2). Retrieved from http://web.archive.org/web/20000816033647/http://www.nogatekeepers.org/newsletter/940623392.shtml.

News. (2000a, January 7). *Broadband in the Public Interest, 1*(6). Retrieved from https://web.archive.org/web/20000816033623/http://www.nogatekeepers.org/newsletter/947263717.shtml.

News. (2000b, February 10). *Broadband in the Public Interest, 1*(7). Retrieved from https://web.archive.org/web/20000815073407/http://www.nogatekeepers.org/newsletter/950207389.shtml.

Newton, C. (2019). Europe is splitting the internet into three. *The Verge.* Retrieved from https://www.theverge.com/2019/3/27/18283541/european-union-copyright-directive-internet-article-13.

Nik-Khah, E. (2005). *Designs on the mechanism: Economics and the FCC spectrum auctions.* PhD dissertation, University of Notre Dame.

Noam, E. (1994). Beyond liberalization II: The impending doom of common carriage. *Telecommunications Policy, 18*(6), 435–452.

Noam, E. (2006, August 29). A third way for net neutrality. *Financial Times.*

NoGatekeepers.org. (2000a). About us. Retrieved from http://web.archive.org/web/20000815073241/http://www.nogatekeepers.org/about.

NoGatekeepers.org (Producer). (2000b). Past headlines and document archives. Retrieved from http://web.archive.org/web/20000815073241/http://www.nogatekeepers.org/archive.

Novet, J. (2017). Google will invest in AI startups and send its engineers to help them out for up to a year. Retrieved from https://finance.yahoo.com/news/google-steps-ai-investments-venture-190000968.html.

Novet, J. (2019, April 22). Apple spends more than $30 million on Amazon's cloud every month, making it one of the biggest AWS customers. *CNBC.com.* Retrieved from https://www.cnbc.com/2019/04/22/apple-spends-more-than-30-million-on-amazon-web-services-a-month.html.

Nuechterlein, J. E. (2009). Antitrust oversight of an antitrust dispute: An institutional perspective on the net neutrality debate. *Journal on Telecommunications and High Technology Law, 7*, 20–66.

Nuechterlein, J. E., & Weiser, P. J. (2005). *Digital crossroads.* Cambridge, MA: MIT Press.

O'Connell, P. (2005, November 7). Online extra: At SBC, it's all about "scale and scope." *Bloomberg Businessweek.* Retrieved from http://www.bloomberg.com/news/articles/2005-11-06/online-extra-at-sbc-its-all-about-scale-and-scope.

Ojeda-Zapata, J. (1998, August 5). Local Internet providers cry foul over new US West lines. *Saint Paul Pioneer Press.*

O'Neil, C. (2016). *Weapons of math destruction: How big data increases inequality and threatens democracy.* New York: Crown.

Open access: A threat to investment or vested interests? (1999, October 22). *Broadband In the Public Interest, 1*(2). Retrieved from http://web.archive.org/web/20000816033647/http://www.nogatekeepers.org/newsletter/940623392.shtml.

Open access advocates suffer reverses in Va. and Mass. (2000, May 8). *Warren's Cable Regulation Monitor.*

Open access setbacks in Plymouth Township, Seattle, Richmond, Dearborn. (1999, November 19). *Broadband in the Public Interest, 1*(4). Retrieved from http://web

.archive.org/web/20000816033633/http://www.nogatekeepers.org/newsletter/943041241.shtml.

Open access suit filed. (1999, November 15). *Television Digest.*

Open bridges to cyberspace: FCC should insist that the public's access to the Internet not be restricted or monopolized by an AT&T-TCI merger [Editorial]. (1998, December 14). *The Oregonian.*

Open Internet Coalition. (2010). *Comments of the Open Internet Coalition in the matter of Preserving the Open Internet, GN Docket No. 09-191, Broadband Industry Practices, WC Docket No. 07-52, and Further Inquiry into Two Under-Developed Issues in the Open Internet Proceeding, DA 10-1667.* Retrieved from https://www.ccianet.org/wp-content/uploads/library/OIC%20NN%20Comments%20in%20Response%20to%20DA%2010-1667%2010-12-10%20FINAL.pdf.

OpenNET Coalition welcomes AT&T acceptance of Open Access "in principle"; Questions delay and uncertainty of implementation. (1999, December 6). *Business Wire.*

Open Technology Institute. (2014). *Beyond frustrated: The sweeping consumer harms as a result of ISP disputes.* White paper. Retrieved from https://na-production.s3.amazonaws.com/documents/Beyond_Frustrated.pdf.

Orcutt, M. (2016, August 19). Three big questions hanging over net neutrality. *Technologyreview.com.* Retrieved from https://www.technologyreview.com/s/602182/three-big-questions-hanging-over-net-neutrality.

Oreskes, N., & Conway, E. M. (2010). *Merchants of doubt.* New York: Bloomsbury Press.

O'Rielly, M. (2016a). *Dissenting statement of Commissioner Michael O'Rielly, in Notice of Proposed Rulemaking in the matter of Protecting the Privacy of Customers of Broadband and Other Telecommunications Services, WC Docket No. 16-106.* Washington, DC: Federal Communications Commission.

O'Rielly, M. (2016b). *Dissent of Commissioner Michael O'Rielly, in Report and Order in the matter of Protecting the Privacy of Customers of Broadband and Other Telecommunications Services, WC Docket No. 16-106.* Washington, DC: Federal Communications Commission.

O'Rielly, L., & Stevens, L. (2018, November 27). Amazon, with little fanfare, emerges as an advertising giant. *Wall Street Journal.* Retrieved from https://www.wsj.com/articles/amazon-with-little-fanfare-emerges-as-an-advertising-giant-1543248561.

Owen, B. (2007, Fall). Antecedents to net neutrality. *Regulation,* 14–17.

Oxman, J. (1999). *The FCC and the unregulation of the Internet.* Working Paper No. 31. Washington, DC: Office of Plans and Policy, Federal Communications Commission. Retrieved from https://transition.fcc.gov/Bureaus/OPP/working_papers/oppwp31.pdf.

Oyedele, A. (2016). CenturyLink is buying Level 3 Communications for $34 billion. *Business Insider*. Retrieved from http://www.businessinsider.com/centurylink-buys-level-3-communications-2016-10.

Pai, A. (2014). *Dissenting statement of Commissioner Ajit Pai, in Notice of Proposed Rulemaking In the Matter of Protecting and Promoting the Open Internet, GN Docket No. 14-28*. Washington, DC: Federal Communications Commission.

Pai, A. (2016a). *Dissenting statement of Commissioner Ajit Pai, in Notice of Proposed Rulemaking in the matter of Protecting the Privacy of Customers of Broadband and Other Telecommunications Services, WC Docket No. 16-106*. Washington, DC: Federal Communications Commission.

Pai, A. (2016b). *Dissent of Commissioner Ajit Pai, in Report and Order in the matter of Protecting the Privacy of Customers of Broadband and Other Telecommunications Services, WC Docket No. 16-106*. Washington, DC: Federal Communications Commission.

Pai, A. (2017a). *Remarks of FCC Chairman Ajit Pai at the Hudson Institute: The importance of economic analysis at the FCC*. Washington, DC: Federal Communications Commission. Retrieved from https://apps.fcc.gov/edocs_public/attachmatch/DOC-344248A1.pdf.

Pai, A. (2017b). *Remarks of FCC Chairman Ajit Pai at the Newseum, "The future of Internet freedom."* Washington, DC: Federal Communications Commission. Retrieved from https://transition.fcc.gov/Daily_Releases/Daily_Business/2017/db0427/DOC-344590A1.pdf.

Pasquale, F. (2015). *The black box society*. Cambridge, MA: Harvard University Press.

Peck, J. (2010). *Constructions of neoliberal reason*. New York: Oxford University Press.

Peha, J. M. (2007). The benefits and risks of mandating network neutrality, and the quest for a balanced policy. *International Journal of Communication, 1*. Retrieved from http://ijoc.org/ojs/index.php/ijoc/article/view/154.

Peha, J. M., Lehr, W. H., & Wilkie, S. (2007). Introduction: The state of the debate on network neutrality. *International Journal of Communication*. Retrieved from http://ijoc.org/ojs/index.php/ijoc/article/view/192/100.

Phillips, E. E. (2018, October 8). Alexa heads to the warehouse. *Wall Street Journal*. Retrieved from https://www.wsj.com/articles/alexa-heads-to-the-warehouse-1539000126.

Phillips-Fein, K. (2009a). Business conservatives and the Mont Pèlerin Society. In P. Mirowski & D. Plehwe (Eds.), *The road from Mont Pèlerin: The making of the neoliberal thought Collective* (pp. 280–301). Cambridge, MA: Harvard University Press.

Phillips-Fein, K. (2009b). *Invisible hands: The businessmen's crusade against the New Deal*. New York: Norton.

Pickard, V. (2010). "Whether the giants should be slain or persuaded to be good": Revisiting the Hutchins Commission and the role of media in a democratic society. *Critical Studies in Media Communication, 27*(4), 391–411.

Pickard, V. (2011). The battle over the FCC Blue Book: Determining the role of broadcast media in a democratic society, 1945–8. *Media, Culture & Society, 33*, 171.

Pickard, V. (2014). *America's battle for media democracy: The triumph of corporate libertarianism and the future of media reform*. New York: Cambridge University Press.

Pickard, V., & Berman, D. E. (2019). *After net neutrality: A new deal for the digital age*. New Haven, CT: Yale University Press.

Pickard, V., & Popiel, P. (2018). *The media democracy agenda: The strategy and legacy of FCC commissioner Michael J. Copps*. Evanston, IL: Benton Foundation.

Picket, K. (2015, February 23). Obama's move to reguate Internet has activists' 'fingerprints all over it'. *Dailycaller.com*. Retrieved from http://dailycaller.com/2015/02/23/obamas-move-to-regulate-internet-has-activists-fingerprints-all-over-it.

Picot, A., & Krcmar, H. (2011, May). Interview with Marvin Ammori and Christof Weinhardt on "Network neutrality and the future of telecommunication." *Business & Information Systems Engineering*.

Plehwe, D. (2009). Introduction. In P. Mirowski & D. Plehwe (Eds.), *The road from Mont Pèlerin: The making of the neoliberal thought collective* (pp. 1–42). Cambridge, MA: Harvard University Press.

Pool, I. d. S. (1983). *Technologies of freedom: On free speech in a digital age*. Cambridge, MA: Belknap Press of Harvard University Press.

Portland drafts omnibus franchise. (2000, July 10). *Television Digest*.

Powell, A., & Cooper, A. (2011). Net neutrality discourses: Comparing advocacy and regulatory arguments in the United States and the United Kingdom. *The Information Society: An International Journal, 27*(5), 311–325.

Powell, M. K. (1998). *Separate statement of Commissioner Michael K. Powell in the matters of deployment of wireline services offering advanced telecommunications capability (CC Docket No. 98-147), Petitions of Bell Atlantic Corporation, US West, and Ameritech for relief from barriers to deployment of advanced telecommunications services (CC Docket 98-11, CC Docket 98-26, CC Docket 98-32), Petition of the Alliance for Public Technology requesting issuance of notice of inquiry and notice of proposed rulemaking to implement Section 706 of the Telecommunications Act (CCB/CPD No. 98015 RM 9244), Petition of the Association for Local Telecommunications Services (ALTS) for a declaratory ruling establishing conditions necessary to promote deployment of advanced telecommunications capability under Section 706 of the Telecommunications Act of 1996 (CC Docket No. 98-78), Southwestern Bell Telephone Company, Pacific Bell, and Nevada Bell petition for relief from fregulation pursuant to Section 706 of the Telecommunications Act of 1996 and 47 U.S.C. § 160 for ADSL infrastructure and service (CC Docket No. 98-81)*. Washington, DC: Federal Communications Commission.

Powell, M. K. (2000). *Concurring Statement of Commissioner Michael K. Powell In the Matter of Applications for Consent to the Transfer of Control of Licenses and Section 214 Authorizations from MediaOne Group, Inc., Transferor To AT&T Corp., Transferee, CS Docket No. 99-251*. Washington, DC: Federal Communications Commission.

Powell, M. K. (2001). *Statement of Commissioner Michael K. Powell, concurring in part and dissenting in part in the matter of applications for consent to the transfer of control of licenses and Section 214 authorizations by Time Warner Inc. and America Online, Inc., transferors, to AOL Time Warner Inc., transferee, CS Docket No. 00-30*. Washington, DC: Federal Communications Commission.

Powell, M. K. (2004). *Preserving Internet freedom: Guiding principles for the industry*. Paper presented at the Silicon Flatirons Symposium on "The Digital Broadband Migration: Toward a Regulatory Regime for the Internet Age," University of Colorado School of Law, Boulder, CO.

Powers, S. M., & Jablonski, M. (2015). *The real cyber war*. Urbana: University of Illinois Press.

Progress and Freedom Foundation. (2006). *Digital Age Communications Act: Report from the Working Group on Institutional Reform*. White paper. Washington, DC. Retrieved from http://www.pff.org/issues-pubs/books/061114dacainstitutionalreform1.0.pdf.

Results International. (n.d.). Number of mergers and acquisitions in the marketing technology sector worldwide from 1st quarter 2013 to 2nd quarter 2018. *Statista—The Statistics Portal*. Retrieved October 21, 2018, from https://www-statista-com.proxy.emerson.edu/statistics/655247/marketing-technology-mergers-aquisitions.

Rhinesmith, C. (2017). Digital inclusion and meaningful broadband adoption initiatives. Retrieved from https://www.benton.org/inclusion-adoption-report.

Rice, A. (2018). This is Ajit Pai, nemesis of net neutrality. *Wired*. Retrieved from https://www.wired.com/story/ajit-pai-man-who-killed-net-neutrality/.

Riley, M. C., & Scott, B. (2009). Deep packet inspection: The end of the Internet as we know it? Retrieved from https://www.freepress.net/sites/default/files/legacy-policy/Deep_Packet_Inspection_The_End_of_the_Internet_As_We_Know_It.pdf.

Rogoway, M. (1999, April 22). TCI fights order to open access to Portland. *The Columbian*, p. C2.

Rogoway, M. (2012, June 6). David Olson's exit closes a chapter in Portland's crusade against cable industry. *The Oregonian*. Retrieved from http://www.oregonlive.com/silicon-forest/index.ssf/2012/06/david_olsons_exit_closes_a_cha.html.

Romm, T. (2015, February 23). Net neutrality: A lobbying bonanza. *Politico*. Retrieved from https://www.politico.com/story/2015/02/net-neutrality-a-lobbying-bonanza-115385.

Rorty, J. (2004). The business nobody knows. In R. W. McChesney & B. Scott (Eds.), *Our unfree press: 100 years of radical media criticism* (pp. 132–137). New York: New Press.

Rosenberg, E. (2017, November 22). Investigation of fake net neutrality comments stymied by FCC, NY attorney general says. *Chicago Tribune*. Retrieved from http://www.chicagotribune.com/news/nationworld/politics/ct-fake-net-neutrality-foes-fcc-20171122-story.html.

Rosenworcel, J. (2017). *Dissenting Statement of Commissioner Jessica Rosenworcel Re:Declaratory Ruling, Report and Order, and Order, WC Docket 17-108, In the Matter of Restoring Internet Freedom*. Washington, DC: Federal Communications Commission. Retrieved from https://apps.fcc.gov/edocs_public/attachmatch/DOC-347927A1.pdf.

Ross, P. (1999, December 22). Internet over leased access subject of last-min. rescue attempt. *Communications Daily*.

Rossiter, N. (2016). *Software, infrastructure, labor: A media theory of logistical nightmares*. New York: Routledge.

Ruggie, J. G. (1982). International regimes, transactions, and change: Embedded liberalism in the postwar economic order. *International Organization, 36*(2), 379–415.

Sadowski, J., & Pasquale, F. (2015). The spectrum of control: A social theory of the smart city. *First Monday*. Retrieved from http://firstmonday.org/ojs/index.php/fm/article/view/5903/4660.

Saltzer, J. H. (1999). *"Open access" is just the tip of the iceberg*. Retrieved from http://web.mit.edu/Saltzer/www/publications/openaccess.html.

Sandvig, C. (2006). The structural problems of the Internet for cultural policy. In D. Silver & A. Massanari (Eds.), *Critical cyberculture studies* (pp. 107–118). New York: New York University Press.

Sandvig, C. (2007). Net neutrality is the new common carriage. *Info, 9*(2/3), 136–147.

San Francisco delays cable open access vote, Broward County sued. (1999, August 2). *Warren's Cable Regulation Monitor*.

Sassen, S. (2006). *Territory, authority, rights*. Princeton, NJ: Princeton University Press.

Scheer, R. (2015). *They know everything about you: How data-collecting corporations and snooping government agencies are destroying democracy*. New York: Nation Books.

Schiller, D. (2000). *Digital capitalism: Networking the global market system*. Cambridge, MA: MIT Press.

Schiller, D. (2007a). The hidden history of US public service telecommunications, 1919–1956. *Info, 9*(2/3), 17–28.

Schiller, D. (2007b). *How to think about information*. Urbana: University of Illinois Press.

Schiller, D. (2007c). Making public-service telecommunications: past and present challenges for networked information infrastructures. *Info, 9*(2/3), 3–5.

Schiller, D. (2014). *Digital depression: Information technology and economic crisis*. Urbana: University of Illinois Press.

Scholz, T. (Ed.). (2012). *Digital labor: The internet as playground and factory*. New York: Routledge.

Schön, D. A., & Rein, M. (1994). *Frame reflection: Toward the resolution of intractable policy controversies*. New York: Basic Books.

Schwartzman, A. (1999). *Letter to Chairman William E. Kennard, December 6, 1999*. Retrieved from http://web.archive.org/web/20000816033804/http://www.nogatekeepers.org/archive/944500938.shtml.

Schwartzman, A. (2000). *Statement of Andrew Jay Schwartzman, Submitted to the Federal Communications Commission (Public Forum February 4, 2000) Re: AT&T/MediaOne Merger, Docket 99-251*. Washington, DC.

Seetharaman, D. (2018, October 8). Facebook launches portal video-chat devices for the home. *Wall Street Journal*.

Selyukh, A. (2014, May 8). U.S. "net neutrality" plan faces heat from venture capitalists. *Reuters*. Retrieved from https://www.reuters.com/article/us-usa-internet-fcc/u-s-net-neutrality-plan-faces-heat-from-venture-capitalists-idUSBREA4711820140508.

Shore, C. (2012). Anthropology and public policy. In R. Fardon, O. Harris, T. H. J. Marchand, C. Shore, V. Strang, R. Wilson, & M. Nuttall (Eds.), *The SAGE Handbook of Social Anthropology* (pp. 89–104). Los Angeles: SAGE.

Sidak, J. G. (2006). A consumer-welfare approach to network neutrality regulation of the Internet. *Journal of Competition Law and Economics, 2*(3), 349–474.

Sidak, J. G., & Teece, D. J. (2010). Innovation spillovers and the "dirt road" fallacy: The intellectual bankruptcy of banning operational transactions for enhanced delivery over the Internet. *Journal of Competition Law and Economics, 6*(3), 521–594.

Singel, R. (2018). *Filtering out the bots: What Americans actually told the FCC about net neutrality repeal*. White paper. Stanford University, Center for Internet and Society. Retrieved from https://cyberlaw.stanford.edu/files/blogs/FilteringOutTheBotsUnique2017NetNeutralityComments.pdf.

Sloss, B. T. (2018). Expanding our global infrastructure with new regions and subsea cables. *Google blog.* Retrieved from https://www.blog.google/products/google-cloud/expanding-our-global-infrastructure-new-regions-and-subsea-cables/.

Smythe, D. (2014). Communications: Blindspot of Western Marxism. In L. McGuigan & V. Manzerole (Eds.), *The audience commodity in a digital age: Revisiting a critical theory of commercial media* (pp. 29–54). New York: Peter Lang.

Sohn, G. (2017). How to write an impactful net neutrality comment (which you should definitely do). *Mashable.com.* Retrieved from https://mashable.com/2017/06/15/how-to-write-a-good-fcc-comment/.

Special feature: Interview with Chris Grace. (1999, October 22). *Broadband In the Public Interest, 1*(2). Retrieved from http://web.archive.org/web/20000816033647/http://www.nogatekeepers.org/newsletter/940623392.shtml.

Sridhar, A. (2010, March 8). *The truth about the third way: Separating fact from fiction in the FCC reclassification debate.* Free Press white paper. Retrieved from https://www.freepress.net/sites/default/files/legacy-policy/The_Truth_About_the_Third_Way.pdf.

Srnicek, N. (2017). *Platform capitalism.* Malden, MA: Polity Press.

Starr, P. (2004). *The creation of the media.* New York: Basic Books.

State and local actions. (2000, January 31). *Warren's Cable Regulation Monitor.*

State's largest car dealer launches web superstore. (2000, January 28). *Capital Times,* p. 1E.

Steiner, Y. (2009). The neoliberals confront the trade unions. In P. Mirowski & D. Plehwe (Eds.), *The road from Mont Pèlerin: The making of the neoliberal thought collective* (pp. 181–203). Cambridge, MA: Harvard University Press.

Stephens, H. (2000, November 20). Access forum breaks out at D.C. hearing *Multichannel News,* p. 32.

Stills, L. (2006). CBC Monitor Report: Rep. Bobby Rush, AT&T's million dollar man. *BlackCommentator.com.* Retrieved from http://www.blackcommentator.com/181/181_cbc_monitor_bobby_rush.html.

Streeter, T. (1996). *Selling the air: A critique of the policy of commercial broadcasting in the United States.* Chicago: University of Chicago Press.

Streeter, T. (2011). *The net effect: Romanticism, capitalism, and the Internet.* New York: New York University Press.

Streitfeld, D. (2018, September 7). Amazon's antitrust antagonist has a breakthrough idea. *New York Times.* Retrieved from https://www.nytimes.com/2018/09/07/technology/monopoly-antitrust-lina-khan-amazon.html.

Stucke, M. E., & Grunes, A. P. (2016). *Big data and competition policy*. New York: Oxford University Press.

Sum, N.-L., & Jessop, B. (2003). On pre- and post-disciplinarity in (cultural) political economy. *Economies et sociétés, 37*(6). Retrieved from http://eprints.lancs.ac.uk/229/01/E-2003c_sum-jessop2003.pdf.

Sundararajan, A. (2016). *The sharing economy: The end of employment and the rise of crowd-based capitalism*. Cambridge, MA: MIT Press.

Svrluga, S. (2019, March 21). Trump signs executive order on free speech on college campuses. *Washington Post*. Retrieved from https://www.washingtonpost.com/education/2019/03/21/trump-expected-sign-executive-order-free-speech/?noredirect=on&utm_term=.d87879ebcf7f.

Swanson, D. (2005, July 16). How Comcast censors political content: Or why my Comcast horror story is better than yours. *Afterdowningstreet.org*. On file with author.

Tady, M. (2010). Free Press ad warns against industry takeover of open Internet. *FreePress.net*. Retrieved from http://conference.freepress.net/blog/10/06/23/free-press-ad-warns-against-industry-takeover-open-internet.

Taylor, K. (1997, November 3). Future DSL deployers are waiting on the carriers. *Network World*.

Tedesco, R. (1998, December 14). Disney, Infoseek give green light. *Broadcasting & Cable*.

Telecommunications Act of 1996. 47 U.S.C. 12 §1302 (a) Stat. (1996).

Terranova, T. (2000). Free labor: Producing culture for the digital economy. *Social Text, 18*(2), 33–58.

Terranova, T. (2012). Free labor. In T. Scholz (Ed.), *Digital labor: The internet as playground and factory* (pp. 33–57). New York: Routledge.

Thierer, A. (2005). Are "dumb pipe" mandates smart public policy? Vertical integration, net neutrality, and the network layers model. *Journal of Telecommunications & High Technology Law, 3*, 275–308.

Thompson, M. W. (2001). *Concurring statement of Commissioner Mozelle W. Thompson in the matter of America Online, Inc. and Time Warner Inc., Docket No. C-3989*. Washington, DC: Federal Trade Commission.

Tongia, R., & Wilson, E. J. I. (2011). The flip side of Metcalfe's Law: Multiple and growing costs of network exclusion. *International Journal of Communication, 5*, 665–681.

Toonkel, J. (2019). Inside AT&T's effort to revolutionize TV advertising. *The Information*. Retrieved from https://www.theinformation.com/articles/inside-at-ts-effort-to-revolutionize-tv-advertising?

Torres, J. (2017, May 12). Voices for Internet Freedom in L.A.'s Skid Row lifts up community voices. *FreePress.net*. Retrieved from http://conference.freepress.net/blog/2017/05/12/voices-internet-freedom-forum-las-skid-row-lifts-community-voices.

Torres, J., & Cyril, M. (2017, March 16). The resistance must be digitized. *FreePress.net*. Retrieved from http://conference.freepress.net/blog/2017/03/16/resistance-must-be-digitized.

Tribe, K. (2009). Liberalism and neoliberalism in Britain, 1930–1980. In P. Mirowski & D. Plehwe (Eds.), *The Road from Mont Pèlerin: The making of the neoliberal thought collective* (pp. 68–97). Cambridge, MA: Harvard University Press.

Tristani, G. (1999). *Separate Statement of Commissioner Gloria Tristani, Dissenting in Part, In the Matter of Applications for the Consent to the Transfer of Control of Licenses and Section 214 Authorizations from Tele-Communications, Inc., Transferor To AT&T Corp., Transferee, Memorandum Opinion and Order, CS Docket No. 98-178*. Washington, DC: Federal Communications Commission.

Tristani, G. (2000). *Concurring statement of Commissioner Gloria Tristani, In the Matter of Applications for Consent to the Transfer of Control of Licenses and Section 214 Authorizations from MediaOne Group, Inc., Transferor To AT&T Corp., Transferee, CS Docket No. 99-251*. Washington, DC: Federal Communications Commission.

Turner, S. D. (2006). *Broadband reality check II: The truth behind America's digital decline*. Free Press white paper. Retrieved from http://conference.freepress.net/sites/default/files/fp-legacy/bbrc2-final.pdf.

Turner, S. D. (2016, December). *Digital denied*. Free Press white paper. Retrieved from http://www.freepress.net/sites/default/files/resources/digital_denied_free_press_report_december_2016.pdf.

Turner, S. D. (2017). *It's working: How the Internet access and online video markets are thriving in a Title II era*. Free Press white paper. Retrieved from https://www.freepress.net/sites/default/files/resources/internet-access-and-online-video-markets-are-thriving-in-title-II-era.pdf.

Turner, S. D. (2019). Tall tales and Title II. *FreePress.net*. Retrieved from https://www.freepress.net/our-response/expert-analysis/insights-opinions/tall-tales-and-title-ii.

Turow, J. (2011). *The daily you: How the advertising industry is defining your identity and your worth*. New Haven, CT: Yale University Press.

Turow, J. (2017). *The aisles have eyes: How retailers track your shopping, strip your privacy, and define your power*. New Haven, CT: Yale University Press.

Turow, J., McGuigan, L., & Maris, E. R. (2015). Making data mining a natural part of life: Physical retailing, customer surveillance and the 21st century imaginary. *European Journal of Cultural Studies, 18*(4), 464–478.

United States Telecom Association v. Federal Communications Commission and United States of America, No. 15-1063 et al. (D.C. Circuit, 2016).

United States Telecom Association v. Federal Communications Commission and United States of America, On Petitions for Rehearing En Banc [Dissenting statement of Judge Kavanaugh], No. 15-1063 et al. (D.C. Circuit, 2017).

Utah law raises open access questions. (1999, November 19). *Broadband in the Public Interest, 1*(4). Retrieved from http://web.archive.org/web/20000816033633/http://www.nogatekeepers.org/newsletter/943041241.shtml.

Vaidhyanathan, S. (2011). *The Googlization of everything (and why we should worry).* Berkeley: University of California Press.

Vaidhyanathan, S. (2018). *Anti-social media: How Facebook disconnects us and undermines democracy*. New York: Oxford University Press.

Van Horn, R., & Mirowski, P. (2009). The rise of the Chicago School of Economics and the birth of neoliberalism. In P. Mirowski & D. Plehwe (Eds.), *The road from Mont Pèlerin: The making of the neoliberal thought collective* (pp. 139–178). Cambridge, MA: Harvard University Press.

van Schewick, B. (2007). *Towards an economic framework for network neutrality regulation.* Paper presented at the 33rd Research Conference on Communication, Information and Internet Policy (TPRC 2005), National Center for Technology and Law, George Mason University School of Law, Arlington, VA.

van Schewick, B. (2010). *Internet architecture and innovation.* Cambridge, MA: MIT Press.

van Schewick, B. (2015). Network neutrality and quality of service: What a nondiscrimination rule should look like. *Stanford Law Review, 67*(1), 1–166.

Verizon. (2017). *State of the market: Internet of things 2017: Making way for the enterprise.* Retrieved from https://www.verizon.com/about/sites/default/files/Verizon-2017-State-of-the-Market-IoT-Report.pdf.

Verizon. (2018). *Giving people the ability to do more: 2017 Annual report.* Retrieved from https://www.verizon.com/about/sites/default/files/annual_reports/2017/index.html.

Verizon layoffs indicate a wise shift in focus. (2019, February 2). *ICT Monitor Worldwide.*

Verizon looking to bundle third-party OTT video with 5G rollout. (2018, November 22). *ICT Monitor Worldwide.*

Verizon Media and Microsoft expand global native advertising partnership. (2019, January 4). *ICT Monitor Worldwide.*

Verizon's next-gen services are poised for growth. (2018, August 7). *ICT Monitor Worldwide*.

Verizon v. FCC, F.3d 623 (D.C. Circuit, 2014).

Vogel, K. P. (2017, August 30). Google critic ousted from think tank funded by the tech giant. *New York Times*. Retrieved from https://www.nytimes.com/2017/08/30/us/politics/eric-schmidt-google-new-america.html.

Wedel, J. R., Shore, C., Feldman, G., & Lathrop, S. (2005). Toward an anthropology of public policy. *Annals of the American Academy of Political and Social Science, 600*, 30–51.

Weiser, P. J. (2009). Institutional design, FCC reform and the hidden side of the administrative state. *Administrative Law Review, 61*, 675–722.

Wholesale broadband access via cable, Paper as approved by the ERG12-Plenary on 11 Febr. 2005 for public consultation. (2005). Retrieved from https://berec.europa.eu/doc/publications/consult_add_cable_netw_chapter/erg0419rev1_wholesale_broadband_access_via_cable.pdf.

Williams, R. (1977). *Marxism and literature*. Oxford: Oxford University Press.

Wilson, H. (Producer). (2014, December 2). Update on FFTF and the net neutrality fight. [Email communication].

Wilson, J. Q. (1978). Social sciences and public policy: A personal note. In L. E. J. Lynn (Ed.), *Knowledge and policy: The uncertain connection* (pp. 82–92). Washington, DC: National Academy of Sciences.

Winseck, D. (2017, July 11). "Curious and curiouser: As economists' anti–common carriage (#NetNeutrality)/FCC case crumbles, industryadvocacy group lawyers threaten Armageddon." *Mediamorphis* (blog). Retrieved from https://dwmw.wordpress.com/2017/07/11/curious-and-curiouser-as-economists-anti-common-carriage-netneutrality-cases-collapse-lawyers-threaten-journal-university-of-southern-california-and-indy-academics/.

Winseck, D., & Pooley, J. D. (2017). A curious tale of economics and common carriage (net neutrality) at the FCC: A reply to Faulhaber, Singer and Urschel. *International Journal of Communication, 11*, 2702–2733.

Winship, M. (2017). Former commish Michael Copps: "Maybe the worst FCC I've ever seen." *Moyers & Company*. Retrieved from http://billmoyers.com/story/michael-copps-fcc-ajit-pai-worst-ever.

Wolfson, T. (2014). *Digital rebellion: The birth of the cyber left*. Urbana: University of Illinois Press.

Wu, T. (2003). Network neutrality, broadband discrimination. *Journal on Telecommunications and High Technology Law, 2*, 141–179.

Wu, T. (2007). Wireless Carterfone. *International Journal of Communication, 1*, 389–426. Retrieved from http://ijoc.org/ojs/index.php/ijoc/article/view/152.

Wu, T. (2011a). Agency threats. *Duke Law Journal, 60*, 1841–1857.

Wu, T. (2011b). *The master switch*. New York: Alfred A. Knopf.

Wu, T., & Lessig, L. (2003). Re: Ex Parte Submission in CS Docket No. 02-52. Retrieved from http://apps.fcc.gov/ecfs/comment/view?id=5509836619.

Wu, T., & Yoo, C. S. (2007). Keeping the Internet neutral? Tim Wu and Christopher Yoo debate. *Federal Communications Law Journal, 59*(3), 575.

Wyatt, E. (2014, November 10). Obama asks FCC to adopt tough net neutrality rules. *New York Times*. Retrieved from https://www.nytimes.com/2014/11/11/technology/obama-net-neutrality-fcc.html.

Yim, S.-J. (1998a, December 30). AT&T, TCI reject Portland, Ore., regulators' condition on local deal. *The Oregonian*.

Yim, S.-J. (1998b, December 14). Bad reception for AT&T. *The Oregonian*, pp. C1, C5.

Yim, S.-J. (1999, January 21). In Oregon, AT&T, TCI sue volunteer regulators, Portland and Multnomah County. *The Oregonian*.

Yoo, C. S. (2004). Would mandating broadband network neutrality help or hurt competition? A comment on the end-to-end debate. *Journal on Telecommunications and High Technology Law, 3*, 23–68.

Yoo, C. S. (2005). Beyond network neutrality. *Harvard Journal of Law & Technology, 19*(1), 1–77.

Yoo, C. S. (2006). Network neutrality and the economics of congestion. *Georgetown Law Journal, 94*, 1847–1908.

Yoo, C. S. (2007). What can antitrust law contribute to the network neutrality debate? *International Journal of Communication, 1*, 493–530. Retrieved from http://ijoc.org/ojs/index.php/ijoc/article/view/153.

Yoo, C. S. (2013). Is there a role for common carriage in an Internet-based world? *Houston Law Review, 51*, 545.

Yoo, C. S. (2014). *Modularity theory and Internet policy*. University of Pennsylvania, Institute for Law & Economics Research Paper No. 13-15, TPRC 2012. Retrieved February 11, 2016 from http://ssrn.com/abstract=2032221.

Yoo, C. S. (2017). Avoiding the pitfalls of net uniformity: Zero rating and nondiscrimination. *Review of Industrial Organization, 50*, 509–536.

Zapler, M. (2010, July 25). FCC chief Genachowski brings Silicon Valley mindset to the job. *San Jose Mercury News*.

Zhou, J. (2014). Tim Wu against the Internet cartel: If elected, Wu would use his office of lieutenant governor to fight Comcast's merger with Time Warner Cable. *Epoch Times*. Retrieved from https://www.theepochtimes.com/tim-wu-against-the-internet-cartel_805919.html.

Zuboff, S. (2015). Big other: Surveillance capitalism and the prospects of an information civilization. *Journal of Information Technology, 30*, 75–89.

Zuboff, S. (2016, March 5). The secrets of surveillance capitalism. *Frankfurter Allgemeine Zeitung*. Retrieved from https://www.faz.net/aktuell/feuilleton/debatten/the-digital-debate/shoshana-zuboff-secrets-of-surveillance-capitalism-14103616.html.

Zuboff, S. (2019). *The age of surveillance capitalism: The fight for a human future at the new frontier of power.* New York: PublicAffairs.

Index